INDEX
TO
OHIO
PENSIONERS
OF 1883

Compiled by
W. Louis Phillips, C.G.

HERITAGE BOOKS
2011

HERITAGE BOOKS

AN IMPRINT OF HERITAGE BOOKS, INC.

Books, CDs, and more—Worldwide

For our listing of thousands of titles see our website
at
www.HeritageBooks.com

Published 2011 by
HERITAGE BOOKS, INC.
Publishing Division
100 Railroad Ave. #104
Westminster, Maryland 21157

Other Heritage Books by the author:

Annotated Bibliography of Ohio Patriots: Revolutionary War and War of 1812
Franklin County, Ohio Adoptions, 1852–1901
Index to Franklin County, Ohio Guardianships and Estates, 1803–1850
Index to Ohio Pensioners of 1883
Jurisdictional Histories for Ohio's Eighty-eight Counties, 1788–1985
Ohio City and County Directories
Warren County, Ohio Apprenticeship and Indenture Records, 1824–1832, 1864–1867
Washington County Northwest Territory, Court of Common Pleas Index, 1795–1803

International Standard Book Numbers
Paperbound: 978-1-55613-056-4
Clothbound: 978-0-7884-8609-8

INTRODUCTION

This is an index to the list of pensioners, male and female, who were residing in Ohio as of 1 January 1883. Complying with a requirement set forth in a United States Senate resolution dated 8 December 1882, the Secretary of the Interior compiled a list of pensioners in the United States, and throughout the world, who were receiving federal funds. The work was originally published in 1883 in five volumes or parts entitled: *Senate Executive Document 84, Parts 1-5, 47th Congress, 2nd Session* (serial numbers 2078-2082), and was reprinted in 1970 by the Genealogical Publishing Company of Baltimore, Maryland. Entries for Ohio appear in Volume 3, pages 3 through 367.

In the original publication and reprint, the pensioners are listed according to the county in which they resided, and the counties are arranged alphabetically within states. Within each county, the pensioners were grouped according to their post-office addresses which appear alphabetically. Prior to the present index, it was impossible to locate a pensioner unless his county of residence was known. Page 3 of Volume 3 is reproduced here as a sample of the 1883 pension list. All page numbers in this index reflect pagination used in the 1883 pension list.

There are six columns of information in the 1883 list of pensioners: (1) number of certificate (pension number), (2) name of pensioner, (3) post-office address, (4) cause for which pensioned, (5) monthly rate, and (6) date of original allowance. Anyone desiring copies of pages from the pension list should contact the author who will provide such for a slight fee.

Most of the pensioners as of 1883 were Civil War veterans or their widows, but numerous War of 1812 entries were also noted - mostly widows, but also some survivors. The War of 1812 entries are clearly identified as such in the pension list, but not in this index. Copies of the actual pension records can be obtained from the National Archives in

Washington, D.C., by supplying them with the name of the pensioner, his or her certificate or pension number, state of residence and whether the person was a Civil War or War of 1812 veteran or widow. The form currently being used for placing such orders is NATF Form 80 which can be obtained by writing to:

Reference Services Branch (NNIR)
National Archives & Records Service
8th and Pennsylvania Ave., NW
Washington, D.C. 20408

As most researchers are fully aware, pension records can provide extremely helpful information, not only for the veteran, but also for his widow and children, and sometimes parents. It would not be an understatement to say that pension records are some of the most beneficial records a genealogical researcher will ever encounter. It is common to find the following types of data in pension records: places of residence prior to and after military service; birth and death dates and places; marriages; children; military service and exploits; physical ailments; physical descriptions (height, complexion, hair and eye color); occupations; places of burial; affidavits of persons acquainted with pensioners; etc. Every entry in this index represents a potential genealogical goldmine just waiting to be tapped.

As with any index, the user should be aware of possible spelling variations for his or her person of interest. As an example, on page 266 of the pension list, Jerome Broukar and Sarah Bronkar appear as pensioners in Muskingum County. It is quite likely that both had the same surname, the difference probably arising from an 1883 compiler's error in interpreting script. On pages 286 and 287, the following surnames were noted in Preble County: Eikinbary, Eikenbary and Eikenberry. All three surnames probably pertain to one family, whatever the correct spelling may be.

Some entries in the 1883 pension list seem to have been reversed - the first name having been recorded as the surname. For instance, on page 48, a Rosson William was noted in Clermont County. Perhaps this should have read William Rosson? It would be wise to check for possible first and surname reversals, especially if your person of interest had a surname that frequently serves as a first name. For instance, if you can't find John Paul, also check for Paul John.

There are a large number of entries for Montgomery County, more so than for any other county. This is because

iv

thousands of veterans from throughout Ohio resided at the soldiers home at Dayton, an institution that is still functioning. Two entries in the pension list had no surnames and these appear at the end of this index.

I would like to acknowledge my parents, William M. and Luella V. Phillips of Newark, for assisting in alphabetizing. For some peculiar reason, my father seemed to enjoy the task. Mrs. Fern Botzenhart of Columbus provided some copying assistance, but most of the actual labor of recording data onto index cards was performed by Mrs. Juanita Hux of Sugar Grove. Without Mrs. Hux's involvement in this project, this index would never have been completed, hence, a special thanks to Juanita.

W. Louis Phillips, C.G.
P.O. Box 24111
Columbus, OH 43224

COUNTY ABBREVIATIONS

Adam	Adams	Lick	Licking
Alle	Allen	Loga	Logan
Ashl	Ashland	Lora	Lorain
Asht	Ashtabula	Luca	Lucas
Athe	Athens	Madi	Madison
Augl	Auglaize	Maho	Mahoning
Belm	Belmont	Mari	Marion
Brow	Brown	Medi	Medina
Butl	Butler	Meig	Meigs
Carr	Carroll	Merc	Mercer
Cham	Champaign	Miam	Miami
Clar	Clark	Monr	Monroe
Cler	Clermont	Mont	Montgomery
Clin	Clinton	Morg	Morgan
Colu	Columbiana	Morr	Morrow
Cosh	Coshocton	Musk	Muskingum
Craw	Crawford	Nobl	Noble
Cuya	Cuyahoga	Otta	Ottawa
Dark	Darke	Paul	Paulding
Defi	Defiance	Perr	Perry
Dela	Delaware	Pick	Pickaway
Erie	Erie	Pike	Pike
Fair	Fairfield	Port	Portage
Faye	Fayette	Preb	Preble
Fran	Franklin	Putn	Putnam
Fult	Fulton	Rich	Richland
Gall	Gallia	Ross	Ross
Geau	Geauga	Sand	Sandusky
Gree	Greene	Scio	Scioto
Guer	Guernsey	Sene	Seneca
Hami	Hamilton	Shel	Shelby
Hanc	Hancock	Star	Stark
Hard	Hardin	Summ	Summit
Harr	Harrison	Trum	Trumbull
Henr	Henry	Tusc	Tuscarawas
High	Highland	Unio	Union
Hock	Hocking	VanW	Van Wert
Holm	Holmes	Vint	Vinton
Huro	Huron	Warr	Warren
Jack	Jackson	Wash	Washington
Jeff	Jefferson	Wayn	Wayne
Knox	Knox	Will	Williams
Lake	Lake	Wood	Wood
Lawr	Lawrence	Wyan	Wyandot

OHIO COUNTIES
AND
COUNTY SEATS

PENSIONERS ON THE ROLLS JANUARY 1, 1883.

OHIO.

ADAMS COUNTY

No. of certificate	Name of pensioner	Post-office address	Cause for which pensioned	Mon.	Date of original allowance
	Jack, Deborah	Bearley's Fork	widow 1812		Jan., 1879
23,061	Cooper, Nancy	do	do		Apr., 1879
90,160	Bradford, Eliza	do	shell w. r. leg		
11,546	Lawrence, Christian	Bentonville	widow 1812		Nov., 1878
167,691	Stephens, Geo.	do	dis. heart, chr. rheum		Apr., 1880
52,588	Thompson, Thos	do	w. l. hand		
73,400	Shelton, Lewis	do	loss r. eye, inj. face & results		Nov., 1871
2,908	Stephens, Elizabeth	do	widow 1812		Nov., 1879
240,058	Bryan, Delila	do	do		Jan., 1879
98,929	Moore, Joseph S	do	w. r. thigh		
178,900	Richmond, Amos	do	dis. kidneys, scurvy		Nov., 1880
113,209	Lewis, James M	do	paraplegia		
169,651	Bryan, John	do	chr. diarr., dis. lungs		June, 1880
34,687	Roush, Furmon	do	dis. lungs		
97,153	McNut, John H	do	w. r. lung		
290,117	Edgington, Lindsey L	do	inj. back, dis. kidneys		1882
166,294	Edgington, Mary Ann	do	widow		May, 1880
80,932	Pointer, Isaac A	do	dep. mother		Apr., 1866
74,473	Maxwell, Sarah A	do	widow		
125,672	Bowman, Ephraim	do	dis. lungs		
221,501	Adamson, Joseph	do	chr. diarr., & dis. of abdomen		Dec., 1882
219,374	Stark, Asa	Blue Creek	chr. diarr. & debility		Aug., 1882
80,931	Knapp, Ebenezer	do	w. l. hip		
98,343	Hazelbaker, Andrew J	do	loss r. leg		Mar., 1886
25,756	Altman, Margaret	do	widow 1812		Aug., 1879
25,664	Thompson, Tamera	do	do		July, 1879
67,163	Grimes, Margaret	do	widow		
141,509	Lewis, Geo. W	do	lu. eyes		
173,971	Martin, Horace H	do	g. s. w. r. arm, varicose veins		Feb., 1869
168,169	Lewis, Philip S	do	dis. heart		May, 1880
127,690	Rodgers, Samuel J	do	w. r. thigh		
89,804	McManus, Garrett	do	w. r. arm		
205,313	Fields, Wm. H	do	dis. eyes		Apr., 1882
147,002	Gwynn, Thos. M	do	w. l. arm		Aug., 1876
14,802	McGin, Mary	do	widow		
374,373	Newman, Jas. K. P	do	dis. lungs		Sept., 1880
171,852	Colvin, Francis	do	chr. diarr., dis. debility		Oct., 1880
162,617	Miranda, Katharine J	do	widow		Aug., 1871
176,758	Shelton, Darius	Dunkinsville	kidney, lungs & heart		Sept., 1880
359,504	Scott, John W	do	dis. throat, lungs & heart		May, 1883
184,289	Scott, Moses A	do	dis. of abd., inj. testicle		Apr., 1881
126,910	Shelton, Wm. J	do	g. s. w. l. leg		Apr., 1881
207,854	Smith, Saml. W	do	chr. rheum., colic, abd. vis.		Aug., 1882
333,914	Scott, John A	do	pulmonary catarrh		
9,419	Boone, Margaret	do	widow 1812		Sept., 1878
5,781	Beam, Isabella	do	widow		
218,065	Mitchell, Joseph	do	dis. lungs, liver & stomach		Sept., 1882
25,762	Ciconler, Wm. M	do	w. l. leg		Jan., 1869
196,844	Lowe, Thos. D	do	chr. diarr. & results		June, 1881
149,292	Gretton, Thos. F	do	chr. diarr. & results		Nov., 1882
209,930	Campbell, Louisa	do	widow		Dec., 1875
136,763	Tracy, John K	do	w. r. arm		Mar., 1884
16,481	Stroker, Aaron	do			
93,975	Patterson, Annie J	do	dis. lungs & liver		Aug., 1881
186,592	Palmer, Perry	do			Apr., 1878
152,334	Dunkel, John	do			
139,323	Strode, Benj. Geo.	do			Mar., 1882
39,310	Silcumson, Eliza	do	do		
117,924	Miller, Wm. H	Buck Run			Oct., 1880
98,905	Vanderson, Angelo	do	loss r. foot		Mar., 1890
43,732	Clemer, Thos. A	do	g. s. w. l. hand		

AARON			**ACKER** (cont)			
Muck	Knox	173	Lewis	Mont	247	
ABBEY			**ACKERMAN**			
Frank	Hami	133	Louis	Defi	080	
ABBOTT			**ACKLEY**			
Edgar G	Cosh	061	Ariadney	Ross	299	
Edward A	Cuya	074	John A	Cuya	074	
Elijah	Adam	006	Montroville	Hami	133	
Geo W	Clar	047	Rachel	Monr	223	
Harlin	Mont	249	Susan	Meig	212	
Henry P	Cuya	067	Theodore	Mont	238	
Jesse M	Cham	041	**ACTON**			
John B	Clin	053	Isabella	Ross	300	
Lafayette	Fair	089	**ADAIR**			
Lucinda	Luca	197	Cornelia	Guer	118	
Nelson	Adam	006	Henry S	Madi	203	
Squire	Rich	295	Lavina	Cuya	073	
William	Wash	346	William C	Will	356	
William	Wash	349	**ADAM**			
William H	Clin	052	John C	Clar	046	
ABBY			**ADAMS**			
Roxanna	Cuya	065	Albert	Warr	342	
ABEL			Alfred B	Fran	099	
Andrew	Loga	189	Anthony W	Wood	358	
Christopher C	Carr	040	Caleb H	Defi	081	
William	Lora	194	Chas N	Paul	272	
ABELE			Cynthia Ann	Clin	053	
Michael	Erie	087	Elijah B	Fran	099	
ABELL			Eliza	Fran	096	
Lucretia	Trum	325	Elizabeth	Musk	263	
Rebecca	Clin	053	Frank B	Summ	322	
ABENDSHAW			Frederick H	Port	284	
Jacob	Wash	349	Frederick M	Henr	153	
ABER			Henry	Fran	099	
James M	Ross	300	Herman C	Fult	105	
ABERNETHY			Horace B	Loga	189	
Sarah B	Hami	122	James	Morg	256	
ABRAHAM			James	VanW	337	
Eliza J	Hami	128	John	Mont	255	
John Q	Will	355	John	Star	317	
ABRAMS			John	Warr	343	
McKenzie	Scio	307	John E	Fair	089	
ACALY			John W	Mont	240	
Mary	Sene	314	Joseph J	Dela	084	
ACHENBACH			Kitty A	Port	284	
Edward	Fran	099	Leonora	Lick	185	
ACHER			Lucy	Adam	006	
Martin	Musk	263	Maria L	Mont	231	
ACHOR			Martha	Dela	082	
Lewis	Clin	053	Martin	Sene	310	
ACHUFF			Mary	Lick	184	
Ezekiel A	Hami	139	Mathew W	Colu	057	
ACKER			Michael	Musk	263	
Geo D	Sene	311	Nelson G	Gree	114	

1

ADAMS (cont.)				AGLER		
Newton P	Athe	020		Amelia	Hami	135
Polly	Lakc	178		AGY		
Priscilla	Lawr	180		Napoleon B	Belm	029
Richard	Musk	267		AHLERS		
Sam'l N	Gree	115		Adolph	Mont	250
Sarah G	Dela	082		Mary	Mont	231
Thos	Mont	233		AHLUM		
Thos	Monr	224		Mariah	Sene	314
Thos C	Adam	006		AHRENS		
Thos C	Erie	086		Fred'k	Hami	139
Virginia H	Ross	299		AIKEN		
William	Hami	133		Caroline L	Clin	054
William G	Mont	248		Geo W	Hami	136
ADAMSON				James	Harr	150
Isaac	Guer	117		AILES		
Joseph W	Adam	003		Hezekiah	Shel	315
ADCOCK				AILSHIRE		
Henry S	Hock	159		John	Ross	299
ADDIS				AINLIN		
Mary Eliz	Wash	345		James	Miam	220
Thomas B	Lawr	181		AINSWORTH		
ADDLESPEIGER				Caroline	VanW	339
Eliz	Wash	348		Robert	Miam	220
ADDY				William H	Mont	241
John	Cosh	060		AIRD		
ADELL				Andrew	Mont	247
Thos	Erie	086		AKENS		
ADKINS				John	Asht	017
Charles I	Dela	083		AKERS		
Marion	Lawr	182		Alonzo G	Huro	164
Richard	Lawr	179		Nancy J	Rich	295
ADKINSON				Napoleon B	Cosh	061
Mary J	Loga	190		William	Lawr	180
ADUDDELL				AKINS		
Joseph	Pike	280		Sarah	Jeff	169
ADY				ALBACH		
Joshua	Monr	224		Riley	Morr	261
Lavosier	Monr	224		ALBAN		
AERY				Henry H	Hanc	141
Margaret	Gree	115		James A	Wash	346
AFFOLDER				ALBAUGH		
Gottleib	Tusc	332		Cath	Carr	040
AGATE				David	Lick	188
Franklin	Lora	193		Felix	Mari	208
AGER				ALBERSDORFER		
George	Mont	250		Equatz	Mont	249
AGIN				ALBERT		
James	Monr	226		Amos M	Perr	277
AGLAR				John Q	Sene	311
Nath'l H	Hami	136		John S	Wyan	365
AGLE				Joseph	Wyan	365
Mary J	Fult	107		Lantz	Tusc	332
				Sarah A	Butl	036

2

ALBERT (cont.)			ALEXANDER (cont)		
William L	Adam	004	James	Morg	257
ALBERTI			James J	Unio	336
Wilhelm F	Mont	237	James S	Summ	323
ALBERTSON			Jno W	Meig	216
James	Holm	161	John M	Brow	031
James G	Wayn	352	John M	Gall	109
John J	Holm	161	Joseph C	Dela	083
Joshua	Warr	343	Joseph P	Clar	044
ALBIN			Margaret	Harr	148
Mary	Clar	046	Mary	Adam	008
ALBON			Mary M	Preb	288
Constance	Huro	161	Melville W	Miam	220
ALBOTT			Robert E	Hami	138
Mary L	Wood	358	Sarah	Fair	092
ALBRECHT			Stephen	Pick	278
Fred'k	Mont	250	Susan L	Faye	094
ALBRIGHT			William	Guer	119
John	VanW	339	William	Loga	192
Lucinda	Guer	117	William T	Mont	228
Nichael	Mari	208	ALEY		
Rebecca	Ashl	013	Simon P	Mont	231
Sarah	Ashl	013	ALF		
ALBRITAIN			Marcus	Mont	237
Richard L	Fran	095	ALFKIN		
ALCOTT			Alfred	Mont	250
Sarah M	Loga	192	ALGIER		
ALDEN			Frederick	Maho	207
Mary C	Hami	128	ALKIRE		
ALDERMAN			Mary C	Morr	260
Lura	Asht	019	Thomas	Tusc	333
Phares	Asht	019	ALLAMAN		
ALDRICH			Samuel	Mont	227
Elias	Morr	261	ALLAN		
Eliza	Dela	082	Thomas	Hami	137
Reuben	Morr	261	ALLBAUGH		
Samuel	Mont	233	David	Preb	288
ALDRIDGE			ALLBRIGHT		
Esther	Pike	282	John W	Musk	264
Hammond W	Scio	307	ALLEMANG		
John P	Mont	245	Erie	Scio	305
ALESHIRE			ALLEN		
Maryland	Jack	166	Amos H	Asht	016
Michael	Lawr	179	Ann	Asht	019
ALEXANDER			Asa W	Colu	058
Amanda	Athe	020	Augustus	Meig	215
David	Asht	019	Betsy	Lora	195
Eliza J	Loga	190	Cath	Monr	224
Ephraim K	Fran	099	Cath	Mont	233
Francis T	Mont	250	Chas L	Fult	105
Fred	Star	318	Chas W	Luca	201
Geo W	VanW	339	Comfort	Brow	033
Hiram	Lawr	181	David K	Belm	028
Hosea W	Dela	083	Don O	Cuya	075

3

INDEX TO 1883 PENSIONERS OF OHIO

ALLEN (cont)				ALLINGER		
Edward	Mont	249		John	Maho	207
Eleanor	Madi	202		ALLION		
Eliza	Faye	094		Lewis	Luca	202
Elizabeth	Putn	290		ALLISON		
Elkana	Clin	054		Benj F	Clar	046
Geo L	Summ	323		Edward H	Preb	287
Henry H	Perr	276		Eliza	Belm	030
Isaac	Putn	289		Elizabeth	Carr	040
Isaac B	Clin	055		James	Faye	093
James	Star	320		James C	Mont	232
James W	Lick	185		Jesse H	Clin	053
Jeptha	Jack	168		Lydia	Morg	257
John	Ross	300		Mary	Gree	114
John B	Fran	095		Rebecca	Gall	109
John T	Guer	117		ALLREAD		
Joseph	Putn	290		Esther	Dark	079
Joseph H	VanW	337		ALLSHOUSE		
Josiah B	Fran	099		William	Maho	205
Louisa	Defi	081		ALLSPAN		
Lyman S	Mont	239		Margaret E	VanW	340
Margaret	Hanc	142		ALLSTEPPER		
Margaret	Loga	192		Peter	Mont	240
Martin	Mont	240		ALLSTETTER		
Martin C	Scio	308		Jacob	Putn	289
Mary	Erie	087		ALLTOP		
Mary F	Lawr	180		Ruth	Lawr	179
Merab	Miam	220		ALLWINE		
Moses	Paul	274		James H	Fair	088
Nancy A	Brow	032		ALSHOUSE		
Nathan	Mont	230		William	Geau	112
Patty	Sand	304		ALSPAUGH		
Racena	Fult	105		Michael	Sene	312
Rebecca C	Faye	094		ALTAFFER		
Serena	Lake	176		Isaac M	Sene	309
Sidney S	Sene	311		ALTENBERGER		
Silas D	Putn	289		Joseph	Wyan	367
Thos	Clar	047		Philip	Pick	278
Thos	Cuya	076		ALTHEN		
Thos	Mont	242		Ann E	Fran	095
Washington	Jeff	171		ALTHON		
Wilber W	Asht	019		Geo	Fran	102
ALLENAN				ALTHOUSER		
Leonard	Henr	152		Fred	Wyan	367
ALLENBAUGH				ALTICK		
David	Ashl	013		John P	Miam	221
ALLENDER				ALTMAN		
Geo W	Guer	120		Frank	Mont	229
John B	Fran	102		Margaret	Adam	003
ALLGOWER				Michael W	Cler	048
Chas F	Mont	250		ALTON		
ALLIN				Helen C	Cuya	073
Calvin J	Madi	202		ALTSMAN		
				Alexander	Scio	306

4

ALWARD			AMOS (cont)			
Mary	Lick	186	Thomas K	Nobl	270	
ALWES			AMSBAUGH			
Elizabeth	Athe	024	Christ'r C	Knox	176	
ALWOOD			AMSDEN			
Elizabeth	Will	356	Eliza E	Erie	086	
Simon	Tusc	333	Harriet	Sand	303	
AMAN			Luzerne	Huro	163	
Frederick	Mont	249	AMSLER			
AMANN			Melchoir	Mont	241	
Charles	Scio	306	AMY			
AMBLER			Harriet	Lick	184	
Sarah	VanW	339	ANDELFINGER			
AMBRECHT			Frank	Luca	196	
Dora	Hanc	142	ANDERS			
AMBRICK			David	Athe	023	
Thomas	Fran	099	ANDERSON			
AMBROSE			Abraham	Pick	280	
Benj	Musk	263	Andrew M	Dela	083	
Honora	Hami	134	Ann	Mont	232	
Patrick	Mont	247	Cordelia	Gree	115	
AMBROSIER			David W	Defi	080	
Daniel	Craw	064	Dewittfield	Fran	099	
AMBROSIUS			Edward L	Geau	111	
Carolina	Cuya	073	Eliza	Cuya	074	
AMBURG			Elizabeth	Miam	222	
William	Mont	238	Elizabeth	Morg	258	
AMERINE			Elizabeth J	Adam	004	
Mariah	Merc	218	Frances E	Belm	030	
AMERMAN			Geo	Mont	249	
Aaron V	Summ	322	Geo S	Asht	019	
AMES			Harrison	Alle	008	
David S	Mont	247	Isaac R	Butl	039	
Dillen	Sene	311	Isaiah	Knox	172	
Eliza	Defi	081	Isaiah	Rich	293	
Harrison	Huro	162	James	Defi	082	
Holiday	Ashl	011	James	Perr	276	
Oscar C	Hanc	141	James	Pike	281	
AMIDON			James H	Sand	302	
Nathaniel D	Asht	014	James M	Tusc	333	
AMLIN			James O	VanW	338	
Hannah	Dark	079	Jennie	Faye	094	
AMMON			John	Defi	080	
John	Lora	194	John	Wood	363	
AMON			John T	Lawr	183	
Stanton	Mont	252	John W	Clin	052	
AMONS			Joseph A	Belm	027	
Cath A	Colu	057	Joseph E	Huro	165	
AMOS			Joseph G	Nobl	267	
David	Mont	250	Lorenzo D	Dela	084	
Joseph	Fran	099	Margaret	Gree	115	
Mary A	Miam	220	Margaret	Gree	115	
Nancy J	Gall	107	Margaret	Mont	256	

ANDERSON (cont)				ANDREWS (cont)		
Margaret	Morg	259		Sarah A	Port	284
Martin	Clar	046		William	Ashl	014
Mary	Luca	197		William L	Hami	133
Mary	Mont	256		ANDRIX		
Mathias C	Guer	117		Henry	Henr	153
Matilda	Cuya	073		ANEY		
Nancy	Cham	042		Theodore L	Mont	239
Rachel	Shel	316		ANGEL		
Rebecca	Cuya	075		Athraida C	Wood	359
Sarah	Guer	117		Henry	Harr	149
Sarah	Jack	167		ANGELL		
Sarah A	Hami	139		Ruth J	Meig	214
Sarah A	Vint	341		William G	Cuya	074
Sarah J	Fair	092		ANGERSON		
Thomas	Meig	212		Samuel	Lick	186
Thomas S	Madi	203		ANGLE		
Watson	Meig	214		Malichi	Cosh	061
William	High	155		ANGUS		
William	Sand	304		Frederick R	Otta	271
William B	Harr	150		Margaret A	Harr	149
ANDERTON				ANITELOPPE		
Chas	Mont	227		Nicholas	Cuya	067
ANDREGG				ANKERMAN		
John	Fair	088		William S	Cham	042
ANDRESS				ANKNEY		
Erasmus H	Erie	086		Geo	Paul	273
William H	Huro	163		Joshua	Defi	081
ANDREW				ANKROM		
Elizabeth	Madi	203		William	Ross	300
Isaac	Alle	009		ANKRUM		
Jos	Medi	211		Archibald	Guer	120
William	Butl	036		ANNAH		
ANDREWS				Lillie	Cuya	065
Albert A	Luca	200		ANNEN		
Alpheus B	Rich	293		Michael	Star	320
Andrew	Luca	200		ANNESS		
Caroline	Fair	091		William R	Butl	038
Chancey L	Asht	016		ANNESSER		
Charles	Athe	023		John	Augl	025
Edwin R	Cuya	075		Joseph	Putn	290
Geo	Defi	080		ANNON		
Geo D	Mont	249		Jesse	Athe	021
Henry M	Putn	290		ANSBAUGH		
Hugh	Gree	115		David R	Rich	292
Isaac	Jack	167		ANSEL		
John H	Mari	208		Joseph	Perr	274
Mary F	Gall	109		Mary A	Vint	340
Mary L	Mont	230		Walter	Meig	212
Mary L	Mont	230		William	Perr	277
Perry	Jack	168		ANSLEY		
Rebecca A	Clar	044		James L	Colu	055
Robert D	Meig	214				
Samantha M	Gree	116				

ANTENSEIB			ARCHER (cont)		
John	Hami	133	Wilson	Guer	117
ANTER			ARCHERD		
Rebecca	Fran	097	Maria A	Hami	128
ANTHONY			ARDIS		
Eliza	Musk	265	John	Hami	133
John C	Cuya	067	ARGO		
Miller	Pick	278	Solomon D	Scio	308
Patrick	Mont	249	ARICK		
Rachel	Luca	197	Margaret	Wayn	352
Williams	Wash	345	ARMBRUSTER		
ANTLE			August	Craw	062
Anna	Athe	023	ARMENTROUT		
ANWAY			Abraham	Ashl	012
John E	Huro	162	ARMISTEAD		
APGER			Edward F	Mont	249
George A S	Hanc	142	ARMS		
Henry B	Hanc	142	Emeline E	Maho	206
APLAS			ARMSTEAD		
David	Alle	009	Mary J	Butl	037
APLIN			ARMSTRONG		
Edward W	Cuya	066	Bruce H	Maho	207
Peter	Mont	231	Burton	Geau	112
APPELFELLER			Clinton L	Hami	133
Christian	Unio	334	Elizabeth	Cler	049
APPENZELLEN			George W	Knox	175
Cath	Mont	232	James	Musk	262
APPLE			Jemima	Belm	030
John	Wood	361	John H	Rich	295
Louis	Cosh	060	John S	Gree	116
APPLEGARTH			John W	Sene	309
Robert	Belm	029	Joseph	Cler	048
APPLEGATE			Joseph M	Tusc	333
Chas	Otta	271	Laura	Jeff	170
Charlotte	Fair	089	Lewis	Fran	099
Dorcas	Butl	038	Mary	Geau	112
Gilbert	Luca	197	Mary A	High	154
John	Rich	292	Nancy	High	153
Thomas	Butl	035	Napoleon	Cuya	065
APPLEMAN			Nelson	Wood	364
Cath	Vint	341	Robert	Hami	133
ARBERTS			Samuel	Madi	202
William	Clar	044	Samuel F	Dark	077
ARBOGAST			Samuel M	Rich	295
George W	Hard	148	Thomas	Cuya	076
ARCHER			William C	Summ	324
Aaron	Loga	191	William P	Otta	271
Edwin W	Hami	133	William T	Hami	133
Enoch	Guer	117	ARNDT		
Ezekiel	Mont	250	Nancy A	Perr	276
John	Pick	280	ARNETT		
John R	VanW	337	Geo	Clar	046
Julia A	Medi	210	Sarah	Hami	128
William A	Loga	191			

ARNEY			ASCHBACKER			
John H	Fair	092	Mary A	Cosh	061	
ARNOLD			ASH			
Cath	Cuya	073	William	Wyan	365	
Elizabeth C	Ashl	013	ASHBAUGH			
Henry	Cuya	066	Elizabeth	Holm	160	
Henry	Hami	133	Emeline R	Fran	101	
Henry J	Miam	222	James R	Fran	099	
John	Lora	194	ASHBROOK			
John	Madi	203	Charity	Gree	116	
John	Rich	292	Tunis P	Fair	089	
John J	Cham	042	ASHBURN			
Joseph	Clin	054	Moses	Augl	025	
Joseph C	Mari	208	ASHBY			
Keziah	Asht	016	Thomas	Mont	242	
Margaret	Sene	312	ASHCRAFT			
Martha O	Morg	257	Jonathan	Cosh	062	
Phebe	Summ	323	Joshua	Lawr	181	
Rebecca	Wyan	366	ASHENBACH			
Richard	Knox	173	Jacob	Wayn	354	
Thomas W	Hard	145	ASHER			
William A	Nobl	269	John S	Paul	274	
William H	Maho	205	ASHFORD			
ARONS			Maria	Scio	308	
Theodore C	Loga	191	ASHLEMAN			
ARPP			John	Tusc	332	
Jacob	Butl	037	ASHLEY			
ARRANTS			John	Scio	305	
Elizabeth	Defi	081	Mary A	Dark	077	
ARRASMITH			Reuben L	Lake	178	
William R	Clin	054	Thomas J	Guer	118	
ARRICK			ASHMAN			
Andrew	Morg	257	Lydia W	Summ	321	
ARTHANIA			ASHTON			
William	Monr	225	Felix L	Cler	048	
ARTHUR			Mary P	Miam	220	
Anna	Augl	025	ASKAM			
Azariah	Jack	168	John H	Putn	290	
Cornelia M	Hami	131	ASKEW			
James H	Mari	209	Cyrus H	Rich	293	
Lewis	Scio	305	ASKINS			
Mary	Perr	275	Margaret	Fair	089	
Millie	Lawr	183	Sarah	Wood	359	
Minutha	Scio	307	ASPEN			
Silas M	Jack	166	Nicholas	Mont	247	
Thomas	Jeff	169	ASPER			
ARTHURS			Amelia C	Trum	329	
Rebecca	Preb	286	ASSMAN			
ARTIS			Conrad	Hami	133	
Angeline	Loga	192	ATCHESON			
ASBURG			Alfred P	Summ	324	
Elizabeth	Vint	341	Nancy	Rich	294	

8

ATER			AUKENG			
Geo	Pick	278	Sabra	Guer	120	
Margaret	Ross	299	AULD			
ATHA			David L	Harr	148	
Abigail	Loga	190	AULT			
ATHERTON			Daniel	Shel	315	
James C	Butl	035	Josiah C	Jeff	171	
John F	Musk	267	Valentine H	Mont	233	
ATHEY			AUNGST			
Malinda	Cham	043	Alex	Rich	293	
ATHONY			AUST			
Mark	Dark	078	Theodore	Fran	099	
ATHWELL			AUSTIN			
Mary A	Belm	030	Alonzo	Cuya	067	
ATKIN			Chas E	Cuya	067	
Thomas S	Lake	178	Edith A	Musk	267	
ATKINS			Elizabeth	Musk	264	
Ira	Geau	113	Harvey K	Summ	323	
Michael	Mont	255	Jeremiah	Dela	083	
Sally	Geau	113	William E	Lora	194	
ATKINSON			AUTENREATH			
Elizabeth	Cuya	073	Geo	Luca	201	
James W	Vint	341	AUTENREITH			
Letitia S	Jeff	170	Chas	Mont	250	
Mary A	Meig	213	AUTHES			
Nancy	Athe	024	Christiana	Hami	133	
Samuel S	Monr	224	AUVRAY			
Sarah A	Carr	039	Augustus	Adam	005	
ATTERHOLT			AUXER			
James	Ashl	012	John H	Geau	113	
ATWATER			AVERY			
Lydia S	Tusc	332	Andrew J	Cler	050	
Samuel C	Otta	271	Caroline	Huro	162	
ATWOOD			Jemima C	Medi	211	
Freeman	Mont	249	Joshua O	Wood	359	
Newton J	Summ	322	Martha E	Fran	103	
AU			Mary D	Rich	293	
Charlotte	Star	318	William	Hami	133	
AUBLE			AVEY			
Mary	Medi	211	Mariam	Shel	315	
AUCKERMAN			AVIS			
Daniel	Lawr	181	Teresa	Fran	101	
AUER			AXLINE			
Geo	Mont	249	May J	Musk	264	
Mathias	Mont	245	AXTELL			
AUFTERHEIDE			Ann	Vint	341	
Cath S	Hami	128	John W	Unio	336	
AUGHEE			AYERS			
Sarah	Preb	288	Amanda	Dela	084	
AUGHEY			Andrew	Ashl	012	
Cath	Mont	227	David	Warr	344	
AUGUSTINE			Harrison C	VanW	338	
Jno	Wash	347	Virginia	Clin	053	

9

AYLES		
Adaline	Otta	271
AYRES		
Elizabeth	VanW	339
Jacob	Dela	085
Rachel	Adam	006
Samuel D	Putn	289
AZDELL		
James	Colu	056
BAARS		
William	Mont	243
BABB		
Hannah E	Merc	216
Solomon	Summ	324
William R	Clin	055
BABBATT		
Charles	Huro	162
BABBITT		
Albert T	Luca	201
BABBOTT		
Lewis	Sene	310
BABBS		
Isaac V	Knox	172
Lucina	Knox	173
BABINGTON		
James A	Colu	057
BABCOCK		
Benj N	Asht	018
Daniel	Sand	301
(alias Daniel James)		
Geo	Medi	210
Geo C	Fult	104
Henry M	Paul	274
Jacob R	VanW	337
James(?)	Sand	301
John B	Henr	153
Margaret E	Sene	311
Mary A	Henr	152
William	Meig	213
BABCOX		
Maria	Asht	016
BACHMAN		
Eliza	Fran	100
John	Hami	134
BACK		
Ferdinand C	Cuya	065
BACKER		
Elias	Wayn	355
Eliza	Butl	037
Johanna	Hami	127

BACKERSTATT		
Frank	Hami	134
Frank	Hami	135
BACKUS		
Andrew	Fran	096
BACON		
John A	Scio	305
Joseph	Lora	196
Lucy C	Lora	193
Mariel	Asht	016
Randall G	Luca	201
William	Colu	055
BADDERS		
Nancy A	Lawr	183
BADENBORUCK		
Susan	Asht	019
BADER		
Peter	Fran	098
BADGELY		
Charlotte	Craw	063
BADGER		
Ansel V	Medi	211
Archey J	Fran	098
Austin	Medi	211
Martha	Jeff	172
Nathaniel L	Lake	178
BADGLEY		
George H	Cler	050
George W	High	155
BADGSLEY		
Perry	Clar	044
BADMAN		
Sarah	Putn	290
BAECHLE		
Lorenzo	Lick	187
BAEHR		
John	Trum	329
William	Hami	135
BAER		
David	Craw	062
Samuel	Henr	153
BAGFORD		
John	Miam	218
BAGGOTT		
Mary	High	156
BAGGS		
Conoway G	Mont	251
David K	Morr	260
Martha	Belm	028
BAGLEY		
Geo B	Medi	211
BAGLIN		
Harriet	Ross	298

10

BAGUE			**BAINS**		
Alonzo	Geau	112	James	Hami	133
BAHEN			**BAINTER**		
John	Mont	243	Mary E	Morg	256
BAKEHORN			**BAIR**		
William H	Alle	009	Elizabeth	Star	318
BAKERSTAFF			Geo	Sene	311
Henry	Fran	099	Mary	Craw	062
BAIER			**BAIRD**		
Andreas	Mont	252	Aaron D	Geau	111
BAIGLEY			Albert B	Hami	133
Joseph	Jeff	169	Amos	Hock	157
BAIL			Anne M	Star	318
Charles P	Geau	112	Asa	Wood	358
BAILEN			Charles C	Wood	361
William	Mont	228	David	Wood	358
BAILES			Eliza L	Jack	167
Jesse M	Musk	263	Mary	Maho	207
BAILEY			Rachel	Guer	120
Amanda	Asht	015	Sarah	Faye	094
Anderson	Lawr	183	William	Hami	135
Ann	Perr	277	**BAIRN**		
Annie	Sand	302	Mary Jane	Jeff	170
Apphia B	Lake	176	**BAKER**		
Brayton C	Luca	198	Adam	Mari	209
Chesney W	Hami	138	Alpheus	Wash	348
Elizabeth	Cuya	066	Amos	Knox	174
George	Pike	281	Andrew J	Lick	188
Girard	VanW	340	Andrew L	Sene	313
Hannah	Augl	026	Augusta R	Hami	132
James	Vint	341	Caleb J	Meig	212
James M	Wayn	353	Charles W	Dark	077
James W	Perr	277	Charlotte	Lick	188
Jane	Pick	279	Clarissa	Clar	045
John C	Hard	146	Daniel	Dela	082
Joshua	Mont	238	Daniel	Lick	185
Judith	Meig	216	Daniel	Lick	187
Lovinah	Pike	283	David	Monr	226
Mary	Gree	116	David	Wyan	367
Mary	Knox	176	Edwin N	Lake	177
Morton	Meig	214	Elijah	Geau	112
Nancy	Mari	208	Eliza R	Colu	058
Nancy	Ross	300	Elizabeth	Cuya	076
Sarah A	Meig	215	Eve	Maho	205
William	Wood	363	Hannah	Preb	287
William J	Wood	360	Harriet	Ross	298
BAILLIE			Harvey D	Wood	360
John	Colu	058	Henry	Ross	300
BAIN			Henry	Monr	226
Amanda A	Morr	260	Henry	Wood	360
Martha	Guer	119	Hugh	Alle	010
BAINES			Isaac	Rich	292
James	Mont	237	James	Hami	133

11

BAKER (cont)			BALDWIN (cont)		
James M	Mont	245	Annie E	Will	357
Jno	Meig	213	Augustus R	Geau	113
John	Hami	133	Chas H	Hami	134
John	Mont	255	Edward	Port	283
John	Paul	272	Geo E	Ross	298
John	Wood	359	Isaac A	Hanc	140
John Q A	Wash	345	Isabella	Lick	183
Leander	Carr	040	John	Wood	359
Lucretia	Shel	314	John F	Belm	029
Lucy A	Cham	041	John M	Asht	015
Mary	Maho	206	Margaret	Shel	315
Mary A	Athe	023	Mary	Hami	128
Mary A	Warr	342	Mary Ann	Hard	143
Mary F	Lawr	183	Mary M	Cham	042
Mary M	Wayn	354	Nancy	Luca	199
Matilda	Athe	021	Nancy	Shel	315
Nancy	Wash	350	Orlin J	High	154
Nancy J	Tusc	331	Stephen H	Dela	082
Philip S	Lora	194	Thomas P	Clin	052
Russell	High	155	William	Clar	044
Ruth	Lick	184	William C	Trum	325
Samuel	Jack	167	William S	Adam	006
Sarah	Cuya	071	BALE		
Sarah A E	Clin	054	Matilda	Will	357
Sarepta M	Miam	220	BALENTINE		
Simon	Cham	042	Sarah Ann	Wash	350
Simon	Geau	112	BALES		
Susanna	Colu	058	John H	Hard	146
Thomas	Belm	029	Sarah	Gree	115
Thomas	Perr	275	BALHEIMER		
Thomas E	Hock	158	Mary	Colu	056
Thomas R	Lawr	182	BALL		
Valentine	Scio	307	Anna M	Faye	093
Walter R	Mont	252	Caroline	Belm	027
William S	Athe	024	Elisha	Nobl	268
William W	Wood	363	Geo A	Lick	187
Yost S	Wayn	353	Jasper B	Wash	346
BALCH			Joseph	Mont	241
Spencer E	Lake	176	Levi B	Mont	232
William	Lake	176	Lowman A	Colu	057
BALCOM			Maria	Hami	128
Almira	Athe	022	Mary	Knox	173
Lucinda	Star	321	Rosannah	Knox	173
BALDINGER			BALLANTINE		
Theo	Lora	194	Maria	Guer	118
BALDOCK			BALLARD		
Lafayette	Miam	220	John H	Hard	144
BALDRIDGE			BALLENTINE		
James A	Adam	007	John	Luca	201
Nancy A	Hami	139	BALLES		
BALDWIN			Mary	Hami	128
Aceneth C	Trum	325			

12

BALLINGER			**BANSCHEPPER**			
Lewis	Merc	217	Henry	Miam	220
BALLOU			**BAOLINE**			
Martha	Asht	017	John	Hami	132
BALSER			**BAPTIC**			
Ann	Brow	032	John	Geau	111
Sarah	Brow	032	**BARB**			
BALSKING			Gabriel P	Trum	327
Robert	Gree	114	**BARBER**			
BALTZ			Alex	Cuya	065
Frederick	Hami	133	Aquilla	Knox	173
BALVIONE			Barnabas	Dela	083
Elias	Sand	302	Charles	Jack	166
BAMBER			Charles H	Port	284
Curtis L	Wood	359	Edgar W	Erie	086
BAME			Electa	Summ	321
George W	Hanc	143	Elias	Shel	315
BAMENT			Elizabeth	Morr	261
Hannah	Hami	128	Elizabeth A	Cler	049
BANBURY			Geo L	Wyan	366
Solomon	Knox	173	Hugh M	Cosh	060
BANCROFT			Ira G	Mont	244
Adrian L	Fran	099	John L	Huro	165
BANDENISTEL			Mahala	Lawr	180
Cath	Mont	231	Myron H	Summ	323
BANDLE			Orville H	Cham	043
Caleb F	Asht	016	Roxana S	Erie	085
BANER			Samuel	Nobl	268
Conrad	Henr	151	Sarah	Scio	307
BANEY			Seth M	Huro	165
Julia A	Wayn	352	Sophia B	Cuya	073
BANGENTON			Thomas	Faye	094
Maria	Tusc	331	Wilson M	Guer	118
BANGHAN			**BARBOUR**			
Lydia	Pick	280	James M	Wood	358
BANKARD			William H	Mont	228
John	Butl	038	**BARCAFER**			
BANKER			Eliza A	Fran	104
Elizabeth	Hard	148	**BARCH**			
BANKS			Hiram C	Erie	087
John F	Paul	272	**BARCLAY**			
John M	Paul	272	George D	Port	283
Robert E	Jeff	172	Joseph	Mont	247
William D	Meig	213	Martha	Craw	062
William R	Paul	272	**BARCROFT**			
BANMAN			Ann	Vint	340
Jacob	Miam	222	**BARCUS**			
BANNING			Eliza	Colu	059
Alexander	Loga	190	Nancy	Lick	185
BANNISTER			Robert B	Holm	161
Chapin M	Lora	193	**BARD**			
BANOR			Frederick	Port	284
Isadore	Luca	201				

13

BARDEN			BARKLEY (cont)			
Ann	Hami	128	Sarah H	Gree	116	
BARDON			BARKLOW			
Rebecca	Wayn	354	Rosanna B	Rich	294	
BARDSHERE			BARKRINE			
Evaline	Erie	086	Henry	Putn	289	
BARE			BARLAS			
Benj	Hanc	141	Hannah	Lake	178	
George	Scio	308	BARLIN			
BARGE			Elizabeth	Tusc	331	
Slocum B	Morr	260	BARLOW			
BARGER			Eunice M	Cuya	067	
Amos G	Wood	359	Mareha	Wood	363	
Benj F	Mont	229	Marion S	Gall	109	
Elias	Trum	330	Martha	Wood	363	
BARHOLTT			Sarah	Hard	146	
Fred	Cuya	071	BARNABY			
BARINGER			Laura	Colu	058	
Adam	Hami	133	BARNARD			
BARIO			Delilah	Monr	223	
John	Mont	237	Henry C	Huro	161	
BARKALOW			Katharine	Trum	326	
Mary	Butl	036	BARNES			
BARKELOO			Adin	Clar	045	
Jacques	Butl	038	Cath	Brow	035	
BARKER			Cath	Fult	105	
Ann M	Musk	267	Cath	Vint	340	
Arthur W	Wood	362	Clinton	Gree	116	
Cath	Colu	058	Cynthia	Vint	340	
Edmund J	Cuya	076	David	Star	317	
Elizabeth J	Shel	314	Francis M	Fult	107	
Isabel	Fran	104	Frederick C	Luca	201	
James	Monr	225	George W	Knox	173	
James G	Wash	348	Isaac	Merc	217	
John	Huro	165	James A	Belm	030	
John	Mont	255	James B	Lake	177	
Joshua	Shel	316	James W	Sand	304	
Judith	Belm	030	James W	Will	355	
Leander R	Sene	312	John W	Unio	334	
Levi	Scio	304	Joseph	Morr	261	
Michael	Hami	136	Louisa	Cosh	061	
Polly	Shel	316	Maria	Nobl	268	
Samuel H	High	154	Mary	Hami	140	
William	Huro	163	Mary A	Clin	055	
William H	Cler	051	Milton	Fran	104	
BARKES			Phebe F	Lick	188	
Mary J	Colu	056	Philander Y	Port	285	
BARKHURST			Sarah	Guer	119	
Jno W F	Cosh	061	Sarah A	Fair	090	
BARKLEY			Sophia	Nobl	269	
Andrew	Tusc	333	Stewart	Fair	092	
Hugh	Mont	249	Sylvester	Defi	081	
Sarah	Cuya	071				

BARNES (cont)		
Wester A	Fran	097
(alias Wester A McDaniel)		
William H	Belm	027
William H	Hami	134
William M	Cler	051
Wilson	Knox	173
BARNETT		
Anna	Putn	288
Calvin	Mari	208
Geo W	Musk	265
Geo W	Tusc	332
Henry	Mont	227
John K	Faye	094
Mary A	Pike	282
Sarah	Musk	264
Thomas J	Craw	062
BARNEY		
Elmer	Cuya	065
Sylvanus	Vint	340
BARNGROVER		
Cath	Brow	031
BARNHARD		
Cynthia	Alle	008
BARNHART		
Elizabeth	Hard	148
Jacob	Henr	153
John A	Will	357
Martin	Mari	208
Nancy	Morg	256
William M	Wash	350
BARNS		
John H	Clin	054
BARNUM		
Herbert	Lora	195
Martha K	Trum	328
Philo B	Hami	133
Richard S	Medi	211
BARONET		
Conrad F	Musk	264
BAROUSKY		
Charles	Mont	255
BARR		
Amos	Fran	095
Andrew J	Cler	049
Anna H	Colu	059
Benj D	Pike	282
Brazilus	Clar	046
Henry N	Ashl	011
James	Mont	242
John C	Alle	009
John F	Knox	176
Leafy	Cuya	076

BARR (cont)		
Nicholas M	Miam	220
Richard	Rich	296
Robert	Rich	292
Samuel A	Gree	114
Thomas	Clin	053
Thomas L	Rich	295
William J	Henr	151
BARRACK		
Mary E	Adam	004
BARRACLOUGH		
Geo	Luca	198
BARRATT		
William	Hami	135
BARREL		
William A	Morg	257
BARRELL		
John	Morg	258
BARREN		
Araminta	Clin	053
BARRERE		
John M	High	155
BARRETT		
Cath	Adam	006
Dallas	Clin	053
Daniel A	Lake	178
Dominick	Mont	243
Edward	Jeff	171
Edwin P	Miam	222
Eliada	Huro	163
George W	Port	285
Isaac	Gall	110
Isaac D	Cuya	071
Jacob	Fult	105
John	Jeff	172
John	Mont	235
John F	Wayn	354
Louisa A	Fran	097
Margaret A	Hami	134
Maria	Musk	262
Mary B	Huro	163
Mary J	Ross	297
Nathan	Belm	029
Ransom	Huro	163
Russell C	Miam	219
Sarah A	Hami	127
Sophia	Cuya	073
William	Jeff	172
BARRICK		
Jane	Lick	183
William	Fair	090
BARRICKMAN		
James	Adam	007

15

BARRINGER				BARTLETT (cont)		
Abraham	Meig	215		John J	Wash	350
John W	Defi	080		John W	Meig	215
BARRINGTON				Laura A	Clar	044
Mary	Luca	199		Lydia B	Luca	198
BARRON				Mary A	Huro	164
Richard	Lawr	180		Mary U	Trum	325
BARROW				Matilda	Sene	312
Isaac	Athe	023		Robert F	Morr	260
BARROWS				William S	Vint	341
Bradley P	Meig	216		BARTLEY		
Clarissa	Lora	192		Beatty	Morg	258
Joseph M	Wash	346		BARTON		
Mary	Dela	084		Anna	Erie	086
BARRY				Barbara	Merc	218
David	Mont	233		Ebenezer	Dela	084
Edward	Mont	247		Edward P	Trum	330
George D	Mont	251		Electra	Jeff	171
Mary	Fran	097		Emeline	Dela	082
Mary	Hami	127		Henry J	Wood	364
Matthew J	Mont	240		James	Jack	167
Thomas J	Mont	243		James R	Luca	201
William	Mont	248		Jonah C	Erie	086
Yelverton P	Morr	260		Lucinda	Dela	083
BARTCH				Margaret E	Dark	078
Elizabeth	Pike	282		Martha J	Jack	167
BARTGES				Nancy	Augl	024
Sarah	Colu	058		Nancy L	Jack	168
BARTH				Sarah A	Dela	082
Frederick	Cosh	059		William	Otta	271
George	Star	318		BARTOW		
BARTHALON				Alvin T	Cuya	075
John W	Guer	119		Seth A	Huro	162
BARTHOLOMEW				BARTRAM		
Cath	Trum	325		Thomas J	Colu	057
Sarah	Morr	261		BARWIG		
William	Luca	197		Henry	Hami	133
BARTHOLOW				BASCH		
Lemuel	Tusc	330		Johannah	Hami	128
Rebecca	Tusc	330		BASFORD		
BARTIMESS				Elijah	Nobl	268
Samuel	Wash	350		Elijah	Nobl	268
BARTLESON				BASH		
Cephas	Sene	312		David	Wood	360
BARTLETT				Eliza	Musk	267
Aaron W	Sand	302		Geo	Musk	267
Albert A	Summ	322		Henry	Lick	188
Chauncey L	Port	285		Josiah	Star	317
David R	Geau	112		Ruth	Fran	101
Eleanor K	Morg	257		BASHAM		
Eliza	Wood	361		Sarah A	Scio	308
Jacob	Fult	107		BASHART		
James C	Lora	192		Constantine	Luca	198

BASHAW				BATIST		
George M	Maho	205		Arada	Mont	234
BASHFORD				BATMAN		
Harriet	Wayn	351		Mary J	Adam	005
BASHORE				BATT		
Solomon	Paul	274		Levi	Wood	363
BASINGER				BATTEN		
John	Morr	259		Thomas	Monr	223
BASOM				BATTENFIELD		
Sarah A	Sene	310		Samuel R	Henr	152
BASOR				BATTERTON		
Henry	Wood	361		Emeline	Gree	116
BASORE				BATTEY		
Maria C	Warr	342		Alfred J	Morr	259
Sarah	Mont	233		BATTIE		
BASQUIN				Mary	Huro	162
Anderson M	Geau	113		BATTIN		
BASS				Margaret C	Harr	149
Bluford D	Mont	247		BATTIS		
BASSARD				Wilkins M	Wash	349
Evert W	Luca	199		BATTLES		
BASSETT				Benj P	Trum	326
Corydon	Lora	195		Luther	Cuya	076
Richard A	Wayn	351		BATTY		
Sabina	Sene	310		Mary	Dark	079
BASSON				BAUER		
August R	Hami	133		Carl A	Mont	252
BASSORE				David J	Lake	176
William W	Wood	359		Geo	Hami	133
BASTEL				Geo	Hami	134
Jacob	Wyan	367		Geo	Mont	242
BATCH				Johanna S D	Cuya	076
Peter	Augl	025		John	Mont	245
BATEMAN				Joseph	Cuya	071
Chris T	Luca	198		Mathias	Mont	240
Samuel	Mont	239		William	Mont	244
BATES				BAUGHAM		
Abram W	Sand	303		Michael	Wood	358
Almira H	Asht	017		BAUGHER		
Christian	Wood	361		George W	Henr	151
Cyrus S	Knox	173		BAUGHMAN		
Eli	Nobl	269		Abraham J	Rich	293
Hiram B	Fran	095		Elizabeth	Madi	203
Jefferson D	Lora	194		Joseph	Perr	275
Leah	Meig	216		Martin L	Rich	292
Meekey P	Gree	115		BAUM		
Randall	Fair	092		John	Will	355
Rufus	Will	356		John W	Hard	148
Solomon	Asht	019		Martha	Musk	262
Thomas	Hami	137		Susan	Will	355
William E	Cuya	067		BAUMAN		
BATEY				Christian	Mont	252
Eliza	Pick	279				

17

BAUMAN (cont)		
Ernest	Mont	245
Lewis	Madi	203
BAUMASTER		
Charles	Fair	090
BAUMGARTNER		
Christian	Hami	134
BAUR		
Jane	Asht	019
Peter	Asht	016
BAVIS		
Ellis	Brow	033
BAWER		
Anna	Hami	121
BAXTER		
Elizabeth	Carr	039
Herod	Dela	082
James	Belm	028
James	Port	285
Lucy	Cham	041
William H	Cham	041
BAY		
Cath	Sand	303
Christian	Hami	134
Jacob F	Maho	205
Mathew W	Nobl	269
BAYARD		
Henry	Mont	243
Samuel A	Cuya	065
BAYES		
Campbell	Fult	107
James	Defi	081
BAYHAN		
Gilead	Pike	282
BAYLESS		
Elizabeth H	Jeff	170
Franklin D	Adam	007
BAYLISS		
Samuel	Luca	197
BAYNE		
Mahala	Brow	034
BAYS		
Esther	Scio	305
BAZER		
Gottlieb	Asht	015
BAZLER		
George	Ross	298
BEACH		
Edwise R	Wood	359
Geo C	Monr	225
John L	Miam	221
John S	Musk	267
Jonathan W	Mont	242

BEACH (cont)		
Joseph	Madi	204
Sophia	Madi	203
BEADLE		
Francis	Mont	241
BEADLING		
Samuel	Guer	118
BEAGLE		
Alva	Hanc	140
Milton	Wash	347
BEAL		
Abraham R	Mont	230
Christina	Rich	291
Ruth W	Pick	279
Thomas	Athe	024
William	Mont	251
BEALE		
James	Mont	251
BEALL		
Charles F	Miam	222
Edwin C	Fran	099
James W	Gree	115
Joseph	Defi	080
Maria M	Alle	009
Mary	Butl	039
Mary	Cosh	060
Mary J	Morr	260
William N	Cler	051
BEAM		
Elizabeth	Lora	195
Henry	Rich	293
Isabella	Adam	003
Solomon R	Merc	217
BEAMER		
Geo W	VanW	338
John	Miam	219
Lewis O	Tusc	332
BEAMERSDERFER		
Cy W	Ross	299
BEAN		
Aaron	Sene	314
Geo H	Meig	216
Hannah	Faye	093
James	Mont	244
John R	Guer	120
Laura L	Athe	022
Margaret	Fair	089
Peter B	Hanc	141
BEANE		
Ezra	Wayn	353
Joseph R	Knox	173
BEANER		
Andrew	Sene	314

BEANS			BEAVERS			
Aaron B	Hard	144	Christina	High	154
Achsah	Port	285	Mary	Scio	305
Joseph	Sene	311	BEAVIRS			
BEAR			Jeremiah	Will	357
Abner	Trum	325	BEAVIS			
Camantha	Lick	185	Geo W	Mont	228
BEARD			BEBB			
Alexander	Wood	362	William J	Alle	008
Eli F	Sene	312	BEBOUT			
Geo	Clar	045	Emily	Meig	212
Jonathan H	Butl	037	Malinda	Knox	174
Josiah	Wood	358	BECHEL			
Martha	Dark	078	Peter	Mont	241
Nancy	Belm	029	BECHERER			
Peter	Mont	254	Samuel	Star	318
Rebecca	Hami	132	BECHMANN			
BEARDMORE			Robert	Butl	036
Maria	Colu	056	BECHOLD			
BEARDSLEE			Geo	Tusc	332
Alfred W	Mont	252	BECHTEL			
BEARDSLEY			Daniel	Wyan	364
Frank A	Asht	015	Isaac C	Wayn	354
Lyman J	Star	316	BECHTELL			
Maria	Asht	018	David H	Fair	088
William E	Summ	323	BECHTOE			
BEARSS			Elizabeth	Will	356
Anna	Otta	271	BECHTOL			
BEASHOR			Ezra E	Will	355
Eliza	Wayn	353	Sophrona J	Cuya	073
BEATON			Susan	Wayn	354
Daniel P	Butl	038	BECK			
BEATTY			Almira	Colu	059
Charles S	Fran	099	Barbara	Hami	134
Eliza J	Harr	150	Christian	Sene	312
Elizabeth	Sene	313	Chs	Monr	224
John L	Lick	184	Daniel, SR	Huro	163
John S	Jack	167	David F	Colu	057
Jonathan	Star	318	Foster	Hami	139
Samuel	Star	319	Geo	Adam	005
Thomas	Jack	168	Geo W	Colu	055
William	Summ	321	John	Sene	313
BEATY			John M	Mont	236
David	Cham	042	Keziah E	Gree	114
Eliza	Alle	009	Martha J	Hami	127
Eliza	Cham	042	Sophia	Wyan	364
Elizabeth E	Faye	093	William	Summ	322
Mary	Cosh	061	William C	Miam	218
BEAU			BECKARD			
Isaac	Fran	103	John	Hami	132
BEAVER			BECKER			
Edith	Lick	185	Chas	Clar	045
Elizabeth	Monr	223	Christian	Mont	252
Sarah	Fran	103	Eliza	Cuya	071

BECKER (cont)			BEECHER			
Frederick W	Hami	133	Betsey	Port	284	
Henry	Hami	133	Mary J	Dela	084	
Jacob	Mont	232	BEECHLER			
John	Erie	087	Sarah	Sene	313	
Joseph	Mont	236	BEEGLE			
Lewis F	Summ	323	Chas D	Holm	160	
Mary	Luca	197	BEEKMAN			
Nicholas	Hami	134	Aaron	Pike	281	
BECKET			Elizabeth	Pike	281	
Michael	Lora	193	Samuel C	Clin	052	
BECKETT			Susan	Pike	281	
Amy	Cler	047	BEELER			
John W	Harr	150	Samuel	Butl	036	
Rachel	Monr	225	BEELY			
BECKFORD			Joseph	Luca	201	
Mary J	Putn	288	BEEMAN			
BECKHAM			Marvin A	Sand	302	
Elijah	Lick	188	Norman	Knox	174	
BECKLEY			BEEMER			
John	Mari	209	Marion	Putn	290	
Michael	Sene	313	BEER			
BECKMAN			Adam	Wyan	366	
Snowden H	Clin	055	Ashbel G	Ashl	011	
Solomon	Sene	311	Eliza	Colu	057	
BECKSTEIN			Levi	Colu	058	
Jacob	Henr	151	BEERBOWER			
BECKWITH			Samuel T	Mari	209	
Chas D	Wood	364	BEERS			
Chas H	Asht	015	Benj	Dark	078	
James	Dela	084	Cyntha	Morr	261	
Mary E	Morg	258	BEERY			
Melita	Lake	177	Christiana	Hami	127	
BEDDOW			John V	Sand	303	
Garrett	Dela	084	Sarah Ann	Hard	145	
BEDEKER			BEESON			
Frederick	Hami	133	Cornelius	Clar	044	
BEDINGER			Mary E	Clar	045	
Lewis	Hami	123	BEEVER			
BEDORTHA			Margaret	Fran	104	
Lydia A	Summ	322	BEEVY			
BEDWELL			Susanna	Shel	315	
Samuel	Unio	334	BEFORE			
BEEBE			Mary	Fair	090	
John M	Trum	327	BEGGS			
John W	Wash	348	Alvin D	Will	357	
Sally	Wyan	364	BEHR			
Temperance	Wyan	364	Mary	Clar	045	
BEECH			BEHRINGER			
James	Augl	025	Jacob	Mont	247	
William	Augl	025	BEHYMER			
			Lovina	Cler	052	

20

BEHYMER (cont)			BELL (cont)		
Margaret	Cler	050	Mary P	Trum	326
Solomon	Lick	188	Milton J	Rich	293
BEHYMEYER			Peter	Mont	240
Freeman	Cler	051	Richard W	Cuya	066
BEIGHLEY			Samuel F	Rich	294
Sidney P	VanW	337	Samuel V	Luca	197
BEIGHT			Sarah J	Morr	259
Agnes	Maho	206	Smith	Cuya	067
BEIL			Susan	Fair	091
Susan	Wash	347	William H	Dark	077
BEILHARZ			William J	Adam	006
Lewis H	Henr	152	William R	Fran	098
BEINZ			BELLER		
Philip	Merc	218	Isaiah V	Fran	100
BELDEN			BELLERY		
Austin H	Trum	330	Kath	Cuya	067
Cornelia E	Lake	178	BELLESFELD		
Henry A	Mont	236	Elisabeth	Rich	293
Lucretia	Asht	019	BELLINGER		
BELFORD			Jemima	Musk	265
James	High	155	BELLOWS		
Mary	Vint	340	Cornelius V	Athe	022
Thomas J	Fran	104	BELLUS		
BELKNAP			Anna	Medi	210
Thomas C	Jeff	169	BELRICHARD		
BELL			Nancy	Hami	136
Alexander	Cosh	061	BELSCHEN		
Annis	Cuya	076	John	Hami	139
Anthony	Putn	291	BELSHER (or BESTLEY)		
Benj F	Defi	081	Jno Thos	Mont	247
Chas L	Meig	215	BELT		
Eliza	Belm	028	Stephen E	Lick	185
Eliza Jane	Faye	094	William O	Monr	224
Eliza Jane	Lawr	182	BELTON		
Emeline M	Colu	056	Mary E	Wash	350
Ezra P	Rich	292	BELTZ		
Famer	Hami	132	Daniel	Hard	148
Fred R	Cuya	072	Lewis J	Hard	145
Geo W	Clin	054	William H	Star	317
James	Putn	289	BELVILLE		
James B	Dark	077	John Q	Lawr	180
James L	Musk	267	BEMIS		
James N	Warr	343	Mary J	Erie	086
James R	Guer	118	Shepard	Wood	360
James R	Morg	257	BEMISDERFER		
Jane	High	154	Simon P	Sene	309
John	Putn	289	BEMUS		
John	Wood	359	Lucy M	Erie	086
John H	Hami	134	BENADUM		
Joseph	Perr	278	Elizabeth	Fair	091
Levi	Nobl	269	Sarah	Fair	088
Lorenzo D	Holm	161			

BENDER

Barbara	Hanc	142
David	Rich	294
Edward	Maho	205
Elias	Dark	078
Henry	Star	318
Jackson	Sand	304
Martin J	Cuya	071
Simon	Luca	197
Valentine	Mont	252
William	Cosh	059
William	Cuya	066

BENEDICT

Charles W	Putn	289
Christian	Otta	272
Elisha N	Meig	213
Eliza	Cham	041
Henry	Dela	085
Julia A	Unio	336
Sarah	Harr	149

BENEDUM

| Mary | Tusc | 333 |

BENHAM

David M	Hanc	142
Geo	Sene	311
John	Miam	221
Melvin L	Wayn	353

BENJAMIN

| Cyrus J | Port | 283 |
| Elizabeth | Musk | 267 |

BENKER

| Elizabeth | Summ | 322 |
| Henry | Cuya | 071 |

BENN

| Joseph L | Hami | 138 |
| Mary L | Hami | 138 |

BENNEMEYER

| William B | Hami | 134 |

BENNER

| Sarah | Dark | 079 |

BENNERT

| David | Mont | 256 |
| Michaell | Mont | 256 |

BENNETT

Alonzo	Hanc	143
Cath	Ross	300
Chas	Pick	279
Chas	Pick	279
Charles H	Sand	304
Christina	Wash	350
Columbus P	Hami	138
Daniel	Mont	251

BENNETT (cont)

David A	Wyan	364
Eli W	Hami	139
Elizabeth	Pike	282
Elizabeth	Warr	344
Elmer J	Lake	178
Ethan A	Fran	099
Francis	Pike	282
Franklin	Wayn	352
George	Scio	308
George S	Knox	175
Henry P	Knox	175
Isaac D	Preb	287
James F	Otta	272
James H	VanW	337
Jennie	Wood	358
John	Hami	132
John A	Paul	273
Lewis S	Pike	281
Louisa E	Hami	128
Margaret	Guer	120
Margaret	High	156
Mary	Butl	037
Mary	Erie	088
Mary	Geau	113
Mary A	Hami	128
Nehemiah	Shel	316
Phebe	Athe	020
Ralph	Fran	102
Rebecca	Guer	117
Sarah	Lake	177
Simon C	Morr	260
Thomas S	Augl	026
Willard F	Dela	082
William, Jr	Unio	335
William H	Guer	120
William H	Medi	211

BENNINGER

| Chas | Hami | 133 |

BENNINGHOF

| John R | Ashl | 011 |

BENNINGTON

| James | Wyan | 366 |
| John C | High | 156 |

BENSE

| James | Hami | 123 |

BENSKIN

| Thomas | Luca | 199 |

BENSLEY

| Fred | Mari | 210 |

BENSON

| James W | Geau | 112 |
| Mary | Hami | 134 |

22

BENSON (cont)		
Ruth	Craw	062
William	Unio	336
William A	Hami	139
BENSTER		
Solomon	Luca	198
BENT		
Nathan	Mari	208
BENTELSPACHER		
Gotleid	Mont	251
BENTLE		
Sarah J	Ashl	013
BENTLEY		
Almon G	Cuya	075
Barbara A	Adam	006
John E	Trum	325
Margaret	Huro	164
Mary E	Huro	165
William	Athe	020
BENTON		
Albert	Trum	326
Alfred	Paul	274
Alzada	Asht	015
Carl	Meig	213
Charles	Luca	196
Julia	Lake	177
Leroy B	Pike	281
BENTZ		
Adam	Meig	214
Geo W	Medi	211
BENZING		
Fredericka	Hami	128
BEOUGHER		
William D	Hock	159
BEPPLER		
Theo	Hami	135
BERCAN		
Silas W	Sene	309
BERENS		
Otto	Mont	233
BERG		
Anna M	Hami	140
Leonard	Ross	297
DERGE		
Mary A	Wood	360
BERGER		
John	Fair	089
John	Mont	241
BERGES		
William G	Hard	146
BERGHOFER		
Adam	Mont	229

BERGIN		
John	Port	285
Walter B	Knox	176
BERGMAN		
Emil F	Mont	236
BERGMANN		
Martin	Mont	236
BERGOLD		
Carrie	Star	319
BERGSICKER		
Anna M E	Cuya	071
BERKEY		
Jacob	Star	317
BERKHEMER		
Chas	Hami	133
BERKSHIRE		
Bethel	Tusc	331
BERLEW		
Jane	Cler	048
BERLIN		
Cath	Star	317
BERNARD		
William	Guer	119
BERNER		
Anna M	Cuya	065
BERNHARD		
Henry	Erie	088
BERNHEISEL		
Jacob S	Hard	145
John W	Preb	287
BERNAY		
Leon D	Knox	174
(alias Rollin Deal)		
BERNITT		
Christian	Hami	136
BERRY		
Cath A	Rich	292
Daniel	Nobl	269
Henry	Wayn	353
Isaac	Cler	051
John C	Adam	004
Josephine	Wash	347
Martha	Wood	360
Mary	Knox	175
Michael	Musk	267
Miriam	Musk	263
William A	Mari	208
William C	Wayn	351
BERSCHIG		
Augustus	Hami	136
BERSTLE		
John H	Craw	064

BERTHOLD		
Rachel	Ross	297
BERTILSMAN		
William	Hami	123
BERTRAM		
Joseph	Hami	132
BERTSCH		
Julius	Hami	132
Matthew	Fran	099
BESSER		
William	Athe	021
BEST		
Geo B	Musk	266
Joseph	Hami	132
Sylvester	Knox	173
BESTLEY (or BELSHER)		
Jno Thos	Mont	247
BESWICK		
Sarah L	Cuya	065
BETCHEL		
Charles	Knox	174
BETHARD		
James S	Putn	290
BETHEL		
Claiborn R	Henr	153
BETTLE		
Sarah	Cler	050
BETTORF		
George	Holm	161
BETTS		
Boston	Perr	277
Frederick	Musk	262
Jonathan	Paul	274
Willis	Trum	327
BETTSCHEIDER		
Margaretha	Hami	128
BETTY		
Rachel	Carr	040
BETZ		
Frank	Hami	129
Isaac C	Fair	091
William	Jeff	169
BEVAN		
Jane	Morg	258
Sarah A	Wash	350
BEVARD		
Henry	Star	317
BEVERAGE		
Lewis H	Athe	020
Rufus M	Athe	022
BEVERIDGE		
John	Rich	295

BEVERLY		
Philanda F	Fran	099
BEVERSON		
William	Sene	311
BEVINGTON		
Jane	Miam	219
Peter A	Ashl	013
Samuel	Miam	219
BEWER		
Richard	Erie	086
BEYREISS		
Louis	Hami	137
BIAS		
Martha	Lawr	182
BIBLE		
Harrison	Alle	009
BIBLER		
Maria J	Fair	089
BICE		
Eliza	Port	285
Joseph S	Mont	228
BICKERSTAFF		
Enos	Jeff	171
BICKFORD		
Benj	Morr	260
BICKHART		
Jacob	Clin	053
BIDDINGER		
Henry W	Alle	010
BIDDISON		
Thomas	Athe	024
BIDDLE		
Dan T	Fult	105
Daniel	Star	320
Maria	Wash	350
BIDWELL		
Ada (Adalaide)	Hami	128
Adaline	Madi	203
Jane A	Clar	045
John T	Fran	099
Mary M	Alle	010
BIEDERMAN		
John	Hami	132
BIEMERT		
Geo	Hami	123
BIER		
Eliza	Brow	032
BIERCE		
Philo	Port	285
BIERLEY		
Frederick	Brow	031

BIGBEE			**BINGHAM**		
William H	Knox	174	Benj	Asht	018
BIGELOW			Julius A	Medi	211
Albert	Cuya	067	Nancy	Rich	295
Henry W	Luca	201	S Antoinette		
William G	Wayn	352		Port	285
BIGERTON			**BINGMAN**		
Sarah	Fair	089	Richard	Hami	134
BIGGER			**BINKLEY**		
Mary J	Wyan	365	Henry S	Fran	095
Thomas	Mont	232	Melanchton	Sand	303
BIGGIN			Samuel	Otta	270
Job	Trum	328	Sophia C	Alle	008
BIGGINS			William	Alle	008
John	Henr	153	**BIRAM**		
BIGGS			Amy	Meig	213
Jerusha	Wash	348	Hannah	Meig	213
John C	Lora	193	**BIRCH**		
R.	Pick	279	Chas	Paul	273
(alias R Holmes)			Eliza A	Maho	207
Samuel	Hanc	141	Pem B	Shel	315
BIGHAM			Robert	Colu	059
William	Huro	162	William	Mont	234
BIGLEY			William	Mont	255
Andrew J	Paul	274	**BIRCHER**		
BILLER			Jane	Nobl	270
Elijah	Musk	266	**BIRD**		
BILLINGS			A Johnson	Dela	085
Ann	Hami	135	Amelia	Belm	027
Lyman C	Fult	105	Chas C	Morr	261
Mary	Lake	176	James	Unio	333
BILLINGSLEY			John	Loga	189
Sarah E	Perr	277	Mary	Summ	324
BILLIS			Sparks, Jr	Ashl	013
Anna	Maho	204	**BIRDSELL**		
BILLMAN			Harriet	Butl	038
Frederick	VanW	338	**BIRDSTADT**		
Henry	VanW	338	Charles	Mont	252
Mary A	Wood	362	**BIRELY**		
BILLOW			William H	Dark	077
Geo W	Clar	046	**BIRK**		
Milton S	Miam	221	Geo W	Mont	228
BILLS			**BIRKLE**		
Almira	Star	319	Casper	Mont	235
BILLSBEY			**BIRMINGHAM**		
Charles	Mont	248	James M	Mont	234
BINET			**BIRNEY**		
Theodore	Mont	252	Nelson L	Tusc	333
BING			**BISCHOFF**		
Mary A	Medi	210	Henry	Mont	236
BINGAMON			**BISDEE**		
Allen	Clin	053	William	Mont	249

BISDORF			BLACK (cont)		
Henry	Butl	036	Bernard	Butl	036
BISHER			Clarissa	Gall	110
Jonathan	Mont	243	Dorcas	Cler	047
BISHOP			Eliza	Gree	115
Albert M	Port	284	Elizabeth	Dark	078
Alonzo T	Huro	165	Elizabeth	Luca	202
Amy A	Clin	054	Ezekiel	Morr	261
Andrew	Cuya	072	George A	Knox	174
Austin	Port	285	George W	Hard	144
Chas	Mont	232	Hetta	Vint	341
Chas M	Maho	206	James	Athe	020
Charlotte	Morr	261	James H	Guer	119
Henry A	Musk	266	James R	Lick	186
Isadore	Colu	055	John	Butl	037
Joab	Belm	031	John	Erie	088
Louisa A	Loga	192	John A	Maho	207
Martha E	Cuya	071	John H	Hard	144
Mary A	Warr	344	John W	Alle	009
Rebecca	Cler	051	Joseph	Ross	298
Sherman	Medi	212	Marietta	Luca	202
Stephen E	Summ	321	Mary	Hami	127
Susan P	Colu	058	Milton	Asht	017
William F	Hard	145	Nicholas	Dela	083
BISSELL			Ransom B	Cosh	060
Harriet	Medi	210	Robert	Hard	144
Lorenzo	Asht	016	Robert M	Carr	039
BISSENWAIER			Samuel S	Preb	288
Robert	Hami	133	Thomas S	Musk	265
BISSERT			William G	Brow	034
John	Hami	132	BLACKBURN		
BITTER			Ann E	Clar	045
Sophia	Hami	132	Eliza F	Butl	037
BITTERMAN			Geo R	Ashl	013
Christina	Summ	324	Geo W	Augl	026
John	Defi	080	Homer M	Morg	258
BITTINGER			James K	Cler	049
Jacob G	Wayn	351	Mary E	Carr	040
BITTNER			William P	Craw	063
Cath	Hami	134	BLACKEMAN		
BITZER			Mason A	Henr	152
Anthony G	Ross	296	BLACKFORD		
BIXBY			John	Miam	219
John	Erie	088	Mahala	Harr	149
Jonah E	Defi	080	BLACKMER		
Mary J	Erie	087	Jane	Clin	055
BIXLER			BLACKSTON		
Nancy	Sand	303	William	Craw	063
BIZZELL			BLACKSTONE		
William	Gree	116	John	Pike	281
BLACK			BLAIN		
Adam	VanW	339	Francis	Meig	215
Andrew H	Gree	116	Hannah	Pike	281

BLAIN (cont)		
Ruth	Madi	204
Solomon	Paul	274
William	Mont	255
BLAIR		
Alexander L	Guer	118
Andrew T	Lawr	182
Cath	Cler	047
Charles W	Madi	204
Christopher	Cler	050
David	Gall	110
Dianah	Faye	093
Emor Jane E	Luca	201
James	Butl	035
James	Butl	037
John	Clin	053
William H	Lora	195
BLAKE		
Caroline	Ross	300
Cincinnatus B		
	Gall	109
Eliza	Jeff	170
John C	Wood	359
Lizzie	Lora	193
Margaret J	Athe	020
Mary J	Unio	335
Miles L	Gall	108
Moses H	Unio	334
Nancy	Adam	007
Nancy	Gall	109
Peter	Mont	254
Sarah	Faye	093
Thomas H	Warr	343
Thomas R	Athe	023
Zachariah	Lawr	179
BLAKELEY		
Harlow	Lake	176
William H	Jeff	169
BLAKEMAN		
David S	Putn	290
BLAKESLEE		
Geo	Cuya	065
BLAKESLEY		
Chas B	Cuya	072
BLAKLEE		
Cynthia R	Cuya	069
BLALOCK		
Wesley	Cler	051
BLANCHARD		
Allen M	Mont	237
Freeman M	Asht	018
John	Lora	193
Oliver C	Medi	211

BLANCHETT		
Elizabeth	Lora	192
BLAND		
Georgia A	Fair	089
Martha	Wyan	365
Mary	Sene	312
BLANDER		
Geo	Erie	086
BLANFIELD		
Elizabeth	Tusc	331
BLANK		
William	Augl	026
BLANKENBUHLER		
Geo	Morg	257
BLANKENSHIP		
Hannah	Lawr	183
John	Jack	168
William F	Lawr	182
BLANKNER		
Margaretta	Fran	097
BLANVELT		
John W	Mont	228
BLATTEAU		
Margaret	Merc	217
BLATZ		
Agata	Huro	164
BLAZER		
Susanna	Monr	224
BLEIBLER		
Lewis	Fran	098
BLEILE		
Eliza	Fran	100
BLESSING		
Frank M	Mont	229
Lucy	Mont	232
BLISH		
Joel	Huro	164
BLISS		
Charles H	Asht	015
James H H	Vint	340
Julius E	Huro	164
Nathaniel	Dark	077
Timothy S	Wash	351
BLIZZARD		
Wesley	Fair	089
BLOCK		
Franklin	Defi	080
BLOCKFORD		
Elizabeth	Cuya	067
BLOCKINGER		
John	Wyan	366
BLODGETT		
Martin	Putn	290
Richard	Lake	178

BLOHM		
John	Hami	132
BLOND		
Lafayette L	Merc	217
BLOOD		
Sarah L	Summ	324
BLOOM		
Jacob	Alle	008
James L	Wood	361
John H	Preb	286
Lydia	Will	355
Samuel L	Defi	082
BLOOMER		
Albert S	Fult	107
Eliza	Faye	094
Robert A	Huro	165
BLOONFIELD		
Susan	Preb	287
BLOOR		
Mahalah E	Rich	294
BLOSER		
Samuel P	Rich	293
BLOSSER		
Frederick	Hock	157
John	Defi	081
Samuel	Sand	301
William H	Perr	277
BLOTNER		
Jno	Dark	079
BLOUGHT		
Henry	Meig	213
BLOWERS		
Cath	Lawr	180
Chas M	Monr	226
John L	Erie	088
Mary	Lawr	183
Samuel S	Craw	062
BLUE		
Abraham	Monr	223
Eve	Knox	172
Margaret	Cham	042
Reuben R	Shel	316
BLUNDELL		
Jos M	Hami	134
BLUNT		
Hannah	Musk	262
Thomas W	Lick	188
BLUSH		
Clarissa E	Cuya	065
BLY		
Nancy	Dark	078
BLYSTON		
David	Knox	173

BLYTHE		
John	Craw	063
BOADARMA		
Susannah	Huro	164
BOALS		
John F	Harr	149
BOARDEN		
Sarah	Perr	275
BOARDMAN		
Robert	Mont	245
BOATMAN		
Barney	Gall	110
Isaac W	Butl	039
BOBB		
Mary	High	156
BOBBITT		
Mildred	Clin	053
Nathan	Ross	297
BOBENMYER		
Sarah	Paul	273
BOBO		
Mary	Vint	341
Prince B	Athe	020
BOCKEY		
Franklin	Otta	271
BOCKLET		
Conrad	Mont	255
BOCKMAN		
Nicholas	Butl	038
BODEMAN		
Christian	Mont	252
BODENSCHATZ		
Chris'r	Mont	251
BODLE		
Elizabeth	Lick	188
BODY		
John	Knox	173
BOEHM		
Eva	Cuya	071
Henry	Mont	247
BOEHME		
Franz	Mont	229
BOERNER		
Martin	Fran	098
BOERSTLER		
Eliza	Fair	091
BOESCH		
Jacob	Cuya	065
BOETCHER		
George H	Guer	117
BOETTICHER		
Charles	Monr	224

BOGAN				BOISE		
Eliza	Clin	052		William	Colu	059
John A	Craw	064		BOISOL		
Sarah E	Clin	052		Elizabeth S	Jeff	170
BOGART				BOKER		
Isaac	Putn	289		James	Musk	262
Jesse W	Defi	080		Joseph	Hami	123
BOGER				Reason	Jeff	171
Magdalena	Shel	315		BOLAND		
BOGGS				Bridget	Hami	128
Elizabeth	Jack	168		Susan M	Fran	101
Elizabeth	Musk	266		BOLANDER		
Geo W	Otta	270		John E	Hard	146
Isabell	Morr	260		William	Hanc	141
James M	Defi	079		BOLEN		
Jane	Otta	271		Ann	Athe	021
John	Gall	110		Ann	Athe	022
Mary	Loga	190		Maria	Belm	028
BOGMYRE				Martha M	Wood	361
Henry	Hami	133		Rachel	Gree	115
BOGUE				BOLENBAUGH		
Rachel	High	154		Abram	Hard	146
BOHAM				David D	Fran	099
Burr	VanW	338		BOLES		
Mary C	Dela	082		James	Mont	251
BOHART				BOLGER		
Margaret	Hanc	143		Maurice J	Mont	242
BOHEIM				BOLL		
Henry	Hami	138		Gerhard	Mont	251
BOHEN				BOLLING		
John	Jack	167		Margaret	Hami	128
BOHLEN				BOLLINGER		
Samuel	Monr	225		Anthony	Musk	267
BOHLENDER				Jacob	Dela	083
Christene	Hami	128		Jos	Cham	042
BOHLER				BOLLMAN		
Peter	Sand	303		Elanor	Hanc	140
BOHLMAN				Samuel	Rich	293
Elizabeth	Hami	134		BOLMER		
BOHM				Rebecca M	Dela	082
Edward H	Cuya	071		BOLON		
BOHN				John C	Belm	027
John	Mont	239		BOLSBY		
Margaretta	Hami	127		Martha	Shel	315
BOHNER				BOLSTER		
John	Will	357		William	Athe	020
BOHRER				BOLT		
Appollonia	Cuya	065		Simon M	Wayn	351
BOICE				BOLTON		
Lemuel	Meig	213		Herman	Erie	088
Melvin	Gall	109		Sophronia	Meig	216
BOILEAN				BOLTZ		
Joseph	Athe	023		Geo	Tusc	332

BOLYARD		
Chas	Wyan	365
BOMAN		
James H	Fran	099
Jno C	Mont	233
BOMBERGER		
Cath	Mont	231
BONAKER		
Joseph F	Preb	286
BONBRIGHT		
Daniel	Mont	239
BONCHER		
Cath	Ross	296
BOND		
Emeline	Guer	119
George	Cler	050
Jesse M	Scio	306
Mary	Cham	041
Silas	Merc	216
Susan	Geau	111
William	Miam	220
BONDFOOT		
John	Wood	359
BONE		
Alfred E	Harr	149
Doctor H	Lawr	183
Elias L	Warr	342
Oscar T	Warr	343
Pinkney	Jeff	170
William H	Warr	343
BONEBRIGHT		
John	Ashl	011
BONER		
John	Belm	027
Phila A	Rich	295
BONESTEEL		
Levi	Cuya	066
BONEWELL		
Benj A	Port	285
BONHAM		
Hannah	Unio	335
Isaac	Hanc	141
Robert	Hanc	141
BONHOTAL		
James A	Maho	207
BONIFACINE		
Schiessele	Mont	230
BONNELL		
Christian	Sene	311
Daniel V	Butl	037
John F	Guer	118
Moses	Sene	310
William T	Mont	237

BONNER		
Anna M	Hami	128
Patrick	Port	284
William	Hami	135
BONNETT		
William H	Unio	334
BONNEY		
James W	Huro	164
William	Henr	153
BONOUN		
William	Monr	223
BONSEL		
Geo W	Wyan	367
BOODS		
George	Hard	146
BOOKER		
Daniel D	Morr	261
BOOKERT		
John A	Ashl	011
BOOKHEIMER		
Jacob	Mont	245
BOOKS		
Samuel H	Ross	298
BOOMER		
Jeremiah M	Geau	111
BOON		
Cath	Will	356
John	Brow	031
BOONE		
Henry H	Adam	006
Margaret	Adam	003
William	Hami	123
BOOR		
William H	Harr	148
BOORE		
William	Mont	233
BOORY		
Alpheus	Star	320
BOOSE		
John	Butl	036
BOOTH		
John	High	157
John T	Hami	140
Maria	Lick	186
Mary M	Sand	301
BOOTON		
Ira W	Gall	109
BOOTS		
James M	Will	356
BOPE		
Conrad	Wyan	364
Jacob A	Gree	113
James A	Hanc	141

BORDEAUX			BOSTATER (cont)		
Ara	Luca	201	Geo	Will	357
BORDEN			Jacob G	Will	356
Edwin	Preb	286	BOSTER		
BORDNER			Francis M	Gall	110
Hiram	Wood	358	BOSTIC		
BOREN			John M	Gall	108
Hannah S	Scio	305	BOSTION		
Robert W	Scio	305	Philip	Dela	085
BORER			BOSTON		
Peter	Rich	295	Evaline	Guer	118
Stephen	Sene	314	James P	Wyan	366
BORGMAN			Samuel	Mont	252
John B	Hami	133	BOSTWICK		
BORING			Ann M	Pick	279
George W	Guer	117	Geo F	Morr	261
BORLAND			Mary	Hard	146
William R	Madi	204	Newton H	Geau	111
BORLEIN			William E	Lick	187
Maria T	Huro	164	BOSWELL		
BORMUTH			Albert	Warr	343
Adam	Sene	313	Albert T	Brow	031
BORN			Mary	Wash	346
Esther	Tusc	332	BOSWORTH		
John U	Hard	146	Fenner	Cuya	076
Samuel F	Shel	315	BOTKIN		
William G	Hard	146	Sarah	Augl	025
BOROFF			BOTSFORD		
John	Merc	217	Horace	Mont	241
BORONAY			Lucy A	Gree	116
William	Star	318	BOTTLES		
BORROR			Geo W	Belm	030
Absolom	Fran	104	BOTTORFF		
BORTEL			David	Miam	219
Allen	Wood	364	BOTTS		
Levi	Wood	359	Cath	Clin	054
BORTLI			Elizabeth	Hami	128
Henry C	Wood	359	Shim	Cler	048
BORTON			BOUCHER		
Bethuel	Guer	117	Benj	Ross	296
Martha	Scio	304	Chauncey A	Will	355
BORTZ			BOUDINOT		
Jacob	Miam	221	John	Knox	175
Jonas	Miam	221	BOUGHAN		
BOSCH			James M	Faye	094
Edward	Mont	230	BOUGHNER		
BOSS			John M	Monr	223
Frederick J	Hami	134	Mary B	Mont	232
BOST			BOUGHTON		
Abraham	Henr	153	Elon G	Huro	165
Samuel	Henr	153	Harriet	Huro	163
BOSTATER			BOULBY		
Abram	Defi	081	Salamis	Hanc	143

BOULDEN			BOWERFIELD		
John A	Cuya	071	John	Mont	255
BOULWARE			BOWERMAN		
Leonidas	Cler	051	Rebecca	Sene	312
BOUNEY			BOWERMASTER		
Harvey	Lora	196	Geo W	Gree	113
BOURE			Samuel A	Gree	113
William H	Wyan	366	BOWERS		
BOURELL			Alex C	Fran	104
Geo	Merc	217	Cath	Musk	265
BOUSMAN			Eliza	Wayn	354
Samuel A	Mont	233	Eliza J	Paul	274
BOVERY			Geo	Pick	280
Valentine	Hami	136	Geo F	Mont	237
BOWDEN			Jacob A	Wash	348
Edward	Mont	255	James F	Clin	055
BOWE			Jefferson	Mont	239
Jerusha H	Port	284	John	Huro	162
BOWEN			John	Huro	162
Anson T	Huro	165	John	Tusc	331
Barbara	Ross	300	Jno W	Wash	347
Bednego	Meig	214	Josiah	VanW	336
Chas H	Fran	096	Lucinda	Pike	282
Chas R	Luca	201	Mary	Cham	041
Cyrus	VanW	338	Mary	Musk	265
Daniel	Mont	249	Mary Ann	Jeff	170
Frank	Dela	085	Michael	Mont	239
John W	Fran	095	Pierce	Mont	243
Lavina	Henr	152	(alias Pierce Powers)		
Mary	Trum	327	Samuel	Alle	009
Rachel	Vint	341	Samuel	Luca	201
Solomon	Luca	197	Valentine	Wash	346
William	Wyan	364	Watson W	Asht	016
BOWENS			BOWERSOCK		
William	Luca	201	Ann C	Hami	128
BOWER			BOWERSOX		
Cassandra	Maho	206	David B	Sene	314
Cordelia	Geau	112	BOWERY		
Elijah	Maho	206	Robert	Monr	224
Emanuel W	Merc	218	BOWIE		
Jacob	Fran	095	Benson	Unio	335
Jacob	Wash	351	BOWKER		
James M	Guer	118	Amanda	Warr	343
John	Mont	249	Emily E	Defi	081
Josiah A	Nobl	268	BOWLBY		
Leonard	Fran	099	Eliza	Hock	158
Linfred	Lick	187	Louisa A	Hami	139
Margaret	Star	319	BOWLER		
Reuben T	Hard	144	Dickerson	Wood	360
Sarah J	Wyan	365	BOWLES		
Thomas C	Belm	029	David	Miam	220
William D	Sand	303	Euritta	Meig	215

BOWLES (cont)			BOYD (cont)		
Jacob	Lawr	180	James T	Sene	310
John	Scio	307	John	Hami	132
John H	Pike	282	John, Jr.	Ashl	011
BOWLIN			Julia Ann	Port	285
Isabella	Star	319	Martha A	Pick	279
BOWLING			Narcissa G	Ashl	011
Elizabeth Jane			William	Belm	031
	Fair	089	BOYDSTUN		
George W	Harr	150	Orah	Scio	306
Nicholas	Pick	278	BOYER		
BOWMAN			Jacob	Mari	209
Aaron	Colu	057	John H	Musk	264
Alexander	Lake	178	Levi	Guer	118
Alfred	Medi	212	Rebecca	Sene	309
Amelia	Colu	058	Sarah	Ashl	011
Benj F	Hard	146	Solomon	Morr	260
Cath	Star	317	Susannah	Tusc	332
Chas	Alle	009	William	VanW	337
Christian	Wash	345	BOYHAM		
Eli	Star	319	Andrew	Mont	247
Elizabeth	Perr	276	BOYINGTON		
Ephraim	Adam	003	Robert J	Morr	261
Frederick	Mont	243	BOYLE		
Geo R	Mont	244	John	Mont	235
John	Mont	235	Thomas	Mont	247
Lewis	Lick	184	Thomas	Wyan	366
Margaret	Meig	213	William	Brow	032
Martin	Putn	289	BOYLES		
Samuel C	Miam	220	James M	Adam	007
William	Trum	327	BOYNS		
BOWMASTER			Sarah	Unio	335
Frank	Gall	109	BOYNTON		
BOWN			Charles	Scio	305
Rachel	Cosh	061	BOZMAN		
BOWSER			James	Perr	278
Henry W	Fran	103	Maria	Morg	257
BOWSHER			BRABHAM		
Nancy	Alle	010	Jno W	Wash	348
BOXWELL			Mary J	Mont	230
Joseph N	Putn	289	Stanton L	Wash	347
BOY			BRABSON		
Christina	Luca	201	Susanna	Loga	190
BOYCE			BRACE		
Albert	Hard	147	Mary	Cler	048
Andrew J	Colu	056	BRACKEN		
James C	Medi	211	Cath	Fult	104
Theodore	Miam	221	Clarissa H	Trum	327
BOYD			BRACKETT		
Andrew	Mont	252	Frank J	Lick	184
Elizabeth	Summ	324	BRADBURY		
Farnata	Hami	127	Hamer	Hami	134
James H	Meig	215			

BRADDISH			BRADY (cont)		
Henry	Cuya	071	John	Mont	236
BRADDOCK			Oliver	Star	318
Sarah J	Wash	349	Thomas	Cuya	074
BRADEN			BRAGDON		
Walter	Mont	233	Laura	Cler	049
BRADFIELD			Leonard H	Luca	197
Eliza J	Meig	216	BRAGG		
Jos K	Morr	261	Joseph	Warr	344
BRADFORD			William	Lawr	179
Almon	Clar	044	BRAHAM		
Andrew	Meig	216	James	Mont	242
Edwin W	Clar	046	BRAINARD		
Elijah	Adam	003	Frank E	Summ	323
Ellen H	Adam	005	Mrs Frank E	Summ	323
James	Mont	237	Hannah	Asht	017
James G	Hami	136	BRAINERD		
John	Gree	113	Hezekiah	Geau	112
Miranda	Putn	291	John A	Cuya	071
Rebecca	Rich	294	BRAKE		
Sarah J	Loga	190	Geo	Asht	015
Stephen R	Adam	006	Geo	Monr	224
William	Brow	031	James H	Asht	015
BRADLEY			Mehitable	Asht	015
Ann	Ross	299	Nellie	Asht	014
Edwin D	Will	357	Oliver R	Fran	099
Emily	Erie	088	BRAKEMAN		
Francis P	Maho	206	Ann	Lake	176
Geo	Rich	292	Francis P	Will	356
Isaac S	Mont	231	Mary A	Lake	177
James W	Adam	005	BRALEY		
Louisa	Cuya	066	Joshua	Mont	244
Patterson	Putn	289	Mary A	Gree	114
Polly	Lick	186	Thomas	Meig	213
Thomas J	Meig	214	BRALT		
Thomas T	Hami	138	Angus	Colu	056
William W	Hami	138	BRALTON		
BRADRICK			William J	Belm	028
Thomas H	Ross	297	BRAMAN		
BRADSHAW			Benj	Fair	090
Cath	Tusc	331	Patrick	Mont	240
Elisha	Meig	214	Ranson E	Lora	193
Francis M	Perr	274	BRAMHALL		
Hannah	Scio	308	Edward R	Nobl	270
Mary	Perr	274	BRAMMER		
Patrick	Perr	278	Francis	Lawr	182
BRADT			William	Brow	035
John R	Mont	239	BRANAM		
BRADY			Wesley	VanW	338
Abraham C	Mari	209	BRANCH		
Eliza	Butl	038	Martha	Hami	128
Geo F	Huro	165	Phila	Huro	164
John	Mont	233	Sophia	Cuya	069

BRANDBERRY			BRATTON (cont)		
John H	Athe	021	Hannah	Will	356
BRANDENBURG			John T	Mont	243
Geo	Butl	038	Mary	Hard	144
BRANDHOEST			BRAUN		
Sophia	Hami	127	Louisa	Hami	128
BRANDHORST			BRAY		
Frederick	Hami	134	James W	Loga	189
BRANDON			Nancy	Vint	340
Iven	Belm	028	BRAYTON		
James D	Cuya	066	Christiana	Otta	271
John	Otta	270	Rufus M	Hard	148
Richard W	Miam	221	BRAZELL		
Samuel H	Miam	221	Michael	Hami	132
Sanford	Dark	079	BREACH		
Sophia	Summ	321	James S	Wash	345
BRANDS			BRECKENRIDGE		
William	Nobl	269	Emily	Hami	128
BRANDT			Geo A	Morr	261
David	Augl	024	BRECOUNT		
Lydia A	Tusc	331	Solomon G	Cham	042
Maria C	Hami	128	BREDINGER		
Philip	Mont	227	Peter, Jr	Hami	136
BRANHAM			BREDWELL		
James H	Mont	236	Laura F	Cler	048
BRANNAN			BREEDLOVE		
Jos	Clar	045	Thomas H	Cham	043
BRANNGART			BREER		
Geo	Gree	114	Henry	Mont	256
BRANNINGER			BREESE		
William	Mont	235	Eliza	Paul	273
BRANNON			Osa	Butl	038
Christiann	Star	319	BREIDENBACH		
Elenor	Cuya	071	Chas	Cuya	074
Lorenzo Dow	Scio	308	BRELSFORD		
Mary Ann	Unio	334	Horace	Shel	315
BRANSCOM			BREMMER		
Tabitha	Jack	168	Anthony	Mont	242
BRANSLEY			BRENBERGER		
Theodore S	Mont	236	Henry	Dark	078
BRANSON			BRENDELL		
Elizabeth	Adam	007	Michael	Augl	025
BRANT			BRENDLE		
John	Wayn	352	Geo	Sene	313
John	Wyan	367	BRENIZER		
Jos	Ross	298	Geo	Wayn	353
Nancy A	Clar	047	William	Morr	260
BRANTZ			BRENNAN		
Joseph	Mont	243	Hannah	Fran	101
BRASHEAR			Luke	Hami	132
Hannah	Guer	120	Michael	Gree	115
BRATTON			Sarah	Harr	149
Eliza	Brow	035	Thomas	Summ	322

BRENNEIS		
John	Cuya	071
BRENNEMAN		
William	Colu	055
BRENNER		
Matilda	Mont	227
BRENNIES		
Geo	Cuya	071
BRENSTIEHL		
Chas	Adam	006
BRENT		
Charles	Mont	238
Edward V	Knox	174
Flora D	Fran	101
BRENTHINGER		
George	Knox	175
BRENTLINGER		
Harriet	Alle	009
BRENZEL		
George H	Mont	247
BRESH		
Delilah	Sene	313
BRESLER		
Hester	Fair	091
BRESSALARE		
Vincent	Hami	135
BRESSIN		
Celestine	Mont	229
BRETSFORD		
David M	Fran	099
John H	Fran	099
BRETT		
Thomas	Cuya	072
BRETZ		
Amos W	Sene	308
Regina	Erie	087
BREUNLING		
Andrew	Mont	233
BREWER		
Abram T	Cuya	067
Amos P	Hock	159
James	Putn	289
Lavinia	High	156
Mary	Morr	259
Thomas J	Faye	093
William F	Athe	023
BREWSTER		
Chas F	Cuya	072
Ira	Meig	216
Lewis E	Luca	201
Oscar	Summ	323
BREYFOGLE		
Mary	Dela	083

BREYFOGLE (cont)		
Wesley	Athe	022
BREYMAN		
Mallon	Sene	312
William H	Hanc	143
BREZETT		
George	Tusc	330
BRIAN		
Sophia	Hock	157
BRIANT		
Geo W	Cosh	061
BRIARMANN		
John	Star	319
BRICE		
Simmons	Monr	225
BRICELY		
Albert	Hard	146
BRICK		
Margaret	Cuya	073
Samuel W	Merc	217
BRICKEN		
Henry	Erie	083
BRICKER		
Benj	Meig	216
George W	Lick	188
Hiram	Lick	188
Jacob	Cham	042
Stephen	Guer	118
Susan	Rich	294
Susannah	Cuya	065
BRICKETT		
Esther K	Hami	134
BRIDEGROOM		
Christ'n F	Monr	224
BRIDENBAUGH		
Sarah	Hanc	142
BRIDGE		
Eramus	Warr	342
John	Brow	032
BRIDGEFORD		
Eliza J	Butl	038
James M	Butl	038
BRIDGES		
Amanda	Hami	128
Eliza	Hami	139
BRIDWELL		
Matilda A	Tusc	332
BRIEN		
Hannah O	Luca	198
BRIERLY		
Jane	Meig	215
BRIGDEN		
Charles A	Trum	327

BRIGEL			BRISTER (cont)		
Otto	Hami	139	Isaac	Maho	207
BRIGGAMAN			John J	Lora	194
Caroline	Fran	100	BRISTOL		
BRIGGS			Geo H	Fran	096
Abner	Clin	053	BRITIGAN		
Benj B	Guer	119	Albert	Merc	217
Newton H	Huro	163	BRITT		
Samuel B	Cham	042	Elizabeth	Hami	134
Sarah M	Huro	163	BRITTINGHAM		
BRIGHT			Cath	Madi	203
Austin H	Trum	325	James H	Adam	007
Josiah	Henr	151	BRITTON		
Mary J	Mont	233	Eda	Nobl	268
BRILL			John	Mont	251
Chas	Rich	294	Martha J	High	157
Elizabeth	Guer	120	Mary E	Wash	349
George W	Nobl	269	William	Mont	228
BRILLHART			BROA		
William R	Knox	174	William	Cuya	075
BRILLMAN			BROADRICK		
John	Luca	201	Isaac	Morg	256
BRINDLEY			BROADRUP		
Philip	Jeff	170	Abigail	Mont	230
BRINER			BROADWELL		
Eliza	Pick	279	William	Lora	193
BRINGMAN			BROBECK		
William H	Butl	039	George	Putn	290
BRINK			John H	Colu	056
Cath	Rich	295	BROBST		
Gilbert W	Fran	103	Franklin S	Sene	310
Herman	Hami	133	BROCEUS		
John W	Fran	099	Simon	Perr	278
BRINKER			BROCH		
John	Mari	208	William	Cler	051
Simon P	Defi	081	BROCHES		
BRINKERHOFF			Samuel	Hard	144
Eliza	Fran	104	BROCK		
Sarah	Sand	304	Elizabeth L	Madi	204
BRINKMAN			Henry	Cuya	072
Bernardine	Hami	134	John W M	Monr	226
BRINN			Margaret	Dark	078
Cornelius	Mont	243	Thomas	Scio	308
BRINNON			William	Knox	174
Eliza	Cham	041	William P	Dark	076
BRINTON			BROCKETT		
Joseph	Ashl	011	George D	Trum	326
BRION			Roxanna	Cuya	071
Norman	Wood	362	BROCKHAUS		
BRISBIN			Elizabeth	Hami	127
Eugene	Wood	364	BROCKWAY		
BRISTER			Darwin G	Trum	326
Elizabeth Ann			Franklin M	Lake	178
	Cosh	060			

BRODEN			BROOKS (cont)		
William H	Guer	120	Norman	Athe	022
BRODERICK			Phebe	Jack	168
John	Mont	236	Samuel	Fair	090
Patrick	Mont	233	Samuel E	Cuya	075
BRODNIX			Spencer	Pick	278
James B	Paul	274	William	Adam	006
BROKAN			William, Jr	Morg	258
Sarah	Harr	150	William C	Athe	024
BROKAW			Zebedee	Athe	023
Geo	Belm	029	BROOM		
Henry	Rich	291	Judson W	Guer	120
BROLLIER			BROOMHALL		
Sarah A	Rich	291	John C	Brow	033
BRONKAR			BROOS		
Sarah	Musk	266	Joseph	Mont	238
BRONKE			BRORON		
August	Hami	134	Martha E	Ross	296
BRONSON			BROSIUS		
John B	Luca	201	Harper	Summ	321
Rebecca L E	Hard	145	BROTHERS		
BROOKE			Andrew	Colu	059
Benj F	Belm	030	Austin	Gall	109
BROOKER			Austin	Star	320
Jacob	Mont	234	Edward	Mont	251
Jacob	Scio	307	John	Gall	109
BROOKEY			John	Gall	110
Geo	Mont	228	Joseph	Lick	186
BROOKINS			BROUGH		
Christena	Mont	227	Abigail W	Wash	350
Hannah S	Jack	167	BROUKAR		
Soronos T	Lake	176	Jerome	Musk	266
BROOKOVER			BROUNE		
Alice	Lick	185	Lydia	Monr	224
Geo W	Brow	031	BROUSE		
BROOKS			Harvey	Lora	195
Albert E	Cuya	066	John	Cuya	071
Daniel	Butl	038	BROWDER		
Daniel N	Mont	246	Thomas F	High	154
Delilah	Athe	024	BROWER		
Edwin H	Fran	103	Albert	Preb	288
Elizabeth	Hanc	143	Celena	Putn	290
Emerson P	Meig	213	Elizabeth	Preb	286
Geo W	Fran	098	BROWN		
Giles	Monr	223	Abraham	Hanc	140
James C	Tusc	333	Abram	Fran	098
John	Nobl	269	Adnah	Wash	347
John J	Scio	305	Albert A	Butl	036
Lydia A	Athe	024	Alexis	Hami	139
Martha	Harr	150	Alfred	Lawr	179
Martha A	Morg	258	Alonzo R	Cler	048
Martha W	Musk	265	Altha	Fran	104
Nelson	Musk	266	Amos	Unio	334

BROWN (cont)				BROWN (cont)		
Amos	Wood	358		Henry	Cuya	071
Ann	Musk	264		Henry	Huro	165
Ann A	Asht	019		Henry	Mont	237
Ann L	Lora	196		Henry	Mont	240
Anna M	Loga	191		Ira J	Paul	274
Benj	Gree	115		Isaac	Lora	195
Benj S	Perr	275		Isaac	Ross	298
Bernard	Perr	275		Isaac N	Wood	364
Biglow W	Faye	094		Jacob	Cuya	071
Caroline F	Clar	045		James	Gree	116
Caroline M	Hami	128		James	Maho	207
Cath	Huro	165		James	Summ	321
Chas	Cuya	072		James C	Warr	342
Chas E	Hami	133		James H	Asht	016
Christiana	Asht	016		James M	Lick	186
Clifton	Madi	204		James M	Wood	362
Clinton	Preb	287		James P	Pike	281
Courtland	Cler	048		James S	Colu	058
Cyrus J	Hanc	143		James W	High	155
Daniel N	Nobl	268		James W	Monr	223
David	Craw	062		Jane	Guer	117
David J	Pike	281		Jane	Luca	197
David M	Belm	031		Jane G	Fran	097
David N	Wood	359		Joel P	Guer	118
Deliverance	Paul	274		John	Faye	093
Edgar C	Meig	215		John	Hami	132
Edmond A	Monr	224		John	Huro	165
Edwin A	Athe	022		John	Lick	184
Edwin F	Mont	229		John	Luca	198
Edwin H	Huro	161		John	Mont	241
Elijah J	Paul	274		John	Mont	247
Eliza	Butl	039		John	Tusc	331
Elizabeth	Loga	190		John C	Jeff	172
Elizabeth	Musk	264		John H	Mont	227
Elizabeth A	Guer	118		Joseph	Defi	080
Elizabeth J	Pike	282		Joseph	Musk	262
Elizabeth R	Trum	329		Joseph N	Ashl	011
Emeline	Morr	260		Joseph W	Monr	226
Emeline M	Monr	224		Joshua	Hanc	143
Erbin	Putn	289		Josiah A	Warr	343
Ezra	Summ	323		Josiah L	Sene	312
Frederick	Hami	134		Julia A	Fran	097
Frederick G	Lora	195		Justin F	Henr	152
Geo	Wyan	364		Laura M	Morr	260
Geo N	High	154		Lewellyn G	Cham	042
Geo W	Hanc	143		Lillis C	Wayn	354
Geo W	Luca	197		Louis A	Luca	196
Geo W	Star	316		Lucinda	Meig	216
Hannah	Shel	316		Lucinda	Warr	344
Hannah	Wyan	364		Lucius	Morg	258
Harriet N	Luca	196		Margaret J	Ross	299
Henrietta P	Ross	300		Margaret M	Cler	050

BROWN (cont)			BROWN (cont)		
Martin L	Miam	218	Thomas B	Hard	146
Mary	Cosh	061	Thomas J	Hock	158
Mary	Pick	280	Thomas J	Musk	266
Mary	Unio	336	Ursula	Luca	198
Mary A	Brow	034	Wesley	Pike	281
Mary A	Ross	297	William	Cuya	066
Mary A	Wash	349	William	Mont	237
Mary G	Trum	327	William	Wood	360
Mary Jane	Hard	146	William A	Mont	237
Mary S	Defi	081	William B	Mont	240
Matilda	Harr	149	William F	Dela	083
Matilda W	Nobl	270	William H	Belm	031
Maurice D	Hami	123	William H	Cler	048
Milton	Warr	343	William H	Hanc	140
Nancy	Gree	116	William H	Rich	293
Nancy	High	155	William H	Rich	295
Nancy	Mont	232	William I	Colu	057
Nancy	Morg	259	Wilson	Unio	334
Nancy	Preb	288	Wilson W	Wood	362
Nelson	Asht	019	BROWNELL		
Nicholas	Lick	188	David	Mont	251
Norman	Warr	343	David S	Faye	095
Norman K	VanW	338	Oscar E	Summ	322
Olcott K	Wyan	366	BROWNELLER		
Oliver M	Lora	195	Geo	Wood	358
Peter	Ross	296	BROWNER		
Philip	Jack	167	Charlotte	Jeff	172
Quincy A	Cler	048	BROWNING		
Richard	Musk	264	Edwin P	Wash	345
Richard J	Alle	010	Jeremiah	Mari	209
Robert B	Musk	267	Samantha	Meig	215
Robert C	Rich	292	William J	Unio	334
Robert H	Guer	120	BROWNMILLER		
Samuel	Tusc	332	Joseph	Dela	083
Samuel	Wayn	353	BROYLES		
Samuel E	Henr	153	Henry	Gall	110
Samuel G	Clar	045	John W	Fair	089
Samuel W	Nobl	268	BRUBAKER		
Sarah	Carr	039	David	Rich	292
Sarah	Clin	052	John	Belm	028
Sarah	Cuya	073	William	Will	356
Sarah	Hock	159	BRUCE		
Sarah	Preb	287	Andrew A	Adam	008
Sarah	Wayn	352	Cath	Monr	225
Sarah E	Adam	006	Charles	Loga	191
Sarah E	Clar	045	Jane B	Faye	095
Seymour	Asht	016	Jeremiah	Lawr	180
Silas S	Erie	086	Lewis L	Loga	192
Susannah	Belm	030	Perry G P	Scio	307
Thomas	Guer	120	Robert	Wash	348
Thomas	Hanc	142	William	Loga	191
Thomas	Jeff	172	BRUCHER		
			Sarah	Cuya	066

BRUCK		
Conrad	Butl	036
BRUEN		
Augusta	Mont	231
Mary	Butl	035
BRUETHABER		
Charles B A	Luca	201
BRUGGEMAN		
Anna M	Augl	025
BRUGGERMAN		
Herman	Hami	137
BRUMBAUGH		
Daniel W	Medi	211
William G	Rich	293
BRUMBY		
John H	Ashl	014
BRUMFIELD		
Rufus B	Lawr	180
Sloan	Lawr	182
BRUMM		
Charles	Hard	146
BRUMMER		
Joseph	Mont	243
BRUNER		
Charlotte	Hami	136
BRUNING		
Fred W	Butl	036
Harriet	Paul	272
BRUNNER		
Frederick	Hami	133
John	Fair	089
BRUNNI		
Rejina	Wyan	366
BRUNT		
Cally	Pike	282
BRUSH		
Israel	Brow	033
James H	Merc	217
(alias Jesse L. Judd)		
Mary A	Cler	049
William	Mont	251
BRUSMAN		
John H	Hami	123
BRUST		
Josephine	Shel	315
BRYAN		
Beal H	Tusc	333
Calista G	Lick	184
Delila	Adam	003
Harriet	Cuya	067
John	Adam	003
John W	Unio	335
Luke	Cham	043

BRYAN (cont)		
Martha W	Meig	213
Ruth A	Monr	225
William	Fran	095
William	Luca	197
William B	Cosh	060
BRYANT		
Ann M	Wyan	364
Caleb L	Rich	291
Eliza J	Mont	231
Isaac Z	Wyan	365
Isabell M	Hanc	142
Mary	Cler	050
Nancy	Miam	222
Oscar F	Ashl	011
Thomas W	Ross	296
BRYNDS		
James P	Paul	273
BUCEY		
Hiram	Jeff	170
BUCHAN		
John	Ashl	011
BUCHANAN		
Anne	Guer	120
Asenath A	Hami	139
Christinus	Perr	276
Elijah	Ross	296
Elizabeth	Harr	150
James	Mont	243
James	Ross	299
Nathan	Hock	159
Rachel	Athe	024
Sampson A	Hami	139
Samuel E	Hami	133
Sarah	Dark	079
William	Mont	236
William H	Carr	040
BUCHANNAN		
Rachel	Dark	078
BUCHER		
Solomon J	Summ	321
BUCHLER		
Adam	Ross	301
BUCHUEE		
Geo H	Butl	037
BUCK		
Alfred H	Hock	159
Alphonzo	Asht	018
Emmons	Cuya	072
Martin	High	155
Mary	Jack	166
Priscilla M	Star	316
William C	Wash	348

BUCKALOO			BUEHLER		
Israel	Musk	263	Christian	Wayn	351
BUCKHANAN			BUEL		
Lucretia	Nobl	268	Frederick	Carr	040
BUCKHART			Henry	Carr	040
John	Mont	235	BUELL		
BUCKINGHAM			Chas L	Asht	014
Cath	Jeff	170	Geo W	Alle	009
Chancy	Fran	095	Grandley O	Fran	102
Harvy	Dark	078	Henry M	Geau	112
William D	Hock	159	BUEREN		
BUCKLER			Henry	Hami	134
Nathan	Cosh	060	BUESA		
BUCKLES			Conrad	Mont	237
Daniel B	Gree	114	BUFF		
Sarah	Cham	042	William	Athe	022
Thomas B	Cham	041	BUFFINGTON		
BUCKLEW			Elizabeth	Athe	020
Benj F	Holm	160	John O	Tusc	333
BUCKLEY			BUGBEE		
Aaron	Ashl	013	John D	Asht	017
Alonzo	Mont	237	BUGH		
Bridget	Hami	134	Matilda	Perr	278
Cynthia A	Madi	203	BUHL		
Daniel	High	154	David	Carr	040
John	Cuya	066	BUHR		
John	Mont	240	Frederick	Augl	025
Michael	Mont	247	BUHRER		
Rebecca	Port	285	Andrew	Fult	105
Thomas E	Rich	295	BUISCHLEN		
William	Mont	251	Christian	Star	318
William N	Wayn	352	BUKEY		
BUCKLIN			William	Dark	079
Benj F	Summ	323	BULFINCH		
BUCKMASTER			Elizabeth H	Asht	017
Richard W	Morr	261	BULGER		
Sarah A	Defi	079	James	Shel	315
William	Putn	290	John B	Belm	027
BUCKNER			Sarah	Belm	027
Robert	Mont	228	BULGERS		
BUCKNEY			John	Mont	239
David C	Luca	199	BULL		
BUCKS			Caroline	Cler	048
Magdalena	Colu	058	Louisa	Fran	097
BUCKSENSHULTZ			BULLARD		
Cath	Musk	265	Lorenzo D	Cuya	071
BUCKWALTER			BULLOCK		
Isaac E	Cuya	071	Nelson	Mont	244
BUDD			BUMCROTS		
James	Ashl	013	John M	Perr	277
John	Rich	293	BUMP		
Mahala	Ashl	012	Louis	Hami	139

BUMPUS				BURCHAM		
Alexander	Knox	174		Henry	Port	284
James I	Will	357		BURCHARD		
BUNCE				Fred	Paul	272
Chas H	Otta	271		William	Lawr	181
Chester	Medi	211		BURCHFIELD		
Mary	Gall	107		Martin M	Tusc	330
BUNCH				BURCHNELL		
William	Fran	103		William W	Pick	279
BUNDENTHAL				BURD		
Theodore	Luca	198		William	Mont	235
BUNDY				BURDEN		
Chalkey S	Morg	257		Eliza A	Augl	026
Leartus	Geau	112		Geo W	Alle	010
Mary	Fult	105		BURDETT		
BUNHARDT				Bentley	Tusc	331
Magdalena	Hami	134		John	Hard	148
BUNKER				Mary Ann	Guer	117
Elwood	Morr	259		William J	Wood	363
Evaline	Mari	209		BURDICK		
BUNN				Mary A	Lake	177
Elizabeth	Jack	168		BURDO		
Mary A	Ross	297		James H	Luca	197
Susan	Wyan	365		BURDSAL		
BUNNELL				Martha B	Hami	139
Chas	Hami	139		BURDUE		
Chester A	Huro	166		Henry	Wood	364
William D	Mont	242		BURGE		
BUNNER				Henry	Warr	342
James	Brow	032		Mary A	Luca	199
BUNTAIN				William C	Clin	052
Mary	Clin	054		BURGELT		
BUNTE				John V	Brow	032
Josephine	Putn	289		BURGENMAYER		
BUNTING				Karol'a	Cler	050
Geo W	Wayn	353		BURGER		
BUNZ				Chas W	Dark	079
Barbara	Miam	220		Frank	Mont	237
BURBAGE				BURGESS		
Elijah L	Adam	007		Elizabeth A	Huro	163
BURBRICK				Dr Franklin	Cuya	065
Arthur	Colu	055		Robert	Putn	290
BURBRIDGE				Roswell S	Sand	303
Charles	Mont	239		BURGET		
Sarah	Butl	036		Andrew	Fran	103
BURCAW				Anna Maria	Hami	128
William	Colu	058		Cath	Fran	103
BURCH				BURGETT		
Asa	Preb	286		Almarin M	Asht	017
Chester	Lawr	183		Hiram	Asht	017
Elizabeth	Hard	144		Nancy	Alle	011
Margaret	Cuya	067		BURGHARD		
Roberson G	Merc	217		Henry	Mont	227

43

BURGHARDT				BURLINGHAME		
Michael	Mont	247		Ferdin'd	Nobl	269
BURGHER				Harrison	Nobl	268
John	Mont	247		BURNELL		
BURGLORF				James D	Trum	328
Sophia	Hami	132		BURNETT		
BURGOON				Calvin	Summ	321
Wilson S	Unio	336		Jesse H	Faye	093
BURK				Mary Ann	Trum	326
Cath	Clar	044		Nathan S	Mont	248
Cynthia	Gall	108		Newton J	Clar	047
Henry	Mont	247		Sally Ann	Wash	346
James	Lake	178		Samantha	Lake	178
James E	Loga	191		Sarah	Hanc	142
John	Hami	132		Wilson S	Colu	059
Joseph	Mont	238		BURNHAM		
BURKE				Abner	Wood	361
Isaac	Wyan	364		Lewis	Cuya	075
John	Mont	238		BURNISON		
John	Mont	241		Alex	Craw	063
Margaret M	Miam	222		William	Craw	063
Nancy	Hami	128		BURNRESTER		
Olive M	Cler	051		Henry	Mont	237
Verena	Paul	273		BURNS		
BURKEMER				Andrew	Vint	340
Jacob	Cuya	076		Andrew J	Ashl	011
BURKET				Charles	Henr	151
Emeline	Otta	271		Elizabeth	Mont	227
Geo	Wood	362		Geo H	Hami	129
Philip	Hanc	143		Geo W	Summ	324
Sophia	Sand	304		Jacob	Preb	287
BURKETT				James	Huro	163
Geo A	Fair	091		James	Trum	330
Jesse	Miam	222		Jennie R	Cuya	065
BURKHALTER				John	Adam	006
Sarah	Sene	313		John	Luca	201
BURKHARDT				John	Mont	228
Mary A	Paul	274		John	Mont	247
Sarah	Madi	204		John	Pick	280
BURKHOLDER				John	Summ	323
Daniel	Fult	106		John B	Otta	271
Hiram	Dark	077		John M	Lawr	183
Joseph L	Putn	290		Margaret	Cuya	067
BURKITT				Margaret	Fran	095
Mary	Scio	307		Martin	Perr	275
BURLEY				Mary A	Adam	004
Eleanor	Vint	340		Mary E	Rich	296
Rachel	Clin	053		Peachey E	Jack	168
Sarah A	Perr	274		Peter	Rich	296
BURLINGAME				Robert	Mont	233
Edwin R	Asht	015		Thomas A	Dark	079
Ira	Cuya	076		William	Mont	242
Stephen	Nobl	270				

BURNSHINE			BURWELL (cont)		
David	Pike	281	Sarah	Adam	007
BURNSIDE			BUSBIE		
Cath A	Colu	058	Cath	Will	355
Nancy	Jeff	169	BUSBY		
BURR			Deborah	Harr	150
Delia R	Adam	006	BUSCHWALLER		
Elizabeth	Putn	290	Anna G	Mont	230
Eunice L	Trum	325	BUSE		
Selden W	Asht	018	Frederick W		
BURRELL				Hami	140
Rhoda	Erie	086	BUSERT		
BURRIDGE			Adam	Alle	008
Elezer	Lake	177	BUSH		
BURRIS			Cath	Cuya	067
Jno H	Perr	277	Elizabeth	Dela	083
John W	Belm	030	Geo	Augl	025
Stinson H	Wash	350	Horace E	Lawr	181
BURROUGH			Jacob	Lick	187
Angeline	Sand	302	Mary	Meig	215
BURROUGHS			Roxana	Erie	087
Egleston	Brow	035	Thomas	Scio	305
Elizabeth	Cler	047	William	Tusc	332
William H	Mont	247	William	Wayn	353
BURROW			BUSHAN		
Anthony	Trum	326	Lethe A	Gree	116
Thomas	Henr	153	BUSHFIELD		
BURROWS			John O	Knox	175
Jerome B	Lake	178	Sarah J	Knox	174
Silvester H	Hami	133	BUSHMAN		
William	Shel	316	Herman H	Shel	315
BURT			Martha	Cler	051
Cath	Guer	117	BUSHNELL		
Daniel	Colu	057	Betsey	Cuya	075
Eveline F	Morr	261	Daniel	Wood	361
James F	Brow	034	Martha	Trum	326
John F	Morr	260	BUSHONG		
Margaret	Asht	017	Geo, Sr	Alle	010
BURTON			Phebe	Hard	148
Abbey P	Cuya	074	William A	Wyan	365
Anthony B	Hami	133	BUSICK		
Cath	Lick	183	Samuel	Fran	102
Ezekiel	Putn	291	BUSKIRK		
Geo	Warr	344	Geo	Will	355
John H	Cuya	071	Joseph H	Monr	224
John W	Fran	099	Mortimer	Monr	225
Mary	Cuya	071	Oliphant	Monr	224
Phebe	Wyan	366	BUSKNET		
Ransom D	Geau	112	Andrew	Mont	238
Sarah C	Alle	009	BUSSELL		
Thompson	Maho	207	Moses	Hami	138
BURWELL			BUSTETTER		
Finis S	Wood	359	Louisa	Shel	315

BUTCHER			BUTTON (cont)		
Chas	Miam	220	Johnson P	Trum	327
Elizabeth A	Gall	108	Justin	Geau	113
Hamilton	Jack	167	Olive A	Vint	340
Jacob	Hard	144	BUTTS		
John S	Gall	110	Martha	Athe	021
Martin	Gall	109	Nelson	Mont	232
Mary	Faye	093	Pardon	Geau	112
BUTLER			BUTZ		
Asa	Ashl	013	Mary	Colu	057
Christian	Musk	265	BUTZMANN		
Geo	Cuya	071	William	Cuya	071
Isabella	Butl	036	BUXTON		
Jacob J	Hanc	143	Sidney	Guer	118
James S	Lora	195	BUZICK		
Jay C	Erie	087	James S	Faye	095
John	Defi	080	BUZZELL		
John	Knox	174	Jeremiah F	Fult	107
John B	Adam	008	Orrin	Fult	107
Levi B	Mont	254	Byan		
Ludlow S	Shel	315	James M	Hanc	141
Margaret	Hami	140	Mary	Wayn	352
Margaret	Holm	161	BYER		
Mary	Port	283	Isaac	Meig	212
Michael	Fran	098	BYERS		
Rachel	Scio	306	Abraham	Wood	358
Sarah	Belm	031	Andrew H	Fran	098
Thomas	Star	318	David	Preb	286
Tirza W	Lake	177	Francis M	Athe	021
BUTRIX			Frank M	Will	355
Elizabeth	Lawr	183	Henry	Sene	309
BUTSCHA			James M G	Maho	206
Gebhard	Fran	099	Jane	Port	283
BUTT			John O	Rich	294
Geo W	Miam	219	Rachel	Dark	077
James L	Perr	277	Thomas P	Meig	215
Mahala	Lick	185	William G	Mari	208
Margaret	Tusc	330	BYLAND		
BUTTER			George T	High	155
Amos	Perr	278	BYNASTER		
BUTTERFIELD			Geo W	Clar	045
Amos	Miam	219	BYRKETT		
Elizabeth	Hami	135	Ahijah B	Miam	222
Isaac C	Fair	089	Francis M	Miam	221
BUTTERWORTH			William F	Miam	222
Abraham	Athe	023	BYRNES		
BUTTLER			Edward E	Asht	018
Albert	Hami	133	Henry H	Trum	326
BUTTNER			BYRON		
Geo	VanW	338	Jno W	Mont	254
BUTTON			Ruth	Athe	024
Albert	Lake	178	BYSEL		
Alley	Preb	286	John	Lawr	181

Name	County	Page
CABASHER		
Maria	Luca	196
CABLE		
Isaac W	Miam	221
CACKLER		
Marion	Dela	083
CADEN		
Luke	Mont	242
CADMAN		
Esther	Hami	139
CADWALLADER		
Abner	Warr	342
Albert	Mont	244
Ezra	Warr	342
CADWELL		
Geo M	Cuya	068
CADY		
Ann Eliza	Hami	135
Caroline	Erie	087
Elizabeth	Pick	280
Martha A	Lick	186
Myron A	Morr	259
Phebe	Lake	176
Rebecca	Meig	213
Robert M	Hami	138
CAFFERTY		
Neil	Mont	236
CAGG		
Julia Ann	Athe	022
CAHALL		
Marion	Brow	033
CAHILL		
Anne E	Tusc	333
Henry E	Summ	322
Philip	Clin	054
Timothy	Lora	195
CAHO		
Anna	Gree	114
Chas H	Mont	227
CAHOON		
Joel B	Cuya	075
CAID		
John K	Mont	247
CAIN		
Andrew J	Will	357
Henry D	Alle	009
Jeremiah	Cham	042
Patrick	Hami	136
Patrick	Morr	259
Samuel W	Adam	007
Sophia	Fran	103
William F	Mont	240
William H	Summ	323
CAIN (cont)		
William W	Putn	291
CAINAN		
John	Rich	292
CAINE		
John	Hami	134
CAIRUS		
Henry B	Henr	151
CAKE		
William M	Sene	311
CALAHAN		
Susan	Pick	280
CALDEN		
Jeremiah	Mont	243
CALDWELL		
David S	Wyan	365
Hugh	Rich	295
Hugh W	Gall	110
James C	Cler	051
James P	Will	355
John	Cuya	068
John D	Pick	279
Lucinda	Sand	303
Margaret	Butl	038
Martha	Wyan	366
Mary A F	Hami	135
Nancy	Musk	264
Samuel S	Cuya	066
Sophronia	Pick	279
Sybil A	Craw	064
William H	High	154
CALEB		
Joseph	VanW	337
CALHOUN		
Abraham	VanW	338
Elizabeth	Cler	051
Margaret	Gall	111
Margaret	Knox	173
CALKINS		
Harvey G	Putn	290
Perrin H	Cuya	067
CALL		
America	Scio	306
Cath	Wash	350
David	Jeff	169
Effaline	Lake	177
Elizabeth	Jeff	169
Margaret	Scio	305
William R	Gall	108
CALLAGHAN		
Patrick	Mont	240
CALLAHAN		
Albert	Maho	205

47

CALLAHAN (cont)		
Chas F	Maho	205
Elizabeth	Maho	205
Ellen	Summ	324
Jacob N B	Hanc	143
Jesse	Brow	033
Joshua	Maho	206
Margaret J	Perr	277
Mathias C	Maho	205
Michael	Madi	203
Patrick	Mont	241
CALLENDAR		
Jos	Ross	299
CALLIN		
James M	Wood	360
CALLISON		
Isaac M	Clar	046
Thomas	Hanc	141
CALROO		
James	Luca	201
CALVERT		
Francis C	Guer	117
William L	Hami	133
CALVIN		
Albert	Wood	359
Elizabeth R	Hami	139
Luther S	Maho	205
Margaret J	Maho	206
CAMBY		
Thomas	Athe	023
CAMERON		
Bridget	Cuya	073
John S	Defi	081
Orrin	Fult	107
Sarah C	Hami	134
William D	Unio	336
CAMFIELD		
Abbie M	Huro	164
CAMP		
Corwin F	Guer	118
Daniel	Fair	092
John	Scio	308
John F	Athe	023
Sarah Jane	Lick	184
CAMPBELL		
Abigail	Hami	138
Alex	Athe	023
Andrew J	Adam	003
Arthur T	Cham	041
Calvin A	Belm	028
Cath M	Colu	056
Charles L	Guer	118
Curran	Perr	277

CAMPBELL (cont)		
Daniel	Carr	040
Daniel H	Wayn	353
Daniel R	Colu	059
David	Mont	247
Edward B	Cuya	068
Eliza	Wyan	364
Elizabeth	Alle	008
Ezekiel G	Colu	059
Geo	Morg	257
Geo	Rich	292
Geo L	Fair	091
Henry	Cuya	067
Hiram H	Adam	006
Isaac	Harr	150
James	Ashl	012
Jane	Hami	122
John	Augl	025
John	Hard	146
John	Mont	241
John H	Mont	227
John H	VanW	336
Joseph P	Mont	228
Keren A	Athe	022
Louisa	Adam	003
Maria E	Guer	117
Mary	Brow	035
Mary	Warr	342
Michael	Mont	240
Peter	Gall	109
Phineas C	Belm	027
Rebecca	Gree	114
Robert	Vint	340
Robert H	Scio	308
Samuel	High	154
Samuel F	Hami	135
Samuel M	Wayn	351
Sarah	Hami	139
Sarah	Scio	308
Sarah L	Brow	031
Siner	Hock	159
Thomas D	Putn	290
William	Mont	243
William C	Meig	216
William J	Brow	031
William K	Putn	290
William O	Summ	323
William P	Belm	030
William V	Cler	048
CAMPTON		
James F	Adam	004
John R	Dela	082
Robert F	Adam	004

CAMREN			CAPEN			
Boyd	Tusc	331	Geo J	Henr	153	
CANADY			CAPLENGIR			
Elvira	Clar	044	Baron De K	Wayn	351	
Mary	Cham	041	CAPLES			
CANAN			Joseph	Tusc	333	
Sophia	Will	356	Nancy	Tusc	332	
CANDLE			CAPP			
Jacob	Clin	055	Susan	Hami	121	
CANDY			CAPPEL			
David	High	156	Caroline	Ross	298	
CANE			Peter	Hami	135	
Samuel	Sand	304	CAPPER			
CANFIELD			Geo	Defi	080	
Bede	Medi	210	John	VanW	336	
Dennis K	Huro	162	Malinda E	Carr	040	
Henry A	Trum	326	CARBERY			
Henry C	Wyan	367	Preston	Brow	032	
James	Cuya	068	CARDEN			
Joseph A	Mont	235	Alfred	Mont	256	
Mary J	Cuya	066	CARDER			
William R	Otta	270	John H	Hard	146	
CANN			Oliver M	Musk	264	
Philip	Erie	088	CARDINELL			
CANNON			Francis	Port	283	
Ann	Fran	095	CARENS			
Cassius	Fair	089	Ellen	Mont	231	
James	Trum	326	Sarah A	Musk	265	
John	Gree	116	CAREY			
Laura	Port	283	Cornelius	Athe	021	
Louisa J	Putn	290	Edward M	Brow	034	
Mary A	Fair	091	Henry C	Asht	018	
Michael	Mont	244	Mary J	Scio	307	
Patrick	Scio	307	Reuben	Wood	360	
Richard M	Shel	315	CARGE			
Robert	Gree	115	William	Mont	241	
CANNY			CARHARTT			
Cath J	Preb	286	John	Cosh	061	
CANOMAN			CARICORN			
John	Mont	243	Peter	Sand	302	
CANTER			CARIER			
Barney	Jack	168	Betsey	Port	283	
Cornelius	Jack	168	CARL			
David H	Clin	053	Cyrus	Unio	336	
CANTLE			James	Merc	218	
Jacob	Warr	342	Lafayette	Port	285	
CANTLEBERRY			William	Mont	233	
Sarah J	Pick	279	CARLE			
CANTLEBERY			Alfred	Butl	036	
William	Holm	160	Harriet	Butl	039	
CANTWELL			Ludwig	Mont	253	
Sarah S	Hard	147	CARLETON			
			Rachel	Monr	225	

CARLEY			CARNEY			
John	Sand	302	George W	Trum	325	
CARLILE			James	Mont	247	
Jacob	Colu	058	Martin	Hami	133	
CARLIN			Mary Ann	Maho	207	
Eliza	Merc	216	Michael C	Perr	276	
James	Wayn	351	CARNICORN			
Thomas J	Asht	016	Jacob	Lick	185	
CARLISLE			CARNS			
Elizabeth	Sene	310	Amos S	Carr	040	
Theo G	Sene	310	Jane	Dela	082	
CARLOCK			CAROTHERS			
Henry C	Lick	184	Margaret	Harr	149	
CARLON			CARPENTER			
William S	Maho	205	Alason	Sand	303	
CARLTON			Benj F	Dela	083	
Clarissa	Port	284	Cath	Hock	159	
Electa	Geau	111	Elizabeth	Rich	292	
Mary J	Medi	212	Ezra J	Hami	133	
CARLYLE			George	Knox	174	
Robert	Wyan	365	George H	Cuya	067	
CARMACK			George W	Luca	201	
Cath	Wayn	353	George W	Meig	216	
Mary	Wayn	353	Grace	Colu	058	
CARMAN			Henry	Paul	273	
Howard	Wood	362	Jacob	Wash	349	
Jane	Warr	344	James J	Morg	256	
John	Jeff	172	Jasper	Scio	304	
William C	Fran	097	Jeremiah	Craw	063	
CARMANY			Joseph	Athe	020	
John	Colu	057	Levi A	Sene	309	
CARMER			Louisa C	Putn	289	
Henry G	Port	284	Lyman	Defi	080	
CARMICHAEL			Marietta M	Warr	344	
Franklin	Rich	295	Martha	Wash	346	
Nancy	Monr	226	Mary	Monr	223	
Susan	Will	357	Mary A	Sand	303	
Thomas	Mont	236	Mary A	Sand	304	
Thomas J	Merc	217	Mary E	Fran	101	
CARMODY			Milton A	Belm	029	
Chas H	Mont	242	Rebecca	Meig	216	
Mary	Luca	201	Samuel A	Cuya	076	
CARMON			Sarah	Cler	049	
John	Luca	201	Sidney	Huro	162	
CARNAHAN			Susannah	Knox	175	
Aaron T	Clin	052	Thomas	Belm	031	
Elias D	Hami	138	Thomas	Wash	346	
Elizabeth J	Holm	160	Thomas F	Dela	082	
CARNELL			Wash J	Asht	014	
Charles	Holm	160	William H	Meig	214	
CARNES			CARPER			
Rhoda	Loga	189	James	Sene	309	
Wilson	Mont	248	Jane M	Dela	083	

CARR				**CARSON**			
Alexander	C	Mont	239	Abraham		Mont	244
Alonzo		Cler	050	Ed		Hami	136
Celia		High	156	(alias Edgar K Clemmer)			
Eliza J		High	154	Erskine		High	155
Elmira		Hanc	142	Jacob W		Trum	327
Henry		Huro	163	James		Hami	137
Isaiah		Musk	264	James R		Wayn	352
James		Brow	034	Jane O		Loga	191
James		Mont	235	John R		Craw	063
James C		Athe	020	John W		Clar	046
James C		Hami	132	Susan M		Jeff	171
James M		Dark	078	Thomas C		Geau	111
John		Faye	093	William		Vint	341
John M		Wood	361	**CARTER**			
Julia A		Jack	167	Adaline		Ross	299
Lavinia		Hanc	143	Betsey		Unio	334
Samuel H		Clar	044	Chloe M		Trum	327
Stephen		Perr	277	Edward N		Jeff	170
Susannah		Guer	118	Elijah		Pike	281
CARREL				Elizzie		Rich	294
John		Nobl	269	Eunice		Fult	106
Lebbeus		Hock	159	Geo M		Fran	102
CARRELL				Hannah		Jeff	171
Chas T		Hami	133	Harriet R		Morr	259
Jane		Hami	135	James		Cosh	061
CARREY				James		Lawr	182
Mortimer		Madi	203	James H		Hami	140
CARRIGAN				James M		Athe	021
Mary		Jack	167	Jane		Summ	323
CARRINGTON				John		Gall	110
Joseph		Jack	167	John		Hard	148
Julius M		Cuya	068	John H		Putn	290
CARROLL				John W		Dark	077
Ellen		High	155	Joseph		Harr	149
Eugene		Mont	247	Joseph B		Summ	325
Foster		Pike	281	Margaret		Fult	106
Francis		Warr	344	Margaret A		Butl	036
Geo W		Fair	089	Mary S		Fult	105
John		Dela	083	Milton H		Musk	266
John		Fran	097	Riley		Trum	327
John		Mont	227	Samuel		Cuya	067
John		Mont	255	William		Belm	031
Jos		Carr	040	William		Gall	109
Sarah J		Warr	344	William		Guer	119
Thomas		Faye	093	William		Harr	149
Thomas R		Maho	205	William N		Trum	325
Vincent		Dark	079	**CARTHRIGHT**			
CARRON				Erwin H		Lick	187
Ailcey		Warr	342	Richard		Lick	187
CARROTHERS				**CARTRIGHT**			
George		Hanc	141	Harmon B		Huro	162
John C		Rich	293				

CARTWRIGHT			**CASNER (cont)**			
Henry G	Clin	055	Matilda	Cosh	060	
Joseph	Jack	166	**CASS**			
Josephine	Huro	162	Isaiah	Mont	253	
CARTZDAFNER			Theo	Belm	027	
Maria	Madi	202	**CASSADY**			
CARUTHERS			James H	Wayn	355	
William L	Luca	196	**CASSAVANT**			
CARVER			Louis	Hami	135	
Geo	Mont	228	**CASSEL**			
Morgan P	Scio	307	Daniel O	Craw	063	
Robert	Scio	307	Elizabeth	Musk	262	
CARY			Henry	Mari	208	
Harriet W	Henr	153	Jacob	Will	357	
Robert	Defi	080	**CASSELL**			
CASE			Levi	Belm	027	
Augustus	Wash	349	Levi	Knox	173	
Cath	Dela	082	**CASSIDAY**			
Chas N	Summ	324	Geo	Unio	336	
Esther C	Wayn	352	**CASSIDY**			
Frank S	Loga	189	James H	Medi	211	
Harlow W	Luca	197	John	Star	317	
James E	Lora	196	**CASSILL**			
Jason	Trum	326	Alexander	Knox	175	
John M	Fran	098	**CASSON**			
Margaret	Dela	085	Huldah	Fran	097	
Mary	Dela	084	**CASTATER**			
Mary E	Harr	150	Daniel	Butl	036	
Matilda	Lick	184	**CASTEEL**			
Nancy	Wyan	367	Geo W	Wash	349	
Penelope	Morr	260	John A	Vint	342	
Sarah A	Adam	006	Susannah	Cosh	062	
Thomas	Preb	286	William	Augl	025	
CASEBOLT			**CASTEL**			
Thomas	Gall	110	Mary	Hami	134	
CASEY			**CASTLE**			
Edward	Lawr	181	Annie S	Cuya	066	
John	Mont	247	Elizabeth	Lick	184	
William	Mont	238	Elizabeth	Wood	360	
CASH			Phebe Ann	Craw	062	
Mary J	Ross	300	Price	Loga	191	
Nathan	Tusc	333	Robert	Putn	290	
CASHIN			Rosalinda	Asht	014	
Patrick	Cuya	068	William M	Fair	091	
CASHNER			**CASTNER**			
Jonathan	Sene	309	John W	Knox	173	
CASKEY			**CASTO**			
Ann	Mont	227	James M	Clin	052	
John G	Summ	322	**CASTOR**			
Lewis H	Craw	063	John	Holm	160	
Margaret	Summ	323	Philander S	Musk	264	
CASNER			**CASWELL**			
Geo W	Guer	120	Eleanor	Erie	086	

CASWELL (cont)			CECIL			
Emiline	Summ	324	Elizabeth	Monr	226	
Lucinda	Wood	362	John W	Harr	149	
CATE			CEEDLE			
Eliza	Cuya	067	Eliza	Hard	148	
CATERAL			CELIO			
Jesse H	Carr	040	Floriani	Otta	271	
CATHRIGHT			CERBE			
Maria	Lick	184	Philip	Erie	087	
CATLIN			CERR			
Ellen	Huro	164	William	Craw	063	
Jonathan A	Trum	326	William	Mont	235	
Victor	Huro	162	CEST			
William H	High	156	Jane	Hami	138	
CATLIP			CETONE			
Penelope	Pike	281	Henry S	Mont	227	
CATT			CHADWICK			
Margaret	Lick	185	Harriet N	Asht	018	
CATTANACH			William	Perr	275	
William	Mont	243	CHAFFEE			
CATTELL			Hannah	Geau	113	
Delarma S	Paul	274	James	Trum	327	
CAUFMAN			James M	Huro	163	
William	Mont	244	John A	Trum	327	
CAUGHLIN			Lydia C	Asht	017	
Thomas	Mont	248	Marion	Mont	241	
CAVANAH			Sherburne H	Trum	326	
Arthur A	Cuya	068	CHAIN			
CAVANAUGH			Henry	Maho	206	
Geo E	Mont	237	CHALFANT			
John	Mont	245	Finley D	Scio	306	
Robert	Mont	247	Geo W	Jeff	172	
CAVANEY			CHALLENDER			
John	High	154	Chas A	Clin	052	
CAVE			CHAMBERLAIN			
Benj E	Hock	159	Devalus	Morg	258	
CAVIN			Mary	Madi	202	
Clarissa	Gall	109	Nor H	Will	356	
CAVINDER			William	Warr	343	
Harriet A	Mari	209	CHAMBERLIN			
CAVINEE			Andrew	Mont	231	
John	Fran	103	Cath	Wood	360	
CAW			Elizabeth	Jeff	172	
William	Musk	262	Isaiah	Wood	361	
CAYLER			Orlando R	Geau	112	
Gertrude	Star	318	William E	Summ	322	
CAYLOR			CHAMBERS			
Mary H A	Mont	230	Amelia	Mont	232	
CAYSE			Daniel	Asht	015	
Sarah E	Mont	231	Hannah A	Summ	324	
CAZEAU			Joseph	Colu	059	
Louis J	Huro	164	M V B	Maho	207	
CEASE			Nancy	Guer	119	
John	Mont	228	Nancy	Warr	343	

CHAMBERS (cont)		
Polly	Trum	326
Rachel	Wayn	353
Uriel B	Clin	052
William	Mont	235
William W	Athe	024
CHAMBLEN		
Sarah	Wood	359
CHAMBLIN		
Jane E	Adam	005
CHAMPENO		
William	Mont	236
CHAMPION		
William J	Hanc	143
CHAMPLAIN		
Ebenezer	Trum	328
CHAMPLIN		
Rachel	Vint	340
CHANCE		
Lewis D	Butl	037
Mary A	Huro	163
Mathew H	Sene	311
Thomas H	Sene	310
William	Belm	028
CHANCEY		
Corrydon	Lora	195
CHANDLER		
Adolphus N	Trum	330
Albert	Wash	345
Benj	Cuya	068
Charles	Trum	330
Fanny	Cuya	066
Jane N	Musk	262
Philander	Harr	149
Sarah E	Cuya	068
CHANDLEY		
Julia A	Ross	298
CHANEY		
Cath	Meig	216
Chas J	Sene	313
Jos J	Ross	298
Mary A	Paul	273
Samuel	Paul	274
Thomas	High	155
William H	Sene	314
CHAPEL		
Cynthia L	Ashl	013
Elias S	Geau	112
CHAPELL		
John	Asht	017
CHAPIN		
Adaline	Wyan	365
John H	Fran	098

CHAPIN (cont)		
John V	Fran	104
Leonard B	Erie	087
CHAPLIN		
Edward M	Clin	052
CHAPMAN		
Abigail	High	155
Augustus A	Gall	108
Azuba	Medi	211
Calvin	Miam	219
Daniel	Lora	196
Daniel S	Asht	016
Edward	Lora	195
Eliza	Brow	034
Elizabeth	Meig	213
Ellen	Holm	159
Ezra A	Wash	345
Harlan P	Lora	194
Henry L	Henr	153
Hiram A	Wash	346
James F	Sand	302
Jemima	Port	285
Jerusha	Summ	324
John S	Clar	046
Joseph A	Asht	017
Justin H	Mont	238
Leroy M	Port	283
Margaret	High	156
Maria	Jeff	172
Martha	Cuya	071
Mary A	Vint	341
Mary A S	Belm	031
Rachel	High	155
Rufus T	Cuya	075
Susannah	Unio	336
Thomas H	Unio	336
William B	Cuya	067
CHAPPELEAR		
Elizabeth	Lick	185
Geo J	Morg	258
Nancy	Perr	276
Susan	Perr	276
CHAPPELL		
Chas W	Wood	362
John W	Wood	361
CHARD		
Ann	Cuya	067
CHARLES		
Alman	Sand	304
Coltron	Luca	197
Hiram	Wood	362
Samuel	Adam	005
Thomas	Maho	207

CHARLESWORTH			CHEESMAN		
James F	Belm	030	Margaret	Fair	092
CHARLTON			CHELLIS		
John	Hock	157	John C	Geau	111
John R	Hami	134	CHEMIDLIN		
Joseph	Rich	293	Nicholas	Mont	237
Samuel	Ashl	012	CHENAULT		
William W	Ashl	012	Elizabeth	Pike	282
CHARPIER			CHENEY		
Peter	Shel	316	Alpheus	Meig	215
CHARTER			David J	Mari	208
Mary	Luca	197	William H	Mont	253
Samuel	Luca	197	CHERINGTON		
CHASE			David W	Jack	167
Christie S	Lick	185	Summerfield	Gall	108
David R	Miam	222	CHERRY		
Edward H	Luca	200	Anna	Luca	198
Edwin A	Hami	138	Elizabeth	Gree	114
Elisha W	Unio	336	Hannah R	Fran	097
Esther	Meig	216	Joseph M	Sene	314
Geo D	Wood	361	Susan E	Erie	087
Hosmer	Athe	024	Susannah	Unio	336
John M	Meig	216	William	Luca	198
Jno W	Wash	349	CHERRYHOMES		
Otaway C	Wood	361	Thomas S	Ross	296
Sarah M	Cuya	068	CHESER		
Simon C	Faye	094	Sarah	Hock	158
Susan	Lick	185	CHESNEY		
William	Warr	344	Adam	Cham	041
William W	Asht	016	CHESSER		
CHATFIELD			Martha M	Lawr	179
Harriet	Luca	199	CHESTER		
CHATMAN			Simon	Ross	299
Ransom	Gree	115	CHESTNUT		
CHATTERDON			Daniel	Pick	278
Ezra	Cler	051	Elizabeth	Scio	304
CHAVERS			CHEVENON		
Griffin	Jack	167	Oliver	Mont	239
CHAVONS			(alias Oliver Chebenon)		
Herbert	Unio	336	CHEWROUT		
CHEADLE			Sarah	Meig	215
Richard H	Morg	257	CHICHESTER		
CHEATHAM			Alice A	Cuya	073
Nancy	Gall	108	Polly	Will	357
Robert	Meig	214	CHIDESTER		
CHEBENON			Cath	Fran	104
Oliver	Mont	239	William B	Wash	345
(alias Oliver Chevenon)			CHILCOAT		
CHEEK			Joseph S	Sene	311
Adaline	Lick	188	CHILCOATE		
Elizabeth	Lick	185	Elizabeth	Perr	278
CHEESEMAN			CHILCOT		
William	Wash	348	Geo S	VanW	338

CHILCOTE			CHRISTMAN (cont)		
James M	Will	356	Peter	Hami	135
John W	Sene	311	Wilhelmina	Musk	267
Perry C	Wood	363	CHRISTOFEL		
Samuel M	Wood	358	Nancy	Ashl	011
CHILDERS			CHRISTOPHER		
Keziah	Pick	279	Caroline	Paul	273
CHILDS			Chas W	Holm	161
Silas M	Cuya	065	Conley	Monr	225
CHINEWORTH			John W	Alle	010
John L	Clin	052	Joseph	Holm	160
CHIPPINGER			William H	Hard	144
Delbert L	VanW	338	CHRISTY		
CHISHOLM			Alma	Tusc	331
Isaac W	Musk	264	John	Belm	030
CHISM			Martha E	Gree	116
James	Mont	237	Samuel	Clin	052
CHISMAN			CHRONINGER		
David R	Madi	202	Susanna	Sand	304
CHITTENDEN			CHRYSTIE		
Walter	Port	285	Mary S	Colu	057
CHITTURN			CHURCH		
Sarah S	Pick	279	Anna M	Nobl	269
CHOATE			Calvin	Madi	202
Elizabeth	Dark	077	Clarence L	Lora	195
Rosina M	Henr	152	Emeline	Lake	177
CHOFFIN			George	Loga	190
Frances	Star	318	Harry A	Lick	185
CHOLLET			James P	Augl	024
Henry F	Mont	242	Peter	Mont	238
CHORD			CHURCHILL		
Sophia	Hami	134	Calvin W	Preb	286
CHORT			CHURCHMAN		
Frederick	Belm	029	Alex	Butl	038
CHRIST			CHUTE		
Ann M	Asht	017	Mary	Perr	276
Joseph	Hami	135	CILLEY		
Joseph	Mont	235	Greenleaf	Hami	133
Rinehart	Hami	121	CLABAUGH		
William	VanW	337	Joseph	Wood	363
CHRISTIAN			Levi W	Sene	311
Frederick	Star	317	Thomas H	Fair	092
Garst	Will	355	CLADEN		
J	Wood	362	Morand	Hami	139
John	Cuya	065	CLAGG		
Lucy	Harr	150	Frances	Gall	109
May	Belm	030	CLAGGETT		
CHRISTIE			Caroline	Rich	295
John	Musk	266	Elizabeth	Morr	260
Mary C	Pick	280	CLAGUE		
CHRISTMAN			Thomas	Wood	359
Daniel	Perr	277	CLAIR		
Lewis	Brow	031	Samuel W	Wood	363
			Thomas	Cuya	067

56

CLAIRBORNE			CLARK (cont)		
Cecilia	Scio	307	Hannah	Butl	037
CLAIRE			Harrison M	Belm	029
Joseph	Fult	105	Harvey M	Hanc	142
CLANCY			Israel D	VanW	338
Ellen	Hami	122	J W	Hami	128
John	Mont	237	(alias John W Leguer)		
Michael	Mont	247	Jacob	Hard	144
CLAPP			James	Mont	247
Isaac	Miam	221	James A	Gall	110
Phebe M	Port	284	James J	Hami	134
Richmond	Lake	177	James V	Fran	097
CLAPPER			James W	Meig	213
Henry	Rich	295	James W	Sene	311
Minerva	Pike	282	Jane S	Cuya	073
CLARE			John	Alle	009
George	Cler	048	John	Faye	093
CLARISSA			John	Hami	135
Benj	Madi	202	John D	Putn	288
CLARK			Jno H	Wash	350
Abner M	Wood	360	John J	Mont	239
Alexander	Guer	118	John M	Warr	344
Alexander	Wash	346	John S	Cuya	067
Alia A	Wash	345	Johnson E	Star	320
Alta M	Asht	018	Jonathan J	Butl	036
Amaziah	Fult	107	Jos	Merc	217
Andrew J	Athe	024	Joseph	Morg	256
Andrew J	Butl	036	Joseph B	Cuya	067
Angelica M	Lake	177	Leander	Sand	303
Anthony W	Lawr	183	Leroy E	Luca	197
Arthur	Lick	186	Lettice	Clin	053
Augustus A	Mont	247	Lewis H	Dela	083
Azel J	Madi	203	Lucy	Meig	214
Baldwin H	VanW	339	Major E	Lora	194
Benj F	Summ	322	Marcus B	Trum	328
Byron	Hami	133	Margaret J	Tusc	330
Cordelia	Fran	102	Marilla	Port	283
David	Mont	239	Mary	Brow	034
Divdate	Cuya	073	Mary	Gall	109
Electa A	Luca	199	Mary	Merc	217
Elizabeth	Cler	048	Mary A	Hami	123
Elizabeth	Cler	049	Mary A	Huro	164
Elizabeth	Hock	158	Mathew D	Summ	322
Elizabeth	Summ	321	Matson N	Morr	259
Esther	Asht	017	Matthias	Clar	046
Esther	Pike	282	Michael	Trum	326
Francis T	Asht	016	Milton W	Port	284
Franklin F	High	156	Nancy	Medi	210
Gardner	Belm	028	Nathan	Mari	208
Geo A	Asht	017	Phineas	Fran	104
Geo W	Cham	043	Rachel A	Belm	027
Geo W	Gall	110	Ralph A	Adam	004
Geo W	Lick	186	Reuben	Cham	041
Geo W	Vint	340	Robert	Mont	238

CLARK (cont)		
Rolan M	Butl	037
Rosannah	Miam	219
Roxanna	Lick	183
Samuel	Medi	211
Samuel H	Hami	133
Samuel R	Meig	215
Samuel W	Adam	007
Sarah A	Adam	006
Sarah J	Hami	138
Sarah J	Mari	208
Stephen L	Will	357
Susan	Defi	079
Susan	Luca	201
Sylvester	Clin	053
Thomas P	Athe	023
Thomas S	Warr	342
Vernon	Luca	196
William	Cler	047
William	Erie	088
William A	Hami	135
William M	Hock	159
William R	Cler	049
William R	Wood	362
William T	Fair	088
CLARKE		
Frances E	Fair	091
Robert	Mont	242
Thomas J	Mont	236
Sarah	Cham	042
CLARY		
Eliza	Nobl	269
James	Mont	249
John	Wood	362
Nicholas G	Athe	023
CLASKEY		
Geo H	Cuya	068
CLASON		
Annie M	Dela	082
CLASPILL		
Chas H	Musk	267
CLASS		
Barney	Hanc	143
John C	Miam	219
CLAUSER		
Harriet	Cuya	076
CLAUSING		
Henry	Faye	093
CLAUSON		
David F	Fult	106
CLAWSON		
Cath	Faye	093
Garrah B	Huro	164
Perry	Shel	315

CLAY		
Ann M	Pike	282
Bursey	Wash	347
Frenica	Holm	160
Henry	Will	357
Henry C	Dela	083
Jane	Summ	324
Mary	Hami	135
CLAYLON		
Malinda	Ross	301
CLAYTON		
Jasper N	Merc	217
Jonathan	Hard	146
Mary C	Hanc	142
CLEAR		
George	Jack	167
William L	Jeff	170
CLEGG		
James F	Hami	132
John E	Monr	223
Thomas	Belm	027
Thomas	Hami	139
Thomas J	Monr	224
CLEM		
Christopher, Sr		
	Warr	343
CLEMENS		
Alexander	Otta	272
Joseph B	Faye	094
Joseph W	Gree	116
CLEMENT		
Ann	Lake	178
CLEMENTS		
James	Clin	052
Jane	Morg	258
Philip W	Pike	282
Ransom	Fran	104
CLEMER		
Thomas A	Adam	003
CLEMMENS		
John S	Athe	023
Warren	Cosh	060
CLEMMER		
Edgar K	Hami	136
(alias Ed Carson)		
John S	Colu	058
Nathan B	Hami	135
CLEMMONS		
Peter	Huro	163
CLEMONS		
Franklin C	Hami	138
Mary J	Fran	101
Thomas M	Hard	146

CLENDENEN		
Louisa	Wash	345
CLENDENIN		
James C	Jeff	172
Robert	VanW	338
CLERC		
Mary	Fult	105
CLEVELAND		
Mary W	Dela	085
CLEVENGER		
William	Clin	052
CLICK		
David	Mari	208
CLIEVLAND		
Elizabeth	Asht	018
CLIFFORD		
Elizabeth	Scio	305
Ellen	Hami	122
Joseph	Cuya	075
Nancy E	Monr	223
CLIFTON		
Elizabeth	Ross	301
Mary C	Miam	221
Mary E	Lick	188
James W	Hami	137
(alias Geo W Torrence)		
John	Fran	102
CLINE		
Benj F	Rich	295
Cath	Hami	132
Geo R	Ross	298
Hannah	Will	355
Hiram D	Gree	113
Jonas C	Unio	335
Joseph	Adam	006
Leonard	Monr	225
Mary B	Lake	177
Matilda	Rich	294
Peter	Butl	036
Rachel	Mari	209
Roseberry	Monr	225
Samuel S	Mont	240
Thomas	Monr	225
Wilson S	Hard	148
CLINEFELDER		
Sarah A	Sand	301
CLINESMITH		
Rachel	Athe	023
CLINGER		
Daniel	Wyan	365
CLINGERMAN		
Jacob C	Hard	144
CLINGMAN		
Ann M	Cuya	067

CLINK		
James	Craw	062
Russell V	VanW	337
CLINTON		
Alexander M	Mont	243
James H	Cuya	067
John	Hami	134
William	Cham	040
CLIPP		
Polly	Wayn	353
CLIPPARD		
John	Warr	342
CLIPPINGER		
Marion L	Alle	009
CLODFELTER		
Frederick	Wayn	355
CLOM		
Ogden M	Mont	233
CLONEY		
William B	Mont	238
CLOSE		
Candace	Lora	194
Harvey	Craw	064
Michael	Alle	008
CLOSSON		
James W	Dela	082
Josiah M	Paul	273
CLOUD		
Mary Ann	Madi	202
Samuel	Wood	361
CLOUGH		
Jonathan W	Fult	106
CLOUSE		
Michael	VanW	337
William M	VanW	337
CLOUSER		
Simon	High	155
William B	Hami	129
CLOVER		
Russell B	Fran	095
Willis	Fran	103
CLOWE		
Craven W	Hock	158
CLOYNE		
Bridget	Luca	202
CLUCKEY		
Betsey	Luca	199
Edward	Otta	272
CLUFF		
Judah	High	155
CLUM		
Samuel	Tusc	331
CLUNK		
James	Colu	059

CLUSE				COCHRAN (cont)		
Joseph	Perr	277		William H	Colu	056
CLUTCHER				COCK		
Mary A	Luca	197		Geo B	Star	318
CLUTTER				COCKERILL		
Deblanan W	Alle	009		Daniel T	Brow	034
Harriet	Brow	035		Nannie J	Hami	137
CLYDE				William S	Faye	094
Jane B	Pick	279		COCKRELL		
CO				Mary A	Ross	298
James	VanW	339		William H	Dela	084
COADY				COCKRILL		
Thomas	Mont	237		Cath	Ross	297
COAKENHOUR				CODER		
Moses	VanW	338		Noah	Luca	201
COALMAN				Simon	Unio	333
Bartholomew	Tusc	331		CODY		
Nancy	Morg	257		Richard	Summ	324
COALTRAP				William J	Hami	135
James W	Guer	119		COE		
COALWELL				Emily	Athe	022
William H	Otta	271		Lucius L	Port	283
COATES				Ruth Y	Port	284
Ellen V	Star	316		COEN		
John S	Musk	267		Edward C	Hami	122
COATS				Emeline	Wood	363
Henry	Meig	213		Lawrence	Cham	042
Reuben	Huro	164		COEY		
Stephen J	Hanc	141		Thomas	Ross	299
COBB				COFFEE		
Cath	Maho	205		William	Mont	245
Diantha	Luca	202		COFFELT		
Fanny J	Carr	039		Agnes T	Loga	189
George	Adam	006		COFFET		
Mary J	Meig	216		Geo	Paul	272
Nancy J	Meig	216		COFFEY		
COBLE				Mary Jane	High	154
Christian	Pick	279		COFFIN		
COBLER				Admiral B	Luca	197
Sarah A	High	156		Phebe	Ashl	011
COCHENOUR				COFFMAN		
Mahlon	Ross	300		Samuel S	High	156
COCHRAN				William H	Lick	187
Alice	Mont	231		COFNERT		
Eliza	Alle	009		Michael	Mont	238
Harrison	Monr	224		COGSWELL		
John	Mont	247		Lydia A	Mont	231
Permenia C	Ross	299		COGWILL		
Robert M	Adam	004		Elisha	Morg	257
Sarah	Shel	315		COHEN		
Sarah A	Clin	054		Geo W	Hami	133
Susannah	Cosh	062		COIL		
Thomas	Belm	027		David	Ross	299
Thomas	Lick	187				

COILEY		
Charles	Trum	327
COINES		
Geo T	Augl	025
COIT		
Elizabeth M	Maho	205
COLAWAY		
Geo W	Mont	241
COLB		
Michael	Vint	340
COLBE		
Lewis	Lawr	183
COLBERT		
Anna	Cham	043
Stephen B	Warr	343
COLBORN		
William A	Perr	276
COLBURN		
Bruno	Cuya	069
Cath N	Perr	276
John E	Cuya	068
Julia L	Asht	015
Lydia M	Trum	325
Thomas	Mont	231
COLBY		
Lucius	Hami	133
COLE		
Amos B	Scio	306
Charlotte D	Summ	321
Chas C	Ross	298
Daniel B	Athe	021
Elias	Dela	082
Farlin B	Harr	150
James A	Scio	306
Jno	Meig	216
John D	Lora	194
Joshua	Fran	097
Joshua V	Trum	326
Joshua W	Jeff	170
Leonard G	Sene	314
Lewis A	Wyan	367
Lyman M	Asht	017
Mahala	Asht	017
Martha	Cosh	062
Mathew S	Harr	149
Moses	Trum	328
Nancy J	Clin	054
Nancy M	Geau	112
Nathan W	Merc	217
Peter P	Fult	106
Priscilla	Musk	262
Sarah M	Cham	043
Sophia	Summ	323

COLE (cont)		
William C	Merc	218
William H	Fult	105
William H	Huro	164
William H	Wyan	367
COLEMAN		
Arnold S	Shel	315
Daniel	Fran	095
Jane	Cler	049
John	Lawr	183
John C	Athe	023
Julius A	Miam	221
Letha A	Hami	123
Marion	Meig	215
William A	Lake	178
COLER		
David	Ross	296
Jeremiah	Henr	151
COLERICK		
Seneca	Morg	259
COLES		
Sarah	Jack	168
COLGROVE		
Benj F	Scio	308
COLL		
Michael	Fult	107
COLLAR		
Martha S	Trum	327
COLLER		
William	Wood	359
COLLETT		
Henry	Dark	077
COLLEY		
Allen	Scio	304
COLLIER		
Charles	Hard	146
Eunice	Jeff	171
Harriet	Gree	116
James T	Sene	314
Mary A	Adam	007
Selinda	Wood	361
COLLIFLOWER		
Susannah	Guer	120
COLLINS		
Absalom G	Preb	287
Ann E	Hock	158
Archibald	Gree	115
Bridget	Tusc	331
Clarissa P	Shel	316
Cyrus W	Brow	035
Eliza	Clin	052
Geo B	Miam	221
Harvey	Fult	105

COLLINS (cont)		
Howard	Port	283
Isaiah	Tusc	332
James	Mont	236
James A	Loga	191
Jane	Hami	123
John	Hami	140
John	Mont	247
John	Sand	302
John Q	Gree	115
Julia	Cler	050
Lydia	Shel	315
Mary	Hami	123
Mary A	Loga	190
Mary L	Craw	064
Ogro W	Geau	112
Phebe	Miam	220
Robert	Adam	007
Samuel A	Gree	116
Sarah	Hanc	143
Tabitha	Preb	287
Thomas J	Luca	201
William	Adam	007
William	Miam	221
COLLUM		
Russell	Unio	336
COLLVER		
David J	Cuya	068
COLMAN		
Harriet P	Mont	230
COLSHEAR		
Lucinda	Hami	136
COLSON		
Mehitable	Cuya	065
COLTER		
Ewing	Lick	184
Thomas	Hami	139
COLTHAR		
James F	Brow	033
COLTON		
Sheldon	Fran	097
COLUMBER		
Richard	Hard	146
COLVILLE		
Leah	Lick	186
COLVIN		
Dennis	Trum	326
Francis	Adam	003
John G	Preb	287
Margaret	Faye	095
Martha	Scio	306
Melevy	Belm	028
Oscar B	Huro	164

COLVIN (cont)		
Samuel	High	156
Susannah	Harr	149
Theo M	Clar	047
COLWELL		
Betsy	Scio	305
Eliza	Cham	043
James	Morg	258
Jonathan T	Lake	177
Kerrilla	Athe	020
Mary E	Defi	079
Mary L	Clar	045
William	Wash	348
COMBS		
Alfred S	Wash	345
Ann	Musk	265
Culberton	Fran	098
Henry	Trum	327
James M	Cler	048
Joseph	Luca	201
Wesley A	Cler	051
COMELY		
Frederick	Trum	326
COMER		
Robert	Jack	168
COMMANDER		
Joseph	Scio	307
COMPTON		
Abraham	Hami	140
Chas	Clar	046
John E	Cler	049
Margaret	Warr	342
Mary	Warr	344
Susannah	Cham	041
William	Putn	289
COMSTOCK		
Abel	Wood	358
Lurinda T	Lora	195
Mary E	Star	319
CONANT		
Agnes	Lake	178
Chas P	Cuya	067
CONARD		
Geo R	Clin	053
John	High	155
CONAWAY		
Betty	Harr	150
Charlotte	Putn	290
George	Lawr	182
Lucinda	Belm	028
CONCHAINE		
Andrew W	Otta	272
Felix H	Otta	272

CONCKLING			CONLEY (cont)			
Mary L	Fult	105	Eliza P	Wash	350	
CONDEE			Ellen	Ross	298	
Julia	Meig	214	Ira C	Sene	310	
CONDIT			Jesse	Monr	226	
Nancy	Lick	185	Pat	Jeff	170	
Polly	Dela	082	CONLIN			
CONDON			Peter	Mont	248	
James	Lora	193	Thomas	Lick	183	
Patrick	Mont	241	CONLON			
William	Mont	228	Patrick	Mont	239	
CONE			CONN			
Armenal.	Sand	303	Clemens	Musk	266	
Mary A	Gree	116	Hiram R	VanW	338	
Sylveanus G	Lake	178	Jesse	Morg	257	
CONES			John C	Jeff	171	
Phebe	Hami	128	John N	Musk	263	
CONFER			Robert	Perr	275	
Geo	Gree	116	Robert R	Henr	152	
CONGDON			CONNEL			
Buell	Fran	097	Michael	Mont	239	
James W	Wash	348	CONNELL			
CONGER			Jane K	Fair	091	
Charles H	Luca	201	John	Fran	097	
David	Huro	164	Rhoda A	Adam	007	
David	Monr	224	William T	Adam	006	
John	Monr	224	Zachariah	Fran	097	
John	Morr	259	CONNER			
Mary	Wash	347	Andrew J	Mont	239	
William B	Wyan	365	Anna	Fair	089	
CONGILL			Geo W	Gree	116	
Cynthia L	Musk	263	James	Hami	139	
CONGROVE			James S	Guer	119	
Rufus	Mont	239	John	Faye	093	
CONKLE			John	Ross	296	
Rachel	Hock	158	Joseph	Monr	225	
CONKLIN			Mary	Rich	291	
Alfred G	Hard	145	Mary C	Colu	059	
Cath E	Unio	336	Patrick	Fran	097	
Chloe D	Will	355	Patrick	Hard	143	
Gilbert J	Morr	259	Rodger	Gree	113	
Hiram M	Mont	231	CONNETT			
Jacob W	Fran	103	Matilda	Hock	158	
Martin	Fult	106	CONNOLLY			
Miranda B	Hami	135	Joseph	Mont	245	
Orra	Morr	261	Mary	Madi	204	
Peter A	Cuya	067	CONNOR			
Samuel J	Shel	315	Bernard	Cuya	068	
CONKLING			Jacob	Hard	146	
Barrett E	Will	356	Michael	Hami	133	
CONKLYN			Phineas S	Hami	135	
Mary E	Hami	128	Robert	Warr	344	
CONLEY			Thomas	Unio	335	
Dennis	Mont	241				

CONOLY			COOK (cont)			
Harry	Mont	235	Clark	Sene	312	
James	Huro	165	Collins C	Huro	162	
CONOVER			Daniel	VanW	337	
Elias	Cler	048	Eliza	Cuya	065	
Geo W	Brow	033	Eliza	Loga	190	
CONRAD			Elizabeth	Scio	305	
B Franklin	Hami	133	Erwin A	Hanc	142	
Elizabeth	Hami	136	George A	Mont	247	
Frederick	Defi	080	George H	Cuya	068	
George B	Dela	083	Guirdon E	Will	356	
Henry	Mont	233	Hannah A	Wash	350	
John	Mont	234	Harriett	Wood	361	
Mary A	Miam	220	Henry A	Mont	253	
Nathan B	Henr	152	Hiram	Pick	278	
Samuel	Perr	275	Horace M	Asht	015	
Thomas	Gree	116	Irving	Scio	306	
CONRADI			Jacob	Gree	115	
Henry	Hami	133	Jacob	Mont	236	
CONREY			James S	Port	284	
Mary	Warr	343	John	Craw	063	
CONSOLVER			John B	Alle	010	
Allen	Shel	315	Joshua	Wyan	365	
CONSTABLE			Laura M	Fran	103	
Emanuel	Wood	359	Lloyd A	Sene	312	
John	Warr	344	Lucinda	Belm	030	
CONTER			Lucinda	Wood	362	
Sarah	Knox	173	Lucy	Asht	014	
CONTNER			Luvina	Athe	022	
William	Wash	349	Mahala	Hami	136	
CONVERSE			Marcia a	Asht	017	
Daniel H	Miam	221	Margaret A	Hami	127	
John Q	Madi	203	Mary E	Monr	226	
CONVEY			Mary T	Putn	288	
James A	Cler	051	Nancy	Jack	167	
CONWAY			Robert G	Lora	196	
Cath	Hami	136	Roxanna	Cuya	069	
John	Madi	203	Ruth A	Colu	058	
John	Mont	247	Samuel	Preb	287	
Patrick	Clar	044	Samuel W	Hard	145	
Peter	Lora	196	Sidney H	Asht	017	
Thomas	Hami	135	Silas	Craw	063	
CONWELL			Theo	Belm	030	
Matthew	Mont	248	Thomas	Athe	023	
COOK			Watson R	VanW	339	
Alden A	Clar	046	William	Butl	037	
Alice A	Dela	084	William	Wood	358	
Allen	Wood	362	William H	Hami	130	
Amarillo	Guer	118	William H	Putn	289	
Charles	Asht	019	William H	Ross	299	
Chloe	Asht	018	COOKE			
Chloe	Port	286	James M	Wash	350	
Clark	Hanc	143	Rodney R	Fran	095	

COOLAHAN			COOPER (cont)		
Michael	Mont	253	George B	Colu	059
COOLEY			George I	Luca	202
Beulah	Clar	044	George W	Adam	004
Carlos S	Geau	112	Henry	Luca	201
Charles P	Wood	363	Ira A	Mont	242
Frances A	Athe	021	Isaac W	Perr	277
Harry	Mont	253	Isabella	Cuya	065
James	Unio	334	James	Jeff	172
Lorinda	Morr	260	James A	Clar	046
Mary A	Lick	184	James B	Cosh	062
Milton B	Athe	020	James H	Athe	023
Sarah	Athe	022	John	Miam	222
Susan	Henr	153	John	Unio	335
William H	Monr	226	John M	Mont	240
COOLIDGE			Jonathan	Scio	307
Calvin	Cuya	075	Joseph	Port	285
COOMBS			Joseph L	Athe	024
Horace D	Mont	238	Josephus	Hock	159
Isabel	Clar	046	Ludlow H	Cosh	060
COON			Mahala J	Monr	226
Anthony	Belm	029	Mary	Loga	190
Isaac	Alle	009	Nancy	Adam	003
Jesse D	VanW	339	Samuel	Wyan	367
John	Alle	010	Samuel F	Mari	209
Louisa	Shel	315	St Clair	Mont	239
Oshea W	Luca	197	Vincent	Lawr	182
Philip R	Mont	249	William	Hard	148
Phoebe J	Augl	026	William H	Fran	097
Rachel E	Wash	346	William H	Gree	117
COONEY			William H	Preb	286
John C	Vint	341	William P	Scio	306
COONIC			COOVER		
Mary	Sene	313	Elizabeth	Loga	191
COONROD			COPAS		
Sarah	Sand	304	Margaret	Pike	281
COONS			COPE		
Cath	Guer	120	John	Harr	148
Jacob A	Hanc	141	Morris	Belm	028
John	Faye	093	COPELAND		
John H	Mont	256	Eliza A	Nobl	270
Joseph	Wyan	366	Geo H	Augl	025
COOPER			John W	Colu	057
Alexr J	Mont	241	Sam	Jeff	172
Alva	Adam	005	Thomas W	Harr	151
Amos	Perr	276	William	Adam	004
Calvin	Athe	022	COPEN		
Chas B	Otta	271	Caroline	Scio	308
Daniel	Preb	286	COPLEY		
David G	Lawr	181	Mary A	Sene	310
Ellen J	Summ	323	COPLIN		
Erasmus M	Perr	277	Elias	Summ	322
Florence	Cler	051			

COPP			CORIGAN		
Lewis	Mont	231	Peter	Sene	311
Rachel	Huro	162	CORL		
COPPERNOLL			Simon	Star	320
Nancy	Cuya	074	CORMANY		
COPUS			Henry P	Star	318
John H	Wood	361	CORN		
CORANS			Amos	Pike	281
John	Ashl	011	Jeremiah	Gall	111
CORBET			Peter	Lawr	182
James	Mont	227	Sarah	Lawr	179
CORBETT			CORNELIUS		
Elizabeth	Hami	122	Valentin	Hami	133
Margaret	Hami	123	CORNELL		
William	Luca	201	Charles	Defi	079
CORBIN			Charles W	Fult	107
Benj F	Fran	102	Mary	Ashl	013
William H	Wood	359	Rebecca	Lawr	179
CORBIT			Stephen S	Star	318
William	Musk	266	CORNER		
CORBITT			Lewis	Scio	305
Geo	Asht	017	CORNETTER		
CORCORAN			Sarah Jane	High	156
Elizabeth	Hami	136	CORNING		
Michael	Port	284	James H	VanW	337
Patrick	Hami	133	CORNS		
CORDELL			James H	Alle	009
Harriet	Lawr	182	CORNTHWAIT		
Martha	Dark	078	David	Butl	038
Samuel	Lawr	181	CORNWELL		
CORDER			Adam	Clar	046
Jane S	High	154	CORNYN		
CORDERMAN			Helen L	Fair	091
Willard A	Hami	133	COROTHERS		
CORDERY			Philip C	VanW	338
Lavinia	Tusc	331	CORRELL		
CORDIN			Henry	Mont	240
Francis	Huro	166	CORREY		
CORDRAY			Mary N	Maho	205
Elizabeth	Lick	186	CORSON		
James	Mont	253	Amanda	Hami	121
William	Musk	262	Geo F	Cuya	068
CORDREY			Huldah	Fran	097
Mary	Brow	033	Mary	Hami	139
CORDRY			CORTMAN		
William	Cler	051	Elizabeth	Hami	136
CORE			William	Hami	135
Caleb	Ross	300	CORWIN		
CORELL			Cyrus W	Morr	261
John B	Cuya	075	Hannah	Hanc	142
CORIELL			Robert B	Warr	343
Elias	Scio	308	Sarah	Morr	261

CORY			COTTRILL			
Daniel F	Unio	336	Mary	Vint	341	
Edwin	Defi	081	William J	Fair	088	
Joseph P	Butl	036	COUCH			
Robert W	Craw	064	Margaret J	Faye	093	
CORZALT			COUDON			
John	Clin	053	Eliza	Ross	296	
CORZILLIUS			COUFER			
Peter	Defi	080	Henry	Clar	044	
COSFORD			COUGHLAN			
David	Knox	173	John	Faye	094	
COSLER			COULSON			
Susan V	Gree	116	Almeda	Musk	265	
COSLET			Eli G	Morg	258	
William C	Will	357	Mary E	Morg	258	
COSNER			Mary H	Morg	258	
John	Hanc	142	COULTER			
COSS			John A	Loga	189	
Benj	Monr	224	Laura F	Cham	043	
Geo	Belm	028	Mary	Monr	225	
Rebecca A	Belm	028	Susannah	Belm	027	
COST			COULTHARD			
Geo T	Gree	115	John	Hami	140	
John W	Clar	044	COULTRIP			
COSTELLO			William	Erie	086	
Ephraim	Clin	052	COUNTRYMAN			
Mary	Hami	123	Owen S	High	154	
COSTLEY			Philanda	Adam	004	
Jane	Unio	334	COUPLIN			
COTAPES			James O	Guer	120	
John	Cuya	064	John	Guer	120	
COTHRELL			COURCEY			
Andrew J	Mont	238	Elvira	Wash	346	
COTHRON			COURSEY			
Thomas	Wyan	366	Hugh D	Gree	116	
COTRAL			COURTER			
William	Mont	228	Geo H	Fult	105	
COTTER			Pell T	Dela	083	
John H	Mont	236	Robert	Cosh	061	
William	Mont	237	Ward C	Dela	083	
COTTERMAN			COURTNEY			
John	VanW	339	John C	Wood	359	
COTTINGHAM			Margaret	Meig	214	
Edward	Preb	286	Susannah	Maho	205	
COTTLE			COURTRIGHT			
Simeon H	Hami	135	Daniel	Henr	153	
COTTON			COURTWRIGHT			
Francis	Trum	327	Phebe	Merc	218	
Thomas B	Knox	176	COUSINS			
COTTONBROOK			John J	Pike	282	
John G	Musk	266	COUTS			
COTTRELL			Jacob	Craw	062	
Jacob	Fult	105				

COVAN			**COWPE**		
Marice M	High	155	Ellen	Huro	165
William T	High	155	**COX**		
COVAULT			Abigail	Tusc	333
Jeremiah F	Merc	218	Andrew J	Hami	138
Nancy Ann	Merc	217	Ann	Lawr	180
COVELL			Anna T	Cuya	074
Harvey J	Asht	019	Benj F	Wood	363
COVENHOVEN			Charlotte E	Trum	327
James	Lora	194	Credilla	Athe	023
COVENTRY			Edward R	Musk	264
Martha E	Belm	027	Elenor	Mont	232
COVER			Elizabeth	Cosh	062
Adam	Ashl	014	Elizabeth	Preb	288
Geo W	Ashl	014	Elsey	Pike	282
Louisa J	Wyan	366	Geo	VanW	337
COVERT			Geo W	Paul	274
Henry W	Lake	179	Hannah	Shel	316
Rachel	Butl	038	Jackson	Monr	224
Rachel	Sand	302	James	Gall	109
Thomas M	Asht	018	Lucy V	Musk	265
William A	Preb	286	Martha	Pick	280
COVVERTS			Mary	Gree	116
John H	Preb	288	Myron R	Hard	145
COWAN			Nancy A	Will	356
John H	Colu	058	Noah W	Wood	362
Lydia	Warr	343	Patrick	Trum	329
William H	Lake	179	Peter J	Cuya	075
COWDEN			Richard	Cosh	061
Henry N	Lake	178	Samuel S	Preb	288
Louisa	Wood	361	Samuel T	Harr	151
Maria	Maho	205	Simeon	Clin	053
Robert	Craw	063	Smith	Scio	304
COWDERY			Thomas	Lake	179
Eliza B	Cuya	069	**COXEN**		
COWELL			Cath	Star	318
Edwin	Paul	272	John B	Star	319
Martin	Erie	088	**COY**		
COWEN			James W	Wood	363
John	Summ	323	Jesse	Colu	057
COWEY			Lafayette	Star	317
Robert	Athe	023	Lawrence	Hanc	143
COWGILL			Margaret	Meig	212
Milton	Sene	314	Mary	Warr	344
COWHICK			Mary Ann	Musk	262
William P	Wayn	351	Silas	Maho	205
COWLES			**COYLE**		
Henry E	Wood	363	John	Lawr	179
Ruth C	Hami	121	John	Mont	235
COWLING			**COYNER**		
Carolines	Perr	277	Francis	Ross	300
COWNE			**COZAD**		
Mary A	High	155	Elizabeth L	Guer	119

COZARD			CRAIG (cont)		
Woodward	Dark	079	Priscilla	Ross	299
COZIER			Samuel W	Hami	135
Margaret	Loga	191	Susan	Belm	030
CRAB			Susan	Tusc	330
Jeremiah	Mont	248	Wesley	Trum	325
CRABB			CRAIN		
Louden H	Cler	051	Caroline	Alle	008
Nancy	Hami	123	Emma J	Dela	085
Thomas W	Madi	203	Geo	Cuya	067
CRABLE			Lewis G	Athe	023
Josie	Rich	294	Tabitha	Colu	059
CRABTREE			CRALL		
Charles	Pike	280	James S	Rich	293
Edward	Scio	304	Simon	Craw	064
Gideon	Merc	217	CRAM		
Jacob	Jack	167	Caroline V	Wash	350
Joseph S	Scio	308	Electa	Wyan	366
Lorana	Unio	333	Ruth	Trum	327
Tillberry	Pike	280	CRAMBLIT		
CRAFT			Thomas E	Jack	168
John	Augl	025	CRAMER		
Lavinia	Trum	328	Adam	Sene	311
William N	Merc	218	Clarenda	Brow	035
CRAGLOW			David	Wyan	367
Rees I	Wyan	365	Elizabeth A	Cler	051
CRAGO			Elliott	Cler	051
Jesse V	Cosh	061	Israel K	Luca	201
Sarah	Ross	296	Jacob T	Lick	187
William	Cosh	060	James W	Madi	202
CRAIG			John	Fran	103
Cath	Defi	079	Joseph B	Lick	185
Cath R	Wyan	366	Reason	Alle	008
David	Mont	255	Richard	Wood	358
David	Perr	274	Wesley	Fran	097
Eliza M	Erie	087	CRANDAL		
Francis E	Hami	136	Marshal	Sand	302
Francis W	Wash	350	CRANDALL		
George T	Putn	289	Elizabeth	Lake	177
Hannah	Butl	039	Walter M	Lora	195
James	Lawr	181	CRANE		
James	Rich	294	Chas	Warr	344
James M	Star	318	Cyrus G	Wayn	351
Joseph	Star	318	Esther	Wood	363
John	Faye	094	Ezekiel	Hami	136
John	Guer	118	Henry J	Luca	196
Joseph	Star	318	Hester S	Cuya	073
Joshua B	Monr	223	James	Port	284
Juliet	Lick	185	Lewis	Summ	323
Leonard	Nobl	268	Margaret	Warr	343
Leroy S	Perr	275	Melinda	Warr	344
Lewis	Nobl	269	Sarah S	Mont	230
Peter	Hami	121	Squire A	Mont	245
Polly	Knox	174			

CRANER		
Christian	Craw	064
CRANKER		
Peter	Luca	201
CRANMER		
Asaph O	Mari	209
Jane H	Summ	324
CRANN		
Henrietta	Sand	301
CRANSTON		
William	Wash	347
CRAPSEY		
Jacob	Miam	220
CRARY		
Mary G	Hami	128
CRASBY		
Laura A	Luca	201
CRASE		
Henry	Dark	078
(alias Henry Seas)		
CRATER		
Almonte D	Asht	018
CRATES		
Henry	VanW	338
John G	Cuya	067
CRATTY		
John	Dela	085
Robert	Mari	209
CRAUN		
John	Sene	308
Leander M	Sand	301
CRAVER		
David	Mont	256
Mary A	Trum	328
CRAWFORD		
Andrew	Hami	133
Axcah	Tusc	331
Cath M	Wood	358
Croco H	Holm	160
Daniel A	Augl	025
David	Adam	004
David	Clin	053
David	Gree	114
Delivera'e A	Warr	342
Eliza	Wyan	364
Emery	Lake	178
Fanny V	Medi	211
George H	Lawr	183
George W	Adam	006
Isaac N R	Holm	160
James	Adam	007
James W	Belm	029
Jane	Adam	007

CRAWFORD (cont)		
Jesse	Hanc	141
John H	Huro	165
Johnson	Clin	053
Lewis S	Tusc	332
Lucretia	Gree	114
Martha	Carr	040
Mary	Lick	186
Mary	Otta	272
Mary M	Mont	232
Peggy A	Huro	164
Richard B	Star	319
Sarah		
(see Sarah Orawford)		
Thomas J	Carr	039
William H	Brow	034
William H	Fran	103
CRAXFORD		
Octa	Huro	166
CREAGER		
William H	Warr	342
William O	Mont	232
CREAMER		
Mahala	Faye	093
Wesley M	Unio	336
CREATH		
Harriet E	Madi	204
Wiley	Madi	202
CREBBIN		
Edward K	Mont	247
CREDIT		
James	Adam	007
CREED		
William J	Fran	097
CREEKS		
Jeremiah	Musk	264
CREGO		
Abigail	Madi	204
George R	Madi	203
CREIGHTON		
Eleanor L	Cuya	073
James	Monr	223
Samuel	Athe	023
Sarah	Belm	028
CREMBLEBINE		
John	Hard	147
CREMEAN		
Mary	Alle	008
CREMEANS		
Linsey	Jack	166
CREMMERING		
Lawrence	Mont	253
CREPPS		
Isabell	Faye	094

CREPS				CRITES		
Eliza	Maho	206		Daniel L	Alle	008
Joseph A	Wood	363		Jonah	Wayn	352
CREQUE				CRITTENDEN		
Ferdinand	Summ	322		Alfred B	Asht	016
CRESPIN				CRITZER		
Mary E	Clar	045		Amelia	Fult	104
CRESS				CROCKER		
Eliza A	Miam	222		Edwin	Cuya	065
William T	Paul	273		CROFOOT		
CRETZ				Ansel	Lake	177
Frank	Hami	139		CROFT		
CREVISTON				James	Cham	043
Mary A	Paul	274		Nancy A	Rich	294
CREW				Samuel	Mont	242
Michael	Mont	241		CROFUTT		
CREWWELL				Charles H	Geau	112
William C	Rich	295		CROGHAN		
CRICK				Aquilla	Merc	218
William	Wayn	353		CROGO		
CRICKET				Geo W	Ross	299
James	Dela	083		CROMAN		
CRIDER				Josiah	Pick	280
Reuben	Augl	024		CROMER		
CRIGER				Ada	Rich	292
Hermon	Tusc	333		John E	Rich	293
CRINYAN				CROMWELL		
James	Mont	241		William	Geau	113
CRIPPEN				CRONAN		
Betsey M	Athe	021		Hanoria	Cuya	067
Earl	Wash	347		CRONENBERGER		
Flora	Athe	021		Nancy	Cuya	074
CRIPPIN				CRONINGER		
Elizabeth	Dela	085		Jacob	Craw	064
CRISE				Lorenzo	Wood	360
James	Star	321		CRONK		
CRISPELL				Geo F	Cuya	065
Cinthia	Asht	018		Sarah R	Cuya	075
CRISS				CRONLY		
Hugh	Star	318		Martin	Hard	147
James	Fran	102		CROOK		
Lydia Ann	Star	320		John W	Fair	089
CRIST				Mary	Monr	226
Alex	Unio	334		Thomas	Mont	248
Andrew	Putn	290		CROOKE		
Ann E	Mont	233		Joseph	Mont	243
CRISWELL				CROOKS		
Jehu	Tusc	330		Geo M	Musk	264
Mary J	Lick	184		CROOSE		
CRITCHFIELD				Job	Mont	249
John	Hami	139		CROPPER		
Lyman R	Defi	081		Reuben O	Adam	005
Roland	Knox	174		CROSBIA		
William P	Wayn	353		Anna	Lick	184

CROSBY			CROUT		
Jeremiah	Mont	238	Geo W	Fult	105
CROSGROVE			Marintha	Fult	106
Eliza J	Ross	297	CROW		
CROSHAW			Ann	Luca	201
Spencer	Wood	364	Barbara	Medi	210
CROSIER			Elizabeth	Faye	093
Abbie	Rich	296	Ezram B	Hard	148
James W	Musk	266	Joseph E	Mari	208
CROSKEY			Mary	Lawr	183
Jasper N	Harr	149	Thomas	Mont	253
CROSLEY			William H	Defi	080
Mary F	Lake	176	CROWDER		
Rosan	Hanc	143	Isabella G	Geau	113
CROSS			CROWE		
Eliza	Star	320	Geo	Hami	133
Elizabeth	Adam	006	John	Knox	175
Elizabeth A	Summ	324	CROWELL		
Eve	Adam	006	John B	Mont	240
Geo W	Unio	333	Milton	Preb	288
Hamilton J	Sene	312	Moses	Star	320
Israel P	Lawr	182	Peter	Alle	010
Jackson	Wash	347	Ruth	Vint	341
Martin	Erie	087	Silas	Clar	047
Reason	Ross	301	William H	Fran	097
Robert	Gree	116	CROWLEY		
Sophia	Hami	128	Emerson	Mont	249
Thomas	Colu	059	Sarah	Cosh	059
CROSSEN			CROWN		
Jacob	Athe	022	Ann Eliza	Jeff	172
John C	Guer	120	Thomas	Tusc	333
Jno J	Perr	275	William B	Jeff	171
CROSSER			CROWNER		
Amanda	Wood	361	David F	Ashl	012
William	Scio	305	CROWTHER		
CROSSHAN			Holt	Mont	236
Eleanor	Wood	363	CROZIER		
CROSSLEY			Elizabeth	Belm	027
Sarah F	Lawr	180	Julia A	Trum	328
Thomas	Meig	214	CRUBAUGH		
William H	Hami	121	John	Mont	240
CROSSMAN			CRUGAN		
John J H	Wayn	353	Mary A	Warr	343
CROSSON			CRUGER		
Annie	Dela	083	Sarah E	Hami	123
CROTTY			CRUISE		
Edward	Hami	133	Allen	Fran	098
John	Hami	133	CRULL		
CROUSE			Abigail	Scio	305
Ethelbert	Paul	272	CRUM		
Isaac	Craw	064	Mary	Butl	037
Michael	Putn	289	Wilson S	Erie	086
Napoleon	Wyan	367			

CRUMBAUGH
Clara	Gree	115

CRUMLEY
Geo W	Fair	089
Henry B	Clin	053
Josias	Colu	059
Mary	Gree	114

CRUMLY
Azel E	Clin	055

CRUMM
Henry	Maho	204

CRUMMEL
John	Wayn	351

CRUMP
Alfred	Holm	161

CRUPPER
Elisha	Hock	159

CRUSER
Henry	Guer	119

CRUTE
Elizabeth	Adam	005
Jane	Brow	032

CUBBAGE
John W	Gall	109

CUDDOHA
Honorah	Paul	273

CUFF
James	Hami	132

CULBERTSON
Ann H	Musk	267
Geo H	Rich	294
Jane	Wayn	353
Jane W	Hami	135
Rhoda J	Miam	222

CULIN
John D	Mont	245

CULLEN
David C	Augl	025
Robert	Hami	135

CULLER
George	Holm	161
Melancthon	Rich	292

CULLEY
Frank C	Defi	080
Robert H	Luca	201

CULLISON
Joseph	Guer	119
Roseann	Knox	174
Zephaniah B	Lick	188

CULLOM
Nancy	Hami	140

CULLUMS
James H	Athe	020

CULLY
Sarah H	Lick	186
Thomas	Wayn	351

CULNON
Mary A	Colu	059

CULP
Columbus D	Rich	292
Jacob	Fair	091
John B	Morr	261
Miles J	Will	357

CULPS
Nancy	Pick	280

CULVER
Alva	Asht	015
Samuel	Sene	314

CUMMING
Cath	Shel	316

CUMMINGS
Anne	Carr	039
Jno H	Meig	213
John W	Harr	149
Joseph B	Gree	115
Julia L	Clar	045

CUMMINS
Francis M	Warr	344
Hannah	Warr	344
Joel B	Pike	282
John C	Hanc	141
Lucretia	Fran	097
Nancy R	Butl	039
Paul	Athe	023
Samuel	Musk	264

CUNARD
Leare	Jack	166

CUNNINGER
Chas	Medi	211

CUNNINGHAM
Alex	Cuya	067
Benj	Carr	039
Francis G	Nobl	270
Geo W	Morr	257
Hugh	Dela	083
James	Luca	201
John A	Alle	010
John T	Monr	225
Julia E	Fran	101
Levi F	Dark	077
Luc'da J	Hami	139
Mary E	Nobl	270
Nancy	Athe	021
Patrick	Mont	248
Peter	Clar	047
Thomas	Mont	248

CUNNINGHAM (cont)			CURTIS			
Warren	Huro	162	Abigail E	Huro	164
William	Belm	028	Amanda	Alle	008
CUNNINGHAN			Andrew J	Belm	026
Maria	Preb	287	Charles C	Knox	175
CUPP			Elijah	Dark	079
Eliza	Mari	208	Erastus R	Hard	144
Hannah	Fran	104	Henry	Mont	242
CUPPLES			Joel B	Mont	253
Jacob	Wayn	353	John	Mont	245
CURL			John W	Nobl	270
Charles H	Hard	146	John W	Ross	299
Lusetta	Warr	344	Leonard H	Cuya	067
Thomas B	Hard	146	Mary	Wash	349
William H	Loga	190	Mary A	Fult	106
CURLEY			Mary E	Cuya	068
Honora	Hami	127	Mary E	Mont	232
Michael	Mont	241	Michael	Meig	214
CURLINS			Robert G	Augl	025
Mary	Musk	265	Samuel	Miam	222
CURLIS			Simon	Meig	214
Susan E	Cler	047	CURTISS		
CURNELL			Augustis	Summ	322
Samuel	Adam	006	Geo W	Huro	164
William	Lawr	182	Harriet	Lake	177
CURRAN			Lewis A	Mont	249
Andrew J	Perr	276	Thomas	Mont	229
Daniel	Cosh	061	CURTNER		
John	Mont	253	Andrew H	Dark	077
Joseph F	Dela	083	John	Dark	077
Peter D	Wood	360	CURTS		
CURREN			Angeline	VanW	339
Allen M	Craw	062	CUSAC		
Cath	Vint	340	Isaac	Hanc	142
Elizabeth	Morr	261	CUSHING		
Mary A	Rich	295	Margaret	Pick	280
Thomas S	Huro	164	CUSHION		
CURRENT			Thomas J	Mont	236
John	Wood	360	CUSHMAN		
CURRIE			Almeda A	Cham	043
Hannah E	Scio	307	Tabitha	Cuya	074
CURRIGAN			CUSICK		
Edward	Sene	314	Jane	Clin	052
CURRY			CUSINE		
Alzina S	Ashl	013	Eli	Luca	198
Evaline	Ross	297	CUSSINS		
Marion	Will	356	Lucian A	Preb	287
William	Preb	287	CUSTER		
William L	Unio	334	Geo H	Rich	292
CURSCHMANN			William W	Perr	275
Fred W	Mont	239	CUSTIS		
CURTIN			Mary	Clin	054
Jeremiah	Mont	247			

CUTCLIFFE		
Samuel D	Erie	088
CUTHBERT		
Sherlock B	Port	283
CUTHER		
Sabina M	Asht	019
CUTLER		
Anna M	Cuya	073
Carsena	Asht	019
Eliza	Medi	210
Eliza	Port	285
Jos N	Cham	042
Prudence	Lora	194
CUTSHALL		
Jacob	Cosh	062
CUTSHAW		
Ellen	Fair	091
Jas	Perr	276
CUTTER		
Jas E	Paul	273
John	Wayn	353
CUTTING		
Alanson P	Hard	146
DABNEY		
Chloe	Trum	325
Narcissa A	Gall	109
DABUS		
Leonard	Miam	219
DAGE		
Hamilton	Paul	274
DAGNAN		
Peter	Lora	195
DAGUE		
Abashaba	VanW	340
Mary J	Wood	360
DAILEY		
Elizabeth	Gree	114
George K	Wood	362
George W	Athe	021
John	Lawr	181
John H	Ross	299
Vincent	Gall	108
DAILY		
Elizabeth	Jeff	172
Samuel	Wood	358
DAINS		
Ebenezer J	Mari	208
Rebecca	Meig	212
Sarah J	Meig	212
DAIRY		
Henry	Mont	238

DALE		
Armsted M	Brow	034
James W	Gall	109
DALEY		
Hannah M	Huro	165
Michael	Mont	249
DALLAS		
Marg	Jeff	169
DALLY		
James G	Monr	224
DALRYMPLE		
Hiram	Asht	019
Margaret	Cuya	071
Nancy	Morr	260
Oliver S	Mont	232
DALTON		
Martha	Hami	136
DALY		
Francis	Mont	253
Jno	Mont	253
DALYN		
Paul	Mont	248
DAMBACK		
Fred	Cuya	067
DAMON		
Elvira	Medi	210
John	Hanc	143
Mary E	Medi	210
DAMOURNE		
Frank	Mont	253
DANA		
Mary Jane	Trum	326
DANECKER		
Barbara	Mont	231
DANFORTH		
Charles	Geau	112
DANGLER		
Sarah	Star	320
DANHAUER		
Alvia	Perr	276
DANIELS		
Camilla	Scio	308
Cath M	Erie	086
Henry	Defi	080
Mary	Cuya	066
Mary E	Huro	162
Samuel	Mont	248
Thomas	Holm	160
Thomas	Meig	214
William W	Lawr	183
DANLEY		
John W	Wash	345
Martha J	Fran	101

DANNALS			DAUGHERTY			
Matilda	Colu	059	Anna	Athe	023	
DARBY			Eli	Augl	025	
Albert	Knox	175	Francis A	Warr	343	
Terniah B	Erie	088	Gibson	Athe	024	
DARLING			Jno	Mont	253	
Eliza	Alle	009	Mary	VanW	339	
Fannie A	Asht	016	Patrick S	Guer	117	
Freeman E	Cuya	069	Samuel U	Mont	229	
Geo H	Adam	007	DAUGHMAN			
James C	Lawr	181	N A M	Hami	139	
John	Morr	260	DAULTON			
John J	Unio	335	Amanda	Brow	034	
Lucina	Huro	162	Martha	Brow	034	
Nancy	Hami	137	DAUM			
Peter	Fran	098	Margaret	Luca	202	
DARLINGTON			DAVEE			
William	Scio	307	Isabell	Cosh	061	
DARNELL			DAVENPORT			
Mary	Fran	102	David S	Shel	315	
DARNES			Geo	Wash	350	
John W	Cosh	060	Martin S	Wood	359	
DAROADS			DAVEY			
Samuel F	Star	317	Lydia	Rich	294	
DARR			DAVID			
David	Wayn	353	Cath	VanW	337	
Henry H	Wayn	354	Daniel R	Mont	230	
Martha	Star	318	DAVIDSON			
Mary	Tusc	330	Delilah	Nobl	269	
Mary A	Fair	092	Edwin	Cuya	067	
DARRAGH			Elizabeth J	Dark	079	
James	Jeff	172	Henry T	Geau	112	
Nancy	Jeff	171	James H	Sene	309	
William	Mont	242	James W	Hanc	141	
DARROW			Jeremiah	Lawr	181	
Lorenzo D	Trum	330	John	VanW	339	
DARST			John S	Knox	175	
Eleanor	Gall	108	Martha	Merc	217	
Jacob	Tusc	332	Martha E	Monr	223	
James	Shel	315	Nancy	Colu	056	
John S	Hard	144	Polly	High	156	
Samuel	Gall	109	Robert S	Wood	363	
DART			Samuel	Knox	172	
Elanor	Erie	086	William	Tusc	331	
DARTT			DAVIE			
Harrison	Meig	212	William	Erie	087	
DASLER			DAVIES			
George	Mont	238	John	Mont	253	
DASSON			Thomas D	Fran	098	
James	Guer	119	DAVIN			
DAUB			Thomas	Unio	336	
Jacob	Maho	205	DAVIS			
			Abraham	Star	320	

76

DAVIS (cont)			DAVIS (cont)		
Adam	Guer	119	Jacob	Musk	267
Alonzo H	Athe	022	James D	Mont	248
Amaziah	Hock	157	James H	Cuya	067
Ambrose	Clar	046	James M	Lawr	181
Andrew	Wash	347	Jane	Colu	056
Andrew J	Brow	034	James C	Paul	273
Ann	Pike	280	James F J	Cuya	067
Anna	Will	356	Jefferson	Scio	307
Anthony F	Alle	010	Jefferson P	Fran	098
Asa	Fran	102	Jesse	Clar	046
Benj F	Athe	024	John	Alle	011
Caroline R	Hami	127	John	Cler	052
Cath	Gall	108	John	Mont	228
Charles C	Wash	349	John	Mont	238
Charles J	Tusc	331	Jno	Mont	253
Charles R	Hanc	143	John	Morg	258
Charles R	Sene	311	John	Scio	305
Charls	Sand	303	John C	Ashl	012
Daniel	Ross	299	John C	Mont	239
David	Lawr	182	John E	Cham	041
David	Will	356	John G	Mont	235
David R	Putn	290	John G	Wood	358
David W	Wash	350	Jno H	Perr	275
Delilah	Rich	294	John L	Star	320
Echmina	Trum	327	John W	Belm	030
Edwin	Cuya	067	John W	Hanc	141
Eldridge	Tusc	331	John W	Henr	151
Elias W	Harr	151	John W	High	154
Elizabeth	Clar	044	John W	Nobl	270
Elizabeth	Lawr	180	Joseph W	Cham	041
Elizabeth	Perr	277	Joshua	Pike	282
Elizabeth A	Hard	144	Julia A	Putn	290
Emor M	Hami	135	Julia Ann	Athe	021
Ephraim W	Wyan	365	Julia R	Fran	101
Fielding	Knox	173	Lavina	Brow	032
Francis	Sand	303	Leander	Belm	030
Francis A	Morg	257	Lewellyn R	Cuya	067
Francis M	Musk	263	Lewis	Monr	224
George	Fran	098	Lewis	Rich	295
George R	Athe	021	Lewis M	Hard	144
Hannah	Mont	231	Lodwick D	Fran	098
Harriet A	Fran	101	Lois A	High	155
Harriet B	Luca	198	Lorenzo	Harr	149
Harriet J	Belm	027	Lucinda	Nobl	268
Henry	Hock	157	Malissa J H	Hami	139
Henry	Meig	213	Maria	Henr	151
Henry C	Faye	093	Maria	Wash	350
Henry C	Hami	134	Mary	Butl	038
Henry H	Shel	315	Mary	Hock	158
Henry M	Morg	258	Mary	Lick	186
Herman E	Wash	347	Mary	Pick	279
Hildreth	Wash	347	Mary	Pick	279

DAVIS (cont)		
Mary	Putn	290
Mary J	Lawr	183
Matilda	Pick	278
Nancy	Meig	213
Nancy J	Scio	306
Nathan G	Guer	117
Obadiah	Brow	034
Olive	Wash	347
Oscar	Wyan	365
Paul W	Wash	347
Permelia	Nobl	268
Pharis	Will	355
Robert T	Hock	159
Rollin W	Asht	019
Rosanna	Scio	308
Russell T	Meig	214
Samuel	Belm	030
Samuel	Ross	298
Samuel	VanW	337
Sarah	Lawr	180
Sarah	Luca	196
Sarah	Morr	260
Sarah	Ross	300
Sarah	Warr	344
Sarah	Wash	350
Sarah A	Cuya	067
Sarah A	Jack	166
Sarah J	Cuya	071
Simeon A	Dela	084
Susan	Jack	168
Theo	Mont	229
Theophilus	Hami	135
Thomas	Nobl	269
Thomas J	VanW	338
Thomas L	Clin	053
W B	Vint	340
Washington	Unio	336
Willard	Wash	346
William	Belm	027
William A	Perr	276
William B	Pick	280
William D	Jack	166
William H	Cosh	060
William H	Hami	135
William H	Unio	333
William K	Belm	028
William M	Morg	257
DAVISON		
Olive M	Lake	178
Sarah J	Adam	004
DAVISSON		
David	Madi	203

DAVISSON (cont)		
Sarah	Clar	044
DAVY		
Ezra J	Morr	260
John	Mont	228
John L	Dela	085
DAWES		
Ephraim C	Hami	135
Margaret	Jeff	169
DAWSON		
Edward H	Henr	153
Eliza A	Tusc	332
Jacob	Ross	300
James	Ross	300
James M	Lawr	182
Nancy	Asht	014
Nancy	Scio	307
Robert	Hami	135
Samuel	Jeff	170
William	Morg	258
William	Unio	335
Willson	Paul	272
DAY		
Alpheus D	Star	320
Anderson	Hami	133
Charles A	Henr	153
Cincinnatus N		
	Meig	213
Deming W H	Wood	359
Eli H	Defi	080
Eliza	Summ	323
George W	Mont	253
Isaac	Brow	031
John	Mont	253
John C	Dela	084
John H	Lick	185
Joseph	Loga	189
Joseph A	Cuya	076
Mary	Belm	027
Mary	Port	284
Minor L	Huro	163
Rebecca	Jack	168
Sarah A	Harr	149
William Henry		
	Hami	135
DAYTON		
James	Dela	085
James	Pick	278
Phebe	Asht	019
DAYWALT		
William J	Sene	313
DEADY		
Jeremiah	Fran	098

DEAL			DEBOLT (cont)		
David	Sand	303	William	Lick	188
John P	Luca	200	DE BRA		
Philip	Sene	313	Daniel W	Miam	221
Rollin	Knox	174	DE CAMP		
(alias Leon D Bernay)			Jno M	Meig	212
DEAMUDE			William M	Mont	235
Eliza A	Musk	263	DECHENHAUSEN		
DEAN			Ernst	Mont	253
Alfred	Wood	360	DECK		
Andrew	Unio	335	Henry C	Clin	053
Anthony	Mont	250	DECKER		
Charles C	Wash	347	Claiborn S	VanW	338
Elizabeth	Cosh	060	Elizabeth	Wash	347
Gulliver	Athe	020	Jacob	Sene	309
Isaiah	Scio	308	Jacob H	Hanc	142
James T	Wood	360	James	Hanc	141
John H	Luca	200	Jerome	Hanc	141
Josiah S	Meig	213	John G	Musk	264
Maria	Henr	151	John M	Cuya	067
Mary J	Erie	086	Lester	Luca	197
Norman F	Hami	134	Moses	Dela	083
Peter L	Lick	187	Nancy A	Fran	101
Samuel F	Belm	029	Peter	Hami	134
Sarah	Cler	048	Polly	Unio	335
Thomas	Meig	213	DEEBLE		
William B	Mont	239	Margaret	Wash	350
DEAR			DEEDS		
Israel S	Mont	231	Hiram B	Summ	323
DEARDOOFF			DEEGAN		
Charlotte	Tusc	331	Bernard	Mont	249
DEARDOURFF			DEEM		
David	Dark	077	Eliza	Star	319
DEARTH			DEEMAR		
Abraham	Ross	298	Albert	Hami	136
Prudence	Hard	144	DEEMS		
DEASY			Mary	Rich	294
Luke	Wash	347	DEERING		
DEATLEY			Henry	Fair	091
Henry	Pike	282	DEERWESTER		
DEATS			John	Loga	190
Henry	Mont	248	DEESER		
DE BECK			William	Tusc	330
Jesse P J	Hami	135	DEETS		
De Bee			Addison	Fair	092
George	Colu	056	DEFFENBAUGH		
De Bell			David	Madi	202
Phebe	Summ	321	DEFOE		
DEBERGER			James	Lawr	182
Adolph	Mont	249	DE FOREST		
DEBOLT			Theresa	Cuya	071
Mekon	Paul	273	DE GARMO		
Silas	Wyan	367	Adaline S	Lora	193

DEGENFELD			DELL			
Frances	Erie	087	John	Rich	292
DEGLER			William F	Hami	134
Jacob	Holm	159	DELLAR		
DEGOOD			Frank	Hami	134
Thomas R	Unio	335	DELONG		
DEGUARIM			Cath	VanW	339
Ann	Morg	258	Edmund	Belm	031
DEHART			Edward	Perr	276
Sarah	Gree	116	George	Lora	195
DEHAVEN			Martha	Mont	231
Malinda	Hock	158	Owen	Nobl	268
DEHNEL			Sarah	Adam	004
Henry	Erie	087	William	Madi	203
(alias Siedkie)			DELP		
DEHUFF			Louis	Hock	158
Margaret	Cosh	060	DELRYMPLE		
DEIS			Jerusha	Asht	018
Martin	Mont	240	DE LUSIA		
DEISLANG			Christopher	Luca	200
Chas	Mont	250	DELYE		
DEISLER			Oliver	Luca	196
Michael	Mont	253	DEMALINE		
DEISMAN			Saul	Lora	193
William H	Cuya	065	DEMANDER		
DEITERS			George A	Mont	248
John	Butl	036	DEMARIS		
DEITRICK			Jacob B	Cler	049
Delormay	Trum	327	DEMINGS		
John	Brow	032	William	Mont	254
DE LAMATER			DEMINT		
Harriet F	Rich	292	Eliza	Butl	038
John C	Cuya	067	Mary	VanW	339
Merrick L	Will	355	DEMORE		
DELAND			Cornelia E	Asht	017
James B	Summ	323	DEMOREST		
DELANEY			John P	Unio	336
Mary	Lora	195	DEMORET		
Patrick C	Mont	240	William	Butl	039
DELANO			DEMOS		
Joel A	Mont	243	Chas W	VanW	339
DELANTY			DEMPSEY		
James	Luca	201	Edw	Mont	250
DELANY			Laurence	Mont	231
Jasper N	Putn	289	Luke	Mont	235
Mary	Belm	029	DEMPSTER		
Mary	Cuya	071	George W	Mont	239
Melinda	Huro	164	Wilberforce C		
DE LA RUE				Hami	135
Octave	Hami	134	William	Morg	258
DELAWTER			DEMUTH		
Sarah	Mont	232	Lewis A	Tusc	331
DELGEN					
Henry	Cuya	067			

DENBOW			DENNISTON (cont)			
William	Monr	226	William M	Brow	032
DENHAM			DENNY			
Henry	Warr	343	Cath	Monr	224
Sarah	Cler	048	DENSLOW			
DENIAS			Julia A	Asht	019
Caroline	Sene	310	DENSMORE			
DENISON			Richard	Meig	214
Andrew	Wayn	352	DENSON			
Joel M	Perr	275	Sarah	Ross	297
DENMAN			DENTON			
Edward P	Paul	274	Caroline	Fair	091
Esther	Merc	218	Susan	Cler	049
Jos	Miam	220	DEPEW			
DENNARD			Anna	Wyan	367
Mary	Hami	138	DEPOY			
DENNERLE			Chas	Ross	300
Lawrence	Cuya	066	DEPRETZ			
DENNEY			Cath	Hami	127
George	Gall	108	DEREMER			
Harvey	Gall	111	Abram	Loga	192
DENNIN			DERHAMMER			
Michael	Mont	248	Amandis	Medi	211
DENNING			DERING			
Lucius	Geau	111	Henry	Augl	025
Newton	Harr	150	DERINGER			
Rebecca	Adam	005	David M	Cosh	061
William	Jeff	171	DERISMORE			
DENNIS			Grizzel	Ashl	013
Charles I	Luca	196	Jas R W	Ashl	013
Eben J	Erie	087	DERLEY			
Eliza	Colu	059	David B	Asht	014
Harvey	Guer	119	DERLIN			
James	Colu	058	John	Mont	248
Jeremiah	Morr	260	DERMODY			
Lloyd	Hami	135	John	Mont	249
Martha S	Fult	106	DE RODES			
Mary	Perr	277	Henry C	Wood	361
Michael	Fult	106	DERR			
Nancy	Jeff	169	Eliza A	Fran	101
Nancy	Meig	213	Jacob N	Cosh	061
Robert J	Belm	027	John S	Morr	261
Sarah	Madi	203	Thomas J	Hock	158
Valentine	Sene	309	DERRICK			
William	Dela	083	Andrew	Hami	133
Willis	Putn	289	Hugh	Colu	058
DENNISON			DERROUGH			
Isabella	Madi	203	Lewis	Scio	305
Jonathan	Lawr	179	DERRY			
Margaret	Madi	203	George S	Vint	341
Mary	Henr	151	Jacob M	Harr	149
DENNISTON			Michael	Knox	174
Geo C	Lora	193	Nancy	Hard	144

DESELMS				DEWALDT		
James	Guer	119		August J	Erie	088
DESHONG				Joseph	Erie	088
John B	Mari	208		DEWALT		
DESTELZWEIG				William	Craw	063
Benedict	Fran	098		DEWAR		
DETAMORE				Eliza	Lick	187
Simeon A	Preb	287		Thomas	Lick	186
DE TAMPLE				DEWEES		
Joseph	Erie	087		Joshua	Belm	027
DETCHON				DEWESE		
Alfred	Maho	206		Anna	Wood	363
DETRICK				DEWEY		
Geo F	Miam	220		Amy	Mont	232
DETTWILER				Jehial D	Asht	016
Eliza	Belm	028		DE WITT		
DETWILER				Ellison	Faye	094
Martin L	Hanc	141		Henry	Fult	107
Sarah	Mont	231		Henry	Holm	160
DEVALL				Jacob	Preb	286
James	Lick	187		John	Knox	174
DE VASS				Margaret	Rich	295
Joseph	Pike	282		DE WOLF		
DEVER				Horatio	Trum	327
Jos S	Clar	046		DEWWESE		
DEVERS				William	Shel	315
Mary A	Cham	041		DEWYANT		
DEVIES				Michael	Sene	313
Beniwell L	Ashl	013		DE YARMETT		
DE VINCE				Chas H	Fran	098
King	Pike	281		DEYO		
DEVINE				Caroline	Pick	279
James	Mont	243		Edson	Fran	103
James	Rich	294		Nelson J	Asht	017
John	Fran	098		DEYR		
DEVISH				Caroline	Pick	279
Luther	Star	318		DEYSLEE		
DEVLIN				Samuel	Tusc	333
Thomas	Mont	254		DIAL		
William	VanW	337		Absalom S	Mont	240
DEVOE				Elizabeth	Knox	174
Henry L	Cuya	076		Lewis	Mont	241
DEVON				Nancy	Holm	161
Mary	Butl	036		DICAS		
DEVORE				Joshua	Putn	289
Alexander	Perr	277		DICE		
Isaac	Hock	158		John	Wayn	354
John W	Guer	120		DICK		
Lydia A	Tusc	330		Geo F	Will	357
DEW				John D	Wash	349
Andrew	Perr	275		Robert W	Sene	313
DEWALD				Sarah	Hami	127
Carrie S	Hami	127		DICKASON		
				Alexander	Jack	167

DICKASON (cont)				DIEHL		
Martha	Jack	168		Aaron J	Colu	057
Mary	Medi	211		Henry	Morg	257
DICKEN				John M	Trum	329
Asias W	Lick	186		Louis	Fran	103
John W	Sene	311		Samuel	Defi	081
DICKENS				DIEHLMAN		
Jesse S	Sene	310		Geo	Fult	104
DICKENSON				DIEMER		
Chancellor	Brow	034		Philip	Mont	254
Phebe	Loga	192		DIENER		
DICKERSON				Thomas	Mont	254
Ephraim	Musk	267		DIER		
John	Gall	107		Erhard	Hami	135
Joshua	Harr	149		DIERKES		
Manuel W	Rich	296		Elizabeth	Monr	225
Matilda	Mari	209		DIES		
Rachel	Musk	265		Sophia	Summ	321
Silas	Mari	209		DIESTER		
Wisula	Loga	191		Cath	Mont	230
DICKEY				DIETER		
Daniel D	Putn	289		Chas W	Mont	227
Elizabeth	Putn	290		DIETRICK		
Ellen E	Cuya	071		Frank	Hami	135
Geo	Butl	037		DIETZ		
James	Musk	263		Andrew	Mont	250
Martha	Preb	286		Ernest	Hami	135
DICKHUT				Philip	Hanc	141
George	Mont	253		DIFENBACH		
DICKINSON				Chas	Mont	249
Ann M	Cuya	067		DIKER		
Ann M	Gree	116		Charles	Hami	138
Chas T	Lick	187		DILBONE		
Chloe	Asht	014		Isaac	Merc	218
Christopher	Star	319		DILDINE		
Daniel	Luca	202		Albert M	Sene	311
George S	Mont	253		Lydia G	Sene	310
DICKMAN				DILENSCHENIDER		
Henry W	VanW	337		Jos	Sand	303
DICKS				DILG		
Mary	Craw	064		Christian	Hami	134
DICKSON				DILGER		
Jas R	Maho	205		Mathias J	Fair	089
John	Hard	146		DILKS		
Martha L	Hami	127		Chas H	Mont	250
Mathew M	Summ	322		DILL		
Nancy	Butl	036		Ann	Hami	140
Robert	Mont	248		Ann	Shel	314
Samuel A	Fair	092		Geo	Hami	135
Samuel	Musk	264		Geo H	Fran	098
DIDAY				Lewis	Miam	220
John	Craw	063		Mary	Butl	038
DIEFENDORFF				Rachel	Clar	045
Menzo H	Summ	323				

DILLE			DINGES			
David R	Athe	020	Conrad	Rich	294	
Mary A	Wash	345	DINGESS			
Rachel	Athe	020	William A	Gree	114	
William	Morg	258	DINN			
DILLEHAY			Frederick	Mont	241	
John W	Guer	117	DINSMORE			
DILLEY			Matilda	Lick	185	
James	Trum	325	DIRR			
James L	Guer	120	Bernhard	Hami	133	
DILLINGER			William	Luca	200	
George	Jack	168	DISAGA			
Leonard	Faye	093	Franz J	Mont	239	
Mary	Jack	168	DISBRO			
Mary J	Adam	004	Abram J	Huro	166	
DILLINGHAM			Edward G	Mont	253	
Samuel	Mont	243	Jane	Rich	294	
DILLION			DISBRON			
James M	Monr	226	David J	Fult	107	
William	Lawr	181	DISBROW			
William	Monr	224	Lucy	Fult	105	
DILLMAN			DISCUS			
Simon P	Mont	254	James F	Hanc	143	
DILLON			DISERENS			
Hamilton	Monr	224	Elizabeth	Hami	139	
Hiram B	Lawr	183	DISHER			
Isaac E	Cler	049	Christian	Luca	196	
James	Clin	053	DISINGER			
John	Mont	233	Samuel	Wood	361	
Lewis M	Cuya	066	DISNEY			
Peter	High	155	Dorson V	Knox	173	
Thomas	Monr	226	DISTER			
DILLOW			Joseph	Mont	228	
Thomas	Lawr	181	DITCH			
DILLSAVER			Geo	Mari	208	
Jonathan	VanW	337	DITER			
DILTS			Cath	Cuya	067	
Llewellyn G	Dark	077	DITTENHAFER			
DILTZ			Harvey	Star	318	
David	Miam	219	DITTER			
DILWORTH			Thomas	Musk	263	
Lois A	Putn	290	DITTMAR			
DILYARD			Frank	Mont	253	
Geo	Dark	078	Jacob	Fair	089	
DIMMICK			DITTO			
Jonathan C	Asht	018	Elizabeth	Sene	313	
Orlando	Geau	111	Matilda	Tusc	331	
DIMPSEY			DITTS			
James	Mont	235	James	Paul	273	
DINE			DIVAN			
Wilson	Star	318	Mary	Lick	184	
DINES			DIVINE			
Maria	Ross	296	Uduy L	Tusc	332	
Phillip	Geau	112				

84

DIX				**DODES**		
Charles E	Fran	098		Isaac	High	155
DIXON				**DODGE**		
Adam	Mont	229		Hester	Asht	016
Alanson R	Lake	177		Margaret	Scio	305
Benoni	Hami	133		**DODSON**		
Eurotus	Cuya	067		Malinda	Scio	307
Francess	Cler	049		Martha E	Cham	042
Jacob	Henr	151		Philip	Meig	214
Jane	Ross	297		**DODVILL**		
John K	Scio	306		Mary	Gall	107
Joseph	Vint	341		**DOEBLER**		
Mary	Athe	024		Michael	Mont	237
Mordecai P	Craw	062		**DOERR**		
Walker L	Dela	084		Cath	Cuya	067
William F	Musk	266		**DOERSH**		
DOAK				Lorenzo	Craw	064
James	Shel	315		**DOGGETT**		
DOAN				Benj	Adam	006
Edward	Athe	021		Eliza	Faye	093
Lyman	Loga	190		Elizabeth	High	154
DOBBINS				**DOHERTY**		
Adaline	Musk	266		John W	Monr	226
Sarah	Wash	345		Thomas	Dela	083
William I	Ross	298		**DOHNER**		
DOBIE				Isaac Z	Will	356
Andrus J	Loga	191		**DOKIN**		
Priscilla	Augl	025		Barkley L	Warr	342
DOBNEY				John W	Warr	342
Margaret	Huro	163		**DOLAN**		
DOBYNS				Thomas	Jack	169
Wesley	Hami	121		**DOLBY**		
DODD				David	Luca	198
Cath	Cuya	071		Luther	Cler	051
Forman	Mont	245		Nathaniel	Pike	282
Lois	Star	317		**DOLE**		
Thomas	Lake	178		John	Jack	167
DODDRIDGE				Martha V	Asht	015
Harry C	Adam	006		Robert D	Will	356
Thomas	Meig	216		**DOLEN**		
DODDROE				Mary	Faye	094
Anna	Fair	090		**DOLL**		
DODDROL				Christiana	Craw	062
James C	Fair	092		Michael P	Rich	293
DODDS				**DOLLINGER**		
Clarissa	Gree	113		Geo S	Miam	219
George	Luca	197		John S	Miam	219
Joseph O	Hard	146		**DOLLISON**		
Josephus	Shel	315		Ann Jane	Fair	091
Margaret	Adam	006		Silas	Miam	222
Samuel	Gree	113		**DOLOHAN**		
Susannah	Scio	306		James M	Ross	298
William C	Scio	308		**DOLPHIN**		
				Joseph	Preb	286

DOLTA			DONNELL (cont)		
John C	Mont	248	Joseph S	Mont	250
DOMAN			DONNELLAN		
Geo W	Belm	030	Charles E	Preb	288
DOME			DONNELLY		
Samuel	Wyan	365	Joseph	Star	319
DOMER			Nancy	Wayn	354
Joseph M	Wood	359	William	Clar	046
DONAFIN			DONNERSBACH		
Julia G	Defi	081	John	Hanc	141
DONAHUE			DONOHOE		
Alfred	Pike	281	Jno	Mont	233
DONAKER			DONOHOO		
Mary	Cosh	061	Jane B	High	154
DONALD			DONOHUE		
Isaiah K	Ashl	012	Cath	Erie	087
James	Holm	161	Daniel	Mont	250
Virginia	Gall	108	James	Meig	212
DONALDSON			(or Donohue James)		
Balee	Holm	161	John	Morg	257
Charity	Jeff	170	DONOVAN		
Chas W	Mont	250	Cath	Luca	202
Francis	Ross	301	Ephram	Mont	255
Isabel	Wash	345	Florence	Mont	229
Jacob C	Fran	098	John	Colu	056
Levi J	Port	283	John	Harr	149
Solomon	Nobl	268	John E	Clar	047
William	Harr	148	DOOLAN		
William B	Dark	077	Nancy	Shel	315
DONARD			Patrick	Clar	046
John A	Hard	144	DOOLEY		
DONEL			Mathew	Brow	033
Samuel B	Wyan	367	DOOLY		
DONELLY			William	Mont	233
Mariah	Cler	050	DOPP		
DONER			Frederick	Knox	174
Abraham R	Clar	044	DORAN		
DONEY			Bridget	Lawr	180
James B	Pick	278	Felix	Mont	256
DONGES			John V	Sene	314
Eliza	Butl	036	DORCAS		
DONGLESS			Mary A	Fran	104
Hiram	Madi	203	DORE		
DONHAM			William	Cler	051
Elizabeth	Cler	047	DORMA		
Jacob	Cler	049	Jacob	Hami	128
DONITHEN			DORNBUSCH		
Alfred S	Mari	210	Henry	Mont	227
DONLEY			DORNEY		
William W	Cham	041	Robert	Hanc	140
DONNAHOO			DORNON		
Michael	Alle	010	Lorenzo	Lawr	183
DONNELL			DORR		
James	Sand	304	Ferdinand	Hami	134

DORRIES			DOUGLASS		
Charlotte	Lawr	180	Charles	Augl	025
DORSEY			Charles C	Star	320
Elizabeth	Guer	120	John	Colu	056
Susan	Musk	265	John	Holm	160
DORWART			Leah	Nobl	268
Henry	Fran	098	Mary A	Pick	278
DOSS			Rebecca	Guer	119
Cinderella	Vint	341	Robert	Belm	029
DOTSON			Thomas	Mont	251
Anna J	Cham	041	Thomas E	Rich	294
Jos	Wash	349	William	Miam	218
Mary E	Guer	120	William	Tusc	332
Samuel	Jack	167	DOULON		
DOTY			James	Mont	246
Caroline	Dela	084	DOUTAZ		
George W	Dela	082	Frank	Cuya	074
George W	Lake	177	DOVE		
Josephus F	Dela	083	Dennis	Ashl	011
Martha	Dark	078	Maria L	Belm	027
Mary	Brow	033	William C	Preb	287
Stephen	Cham	042	DOVER		
DOTZE			Martha M	Merc	217
Augustus	Clar	046	DOW		
DOUBLER			Sabra A	Ashl	011
Adam	Miam	222	DOWD		
DOUDNA			Edward B	Will	356
Geo W	Gree	115	Jas O	Morr	260
DOUDS			DOWELL		
John	Jeff	169	Andrew J	High	156
DOUGHERTY			David	Fult	105
Daniel	Fran	097	Hannah	Monr	223
Joseph	Hard	144	DOWER		
Julia A	Nobl	269	Michael	Mont	240
Julius	Cuya	067	DOWLAR		
Margaret	Cuya	076	Amos	Ross	296
Mary	Tusc	330	Uriah	Dark	078
Solomon	Mont	237	DOWLING		
William	Cler	048	Ann	Lake	177
William S	Guer	117	Bridget	Lawr	180
DOUGHLEBY			James	Mont	255
William	Ross	300	Joseph	Mont	253
DOUGHMAN			Patrick H	Luca	200
Thomas J	Cler	049	William	Mont	235
Valentine	Warr	342	DOWN		
DOUGHTER			Isaac	Sand	304
Elizabeth	Morg	258	DOWNARD		
DOUGHTY			Margaret	Harr	149
Adaline M	Pick	279	Mary	Jack	168
Enos	Mari	208	Rachel	Musk	266
DOUGLAS			DOWNER		
Josiah	Cham	041	Andrew	Guer	117
Nelly	Rich	292	John	Trum	328
William	Mont	228	Lucinda	Trum	327

DOWNES
William	Cosh	061

DOWNEY
John	Mont	239
Katie	Hami	137
Lewis	Gree	113
Mary A	Hami	127
Mary A	Pike	281
Sarah	Gree	115

DOWNING
Darius	Huro	162
Eli	VanW	338
Eliza M	Adam	007
Elizabeth J	Adam	005
Henry	Adam	004
Jasper E	Loga	189
John	Musk	263

DOWNS
Lewis	Luca	202

DOYLE
James	Lick	186
John	Hami	135
Patrick	Hami	135
Patrick	Mont	229
Thomas	Fran	098
William	Mont	248

DOZER
Henry	Perr	277
Lyman	Musk	264

DRAEGER
Johanna	Cuya	071

DRAGER
Fred	Cuya	067

DRAGGOR
Cath	Hami	121

DRAGO
Henry	Luca	197

DRAIN
Joseph	Hami	134

DRAIS
Felix M	Faye	093
Lawson	Faye	094

DRAKE
Abraham	VanW	339
Asa	Sene	313
Benj C	Nobl	269
Charles	Huro	162
Eliza E	Ross	296
Elmer M	Brow	034
Francis M	Brow	032
Frederick F	Mont	256
George B	Erie	088
George F	Huro	163

DRAKE (cont)
James B	Fran	098
James H	Cler	049
Jerusha	Lick	184
John	Ross	298
John	Wash	351
Louisa	Fran	101
Margaret B	Lawr	180
Mary	Warr	342
Oliver P	Wood	358
(alias Perry O Drake)		
Paul W	Holm	161
Perry O	Wood	358
(alias Oliver P Drake)		
Sarah	Mont	232
William	Ross	300

DRATT
Maria	Loga	191

DREA
James	Cuya	067

DREDGE
James	Mont	242

DREIBELBERS
William H	Cuya	067

DRENCHER
Arthur	Loga	189

DRENNAN
Phebe	Hami	136

DRESEL
Alois	Mont	248

DRESSER
Levi	Summ	324

DRESSLER
William	Scio	306

DREVE
Julianna	Hami	136

DREW
Horace H	Cuya	067
James	Dark	077
Solomon	Alle	009

DRIGGS
George	Athe	021
John D	Monr	226
Nelson	Guer	120
William	Athe	021

DRIMEIRER
Henry	Mont	253

DRINKWATER
William	Perr	276

DRISCOL
Geo B	Wash	348

DRISCOLL
Edward M	Hami	133

DRISCOLL (cont)			DUCLOS		
Margaret M	Hami	136	Michael	Jeff	170
Patrick	Faye	094	DUCY		
Patrick	Mont	242	William	Faye	093
DRISKILL			DUDEN		
Stukely	Wash	347	John A	Augl	026
DRONILLARD			Robert S	Dela	082
Joseph	Gall	108	DUDGEON		
DRUDON			Nancy B	Fair	091
William C	Pick	280	DUDLESON		
DRUGGAN			Henry	Vint	340
Sarah	Athe	020	DUDLEY		
DRUHOT			Clara	Mont	249
John	Holm	160	Fanny	Clin	052
DRUM			Joseph	Nobl	269
Elizabeth	Clar	046	Lyman	Cuya	068
Jas	Wash	346	DUDSON		
Maria J	Fair	091	Joseph	Mont	239
William R	Monr	226	DUER		
DRUMM			Dillon P	Asht	019
Geo W	Unio	336	Eleanor	Holm	161
DRUMMOND			DUERR		
John	Wood	364	Jos	Hami	135
Rodman M	Ross	299	DUESLER		
DRUMMUND			Louisa	Sene	314
Lewis	Gall	109	DUFF		
DRURY			Mary	Jeff	172
Augustus D	Trum	326	DUFFEY		
Harriet E	Miam	222	John	Wayn	352
Jno T	Mont	253	Michael	Mont	254
DRUSCHEL			William	Gree	113
George	Hard	146	DUFFIELD		
DRYDEN			Christina H	Harr	149
Harriet	Cuya	076	DUFFNER		
John	Adam	003	John	Rich	294
Joseph	Brow	031	DUFFY		
Lemuel F	Adam	006	Edward	Jack	168
DUANE			James	Mont	255
Ann	Clar	045	James J	Perr	276
DUBOIS			James P	Mont	253
Abraham	Asht	015	John	Mont	228
Ezekiel	Fran	095	Josephine R	Lawr	180
Nancy A	Belm	028	Patrick	Mont	245
DUBRIE			Patrick	Sene	310
Gabriel	Otta	271	Thomas	Mont	244
DUCK			William	Hami	135
John	Luca	202	DUGAN		
DUCKER			Henry P	Mont	235
Martin V B	Fran	098	John	Jeff	172
DUCKINS			John	Mont	254
Jerry	Brow	032	Richard H	Musk	266
DUCKSON			William C	Guer	117
Robert	Dark	077	DUGANS		
			John J	Mont	235

89

DUGGAN		
Thomas	Mont	229
DUGLE		
Oliver	Adam	006
DUGNAY		
George	Cuya	074
DUKE		
John K	Scio	306
Persis	Lick	185
DULANEY		
Thomas J	Madi	202
DULIN		
Clemence	Fran	103
Kingsbury	Meig	212
DULL		
Dar	Fult	105
DULTZ		
Michael	Musk	267
DUMAS		
Jane	Hami	127
John	Mont	237
DUMERIEL		
James M	High	155
DUMFORD		
John R	Cler	048
Margaret	Warr	343
DUMM		
Peter	Ross	296
Rebecca A	Wyan	366
DUMMOND		
Samuel	Gall	109
DUMOND		
France	Scio	305
DUNATHAN		
David P	VanW	338
DUNAWAY		
Thomas	Lick	187
DUNBAR		
Boyd	Henr	153
David	Wash	346
Isabell	Hami	137
Jane	Holm	160
Lucy	Cuya	065
Mary A	Fult	107
Robert S	Jeff	170
DUNCAN		
Henry	Gree	117
Jane	Adam	007
Sam	Fult	106
Thomas M	Clin	053
William	Miam	222
DUNDORE		
Sarah	Wyan	366

DUNFEE		
Earlwine	Lawr	183
DUNGAN		
Robert H	Carr	040
DUNHAM		
Albert	Cuya	065
Ann	Cuya	066
Huldah H	Dela	084
James C	Miam	219
Jos	Wayn	351
Luther S	Mont	233
Margaret	Dark	078
Nancy	Cham	042
DUNIGAN		
James	Mont	247
DUNILON		
Peter	VanW	339
DUNKEL		
Elizabeth	Erie	087
Julia A	Gree	116
DUNKIRT		
John	Mont	248
DUNKLE		
Benj F	Wayn	352
Jacob	Hock	157
Joseph F	Mont	228
DUNLAP		
Albert	Lick	188
Ann E	Pick	279
Benj	Craw	064
David	Scio	304
Eliza	Colu	058
Emily	Cham	042
Geo	Adam	004
Jas W	Hami	135
John A	Colu	057
Rebecca	Hami	127
William R	Mont	242
DUNLEVY		
Anthony H	Warr	343
DUNMIRE		
Jas H	Craw	063
DUNN		
Christiana	Summ	321
Cynthia A	Knox	174
Elizabeth	Jack	168
Fanny	Hami	127
James	Perr	276
James N	Cham	041
John	Mont	245
Jno	Perr	275
John S	Morg	258
John W	Cuya	067

DUNN (cont)			DURKIN (cont)		
Joseph	Mont	253	Michael	Cham	042
Lewis	High	153	DURLER		
Mary Ann	Hami	137	Christian	Holm	160
Nathan S	Brow	035	DURM		
Rebecca	Loga	192	Alexander	Scio	305
Richard	Mont	241	DURR		
Sarah	Ross	298	Amaly	Sene	313
Thomas	Hami	135	DURRANT		
Thomas	Mont	238	Joseph L	Musk	263
William J	Luca	201	DUSCH		
DUNNIFON			Abraham	Mont	250
Geo	VanW	338	DUSCHENES		
DUNNING			Jacob	Mont	239
John J	Huro	164	DUSENBERRY		
Leroy	Cuya	065	Henry	Perr	275
DUNNINGTON			Rebecca	Perr	276
James N	Musk	264	DUSTAN		
DUNSON			Volunia	Athe	020
James C	Madi	204	DUSTMAN		
Lewis	Hard	146	Helen C	Dela	082
DUNTON			Solomon	Trum	327
Sarah L	Cuya	075	DUTCHER		
DUPEE			Albert V	Trum	326
Cath	Morr	261	DUTENHAVER		
DUPLER			John	Carr	039
Elizabeth	Athe	024	DUTIEL		
DURALL			William	Scio	305
William L	Dark	076	DUTTERER		
DURANT			Susan	Defi	081
Malinda	Athe	022	DUTTON		
Mary	Fran	101	Amanda	Dela	084
Nelson	Lick	184	F Ella	Cuya	071
DURBIN			Melvin J	Meig	213
John P	Hard	146	DUVAL		
Margaret	Will	357	Daniel	Henr	153
DURELL			Jane A	Knox	174
Elizabeth	Defi	079	Rachel	Hami	127
DURFEY			Washington L		
Alcy C	Lick	184		Musk	264
Benj	Dela	083	DUVALL		
Dexter	Unio	336	August	Augl	025
Ekwin C	Paul	273	Edmund F	Musk	267
Elisha A	Luca	201	Isaiah	Morg	258
Henrietta	Dela	085	Jane	Wash	351
DURFLINGER			Priscilla	Hami	135
Sylvester W	Madi	203	DWIRE		
DURHAM			Hiram	Wyan	366
William H	Lora	195	DWYER		
DURKEE			Richard	Hami	135
Minerva	Alle	008	Rufus A	High	156
Sally	Geau	112	Timothy	Mont	248
DURKIN			DYAR		
James	Mont	227	Jos	Wash	349

DYARMAN			**EARHART**		
Orlando	Defi	080	Anna R	Hami	138
DYE			Francis M	Brow	035
Ary	Monr	223	Herman	Mont	229
Eliza	Morg	257	Judith E	Hami	135
James A	Athe	022	**EARHEART**		
John W	Jack	168	Jacob M	Hami	136
Joseph	Hard	145	**EARICK**		
Josiah	Fult	106	George W	Butl	038
Mary	Athe	022	**EARL**		
Matilda	Cham	043	John	Port	285
DYER			Susannah	Sene	313
Benj	Nobl	268	William H	Lake	177
David	Nobl	268	**EARLES**		
Hebron	Nobl	268	Elliott N	Lawr	182
Isaac P	High	154	**EARLEY**		
Lucy	Wayn	351	Alfred	Monr	227
Lydia	Monr	225	Geo W	Wash	347
Maria	Lake	177	**EARLSTON**		
DYHE			Emily	Will	355
William H H	Pike	282	**EARLY**		
			Elbridge T	Asht	016
			Isaac	Morr	261
			Mary	Colu	059
EACHES			Moses D	Belm	029
Joseph C	Knox	176	Timothy	Guer	119
EADS			**EARNHART**		
Temperance	Gree	115	Cyrus M	Warr	344
EAGAN			**EASTABROOK**		
Cath	Preb	288	Marshall	Geau	112
Martin	Mont	251	**EASTER**		
Thomas	Mont	248	Milton	High	154
EAGEN			Sarah	Adam	004
Patrick	Merc	216	William J	Adam	004
EAGLE			**EASTERBROOK**		
Harriet	Fair	088	Thomas	Sene	312
EAGLETON			**EASTERWOOD**		
John W	Mont	249	Charles	Sand	303
EAGON			**EASTMAN**		
William	Cosh	060	Emery M	Dela	083
EAGY			Emily	Medi	211
Mary	Carr	040	Harriet A	Preb	288
EAHOLTZ			James W	Wood	358
Martin H	Colu	057	Nancy	Madi	204
EAKIN			**EASTON**		
Joseph A	Vint	341	Elizabeth	Cosh	060
Joseph H	Star	320	**EASTWOOD**		
Samuel S	Colu	055	Henry	Pick	280
EALAND			**EATINGER**		
Edmond	Rich	295	Hannah	Port	285
EAMES			**EATON**		
Cornelius	Rich	292	Alex H	Sene	309
William M	Asht	015	Azur	Fult	105

EATON (cont)			ECKERMAN			
Chas H	Clar	045	Chas	Cuya	073	
Delilah	Monr	224	Daniel C	Fair	089	
Elizabeth	Pike	281	Henry L	Cuya	073	
Henry Z	Luca	199	ECKERT			
Hester	High	155	Almira	Dela	085	
Marcus	Pick	278	August	Cuya	073	
Mary	Wayn	352	John	Tusc	332	
Mary H	Sand	301	ECKFELD			
Nathaniel	Cuya	072	John N	VanW	339	
Richardson	Huro	165	ECKHARDT			
William	Mont	248	Chas	Tusc	333	
EBERFIELD			ECKHART			
Bernardina	Lawr	180	Charles	Lawr	179	
EBERHARD			Jacob	Jack	166	
William	Summ	322	ECKLE			
EBERHARDT			Mary E	Ross	298	
August	Mari	209	ECKLES			
EBERHART			Ann C	Cham	043	
John M	Ashl	013	ECKLEY			
EBERLE			Barbara	Fult	104	
Frederick	Belm	028	ECKMAN			
EBERLY			Serena	Meig	213	
Benj F	Wood	358	Susannah	Hami	122	
Eliza J	Gree	116	EDDLEBUTE			
EBERSOLE			Jacob	Morg	259	
Jacob	Star	317	EDDY			
EBERT			George S	Lake	178	
George	Hard	145	John K	Belm	027	
John H	Cuya	074	Peter	Luca	197	
EBERTH			Sally	Geau	112	
John H	Craw	062	EDEL			
EBLE			Lorenz	Cuya	072	
Julia	Hami	122	EDELBLUTE			
EBLIN			Jacob	Unio	335	
Jacob	Pike	281	Lewis	Dela	083	
EBLING			EDGAR			
Addi	Hanc	141	Eleanor	Knox	173	
EBRIGHT			Richards	Huro	166	
Ewin M	Mont	240	Squire L	Wood	361	
William	Defi	080	Susan	Cosh	059	
EBY			William D	Hard	145	
Joseph	Cuya	072	EDGERLY			
ECCLESTON			Charles H	Summ	322	
William F	Lora	196	EDGINGTON			
ECHELBERRY			Anthony	High	154	
Lewellyn	Musk	267	Chas	Morr	259	
ECHELBERY			David	High	157	
Peter	Sene	309	Lindsey L	Adam	003	
ECHLEY			Mary Ann	Adam	003	
Isaac	Fult	106	Nancy	Luca	200	
ECKELBERRY			Salome	Wyan	367	
Cath	Monr	223				

93

EDGINTON			EGAN (cont)		
Nathan	Scio	308	John	Mont	250
EDINGTON			EGGERMAN		
Mary M	Monr	223	Elizabeth	Hard	144
EDLER			EGGERT		
John	Gall	110	Maria	Hami	122
EDMESTON			EGGLESTON		
David	Huro	165	Foster W	Asht	015
EDMONDS			John	Fran	100
David D	Rich	295	Rebecca	Paul	273
Sarah A	Wash	346	Tryphena	Athe	021
EDMUNDS			EGLEY		
Cassius	Scio	306	Jacob A	Hami	122
EDNEY			EGLI		
Chas	Colu	058	Jacob	Sene	309
EDSON			EGNER		
Daniel B	Belm	027	Freeman	Rich	296
EDWARD			EHA		
Sarah	Brow	031	Sophia	Hami	122
EDWARDS			EHLERS		
Alex	Brow	035	Hannah	Rich	294
Andrew J	Hami	122	EHNI		
Cath	Knox	173	Geo J	Perr	275
Daniel	Fair	089	EHRMAN		
David J	VanW	340	William H	Hami	122
Elisha	Hanc	141	EIBERT		
Elizabeth	Fair	091	Henry	Ross	297
Elizabeth A	Musk	265	EICHELBERGER		
Elizabeth E	High	156	Geo	Dark	079
Evan	Maho	207	EICHELBORGER		
Fielding	Fair	089	Joseph	Dark	077
Hannah H	Luca	201	EICHELE		
Harlan	Clin	054	Frederick	Hami	122
Henry P	Wyan	367	EICHER		
Jacob J	Madi	204	Jacob M	Paul	273
John B	Rich	291	EICHLER		
Joseph	Cuya	074	Julia	Mont	231
Joseph	Henr	151	EICHOLTZ		
Lavinia	Colu	055	Sigmond	Warr	344
Louisa	Medi	211	EICHOTTZ		
Lucinda	Star	320	Mathia	Dark	077
Martin	Henr	152	EICKE		
Moses	Clin	053	Lewis	Monr	225
Paul	Luca	199	EIDENIRE		
Sarah L	Erie	086	Philip	Colu	057
Thomas	Clin	054	EIDSON		
Wallace D	Port	285	Caroline	Henr	152
William	Hanc	142	Rachael	Preb	287
William H	Paul	274	EIGHNEY		
William H H	Brow	035	Cath	Asht	016
EFFING			EIKELBERRY		
Harmon	Hami	122	Abraham	Monr	223
EGAN			Cath	Monr	225
Hubert W	Cuya	066			

EIKENBARY			ELKINS		
John	Preb	286	Stephen H	Butl	036
Peter S	Preb	287	ELLEFORD		
EIKENBERRY			William	Wash	348
Abraham	Preb	287	ELLEN		
EIKINBARY			Gallivan	Shel	316
Joseph	Preb	286	ELLENBERGER		
EINHART			Louisa	Tusc	330
John B	Medi	211	ELLENWOOD		
EISANBISE			Abigail	Summ	321
John	VanW	336	Rebecca E	Warr	344
EISELE			Washington	Port	284
Cath	Butl	036	ELLER		
Margaret	Star	319	Rachel	VanW	339
EISENHARD			ELLIFRITZ		
Mary	Will	356	Geo W	Wash	350
EISENHUT			ELLIOTT		
George	Shel	315	Alex C	Maho	206
EISENHUTT			Christopher		
Valentine	Hami	122		Mont	247
EISENMAN			Daniel	Cuya	072
Martin	Star	319	Drusy Ann	Monr	225
EITEL			Eliza	Adam	008
William F	Mont	253	Emory B	Defi	081
ELARTON			George	Trum	328
Margaret	Henr	152	Isaac C	Hami	139
ELBEN			James G	Jack	167
Caroline	Star	318	James S	Mari	208
Levi	Cosh	061	John	Fran	100
ELBERGER			John	Mont	255
Jacob B	Mont	251	John	Trum	329
ELBON			Louisa	Brow	032
John H	Clin	053	Margaret	Cham	042
William E	Lick	185	Martha J	Monr	226
ELDER			Mary	Athe	024
David L	Craw	063	Miles W	Hami	122
James A	Guer	119	Priscilla	Knox	174
John W	Perr	274	Robert	Mont	239
Thomas J	Carr	040	William A	Jeff	171
ELDERS			William J	Fran	100
Rebecca	Rich	292	ELLIS		
ELDRAD			Alexander C		
Zenas	Asht	018		Loga	191
ELDRED			Anna	Huro	163
Mary J	Erie	086	Clarissa	Athe	021
ELDRIDGE			Delilah	Athe	021
James H	Trum	325	Edward W	Loga	189
ELECTA			Elias C	Hami	139
Sheldon	Knox	176	Elizabeth	Lick	184
ELER			Geo W	Cuya	072
Sylvester	Butl	036	James	Musk	267
ELIMILLER(?),			Jesse B	Belm	026
Minerva J	High	154	John W	Clin	053

ELLIS (cont)			ELWELL (cont)		
Jonathan	Faye	094	John J	Cuya	072
Joseph	Mont	255	Lewis	Perr	275
Joshua	Clin	054	Maria	Geau	112
Lyman	Knox	174	William T	Knox	175
Margaret	Musk	267	ELWOOD		
Margaret	Tusc	331	Nancy	Hard	144
Mary	Gall	109	Reese B	Pick	280
Milo D	Mont	230	ELY		
Mitchell	Pick	278	Alfred S	Gall	110
Nancy	Brow	031	Chas S	Sene	313
Sabbina	Brow	031	Eliza	Cuya	073
Sarah C	Cler	048	Geo W	Miam	221
Sarah D	Musk	262	Ira	Lake	176
Simon B	Brow	031	Ira W	Lake	178
William	Morg	259	John	Port	284
William M	Hard	147	Thomas	Port	284
ELLISON			ELZAY		
Andrew	Adam	007	Francis M	VanW	338
Parthenia	Adam	004	EMAHISER		
William G L	Scio	305	Emanuel	Morr	262
ELLSWORTH			EMBRIC		
Charles	Asht	019	John	Lawr	179
Hezekiah	Port	285	EMCH		
Jane	Wood	361	Nicholas	Cuya	076
Sarah A	Port	284	EMENEKER		
ELMORE			Matthias	Mont	253
Sarah J	Adam	004	EMENS		
ELMS			John R	Preb	287
Nancy	Hanc	142	EMERSON		
ELROD			Andrew	Erie	085
James	Monr	223	David W	Summ	322
Mary Jane	Cler	051	Esther G	Dela	083
ELSASSER			Franklin	Paul	274
Louis	Hard	147	James	Mont	251
ELSEON			Josiah D	Loga	190
John	Paul	274	Mary	Hami	135
ELSEY			Melita	Cuya	067
Phebe M	Dela	082	Minerva	Star	317
ELSING			William H	Sene	312
Henry	Hami	122	EMERY		
ELSON			Geo	Ashl	013
Mary J	Tusc	330	John B	Maho	207
Parker A	Jeff	172	Julia	Cler	049
ELSTNER			Robert G	Henr	151
Mary	Hami	134	EMMENS		
ELSTON			Eliza	Ashl	013
John H	VanW	340	EMMING		
ELSWICK			William	Hami	122
William T	Lawr	181	EMMONS		
ELSWORTH			Alcitia	Geau	112
Mary	Cham	043	Alonzo J	Lora	193
ELWELL			Asenath	Geau	113
Geo F	Otta	272	Lorenzo	Sene	310

EMMONS (cont)			ENGLISH (cont)		
Sarah	Colu	057	Josiah G	Gree	116
William	Brow	034	Lewis J	Augl	025
EMRICH			Rebecca	Scio	306
John	Miam	221	Susan	Fair	090
EMRICK			ENNES		
Henry	Summ	323	Anna	Loga	192
Susannah	Miam	222	ENNIS		
ENCK			Cath	Mont	230
Joseph	Ashl	012	David	Erie	086
ENDERLIN			Dennis	Hami	122
Richard	Ross	298	John B	Sene	312
ENDERS			Michael	Augl	025
Anton	Mont	245	Olive J	Hami	122
ENDRES			ENO		
Sebald	Mont	253	Matilda	Gall	110
ENERINGHAM			ENOCHS		
John	Erie	086	Rebecca A	Nobl	269
ENGEL			ENRIGHT		
Frank	Mont	249	Thomas	Alle	010
John	Fran	097	ENSEY		
Lewis	Luca	199	Abraham	Mont	231
Louisa	Hami	122	ENSOR		
ENGELBERT			John B	Fair	091
John	Mont	251	ENTERLINE		
ENGELHARDT			Reuben	Will	357
Martin	Port	285	ENTMAN		
ENGHANSEN			James	Mont	238
Mary Ann	Hami	134	ENTREKIN		
ENGLAND			Brinton	Colu	057
Hezekiah	Ross	298	John E	Ross	298
William	Jeff	172	ENTSMINGER		
ENGLE			Elizabeth	Meig	213
Chas F	Ashl	013	James R	Summ	323
Elizabeth	Pick	280	EOBBS		
Henry	Nobl	269	John	Mont	251
Joseph G	Hard	144	EOFF		
Orestes V	Asht	019	Sardine	Wash	350
Phebe J	Mont	231	EPP		
ENGLEHART			Peter	Huro	164
Cath	Luca	199	EPPERT		
Elizabeth	Guer	120	Elizabeth	Cler	049
Fred	Cuya	073	EPPS		
ENGLEMAN			Almeda	Unio	334
William	Trum	329	ERBEL		
ENGLERT			Fred	Mont	231
Bernard	Cuya	072	ERDEMILLER		
ENGLISH			Margaret E	Miam	222
Alford	Loga	189	ERINGTON		
Ellen	Cler	048	Rachel	Vint	340
John	Craw	063	ERISMAN		
John W	Augl	025	Elizabeth	Rich	291
John W	Hami	136			

ERKENBRECHER			ESTEP		
Chris'n	Mont	249	Edwin	Summ	322
ERNE			ESTES		
George	Mont	250	James H	Lawr	179
ERNST			Reuben	Lawr	181
Charles	Hami	128	ESTILE		
Christiana	Geau	113	Mary R	Knox	173
Frederick	Mont	250	ESTILL		
John C	Erie	087	Mary	Scio	306
ERSKIN			ESTLE		
Adam	High	154	James L P	Pike	281
Jacob	High	154	William	High	155
ERTEL			ESTY		
Daniel	Mont	249	James H	Miam	221
Sarah	Warr	344	ESWORTHY		
ERVEY			Mary A	Musk	263
Winfield S	Mont	253	ETHER		
ERVIN			John G	Preb	287
Craton	Madi	204	ETTER		
David	Hami	138	Levi	Miam	218
Sarah	Clar	044	ETTINGER		
ERWIN			Josiah	Athe	021
Augustus M	Port	284	ETZEL		
Benj F	Clar	045	Christian	Hami	122
Elizabeth	Faye	094	ETZLER		
Thomas J	Musk	266	Maranda	Belm	028
ESALY			EUBANKS		
John	Monr	226	Elizabeth G	Gall	111
ESHLEMAN			EULER (or Ihler)		
Elizabeth	Hard	146	Joseph	Lora	193
ESKER			EURCH		
Caroline	Ross	297	John	Luca	199
Frank	Ross	298	EVANS		
ESLEBE			Alfred H	Musk	265
Geo	Otta	270	Allen	High	154
ESPENSHEED			Andrew G	Cuya	072
Henry	Tusc	332	Angelina	Athe	020
ESPY			Anthony	Adam	005
Jacob B	Wayn	354	Benj	Colu	059
ESSERT			Charles	Hami	122
Martin	Hami	122	Charles	Madi	203
ESSES			Charles	Maho	207
Jacob	Hami	122	Christian	Luca	199
ESSEX			Columbus	Jeff	170
Amaziah	Adam	006	Columbus D	Fran	100
Andrew	Wash	347	Cordelia	Asht	016
Louisa	Fran	097	Daniel	Gall	111
ESSIG			David	Adam	004
Jas	Carr	039	David	Cosh	062
ESTABROOK			Edwin M	Mont	250
Harriet	Rich	294	Elizabeth	Cosh	061
ESTELL			Elizabeth	Hock	157
Alva	Musk	264	Elizabeth	Ross	301

EVANS (cont)			EVERETT		
Elizabeth	Sand	303	Clayton H	Luca	199
Elizabeth	Summ	323	David W	Tusc	331
Ezeriah	Star	320	Hannah	Medi	210
Geo W	Cuya	072	Jane	Summ	323
Henry	Ross	298	Mary	Cham	042
Henry	Unio	335	Peter	Rich	295
Henry A	Maho	207	William D	Tusc	331
Henry C	Fran	100	EVERHARD		
Hugh	Brow	034	Elizabeth J	Will	357
Isaac T	Fran	100	Philip M	Hami	122
Jane W	Musk	264	EVERHART		
John A	Brow	031	Andrew	Ross	296
John E	Fran	102	Jacob	Hard	147
John F	Fran	100	John	Summ	322
John W	Clar	047	EVERICH		
John W	Lick	185	Jacob	Mont	251
Jonas G	Dela	083	EVERITT		
Julia S W	Cuya	073	Ambrose	Craw	064
Leroy J	Brow	035	Edson S	Trum	325
Lewis	Mont	229	EVERROLE		
Line	Perr	277	Luania	Otta	270
Lotwig	Star	318	EVERS		
Margaret S	Hock	157	Chas W	Wood	358
Martha J	Will	355	Milton B	VanW	338
Mary A	Fran	097	EVERSMANN		
Mary A	Huro	164	Henry	Hami	122
Mary P	Gall	111	EVERSOLE		
Miranda	Huro	163	David	Perr	275
Nancy A	Cuya	066	William	Mari	209
Oliver	Fran	100	EVERSON		
Rachel	Lick	186	James A	Hami	122
Ransom H	Merc	217	EVERSTIEN		
Richard	Cuya	073	William	Mont	242
Robert	Brow	031	EVERTON		
Rowland W	Unio	335	Thomas E	Adam	003
Sarah	Asht	016	EVNER		
Sarah	Monr	223	John	Athe	020
Stephen D	Hami	122	EWAN		
Sylvester G	Fran	103	Joseph W	Musk	263
Thomas	Miam	220	EWERS		
Thomas L	Jack	168	Harriet	Perr	275
Thomas S	VanW	339	Mary A	Wash	347
William	Colu	056	EWING		
William A	Miam	221	Abner	Nobl	269
William T	Jack	167	Armstrong	Mont	242
EVELAND			David	Fair	091
Byerla	Morg	257	Edward H	Augl	025
EVELETH			Elmore	Ashl	011
Isaac N	Mont	247	Elmore E	Scio	306
EVENS			Hugh	Fair	089
Loring C	Mont	229	Jane	Mont	227
EVERCATT			John	Tusc	330
Geo	Hami	136	Lucinda	Gall	108

FALLON			FARNAM (cont)		
Cath	Belm	027	Darwin	Port	284
FALLS			FARNBACH		
Samuel D	Mont	252	John	Otta	270
FALLWILER			FARNS		
Leonard	Meig	214	John	Morg	256
FALSON			FARNSWORTH		
James D	Wood	361	Joseph	Belm	028
FANCHER			Martha	Musk	263
Evaline	Fran	104	Sarah J	Medi	211
FANNING			FARR		
Richard J	Cuya	072	Louisa M	Summ	321
Roxanna	Hami	134	FARRALL		
Thomas W	Hami	129	John	Clar	047
FANSHEAR			FARRAN		
Walter	Loga	189	James	Hami	122
FAQUETTE			FARRAND		
John W	Luca	198	Eliza	Fran	101
FARDEN			William H	Cuya	072
Jane	Ross	298	FARRAR		
FAREN			Asa A	Jack	166
Alpheus	Mont	246	Miranda C	Lora	194
Peter	Mont	229	FARREL		
FARION			Lock	Mont	252
John	Scio	304	FARRELL		
FARIS			Dennis	Mont	243
Huldah	High	156	John	Mont	238
Lafayette	High	156	John	Mont	241
Rachel	High	156	William	Geau	113
FARLEY			William H	Mont	248
Charles W	Nobl	270	FARRINGTON		
Elizabeth	Wash	345	Abigail	VanW	339
George	Dela	082	Floyd	Geau	113
George	Wash	345	FARRIS		
Nancy	Knox	173	Eliza	High	156
FARLING			Eliza A	Morg	257
Henry	Miam	221	FARSHT		
FARLOW			Jane	Luca	196
Elizabeth	Ross	299	FARWELL		
Mary C	Preb	287	Benj J	Cuya	076
FARMER			Franklin A	Cuya	072
Antoinette	Huro	166	FARWICK		
Geo E	Colu	057	Henry	Hami	129
Hannah M	Cuya	073	FASER		
Henry	Lora	193	Mary	Lora	195
John	Wash	347	FASHBAUGH		
Jos	Miam	220	John Q	Fult	105
Loammi	Hanc	143	FASIG		
Margaret	Wash	347	Albert	Ashl	011
Samuel	Monr	225	FASING		
Sarah	Meig	214	Margaret	Ashl	011
FARNAM			FASSLER		
Asa D	VanW	338	Caroline	Clar	044

FENICAL				**FERRELL** (cont)		
Noah	Craw	063		Margaret	Tusc	332
FENIMORE				Thomas C	Tusc	332
John H	Will	357		**FERREN**		
FENNER				Margaret	Belm	030
Mary	Tusc	332		**FERRES**		
FENSTERMAKER				Dana B	Cuya	076
William H	Hanc	142		**FERRIER**		
FENT				Thomas	Mont	249
Lewis W	Madi	202		**FERRIMAN**		
FENTON				Amanda	Summ	323
Alpheus A	Asht	018		**FERRIS**		
Arthur E	Lake	178		Charles G	Lick	188
John	Cham	043		Jacob	Hami	139
Solomon P	Cuya	073		Lewis	Defi	081
William W	Trum	328		Mary	Sene	311
FERGESON				Nancy	Mont	232
William	Sand	303		Oliver	Hock	158
FERGUSON				**FERRISS**		
Alexander	Mont	235		Harrison	Knox	173
Cath	Hami	134		**FERRY**		
Charles W	Luca	202		Mary	Defi	081
Daniel	Mont	253		**FERRYMAN**		
Edward R	Erie	086		John	Guer	118
Geo E	Hami	122		**FERSON**		
Henry B	Paul	273		Samuel	Dela	084
Herman R	Sene	312		**FERWILLIGER**		
James	Gree	116		Amos	Huro	164
John	Mont	244		**FESLER**		
Joseph	Huro	161		George L	Mont	253
Joseph J	Star	317		John M	Erie	088
Margaret	Trum	326		**FESSLER**		
Martha O	Rich	292		William	Summ	321
Mary E A	Clar	044		**FESTER**		
Nancy	Alle	010		William	VanW	338
Nancy H	Lawr	183		**FETHERKILE**		
Nathan P	Dela	084		Margaret	Adam	006
Robert J	Port	285		**FETHERLIN**		
William	Star	317		Jacob	Faye	093
William A	Guer	119		**FETTERLY**		
William J	Scio	306		Alex	Alle	010
FERNEAN				**FEX**		
John F	High	156		Charles	Mont	253
FERON				**FEZER**		
James O	Lake	178		Herman	Mont	236
FERREE				**FIANT**		
Joel W	Jeff	171		Cath	Morr	259
FERREL				Joel	Mont	236
Anny	Tusc	332		**FICKEL**		
Jas D	Monr	223		Geo	Musk	263
FERRELL				James	Fair	091
Charles H	Fran	100		**FICKLE**		
David L	Cuya	072		Alfred	Fran	103

FIDLER			**FIGLEY** (cont)		
Joseph	Mont	237	William M	Nobl	268
FIEDLER			**FIKE**		
August	Mont	253	Jacob	Will	355
John	Hami	122	John A	Luca	197
FIELD			**FILBURT**		
John	Paul	274	Antoni	Mont	255
John F	Fran	100	**FILHART**		
Luna A	Lora	195	David	Alle	008
William	Lick	186	**FILLEY**		
FIELDING			Benj	Paul	272
Elizabeth	Shel	316	Betsey A	Summ	321
Sarah	Sene	312	**FILLIS**		
FIELDS			James	Mont	235
Albert	Fran	103	**FILLMORE**		
Amanda	Harr	150	Conrad	Hard	146
Ann	Cham	042	Hattie A	Musk	265
Ann	Erie	086	Hester A	Gall	108
Cath	Summ	321	Laura E	Gall	109
Edward	Otta	271	**FINCH**		
Geo W	Adam	007	Cyrus M	Scio	306
Henry E W	Unio	335	Eliza A	Hami	122
Hiram	Otta	270	Henry	Wash	347
John W	Belm	028	Hosea	Wyan	365
John W	Fran	100	Sarah	Star	320
Sarah	Cler	047	**FINCK**		
Sarah A	Jack	167	Frederick	Mont	248
Simon M	Adam	007	**FIND**		
William	Mari	209	Isaac N	Jack	166
William H	Adam	003	**FINDLEY**		
FIERBAUGH			Eliza	Wayn	353
John	Gall	109	James	Mont	248
Robert	Gall	109	William	Gree	114
FIERCE			**FINFROCK**		
Geo W	Athe	023	Henry	Shel	315
FIERSTONE			**FINGER**		
Isaac	Will	356	Rachel	Morr	262
FIET			**FINIGAN**		
Julianna	Star	319	Elizabeth A	Gall	109
FIFE			**FINISY**		
Cath	Colu	059	David	Butl	039
Susannah	Colu	059	**FINK**		
William B	Guer	118	Daniel Y	Sene	309
FIFIELD			Jerusha J	Otta	271
Amos K	Asht	016	John F	Sene	309
Emeline	Lake	177	Lewis	Wood	362
FIGHT			Margaret	Fult	107
Milly	Brow	033	Mary	Wayn	352
FIGLEY			Neoma N	Hami	122
Jacob	Musk	266	William H	Knox	175
Phebe	Nobl	268	**FINKBEINER**		
Simon	Mont	238	Christopher	Wood	361
William F	Colu	057			

FINLAN			**FISHER (cont)**		
Nancy	Meig	215	Cyrenius	Paul	273
FINLEY			Daniel	Preb	288
Henry	Mont	253	David	Hami	135
Henry S	Musk	263	David W	Sene	309
Henry T	Athe	022	Elnora	Ashl	012
FINN			Frank M	Unio	334
Charlotte	Fran	101	Franklin	Wayn	354
Frank	Mont	234	George	Rich	295
Mary	Warr	343	George W	Monr	225
FINNEGAN			Hannah A	Asht	016
Patrick	Mont	252	Henry	Brow	034
FINNEY			Henry	Mont	237
Jacob	Henr	152	Herman	Mont	253
John J	Jeff	172	Huldah E	Madi	203
Rachel	Tusc	331	Jacob	Mari	208
Sarah	Clar	045	James B	Madi	204
FINSTERWALD			John	Fair	089
Samuel	Perr	277	John B	Defi	080
FINSTERWALL			John G	Carr	039
Charles	Athe	020	Jonathan	Alle	008
FIREBEND			Joseph	Will	357
Solomon	Rich	295	Joseph H	Mont	253
FIRESTONE			Joshua W	Clin	054
John L	Colu	058	Lloyd	Cuya	075
FIRMAN			Louis	Hock	158
Charity	Morr	260	Margaretha	Hami	122
FIRMANN			Mary	Cler	050
Charles	Hami	122	Mary	Merc	217
FIRST			Mary	Monr	224
James M	Rich	292	Preston B	Mont	256
FISCHER			Rebecca	Adam	004
Frederick	Hami	122	Rebecca A	Loga	192
John	Butl	036	Rolandes E	Hami	122
FISCUS			Sabastian	Lawr	181
Chas W	Brow	033	Samuel	Wyan	365
FISH			Sarah	Cham	042
Betsey	Cuya	074	Shepler	Loga	190
Charles	Knox	174	Theodore	Mont	252
Daniel	Cuya	065	Thomas	Guer	118
George L	Huro	162	William	Monr	225
Lydia A	Huro	164	William	Will	357
Mary H	Cuya	065	William R	Jeff	172
Samuel H	Wash	346	**FISHLEY**		
FISHEL			Charles H	Scio	317
Rebecca	Star	320	**FISHPAW**		
Samuel	Trum	328	Chas H	Fran	103
FISHER			**FISK**		
Albert W	Luca	199	Jonathan	Mont	238
Barbara	Putn	289	Samuel	Lora	194
Benj M	Merc	217	**FISKE**		
Caroline E	Fair	089	Henry B	Cuya	072
Chs	Huro	165			

FISSEL		
Angeline	Rich	291
FISTE		
Samuel F	Gree	113
FISTER		
Frederick	Ross	298
FITCH		
Chloe A	Meig	214
Henry	Scio	306
James	Huro	163
John G	Sand	303
Lourana	Morg	257
Martin L	Asht	016
Mary B	Trum	327
Orsamus	Trum	325
Sanford H	Lake	178
Sarah	Wayn	352
Van F	Maho	206
William T	Lake	176
FITE		
Bathsheba	Adam	005
Jesse	High	154
FITZ		
Geo W	Sene	312
FITZER		
James H	Lawr	181
FITZGERALD		
Eleanor	Defi	081
Eliza	Hami	122
Garrett	Mari	209
John	Luca	201
Michael	Lake	178
Nancy	Gree	116
Priscilla	Vint	340
Robert	Cuya	072
Thomas	Mont	237
Thomas W	Madi	203
FITZGIBBON		
Ann	Hanc	142
FITZGIBBONS		
Gerard	Mont	253
Patrick	Mont	248
FITZIMONS		
George W	Ross	298
FITZPATRICK		
James W	Athe	023
Joseph F	Mont	242
FITZSIMMONS		
Ann E	Craw	062
FIX		
Joseph	Musk	265
FLACK		
Andrew	Mont	253

FLACK (cont)		
Jane	Ashl	013
Nancy	Maho	205
William R	Preb	288
FLAGG		
Cath	Cosh	060
William C	Wash	347
FLAHARDA		
George W	Madi	204
Rodney	Musk	263
FLAHERTY		
Geo A	Rich	291
Martin	Loga	191
Patrick	Mont	248
FLAISIG		
Nathan W	Mont	252
FLAMMER		
Bernhard	Miam	219
FLANAGAN		
James	Athe	024
John	Mont	237
Peter	Cuya	073
FLANDERS		
Joseph	Morg	258
FLANGHER		
Jacob	Brow	031
Jos H	Maho	205
FLANIGAN		
Andrew	Mont	248
FLATH		
Philip	Alle	010
FLATTER		
Barbara	Gree	116
FLAUX		
Mary	Lora	192
FLEAHMAN		
John A	Monr	226
FLECK		
Frank	Luca	198
Thaddeus	Unio	334
FLECKNER		
Henry	Dela	085
FLEHARTY		
Perry A	Erie	087
FLEIGHT		
Levi	Geau	112
FLEMING		
Aliva	Morg	259
Caleb W	Dark	079
Garrett	Fair	089
Henry C	Loga	190
Henry H	Meig	215
Jacob S	Jeff	169

FLEMING (cont)			FLOOD (cont)			
James	Port	285	Elizabeth	Nobl	268	
Jno	Perr	277	Franklin	Lake	178	
John P	Erie	086	Nicholas	Lora	193	
Joseph	Mont	229	FLOONEY			
Lucinda	Port	286	Hugh	Mont	253	
Robert H	Hami	121	FLORA			
Sophia	Craw	063	Jesse	Otta	271	
William	Belm	028	Lydia	Wayn	351	
FLENNER			FLORENCE			
Granville M	Butl	036	William	Port	283	
Mary A	Hanc	142	FLOREY			
FLESH			Roxena	Luca	201	
John	Alle	008	FLORG			
Moses	Miam	220	Joseph	Mont	235	
FLESHER			FLORO			
Alfred	High	155	Zacheus C	Hami	121	
FLETCHER			FLOWER			
Chester B	Miam	219	David	Henr	153	
George C	Musk	267	Stevens W	Luca	198	
Jacob	Knox	173	FLOWERS			
James M	Mari	208	Alfred	Wash	347	
La Quino	Sand	303	Benj F	Fair	092	
Maria	Wash	347	Charls F	Sand	303	
Robert B	Fran	096	Henry	Port	285	
Sarah	Lick	185	Leyman	Musk	267	
William	Erie	088	Mary	Fran	101	
FLEXER			Sarah	Musk	267	
Rebecca J	Star	317	Sarah	Musk	267	
FLICKENGER			William	Cuya	076	
Eliza	Fran	097	FLOYD			
FLICKER			Elmon T	Lawr	181	
Peter	Ross	299	George	Hock	159	
FLICKINGER			Jefferson	Lick	186	
Frances	Star	320	Thaddeus S	Hock	158	
Joseph	Wood	361	FLUHART			
Sarah	Wayn	352	Geo H	Perr	277	
FLIFF			William M	Jack	166	
Jas B	Clar	047	FLUKE			
FLINN			Geo H	Musk	266	
Albert A	Fran	100	FLYN			
John O	Hami	139	Peter	Sene	314	
Sarah A	Hami	122	FLYNN			
FLINT			Ann	Cuya	067	
Mary	Will	356	James	Medi	212	
Mary A	Wash	350	(alias James Quigley)			
Sarah I	Rich	294	Johanna	Fran	097	
FLODING			John	Mont	253	
Sebastian	Colu	057	John D	Mont	249	
FLOHR			Margaret	Knox	175	
John	Summ	324	Michael	Mont	238	
FLOOD			Owen	Guer	118	
Arthur	Mont	244	Patrick	Butl	037	

FLYNN (cont)			FOLLETTE		
Patrick	Mont	241	John T	Hami	121
Peter	Mont	252	FOLLHARBST		
Polly	Alle	009	Clemens	Hami	122
FOBES			FOLMER		
Alfred A	Asht	016	Conrad	Will	356
Marvin E	Asht	018	FOLSOM		
FOGARTY			Osmar W	Port	284
Patrick	Mont	252	FOLTZ		
Sarah A	Hami	122	Abner E	Summ	322
FOGEL			Eliza A	Wayn	353
George A	Star	321	John	Wood	359
FOGG			Philip	Mont	243
Mary	Meig	216	Reuben C	Star	320
FOGLE			FOLWELL		
John	Harr	148	Jane	Lawr	180
Peter	Nobl	268	FONT		
Rufus	Nobl	270	Jasper	Loga	191
FOGLEMAN			FOOT		
Andrew J	Hami	122	Amos H	Wood	360
FOGLESON			FOOTE		
Schiller	Mari	209	Douglass M	Mont	240
FOHES			Geo W	Huro	163
Franklin J	Trum	327	Louisa A	Hami	122
FOLAN			Lydia Ann	Summ	321
Andrew M	Carr	040	FORBERT		
FOLDEN			John J	Morg	257
William G	Meig	213	FORBES		
FOLEY			David W	Fult	106
Christy	Gree	115	Ellen	Belm	031
Harriet	Hami	134	Geo	Clar	047
James W	Summ	324	Mary	Hami	134
John	Fran	099	Mary E	Clar	047
John	Mont	246	Samuel F	Luca	198
FOLGER			William E	Asht	016
Acksa J	Hami	122	FORBING		
Marshall H	Hami	134	Jacob	Hard	147
Webster J	Belm	027	FORCE		
FOLK			Abigail P	Port	285
Daniel	Perr	275	Emory W	Summ	323
Peter	Henr	152	FORD		
FOLKER			Alexander C	Preb	287
Samuel	Miam	222	Alonzo	Mont	249
FOLKS			Amy	Luca	198
Charles B	Cler	048	Arabella	Maho	206
FOLLANSBEE			Athalia	Geau	112
Julia F	Gree	116	Austin K	Fult	105
FOLLAS			Caroline R	Lake	177
Richard	Clar	045	Christopher M		
FOLLEN				Henr	152
Mary Ann	Lick	188	Eber F	Fran	100
FOLLETT			Elizabeth	Cler	048
Susan	Erie	087	Finelia	Asht	018

FORD (cont)		
George F	Luca	196
Henry W	Gree	113
Jackson V B	Fran	103
Johnson	Sene	309
Maley	Cham	041
Martha	Pick	280
Mary	Maho	206
Mary Ann	Athe	021
Patrick	Fran	100
Patrick P H	Rich	293
Robert	Rich	293
Stephen D	Harr	149
Thomas	Belm	031
Thomas	Mont	248
William	Jeff	170
FORDING		
Lloyd	Maho	207
FOREAKER		
Geo S	Monr	224
FOREMAN		
Alfred	Huro	165
Jos S	Carr	040
Josephus	Belm	028
Samuel	Mont	233
William H	Gree	116
FORGRAVE		
Robert	Lick	185
FORNSHELL		
Frank L	Clin	055
FORRER		
John L	Mont	256
FORREST		
James A	Mont	227
Mary A	Rich	291
FORSALL		
Noah	High	156
FORSCHNER		
Eliza	Cuya	073
FORSHAY		
Geo	Wash	347
FORSHEY		
Hester	Nobl	269
FORSTNER		
Paul	Cuya	066
FORSYTH		
Charlotte T	Luca	201
Geo W	Wood	360
FORSYTHE		
James H	Adam	006
John	Star	317
William H	Dela	084
FORTNER		
Casper	VanW	336

FORTNEY		
Augustus	Henr	152
FORTUNE		
Daniel	Cosh	060
Eli	Cosh	061
Elizabeth H	Cosh	062
Malinda	Hock	158
FOSKETT		
Augustus A	Medi	210
FOSNOUCHT		
Emory	Maho	206
FOSS		
Henry	Mont	236
James	Lake	178
FOSTER		
Andrew J	Mont	242
Cath	Wash	350
Eliza	Madi	202
Elizabeth	Summ	324
Fannie E	Lake	176
Florilla A	Port	284
Frank T	Hami	122
Gardner	Geau	111
Geo H	Cuya	072
Henry C	Adam	006
James	Luca	201
James S	Cham	043
Jerden L	Adam	005
John	Otta	270
Jonas	Preb	286
Jonas	Sene	311
Joseph W	Asht	016
Lydia	Lake	177
Margaret	Musk	264
Nancy	Wyan	365
Nellie	Adam	005
Nelson	Pick	278
(alias Nelson Stanley)		
Robert	Belm	028
Robert G W	Luca	201
Romeo W	Erie	087
Sarah	Cham	041
Sarah	Scio	307
Theodore	Wood	361
Watson	Scio	305
William	Hami	121
William N	Geau	111
FOTCH		
John	Medi	210
FOUCHT		
Eve	Perr	275
FOUGHT		
Elizabeth	Hock	157

FOUGHT (cont)				FOX (cont)		
Lydia	Morr	259		James B	Sene	311
Rebecca	Paul	274		John	Fran	100
Simon J	Fran	100		John	Lawr	180
FOULK				John	Lawr	181
Nicholas W	Loga	190		John No 2	Mont	228
Sarah	Dela	084		John A	Tusc	330
FOUNTAINE				John C	Trum	329
Floriane	Mont	239		Joseph	Alle	010
FOURAKER				Lucinda	Maho	206
Le'is K McL	Wash	347		Mary	VanW	339
Margaret E	Wash	346		Michael	Star	319
Richard	Wash	347		Peter	Wayn	351
FOURNACE				Robert	Sene	310
Abraham	Star	318		Sarah	Cler	048
FOUST				Sarah	Mont	256
Abram	Medi	211		Thomas	Mont	229
Amos	Hanc	143		William	Cuya	072
Dorcas	Morr	260		William H	Trum	329
Isaac	Fair	092		FOY		
Sarah S	Maho	207		Geo	Hami	122
FOUT				Patrick	Hami	122
Ann	Lawr	183		FRAAS		
FOUTS				Henry	Fran	100
John	Miam	222		FRACKER		
FOWLER				Eliza J	Hami	132
Augusta L	Asht	018		FRACKLER		
Austin A	Wood	358		Geo W	Gree	115
Benj F	Sand	304		FRADD		
Edward P	Mont	229		John	Lawr	181
Elizabeth	Clar	044		FRAIPOUT		
Francis	Mont	245		Emile	Mont	240
Hannah	Harr	149		FRAKES		
Henry M	Maho	205		Sarah	Nobl	269
Isaac	Pick	278		FRALEY		
Mary B	Cuya	067		Daniel W	Miam	222
Susan C	Lawr	182		George W	Gall	110
Thomas W	Belm	027		FRALISH		
William H	Mont	242		Jacob	Brow	033
FOX				FRAMBS		
Alsey	Brow	034		Mary	Cler	049
Caroline J	Pick	279		FRAME		
Chas W	Mont	242		Elizabeth	Trum	327
Christian	Maho	205		FRAMPTON		
Christiana	Maho	206		Isaac K	Lick	184
Elizabeth	Fair	088		Jonathan	Lick	184
Ellis	Trum	329		FRANCE		
Geo	Tusc	332		Daniel K	Wayn	351
Henry	Guer	118		Eliza	Musk	267
Henry	Lawr	181		George W	Athe	021
Jacob	Hock	158		Marion E	Wayn	354
Jacob J	Luca	198		Wesley D	Rich	291
James	Mont	229				

FRANCES				FRANZKI		
James P	Knox	176		Christian	Rich	295
Michael	Ashl	011		FRANZREB		
William H	Athe	021		Elizabeth	Hami	134
FRANCIS				FRASER		
Alexander M	Mont	242		George	Mont	244
Jacob	Butl	038		James W	Wood	361
Jacob C	Musk	263		FRASIER		
Levinah	Lick	187		Jesse	Meig	214
Mary J	Pick	280		FRAVEL		
Mary S	Hami	122		Gilbert	Dela	084
Minerva	Adam	004		Jane A	Fran	103
Rachel J	Belm	027		Jeremiah	Mont	229
Simon	Musk	263		FRAVOR		
Susannah	Musk	263		John	Sene	309
FRANCISCO				FRAWLEY		
Cath	Sand	303		Patrick	Mont	235
James A	Wyan	367		FRAXLER		
Jams R	Sand	303		Nicholas T	Lora	192
John C	Fair	089		FRAZELL		
FRANIER				Augustine	Madi	204
William W	Guer	117		Minerva	Madi	204
FRANK				FRAZER		
Frederick	High	154		Andrew S	Gree	115
George	Port	285		John W	Hami	122
Henry	Ross	298		Peter	Mont	252
Jacob	Mont	244		FRAZIER		
Mary A	Huro	164		Ashley J	Mont	230
Matilda	Hami	122		David	Guer	118
Robert	Hami	122		Edward	Cler	051
Samuel D	Miam	221		Eli	Merc	217
FRANKBERGER				Elizabeth	Musk	267
Martha E	Cham	041		Evan	Wash	350
FRANKENBURG				Frances M	Cler	048
Geo G	VanW	337		Malinda	Warr	343
FRANKFOTHER				Mary H W	Musk	264
Mary	Maho	206		Nancy	Cler	048
FRANKHOUSER				Samuel	Luca	197
Solomon	Sene	309		William H	Pike	281
FRANKLIN				FREAKER		
Alex G	Sene	310		William	Miam	219
David B	Asht	018		FREAS		
John	Gall	109		John R	Trum	329
Mary	Merc	218		FREATENBOROUGH		
Rose A	Clar	045		Cath	Luca	201
Sarah B	Ross	297		FRECH		
Stephen	Hami	137		Mathew	Sand	303
William L	Clar	045		FRECK		
FRANKS				William	VanW	336
Homer S	Lora	196		FREDERICK		
Owen	Musk	263		Delilah	Sene	313
FRANTZ				Jacob G	Lick	185
Chas	Gree	115		James	Wood	360

FREDERICK (cont)		
William H	Wood	358
William H	Wood	360
FREDERICKS		
George	Henr	151
Sarah J	Luca	199
FREDKAMP		
Henry	Mont	253
FREDO		
Fed'k	Lora	193
FREE		
John	Holm	161
Jno W	Perr	276
FREED		
Geo A	Will	356
Henry	Hard	145
FREEL		
Hannah	Dark	078
FREEMAN		
Albert	Luca	199
Betsey	Cuya	076
Edward R	Mont	248
Edwin	Hami	129
Edwin	Knox	175
Elisha R	Hami	138
George	Scio	306
James D	Jack	168
John	Cuya	074
Oscar D	Port	285
Theodore O	Dela	085
Thompson P	Unio	334
FREER		
Gabriel	Lake	177
FREES		
John W	Sene	311
Sarah	Wood	360
FREESE		
Augustus	Putn	288
FREET		
David	Alle	008
Samuel T	Cosh	061
FREIBERGER		
Jos F A	Merc	218
FREMONT		
Henry C	Hami	137
FRENCH		
Andrew Y	Paul	274
Cynthia	Asht	018
Cyrus	Lake	177
Dianna	Athe	022
Francis M	Lawr	181
Frank D	Lick	186
Grovey	Hard	145

FRENCH (cont)		
James	Mont	243
Jane	Holm	161
Joanna	Lake	177
Lavina	Craw	062
Llewellyn W	Huro	166
Mary M	Putn	288
Simon W	Butl	036
Walter W	Dark	078
FRENIER		
Jane	Lick	187
FRERCHEY		
Isaac	Hami	138
FRESHAM		
Daniel	Ross	297
FRESHER		
Thomas	Trum	329
FRESHMAN		
Geo W	Hami	122
FRESHOM		
Absalom	Ross	296
William	Miam	218
FRESHWATER		
William H	Unio	334
FRETTER		
Thomas O	Luca	202
FRETWELL		
Eliza	Fran	095
FREW		
William	Mont	243
FREY		
Dorothea	Augl	025
FRIAR		
Henry	Sand	304
FRIBLEY		
Susan	Star	320
FRICK		
Magdalena	Sene	313
FRICKE		
Francis	Hami	122
FRICKEL		
Silas W	Musk	264
FRICKER		
Geo	Fair	089
FRICKET		
Jacob	Mont	241
FRIDLEY		
Mary E	Clar	044
FRIED		
Geo J	Hami	139
Henry C	Colu	058
FRIEDERICH		
Adam	Mont	235

FRIEDERICKS			FRIZELLE			
John	Mont	235	Harrison	Medi	210
FRIEL			FRIZZELL			
James	Mont	248	Josiah	Musk	263
Levi J	Lawr	183	FROEBE			
FRIEND			Philip	Dark	078
Adam	Hami	139	FROMM			
Asa	Hock	159	George	Mont	243
John	Hock	159	FRONCE			
FRIES			Jacob	Henr	152
Cath	Tusc	332	John	Ashl	013
Frederick	Mont	245	FRONEFIELD			
John	Mont	248	Joseph B	VanW	338
FRIESCH			FROST			
Salindoo	Star	320	Ansel	Huro	165
FRIESNER			Horatio H	Mont	255
Christena	Hock	158	Martha	Hami	122
FRIGNER			Susan	Athe	022
John W	Musk	264	FROUTHOF			
FRIK			Herman	Mont	253
Jacob	Scio	306	FROUTS			
FRINK			Susan	Morg	257
Charles	Hami	129	FROW			
FRISBERGER			William G	Adam	005
Arnold	Cuya	072	FROWINE			
FRISBEY			Robert	Scio	308
Chas	Morr	260	FRY			
Nathan W	Fran	103	Alfred	Craw	064
FRISBIE			Ambrose	Henr	153
Lorin	Asht	016	Andrew	Brow	033
FRISCH			Cath J	Luca	196
William	Mont	242	Eliza A	Mont	231
FRISINGER			Henry J	Gall	108
Thomas R	Alle	010	Jacob B	Wood	358
FRISSELL			Jane	Knox	173
Thomas B	Geau	112	John	Adam	005
FRIST			Jos A	Ross	297
Robert M	Preb	288	Josephy	Wood	359
FRISTO			Lavissa	High	154
Richard C	Clin	054	Margaret	Cler	048
FRITCH			Mary	Clar	045
Henry	Mont	253	Mary A	Ross	297
FRITCHER			Samuel	Gall	111
Geo W	Sene	311	Samuel G	Unio	334
FRITCHMAN			Sarah A	Hami	140
Jos	Colu	057	Walter	Adam	005
FRITSCH			FRYANT			
Matthias	Hami	136	Margaret	Hami	134
FRITZ			FRYBARGER			
Christina	Cuya	073	William W	Mont	247
George	Mont	248	FRYER			
Joseph	Brow	034	John R	Merc	217
Louis	Hami	122	Matilda C	Scio	306

FRYER (cont)		
Robert	Mont	243
Robert W	Cuya	075
William	Adam	004
FRYMAN		
Rachel	Defi	080
FUCHS		
Andrew	Hami	122
Johanna	Hami	134
Peter	Star	319
FUDGE		
Susan	Gree	113
FUGATE		
Addison R C	Luca	199
Margaret	Will	356
Robert	Meig	215
FUHR		
Henry	Star	317
FUHRMAN		
Margaretha	Cuya	073
FULHABER		
Sydna J	Sene	311
FULK		
Abram	Wyan	364
FULKASON		
Christena	Pick	279
FULKERSON		
Margaret	Perr	277
Philip	Scio	306
FULKERT		
Michael	Otta	271
FULLEN		
William	Pick	279
FULLER		
Abbie F	Hami	122
David	Merc	216
Edwin B	Erie	086
Edwin G	Athe	022
Eliza	Putn	289
Elizabeth	Perr	278
Geo W	Fran	102
Happy	Asht	014
Henry	Cuya	073
Job	Knox	175
Julia Ann	Asht	014
Juliana M	Clar	046
Lucretia	Asht	016
Luman	Lora	193
Moses	Medi	211
Resolved E	Athe	020
Robert	Asht	015
Robert	Mont	252
Stephen	Dela	083

FULLER (cont)		
Thomas	Cham	043
William	Henr	151
William	Wood	363
William H	Hock	158
William L	Jack	166
William S	Trum	330
Willis	Paul	273
FULLERTON		
James H	Scio	306
John	Pike	281
Joseph	Butl	038
FULLIS		
Amanda M	Star	316
FULLMER		
John	Defi	080
FULLWILER		
Ensign	Trum	325
FULMAR		
John	Wayn	352
FULMER		
Dewalt	Ashl	012
Louisa F	Wyan	365
Mary J	Wash	347
FULSHER		
Harriet	Pike	282
FULTON		
Andrew J	Belm	029
Augusta L	Ashl	011
Benj F	Mari	208
Cath	Luca	197
Harrison E	Wayn	353
Henry S P	Mont	227
Jane S	Adam	004
John D	Guer	118
Martha	Athe	021
Mary E	Musk	263
Matthew H	Craw	062
Nancy	Gall	107
Nancy	Gall	108
Nancy	Loga	191
Nelson A	Gree	116
Robert L	Athe	022
Robert M	Belm	029
Robert M	Gall	107
FULTS		
John W	Knox	176
FULTZ		
Isaac	Ross	298
FUNITER		
Edward A	Dela	084
FUNK		
Albert	Miam	221

FUNK (cont)			GABE		
Anna	Miam	221	August	Hami	126
Frederick	Hami	122	GABELIN		
Frederick	Hami	129	Charles	Hock	157
George	Mont	249	GABLE		
George W	Perr	276	Jacob	Musk	267
Jos	Wyan	365	GABRET		
Julia A	Rich	292	Jonas	VanW	338
Katharine	Cosh	060	GABRIEL		
Mary	Pick	279	Elijah	Cham	041
Michael	Pick	280	Esther	Athe	020
FUNKE			Mary E	Mont	233
Margaretta	Hami	134	GADDIS		
FURBANKS			Franklin	Star	321
John	Mont	234	Henry M	Rich	291
FURBAY			Leonard W	Otta	271
Reese	Harr	149	Martha	Wayn	352
FUREY			Sally E	Wayn	352
William	Mont	247	GAES		
FURGESON			Peter	Mont	247
Jane	Meig	216	GAETZ		
Susan	Port	284	William W	Dark	078
FURGISON			GAFFNEY		
John	Cler	049	Ann	Hami	121
FURGUSON			GAGE		
Benj E	Harr	150	Charles F	Asht	015
FURL			GAHAGAN		
James	Lawr	180	Hannah M	Miam	222
FURLONG			GAILY		
Jas	Hami	136	Andrew	Colu	058
Patrick	Mont	244	GAINES		
FURMAN			Annaliza	Paul	273
Geo H	Lora	195	GAITHER		
FURNACE			Henry	Clin	055
Mary	Star	318	GAKENHEIMER		
FURNEY			Lewis	Monr	225
Michael	Henr	152	GALBRAITH		
FURNIER			Elbert P	Alle	009
William H	Scio	304	Freelove	Pike	282
FURNSY			James	Cuya	075
John M	Guer	117	Mary	Morr	259
FURROW			GALBRATH		
Amelia F B	Cham	042	Alvan S	Mont	250
John K	Cham	042	GALE		
FURRY			Geo F	Fran	100
Isaac N	Luca	196	Henry	Sene	312
Jacob H	Wood	361	Lyman	Trum	328
Margaret J	Faye	094	Mary J	Meig	216
William	Wood	363	Otho G	Cham	042
FURST			GALEANOR		
Josiah	Tusc	333	Mary	Merc	217
FUSSELMAN			GALEHOUSE		
Jupiter P	Medi	210	Dorothy	Wayn	352

GALEHOUSE (cont)		
Harvey H	Wayn	352
GALES		
Geo W	Gree	115
Matilda	Ross	297
GALLACHER		
Thomas	Mont	234
GALLAGHER		
Franklin	Maho	204
John	Fair	089
John	Mont	228
John	Mont	248
Michael	Wash	346
Nancy	Guer	119
Patrick	Wash	351
GALLAHER		
Alice E	Warr	342
Calvin J	Monr	224
James	Mont	227
GALLANT		
Geo W	Otta	270
William H	Alle	009
GALLEGHER		
Mary	Lawr	180
GALLEHER		
America C	Knox	174
GALLENTINE		
Thomas	Defi	081
GALLIN		
Rebecca	Morg	258
GALLNTINE		
Jas	Wayn	351
GALLOWAY		
Elizabeth	Gree	119
Geo W	Wayn	352
James W	Mont	227
John	Wayn	351
Mary E	Fran	101
Richard	Gree	115
GALLUP		
George D	Guer	118
Naomi	Putn	290
GALOOLEY		
Andrew	Mont	250
GALVIN		
Michael	Mont	251
GAMBEE		
Rhoda A	Erie	086
GAMBLE		
John L	Otta	271
Martha	Jeff	171
Nancy	Fair	092

GAME		
Philip	Fran	095
GAMEL		
Robert	Mont	250
GAMERDINGER		
Mary	Lick	186
GAMES		
Elizabeth	Lick	187
Robert	Unio	335
GAMMIELL		
David	Dela	085
GAMON		
Hannah	Lawr	182
GANABLE		
David W	Carr	040
GANBAUX		
Augustus	Dark	079
GANCKSTADT		
Henry	Luca	199
GANDY		
John J	Monr	225
Sarah	Ross	297
GANEY		
Mary	Cuya	068
GANGI		
Jacob Jr	Augl	025
GANNON		
Barckley	Mont	250
James	Mont	237
Jesse	Lawr	182
Patrick	Mont	247
GANO		
Jacob W	Hami	125
GANT		
John H	Mont	228
GANTZ		
William	Mont	251
GANVEY		
Geo B	Maho	205
GARBER		
Daniel	Rich	291
Geo C	Hami	138
Samuel	Mont	237
GARCH		
Joseph	Cuya	072
GARDENER		
George W	Cler	047
GARDHEFFNER		
Andrew	Star	317
GARDNER		
Ary R	Lick	184
Asa A	Morr	261
Daniel E	Cuya	066

GARDNER (cont)			GARONTTE		
Dewitt C	Port	285	John S	Clin	053
Eliza Jane	Unio	336	GARRELL		
Eliza P	Fran	104	Jas	Will	355
Elizabeth	Hami	131	GARRET		
Elizabeth	Summ	324	John N	Musk	262
Emily H	Carr	040	GARRETSON		
Hannah R	Trum	326	Eli	Belm	030
Harriet M	Gall	109	Ellenor	Wash	349
Jacob M	Butl	036	GARRETT		
Jared	Lora	193	Augustus C	Erie	087
John E	Wyan	365	Charles C	Hard	144
John M	VanW	339	Daniel	Musk	262
John W	Lick	184	Dwight	Augl	025
Joseph	Monr	226	Francis F	Colu	055
Joseph L	Huro	165	Irena	Medi	212
Julia A	Ross	300	Laura M	Rich	295
Lydia A	Guer	120	Mary	Belm	030
Margaret O	Medi	212	Mary	Guer	119
Monroe M	Medi	210	Mary	Summ	323
Robert	Musk	263	Mary E	Clin	054
Thomas F	Faye	094	Priscilla J	Madi	202
William L	Wash	350	Thomas	Belm	028
GARDON			Thomas	Ross	300
Hetta	Gall	109	GARRICK		
GAREN			John	Mont	251
Ireneus A	Fran	100	GARRISON		
GAREY			Franklin	Asht	015
Jas K	Perr	275	James A	Port	285
GARFIELD			James A O	Hami	125
Lucretia R	Cuya	074	John M	Mont	249
William H	Rich	291	Matilda	Hami	121
GARGES			GARST		
William C	Musk	266	Susan	Mont	230
GARIS			GARTHEFFNER		
Mary	Ross	299	Mary	Hami	121
GARLICK			GARTLAND		
Elizabeth B	Unio	334	Patrick	Mont	240
GARLOCK			GARTNER		
William H	Will	355	Jesse	Fult	105
GARLOUGH			GARVER		
Polly	Mont	233	Emanuel	Luca	199
GARMAN			Henry F	Mont	251
Chas P	Mont	227	Lewis C	Dark	076
William	Fult	107	Sophronia	Colu	056
GARMUTH			GARVIE		
Godfrey	Hard	147	George G	Hami	125
GARNER			GARVIN		
Celia A	Unio	333	Cath	Harr	150
James W	High	155	Davis	Harr	149
GARNES			John M	Harr	149
William A	Gall	110	GARWIN		
			Thomas	Mont	239

GARWOOD			**GAUMER**			
Angeline	Cham	041	Magdalena	Cosh	060	
Eliza C	Colu	058	**GAUS**			
Rachel	Paul	274	Jane	Preb	287	
GARY			**GAUZERT**			
Isaac L	Asht	015	Adolph	Lora	195	
John D	Butl	039	**GAVIN**			
GASKILL			Daniel	Cuya	072	
Franklin B	Dark	078	**GAW**			
James	VanW	337	Aaron M	Cuya	072	
Joseph	High	154	**GAY**			
GASKIN			Deloss	Fult	107	
Mariah H	Lora	195	Horace M	Wood	362	
GASKINS			Mary J	Nobl	269	
John R	Adam	005	Polly	Musk	262	
GASPER			Timothy E	Defi	081	
John	Mont	247	William	Lora	194	
GASSER			**GAYER**			
Mary L	Otta	271	Jacob	Mont	229	
GASSNER			**GAYLORS**			
Peter	Cuya	065	Wilbor H	Cuya	074	
GASTON			**GAZELEY**			
Lafayette	Gall	108	Jabez C	Cuya	072	
GATCHELL			**GEAGLEY**			
John B	Morr	260	George	Port	284	
John D	Monr	224	**GEAR**			
GATES			Harrison	Miam	220	
Edwin N	Cuya	072	**GEARAN**			
Geo W	Mont	228	Mary	Jeff	170	
Geo W	VanW	340	**GEARHARSTINE**			
Harriet	Port	285	Rebecca	Huro	163	
Howard	Wayn	352	**GEARHART**			
Isaac	Belm	026	Chas	Mont	228	
John	Cuya	069	Drusilla	Miam	220	
John	Luca	199	**GEARY**			
Margaret	Ross	297	Sarah	Colu	058	
Napoleon	Rich	293	William	Rich	291	
Roswell	Alle	008	**GEBANER**			
Stephen P	Lawr	181	Johanna R	Sene	309	
Stephen P	Mont	245	**GEBHARDT**			
GATTON			Mary S	Mari	209	
Sarah	Rich	291	**GEBHART**			
GATWOOD			Cath	Hami	131	
William R	Musk	265	**GEER**			
GAUCKLER			Armineas	Gall	107	
Cath	Hami	121	Henry	Vint	341	
GAUDY			Jacob	Gall	107	
Clayton L	VanW	337	John J	Cler	051	
GAUFF			Madison	Gall	107	
Charles H	Hami	125	Milo	Fult	107	
David H	Erie	087	Nancy	Gall	107	
GAULT			Sallie A	Cler	051	
Ellen	Asht	016	Thomas	Madi	204	

GEESBURG		
Benedict	Mont	248
GEGHAN		
James	Mont	251
GEIER		
Anna Maria	Dark	078
GEIGER		
Geo	Hami	125
John	Hami	125
GEIGERMAN		
David	Hami	126
GEIL		
Margaret	Ross	297
GEILER		
Frank	Hami	126
GEINER		
Phebe	Dela	082
GEIOGUE		
Mary M	Holm	160
GEIRNIGER		
George	Hami	125
GEIS		
John M	Cuya	066
GEISENDORF		
Harvy	Hami	125
GEISLER		
William E	Cuya	066
GEIST		
Casper	Mont	239
GEISZ		
Casper	Mont	251
GEITHER		
Michael	Cuya	072
GELVIN		
Joseph	Dela	084
GEMBERLING		
David	Huro	161
GEMPELLER		
Fred	Cuya	072
GENAVAN		
Reuben H	Clar	045
GENET		
Joseph	Star	319
GENGER		
John C	Trum	330
GENSEL		
Eliza	Alle	008
GENTES		
Charles	Mont	243
GEOGHEGAN		
James	Miam	220
GEORGE		
Edward	Maho	207

GEORGE (cont)		
Felix	Mont	251
Frank	Dela	085
Henry	Hanc	142
James	Hock	157
James A	Carr	039
Joseph	Sand	302
Kate	Sene	310
Miner	Guer	119
Nancy	Guer	119
Richard	Lick	184
Sarah	Guer	120
Susan	Musk	267
Theodore M	Ashl	012
William B	Fran	099
GEPHART		
Geo	Sand	303
Geo W	Pick	280
GEPPERT		
Thomas	VanW	338
GERARD		
Martha	Athe	023
GERBER		
John	Mont	251
GERBODE		
Louis	Mont	251
GERHART		
Geo	Ross	298
GERNHARD		
Mathias	Otta	270
GERNIG		
John C	Star	320
GERSHBACH		
Magdalena	Cosh	060
GERSTNER		
Gotfried	Hami	125
GERUKE		
Cath	Erie	087
GERVAIS		
Henry	Fran	101
GERWE		
Mary	Hami	121
GESSLER		
Francis	Sene	313
GESSNER		
Conrad	Cuya	065
John	Henr	152
William T	Dela	082
GETTY		
Ebenezer	Asht	016
GETTYS		
Samuel A	Ross	298

GETZ		
Adam	Star	320
GEUSTER		
Martin	Lora	195
GEVEEKE		
August	Mont	248
GEYELIN		
George	Summ	322
GEYER		
Margaretta	Hami	131
GEYSER		
William	Fult	106
GHOLSON		
Sarah	Lawr	180
GIBBAN		
Richard	Maho	207
GIBBENS		
Andrew	Will	355
GIBBENY		
Samuel H	Will	356
GIBBONS		
Patrick	Gree	113
Sarah C	Musk	264
William S	Port	285
GIBBS		
Archibald	Meig	215
Chas	Cuya	075
Daniel W	Morr	259
Malisse	Wash	347
GIBERSON		
Allen H	Cuya	072
GIBLIN		
Ann	Madi	202
Thomas	Mont	232
GIBONEY		
Sarah H	Wash	350
GIBSON		
Ann E	High	154
Henry	Sene	309
Jane J	Colu	057
Joel W	Wyan	366
John D	Mont	240
John H	Mont	228
Lydia	High	155
Mary A	Hami	121
Samuel J	Hard	147
Samuel S	Tusc	331
Theo	Wyan	366
Thomas	Star	317
William	Monr	226
William O	Morg	257
Wilson S	Wood	361
GIDDINGS		
Charles	Wash	346
GIEFOY		
Patrick	Mont	242
GIESY		
Jonas	Belm	026
GIFFORD		
James L	Geau	111
James P	Putn	290
Oscar E	Asht	016
GIGOS		
Mary A	Hami	121
GILBERT		
Abel	Morg	258
Andrus J	Rich	293
Daniel	Hanc	143
Edward W	Hard	144
Esther B	Cuya	068
Fuller	Wood	360
George A	Adam	005
Harlow M	Alle	008
James	Lawr	183
John C	Dark	077
John J	Hard	145
Margaret E	Dark	077
Mary	Maho	204
Naomi	Geau	112
Peter Sr	Musk	263
Phebe A	Hard	145
Rebecca	Miam	219
GILBRATH		
Thomas	Lawr	180
GILBREATH		
Samuel F	Lick	189
GILBRETH		
London	Cham	043
Margaret W	Meig	212
GILCHRIST		
David	Perr	277
GILDARD		
Henry B	Cuya	076
GILDEA		
Mary	Guer	120
Patrick	Lawr	181
GILDOW		
Geo W	Ross	298
GILLEAU		
George I	Cler	047
GILES		
Martha	Harr	149
GILGER		
Jacob	Musk	262

GILKEY			GILLMORE		
Ellen J	Trum	326	Duane W	Geau	112
GILKISON			GILLON		
Newton	Rich	292	Jacob	Gall	110
GILL			GILLOW		
Ann	Hami	131	Patrick J	Mont	245
Chas B	Mont	230	GILMAN		
Christena	Meig	213	Charles	Hami	125
Eliza A	Lake	177	GILMORE		
Elyah	Guer	118	Deborah	Ross	299
Geo	Musk	267	Eliza J	Augl	026
GILLAM			Emory	Trum	326
Mary A	Wyan	365	Hugh H	Mont	251
GILLAN			John W	Wayn	353
John	Mont	234	Sarah	Ross	300
GILLEN			William H	Preb	287
Augustus	Hard	145	GILPEN		
GILLENWATER			Marila	Meig	216
Charlotte	Pike	281	GILPIN		
GILLESPEY			Elizabeth	Wash	345
Thomas	Putn	289	James	Ross	296
GILLESPIE			Nancy	Morg	259
Elijah P	Mont	249	Rebecca E	Guer	118
Harrison	Jack	166	Rufus	Morg	257
John W A	Butl	037	GILROY		
Solomon	Morg	258	John	Augl	026
GILLETT			GILSON		
Clarissa L	Will	355	James	Guer	120
Margaret A	Ross	300	John H	Colu	057
Sarah	Luca	197	GILYER		
Sarah E	Medi	211	Frederick	Sand	303
GILLFILLAN			GINDER		
Cath	Ross	297	William H	Hard	147
Mary	Ross	297	GINGERY		
GILLHOFER			Aaron	Fult	105
George	Mont	251	GINGLES		
GILLIAM			Andrew	Mont	248
David T	Fran	101	GINHIEMER		
Hartwell	Clin	052	Frederick	Scio	308
Coleman	Scio	307	GINN		
GILLILAND			Leroy S	Dela	085
Hannah	Jack	167	GINTEN		
Harrison	Jack	168	Horace	Will	357
Lydia	Jack	168	GINTHER		
Rebecca	Jack	168	John	Sand	303
GILLILOUD			GINTNER		
Valentine	Hard	145	Ann M	Perr	277
GILLIS			GIPE		
Allen W	Trum	327	Joshua	Rich	291
Amanda M	Cuya	074	GIPPHARD		
Simeon	Will	355	William	Gall	109
Thomas	Meig	214	GIRARD		
			Durfey	Dela	084

GIRARD (cont)			GLEASON (cont)		
Griffith M	Preb	287	Warren	Fult	107
GISING			William	Mont	251
Mary	Fran	101	GLECKLER		
GITTINGER			William	Lick	186
William H	Sene	312	GLENDENNING		
GITTS			Charles	Geau	111
Peter	Defi	080	GLENN		
GIVEN			Alexander B	Lake	177
Susan	Wayn	354	Andrew	Wood	358
GIVENS			Henry	Huro	161
Jos B	Wash	346	John B	Mont	238
GIVENY			Joseph	Musk	264
Philip	Mont	247	Margaret	Lawr	182
GLADDEN			Mary J	Hard	147
Rachel	Ashl	013	Milton K	Gall	111
William F	Ashl	013	Priscilla	VanW	339
GLANCY			GLENNAN		
Priscilla	Lick	188	Martin	Luca	197
GLANNER			GLENNON		
Mathias	Cham	041	Thomas	Mont	248
GLASGLOW			GLICK		
John H	Cler	048	Cath	Fair	091
GLASGOW			GLIDDEN		
Alex W	Wayn	354	Isaac H	Nobl	270
Cath	Hock	158	GLOSENER		
Mary F	Hami	138	Cath	Jeff	171
GLASPY			GLOSSINGER		
Robert	Belm	028	John	Gree	116
GLASS			GLUCKOWSKI		
Ann E	Cuya	074	Jacob	Hami	125
Charles	Fran	101	GLUE		
Mathew G	VanW	338	William	Jeff	170
Nancy	Perr	276	GLUNT		
GLASSBURN			Cath	Preb	287
Barbara	Jack	167	GLYNN		
GLASSCOCK			Martin	Mont	240
John P	Adam	005	GOBLE		
GLATHART			Leonard	Cuya	072
Aaron J	Hanc	141	GOCHNAUR		
GLAZE			David	Mont	251
Cynthia A	Brow	033	GODDARD		
William	Pike	282	Charles A	Scio	305
William S	Faye	095	Elisha W	Cuya	072
GLAZIER			Elizabeth	Hami	131
Polly	Athe	020	GODDEN		
GLEASON			Bernhard	Mont	246
Andrew J	VanW	337	GODFREY		
David A	Defi	080	John	Guer	118
John	Mont	246	John	Sene	311
Joseph H	Huro	165	GODMAN		
Rebecca	Hami	138	Jas H	Fran	099
Sidney M	Will	355			

GOEBEL			GOLLATUE		
Cath	Cuya	074	Henry	Sene	310
Eliza	Fran	097	GOLLINGER		
Henry	Mont	251	John	Mont	251
Magdalena	Hami	121	GOLLIVER		
GOELLER			Tovanium	VanW	337
William	Hami	136	GOLLUM		
GOETTLER			Ernest	Mont	232
Albert	Hami	125	GOLSCH		
GOETZ			Frederick	Mont	238
John	Mont	255	GOMAN		
GOFF			John B	Fair	089
Job S	Loga	189	GONEY		
John	Harr	150	Michael	Mont	251
Porter A	Otta	271	GONNAN		
Vernum	Hard	147	James	Fran	099
GOFORTH			GOOCH		
N Pool	Hami	121	Emma J	Warr	343
GOGERTY			GOOD		
Patrick	Mont	247	Arabella	Alle	010
GOHN			Daniel	Wyan	365
Franklin R	Clar	045	Emanuel	Wayn	353
GOINS			George	Paul	274
Thomas	Meig	214	George B	Putn	289
COKER			Henry	Will	355
John	Hami	140	Louisa	Maho	205
GOLBRAITH			Lydia	Jeff	171
James	Harr	151	Thomas	Belm	027
GOLDEN			GOODALL		
Benj	Clar	044	Emeline	Lawr	179
			GOODELL		
Caroline G	Sand	301	Bethuel	Henr	151
Ephraim P	Hami	137	George F	Mont	242
H Maria	Summ	321	GOODHART		
Jacob	Morg	258	Samuel	Trum	329
John	Hami	125	GOODIN		
John E	Hami	137	Harriet	Perr	276
GOLDSBERY			William	Wyan	366
Martin	Unio	336	GOODING		
GOLDSBOROUGH			Phebe T	Dela	084
Euph'a	Wayn	352	GOODLING		
GOLDSBURG			Michael B	Mont	251
Emily	Faye	093	William B	Mont	250
GOLDSBURY			GOODLIVE		
Mahala	Gree	115	Adam	Perr	275
GOLDSMIDT			GOODMAN		
Abraham	Trum	328	Benedict	Tusc	330
GOLDSMITH			Oliver	Wood	358
Abigail Jones			GOODRECH		
	Lake	177	Sarah P	Lick	184
Henry B	Star	320	GOODRICH		
Mary A	Lora	192	Cath	Trum	328
Sarah J	Fran	095	Ella	Knox	173

GOODRICH (cont)		
Henry	Mont	238
Henry R	Lake	178
James D	Wood	360
Susan	Fult	107
GOODSELL		
Bridget	Erie	087
Philo S	Cuya	072
GOODWELL		
Ira	Wash	348
GOODWILL		
Bradley C Jr	Star	317
Nancy	Cuya	069
GOODWIN		
Albert	Fran	101
Cynthia	Cuya	074
David C	Putn	289
Geo W	Warr	344
Lewis H	Erie	088
Lucina	Cler	049
GOON		
Jacob	Rich	292
GOORE		
Moses	Henr	152
GOOS		
Elizabeth	Tusc	330
GOOSUCH		
James A	Knox	174
GOPPERTON		
Geo	Adam	004
GORBY		
Benj F	Scio	308
Malinda	Colu	056
GORDAN		
Richard B	Hami	139
GORDON		
Alex	Cuya	064
Andrew J	Morr	261
Cath A	Hard	146
Clinton	Hami	126
David	Hard	147
Edwin A	Wyan	366
George	Gree	115
George F	Port	284
Henrietta	Gree	113
Henry C	Gree	116
Hugh	Fran	100
Jas H	Cham	042
John	Mont	245
John	Mont	247
John N	Fair	090
Malinda	Ashl	014
Martha A	Morr	260

GORDON (cont)		
Parker P	High	156
Perkins A	Erie	087
Priscilla	Belm	030
Rebecca	Hard	148
Robert	Miam	221
Samuel	Wyan	364
Samuel C	Cuya	072
Thomas W	Brow	032
GORE		
Geo W	Cuya	072
GORHAM		
Ethelinda R	Wash	350
GORMAN		
John A	Miam	221
Thomas J	Butl	039
GORMLEY		
Leander A	Mari	209
GORRELL		
Cyrus W	Paul	274
Margaret	Will	355
Maria M	Wyan	364
GORSUCH		
Hannah	Butl	035
Joseph T	Musk	266
Russel B	Otta	271
Thomas	Fult	106
GORTMAN		
William P	Cuya	075
GORTON		
Geo B	Wood	360
GOSHAM		
John	Paul	273
GOSNELL		
Jasper N	Unio	335
GOSNEY		
Elizabeth	Hami	138
William	Hami	138
GOSS		
Reuben	Cuya	065
Sebastian C	Medi	212
GOSSAGE		
Adam	Fult	107
GOSSARD		
Ellen	Alle	011
GOSSETT		
David	Lawr	183
Warden	Nobl	269
GOTSHAL		
Sarah E	Star	320
GOTSHALL		
Rebecca	Star	318

GOTT			GRACY			
Chas	Ross	300	Sarah E	Jeff	170	
GOTTSHOLL			GRADOLPH			
Daniel	Harr	150	John	Butl	036	
GOTTSTEIN			GRADY			
George	Mont	244	Aaron	Ross	300	
GOTWALS			Ann	Cuya	074	
Cath E	Clar	044	Michael	Clin	055	
GOUDY			William A	Wyan	364	
John	Monr	226	GRAETZ			
Mary	Monr	223	Edward T	Lora	195	
GOUGH			GRAFF			
David	High	155	Herman	Erie	088	
GOUIN			Wilhelmina	Hami	131	
Francis	Cuya	072	GRAFT			
GOULD			Chas	Craw	062	
Bradley	Sand	302	GRAHAM			
Daniel W	Harr	150	Amelia	Rich	294	
Edward E	Lake	177	Andrew N	Butl	035	
Elizabeth J	Wood	362	Elizabeth	Preb	287	
Franklin	Cuya	072	Finley	Athe	020	
Lucinda	Cuya	064	Helen Mary	Preb	288	
Margaret E	Cham	042	Henry	Cler	049	
Mary	Brow	033	James	Mont	234	
Nathan	Colu	057	James H C	Faye	094	
Orrin B	Cuya	072	Jasper	Scio	308	
Polly	Ashl	014	Jehiel	Meig	214	
William	Hami	125	John	Jeff	170	
GOULDING			Joseph	Hard	144	
Cath	Musk	265	Joseph	Scio	304	
GOULT			Keturah	Ross	300	
Calvin B	Maho	206	Margaret	Morr	260	
GOUSER			Mary E	Gall	110	
Martin	Hard	144	Mary J	Fran	101	
GOUTER			Michael	Luca	199	
Albert	Wayn	352	Peter	Meig	213	
GOVE			Peter F	Medi	211	
Chas F	Cuya	072	Robert	Wash	345	
GOWIN			Sarah E	Fran	101	
Sarah A	Meig	212	Sydney A	Meig	216	
GOWING			Thomas	Fran	095	
Geo E	Craw	064	Thomas	Fran	101	
GOWITZKI			William	Athe	023	
William	Cuya	076	William M	Shel	315	
GRABB			GRAINGER			
Archibald	Wash	345	Joseph A	Defi	080	
GRABEL			GRAITER			
Nancy	Sand	303	Chas	Cuya	072	
GRABLE			GRAMLICH			
Uriah H	Hanc	141	Sabastian	Fran	100	
GRACE			GRANDSTAFF			
Ferdinand L	Fran	103	Alvin	Lick	184	
Jeremiah J	Mont	229	William W	Lick	185	

GRANER		
John	Wyan	367
GRANFELL		
Mary	Harr	151
GRANGER		
Charles C	Dela	085
Edgar O	Geau	111
Wilbert	Morr	261
GRANNES		
Lenora	Wood	358
GRANT		
Caroline	Asht	015
Charlotte	Hami	121
Eunice	Paul	273
Geo	Lora	194
Hannah	Cuya	065
Henry C	Summ	323
Parkinson	Holm	160
Preservid H	Geau	111
Rebecca L	Nobl	269
Sallie A	Fran	101
GRANTHAM		
Nancy	Clin	055
GRASS		
Henry	Lick	186
William	Wash	348
GRASSER		
William	Lick	187
GRASSMAN		
Charles	Mont	251
GRAVE		
John	Morr	261
GRAVEL		
William H	Mont	235
GRAVELL		
Oswald E	Craw	062
GRAVENITZ		
William	Mont	251
GRAVES		
Betsey	Cuya	065
David	High	154
David	Will	355
Elive	Vint	340
Isabel	Lick	184
James W	Perr	278
Oscar	Meig	213
Thomas A	Paul	272
William	Wood	362
William S	Gall	108
GRAVETT		
Marenda	Cler	051
GRAW		
Gottlieb	Luca	202

GRAW (cont)		
John	Butl	035
GRAY		
Aaron	Mont	248
Ann	Hami	138
Annie	Knox	173
Barbara	Mont	231
Cath	Monr	226
Cornelius	Wash	346
Emeline	Geau	112
George	Lick	185
George B	Cuya	072
Gibbons	Clin	052
Hannah	Cuya	075
Hezikiah T	Morg	259
James N	Monr	226
Jesse	Nobl	269
Magdalena	Wayn	353
Matilda	Musk	265
Nancy	Belm	027
Patrick H	Mont	242
Peggry	Musk	266
Robert	Belm	029
Robert	Maho	207
Roxanna	Lora	193
Samuel	Hami	125
Samuel	Holm	160
Samuel B	Harr	150
Susan J	Clin	053
Thomas J	Butl	036
Thomas J	Hami	125
Thompson D	Mont	251
William	Henr	151
William R	Monr	223
GRAYBILL		
John M	Fair	089
Lydia	Summ	321
GRAYSON		
Lemuel	Fair	091
GREEN		
Albert W	Star	316
Ann O	Ross	301
Bartholomew	Mont	250
Benj G	Lora	195
Cath	Hanc	142
Charles J	Cuya	072
Conrad	Mont	242
Eliza	Colu	056
Elizabeth	Hami	135
Elizabeth	Hock	157
Esther E	Lake	177
Fanny M	Luca	197
George	Miam	221

GREEN (cont)			GREENWOOD		
Henry	Otta	272	George W	Mont	251
Henry S	Cuya	076	John L	Cuya	074
Hester	Hard	148	Mary T	Luca	199
Horace	Paul	274	GREER		
Ira	Fran	100	Alexander	Maho	204
Isaac	Fran	102	Aurelia	Lake	177
James G	Colu	057	Benj A F	Knox	176
Jane	Port	284	Ellen	Cuya	076
Joel V	Tusc	330	Geo S	Alle	009
John	Hami	138	Harriet	Lora	195
John G	Sene	311	James S	Hanc	143
John R	Mont	241	John	Wyan	364
Jonathan	Cuya	076	GREGEOIS		
Margaret	Fair	091	Michael	Hami	125
Margaret	Meig	215	GREGG		
Mary	Clin	052	Calvin W	Loga	191
Mary A	Nobl	269	Elias G	Rich	295
Nancy	Colu	055	Geo W	Pick	280
Nancy	Fran	101	John F	Wyan	366
Nancy E	Athe	021	Lucretia	Erie	087
Nancy J	Unio	333	Perry	Hami	125
Parker	Clin	052	Rebecca	Wyan	365
Samuel	Perr	276	William	Loga	189
Susannah	Henr	152	William J	Nobl	268
Thomas	Huro	165	William S	Belm	028
Thomas	Mont	237	GREGORY		
Thomas C	Fair	090	Aaron H	Ross	301
William	Unio	335	Adam	Vint	340
William C	Lick	188	America	Hami	131
William L	Otta	272	Dulcena	Brow	035
William P	Perr	275	John H	Star	319
William W	Lick	186	Levi	Clin	053
GREENANYER			Marcus E	Lake	178
Chester D	Hami	125	Mary Jane	Lake	177
GREENAWALT			Polly	Huro	163
Elizabeth	Maho	206	GREINER		
GREENAWAULT			Engelbert	Mont	251
Henry H	Ashl	011	Peter	Henr	151
GREENE			GREIS		
Chas W	Musk	266	Peter J	Sene	313
Jacob	Fair	092	GREISINGER		
GREENHO			Geo W	Fult	104
Andrew	Summ	324	GRENLING		
GREENLEE			Henry	Mont	241
David	Belm	028	GRESSNER		
William	Adam	007	Theo	Mont	229
William M	Adam	003	GRETHER		
GREENO			Charles	Cler	050
Maria	Pick	279	GREVING		
Samuel	Wyan	366	Joseph	Rich	291
GREENWALT			GREYSON		
Hannah L	Harr	149	Frank	Cler	049

GRIN			**GRORT**		
Frederick	Monr	224	Geo A	Cuya	072
Nancy	Tusc	333	**GROSCHNER**		
GRINER			Dorothy	Henr	153
Daniel	Hard	144	**GROSS**		
Edward	Pick	280	Chas	Wood	361
Isaac	Hard	144	Christian	Hami	125
GRINNELL			Ephraim	Wood	363
William	Port	285	Jacob	Tusc	333
GRISEN			Jno	Dark	079
Mary M	Erie	087	Lorentz	Athe	021
GRISOT			Louis	Mont	236
Caroline	Hami	121	Theobald	Mont	244
GRISS			**GROSSKLOSS**		
Enos	Wood	362	Jacob	Wash	348
GRISSINGER			**GROSSKOPFT**		
David	Fult	104	Edward	Mont	251
GRIST			**GROSVENOR**		
Thomas E	Maho	205	Ann C	Athe	020
GRISTE			Charlotte G	Wash	349
Luman G	Summ	325	Frances	Miam	222
GRISWOLD			Royal W	Miam	220
Arthur O	Lora	193	Samuel S	Wash	348
Nancy	Paul	272	**GROTE**		
Salem T	High	154	Christopher	Hami	125
GRITZEN			**GROUSE**		
Magdalena	Cuya	065	Benj	Hami	125
GROATT			**GROVE**		
Hannah H	Lora	194	Abraham	Sene	312
GROCE			Cath	Sene	311
Mahlon G	Fran	100	Eve	Clar	044
GROFF			Frederick	Holm	160
Cath	Fair	089	Hezekial	Pike	281
GROFFNEY			John H	Fran	100
Sarah	Musk	265	Joseph	Wood	361
GROFMILLER			Rachel	Tusc	332
Augustus	Rich	295	Samuel	Meig	212
GROGAN			Stephen	Fair	089
Mitchell D	Colu	059	Susannah	Cham	043
GROIN			William S	Harr	149
Mathias	Cuya	072	**GROVENBURY**		
GROLLE			Joseph	Fran	100
Mary Ann	Hami	140	**GROVER**		
GROMES			Harvey B	Summ	322
Samuel S	Otta	271	John A	Dark	078
GROOM			Margaret	Sand	303
Arvin	Paul	273	**GROVES**		
Thomas	Fran	103	Edward	Wash	347
GROOMS			Louisa	Jeff	172
James W	Fran	102	Lucinda	Warr	342
John F	Musk	265	Mary J	Fran	103
Thomas	Adam	004	Samuel S	Mari	208
GROOWIN			Squire C	Hanc	141
Hannah	Hanc	142			

GROVES (cont)		
Thomas	High	156
William O	Asht	017
GROW		
Cath	Jack	167
James W	Mont	244
William	Wayn	352
GRUB		
Jacob	Will	356
GRUBB		
Eliza	Medi	212
Geo W	Rich	295
Isaac N	Defi	080
Wells	Athe	022
William	Unio	335
GRUBBS		
John	Scio	308
Samuel	Perr	277
GRUBER		
Jacob	Mont	248
GRUBS		
Sarah	Sand	301
GRULL		
Mary	Jeff	171
GRUMMEL		
Henry	Sene	313
GRUND		
Conrad	Colu	055
GRUNDEN		
Samuel	Merc	217
GRUNDICH		
Jacob	Wyan	366
GRUNLEY		
Joseph	Dela	085
GRUVER		
John	Sene	309
GSHWEND		
Theresa	Mont	230
GUARD		
Edmonia R P	Hami	138
GUARLECH		
Cath	Luca	199
GUBER		
Hiram E	Merc	217
GUCHES		
John M	Fran	103
GUDGEON		
Charles	Hami	125
GUELLERMER		
Philip	Jeff	170
GUENGERICH		
Daniel	Mont	246

GUENTHER		
August	Hami	125
George A	Mont	251
GUERIN		
Jane	Shel	314
GUESS		
Jason	Hock	158
Sarah	Carr	039
GUILD		
Elizabeth B	Lake	178
Louisa T	Cuya	074
GUILE		
Hiram	Luca	199
GUILFORD		
Geo	Fult	106
GUILLERNE		
Magdalena	Hami	121
GUINAN		
Bernard	Mont	243
GUINN		
Geo W	Meig	214
Mary J	Cham	043
GUISBERT		
Emma D	Sene	311
GUISEBERT		
Dar	Fult	105
GUITON		
William	Madi	204
GUITTE		
Andross	Musk	265
GULDSBAH		
Hugh	Lawr	182
GULLY		
William	Mont	246
GUMP		
Jacob	Miam	219
GUNDER		
Joseph S	Port	283
GUNDY		
Ann	Harr	148
Christop	Wood	363
Isaac	Fair	089
GUNKLACH		
Henr	Hami	125
GUNN		
Cath F	Cuya	074
James D	Luca	198
Julian H	Henr	151
GUNNING		
James A	Faye	094
GUNSAUL		
Cath	Medi	210

GURLEY		
Chas A	Luca	198
GURST		
Geo W	Sand	303
GURTH		
George	Mont	242
GUSEMAN		
Am M	Fair	090
GUSS		
Chas	Otta	270
GUTH		
Leonard	Erie	088
GUTHRIDGE		
Jonathan L	Jeff	170
GUTHRIE		
Amy	Butl	038
Andrew J	Harr	149
Elizabeth	Harr	150
Hugh	Hard	145
James V	Hami	124
Mary C	Belm	029
Nathaniel C	Harr	149
Thomas F	Adam	005
GUTHRY		
John W	Brow	033
GUTKNECHT		
John	Star	317
GUTMAN		
Bertha	Hami	121
GUTSHALL		
Gideon	Harr	150
GUTTER		
Henry	Musk	266
GUY		
Ann	Cler	050
Caroline	Hami	121
Henry	Colu	056
John S	Gall	109
GUYER		
Charles	Mont	251
GUYETT		
Fannie	Luca	197
GUYTON		
Sophia	Clar	047
GWEEN		
Van M	Carr	040
GWINN		
Zale	VanW	337
GWYER		
Emanuel	Henr	153
GWYNN		
Thomas M	Adam	003

GWYNUS		
Samuel	Maho	207
HAAF		
Maria	Hami	131
HAAG		
Mary	Star	318
Samuel C	Henr	153
HAAS		
Christina	Sene	313
Daniel	Tusc	332
John	Craw	063
John	Luca	200
John H	Tusc	332
HABEL		
Chas	Hami	139
HABERMAN		
John	Mari	209
HABLIG		
Tobias	Cuya	070
HACKETT		
Edward	Lora	196
Eliza J	Hami	139
John	Warr	344
Thaddeus W	Huro	165
HACKLEY		
Ann E	Nobl	269
Robert	Ross	298
Samuel	Guer	120
HACKNEY		
Geo W	Musk	262
Mary E	Guer	120
HACKSTRADT		
Geo H	Hami	140
HACKWITZ		
Ernst	Mont	239
HACKWORTH		
Jarret C	Scio	305
William	Scio	307
William P	Lawr	181
HADDIX		
John	Gree	114
HADDOCK		
Jasper	Belm	031
HADLEY		
Jonas M	Luca	196
William	Clin	052
HADLOCK		
Betsey W	Medi	210
John S	Asht	017
Joseph	Asht	016

HAER			**HAGNER**		
Henry	Hami	129	Anthony P	Hami	129
HAFER			**HAGUE**		
Daniel	Rich	295	Sarah	Hard	147
Levi	Rich	296	**HAHN**		
Thomas M	Brow	033	Chas	Defi	080
HAFERTEPHEN			Christian	Paul	274
Geo H	Butl	037	Eliza	Belm	031
HAFFORD			Eliza	Butl	036
James H	Sand	303	Frederick	Sene	312
Sarah	Sand	303	Jacob G	Loga	190
HAFLER			John	Wyan	365
Joseph	Hock	158	John W	Dela	084
HAGAMAN			Mary S	Maho	206
John C	Will	355	Rosina	Hami	124
HAGAN			Samuel	Maho	204
Ellen	Hami	131	Sarah	Maho	206
HAGELBARGER			William M	Rich	294
Henry	Cosh	061	**HAIFLY**		
HAGELE			Aaron	Colu	058
Leonard	Luca	200	**HAINES**		
HAGEMANN			Archibald S	Scio	305
Chas	Mont	247	Cath	Cler	051
HAGEMEYER			Elias	Geau	112
August	Mont	235	Elizabeth T	Mont	230
HAGEN			Henry	Lick	188
Paul	Defi	081	Margaret C	Fair	091
HAGER			Rebecca	Monr	225
Aurelius	Madi	203	Robert H	Hanc	143
Geo	Alle	008	Samuel	Miam	220
Geo	Ashl	013	Samuel	Otta	270
Levi E	Hard	147	Samuel	Will	355
HAGERMAN			Sarah E	Cler	051
Flora V	Wash	345	Thomas	Adam	004
Hiram P	Rich	291	**HAIR**		
Joseph	Augl	025	Joseph L	Mont	233
Mary	Cuya	068	William O	Knox	173
Nicholas	Mont	235	**HAISCH**		
Robert	Mont	230	Christopher	Shel	315
HAGERTY			**HAITSON**		
Jeremiah	Mont	235	Ebenezer	Asht	019
John	Adam	008	**HAKE**		
Saloma	Adam	008	Emos	Trum	329
HAGGARD			Samuel	Trum	329
Thomas	Hard	146	**HAKEAS**		
HAGGENDORN			Jacob	Luca	200
Barbara	Perr	278	**HAKES**		
HAGGERTY			Chas	Paul	274
Blair	Will	356	**HALBAUER**		
John	Mont	241	Jacob	Hami	129
William A	Mont	241	**HALE**		
HAGGOTT			Allen	Sene	310
Mary A B	Butl	037	Elinizer	Lora	193

HALE (cont)		
James T	Gree	114
Rachel E	Guer	120
Ruth	Sene	310
Thomas	Wash	350
HALEM		
Martin	Dark	078
HALES		
Mary	Jeff	170
HALEY		
Bridget	Butl	035
Cath	Hami	121
Cath	Hami	131
James	Hanc	141
James	Henr	152
Jno	Mont	253
HALFHILL		
Lewis	Cler	049
HALL		
Abel	Monr	224
Alfred	Ashl	012
Alice C	Hami	124
Andrew J	Butl	037
Arabell M	Belm	029
Caroline	Lora	193
Cath M	Wyan	365
Chas	Fran	095
Chas F	Mont	229
Chas N	Adam	006
Cybelia H	Port	284
Edward M	Knox	173
Eleazer F	Dark	077
Eli	Luca	198
Elijah	Medi	210
Elisha	Musk	266
Elizabeth	Jeff	170
Elizabeth J	Monr	224
Elvira	Asht	017
Geo	Defi	080
Geo W	Sene	311
Geo W	Wyan	366
Harvey W	Miam	219
James	VanW	336
James C	Monr	224
James J	Lawr	179
James L	Wayn	352
James N	Mont	255
John	Colu	056
John	Cuya	075
(alias John Mullaly)		
John M	Knox	175
John R	Wood	359
John W	Monr	223

HALL (cont)		
Joseph N	Port	284
Josiah C	Hami	123
Josiah W	Wash	349
Julia A	Huro	162
Margaret	Meig	212
Maria	Lawr	179
Martha J	Guer	119
Mary	Fult	106
Mary	Trum	328
Mary A	Harr	150
Mary A	Warr	343
Monroe	Lake	176
Moses	Gree	114
Nancy	Loga	190
Nancy A	Mont	231
Oliver B	Trum	326
Orlando F	Luca	202
Orrin M	Asht	014
Richard A	Hard	143
Riley	Trum	326
Sarah	Trum	326
Sereno E	Asht	018
Thomas R	Lawr	181
Warner	Ross	298
William	Hami	136
William	Perr	277
HALLEMAN		
Malinda D	Cler	048
HALLER		
Chas F	Hami	129
Eliza	Warr	342
William W	High	156
HALLETT		
Howard	Wash	348
HALLEY		
Hugh P	Gall	108
Nancy	Gall	110
William B	Gall	110
HALLIWILL		
John	VanW	339
HALLMAN		
Elizabeth	Meig	215
HALLOWELL		
David	Alle	008
HALM		
William	Fran	098
HALSEY		
Rachel	Dark	077
William F	Luca	201
HALSTED		
John	Trum	328

HALTENNAN		
Samuel	Cham	040
HALTER		
Geo	Meig	216
HALTERMAN		
Eli	Pike	280
HALTERY		
Daniel	Augl	025
HALY		
Joseph J	Henr	153
HAM		
Chas H	Clar	047
David	Asht	014
Ellen	Pick	279
HAMAN		
William	Ashl	013
HAMDEN		
Phyn	Geau	112
HAMEL		
Elizabeth A	Hami	138
HAMERSLEY		
Mary M	Cosh	060
HAMILL		
Leah C	Gree	116
HAMILTON		
Albert G	Wash	348
Bridget	Clin	055
Edward	Carr	040
Eliza	Wayn	353
Elizabeth	VanW	337
Esther	Lick	184
George W	Athe	023
George W	Cham	041
Horatio C	Unio	335
Israel L	Monr	226
Jane	Clin	053
John	Lawr	181
John	Wood	363
John A	Fran	097
John A	Wash	349
Joseph	Mont	235
Joseph B	Nobl	268
Lewis	Paul	274
Mariah	Unio	334
Mary	Hock	158
Mary E	Dela	084
Milton J	Meig	214
Miranda	Otta	270
Peter	Butl	037
Samuel E	Faye	093
Samuel T	Hami	138
Samuel Y	Brow	032
Thomas	Lawr	181

HAMILTON (cont)		
Thomas J	Ashl	012
Wilson	Wood	362
HAMLIN		
Avis	Lora	193
Jacob	Lawr	179
John O	Brow	035
Mary	Star	317
William B	Cuya	064
HAMMAN		
Conrad	Ashl	012
Elizabeth	Maho	207
HAMMAPPEL		
Anthony	Mont	252
HAMMEGER		
William	Wash	346
HAMMEL		
James B	Star	317
Joseph	Hami	129
HAMMELL		
Susanna	Henr	151
HAMMER		
Elisha	Clin	054
George	Mont	234
Lawrence	Hami	129
Michael	Hami	129
HAMMERSLEY		
Henry	Cuya	069
HAMMITT		
Sarah E	Musk	263
HAMMON		
Geo	Hami	129
Jacob	Jack	168
James	Ross	301
Regina	Rich	291
Richard H	Miam	220
HAMMOND		
Albert	Musk	264
Edwin H	Luca	198
Elizabeth C	Asht	018
George F	Hanc	140
Hannah	Wood	358
Harriet E	Guer	118
Henry L	Otta	270
John L	Wash	345
Johnston	Guer	118
Joseph	Mont	228
Martin H	Asht	018
Mary	Tusc	332
Robert	Guer	118
HAMMONDS		
James	Ross	298

HAMPE			HANGER		
Mary	Hami	124	Mary Ann	Preb	287
HAMPHHIRE			HANIFY		
Lucinda	Lick	184	John J	Maho	207
HAMPTON			HANING		
Mary	Wood	363	Elizabeth	Athe	024
Randolph	Loga	189	Eunice R	Athe	020
Taylor W	Gall	109	Lesley	Meig	213
Thomas	Mont	233	HANK		
HANAN			John	Pike	282
John	Jeff	172	Peter M	Clar	044
HANCE			HANKIESON		
Harrison	Will	355	Peter M	Perr	276
Vinson S	Alle	010	HANKS		
HANCHETT			Harriet	Alle	010
Chas H	Henr	153	HANLAN		
HANCY			E Tappan	Belm	026
John	Cuya	069	HANLEY		
HAND			Maria	Hard	144
Hiram H	Mont	245	HANLIN		
HANDLEY			Edward	Mont	245
Michael	Asht	014	HANLON		
HANDLIN			Elizabeth	Jeff	170
David	Mont	245	John	Mont	241
Ephraim L	Lawr	180	Margaret	Wash	345
Henry O	Wash	347	William	Mont	242
HANDSHAW			HANNA		
James J	Hami	129	Eliza	Merc	217
HANDY			Elmira C	Cler	048
Chas F	Fult	106	James	Mont	233
Chas L	Mont	245	James	Wash	346
Eliza	Hami	121	Kezia	Defi	079
Henry	Medi	211	Lucinda	Maho	206
John	Harr	149	Matilda N	Cuya	068
Samuel	Hami	136	Rebecca	Butl	039
HANE			HANNAFORD		
Fernando B	Star	318	Mary J	Cler	049
HANER			HANNAH		
Mary A	Wyan	365	Elijah P	Cham	041
HANES			Harriet R	Gall	110
Elias	Wayn	351	Sheriff P	Vint	340
Norman S	Luca	198	William D	Guei	120
Parmelia E	Will	355	HANNAKA		
HANEY			Charles	Mont	252
Bridget	Gree	116	HANNARD		
Emily	Lawr	182	John W	Merc	217
Jacob	Cler	048	HANNER		
Samuel A	Warr	343	Frederick	Mont	247
HANFORD			HANNGS		
Gains	Luca	202	Benard	Mont	233
HANG			HANNI		
Michael	Mont	241	Rosanna	Maho	206

HANNUM			HARBOUR			
James G	Musk	266	Effa	Cham	042	
HANPRICK			Elizabeth	Gall	110	
William	Mont	239	HARBRECHT			
HANS			Henry	Hami	129	
Gerhart	Ashl	013	HARBROWN			
Margaret	Wood	361	John	Ashl	012	
HANSARD			HARBURN			
Margaret	Cuya	068	Margaret	Luca	199	
HANSELMAN			HARDEBECK			
Jno W G	Mont	254	Harmon	Hami	123	
Peter J	Colu	057	HARDEN			
HANSER			Henry O	Fair	092	
Cath	Otta	271	Pennington	Belm	026	
HANSHER			HARDENBROOK			
John	Vint	341	Aseneth	Cosh	062	
HANSON			HARDESTY			
Jas F	Wash	347	Ezra	Ross	296	
Kate	Madi	202	Isabel	Belm	027	
Mary A	Alle	009	Jane	Guer	118	
Peter	Morg	257	Lucas	Shel	315	
Sarah P	Sand	303	Martha	Summ	321	
Wilder L	Mont	234	Sylvester W	Morg	257	
HANSTEIN			HARDIN			
Peter	Fair	092	Henry	Mont	242	
HANUM			Job	Knox	174	
Mary	Nobl	269	Mary E	Alle	010	
HANVER			HARDING			
Martin	Fran	104	Amos F	Morr	260	
HAPP			Franklin S	Brow	031	
Marcus	Mont	237	Henry S	Musk	266	
HAPWOOD			Mary M	Carr	040	
Henry	Wood	362	Sarah	Brow	032	
HARAN			Vincent	Hami	129	
Adam	Monr	225	HARDMAN			
HARBAUGH			Lyman	Tusc	333	
Asa	Fair	090	Nelson	Clar	046	
David C	Cler	048	Patrick	Mont	254	
Margaret	Paul	273	HARDWICK			
Thomas	Colu	057	Elizabeth	Fair	092	
HARBER			Hugh H	Fair	091	
Aaron	Maho	207	HARDY			
HARBERT			Isaac	Cuya	065	
Elizabeth	Ross	300	James	Trum	326	
HARBESON			Samuel	Lawr	181	
Samuel	Mari	208	Sarah J	Lake	178	
HARBIN			HARE			
Barbary A	Nobl	269	Eliza	Belm	030	
HARBOCKER			Henry	Luca	200	
Hiland H	Lick	184	Mary A	Brow	032	
HARBOR			Shelden P	Clar	046	
Augustus	Pick	279	HARGESHIMER			
			Mary	Fair	091	

HARGO			HARMON (cont)		
Caroline	Lawr	180	Mary A	Tusc	330
HARGRAVE			William	Butl	038
Jeremiah	Madi	203	HARMONY		
William	Clin	055	Mary C	Hami	121
HARK			HARN		
Cath	Mont	230	Mary A	Wayn	354
Cinderella	Miam	220	HARNESS		
HARKER			Geo B	Wyan	365
Amos H	Will	356	HARNLEY		
Sarah	Ashl	013	David	VanW	338
HARKINS			HARNLY		
Dennis	Mont	245	Milla	VanW	339
Mary A	Morg	256	HAROVER		
HARLAN			Francis M	Adam	005
Isaac H	Clin	054	HARPER		
Jesse J	Hami	129	Barbara	Ross	300
Thomas J	Musk	264	Chas L	Will	357
HARLE			Grace	Wash	348
Mary Ann	Hami	131	Isaac N	Nobl	270
HARLEMAN			James L	Fran	096
Sophia	Preb	288	Joanna	Meig	212
HARLETT			Mary J	Unio	335
William	Guer	117	Miron	Meig	212
HARLEY			Samuel A	Gree	114
John D	Sene	311	Thomas	Mont	236
HARLISON			William J	Athe	021
Sarah	Hard	145	HARPOLD		
HARLOFF			Riley	Meig	215
Geo W	Merc	216	HARPS		
HARLOW			Mahlon S	Fair	090
Augustus	Pick	279	HARR		
HARMAN			Thomas	Belm	027
Benj C	Wood	363	HARRIGAN		
Cyrus P	Port	283	Jeremiah	Mont	237
Erastus W	Pick	279	HARRIMAN		
Michael	Luca	201	Geo	Unio	333
Shepard C	Henr	153	Joshua	Loga	190
Wesley	Fair	091	Sarah	Unio	336
William	Sene	309	HARRINGTON		
HARMANN			Benj P	Luca	198
Aerni	Putn	290	Chas W	Mont	229
Henry	Monr	224	Eliza J	Hami	121
HARMER			Elizabeth	Summ	321
Erastus W	Pick	279	Geo W	Mont	247
HARMON			Henrietta	Huro	163
Cynthia	Asht	014	Henry J	Fult	107
Geo W	Ross	296	Irving M	Cuya	064
Jehu	Mont	227	Jane	Wayn	354
John	Mari	209	Mary M	Summ	323
John	Unio	334	Nathan J	Loga	189
Joseph	Dark	077	Norman R	Mont	245
Levi	Tusc	330	William	Geau	112

HARRIOTT			HARRISON (cont)		
Julia	Hard	144	Cynthia M	Faye	093
Mary E	Fult	106	Deborah	Defi	081
HARRIS			Eliza	Brow	034
Alice	Belm	028	Enoch	Holm	161
Andrew L	Preb	286	Frances M	Cuya	074
Arthur	VanW	337	Jefferson	Summ	324
Cath	Clar	045	John	Clin	053
Cath	Guer	119	John	Hami	129
Christian	Will	355	John C	Miam	218
David	Mont	236	John W	Vint	341
David A	Nobl	268	Jonathan C	Jeff	170
Elisha	Holm	161	Marilda	Otta	271
Eliza	Summ	323	Martha	Lick	185
Elizabeth	Cler	047	Peter	Belm	029
Elizabeth	Hami	124	Richard B	Lick	185
Elizabeth	Mont	230	William H	Asht	015
Esaw	Morg	257	William H	Tusc	330
Ezra C	Gree	114	William S	Clin	054
Florence	Paul	273	HARRISS		
Francis M	Morr	261	John	Mari	208
Garland A	Brow	032	HARROD		
George	Unio	334	Cath	Merc	218
Henry	Alle	009	John H	Fran	096
Hiram	Hanc	141	HARROP		
Isabel	Asht	016	Rufus H	Musk	262
James R	Lick	184	HARROUN		
Jane H	Morr	260	Alex D	Cuya	065
John	Nobl	268	Franklin	Dela	084
John J	Clin	052	HARRY		
John W	Pike	282	Abraham B	Star	319
Julius A	Huro	163	Mary	Gree	114
Marion	Clin	052	HARSHA		
Mary	Lick	186	Jas	Hami	139
Mary	Miam	218	HARSHMAN		
Mary	Wash	347	Mary	Preb	287
Mary A	Summ	322	HART		
Milo	Lake	177	Adeline	Mont	230
Roselen	Mari	208	Clinton O	Trum	329
Sampson	Nobl	268	Edward P	Cuya	069
Samuel A	Wash	349	Elijah	Ross	296
Sarah	Mont	230	Francis M	Sene	314
Susan	Sand	302	Frank	Mont	247
Susan	Vint	340	Franklin	Mont	235
Thomas B	Paul	272	Henry C	Alle	010
Thomas M	Jack	166	Homer H	Will	355
Thomas P	Belm	031	James	Meig	212
Thornton	Athe	021	James W	High	157
William	Gree	115	John	Putn	288
William	Hard	144	Jonathan	Dark	078
HARRISON			Lewis	Wash	350
Albert J	Harr	149	Lorenda R	Port	283
Andrew W	Otta	270	Margaret	Fran	103

138

HART (cont)			HARTMAN (cont)		
Margaret	Holm	161	Nancy P	Jeff	169
Maria	Rich	295	Rebecca	Mont	256
Mary A	Summ	324	Robert	Luca	200
Mary A	Will	356	HARTNELT		
Romaine B	Medi	211	Daniel	Henr	153
Rosannah	Trum	329	HARTNETT		
Samuel	Wash	350	James	Mont	237
Samuel	Wyan	364	HARTPENCE		
Sarah E	Trum	326	John W	Hami	139
Susan	Ross	301	William R	Hami	139
HARTER			HARTRAM		
Barton S	Miam	221	Enoch	Lick	188
Daniel H	Wayn	353	HARTRUM		
Elem	Dark	078	Ira	Dela	082
Elias	Lake	176	HARTSHORN		
Jacob	Summ	324	Louisa	Pike	282
James H	Morg	257	Maria L	Pike	283
John H	Craw	064	Thomas	Tusc	331
Margaret	Dark	078	HARTSOCK		
HARTIGAN			Sarah A	Sene	310
David	Hami	129	HARTUPEE		
Patrick	Fran	097	Elnathan C	Rich	292
HARTLE			HARTWELL		
Sarah E	Dark	079	Oliver C	Hard	147
HARTLERODE			Thomas A	Lora	195
Hency C	Port	286	HARTWICK		
HARTLEY			Michael	Erie	086
Eli	Scio	308	HARTWIG		
James	Athe	023	John	Lawr	182
Jno W	Mont	234	HARTZ		
Malissa J	Guer	119	Thomas	Mont	231
Samuel	Madi	203	HARTZELL		
William	Meig	215	Howard F	Otta	270
HARTLIEB			Jackson W	Star	317
Margaret	Hami	124	Margaret	Port	283
HARTLINE			Rachel	Port	283
Samuel	Monr	223	HARTZOG		
HARTLY			Benj	VanW	339
David	Musk	266	HARVEY		
Jesse	Musk	262	Albert	Alle	009
HARTMAN			Bermclia	Cuya	069
Anna M	Cuya	074	Chloe Z	Preb	287
Cath	Fair	089	Geo E	Hami	129
Daniel	Colu	055	Gideon	Jack	167
Gaylord	Fair	089	Hamilton	Mont	256
George	Mont	245	John	Musk	266
Hetty	Dela	083	Nancy	Craw	062
Jacob	Maho	205	Nancy J	Adam	006
Jacob	Ross	298	Nathan	Warr	342
John	Hami	129	Obadiah H	VanW	336
Lewis	Wood	358	Patrick	Mont	241
Mary A	Holm	160	Sophia	Brow	032

HARVY			HATCH (cont)		
Louisa	Harr	150	Nathan S	Athe	022
HARWOOD			Violet	Gree	114
Avery	Trum	326	HATCHER		
HARZ			Abel T	Loga	191
Frederick	Cuya	069	David	Wood	361
HASE			Ramathy	Hami	124
Geo	Craw	064	HATFIELD		
HASEBROOK			Arthur A	Madi	203
Albert	Shel	315	Eli	Fran	098
HASEL			Eliza	Brow	032
George	Wood	360	Gibson C	Fult	106
HASELTON			Margaret J	Pike	281
William	Monr	224	Maria	VanW	339
HASFIELD			Samuel M	Pike	281
Charles	Mont	252	William	Mont	227
HASKELL			HATHAWAY		
Joseph T	Lora	194	Allison J	Trum	329
Phineas B	Hami	129	Elias	Unio	334
HASKIN			Lodema	Cuya	075
Adie G	Wash	349	Nancy J	Wood	360
Martha	Cuya	076	HATTAN		
HASKINS			Isaac W	Musk	266
John	Pick	279	Maria C	Cuya	074
Liberty W	Luca	202	HATTER		
Margaret M	Hanc	142	William M	Defi	082
HASLOP			HATTERY		
Eliza A	Lick	187	Sarah	Alle	010
HASPSTER			HATTON		
Jesse	Wood	359	Abraham	Hock	157
HASS			HAUCK		
Elizabeth	Rich	291	John	Mont	228
HASSEL			HAUGHAWOUT		
Maria A	Hami	124	Barbara	Port	283
HASSENNIER			Mary	Port	285
John C	Augl	026	HAUGHT		
HASSLEMAN			Melinda A	Port	284
Christian	Scio	305	HAUGHTON		
HASSON			Nathaniel	Luca	200
Mariah	Fair	091	Solon	Luca	200
Marvin F	Knox	173	HAUK		
HASTINGS			Monroe	Star	318
Charlotte	Lora	194	HAUPT		
Eliza	Asht	015	Cath	Mont	232
John J	Port	284	Gustav	Lora	194
John R	Colu	055	HAURNER		
Thomas F	Brow	032	Adam	Lora	195
HATCH			HAUSCH		
George	Meig	215	John	Geau	113
Harlan H	Trum	329	HAUSER		
Henry H	Dela	085	Katharine	Hami	124
Mary	Asht	015	HAVE		
Mary	Wood	361	Martin	Fran	095

140

HAVELY			**HAWKINS (cont)**		
Anthony D	Monr	225	Timothy B	Sene	308
Martha J	Monr	225	Ursula	Star	320
HAVEN			William D	Lawr	182
Frank	Butl	038	William H	Monr	223
Maria	Hanc	142	**HAWKINSON**		
HAVENS			Samuel	Lick	186
Alonzo P	Wyan	366	**HAWLEY**		
Andrew J	Pike	281	John S	Mont	243
Clayton	Mont	256	Louisa E	Port	283
Jesse M	Butl	037	Rachel C	Morr	260
Joel	Mont	248	Theodore F	Trum	326
Jno J	Dark	079	**HAWN**		
HAVERLAND			Martha A	Jeff	170
Lovina	Star	318	**HAWS**		
HAVEY			James M	Gree	113
Robert	Gree	114	**HAWTHORN**		
HAVILAND			Alex G	Belm	029
Ann	Belm	027	Geo P	Brow	032
Francis	Mont	235	William A	Brow	032
Sallie A	Clar	044	**HAY**		
HAWES			David B	Mont	229
Amos A	Hami	139	James	Cuya	069
HAWK			Martha E	Warr	342
George W	Vint	341	Samuel H	Colu	056
James	Wayn	353	**HAYCOCK**		
Lewis	Sand	303	Nathaniel	Dela	082
Mary	Athe	022	**HAYDEN**		
Mary	Vint	341	Clara A	Trum	325
Sarah	Faye	093	Elizabeth	Putn	291
Theo	Lora	196	Garret	Perr	275
William	Cosh	059	James	Rich	293
HAWKE			Mary	Fran	101
Anna C	Morg	258	**HAYDON**		
HAWKEN			Oliver	Sand	302
Elizabeth	Hock	158	**HAYES**		
HAWKINS			Abram	Alle	008
Benj F	Port	284	Cath A	Gree	115
Charles H	Star	317	Edwin F	Fult	107
Charles S	Asht	018	Festus C	Tusc	333
Edward	Mont	237	James	Port	283
Elizabeth	Dela	083	Jamos	Wood	362
Eunice E	Trum	329	John	Hami	129
Fanny	Luca	197	John C	Dark	077
Harriet	Fair	091	Jos E	Hami	137
Hosair	Wyan	364	Robert	Mont	241
Isaac N	Ross	298	**HAYMAKER**		
Isabella J	Dela	083	Elizabeth R	Defi	079
John B	Mont	249	**HAYMAN**		
Orrin W	Asht	015	Eliza M	Lawr	180
Reuben	Meig	216	Nancy	Meig	214
Rezin	Cler	050	**HAYNER**		
Samuel B	Star	319	Spencer	Gall	108

HAYNES		
Calvin	Athe	023
Ebenezer	Adam	004
James B	Lick	187
Mary J	Unio	335
Mary R	Fran	097
Orelius	Henr	153
William B	Loga	192
William D	Summ	321
William M	Mont	253
HAYNIE		
Sarah	Clin	053
HAYR		
Kate	Faye	094
HAYS		
Anco	Harr	149
Corkins	Athe	021
Eliza	Merc	217
George P	Trum	326
Geo W	Morg	258
James	Cuya	069
Jno	Wash	350
John C	Faye	093
John W	Belm	026
Joseph	Summ	322
Margaret	Cuya	074
Margaret	Sene	310
Mary A	Tusc	333
Priscilla	Wash	350
Sarah	Pick	280
Wesley H	Pick	280
William	Lawr	180
William	Lawr	180
HAYSE		
Henry	Erie	088
HAYSLIP		
Jane	Adam	006
John	Scio	305
Margaret	Adam	005
HAYSLIT		
James R	Warr	344
HAYWARD		
Betsey	Asht	017
Chas	Asht	015
HAYWOOD		
Edward	Wyan	367
Solomon	Gall	108
HAZEE		
Paul F	Mont	235
HAZEL		
Barnet	Port	284
Frederick	Wash	348
Isabella A	Clar	045

HAZEL (cont)		
John K	Lora	194
Mary	Cham	041
Rebecca	Port	284
HAZELBAKER		
Andrew J	Adam	003
HAZELMEYER		
Barbara	Luca	199
HAZELTINE		
John G	Lake	176
HAZELTON		
Henry	Perr	275
James	Putn	291
HAZEN		
Augustus	Miam	221
Chas D	Wash	348
Jacob	Sene	310
John A	Cuya	074
Maria	Geau	112
HAZENBACK		
Stephen	Cham	043
HAZENBOELER		
Waldburga	Augl	026
HAZLE		
Will	Summ	321
HAZLETON		
Lewis	Wyan	367
HAZLETT		
Ellen	Musk	265
HAZLITT		
Elizabeth	Gall	108
HAZZARD		
Angeline	Will	356
HEAD		
Geo W	Clin	054
HEADINGTON		
Cath A	Knox	174
HEADLEY		
Cath	Athe	024
HEALY		
John E	Wyan	364
Joseph	Summ	324
HEAM		
John	Mont	236
HEARING		
Jacob	Fran	096
HEARLEY		
Thos	Otta	270
HEARN		
Barbara	Harr	148
HEASLEY		
Cath	Unio	334
James C	Unio	334

HEASTON			HEDRICK			
Samuel C	Mont	242	Susan	Rich	294	
HEATER			HEEKMAN			
Henry	Hard	145	Elizabeth	Mont	230	
HEATH			HEENEY			
Benj F	Mont	230	Peter	Hami	123	
Edward E	Sene	312	HEES			
Eliza	Cham	041	John	Henr	152	
Israel R	Belm	027	HEFFELFINGER			
Jacob	Wood	362	James	Craw	063	
Jeremiah	Faye	095	James	Hard	143	
Mary E	Asht	015	Wallace	Ashl	012	
HEATON			HEFFERMAN			
Francis M	Jeff	169	John C	Mont	228	
Jacob	Colu	058	HEFFLEBOWER			
Toliver P	Gree	116	Wm H	Hanc	141	
Townsend	Brow	031	HEFFLEY			
HEAVERLOE			Prudence	Madi	204	
Hannah	Dela	084	HEFFNER			
HEBENTHAL			Joseph	Augl	024	
Lewis	Hard	145	HEFFRON			
HEBER			Patrick	Dela	084	
Uriah	Wyan	365	HEFLEY			
HEBERLING			Eliza	Clin	053	
Leir	Henr	151	HEFT			
HEBNER			Elizabeth	Fair	090	
Andrew	Mont	229	HEGE			
HECK			Jacob H	Cuya	075	
Jacob	Tusc	331	HEHMING			
John H	Dela	084	Heinrich	Mont	247	
HECKART			HEIBLER			
John	Craw	063	Sophia	Luca	200	
HECKATHORN			HEID			
Ann	Colu	056	George	Lawr	181	
Francis M	Mari	209	HEIDEBRINK			
HECKLER			Henry	Hami	129	
Barbara	Hami	121	HEIDELSHEIMER			
Barbara A	Tusc	332	H W	Nobl	268	
Charles F	Fran	096	HEIGES			
John	Will	356	Mary	Geau	112	
John J	Fran	096	HEIL			
Nancy K	Tusc	332	Magnus	Nobl	268	
HECKMAN			HEILBRUM			
Carolina	Cuya	074	Philip	Fran	097	
Geo	Wyan	365	HEILBURN			
Peter	Hami	129	Alexander	Hami	129	
HECOCK			HEILMAN			
Eunice	Lora	193	Geo E	Sene	311	
HEDGES			HEIMBURGER			
Elijah B	Dela	082	Diebold	Erie	086	
Jabez	Pick	280	HEIMKAMP			
HEDINGTON			Maria	Hami	131	
Mary	Luca	199				

HEIMS			**HELLMUND**		
Charles	Cuya	069	Erns't T G	Clar	047
HEINE			**HELLRIGLE**		
Johanna	Hami	124	Ann M	Mont	232
HEINISCH			**HELLWIG**		
Gustav A G	Augl	026	Gottlieb	Hami	130
HEINLEIN			William H	Mont	244
Ellen	Nobl	267	**HELLYER**		
HEINLEN			Handby	Athe	023
Abram	Dela	084	**HELM**		
HEINMELSPECH			Dorotha	Mont	232
Louis	Luca	200	Keziah	Brow	031
HEINMILLER			Noah	Wood	358
Henry	Fran	098	**HELMAN**		
HEINZ			Roena P	Athe	023
John	Fran	097	**HELMERING**		
HEIRY			Charlotte	Cler	050
Thos	Pick	278	**HELMICK**		
HEIS			Fredericka	Erie	087
Margaret	Cuya	074	**HELMKEE**		
HEISER			Jacob	Wayn	353
Edmund J	Ashl	012	**HELMS**		
HEISSERMAN			Aaron	Hard	144
Henry	Sene	314	**HELPBRINGER**		
HEISTAND			William H	Belm	030
Elizabeth	Hanc	142	**HELPMAN**		
HEIT			David	Miam	221
Eliza J	Lawr	180	Perry E	Defi	080
HEITZ			**HELTERBRAND**		
August	Hami	129	Christena	High	157
HELBERG			**HELTZEL**		
Christian H	Henr	152	Daniel	Summ	322
HELBERT			**HELWIG**		
Jacob	Ashl	013	Carrie G	Butl	037
HELD			Casper	Trum	327
Frederick	Scio	305	**HEMAN**		
Jno	Mont	253	Henry	Allc	009
Mary	Hami	124	**HEMDON**		
Pauline	Hami	130	Robert J	Loga	190
Philip, Jr	Hard	146	**HEMEBRIGHT**		
HELFENBEIN			Geo W	Shel	316
John	Pike	282	**HEMENWAY**		
HELFENSTEIN			Mary E	Lake	176
George W	Scio	307	**HEMINGER**		
HELFFELFINGER			Elizabeth A	Unio	334
Samuel	Morr	260	John A	Wood	361
HELFRICH			**HEMINGWAY**		
Nicholas	Clar	046	Geo R	Sene	312
HELLER			Mary	Medi	211
Eliza	Wayn	352	**HEMIS**		
Henry T	Wood	359	Peter	Mont	254
Philip	Hard	145	**HEMLEY**		
HELLMAN			James	Hami	123
Elizabeth	Adam	006			

HEMMEGER		
Alfred	Wash	348
HEMMERLING		
John	Cuya	069
HEMMINGER		
Lewis	Sene	312
HEMMINGS		
John H	Carr	039
HEMPEL		
Nicholas	Hami	121
HEMPEY		
Cath	Fair	092
HEMPHILL		
Rebecca	Faye	093
HEMPLEMAN		
Hannah	Clar	044
HEMPSTED		
Newton	Lawr	181
HEMRICK		
John	Wood	360
HEMRY		
Chas	Summ	323
HEMSTREET		
Edward	Hami	129
HENBERGER		
Haver	Hami	138
HENDEE		
Ambrose L	Clin	053
HENDERNOCK		
Florenz	Hami	129
HENDERSHOT		
Martin V	Cuya	075
HENDERSHOTT		
Martha	Alle	010
Nancy	Loga	191
William H	Loga	191
HENDERSON		
Archibald	Hami	129
Arthur	Asht	015
Chas	Perr	276
David	Wyan	366
George	Morg	256
George G	Henr	152
Henry	Adam	005
Hiram	Henr	152
Hiram E	Hanc	141
Jacob	Adam	005
James	Musk	262
John	High	154
Joseph	Cosh	061
Margaret B	Star	318
Martha	Mari	208
Mary F	Wash	345

HENDERSON (cont)		
Matthew T	Lick	186
Oliver T	Fran	098
Richard	Mont	251
Samuel	Holm	160
Samuel	Mont	239
Sarah	Fran	098
Stewart E	Mont	253
Westley	Carr	040
William	Monr	227
William	Morg	256
William	Nobl	269
William H	Cuya	065
Wilson	Harr	149
HENDGES		
Emma	Lora	192
HENDLEY		
John B	Hami	129
HENDRICKS		
Nathan H	Colu	056
HENDRICKSON		
John W	Fran	096
HENEKE		
Chas	Hami	129
HENERY		
Samuel J	Wash	345
HENIGER		
Margaret	Wash	347
HENKE		
Sophia	Hami	124
HENKLE		
George W	Clar	044
Isaac N	Hard	148
Jos	Merc	218
HENLY		
James C	Fair	090
HENMAN		
Almira J	Cham	042
HENN		
Philip	Mont	240
HENNACY		
William	Colu	057
HENNE		
Cornelius	Maho	207
William	Alle	010
HENNESEY		
Patrick	Mont	245
HENNESS		
John M	Ross	299
HENNESSY		
Cath	Hami	121
HENNESY		
Edward	Cham	043

HENNING			HERBEL		
William	Wash	350	John	Erie	087
HENNINGER			HERBERT		
Jonathan	Butl	037	Edward	Star	320
HENRICHS			Henry H	Adam	005
William	Cuya	069	HERDMAN		
HENRY			Ann	Adam	004
Cyrus	Clin	054	Jemima	Adam	004
Cyrus C	Maho	206	HERFEL		
Deborah	Musk	265	Nicholas	Butl	038
Edward E	Mari	209	HERHANMER		
Eliza	Asht	017	Mary	Hami	124
Emeline	Trum	327	HERINGSHAW		
George	Hami	129	Geo H	Cuya	069
George W	Dela	084	HERLD		
Jane	Maho	205	Sarah	Athe	023
Jesse	Colu	056	HERLING		
John D	Trum	328	Zezelia	Cuya	068
Jno S	Perr	277	HERMAN		
Josiah	Colu	057	Amos T	Summ	322
Lawrence	Huro	162	Cath	Hard	146
Levi	Putn	291	Edward	Mont	243
Lydia C	Preb	288	Englebert	Mont	232
Margaret	Butl	035	Gotlieb	Hock	159
Mark S	Lawr	181	John	Ashl	013
Mathew	Harr	150	John F	Fran	102
Nathan	Clin	054	Samuel	Wyan	364
Rachel	Port	283	HERMANN		
Stephen H	Mari	208	Adam	Mont	242
William	Athe	021	Ferdinand	Ross	301
William	Mont	240	HERNLEY		
Wittenmeyer	Hanc	143	Gustavus	Putn	289
HENRYHAN			HEROLD		
Stephen	Mont	244	David	Mont	238
HENSEL			HERPEG		
Margaret	Fran	101	Thomas	Fran	097
HENSHAW			HERR		
Charlotte L	Summ	324	Geo M	Mont	256
HENSON			Maria	Cuya	065
Chas W	Pike	283	HERREL		
Jemima	Cuya	074	Geo W	Dark	077
John	Pick	280	Sarah E	Hami	124
HENSTCH			HERRELL		
Louis	Mont	251	Richard	Dela	084
HENTHORN			HERREN		
James W	Lawr	181	Cath	Asht	017
John C	Monr	226	HERRICK		
Magaret	Monr	226	Albinah	Belm	028
Mary	Monr	223	Burgess	Lake	178
HEPBURN			Charles R	Fran	099
Dixon M	Belm	031	Edgar	Lora	193
HEPHNER			Walter F	Lora	196
Eliza	Colu	057			

HERRIG			HESS (cont)		
Mathias	Sene	314	Thomas K	Knox	173
HERRING			Vincent	Hami	129
Charles	Mont	252	William	Will	355
Charles	Rich	293	HESSE		
Lydia	Hard	147	Alex	Fran	099
William	Augl	025	Christian	Jeff	171
HERRINGTON			HESSER		
Deloss E	Lora	193	John	Wyan	365
William	Dela	084	Madison W	Star	317
HERRIOTT			HESSLER		
William	Craw	063	Nancy	Scio	308
HERROD			HESSON		
David	Morr	259	John	Mont	256
HERROLD			John	Nobl	268
John	Vint	342	HESTER		
HERSH			Cath	Colu	056
Henry L	Mont	227	HESTON		
Zephania E	Mont	229	John	Guer	118
HERSHEY			Joseph S	Alle	009
Isaac	Hanc	141	HETENHOUSER		
Oliver P	Sand	303	Frederick	Pick	278
HERSHMANN			HETHERINGTON		
Ann	Hami	121	Mary E	Rich	292
HERSHNER			HETHERMAN		
Adam	Craw	063	Michael	Cuya	069
HERVEY			HETRICK		
Robert	Mont	243	Barbara	Colu	055
William	Rich	292	HETSIG		
HERZOG			Rudolph	Luca	200
Felix	Sene	314	HETTINGER		
HESELDEN			Barbara	Pick	280
Jacob	Rich	293	Christina	Lake	176
HESKETT			Susannah	Rich	292
Elmira V	Knox	174	HETZEL		
HESLINGTON			Elizabeth	Guer	117
Thomas C	Sene	313	HETZER		
HESLIP			Matilda	Meig	215
Joseph	Cosh	060	HETZLER		
HESS			Geo	Miam	219
Cath	High	156	Jos N	Merc	217
Christina	Carr	039	Margaret A	Miam	219
David	Harr	150	HEUTER		
Elizabeth M	High	157	John	Huro	162
Geo W	Wyan	365	HEVIN		
Harriet	Otta	272	Robert	Loga	189
Henry C	Henr	151	HEWEY		
Jno	Meig	216	George	Trum	330
Margaret	Hami	124	Thomas H	Trum	330
Mary	Monr	223	HEWINS		
Rebecca	Hanc	140	Elisha M	Mont	252
Samuel N	Wood	358	HEWIT		
Susan	Harr	150	Ervin	Otta	272

HEWITT			HICKS (cont)		
Deborah	Summ	324	Nancy	Nobl	267
Frederick K	Hami	129	Nancy V	Cler	051
George F	Summ	324	Robert	Meig	214
Oscar	Luca	201	Thomas D	Lawr	181
William J	Mont	234	William A	Brow	033
HEYARD			HICKSENHYTZER		
Susanna	Star	319	John J	Miam	219
HEYDORN			HIEN		
William	Cuya	070	Cath	Rich	293
HEYLIN			HIESTAND		
Eliza A	Cham	042	Daniel	Unio	336
HEYMANN			Michael	Fair	089
Mathias	Mont	241	HIETT		
HEYSER			William V	Alle	010
Elias	Rich	291	HIFFRON		
HIALLY			James	Mont	249
James	Mont	248	HIGBEE		
HIATT			Elbert R	Cuya	065
Elihu	Clin	054	Lavina	Brow	033
Elizabeth	Miam	218	Melissa V	Cuya	069
Thomas S	Loga	190	HIGBY		
HIBBS			Chas D	Ross	299
Electa M	High	155	HIGGINS		
HIBLER			Andrew F	Brow	033
Jacob	Cuya	069	Asa	Clin	053
HICKARD			Chas	Hami	129
Daniel	Merc	217	Delilah	Jeff	172
HICKEY			Elizabeth	Gree	115
Charlotte	Musk	262	Fannie M	Mont	231
Patrick	Maho	207	Henry W	Jack	168
Patrick	Mont	254	John	Mont	237
William	Lick	189	Martha	Carr	039
HICKLE			Mary A	Loga	190
Hannah	Fair	091	Rebecca C	Belm	028
Isaac N	Nobl	269	Sarah A	Butl	038
Stephen	Guer	119	Thomas M	Mont	244
HICKLER			William	Defi	080
William	Wood	361	HIGH		
HICKMAN			Lucy E	VanW	336
Eleanor	Colu	056	William H	Wyan	365
James	Fair	092	HIGHFIELD		
John T	Augl	026	Margaret	Belm	027
Phebe	Colu	059	HIGHLAND		
Thomas N	Morr	261	Hugh	Mont	255
HICKOX			Mary Ann	Star	319
William D	Trum	326	Milton	Carr	040
HICKS			Patrick 2nd	Ross	298
Jackson	Gree	115	Patrick	Wash	349
Jas W	Meig	213	Sarah E	Faye	094
Jonathan	Dark	078	HIGHMAN		
Lewis E	Lick	185	Duncan	Monr	224
Lucinda	Belm	029			

HIGHT		
John R	Luca	197
HIGHTON		
Richard	Hami	137
HIGHTOWER		
James P	Fran	096
HIGHWARDEN		
Abram	Dela	084
HIGLEY		
Chauncey	Dela	082
Hezekiah	Sand	302
Lewis	Asht	019
Margaret	Lake	177
Mary	Meig	214
HILBORN		
John	Craw	064
HILDEBRAND		
Henry	Ashl	012
Henry	Faye	095
Henry	Mari	209
Katharine	Mont	232
William W	Wash	348
HILDEBRANDT		
John W	Warr	344
HILDEBRANT		
David	Clin	053
HILDENBRAND		
David	Jack	167
HILDERMAN		
Cath	Mont	232
HILDRETH		
Algery	Cuya	069
Benoni P	Unio	334
Caroline	Knox	174
Franklin	Clin	054
HILER		
Daniel D	Fran	098
HILES		
Jackson	Fair	090
Jackson	Perr	276
Jas	Perr	275
Margaret	Merc	217
Thomas	Fran	097
HILFORD		
Jas M	Mari	210
HILGAMAN		
Fred	Augl	025
HILL		
Andrew J	Wood	362
Barbara	Hami	131
Calvin H	VanW	339
Charlotte E	Butl	036
Clarison	Geau	111

HILL (cont)		
Daniel Y	Wash	348
Daniel Y	Wash	349
David	Erie	086
David	Henr	151
David	Wood	360
Eber B	Mont	232
Elizabeth	Fair	091
Elizabeth	Gall	108
Elizabeth	Hanc	143
Francis	Pick	279
George	Geau	112
Hannah J	Wash	347
Henry M	Wash	348
Isaac	Luca	197
Isaac	Wash	351
Isaac H	Adam	005
Isaac N	Trum	326
Jacob	Hami	129
Jacob A	Hanc	141
James	Ross	298
James A	Cler	049
James W	Cler	048
Jane L	Fair	090
Jefferson H	Hami	140
Joseph	Trum	329
Joseph F	Henr	151
Joseph H	Mont	239
Joseph J	Warr	343
Joshua	Medi	212
Josiah L	Miam	219
Levi G	Perr	277
Lorenzo D	Nobl	269
Margaret J	Vint	341
Margh	Knox	176
Maria A	Lake	177
Maria C	Lawr	180
Mary A	Hami	131
Morris	Wood	359
Patrick	Mont	249
Peter	Unio	333
Peter	Wash	346
Prescott	Wash	347
Rebecca	Cham	043
Rebecca L	Clin	052
Reuben	Lora	194
Robert A	Mont	255
Samuel	Cham	043
Sarah	Faye	093
Sarah	Jack	166
Sarah J	Hanc	142
Susan	Wood	361
Syndester	Jack	167

HILL (cont)			**HINDMAN**			
Thomas C	Huro	164	John M	Wayn	354	
Thomas E	Lake	176	Sarah	Vint	340	
Valentine	Mont	234	**HINDS**			
William	Butl	039	Adam	Wood	363	
William	Lick	186	John	Wash	350	
William	Wash	349	**HINE**			
William	Wood	362	Augustus F	Butl	037	
William A	Vint	341	Eliza	Wyan	364	
William F	Mari	208	Mary S	Lake	177	
William H	Hami	140	Peter C	Fair	092	
William L	Defi	080	**HINEBAUGH**			
William W	Wood	364	Show	Hard	144	
HILLARD			**HINES**			
Mary A	Musk	267	Amos G	High	156	
HILLARY			Angevine	Mont	229	
Eleanor	Perr	275	Christian A	Harr	149	
HILLBRUNNER			Elizabeth J	Mont	227	
Andrew	Lora	192	George W	Harr	149	
HILLEN			Isaac	Asht	014	
Isabella	Hami	124	James H	Mont	230	
HILLERY			Jonathan	Meig	212	
Eleanor	Lick	188	Jonathan A	Adam	005	
HILLES			Priscilla	Hanc	142	
Samuel	Belm	030	Thomas	Sand	302	
Sarah C	Belm	027	**HINKLE**			
HILLHOUSE			Geo	Perr	276	
Lucy	Ross	296	Hannah	Scio	305	
HILLIS			Richard	Fult	106	
William D	Craw	063	**HINKLEY**			
HILLMAN			Addison S	Huro	164	
Ann E	Hami	131	**HINSDALE**			
William P	Musk	263	William E	Cuya	070	
HILLYER			**HINSHILLWOOD**			
Henry	Harr	149	Agnes	Colu	058	
Maria	Huro	163	**HINSHILWOOD**			
HILMAN			Thomas J	Star	317	
Louisa	Otta	271	**HINSON**			
HILT			Cath	Ross	301	
Daniel C	Cham	043	Henry	Pick	278	
HILTABIDDLE			**HINTCHLIFFE**			
Daniel W	Trum	326	Geo T	Colu	057	
HILTON			**HINTON**			
Sarah	Harr	149	George	Fair	088	
HILYARD			Thomas	Mont	235	
Mary	Fair	089	**HIO**			
HIME			Nicholas	Hami	129	
Jacob E	Luca	200	**HIPP**			
John F	Mont	232	Charles	Augl	025	
Lewis	Fran	103	**HIPPEARD**			
Mary	Henr	151	John	Merc	217	
HIMES			**HIPPENHEIMER**			
Margaret	Adam	005	Cornelius	Mont	247	

HIPSHER			HITESMAN		
Henry	VanW	338	John A	Warr	342
HIPSHIRE			HITTLE		
James	VanW	338	Adalia	Musk	262
HIRDY			HITZ		
Jacob	Gall	110	Joseph L	Cuya	069
HIRE			HITZING		
Mary	Erie	086	Fredericka	Hami	124
Thomas W	VanW	337	HIVELY		
HIRN			Jno	Mont	253
Elizabeth A	Pike	283	Margaret	Maho	206
HIRONS			HIXENBURGH		
Samuel	Mont	230	Henry B	Monr	226
HIRSCHFIELD			HIXON		
Edward	Trum	327	Martha	Carr	040
HIRST			HIXSON		
Samuel	Tusc	332	Elijah	Ross	298
Thomas C	Gree	117	Henry G	Wood	358
HISER			Isaac	Clin	052
Eliza	Fran	098	Timothy	High	154
Jacob	Henr	152	HIZER		
HISEY			Ellen	Fran	104
Henry C	Loga	192	HOAG		
HISINGER			Eliza C	Cuya	068
Philip	Clar	044	Ezra N	Wayn	351
HISSOM			HOAGLAND		
James	Monr	226	Joseph	Fran	095
HISSONG			Nelly	Knox	174
Levi	Rich	291	Solomon	Knox	174
HITCHCOCK			HOAR		
Ardelia	Meig	212	Thomas P	Knox	175
James	Putn	290	HOBART		
Keziah	Hard	143	Thomas	Summ	323
Luther C	Fult	105	HOBBLE		
Mary	Pick	279	Edward	Lawr	181
Mary	Wyan	366	HOBBS		
Moses K	Alle	008	Alonzo M	Harr	150
Rachel	Putn	289	Elisha	Gall	108
HITCHENS			HOBERT		
Chas	Morg	258	Chas	Erie	088
Eliza	Hami	121	Lucinda	Unio	336
HITE			HOBLET		
Henry H	Fair	092	William	Mont	228
James J	Alle	009	HOBSON		
Martin K	Wood	364	Elizabeth	Cler	049
Samuel	Lick	186	Samuel N	Athe	024
HITES			HOCK		
David	Craw	064	Cath	Jack	166
Margaret	Hard	148	Ignaz	Hami	129
William	Loga	189	Jess	Will	355
HITESHAW			HOCKINS		
Alfred	Sene	310	John	Mont	253

HOCKMAN			HOFF (cont)		
Delitha	Brow	033	Jonathan D	Meig	214
Harman	Luca	202	Martha	Unio	334
HODDER			Otto	Hami	129
Ellen	Mont	232	HOFFERD		
HODDY			Wilson S	Defi	080
Elizabeth	Ross	299	HOFFLAND		
HODGE			Margaret	Cuya	068
Alexander H	Hard	144	HOFFMAN		
Daniel	Fair	091	Adaline C	Hami	138
James M	Gall	108	Chas	Butl	037
John H	Sene	314	Eliza	Ross	297
John O	Cuya	069	Franklin	Asht	016
William B	Meig	214	Geo	Cuya	069
HODGES			Geo S	Mont	228
Elizabeth	Cler	048	Geo W	Trum	328
James	Scio	307	James H	Gall	108
James B	Dela	084	Johann	Mont	247
Sylvanus	Rich	296	John	Cuya	065
HODGMAN			John F	Butl	037
Francis E	Asht	017	Lazarus	Fran	096
HODGSON			Margaret	Cuya	068
Geo B	Hami	129	Peter	Cuya	069
Thomas	Fair	088	Robert H	Preb	288
HODSON			Susannah	Lick	187
Eli	Clin	054	Thomas B	Harr	148
Laura	Cuya	074	Timothy	Mont	236
Phebe	Clin	053	Valentine	Mont	242
HOEFER			William	Pick	278
Geo	Hami	130	HOFFMIRE		
HOEFNAGEL			John	Fult	104
Frederick	Craw	063	HOFFNER		
HOEGER			Thomas	Hami	139
Gustav	Cosh	059	HOFFRICHTER		
HOEING			Henry	Loga	192
Magdalena	Fult	104	HOFSTETTER		
HOEL			John	Hami	129
Wesley	Butl	037	HOGAN		
HOERR			John	Mont	253
Louis	Luca	200	John	Scio	307
HOESE			John D	Fran	096
Caroline	Hami	121	Joseph P	Hami	129
HOEWERLER			Michael	Mont	237
Geo	Hami	129	Patrick	Cuya	075
HOEWISCHER			HOGARTH		
William	Augl	025	Thomas	VanW	337
HOFER			HOGE		
Margaret	Musk	267	Solomon L	Hard	147
HOFF			HOGLE		
Cath	Hami	121	Elizabeth	Trum	326
Clara	Cuya	068	HOGLIN		
Curtis	Wyan	365	Samuel	Augl	025
George	Mont	247			

HOGUE			HOLGATE		
Aurelia	Summ	324	Elizabeth	Rich	295
HOHNECKER			HOLL		
Jacob	Hami	129	John H	Musk	262
HOISINGTON			HOLLABACH		
Jas E	Mont	247	Mordecai	Rich	295
John G	Cham	043	HOLLABAUGH		
HOLBROOK			Eliza	Sene	311
Josiah	Warr	343	HOLLAND		
Oliver	Luca	200	Geo W	Unio	335
William A	Otta	271	Hannah	Cler	047
HOLCOMB			Joshua	Mont	237
Abijah	Asht	017	Julia A	Preb	288
Eliza M	Sand	301	Thomas B	Paul	274
Elizabeth	Faye	093	William N	Wash	348
George W	Lick	188	HOLLENBAUGH		
John M	Gall	108	Frank	Craw	063
Leroy S	Morg	258	Jacob	Rich	295
Norton B	Asht	016	HOLLENBECK		
Percival	Lora	194	Henry	Jack	168
Robert N	Trum	327	Lucius	Trum	330
Susan	Asht	019	Vincent W	Trum	325
Thomas J	Cuya	065	Wallace	Mont	247
Zara	Gall	111	William H	Wood	362
HOLDEMAN			HOLLENBERRY		
Felix	Dark	076	Hannah	Gree	114
HOLDEN			HOLLENSTULLER		
Abigail	Asht	014	Daniel	Mont	249
Chas H	Port	284	HOLLER		
Christena	Unio	335	Jacob	Mont	229
Elisha M	Wood	359	HOLLERITTER		
Holdridge C	VanW	337	Maria A	Vint	341
John	Mari	209	HOLLETT		
William	Mont	238	Dar	Fult	105
William B	Wyan	365	HOLLEY		
HOLDER			Harriet E	Henr	152
Jas	Carr	039	HOLLIDAY		
HOLDERBAUM			George H	Lawr	181
Henry	Wayn	352	James J	Lawr	183
John W	Holm	161	HOLLIGER		
HOLDERMAN			Frederick	Luca	200
Jacob W	Mont	244	HOLLINGER		
Samuel	Fair	090	Chas	Defi	081
HOLDMAN			Frederick A	Miam	220
Joseph	Dark	079	John J	Wayn	354
HOLDSWORTH			Samantha A	Lick	184
George	Cosh	059	HOLLINGSHEAD		
HOLE			Dan	Warr	343
John L	Mont	228	Lois	Wood	358
John S	Merc	217	HOLLINSHEAD		
HOLETON			Jeremiah	Defi	079
Benj	Asht	015	HOLLIS		
			Cath B	Scio	306

HOLLIS (cont)			HOLODAY		
Sarah	Fran	101	Samuel A	Clin	054
HOLLISTER			HOLSAPLE		
Edwin	Erie	086	Moses	Preb	287
Lydia	Cuya	075	HOLSCHER		
Samantha	Port	283	Henry	Butl	037
HOLLMAN			HOLSER		
William	Fult	106	Fredericka	Fran	098
HOLLMEYER			HOLSINGER		
Henry F	Butl	038	Elizabeth	Meig	213
HOLLODAY			Peter	Meig	006
Joel F	High	156	HOLSON		
HOLLOPETER			Temperance	Clin	054
Benj	Miam	219	HOLST		
Gideon W	Defi	081	Julius	Hami	136
HOLLOWAY			HOLT		
George	Unio	335	Cath	Adam	004
James W	Fran	102	Cath	Hanc	142
Jane	Musk	265	Elias	Scio	307
Jerome C	Ross	301	James	Gree	113
John S	Clin	054	Mary	Morr	260
Margaret A	Hami	124	Milton	Lora	194
Mary A	Fult	105	Nelson	Sene	309
Monroe	Fult	106	William	Holm	160
HOLLY			William S	Luca	197
Hezekiah	Putn	288	HOLTSBERY		
Ledyard B	Wood	362	William	Lick	185
Sarah Jane	Henr	152	HOLTSEY		
HOLM			Geo W	VanW	338
Jacob	Belm	029	HOLTZ		
HOLMES			Ernest	Scio	307
Calvin	Preb	286	HOLTZHOCKER		
Charles	Luca	201	Lewis	Summ	324
Daniel M	Hami	137	HOLWAN		
Geo	Warr	342	Henry	Jeff	171
Geo W	Fair	090	HOLYCROSS		
Gilmon T	Mont	240	John K	Madi	203
Jackson	Unio	333	HOLZER		
Jacob A	Hard	146	Ferdinand	Mont	230
John	Wood	360	HOMAN		
Jonathan	Wayn	353	Jonathan V	Clin	052
Letitia C	Henr	151	Solomon E	Fran	097
Margaret	Faye	093	Ucle	Merc	217
Martha E	Jeff	169	HOMER		
Mary A	Nobl	270	James	Jeff	172
Phineas	Mont	246	HOMMAN		
R	Pick	279	Jno	Perr	277
(alias R Biggs)			HOMMEL		
Sarah	Cosh	061	William	Merc	217
William H	Clin	054	HON		
HOLOBAUGH			Benj T	Adam	004
James	Pike	282	HONADDLE		
			Michael	Summ	322

HONAKER		
Emily J	Mari	209
HONE		
Mary A	Hock	157
HONEOUS		
Peter	Dark	079
HONEYWELL		
William H	Cuya	075
HONNOLDS		
Harm S	Vint	341
HONSEL		
James	Summ	324
HOOBLER		
Henry	Luca	202
HOOD		
Amy	Hock	157
Edward B	Harr	149
Edwin T	Fult	106
James Y	Lawr	182
Maria L	Knox	174
Thomas	Hock	157
HOOK		
Abraham	Ross	299
Alpheus	Lora	196
Angeline	Hanc	143
James	Adam	004
John	Morg	259
Seymour R	Hanc	143
William F	Brow	033
HOOKER		
Rebecca Jane	Cosh	061
William	Morg	258
HOOKINS		
Milton B	Asht	018
HOON		
Rosa	Hami	137
HOONER		
Henry E	Wood	359
HOOPER		
Cath	Hock	158
Frederick	Mont	245
(alias Fridolin Huber)		
George W	Mont	236
John B	Jeff	170
Joseph	Jeff	171
Rachel	Putn	288
Thomas G	Mont	234
William H H	Pike	281
HOOPS		
Phebe	Holm	160
HOORER		
Joseph	Sand	302

HOOSA		
Gratia	Asht	014
HOOT		
Noah	Henr	151
HOOTE		
Conrad J	Sene	314
HOOTMAN		
Susannah	Ashl	012
HOOVER		
Aaron	Lawr	182
Andrew	Paul	273
Ann M	Mont	232
Charles	Lick	186
Euphemia	Asht	016
Geo W	Craw	063
John	Mont	236
John A	Sene	310
John A	Star	318
Mary	Mont	232
Matthias	Augl	024
Samuel	Fran	098
Samuel	Star	317
Sarah F	Preb	287
Susan	Loga	190
Thomas L	Mont	245
William	Craw	063
William	Hard	144
HOPE		
John	Jack	167
HOPKINS		
Cath	Hami	121
Cath	Lora	194
Charles B	Cler	047
Charles W	Otta	271
Delilah	Huro	163
Eliza	Wayn	353
Elizabeth M	Sene	312
Eunice P	Hard	145
Geo	Huro	165
Howell G	Lawr	181
Jacob	Lawr	183
James	Huro	163
John B	Adam	007
Lucius	Will	356
Mary	Lick	188
Nancy	Mari	209
Sarah D	Huro	165
Sophia	Faye	094
Tarcillia	Warr	344
William G	Meig	213
HOPP		
Resetta	Cuya	074

HOPPE			HORPER			
Henrietta	Cuya	074	James	Fair	090
HOPPEL			HORR			
John	Butl	037	Vesalius	Cham	043
William T	Mont	242	HORSEY			
HOPPER			William	Mont	237
James J	Wood	360	HORSINGTON			
HOPPES			Henry H	Lora	195
Henry	Faye	093	HORTON			
HOPPING			Amos B	Medi	211
David R	Gree	114	David A	Pike	281
HORD			Edgar D	Unio	335
Mariam	Ross	300	Hosea W	Asht	015
HORDEN			Laura	Dela	083
Richard	Meig	214	Nancy	Lora	195
HORDMAN			Sally	Cuya	069
Peter N	Clar	046	HOSACK			
HORMER			Lavina	Guer	119
Ira B	Wood	363	Uriah W	Defi	081
HORN			HOSE			
Geleo	Musk	263	Frederick	Star	319
Geo W	Paul	273	HOSFELD			
James W	Defi	081	Andreas	Hami	129
Jonathan A	High	155	HOSFORD			
Mary	Hard	145	Robert H	Ross	299
Nancy	Loga	189	HOSIER			
Otto W	Fran	098	Annie	Faye	093
Thaddeus	Mont	241	William	Mont	234
Thomas A	Defi	081	HOSKINS			
HORNADAY			John H	Monr	225
Noah	Preb	288	Joseph	Monr	225
HORNBACH			Mary	Unio	335
William D	Clar	047	Morris E	Geau	111
HORNBECK			HOSLER			
Norton	Putn	289	Cath	Morr	261
HORNE			Rufus	Ross	298
Fred	Cuya	076	HOSMER			
HORNER			Benj F	Will	357
Calvin M	Medi	210	Lucy	Medi	211
Geo	Mont	232	Olive	Cuya	075
Geo W	Gree	116	HOSPEHAUN			
James W	High	154	Geo	Sene	314
Samuel	Mont	230	HOSS			
HORNEY			John	Clar	044
Deborah	Unio	334	HOSTLER			
James W	Madi	204	Benton	Sene	310
Mary	Gree	116	HOSTOTLER			
Oliver E	Faye	093	David	Meig	216
HORNING			HOTCHKISS			
Christopher	Jack	168	Jarvis M	Colu	056
HORNUNG			Martha A	Lake	178
Anna Maria	Hami	131	HOTT			
			Jackson	Pick	279

HOTT (cont)			HOUSER (cont)			
Jackson	Pick	279	William Fletcher			
(2 Jacksons on this page)				Pike	282	
Joe L	Rich	292	HOUSK			
HOTTES			Jno	Mont	253	
Cath	Augl	026	HOVER			
HOTTINGER			John	Wood	363	
Christopher	Cosh	059	Washington	Loga	190	
HOUCH			HOVERSTOCK			
Susan	VanW	339	Elizabeth	Star	319	
HOUCHINS			HOW			
Mary A	Gree	113	John P	Mont	246	
HOUCK			HOWALD			
Barbara	Musk	265	Otis W	Star	319	
Benj F	Defi	081	HOWALL			
John E	Will	356	Seth	Belm	029	
Melissa A	Augl	026	HOWARD			
Michael	Cuya	070	Almira	Warr	344	
Sol J	Clar	047	Andrew J	Meig	212	
HOUGH			Cyrus	Adam	004	
Amos	Wayn	353	Cyrus W	Adam	008	
Mary M	Rich	295	Derinda A	Morr	258	
HOUGHEY			Edward	Colu	057	
Alexander	Mont	249	Edward L	Maho	205	
HOUGHLAND			Elijah	Fair	092	
Byron	Cuya	074	Elmira A	Hami	121	
Marshall	Wayn	351	Frank D	Dela	084	
HOUGHTON			Henry	Mont	235	
Albert C	Luca	200	Joanna	Hanc	142	
Edith	Cuya	074	Leander	Hami	129	
Eliza	Medi	211	Mary Ellen	Brow	034	
HOUK			Nancy	Warr	344	
Jacob	Medi	210	Perry C	Loga	189	
HOUPT			Peter	Huro	163	
Joseph	Wyan	364	Samuel	Hanc	141	
HOUSE			Theo P	Wood	358	
Charles	Nobl	268	Thomas B	Brow	034	
Edwin L	Cler	050	William	Huro	165	
Henry	Star	320	HOWDYSHELL			
Lydia	Nobl	269	Samuel S	Hock	159	
HOUSEHOLDER			HOWE			
Cath	Clar	046	Albert L	Cuya	070	
Geo	Jeff	169	Eber D	Lake	177	
Robert	Wood	363	Henry	Brow	031	
William L	Jeff	169	Henry G	Scio	307	
HOUSEMAN			Mary B	Summ	321	
Frank	Fult	106	Mercy	Hard	145	
HOUSENER			Rufus	Cuya	070	
Elizabeth	Tusc	332	Salem T	Huro	165	
HOUSER			HOWELL			
Eliza	Merc	217	David M	Harr	150	
Jefferson	Star	318	Edmond	Meig	213	
Solomon	Ashl	012	Eliza J	Wash	346	

HOWELL (cont)		
Geo P	Craw	064
Geo W	Morr	260
John W	Belm	029
Joseph	Adam	005
Martha J	Meig	212
William E	Adam	005
William W	Vint	341

HOWER		
Jeremiah M Jr		
	Cuya	060
Moses L	Star	320

HOWIND		
Hermann	Hami	129

HOWLAND		
Horace M	Luca	196
Margaret	Brow	034
Matilda	Brow	032
Sarah	Brow	034

HOWLEY		
Andrew	Mont	247

HOWSER		
Gasaway	Harr	150
Henry W	Fran	102
Nancy A	Cler	050

HOWSON		
John	Athe	021

HOXTER		
Melvin C	Hami	136

HOY		
Cynthia	Morr	261
Tellitha	Hanc	142
William L	Fair	091

HOYER		
Jno	Mont	253

HOYT		
Chs	Huro	165
Francis A	Cuya	074
Luther E	Asht	017
Lydia L	Huro	162
William B	Scio	307

HOZOR-HUTZ		
Fidelia	Hami	121

HUBACHER		
Jno	Mont	253

HUBBARD		
Alvin	Augl	025
Caroline E	Fran	098
Edgar P	Asht	019
Eliza J	Lora	194
Gerusha	Port	283
John	Pick	280
Julia A	Asht	017

HUBBARD (cont)		
Louisa	Asht	016
Polly L	Asht	018
Robinson B	Paul	273
Sarah	Gree	114
Sarah L	Lora	194

HUBBELL		
Augustus	Lora	194
Daniel	Sene	309
Magdalena	Fran	101
Rebecca S	Huro	163

HUBBERT		
Cordelia	Asht	016

HUBBS		
Sarah J	Wyan	364

HUBER		
Adam	Hami	121
Fridolin	Mont	245
(alias Frederick Hopper)		
Gustav	Hami	136
Henry	Star	319

HUBERT		
Andrew F	Guer	118

HUBERTY		
Nicholas	Star	318

HUBORN		
Samuel	Wood	360

HUCHINS		
Adelia	Morg	257
Shubel	Morg	258

HUCHISON		
Zipporah	Faye	094

HUDDE		
Christian	Brow	032

HUDDLESON		
Andrew	Cham	041

HUDDLESTON		
John A	Hami	121
Mary L	Hami	139

HUDERER		
Michael	Hami	139

HUDGELL		
Henry	Warr	343

HUDLEY		
Joseph	Hami	129

HUDNALL		
John	Hami	129
William	Hami	130

HUDNELL		
Jos	Ross	300

HUDSON		
Amanda	Scio	308
Edmund	Port	285

HUDSON (cont)		
Electa F	Mont	230
Henry C	Port	283
Jason	Erie	086
Jesse T	Augl	025
John	Mont	243
Joseph	Hami	129
Joseph M	Adam	005
Loretta F	Cham	040
Magdalena	Maho	206
Mary Ann	Pike	282
Sarah F	Hard	148
HUENEMANN		
John B	Hami	136
HUETTEL		
August	Mont	231
HUEY		
Cath	Butl	036
Jas	Wash	346
HUFF		
Cath	Alle	010
Lysander G	Madi	203
Michael H	High	155
Sarah	Clin	053
Thomas	Jack	166
HUFFIN		
Moses	Unio	335
HUFFMAN		
Amos	Clin	054
Daniel W	Otta	271
Dorcas	Wash	351
Francis M	Ross	300
Geo W	VanW	338
Godfrey E	Morg	257
Henry	Cham	042
Henry	Fair	092
Henry J R	Augl	024
Hiley	Hock	159
Hiram	Hanc	140
Isaac	Mari	209
Isaac B	Shel	316
Jacob	Wood	359
Jacob M	Monr	225
James C	Musk	266
John Sr	Fran	103
John	Morr	261
John H	Clin	054
Jos	Cham	043
Levi W	Wayn	354
Maria	Rich	294
Michael	Sand	303
Peter	Cuya	076
Samuel	Morg	258

HUFFMAN (cont)		
Simon	Wyan	367
William	Lawr	180
William H	Mont	228
HUFFORD		
Daniel	Dark	079
Geo W	Wood	362
Nicodemus D	Hock	158
HUFFORDS		
John	Shel	315
HUFFSEY		
John	Sene	314
HUFFZKY		
Frederick W	Hami	121
HUFTILE		
Margaret A	Fult	106
HUGES		
William	Huro	163
HUGGERT		
James A	Unio	335
HUGHES		
Andre L	Paul	273
Anna	Rich	296
Calvin	Gall	110
David No 2	Mont	245
David	Shel	314
Edward	Hami	137
Edwin R	Hami	137
Eliza	Cuya	069
Eliza	VanW	337
Emily M	Butl	038
Emily N	Hami	135
Geo W	Mont	245
Hannah B	Paul	272
Henry	Clar	047
Henry J	Gall	107
Hetty	Rich	296
Howard M	Trum	329
James	Cuya	069
James	Mont	238
James M	Hami	129
John	Mont	242
John	Mont	245
John	Mont	253
John D	Cosh	060
John L	Mont	228
Joseph	Guer	117
Joseph A	Harr	150
Louisa	Rich	296
Lydia	Warr	344
Martha	Adam	007
Mary	Pike	281
Mary A E	Monr	226

HUGHES (cont)			HULL (cont)		
Melissa E	Lick	184	John B	Ashl	012
Michael	Cuya	069	John C	Rich	292
Morris R	Cuya	069	Lot D	Madi	204
Nancy	High	154	Louisa	Wash	349
Nancy	Nobl	270	Lucretia A	Athe	022
Nancy	Pike	282	Mary	Hami	138
Nancy	Pike	282	Mary Jane	Athe	022
Rachel	Rich	294	Nancy	Ross	297
Sanford C	Hami	129	Otha H	Henr	152
Sarah	Fair	091	Rachel	Butl	036
Silas	Lawr	183	Stephen F	Athe	022
Thomas G W	Huro	164	Van Ransler J		
Wesley	Adam	006		Cuya	070
William	Paul	273	William A	Ashl	012
HUGHEY			Zenus A	Hock	157
Andrew H	Guer	117	HULLINGER		
Eleanor	Ross	301	Edward	Alle	009
Jas A	Clin	054	HULLS		
Jas M	High	154	John A F	Fran	096
Samuel	Wyan	367	HULS		
William F	Ross	301	William H	Hock	159
HUGHS			HULTS		
Ellen	Ross	297	John F	Dela	084
Samuel H	Mont	232	HUMBERT		
HUGLER			Amos	Knox	174
John	Erie	088	Cath	Summ	324
HUHN			Reuben	Merc	217
Christian	Craw	063	HUMBLE		
Jos S	Ross	299	James	Adam	004
HULBERT			Martha	Guer	117
Lucina	Lora	194	HUME		
HULBMEIER			John	Port	285
Simon	Cuya	070	Phebe	Gree	115
HULBERT			HUMES		
Charles W	Hard	148	Alonzo	Fran	096
HULET			Tabetha R	Adam	007
Rachel	Henr	151	HUMISTON		
HULING			Clarissa	Summ	321
Nancy	Ross	296	HUMMEL		
HULIT			Albert	Cuya	069
Jane	Rich	294	Henry	Cosh	061
HULL			Henry	Dela	084
Abigail	Port	285	Isaac D	Holm	160
Anna	Rich	295	HUMMER		
Eliza	Knox	175	John F	Cosh	059
Elizabeth	Erie	087	HUMPHREY		
Esther	Loga	189	Anne M	Meig	215
George W	Mont	252	Clara	Lora	195
Hiram	Trum	329	Edgar	Athe	021
Horace A	Lake	177	Lucien E	Summ	324
Irving	Cuya	065	Malachi G	Cuya	069
John	Athe	023	Morris	Athe	021

HUMPHREY (cont)		
Nancy A	Lawr	182
Nathan	Belm	028
Seldon	Meig	215
HUMPHREYS		
Cath	Clar	046
Mary	Shel	315
Permelia	Loga	190
Thomas	Mont	238
HUMPHRIES		
Samuel	Mont	235
HUN		
Columbus C	Wood	362
HUNFNER		
Mary	Hami	124
HUNGERFORD		
Zadok	Wood	360
HUNSAKER		
John	Hock	158
HUNSICKER		
Andrew	Summ	322
HUNSINGER		
Margaret	Butl	038
HUNSUCKER		
Henry	Scio	305
HUNT		
Burwick P	Belm	026
Charles J	Henr	151
Ellen	Knox	175
Frank M	Sene	312
Gustavus	Miam	220
Henrietta	Cuya	074
James H	Wood	362
Jane	Warr	343
John D	Cham	041
John M	Cham	040
Jonathan A	Lawr	181
Martha	Cuya	066
Mary C	Hami	124
Nancy	Musk	263
Phauetus	Port	285
Philinda	Star	317
Stephen B	Warr	342
Valentine	Mont	234
William L	Hami	129
HUNTER		
Alex	Cuya	069
Geo B	Cham	043
Henry B	Fair	090
Isabella D	Fran	097
James	Fran	102
James	High	156
James B	Mont	233

HUNTER (cont)		
James M	Mont	241
Jane	Ashl	012
John	Knox	175
Julia A	Cham	042
Margaret	Fran	097
Neal	Mont	239
Newton P	Hami	137
Rebecca	Colu	059
Robert	Mont	235
Robert	Mont	244
Solomon	Fair	090
Thomas	Cosh	059
Thomas	Mont	234
William	Brow	034
HUNTINGTON		
Julian C	Asht	015
Sarah	Musk	267
HUNTLEY		
Calvin W	Trum	325
Mary	Alle	010
Rachel	Hard	145
Roxa A	Huro	164
HUNTOON		
Naomi	Lake	177
HUNTSBERGER		
Isaac D	Wayn	352
HUNTSBERRY		
Urias	Knox	175
HUPEE		
Frederick C	Mont	232
HUPP		
Daniel	Wayn	351
George W	Nobl	268
Zachariah	Wash	348
HURAT		
William F	Mari	208
HURD		
Anna L	Wyan	366
Martin G	Maho	207
Mary	Trum	327
Sarah	Trum	328
HURLBURT		
David E	Asht	017
HURLBUT		
George	Port	284
HURLEBANS		
Gottleib F	Cuya	069
HURLESS		
Hannah	Hock	159
Seny	Harr	150
HURLEY		
Daniel T	Augl	025

HURLEY (cont)		
Harriet	Morr	259
Mary J	Ross	300
HURSE		
Mary	Miam	222
HURSEY		
John	Tusc	331
HURSHMAN		
Mary	Scio	306
HURST		
John M	Loga	189
Martin W	Loga	189
HUSH		
Andrew	Hanc	141
HUSS		
Noah B	Otta	271
HUSSEY		
John	Gree	113
HUSSMAUL		
John	Musk	264
HUSTED		
William H	Jeff	172
HUSTON		
Cunningham	Hard	145
Galon S	Harr	151
John	Cosh	061
Mary E	Cuya	068
Thomas	Lick	186
HUTCHENS		
Lucy	Brow	032
HUTCHESON		
William C	Colu	058
HUTCHINS		
Joseph P	Miam	221
Thomas L	Loga	189
HUTCHINSON		
Amanda M	Belm	029
Cath	Will	357
David	Sene	312
Eliza	Cuya	074
Enoch	VanW	339
Geo M	Fran	102
Henry U	Wash	349
Henry W	Wash	347
John	Hard	144
Joseph M	Hard	145
Margaret	Gall	110
Mary E	Knox	175
Phebe I	Monr	223
Philson	Wood	360
Sally	Cuya	075
Thomas B	Warr	343
William	Will	357

HUTCHINSON (cont)		
William H	Fran	102
William J	Lake	178
HUTCHISON		
Allen C	Lawr	179
Jas A	Merc	217
Thomas	Hock	157
William H	Monr	224
HUTHER		
Nicholas	Huro	163
HUTHRUACKER		
Andrew	Erie	086
HUTSON		
John P	Unio	334
Minerva	Trum	328
Wesley	Gree	114
HUTTENBOCKER		
Michael	Otta	272
HUTTER		
John	Defi	080
HUTTON		
George W	Cler	051
HUTZELL		
Joseph	Lick	185
HUTZELMAN		
Michael	Rich	294
HYATT		
Alonzo H	Medi	210
Alonzo R	Will	357
Elmer	Mont	249
Mary	Fran	101
Rispah	Knox	174
Sarah	Knox	174
William B	Wayn	352
HYDE		
Hannah P	Hanc	142
Patrick	Mont	241
Rachal	Musk	262
Rhoda A	Wood	359
HYDORN		
Josephine	Cuya	073
HYER		
Mary	Ross	299
HYKE		
Emily	Luca	200
HYLAND		
Dennis	Mont	245
HYLER		
Jas	Wash	349
HYNDMAN		
Joseph A	Hami	129
HYNES		
Samuel	Belm	029

HYRE				IMMEL		
Jesse R	Dark	078		Geo	Wash	346
HYSELL				IMON		
Adaline	Meig	215		Felix P	Clin	053
Celestia	Meig	215		INDLEKOFER		
Mary C	Meig	212		Cunigundi	Sand	302
Nancy	Meig	216		INFIELD		
Perry	Meig	214		Phenas	Cosh	060
				INGALLS		
				Abram	Cham	042
				Ann Jane	Summ	323
IAMS				Joshua	Miam	219
Elizabeth M	Nobl	268		Mary	Cler	047
ICKES				INGERSOLL		
Henry	Cham	043		Mary L	Warr	342
IDAN				INGERSON		
Mahlow	Morr	260		John	Mari	209
IDD				Tirza A	Wyan	366
William	Monr	223		INGHAM		
IDDINGS				Smith W	Hami	138
Jefferson D	Miam	221		INGLE		
IGLEBARGER				Isaac W	Henr	152
Martin	Butl	037		William H	Henr	152
IGO				INGLISH		
Daniel	Morr	261		Rachel	Guer	117
John	Mont	242		INGRAHAM		
IHLER (or Euler)				Geo	Cuya	076
Joseph	Lora	193		Tim Jr	Cuya	070
IKE				INGRAM		
Jno M	Dark	079		Jas	Will	356
ILER				John	Mont	228
Anna	Hock	159		INMAN		
Isaac	Sene	314		Harkless K	Wyan	364
ILES				Hiram	Fult	107
George W	Hock	158		William	Rich	292
Mary A	Summ	321		INNES		
Origin M	Morr	260		Jane	Ashl	013
ILGER				INNIS		
Sarah	Ashl	011		Adam R	Fran	098
ILIFF				Isabella C	Fran	097
John F	Faye	094		INSKEEP		
ILLBROOK				Elizabeth	Loga	192
William	Hami	123		Rebecca	Guer	119
IMBODEN				INSLEY		
John	Wayn	351		Martin	Hanc	142
IMBRIE				IRELAND		
Isabella	Maho	205		Eliza	Hami	131
IMES				Elvina	Miam	223
Hiram G	Lawr	182		John	Erie	086
Solomon H	Lawr	182		Nicholas	Wood	361
IMICK				Robert	VanW	337
Jno	Mont	234		William E	Alle	008

IRELING			JACK			
Levi	Wayn	354	Deborah	Adam	003	
IRETON			Jane B	Trum	326	
John N	Hami	123	JACKAWAY			
IRISH			Jos M	Mont	234	
Chas	Lora	194	JACKMAN			
Jackson	Lora	192	Mary J	Henr	153	
IRVIN			JACKS			
Andrew J	Perr	276	Levi	Meig	213	
Jas	Mari	209	Lewis W	Lake	177	
IRVING			JACKSON			
Thomas	Wyan	366	Aaron	Monr	225	
William	Alle	008	Alfred H	Mont	247	
IRWIN			Alonzo	Mont	231	
Cath	Morr	261	Andrew	Athe	021	
Corydon S	Wash	348	Andrew	Hami	140	
Elias B	Alle	008	Anna	Wayn	353	
Geo W	Brow	033	Charles H	Sene	314	
Geo W	Hami	123	Chas L	Cham	041	
Isabella	Ross	300	Cyrus	Morg	257	
Isaiah	Fran	098	Dolly	Ross	297	
Joseph G	Warr	343	Eleanor	Adam	007	
Mary A	Adam	004	Eleanor	VanW	339	
Naomi	Hock	158	Eliphalet	Huro	165	
Russell B	Cler	049	Eliza	Hami	138	
Sarah	Warr	342	Elizabeth	Musk	267	
Valentine	Sene	311	Elwood	Lake	178	
IRY			Frances	Brow	034	
William	Port	284	Geo B	Warr	343	
ISDELL			Geo W	Mont	245	
Geo W	Mont	243	Harriet	Wash	348	
Louisiana	Hami	131	Isaac	Wood	361	
ISENNAGLE			James	Monr	224	
Jacob	Ross	299	James A	Butl	037	
ISERAL			John	Hami	123	
Milton K	Hami	136	John	Holm	160	
ISGRIGG			John W	Knox	174	
Daniel Jr	Hami	140	Joseph	Perr	277	
ISHAM			Joseph M	Trum	330	
Asa B	Hami	123	Joshua	Monr	227	
William R	Cuya	070	Josiah	Holm	161	
ISMALL			Leonard M	Sene	309	
Geo	Hami	123	Marissa	Clar	045	
ISRAEL			Minerva	Rich	292	
Jabez T	Cler	048	Phebe W	Shel	316	
Hannah G	Morg	258	Philip	Wash	347	
Peter	Lawr	182	Rebecca	Morg	257	
IZER			Samuel H	Cler	051	
Ezra	Clar	046	Sarah A	Cuya	069	
			Stiles	Wood	360	
			Susannah	Knox	173	
			Sylvadoe	Knox	175	
			Thomas	Craw	064	

JACKSON (cont)			JAMES (cont)		
Thomas P	Wash	348	Hester	Belm	028
Uriah S	Clin	053	Isaac	Hard	146
William	Mont	243	Jacob	Lawr	182
William E	Hami	123	John	Cuya	070
William H	Butl	037	John	Warr	344
William H	Sand	301	John A	Cuya	070
JACOB			John D	Lawr	182
Christie	Clin	052	John W	Faye	093
Cornelius	Cuya	075	John W	Wash	348
Mary	Cler	050	Manuel C	Mont	256
JACOBAR			Martha	Musk	263
Rudolph	Mont	234	Norval W	Athe	022
JACOBS			Sarah A	Monr	223
Bart	Cler	049	Susan J	Belm	029
Chas	Wash	348	Susannah	Musk	265
Eugene	Hami	123	Taluma	Wood	363
Eva	Hami	140	Wesley	Carr	040
Francis O	Lick	186	William	Mont	228
Harriet	Cosh	059	William J	Hami	123
Henry	VanW	337	William M	High	155
Isaac	Augl	025	William M	Madi	203
Jacob	Mont	234	JAMESON		
John L	Loga	191	Christina	Preb	287
Margaret	Miam	220	Melville	Huro	165
Mary A	Cuya	068	Rush	Alle	008
Nathaniel P	Loga	192	JAMIESON		
Rachel	Maho	206	John	Cler	047
Samuel	Shel	315	JAMISON		
Susannah	Augl	026	Sarah E	VanW	337
William M	Loga	192	William A	Ashl	012
JACOBSON			JANCH		
Isaac	Mont	234	Jacob	Mont	254
JACOBY			JANNEY		
Ann C	Wyan	365	Rebecca A	Clin	055
Henry F	Mont	236	JANUARY		
James	Mari	208	Samuel	High	155
JAEGER			JAQUES		
Adolph	Hami	123	Henry	Will	356
JAHLA			JAQUETH		
John	Mont	244	Lydia	Wyan	366
JAMES			JARBAUGH		
Alexander	Pike	283	William H	Wood	361
Allen M	Hami	123	JARRA		
Arthur	Cler	048	Thomas	Trum	327
Cath	Lora	193	JARRELL		
Charles C	Gall	109	Geo F	Adam	006
Charles C	Jack	167	JARRETT		
Charles E	Ross	300	Jane	Belm	029
David	Lick	186	William	Erie	086
Donohue	Meig	212	JARVIS		
Elias H	Athe	023	Albert	Sand	302
Ephraim	Henr	152	Caroline K	Dela	084

JARVIS (cont)		
Geo B	Athe	020
Geo W	Lora	195
John	High	156
Robert	Jeff	172
Sarah	Wayn	353
JAY		
Chas C	Erie	088
Morris	Mont	254
JAYERMAN		
Andreas	Hami	123
JAYNES		
Elizabeth	Jack	168
JEFFCOATE		
Jno	Mont	254
JEFFERIES		
Geo C	Lora	193
JEFFERIS		
Pious	Belm	027
JEFFERS		
Abraham	Gall	108
Christopher	Wood	363
George W	Hard	148
JEFFERSON		
David E	Luca	198
Job	Preb	287
John A	Erie	086
JEFFERY		
Sarah A	Guer	120
William H	Luca	202
JEFFORDS		
Almira	Asht	019
JEFFREY		
Samuel W	Craw	064
JEFFRIES		
Anne	Monr	225
Harriet	Wayn	352
John	Merc	217
Linneus Q	Wayn	354
Sarah J	Belm	031
JEFFRIESS		
John	Mont	238
JELLIFFE		
Benj Jr	Hami	123
JENKINS		
Alex	Cham	041
Asa	Clin	055
Charles S	Gall	109
Cyrus H	Jeff	169
David R	Putn	290
Edward	Hami	123
Elizabeth	Erie	085
George C	Faye	094

JENKINS (cont)		
Henry	VanW	336
John	Trum	328
Lewis	Cuya	075
Martha A	Morr	261
Mary L	Brow	033
Nimrod W	Hanc	143
Philip	Pick	278
Sarah	Cham	042
Thomas A	Faye	093
William	Cham	042
William J	Jack	167
JENKINSON		
Phebe	Meig	215
JENKS		
David	Clin	054
David	Mont	229
Isaac P	Clin	052
JENNETT		
Elizabeth	Dark	078
JENNINGS		
Ann C	Pick	280
Clarkson	Preb	286
David	Colu	056
Delila	Brow	033
Henry C	Port	283
James	Mont	243
Jane	Colu	055
John	Pike	283
Louisa	Huro	163
Nancy L	Butl	035
Rachel	Maho	206
Silas H	Sene	311
William	Athe	023
William H	Wood	361
William R	Mont	256
JENTS		
John	Luca	198
JENVEY		
Geo K	Wash	348
JEREMY		
Jemima	Lick	184
JEROLEMAN		
Peter	Meig	212
JEROME		
Alfred A	Cuya	075
Henry	Cuya	070
Joseph	Lake	177
JERREL		
Thomas	Maho	207
JERSEY		
Andrew	Cuya	074

JESSELYN			**JOHNSON** (cont)		
Mary	Musk	267	Belinda	Scio	305
JETT			Benj	Hock	157
Jno	Mont	254	Benj F	Port	283
Joseph	Ross	300	Bersheba	Ashl	014
JEWELL			Caroline	Guer	119
Enos	Musk	262	Cath	Fair	089
Eugene W	Athe	021	Cath	Hard	144
Henry C	Lake	178	Cath	Musk	262
Lintha	Erie	086	Cath	Nobl	270
JINKINS			Cath	Will	355
Thomas J	Meig	214	Cath M	Musk	263
JINKS			Charles	Cosh	060
Liberty	Ross	296	Clarissa	Asht	015
JOBE			Crandle	Summ	323
Jas	Wayn	353	Dan S	VanW	338
Mary A	Gree	114	Daniel	Faye	093
Sylvester	Adam	004	David	Hami	123
Thomas B	Gree	116	David C	Asht	019
JOBES			David C	Unio	334
Jno W	Mont	254	David H	Dark	077
William	Meig	213	Elijah	Faye	093
JOHANNE			Eliza	Asht	017
Speidel	Wash	351	Eliza	Butl	038
JOHN			Eliza	Lora	193
Jacob M	Dark	077	Eliza	Unio	333
James S	Cler	048	Elizabeth	Faye	093
Margaret A	Wayn	352	Elizabeth	Harr	150
Peter A	Erie	088	Elizabeth	Hock	159
Seth	Shel	315	Elizabeth	Hock	159
JOHNS			Elizabeth A	Hard	147
Ann	Lawr	180	Erville	Vint	341
Augustus	Fran	099	Fairaby	Loga	190
Dewitt C	Brow	034	Frances A	Dark	078
Elias H	Alle	010	Francis M	Ross	296
Eliza	Holm	160	Frederick	Hami	123
Geo H	Wyan	365	Frederick W	Craw	063
Henry D	Summ	323	Geo	Belm	026
Louisa	VanW	337	Geo	Lora	194
Robert W	Merc	218	Geo L	Adam	006
JOHNSON			Harriet	Summ	321
Adaline M	Lora	194	Harriet H	Otta	271
Alex	Cham	043	Henry	Putn	290
Alex A	Unio	336	Henry P	Nobl	268
Alvira	Lora	193	Hilas R	Gall	108
Andrew	Lora	193	Hiram	Wood	358
Andrew J	Miam	218	Homer B	Lora	195
Ann M	Athe	020	Horatio G	Cham	041
Ann M	Musk	264	Jacob T	Pick	280
Anna	Lick	186	James	Faye	093
Armstrong	Nobl	269	James	Hami	123
Asbury M	Mont	243	James	Mont	247
Austin T	VanW	338	James	Morg	259

JOHNSON (cont)		
James	Wood	360
James S	Mont	242
James W	Preb	287
Jane	Mont	256
Jarrett	High	156
Jno C W	Mont	254
John	Hard	144
John	Hard	145
John	Musk	262
John	Summ	321
John Jr	Lick	184
John M	Hami	123
John R	Gree	116
Johne	Cosh	061
Jonas	Jack	166
Jonathan M	Mont	229
Joseph H	Mont	249
Julia A	Defi	081
Levi M	High	155
Lewis C	Meig	216
Lewis P	Luca	197
Lucinda	Asht	019
Lucius	Fran	099
Lydia	Warr	342
Mahala	Fran	102
Marcia	Geau	113
Margaret	Hami	133
Margaret	Star	316
Mary	Cler	050
Mary	Erie	085
Mary	Perr	277
Mary	Wash	350
Mary A	Medi	210
Mary A	Ross	299
Mary B	Ashl	013
Mary C	Mont	230
Matthew	Mont	238
Milton	Hard	145
Monroe W	Maho	207
Moses	Paul	273
Nancy P	Jeff	171
Newton	Holm	160
Oliver B	Will	357
Philander	Guer	119
Philip	Sene	313
Rebecca	Will	356
Rhoda	Lora	194
Richard K	Cham	043
Robert	Asht	014
Robert	Mont	254
Robert	Putn	289
Robert L	Knox	175

JOHNSON (cont)		
Robet M	Loga	190
Samuel H	Cuya	070
Sarah A	Jack	167
Sarah K	Hami	130
Simeon	Morg	259
Simeon	Ross	300
Theodore	Preb	286
Thomas	Hock	159
Warren S	Wood	363
Weslay B	Paul	273
Willard C	Henr	152
William	Cler	048
William	Cuya	065
William	Miam	220
William	Trum	330
William	Unio	333
William	Wayn	354
William F	Pike	283
William H	Lake	177
William H	Lake	178
William H	Merc	217
William H	Wash	346
William M	High	156
William R	Faye	093
JOHNSTON		
Anthony	Dela	084
Charles	Luca	198
Cynthia	High	156
David	Cuya	076
David E	Trum	325
Deborah	Trum	328
Della	Loga	190
Dycy Ann	Hami	131
Edward P	Jeff	169
Eliza	Medi	211
Elizabeth	Hock	158
Elizabeth J	Wood	363
Ephraim	Hanc	141
Harlon F	Madi	204
James	Cuya	070
James	Gall	109
James	Mont	254
Jehiel	Geau	112
John	Cuya	070
John S	Guer	120
Joseph	Meig	212
Lewis	Monr	227
Margaret	Lawr	180
Moses B	Wash	345
Robert	Warr	342
Robert B	Cuya	070
Sally	Ross	300

JOHNSTON (cont)			JONES (cont)		
Sarah	Shel	316	Eliza	Musk	267
Stephen	Shel	315	Eliza A	Lick	185
Thomas E	Jeff	171	Eliza C	Cham	041
Wallace W	Athe	021	Elizabeth	Gall	110
Wesley	Colu	055	Elizabeth	Morr	260
William L	Colu	056	Elizabeth B	Hami	121
William T	Rich	293	Elmore	Hami	138
JOICE			Enas M	Henr	151
Parish	Lake	176	Enos	Lawr	179
JOINER			Eunice W	Summ	321
Vincent	Fran	099	Evan	Jeff	171
JOLLY			Garrett G	Loga	191
Edward	VanW	340	George	Athe	023
James J	Gall	109	George	Tusc	330
Jared	Wood	359	George C	Cuya	070
Sarah A	Wood	363	George E	Hami	123
JONAS			George E	Hami	136
Hester	Gree	114	George M	Adam	007
Jno	Perr	276	George W	Scio	306
Lydia	Perr	276	Hannah	Port	285
JONES			Harrison W	Mont	237
Absalom	Jeff	169	Henry	Mont	244
Albert	Trum	326	Henry P	Clin	055
Albert G	Cuya	070	Hezekiah	Sand	304
Alice E	Otta	271	Isaiah	Lawr	182
Allen	Trum	327	Isaiah	Mari	209
Amelia	Craw	063	Jabez	Will	355
Andrew J	Lawr	183	James	Perr	275
Ann M	Cler	047	James A	Huro	165
Anna	Fran	098	James B	Fran	099
Arthur A	Geau	113	James L	Mont	227
Azenath	Cuya	068	James W	Mont	239
Benj	Ross	298	Jane	VanW	340
Biddy	Miam	223	Jane S	Gall	111
Byron W	Cuya	066	Janes	Clar	044
Calvin	Wash	350	Jennie C	Asht	017
Cassius C	Wyan	366	John	Athe	024
Charles W	Gall	109	John	Brow	033
Charles W B	Brow	035	John	Gree	115
Clarissa	Maho	205	John	Hock	158
Daniel K	Ross	297	John	Lick	186
Daniel T	Gree	116	John A C	Sene	309
David	Star	320	John B	Alle	008
David A	Mont	254	John E	Mont	246
David J	Lick	187	John H	Fran	099
David M	Henr	152	John J	VanW	339
David W	Fran	099	John L	Butl	039
Dorcas	Asht	016	John N	Pick	280
Edward L	Luca	198	John O	Athe	020
Eleanor	Meig	216	John T	Medi	212
Eli	Ross	300	John W	Fair	088
Elias	Mont	238	John W	Hard	147

JONES (cont)			JONES (cont)		
John W	Hock	158	William B	Hami	138
Joseph H	Belm	028	William B	Jeff	171
Joseph W	Athe	024	William H	Hock	158
Joseph W	Nobl	268	William L	Fran	099
Joshua	Gree	115	William S	Summ	323
Josiah	Perr	275	Zenas B	Cham	043
Louisa M	Henr	152	JOPLIN		
Lucinda	Dark	077	John	Lawr	179
Lucy E	Faye	094	JORDAN		
Lurton D	Mont	229	Barbara A	Holm	161
Luther R	Scio	306	Cath	Knox	174
Margaret W	Jack	168	Corelia M	Fran	098
Martha	Cosh	060	Cornelia E	Morr	261
Martha	Fran	097	David	Adam	006
Mary	Port	285	Edward	Warr	343
Mary A	Warr	343	Elijah	Belm	029
Matilda	Maho	205	George	Unio	334
Micajoh J	Clin	055	Hezekiah	Mont	229
Morris D	Wood	359	John M	Hanc	140
Nancy	Hami	135	La Roy S	Miam	220
Nancy	Hami	137	Margaret J	Shel	315
Nancy	Nobl	269	Mary	Fran	097
Nancy	Wood	362	Michael A	Cham	043
Nathaniel	Butl	038	Peter	Mont	231
Orson H	Wood	359	Phebe	Knox	173
Palmyra	Asht	018	Philip W	Hard	147
Peter	Miam	220	Priscilla	Sene	312
Rachel	Ross	297	Selina	Perr	276
Rachel A	Lick	184	Susan	Fair	091
Ralph G	Summ	323	William	Hami	123
Rebecca	Belm	029	William D	Luca	198
Richard	Hard	146	JOSEPH		
Richard C	Alle	010	Charles	Hami	123
Rollins L	Asht	018	Jacob	Star	319
Samuel	Harr	150	John A	Jeff	172
Samuel	Lawr	182	Jno W	Butl	037
Samuel	Rich	295	Joshua C	VanW	337
Samuel W	Monr	225	JOSLIN		
Sarah	Hard	145	William	Loga	192
Thomas	Jeff	171	JOSS		
Thomas A	Lick	184	Lucy A	Tusc	331
Thomas M	Lick	184	JOSTATT		
Thomas S	Jack	168	Albert	Trum	328
Washington	Cham	040	JOURDAN		
William	Cosh	061	Daniel C	Craw	063
William	Cuya	070	Jno	Perr	278
William	Gall	108	Trougett	Mont	240
William	Mont	242	JOWITT		
William	Morg	256	Ann	Fran	097
William	Star	319	JOYCE		
William	Unio	335	Daniel B	Luca	198
William A	Wood	358	Eliza A	Holm	161

JOYCE (cont)			JUST			
James	Mont	247	Robert F	Luca	198
Mary L	Holm	161	JUSTICE			
JOYNER			Francis	Madi	203
Phebe	Cham	041	Purnell	Ross	299
JUBINVILLE			William	Lawr	182
John	Defi	080	JUSTUS			
JUDD			Caroline C	Hanc	142
Chas H	Lawr	182	Ellen	VanW	337
Elizabeth F	Cosh	060				
Isaac	Star	318				
Jesse L	Merc	217				
(alias Jas H Brush)			KADOW			
Stephen H	Fult	105	Louis	Hami	126
William H	Mont	254	KAENZIG			
JUDY			Christian	Monr	224
Jesse	Loga	189	KAESTNER			
JUKES			Eliza	Wyan	365
Jannett	Hami	139	KAFFEE			
JULI			Lawrence	Wayn	354
Antonia	Fran	098	KAGA			
JULIAN			Abraham	Mont	229
Marion	Clar	047	KAHL			
JULICK			Chas	Craw	063
Nancy	Hami	131	KAHLINE			
JULIEN			Frederick	Lake	178
Joshua	Cler	050	KAISER			
JUMP			Anton	Hami	125
Ira S	Huro	163	Christian	Mont	238
Isaac	Craw	064	Ellen	Ross	297
JUMPER			Philippina	Hami	137
Benj S	Hami	121	KAISERMAN			
William	Putn	289	James	Monr	224
JUMPS			KALAHAN			
John H	Harr	149	Alex	Gree	116
JUNE			KALE			
Edwin M	Huro	162	Martha J	Colu	057
James P	Erie	087	KALES			
Reuben A	Huro	163	William	Jack	166
JUNG			KALY			
Adam	Mont	240	Elizabeth	Fult	106
JUNGBLUTH			KAMMERLING			
John	Lora	193	Cath	Hami	130
JUNGELAS			KANAGY			
Augustus	Mont	229	Joseph	Mont	240
JUNGKURTH			KANCHER			
Lewis	Fair	091	Chas	Mont	250
JUNK			KANE			
Henry C	Pick	279	Christian	Cuya	071
Susan	Faye	093	Henry	Sand	304
JURDON			James	Maho	206
Benj N	Fult	105	Patrick	Mont	249

KANEEN			KAUFFMAN (cont)		
Eliza E	Cuya	068	Elizabeth	Ashl	013
KANTRINER			George	Mont	238
Elizabeth	Jeff	170	Henry	Clar	046
KANTZ			Jeremiah D	Miam	219
John Philip	Brow	031	Mary	Wayn	353
KANZLEITER			Victor	Hami	126
Daniel	Craw	063	KAUFMAN		
KAPP			Adam	Sene	310
Jacob	Brow	034	Christian	Gree	114
KAPPLER			Ida	Star	318
Cath	Mont	230	John	Miam	218
KARCH			KAUP		
John Jr	Mont	227	Emma	Sene	313
KARCHER			KAUTRUN		
Henry	Monr	226	Frederick	Hami	126
KARIS			KAVANAUGH		
Susannah	Craw	064	Edward J	Mont	229
KARL			KAY		
William J C	Hami	137	Lucinda	Butl	039
KARN			KAYLER		
Geo W	Jack	167	Christena	Star	321
John	Otta	272	KAYLOR		
William	Hanc	140	Alfred	Mont	229
KARNES			KAYS		
Elijah	Defi	080	John	Wash	346
Elizabeth	Star	318	KEAN		
KARNS			Joseph C	Morg	259
Andrew W	Vint	341	KEANEY		
Jacob	Merc	218	Cath	Wyan	366
KARPER			KEARNEY		
Frank	Star	316	Terence	Wayn	354
KARPP			KEARNS		
William	Augl	026	Geo W	Clin	053
KARR			Henry	Paul	273
Elizabeth	Jeff	171	James	Paul	274
Franklin H	Otta	272	Jos	Miam	220
Geo	Meig	214	Mahlon	Clin	052
Nathan	Wyan	364	KEASER		
KARRER			Sallie	Paul	273
Thomas	Star	320	KEATH		
KASER			Patrick	Cuya	074
John F	Will	357	KEATING		
KASSON			Alice E	Hami	130
Orange H	Cuya	071	Margaret	Mari	209
KASTEL			KEAVERLO		
John	Hami	125	Mary R	Dela	085
KAUBLE			KEBBLE		
David	Wyan	367	Anselem	Clar	046
KAUFEIS			KECHTER		
Anton	Mont	255	Mathias	Mont	251
KAUFFMAN			KECK		
Adaline	Paul	272	Philip H	Jack	169

KECKELER		
Elizabeth	Hami	130
KEECH		
Thomas B	Mari	208
KEEFE		
Johanna	Clin	053
KEEFER		
Abram	Wood	360
John	Star	318
Susan	Cosh	060
KEEGAN		
Cath	Cuya	068
Michael	Augl	025
KEELER		
Abigail	Huro	164
Alonzo B	Wood	362
Geo	Adam	007
John M	Hami	121
Mary A	Luca	202
William O	Wood	360
KEELEY		
Bridget	Perr	278
Daniel	Tusc	333
KEEN		
Eleanor	Trum	325
James	Butl	037
Vesta A	Geau	112
KEENAN		
James	Mont	237
Sarah	Hard	145
KEENE		
Henry F	Mont	239
Jos R	Mont	251
Sarah B	Fran	103
KEENHARDT		
John A	Mont	236
KEEPERS		
William H	Hami	126
KEEPLINGER		
Martha J	Pike	281
KEERAN		
Jas B N	Unio	335
KEESLER		
Hiram C	Cuya	075
KEEZER		
Rosana	Ross	297
KEFFER		
Peter D	Sene	313
KEHERER		
Louisa	Scio	307
KEHR		
Eliza	Cuya	073
KEIBER		
Jacob	Sene	310
KEIFER		
J Warren	Clar	046
Louis	Mont	245
KEIGAN		
Patrick	Mont	229
KEIL		
William	Sand	304
KEINARDT		
Jno	Mont	241
KEIP		
Frank	Wood	362
KEISCHER		
Charles	Henr	153
KEISER		
Henry	Asht	014
Washington	Star	319
KEISS		
Emanuel	Craw	063
KEITH		
Al M	Jeff	172
Andrew B	Rich	292
Christian	Mont	236
Munson	Fult	105
William D	Warr	344
KELCHER		
John	Mont	240
William J	Mont	251
KELISON		
Daniel F	Pike	281
KELL		
Christian	Mont	237
George	Cler	048
John	Jeff	171
KELLAR		
Jacob	Wyan	365
John L	Knox	174
KELLER		
Ann	Clar	044
Chas A	Cuya	071
Christian	Holm	159
Cornelius	Dark	078
Daniel D	Merc	217
Eli G	Fran	103
Eliza	Wayn	353
Frank S	Fran	101
Fred	Cuya	071
Geo C	Augl	026
Geo W	Wood	359
Harrison S	Craw	063
Isaac N	Luca	197
Jacob L	Hanc	141

KELLER (cont)			KELLY (cont)		
John	Scio	306	Francis M	Sene	310
John B	Fair	089	Garrett	Mont	240
John B	Fran	101	Geo B	Wyan	366
Levi	Sene	309	Henrietta F	Maho	206
Louis	Cuya	069	Henry	Clar	046
Magdalena	Hami	124	Henry	Jeff	171
Martin	Fair	090	Hugh	Tusc	332
Mary A	Hami	130	Jacob	Will	357
Mary E	Rich	294	Jas	Clar	046
Susan G R	Loga	192	John	Dela	084
Thomas J	Rich	294	John	Mont	248
William	Erie	087	John	Mont	251
KELLEY			John	Trum	325
Albert J	Mont	239	John A	Cuya	076
Caroline	Hard	146	John H	Jack	168
Eli	Miam	222	John M	Morg	258
Eli H	Merc	217	Leander C	Mont	233
Eliza	Wayn	353	Mary	Cuya	073
Ephraim	Colu	059	Mary	Faye	094
Harvey P	Scio	306	Michael	Mont	248
Henry C	Dela	083	Patrick	Mont	241
Isaac N	Wood	361	Ruth	Scio	307
James	Gree	114	Solomon W	Shel	316
James	Hami	126	Thomas	Mont	243
John	Clar	046	Vincent P	Mont	255
John	Cosh	059	William	Fran	101
John	Mont	239	William	Wayn	354
Michael	Mont	240	William A	Lawr	182
Nancy	Hanc	142	William B	Cuya	075
Thomas	Lake	178	William N	Gree	115
Timothy	Mari	209	KELSEY		
William	Hami	126	Chas W	Fair	091
KELLNER			Curtis	Hami	125
Henry	Wash	347	James M	Sand	301
KELLOG			KELSO		
Dwight	Huro	164	Elizabeth	Musk	267
KELLOGG			KELTER		
Edwin	Medi	210	Cath	Maho	206
Henry H	Asht	016	KELTNER		
Horace	Huro	165	John	Fran	101
Lyman	Huro	165	Solonius	Hanc	141
Martin H	Fult	106	KEMBLE		
KELLS			Chauncey C	Maho	205
James	Guer	119	Mary E	Colu	058
KELLY			KEMMER		
Amanda	Perr	277	Sophia	Alle	009
Benj F	Hard	148	KEMMLER		
Cath	Mont	232	Mary	Rich	293
Edward	Mont	235	KEMP		
Elizabeth	Vint	340	John	Lick	186
Elizabeth A	High	153	KEMPER		
Francis A	Madi	204	David	Pike	281

KEMPER (cont)		
Elijah S	Lick	185
Lucy	Lick	184
KEMPLER		
John	Wood	360
KEMPTON		
John F	Dela	085
KENAN		
James	Luca	196
KENASTON		
Edward R	Mont	251
KENDALL		
Alonzo P	Hami	140
Andrew J	Hami	136
Eleanor	Gree	115
Elizabeth	Fult	106
Elizabeth	Scio	307
Henry L	Asht	014
Horace E	Rich	294
John	Huro	163
Nancy A	Mari	209
Roxy A	Pick	279
Sarah	Jeff	171
KENDELL		
Madison	Miam	219
KENDRICK		
Amanda	Hami	137
KENEY		
Erastus H	Mont	230
Kitty Ann	Wash	345
KENNARD		
Joshua F	Brow	035
KENNEALLY		
Mary	Hami	132
KENNEDY		
Aaron	Hard	147
Alfred G	Hami	136
Daniel	Preb	286
Edward J	Cuya	065
Esther E	Maho	206
Geo W	Trum	328
Gertrude F	Luca	200
Hester R	Brow	034
James	Cuya	074
John	Mont	243
John F	Cuya	071
John W	Cham	043
John W	Fult	104
John W	High	156
Joseph M	Butl	037
Joseph R	Guer	120
Martha A	Brow	035
Michael	Cuya	071

KENNEDY (cont)		
Philip A B	Hami	137
Richard V	Mont	243
Robert H	Ross	301
Robert O	Erie	086
Ruth	Cham	041
Sarah A	Cuya	075
Sarah J	Medi	211
Sidney A	Asht	015
Thomas	Hami	136
Vene S	Cler	048
William	Hock	159
William	Rich	293
William H	Pick	280
KENNEL		
Edna	Hami	130
KENNEY		
Cornelius	Mont	231
David	Mont	241
William H	Clin	053
KENNY		
Jane E	Asht	017
John E	Mont	234
Joseph	Monr	224
KENOY		
Mary	Hami	130
KENT		
Charles F	Luca	198
Ezra T	Paul	273
Henry A	Gall	110
Israel A	Nobl	268
Olvin	Scio	306
Susannah	Dark	077
KENTFIELD		
David L	Wyan	364
KENWORTHY		
William R	Clin	053
KENYON		
Jas M	Mari	208
KEOWAN		
Thomas	Mont	251
KEPHART		
Mariah	Warr	342
William C	Cuya	071
KEPLER		
Levi W	Preb	287
Rachel	Defi	080
Susannah	Hock	159
KEPPELMEYER		
Frank	Sene	314
KEPPLER		
Christina	Cuya	068

KIDNEY			KILKENNY			
Edward W	Cuya	076	Edward	Knox	174	
John	Hami	137	KILL			
Sarah A	Fran	103	Martha J	Cler	049	
KIEFER			KILLAM			
Lewis	Miam	220	Frederick	Mont	251	
KIEFFER			KILLEN			
Joseph	Star	320	Abner	Putn	289	
KIENZLE			Rebecca	Putn	289	
Frank	Lawr	182	KILLGORE			
KIERCHMEYER			John	Belm	027	
Reinhard	Mont	248	Liney	Adam	005	
KIERNAN			KILLIN			
Michael	Mont	238	Samuel D	Hami	140	
KIERS			KILLINGER			
Henry E	Mont	236	Anna M	Meig	215	
KIESEWETTER			Henry	Cler	050	
Emil	Fran	101	KILLMARTIN			
KIGER			John	Mont	251	
John	Wood	360	KILLOUGH			
Polly	Fair	092	Elizabeth A	Preb	286	
KIGGINS			KILMER			
Samuel J	Belm	028	Caroline	Wyan	366	
KIGHTLINGER			Mary L	Lora	194	
Cath	Wyan	365	KILPATRICK			
Sol L	Cuya	071	George	Mont	242	
William	Unio	334	Letitia	Jeff	170	
KILBOURN			Mary	Henr	153	
Mary A	Guer	119	KIM			
KILBOURNE			Joseph H	Meig	215	
Byron	Mari	208	KIMBALL			
KILBREATH			Benj	Brow	033	
William C	Guer	119	Lafayette	Jeff	171	
KILBURN			Mary A	Otta	271	
Enoch H	Huro	166	Robert	Erie	087	
Flavius J	Erie	085	William H	Fult	107	
KILBURY			KIMBERLY			
Thompson	Madi	203	Jane R	Wash	347	
KILDEA			KIMBLE			
Thomas	Mont	229	Benj F	Wood	360	
KILDON			Julius	Sand	301	
Mary	Musk	264	Nancy	Miam	222	
KILDROW			Sarah Jane	Craw	062	
Eliza E	Belm	028	KIMMEL			
KILE			Chas F	Mont	227	
Horatio P	Asht	014	Jacob A	Hanc	141	
Nancy	Unio	335	Joseph F	Wyan	367	
Oliver W	Wash	347	Rinaldo	Defi	081	
KILGORE			Sarah J	Maho	207	
Mary A	Hami	124	KIMMEY			
KILIANI			Amos	Guer	118	
Elizabeth	Miam	222	KIMMICK			
			Frederick	Medi	210	

KINCAID		
Amiel	Trum	328
Benj F	Rich	292
Chelnisce	Faye	094
Geo W	Rich	291
Isabella L	Maho	206
James P	Brow	035
James W	Mont	227
Thomas	Trum	329
William	Rich	291
KIND		
William	Warr	344
KINDEL		
Sarah A	Hard	144
KINDER		
David	Perr	275
Elizabeth F	Mont	233
Isaiah	Fran	104
Mary Ann	Perr	274
KINDLE		
John S	Mont	227
KINE		
Sarah	Wyan	364
KINERT		
Oscar B	Cosh	061
KING		
Abigail	Cuya	065
Ambrose G	Belm	030
Ann E	Athe	020
Anna M	Fran	101
Cath	Hami	130
Charles	Lawr	182
Charles O	Mont	246
Cyrus	Fair	091
David	Clar	044
David L	Rich	292
Elizabeth J	Hanc	142
Ferd J	VanW	336
Frank C	Lick	188
Frank L	Cler	049
George	Adam	007
George	Clar	045
Hannah	Colu	057
Henry	Hami	125
Henry	Lawr	182
James M	Gree	113
Jane	Hami	135
John	Asht	015
John	Paul	273
Loren G	Preb	288
Lucinda	Scio	307
Manella	Trum	329
Margaret	Musk	263

KING (cont)		
Mark	Lawr	182
Martin V B	Maho	205
Mary A	Cuya	076
Mary G	Asht	019
Mary P	Belm	027
Michael	Hami	124
Miles	Mont	251
Milton	Wash	347
Nancy	Musk	263
Nancy	Trum	329
Newel	Gall	108
Robert P	Colu	058
Sarah A	Musk	263
Silas	Monr	226
Silas W	Brow	033
Silvester	Defi	081
William	Wash	349
William H	Musk	262
William H H	Merc	218
William W	Star	316
KINGERY		
Salina	Paul	273
KINGMAN		
Elizabeth	High	154
KINGREY		
Margaret S	Ross	300
KINGSBURY		
Climena H	Lora	195
KINGSLEY		
Algernon	Asht	019
Betsey M	Asht	016
Henry	Huro	163
Mary P	Lora	195
KINION		
Russell	Wayn	354
KINKADE		
Amanda M	Monr	225
Athalinda	Musk	265
KINKAID		
Sarah	Lick	185
KINKEAD		
Elizabeth	Mont	232
Henrietta	Morg	258
KINKUP		
James S	Port	285
KINLEY		
James	Hami	125
KINMAN		
Chas C	Madi	203
KINMONT		
Thomas C	Defi	081

KINNAMAN				**KIRCHMER**		
William	Asht	015		Jacob	Mont	229
KINNAMON				**KIRCHNER**		
Lavina J	Ross	297		Henry	Mont	245
William J	Star	319		**KIRDENDOLL**		
KINNEAR				James W	Lick	188
John W	Asht	018		**KIREHOFF**		
KINNETT				John	Loga	191
Harvey	Brow	033		**KIRGAN**		
KINNEY				Amanda J	Scio	305
Jane	Hanc	142		Mary	Cler	047
Joel F	Hami	125		**KIRK**		
Michael	Mont	234		Allen M	Belm	029
KINNISON				Bernard	Mont	241
Cath	Pike	280		Emerick	Henr	152
KINSELL				Enos	Ross	301
Richard	Mont	256		Isaac W	Port	285
KINSELLA				John	Tusc	331
Ellen	Hami	124		**KIRKBRIDE**		
KINSELY				Dudley	Cler	051
Cath	Craw	062		Eli T	Monr	225
KINSER				**KIRKENDALL**		
Dianna	Hock	159		Aaron	Jack	166
KINSEY				**KIRKER**		
David	Mont	227		Esther A	Adam	005
Gideon S	Hami	125		**KIRKPATRICK**		
KINSLEY				Cynthia	Wash	350
John W	Unio	334		Elizabeth J	Preb	287
Sarah A	Belm	029		Mahala	Wash	347
William A	Lora	192		Nancy	Brow	034
KINSMAN				Nancy	Nobl	268
John	Trum	329		Rachel	Rich	295
KINTIGH				Rebecca	Miam	218
Isaac E	Defi	081		W H	Trum	329
KINTZ				William	Brow	034
William J	Sene	313		**KIRKUP**		
KION				Chas A	Port	283
Kunigunde	Fran	097		Robert	Hami	125
KIPLINGER				**KIRKWOOD**		
Honor	Wayn	352		Geo	Fair	089
Levi H	Ashl	013		John S	Loga	192
KIPP				**KIRLACH**		
John	Cler	049		Joseph	Hami	138
KIRBY				**KIRLEY**		
Byron	Hami	125		John C	Mont	235
Eliza	Colu	056		**KIRN**		
John E	Craw	064		Christian	Sene	314
Julia A	Cuya	075		**KIRNER**		
William	Mont	228		Theo	Cuya	071
William S	Wyan	365		**KIRSCHNER**		
KIRCHBERGER				Esther M	Cuya	068
Barbara	Hami	124		Jacobina	Hard	147
				Michael	Mont	241

KIRSH		
John	Rich	295
KISE		
Eliza	Mari	209
KISER		
Benj	Lawr	180
Eli	Madi	204
Geo	Dark	079
Hiram	Scio	305
Joseph	Otta	272
Levi A	Merc	218
Lorenzo D	Sene	311
Richard	Scio	308
William	Miam	219
William I	Miam	219
KISHLER		
Mary J	Augl	025
Nelson M	Perr	275
KISKADDEN		
George	Lawr	180
KISLING		
Geo	Sene	309
William	High	157
KISSEL		
Jacob	Hanc	141
Philip	Ashl	013
KISSELRING		
Henrietta	Butl	037
KISSINGER		
Ellen	Jeff	170
Henry	Mont	227
James H	Sene	314
Susan	Star	318
KISSLING		
Jeremiah	High	157
KISTLER		
Andrew J	Mont	248
Theo F	Fran	101
KISTNER		
Christian	Sene	310
KITE		
Ira	Shel	316
Sarah	Cham	042
KITTS		
David	Lawr	182
KLAFINGER		
Samuel Sr	Erie	087
KLAGES		
Augustus	Jeff	171
KLANKE		
Sophia	Hami	130
KLAPPROTH		
Gotfried	Mont	237

KLAUS		
George	Star	319
KLAWITTER		
Fredericka	Luca	198
KLECKNER		
Elizabeth	Star	318
John H	Summ	324
KLEE		
Mathias	Dela	083
KLEEMEIER		
Frederick	Hami	126
KLEESPIES		
Frank	Mont	248
KLEIN		
Christopher	Mont	250
Frederick	Rich	293
Henry	Knox	173
Johanna	Butl	036
John	Hami	126
John	Mont	248
Jno P	Mont	251
Maria	Hami	124
KLEINEGGER		
Francis	Otta	272
KLEINGRIES		
John	Mont	236
KLEINHAUS		
Jacob	Mont	238
KLEINHENN		
Reinhardt	Mont	251
KLEINHENZ		
Jos	Merc	217
KLEINOCHLE		
William	Hami	126
KLEINSCHMIDT		
Agnes	Cuya	073
KLEUBER		
Mary M	Erie	087
KLEVER		
Jacob	Wood	362
KLEY		
Anna	Butl	036
KLINE		
Andrew	Sand	302
Andrew J	Mont	250
Asa	Scio	305
Frank	Madi	204
Jacob	Hami	121
John	Luca	198
John	Mont	240
Knox	Holm	161
Mary M	Mont	230
Ragenia	Lick	187

KLINE (cont)			KNAPP (cont)		
Solomon	Fult	106	Obed	Asht	015
William H	Defi	080	Philemon	Lora	193
KLINEFELTER			KNAUSE		
James H	Putn	290	Susannah	Tusc	330
KLING			KNEADLER		
Anna	Cosh	061	Jacob	Augl	026
Cath	Hami	137	KNECE		
Samuel F	Star	317	Martin	Ross	296
KLINGER			KNECHT		
Chas T	Paul	274	Adam Jr	Mont	229
Jacob	Preb	288	KNEDLER		
Jacob	Wyan	365	Sallie	Ross	297
Rebecca	Ashl	013	KNEE		
KLINGLER			Uriah L	Carr	040
George M	Hard	144	KNEEDLER		
Magdalena	Mont	230	John W	Faye	094
Wilhelm	Mont	251	KNEELAND		
KLINKNER			Horatio H	Fran	101
Joseph	Cuya	071	KNEISLEY		
KLONNE			Joseph A	Ross	296
John	Hami	125	KNEPPER		
KLOOR			John	Colu	056
Henry	Wood	360	KNEPPLE		
KLOPBENSTIEN			John C	Sene	314
Lee	Wood	358	KNERR		
KLOSTERMEYER			Christian	Wood	362
Rozena	Otta	271	KNESS		
KLUSHMAN			Eli	Vint	340
Barbara	Sand	304	KNICELEY		
KNABEL			John	Hard	147
Frederick	Hami	124	KNIFER		
KNAGGS			Edward	Wood	359
James W	Wood	362	KNIFFIN		
KNAPKE			Phebe R	Clar	047
Mary	Hami	124	KNIGHT		
KNAPP			Chas G	Fran	101
Andrew J	Mari	208	Dolly Ann	Meig	212
Benj	Miam	222	Frederick H	Trum	325
Cath	Sand	303	Jonathan	Belm	030
Chas H	Cuya	065	Joseph H	Trum	325
Dorcas	Huro	165	Josiah J	Loga	192
Ebenezer T	Adam	003	Louisa E	Trum	326
Ezra	Meig	213	Margaret	Loga	192
Henrietta J	Lora	194	Nancy	Fran	097
Henry J	Asht	019	Porter	Huro	164
Hiram A	Lora	196	Zelpah A	Clar	047
Jas	Mari	208	KNIGHTON		
Lafayette	Mont	241	James S	Jack	168
Lydia	Mari	209	Josiah A	Faye	094
Lydia A	Gall	108	Winkfield	Ross	301
Mary E	Paul	272	KNIPE		
Mary H	Asht	017	Cath	Vint	341

KNIPPER		
Joseph	Hami	125
KNOBEL		
John	Mont	244
Samuel	Alle	008
KNODE		
John H	Mari	209
KNOER		
George	Hami	125
KNOFFLE		
Samuel	Mont	242
KNOPF		
Aegidins	Hami	126
KNOTT		
John Q	Hami	140
Phebe J	Cler	051
William W	VanW	339
KNOTTS		
Milton	High	155
KNOWLDEN		
Almedia	Musk	265
KNOWLES		
Alexander G	Mont	235
Chas G	Meig	215
Diantha	Lake	178
Eliza A	Loga	191
Susan B	Athe	023
KNOWLTON		
Newton	Asht	019
William A	Cuya	065
KNOX		
Charles	Knox	172
Clark	Maho	206
George M	Summ	321
Hugh T	Unio	335
Margaret A	Merc	218
Mary	Harr	149
Medill	Morg	258
Robert	Perr	277
Samuel	Hami	125
KNOXVILLE		
Peter	Mont	242
KNUST		
Jacob	Mont	231
KNYRIM		
Francis	Mont	237
KOB		
Philip L	Wayn	351
KOBB		
Henry	Hami	139
KOCH		
Herman	Hami	125
Matilda	Sene	312

KOCH (cont)		
Threasa	Hami	130
William	Hami	125
KOCHLER		
Theressa	Star	318
KOEBLER		
John	Asht	018
KOEHLER		
Augustus	Hami	125
Christian	Summ	321
Frederick	Scio	307
Henry	Meig	215
KOEHN		
Hugo	Cuya	071
Theodore	Hami	126
KOENIG		
Julia A	Wash	349
Nicholaus	Mont	251
KOEPPEL		
Gabriel	VanW	339
KOERBER		
Jacob	Rich	296
KOHL		
Magnus	Cuya	071
KOHLBRAND		
Henry	Hami	126
KOHLER		
Andrew	Augl	026
Barbara	Hami	130
KOHLHORST		
William	Augl	025
KOHLMAN		
Amelia	Cuya	073
Henry	Hanc	143
KOHR		
Abram B	Fran	104
KOLB		
Barbara	Wayn	351
KOLBE		
Johanna	VanW	337
KOLLER		
Henry C	Hard	147
Jacob	Monr	224
KOLLMAN		
John C	Lora	194
KOLP		
Nicolas	Star	320
KONSCHAKY		
David	Mont	235
KONTNER		
Isaac D	Hock	158
KONZEN		
Henry	Henr	152

KOO			KRAMB		
John A	Hami	126	Henry J	Sand	304
KOOGLE			KRAMER		
Mary E	Warr	343	Anna M	Lora	193
Milton	Loga	189	Elnora	Lick	186
KOOHEN			George	Mont	228
Jefferson	Sene	310	Henry	Gree	114
KOOKEN			William H	Wyan	366
Joshua	Unio	334	KRANER		
KOOL			Ann	Fran	103
Valentine	Mont	239	Solomon	Hard	147
KOOLEY			KRANTH		
Peter	Cuya	071	Caroline	Mont	230
KOON			KRANTHER		
Clark	Geau	111	Fredericka	Hami	130
Weedon	Wash	349	KRAPS		
Wilson	Wash	346	Cath	Morg	257
KOONS			KRATSCH		
David S	Putn	290	Justine	Holm	161
Elizabeth W	Knox	175	KRATZER		
John T	Otta	271	Lewis	Brow	033
Samuel B	Craw	064	Reason	Brow	035
KOONTZ			Thomas	Brow	035
Aaron F	Clar	046	KRAUTH		
Frederick F	Ashl	012	Adam	Cler	051
KOPF			KRAUTHER		
Michael	Wood	360	Johannetta	Hami	130
KOPLIN			KREAGER		
Aaron	Hard	147	Cynthia	Lick	185
Jacob	Summ	321	KREAMER		
KORGLER			Eliza	Wayn	353
John	Gree	113	KREAR		
KOSHNER			Isabella	Star	319
Abby	Trum	326	KREBS		
Daniel	Trum	326	Eve	Star	318
KOTZBUE			Frederick	Mont	236
Caroline	Fair	091	KREIDLER		
KOUNS			Chas W	Sene	311
Cath	Lawr	183	KREIGER		
KOUNTZ			Mary A	Cuya	065
John	Luca	201	KREITER		
John S	Star	318	Angeline	Tusc	330
KOUTNER			KREPS		
Sylvester	Athe	023	Joseph	VanW	336
KOWLING			KRESS		
Amza	Mont	245	Christian	Cler	051
KRAFFT			Henry	Adam	005
Susan	Colu	055	Peter	Mont	251
KRAFT			KRETSCHMAN		
Charles	Hard	147	Chas W	Hami	126
Levi	Mont	248	KRETZER		
Louis	Fran	101	John H	Ross	297
Mary	Star	317			

KREWSON			KUHN (cont)		
Nellie	Musk	263	John P	Wayn	351
KRIEGER			John W	Tusc	332
Ernest J	Mont	248	Joseph	Cuya	074
KRIM			William	Fran	101
Sarah	Belm	029	KUHNER		
KRING			Jacob	Jack	167
Elizabeth	Athe	024	KULOW		
Lafayette	Hanc	141	John	Athe	022
KRININGER			KUMBER		
Christ	Hami	125	Franklin W	Butl	039
KRISHER			KUMLER		
Benj F	Mont	240	Henry J	Butl	037
KRISKIE			KUMMERO		
John	Mont	255	Ernst	Luca	198
KROGMAN			KUN		
Gertrude	Hami	124	Charles P	High	155
KROHN			KUNCI		
George W	Putn	290	Frederick A	Huro	162
KROLL			KUNEMAN		
Harmann O	Faye	094	Jacob	Star	318
KRONE			KUNKEHMAN		
Henry W	Mont	245	Lucinda	Miam	222
KROUSE			KUNSMAN		
Theo	Defi	080	William W	Will	355
KROUTZ			KUNTZ		
Jacob	Defi	080	Jacob	Mont	237
KRUCK			KUNZ		
Jacob	Ross	298	Cath	Cuya	073
KRUG			Michael	Lora	196
John H	Lick	184	William	Miam	222
KRUGER			KUPFER		
Matilda	Fran	097	Rebecca J	Belm	029
KRUGH			KUPFERSCHMIDT		
Mary	Merc	217	Casper	Hami	125
KRUMBAUF			KURFIS		
Samuel J	Perr	278	Caroline E	Warr	343
KRUZ			KURTIS		
Jacob	Mont	248	Jos	Clar	046
KUANER			KURTZ		
Elizabeth	Musk	265	Anthony	Mont	250
KUBLER			Daniel	Clar	046
John W	Preb	287	Gebhart	Mont	240
KUCHNER			Margaret	Star	320
William	Fran	101	KUSS		
KUEBLER			John F	Medi	212
Anthony	Mont	248	KUSTERER		
KUGLER			Emilie	Hami	130
Amanda	Hami	130	KYES		
KUHN			Patrick	Mont	236
Christopher H			KYLE		
	Mont	255	Caroline	Gree	116
Henry	Scio	305	Elias	Unio	335

KYLE (cont)			LAFLORE			
Elizabeth	Cler	050	Clara	Luca	197
Ira	Mari	208	Dominic	Wood	361
James H	Gree	115	LAFONG			
John	Mont	243	Cassandra	Mont	232
Samuel	Gree	115	LAFONTAINE			
KYNELT			Alfred	Mont	248
Flavius J	Luca	197	LAFORCE			
			Alford	Fran	103
			LAHMERS			
			Chas	Tusc	332
LAAS			LAHNER			
Mary	Fran	097	Valentine	Luca	198
LABBE			LAIR			
Elizabeth	Hami	130	Elizabeth	Ashl	013
LABEW			LAIRD			
David	Perr	275	Alvan	Preb	288
LABNE			Andrew	Rich	295
Cath M	Perr	275	Esther	VanW	339
LA BOUNTY			George F	Star	317
Ashley O	Asht	015	Louisa	Trum	327
LA BRICK			Silas	Preb	288
Peter	Fran	095	LAIZER			
LABRY			Mary A	Belm	030
Frederick M	Mont	238	LAKE			
LACEY			Benj B	Wayn	354
Anderson	Fair	092	Cath	Perr	278
Anna J	Harr	150	Edgar B	Mont	249
Hannah F	Wash	345	Elizabeth	Meig	216
Leroy	Ross	298	Geo C	Guer	119
Matilda	Meig	213	Jarvis N	Preb	286
LACKEY			John	Unio	335
Joseph	Summ	324	John P	Trum	325
Michael O	Gall	111	Lee Ann	Guer	120
LACKS			Mary E	Brow	034
Stephen	Morr	260	Polly A	Port	284
LACOCK			Thomas J	Wood	361
Levi	Brow	034	William B	Hard	146
LACY			LAKEN			
Pollis D	Rich	293	David	Fran	099
Washington	Pick	280	LAKIN			
LADD			Luther	Mont	245
Celinda S	Fult	106	LALLY			
Demaris	Wash	349	Cornelius M	Mont	234
Mary A	Wash	348	Michael	Maho	205
LAEHY			LAMB			
William	Mont	249	David	Mont	236
LAFFELL			Eliza	Jack	168
Rachel	Perr	275	Harrison H	Henr	152
LAFFERTY			Harvey W	Asht	015
James	Rich	291	James D	Loga	189
John L	Rich	291	John H	Trum	329
Nelson B	Adam	004	Joseph	Meig	216

LAMB			LAMPTON			
Julia A	Perr	277	Nancy A	Dela	083
Lemuel B	Harr	150	LANAM			
Nelson M	Lick	186	Martin	Nobl	268
Sarah	Fult	107	LANBERT			
LAMBACHER			Philip	Summ	322
Geo	Cuya	075	LANCE			
LAMBERS			Henry	Huro	163
Mary A	Augl	025	LANDEN			
LAMBERSON			Ada S	Cuya	066
Susannah	Morr	260	LANDER			
William D	Trum	326	Edward	Mont	243
LAMBERT			LANDES			
Angaletta	Madi	204	Carolina	Fran	097
Easter	Shel	315	LANDIS			
Ellen	Butl	038	Emanuel	Mont	234
Evaline	Hami	130	Hiram	Sene	309
Jonathan	Paul	274	Isaac A	Miam	222
Louis E	Cuya	071	Jacob K	Butl	036
Margaret	Scio	308	LANDON			
Paul	Mont	231	Darius	Mari	209
William B	Scio	305	Ellen M	Star	319
LAMBING			Hamilton A	Mari	209
Mary	Mont	230	LANDRUM			
LAMBION			John L	Ross	300
Mar	Scio	307	LANDSDALE			
LAMBORN			Francis K	Cler	051
Ezehiel	Clar	044	LANE			
LAMBRIGHT			Achsah	Musk	262
John F	Wood	363	Henry A	Cuya	073
Lewis	Butl	037	Henry G	Craw	062
LAMMA			Jacob	Will	357
Andrew J	Cosh	060	James A	Scio	306
LAMME			John	Dela	082
Isaac	Gree	113	John C	Lawr	181
Margaret F	Gree	113	John R	Knox	175
LAMMER			John W	Pick	279
Christena	Knox	174	John W	Pick	279
LAMONDA			Marth	Cler	052
John N	Brow	035	Mary J	Loga	190
LAMOTT			Peter	Miam	219
James H	Fair	090	Sherman	Summ	325
Sarah	Fair	090	Thomas A	Hami	128
LA MOTTE			William	Mont	242
Leslie A	Dark	077	LANER			
LAMP			John	Wash	348
John	Fran	099	LANEY			
LAMPHIER			Cath	Fair	088
Esther	Summ	323	Luke H	Wood	359
Sarah	Asht	015	Owen H	Wood	361
LAMPKIN			LANG			
Ellen	Belm	028	Anna	Cler	048
			Emily M	Lawr	180

LANG (cont)			**LANTZ (cont)**		
Herman	VanW	336	Susannah	Craw	062
James	Adam	005	**LANTZENHEISER**		
James W	Hard	146	Aaron	Henr	152
John H	Monr	226	**LANY**		
Louis	Hami	136	Joseph	Hami	138
Margaret	Preb	287	**LANZ**		
LANGAN			Mary	Hami	130
Oliver S	Alle	008	**LAPE**		
LANGDON			Jeremiah	Madi	204
Alonzo	Butl	037	Mary A	Madi	203
LANGERDORF			**LAPENDAHL**		
Sebastian	Luca	196	Nicholas	Henr	153
LANGFITT			**LAPHAM**		
Benj F	Wash	347	Valentine	Mari	209
LANGHAM			**LAPORT**		
Eliza	Fran	103	Zephaniah	Loga	192
LANGLEY			**LAPP**		
John	Trum	328	Jacob	Summ	322
LANGSTAFF			**LARABEE**		
Henry	Musk	262	Orilla	Athe	020
James G	Putn	289	**LAREW**		
Lucy J	Musk	263	Kessiah	Hami	138
LANGSTEIN			**LARGER**		
Joseph	Mont	251	Appalonia	Miam	220
LANGTON			**LARIMER**		
John	Lora	193	David K	Faye	094
LANHAM			**LARIMORE**		
Elizabeth A	Cler	049	Frank C	Knox	175
Fletcher C	Meig	214	**LARISON**		
LANIHAN			John	Athe	023
John J	Hami	128	**LARKIN**		
LANKO			John	Fair	091
Christopher	Mont	248	Mary	Hami	130
LANNING			Philip	Mont	244
Elizabeth	Harr	150	**LARRICK**		
Elizabeth	Tusc	331	Rachel	Nobl	267
James W	Mont	250	Sarah	Ross	296
Lemuel	Perr	276	**LARSH**		
Lucinda	Alle	009	Charles	Preb	287
William	Hard	147	**LARSON**		
LANNON			Alexander	Mont	246
Patrick	Mari	209	Peter	Mont	241
LANSDOWN			**LA RUE**		
Frank M	Loga	189	Geo S	Hami	140
LANSON			**LASLEY**		
Margaret	Colu	056	David H	Fran	099
Thomas B	Meig	214	**LASSIG**		
LANTRY			Julias	Hami	128
Michael	Dark	078	**LASURE**		
LANTZ			Morris W	Gree	114
Benj F	Rich	292	**LATCH**		
J Alexander	Summ	322	William F	Cuya	072

LATHAM			LAUTERMAN			
Calvin M	Fran	103	Henry	Trum	329	
Edward P	Geau	111	LAUTZ			
Henry C	Hanc	142	John A	Hami	128	
James M	Will	357	LAUX			
Rowzee	Hanc	143	Susan	Sene	313	
LATHAN			LA VELLE			
Marcus L	Port	284	Frederick	Port	283	
LATHER			LAVERY			
Frederick	Fult	105	Elizabeth	Morg	257	
LATHRAPE			LAWBAUGH			
Joshua R	Luca	199	Lewis	Ashl	011	
LATHROP			LAWLER			
Chancy A	Huro	161	James	Hami	128	
Lucy	Luca	196	Timothy	Wood	358	
LATHROPE			LAWRENCE			
Walter	Luca	197	Abigail M	Loga	189	
LATIMER			Chas	Mont	248	
James O	Trum	330	Christina	Adam	003	
Olney P	Cuya	065	Clement	Hami	128	
LATIMORE			Ellen	Sene	312	
John S	Hard	147	Harriet M	Cuya	068	
LATTA			James L	Sene	312	
Moses	Ross	299	John	Hami	128	
LATTERMAN			Mark	Belm	027	
Gideon	Lora	194	Miner	Huro	165	
LATTIMER			Norman P	Dark	078	
John M	Huro	165	Patrick C	Hard	144	
LATTIN			Peter	Maho	206	
Quincy	Trum	326	Rachel	Musk	264	
LATURE			LAWSON			
Henry	Mont	248	James S	Pike	282	
LAUBER			Thomas E	Wash	346	
Christina	Hami	130	William	Mont	249	
LAUCHRIST			LAWTON			
Margaret	Sene	313	Austin	Hami	121	
LAUCK			James	Clar	045	
John	Wood	361	Matilda	Trum	329	
LAUGHLIN			LAWYER			
David	Clar	044	Mary	Carr	040	
Joseph S	Shel	315	LAX			
Mary W	Wyan	364	Thomas	Athe	023	
Nancy	Musk	267	LAYCOCK			
LAUGHREY			Rebecca A	Musk	264	
Ida A	Cuya	068	LAYLANDER			
LAUGHRIN			John	Holm	161	
Mary	Trum	329	Mary	Holm	160	
LAUNDON			LAYMAN			
John P	Lora	196	Emeline	Cler	049	
LAUPPE			Fanny	High	156	
Mary	Rich	291	Ragan	Rich	292	
LAUS			Rebecca	High	156	
Thomas	Craw	064				

LAYNE		
John N	Lick	184
Samuel E	Gall	108
William C	Lawr	181
LAZARO		
Chas	Wayn	354
LAZARUS		
Edward M	Port	283
LAZENBRY		
Henry	Henr	153
LAZURE		
Geo W	Adam	007
LAZZELL		
Francis M	Fran	099
LEA		
John B	Wyan	365
Margaret	Musk	267
LEACH		
Cath	Luca	196
Mary	Craw	062
Mary A	Cuya	068
Matthew	Mont	252
Sarah	Ross	300
Sherman M	Port	284
LEADBETTER		
David	High	155
LEAHY		
Edward F	Asht	015
LEAK		
Alfred D	Warr	344
LEAMING		
Samuel	Hami	121
LEANDER		
Wiley	Monr	223
LEANHAM		
Notley	Cler	049
LEAPLEY		
Louisa	Shel	316
Thomas C	Shel	314
LEAR		
Frederick	Gall	110
Valentine	Augl	026
LEARY		
John	Wood	362
Margaret	Luca	200
LEAS		
Henry L	Henr	152
LEASE		
Daniel	Mont	236
Ella	Hanc	140
James N	Faye	095
Nelson P	Trum	329
Priscilla	Faye	094

LEASE (cont)		
Rebecca A	Hard	148
Samuel R	Brow	034
LEASER		
Martin	VanW	338
Sophia	Merc	217
LEASURE		
Geo W	VanW	336
Rudolph	Hami	138
LEATHERMAN		
Hannah	Alle	008
Nancy	Putn	290
LEATHERS		
Weasley	Wood	358
LEAVELL		
Barbara	Miam	222
LEAVITT		
Mary A	Cosh	060
LEBAY		
Frank	Wood	360
LEBEL		
Jacob	Medi	211
LECHBRANS		
Adam	Mont	250
LECHLEITNER		
Aplon	VanW	337
LECHLITNER		
Salome	Maho	206
LECOMPT		
Chas H	Clar	045
LECOMPTE		
Bridget	Cuya	068
LEDBETTER		
Frederick B	Gree	115
LEDGER		
George	Mont	241
LEDWELL		
Eliza	Butl	036
LEE		
Albert W	Harr	150
Ann	Defi	079
Arthur	Mont	245
Austin B	Port	284
Charlotte C	Summ	324
George W	Summ	321
Jacob	Augl	026
Jas M	Colu	056
John	Mont	244
Joseph	Ross	298
Manerva	Adam	007
Margaret	Fran	097
Martha	Miam	221
Mary	Jeff	172

LEITER (cont)				LENTRY		
John	Adam	006		Mary	Cuya	068
Sarah	Luca	200		LENTZ		
LEITH				Mary A	Cham	042
Eliza	Wyan	365		William P	Alle	008
LEITNER				LEONARD		
Andrew J	Sene	314		Alfred	Adam	005
Eliza	Wayn	354		Benj F	Cham	043
Julius	Sene	309		Carline	Clar	045
William	Henr	151		Cath	Maho	205
LEIVE				Cath W	Hami	130
Henry	Scio	305		Charles	Scio	308
LELAND				Ebenezer D	Clin	052
Andrew	Cuya	073		Ellen C	Geau	113
LEMASTERS				Horace A	Asht	018
John W	Tusc	333		Isabella	Maho	205
Sarah	Lawr	183		John	Hami	128
LEMEN				Jonathan R	Sene	311
Edward F	Cham	043		Michael I	Mont	248
LEMERT				Morgan	Miam	219
Sarah A L	Lick	184		Nancy	Dela	084
LEMMON				Sarah A	Adam	005
Jesse H	Colu	058		Thomas	Hami	121
Samuel R	Star	317		Thomas	Mont	244
LEMON				LEONHARD		
David W	Brow	034		Alex	Unio	333
Ezra	Holm	160		LEOPOLD		
Mary A	Loga	191		Michael	Mont	252
Samuel	Brow	034		LEPAGE		
LEMONS				Cornelius S	Guer	118
Pleasant H	Hard	146		LEPARD		
William	Wood	364		Eliza	Cuya	068
LEMPP				Elizabeth	Port	284
Augustus	Mont	234		LEPERT		
LENARDSON				Conrad B	Craw	063
Hezekiah	Luca	196		LEPIRD		
LENEY				Sophia	Augl	024
Thomas	Cuya	076		LEPLEY		
LENHART				George	Knox	174
Jas H	Perr	277		LERCH		
Mary A	Perr	277		John	Hami	128
Samuel	Madi	203		LEROUX		
LENIX				Jane	Asht	016
Chloe	Mont	233		LE ROY		
LENNON				Amanda	Lake	178
John	Cler	050		LESHER		
LENNOX				Jacob	Hanc	143
John	Mont	248		LESLIE		
LENT				Henry A	Musk	266
Daniel H	Miam	220		John	Wyan	365
LENTEL				Joseph	Mont	249
John H	Star	317		Susannah	Gall	108
				William F	Hard	144

LESSER			**LEWIS (cont)**		
Gabriel	Jack	167	Henry	Meig	214
LESSLEY			Henry	Mont	227
Samuel	Ashl	013	Henry	Pike	282
LESTER			Henry J	Maho	206
Cornelius R	Jeff	172	Isabella	Musk	265
Joshua M	Mont	252	Jacob B	Craw	063
Pauline E	Huro	164	James	Lawr	182
LETTERS			James	Lora	196
Thomas F	Belm	027	James	Miam	222
LETTERSTE			James J	Musk	264
Joseph	Pike	282	James M	Adam	003
LETTS			Jerome	Morr	262
Peter	Huro	165	John	Defi	080
LEVALLY			John	Gall	111
Lydia	Clar	044	John	Vint	341
LEVENGOOD			John B	Trum	327
John	Cosh	062	John R	Sene	314
LEVENS			Jonathan	Defi	080
Mary	Hami	131	Jos	Miam	222
LEVET			Joshua	Jack	168
Chas	Medi	211	Laura E	Cler	048
LEVI			Margaret B	Trum	327
Willis	Cler	049	Maria J	Pick	280
LEVINGSTON			Mary	Clar	046
Henry	Hard	144	Mary A	Knox	175
LEVINSTINE			Mary Ann	Hard	146
Frederick	Sand	302	Mary E	Cuya	068
LEWERS			Oren	Sene	313
Sarah	Jeff	169	Orson	Athe	023
LEWI			Philip	Trum	327
Henry	Cuya	073	Philip J	Adam	003
LEWING			Rise A	Alle	009
Cath	Brow	034	Shem	Port	284
LEWIS			Thomas J	Cham	043
Albert	Hami	128	Wallace W	Madi	204
Albert H	Cuya	065	William	Alle	008
Albert W	Adam	007	William	Trum	328
Andrew J	Butl	038	William H	Brow	034
Casper	Wood	364	William H	Mont	244
Cath	Butl	037	William H H	Mont	252
Cath	Trum	326	**LEWMANS**		
Charles A	Jack	167	Elizabeth	Sene	310
David	Brow	034	**LIBIS**		
Dickerson	Luca	196	Lucas	Summ	322
Edwin D	Trum	330	**LIBOLD**		
Elias C	Hami	128	Frederick	Huro	161
Emeline	Asht	019	**LICHTENBERGER**		
Frank	Lawr	182	John	Faye	094
Geo	VanW	338	**LICHTY**		
Geo W	Adam	003	Augusta C	Paul	272
Geo W	Medi	211	Joseph	Defi	081
Harriet	Geau	111			

LICKLIDER			LILES			
David E	Miam	220	Joseph H	Hard	145	
LICTHY			William	Erie	087	
Levi	Paul	273	LILLEY			
LIDDLE			Ellen	Wayn	353	
Arthur	Maho	205	John W	Wyan	366	
LIDDY			Louis	Mont	252	
John	Mont	237	Michael A	Fran	099	
Mary	Cham	042	Susan	Carr	039	
LIDEY			LIMBARGER			
Elizabeth	Perr	278	Isaac	Meig	216	
LIEBERT			LIMBAUGH			
Juliane	Lawr	180	Christian	Sene	310	
LIEBRANDT			LIMBERGER			
Charlotte	Hami	131	Bernardina	Hami	130	
LIEBTAG			Geo	Hami	125	
George	Star	320	LIME			
LIECHTE			Margaret	Wyan	366	
Albert	Hami	121	LIMING			
LIEDEL			Mary	Brow	033	
William	Miam	221	LIMRICK			
LIENHARD			Joseph	Summ	322	
Anne B	Star	321	LINAMENT			
LIESY			John	Fran	104	
John	Lick	187	LINARD			
LIGGET			Mary M	Mont	230	
Henry	Clin	052	LINCH			
LIGGETT			Eliza J	Clin	054	
Eliza	Wayn	354	LINCKERMEYER			
Theodore	Harr	150	Margaret	Hami	131	
William M	Harr	150	LINCOLN			
LIGHT			Hannah U	Lora	195	
Arlenzo S	Luca	196	Joseph	Wood	359	
George B	Putn	289	Spencer D	Dela	085	
William	Clin	052	LIND			
William C	Athe	022	Jacob	Fran	099	
LIGHTER			Philip H	Unio	334	
James	Ross	300	Robert L	Miam	222	
LIGHTFOOT			Thomas N	Hami	138	
Mary	Will	357	LINDEMOOD			
Owen	Ross	300	Edmond	Jeff	170	
LIGHTLE			LINDENWOOD			
Thomas	Pike	282	Christina	Monr	226	
LIGHTNER			LINDER			
John	Hard	146	Edward	Morr	260	
Jno A	Wash	348	Wallace	Unio	335	
Josiah	Harr	150	LINDERGREEN			
William	Belm	030	Henry W	Asht	016	
LIKE			LINDLEY			
Jno	Perr	275	Francis W	Medi	210	
LIKES			LINDNER			
Rhoda	Guer	119	Christian	Mont	240	

LINDSAY		
Chas W	Miam	219
John	Scio	306
Rachel A	Putn	289
Sarah A	Pick	279
Thomas	Belm	029
William	VanW	337
LINDSEY		
Barnet N	Jeff	172
Cath	Hock	158
Elizabeth	Cler	050
John	Brow	032
John M	Knox	176
Maria	Hami	131
Samuel	Mont	252
Thomas J	Faye	095
LINDSLEY		
Dryden	Cuya	073
LINDUFF		
Isaac	Jeff	172
LINE		
Rebecca J	Loga	192
LINES		
Hannah	Fair	089
Ira	Lick	184
LINEWEAVER		
Cath	Knox	174
LING		
Mary A	Holm	161
LINGGEN		
Christian B F		
	Miam	219
LINGO		
Frederick	Hami	128
LINGRELL		
Thomas	Ross	300
LINHART		
John M	Sene	311
LINK		
Eli	Mont	236
Shepley H	Wyan	366
LINKHART		
John	VanW	339
LINKS		
Dorothea	Cuya	075
LINN		
Addis A	Wayn	352
Andrew F	Guer	117
Cornelius W	Rich	294
David	Star	317
Irwin D	Fair	090
Mathew	Musk	263
William H	Fran	099

LINNABURG		
Sally	Paul	273
LINNELL		
Hannah	Lick	184
LINSCOTT		
Thomas B	Athe	020
LINSLEY		
Lucius O	Trum	326
LINTHARDT		
Louise	Luca	200
LINTON		
Geo	Jeff	171
Otho	Jeff	170
Sophia	Monr	224
LINTZ		
Willoughby	Mont	248
LINVILLE		
Howard	Cham	043
LINZEE		
Abigail V	Augl	025
LIPPENCOTT		
Geo H	Preb	287
LIPPERT		
Carie	Hami	130
Emilie	Hami	121
LIPPINCOTT		
Anna	Cham	042
LIPPOLT		
Christiana	High	156
LISBY		
John	Loga	191
Lucinda	Jeff	170
LISLE		
James	Lick	188
John M	Ross	298
LIST		
Cath	Brow	031
LISTEN		
Ann M	Unio	333
LISTER		
Benj	Star	317
Elijah	Unio	335
Samuel	Star	317
LISTMAN		
Andrew	Wood	361
LITEHISER		
Joseph T	Preb	286
LITHERBURY		
John W	Hami	136
LITTEN		
John Jr	Jeff	172
Noah	Monr	226

LITTICK			**LOBAN**		
Phebe	Dela	083	Bridgett	Cuya	074
LITTLE			**LOCHMAN**		
Aaron W	Otta	272	Gustav	Mont	240
Christina	Mari	208	**LOCHRER**		
David B	Guer	117	Rosina	Tusc	332
Geo W	Musk	267	**LOCKARD**		
Geo W	Rich	291	Samuel J	Belm	030
Hezekiah	Clin	054	Sarah A	Jack	167
James	Adam	005	Thomas	Musk	263
Martin V B	Fran	099	**LOCKE**		
Nancy	Colu	056	Chas E	Lora	195
Richard B	Lawr	182	Nathaniel	Luca	198
Susan	Unio	334	**LOCKHART**		
Thomas	Musk	267	Hannah	Clar	044
William	Belm	027	**LOCKWOOD**		
LITTLEJOHN			Addie C	Cham	042
George W	Shel	315	Alvin	Asht	016
LITTLEPAGE			Anthony T	Belm	027
William H	Mont	244	Eliakim E	Knox	176
LITTLER			Emily D	Cuya	068
Archibald	Clar	044	Ira L	Knox	173
LITTLETON			Lucinda	Sand	302
Isaac	Monr	224	Reuben	Defi	080
LITZENBERG			Sarah R	Otta	271
Elizabeth	Lick	188	Stanley B	Lake	178
George	Knox	173	**LODGE**		
LITZINGER			Dan	Jeff	171
Geo O	Star	317	**LODWICK**		
LIVENGOOD			Jonathan	Trum	327
Ellen	Mont	232	**LOEBLIN**		
LIVENSPARGER			Magdalena	Cuya	068
John C	Will	357	**LOESCHER**		
Louis	Sene	309	William	Mont	233
LIVENSPIRE			**LOFTUS**		
Chas E	Wyan	365	Michael	Mont	252
LIVESAY			**LOGAN**		
Eliza	Gall	108	Eliza	Mont	232
LIVINGSTON			Elizabeth	Augl	025
Albert	Harr	151	Elizabeth	Miam	222
Andrew	Clar	045	Elizabeth	Musk	264
James	Fult	106	James	Mont	250
James	Mont	239	James	Sand	303
John	Hami	139	Joseph	Musk	266
Susannah	Wayn	354	Mary V	Faye	094
LLOYD			Rachel	Morg	258
John	Cosh	061	Samuel M	Mont	229
Lydia L	Gree	116	**LOGHT**		
Nathaniel	Mont	236	David	Wyan	365
William	Hard	144	**LOGSDON**		
LOAR			Frank	Knox	174
Elizabeth	Lick	187	**LOGUE**		
George	Lick	187	Edward	Mont	240

LOHR			**LONGLEY**			
Jacob	Rich	295	Cyrenius	Hami	128
LOMAN			**LONGLY**			
Jeremiah	Wood	358	Samuel I	Sene	312
LONDON			**LONGMAN**			
Eva	High	154	Joseph	Butl	038
James	Mont	250	**LONGSDORF**			
LONG			Frederick	Rich	293
Adam	Miam	219	**LONGSHORE**			
Alfred O	Ashl	011	Jemima	Tusc	330
Benj	Meig	214	**LONGSTRETH**			
Cath	Hanc	142	Elizabeth S	Perr	277
Chas W	Lora	195	**LONGSWORTH**			
Daniel	Luca	197	Elizabeth	Tusc	330
Daniel	Tusc	330	**LONGWELL**			
David B	Belm	027	Asbury	Craw	064
Davidson	Will	355	Elizabeth	Dela	084
Eliza	Colu	055	**LONON**			
Elizabeth	Wood	362	Daniel	Belm	031
Francis	Cuya	075	**LOOKER**			
Francis	Knox	174	Ellen	Lick	188
Frank	Paul	273	James R	Lick	185
George	Hanc	142	Moab	Fair	091
George W	Putn	289	**LOOMIS**			
Henry	Clin	052	Ann E	Lake	178
Henry J	Brow	033	Eunice A	Medi	212
Henry L	Wood	359	Robert	Medi	210
Hiram	Merc	217	Russel	Lora	194
Hugh	Wyan	365	Russell J	Hock	157
Isaiah C	Lick	186	Sally	Trum	328
Jacob A	Carr	040	Warren	Asht	019
James	Guer	120	**LOOP**			
James	Wood	359	Elizabeth	Preb	286
James N P	Rich	292	Philip G	Luca	196
John	Fran	099	**LOOTS**			
John A	Geau	112	John	Preb	286
Joseph S	Alle	008	**LOPER**			
Lewis	Trum	325	William J V	Scio	307
Margaret	Belm	027	**LOPPIN**			
Matilda	Sand	303	Elizabeth	Summ	323
Philip	Fran	099	**LORAH**			
Rebecca	Hami	131	Charlotte	Defi	081
Susannah	Wash	345	**LORAINE**			
William	Cuya	073	Jno	Dark	079
LONGABAUGH			**LORANZ**			
Elijah C	Hard	144	Maria Josephine			
LONGANDAFFER				Sene	313
Frank	Craw	063	**LORB**			
LONGFELLOW			Sigmond	Star	319
Carolina	Butl	036	**LORD**			
Cath	Wash	348	Alexander R	Sand	301
LONGHBOTTOM			**LORE**			
John H	Maho	206	John B	Athe	022

LORENZ			LOUGHREY (cont)		
Henry	Hami	128	Thomas B	Cuya	074
Philopena	Cuya	069	LOUIS		
LORETT			Lorenzo T	Luca	198
Joshua	Loga	191	Rachel	Athe	024
LORIE			LOUISCOTT		
John	Monr	223	Jeremiah	Gree	116
LORO			LOUISO		
Geo	VanW	338	Herbert	Hard	146
LOROW			LOUKS		
Franklin	Rich	292	William A	Gall	111
LORTON			LOURY		
Melissa	Clar	045	Hugh	Trum	325
LOSEY			Joseph C	VanW	338
Daniel	Geau	111	LOUSLYN		
Harris P	Geau	111	Sarah	Perr	277
Thomas	Lawr	182	LOUTHAN		
William F	Cuya	073	William M	Miam	221
LOSH			LOVE		
Rebecca	Cham	042	Esther	Colu	059
Sarah A	Loga	191	John	Tusc	333
LOTT			Oliver E	Huro	165
Joseph	Dela	084	Peter	Athe	020
Martha	Ross	301	LOVEGROVE		
LOTTRIDGE			Obadiah	Fran	099
Geo W	Meig	213	LOVEJOY		
Melissa F	Morr	259	Frances A	Asht	014
LOTZ			Mary A	Adam	007
Nancy	Merc	217	Perry G	Belm	028
LOUB			Simeon	Will	357
Daniel	Hanc	141	LOVELAND		
LOUCHER			Edwin R	Trum	327
Elizabeth	Pike	282	Elizabeth	Scio	306
LOUCKS			Lafayette	Morr	260
Martin S	Wood	361	LOVELESS		
LOUDENBACK			Huldah	Trum	327
Eve	Cham	042	James	Trum	328
Mary	Cham	042	LOVELL		
LOUDENSLAGER			Anna	Wood	361
Eliza	Fran	097	LOVERING		
LOUDER			William H	Hanc	141
Geo W	Adam	004	LOVETT		
LOUDERBACK			Benj F	Port	286
Andrew J	Athe	023	Dennis	Luca	198
Imri	Brow	031	Elizabeth A	Gree	113
LOUDERMILCH			Nelson C	Nobl	269
William J	Wyan	366	LOVEWELL		
LOUGH			John	Asht	017
William H	Mont	228	LOW		
LOUGHMAN			George W	Holm	160
Elizabeth	Lick	188	John A	Jack	167
LOUGHREY			LOWE		
Elizabeth K	Scio	305	David G	Mont	242

LOWE (cont)			LUCAS (cont)		
Henson	Nobl	268	Alice	Asht	017
Isaac	Monr	224	Bazil V	Gree	115
James	Hard	148	Cath	Augl	026
Lizzie	Hami	130	Cath	Jack	166
Manerva	Holm	160	Cath	Luca	202
Manora F	Mont	230	Chas R	Perr	275
Orr	Jeff	172	Geo W	Will	357
Thomas D	Adam	003	Henry	Mont	227
Thomas H	Mont	247	Ira	Erie	085
LOWELL			Isaac	Pick	278
John	Vint	342	John M	Monr	225
LOWER			Lavina	Musk	265
Mary	Lora	192	Margaret	Wayn	352
LOWERY			Mary A	Mont	256
Albert A	VanW	338	Mary E	Musk	265
Cath	Fran	097	Napolean B	Preb	287
David	Meig	212	Orita	Brow	031
Geo	Adam	005	Rebecca	Adam	006
Geo W	Henr	151	LUCE		
William	Miam	223	Charles	Asht	015
LOWMAN			Jesse B	Trum	328
Charles E	Cuya	074	Joseph	Warr	343
LOWN			Joseph H	Luca	197
Jacob	Lick	184	Laura A	Asht	018
LOWREY			LUCK		
Geo H	Cuya	075	Chas	Cuya	073
Rosannah	Asht	018	LUCKERT		
Susannah	Erie	085	Christian	Hami	128
LOWRY			LUCKEY		
Alex	Colu	058	Martha	Otta	271
Angeline	Guer	120	LUDER		
Nancy	Faye	095	Jacob	Cuya	073
Richard H	Ross	298	LUDINGTON		
Samuel R	Athe	023	Delilah	Clin	055
Thomas	Athe	023	LUDLOW		
Washington	Ross	298	Edmond	Huro	165
William	Mont	237	LUDLUM		
LOWTHER			James	Warr	344
William M	Monr	224	LUDWICK		
LOY			Charles	Mont	244
Jacob	Mont	256	Christine	Athe	024
John C	Wood	360	Milla	High	156
Martin P	Clar	045	Solomon	High	156
Samuel N	Brow	031	LUDWIG		
LOYNES			Edward	Cuya	072
Chas C	Cuya	076	Eliza A	Sene	313
LOZINIA			Fredericka	Hami	131
Thompson	Shel	316	Henry H	Hanc	140
LUBAR			John	Wayn	352
John	Paul	272	Mary	High	156
LUCAS			Peter	Huro	165
Abigail	Wash	346			

LUDWIGSECK			LUSK		
Arthur	Cuya	074	David	Wood	362
LUEBKE			LUSTER		
Henry	Hami	128	Geo	Cuya	074
LUELLEN			LUTE		
Samuel	Meig	216	Henry	Ashl	012
LUETHY			LUTES		
Ulrich	Butl	038	Mary	Belm	030
LUGENBEAL			LUTGEN		
David	Musk	263	Alvenia	Morg	259
LUGENBEEL			LUTHER		
William A	Ross	300	Elizabeth	Lick	187
LUGENBUCHL			Hathaway	Perr	277
William	Mont	240	Perry	Hard	148
LUKAS			LUTKENHAUS		
Margaretha	Hami	121	Herman	Mont	234
LUKE			LUTTON		
Cath	Belm	029	Morgan	Hami	129
Margaret	Monr	226	LUTZ		
Parmelia	Nobl	268	Byron	Ross	301
Sarah A	Will	356	Frederick	Hami	137
William	Luca	198	George	Mont	233
LUKEMIRE			John	Cler	050
Peter	Cler	050	Lucinda	Dark	077
LUKENS			Nancy	Dark	078
Alfred	Fran	102	Samuel	Pick	280
Eli B	Monr	224	Sophia	Ross	296
Thomas	Hami	128	William	Port	284
LUKINGBEAL			LYBARGER		
Samuel	Mont	232	Edwin L	Cosh	061
LUMAN			Jacob	Knox	174
David	Sene	310	Jasper R	Summ	323
LUMBAR			LYBOLD		
Francis A	Sene	312	Andrew	VanW	338
LUMBARTUS			LYBROOK		
Geo	Monr	226	Henry	Scio	306
LUNCEFORD			LYCURGUS		
Hannah	Lawr	183	Henry	Warr	343
LUNDIS			LYDIA		
William	Mont	236	Switzer	Ashl	013
LUNDRY			(possibly Lydia Switzer)		
Levi	Dark	079	LYDICK		
LUNGARSHAUSEN			John B	Guer	120
Aug	Mont	238	Samuel B	Fran	099
LUPTEN			LYLE		
Israel	Perr	275	Emily E	Vint	341
LUPTON			John	Jeff	171
Elizabeth	Dela	083	Robert	Sene	313
Henry R	Guer	118	LYMAN		
LUSE			Betsey	Asht	018
Algernon	Meig	214	Carlos P	Trum	327
LUSH			Caroline	Alle	009
James H	Wood	362	Frank E	Cuya	065

LYMAN (cont)		
Geo	Medi	212
LYNCH		
Anthony	Mont	244
Cath	Brow	034
Cath	Mont	230
Emily	Cosh	062
Frank	Cuya	073
John J	Gree	113
Larry	Rich	295
Mary	High	154
Michael	Mont	252
Michael J	Mont	241
Patrick	Otta	271
LYNDES		
Anson	Lora	193
LYNE		
James W	Nobl	269
LYNN		
Henrietta	Scio	305
Maria S	Asht	014
Peter	Mont	236
Rebecca	Preb	287
LYON		
Almira B	Hami	124
David	Clin	053
Elizabeth	Warr	343
Emily A	Gree	115
Erwin E	Lora	195
Hannah	Hami	131
John	Lora	193
John H	Summ	323
Nancy	Jeff	172
Sarah J	Hami	130
Susan	Summ	323
William C	Lick	187
LYONS		
Amanda E	Ross	297
David M	Hami	128
Eliza	Athe	023
Elizabeth	High	154
Mathew S	Pike	281
Phebe	Clar	045
Robert	Mont	229
Samuel	Luca	198
Sarah L	Nobl	269
Thomas	Hami	121
William	Will	355
LYTLE		
Hannah	Faye	094
William	Sene	310
LYTTLE		
Geo	Fran	104

LYTTON		
Jas	Meig	214
LYYBARGER		
Porter	Craw	062
McADAMS		
Elizabeth A	Cler	051
Isaac N	Cler	051
McADOW		
Thomas J	Unio	334
McAFEE		
William	Faye	095
McALLISTER		
Gus L H	Faye	093
Isaac	Hock	158
Lany A	Unio	335
Richard	Clin	052
McAMANEY		
Eliza	Wayn	354
McANDREW		
John	Mont	236
McARTEE		
William A	Ashl	013
McARTHUR		
Byron	Hock	158
Kate C	Lick	185
McATAMNY		
Henry	Athe	021
McATEE		
Alfred M	Hard	148
Anna	Loga	192
McAULEY		
Bridget	Erie	086
Hannah	Scio	304
McAVERNLY		
Cath	Luca	200
McBAIN		
John	Carr	040
McBANE		
Philip	Jeff	169
McBARROW		
Henry H	Alle	010
McBETH		
Demaris	Loga	189
McBRIDE		
Alexander	Mont	239
Alexander B	Scio	306
Cath	Holm	160
Elizabeth	Luca	200
Frank	Mont	229
James	Harr	150
James E	Luca	199

McBRIDE (cont)			McCANN		
James N	Geau	111	James	Mont	235
Joseph	Meig	214	John	Mont	248
Louisa	Craw	062	Rachel	Hard	145
Maria L	Gree	116	Sarah	Colu	056
Mary J	Musk	263	Sarah	Morg	257
Rhoda	Asht	018	Sylvester	Hard	145
Richard	Gree	115	Thomas	Ross	298
William H	Cuya	065	William	Jeff	170
McBROOM			McCANNA		
Emily E	Hock	159	Hugh	Cuya	072
McBROON			McCANNON		
Robert	Hock	157	John A	Colu	056
McCABE			McCARLEY		
Henry	Mont	252	Hiram S	Gall	109
Jno	Perr	276	McCARON		
Patrick	Mont	243	Walter O	Luca	199
William	Cuya	072	McCARRAN		
McCAFFERTY			Mary A	Cuya	068
Edward	Mont	245	McCARREN		
McCAFFERY			Henrietta	Brow	032
Manus	Maho	207	McCARRON		
McCAFFREY			Frederick	Rich	296
William S	Lawr	179	McCARTEN		
McCAGER			Mary	Butl	036
Clater	Pike	282	McCARTER		
McCAIN			James	Mont	252
Mary J	Alle	009	McCARTHY		
Sarah	Monr	223	John	Cuya	072
Susannah	Gree	116	Patrick	Mont	235
McCALL			McCARTNEY		
Andrew B	Scio	308	John P	Holm	161
Charles	Mont	242	Joseph	Jack	167
Nancy	Wash	345	McCARTY		
Solomon	Mont	249	Ann S	Hami	137
McCALLA			David	Adam	007
Elias	Paul	273	Elizabeth	Meig	213
Simon	Defi	081	James	Fran	102
McCALLISTER			Jno	Mont	254
Nancy	Ross	297	Joseph	Warr	342
McCALLUM			Josiah	Hami	128
John	Mont	254	Lydia	Gall	109
John F	Maho	207	Mary	Carr	040
McCALMONT			Mary A	Brow	034
Robert	Trum	325	Nathan	Ross	301
McCAMMANT			Oiver C	Ashl	013
Marjary E	Knox	172	Oren L	Trum	328
Rebecca	Knox	172	Peter	Lawr	179
McCANDLESS			Samuel R	Gall	108
Ellen E	Faye	094	William B	Wood	359
Jane	Adam	006	William W	Fran	099
Sarah E	Scio	308	McCASHEN		
William H	Adam	006	Elizabeth	Warr	342

McCAULEY		
Ann	Sene	313
Cyrus T	Colu	057
John W	Colu	055
William	Star	317
McCAULLA		
Oristis A	Madi	204
McCAUSLAND		
Cath	Cosh	060
John	Morr	260
McCAVE		
Peter	Maho	205
McCHELLAW		
Geo W	Dark	078
McCHESNEY		
Robert	Adam	005
McCLAFLIN		
Edwin M	Huro	165
McCLAIN		
Cath	Pike	281
David	Colu	058
Eli P	Gall	108
Mary J	Perr	274
Rebecca	Wyan	366
McCLAMMER		
Nancy	Preb	288
(alias Nancy McClamrock)		
McCLAMROCK		
Nancy	Preb	288
(alias Nancy McClammer)		
McCLANAHAN		
James	Adam	004
McCLARAN		
Thomas M	Lora	196
McCLARREN		
William	Fult	107
McCLARY		
Mary L	Putn	288
McCLAY		
Henry	Ashl	012
William	Rich	291
McCLEAD		
Elias	Wash	350
McCLEARY		
Andrew	Butl	036
McCLELIN		
John P	Mont	254
McCLELLAN		
Luther A	High	157
Lydia	Brow	032
William	Mont	254
William R	Cham	043
McCLELLAND		
David	Lick	188
Drusilla	Medi	210
Geo T	Butl	035
Rachel	Holm	161
Samuel	Hock	159
Thomas	Belm	028
William	High	153
McCLINTICK		
Elizabeth	Fran	102
John O	Clar	045
Marietta	Clar	044
McCLINTOCK		
Eliza J	Carr	039
Milo A	Cuya	065
McCLOSKEY		
Chas	Jeff	172
James	Mont	241
Patrick F	Colu	056
McCLOSKY		
Elizabeth	Gall	110
McCLOUD		
Elias	Hard	147
James M	Madi	204
McCLOY		
David E	Perr	277
Harrison	Lora	193
McCLUNG		
Elizabeth	Preb	287
Jane	Fair	092
John	Adam	005
Mary	Warr	344
Mary J	Shel	316
McCLURE		
Anna S	VanW	339
Eliza	Alle	009
James	Cosh	060
James	Will	355
James F	Shel	315
Jno	Meig	215
Lavina	Wash	345
Moses	Alle	009
Robert	Rich	293
Samuel	Hami	139
Sarah	Henr	152
Thomas W	VanW	339
William H	Wayn	354
McCLURG		
Sarah E	Hard	145
McCLUSKY		
Wilson	Maho	205
McCOLLEY		
John	Wood	363

McCOLLEY (cont)			McCONNELL (cont)		
Josephus C	Rich	293	Eliza	Clin	054
McCOLLISTER			Eliza	Fran	096
Jonathan	VanW	338	Ellen	Belm	027
McCOLLOCH			James B	Hard	147
Ruth	Athe	024	John	Trum	329
McCOLLOCK			Jonathan	VanW	336
George	Loga	190	Sarah	Miam	219
McCOLLOUGH			Thomas	Knox	173
Eliza	Will	357	McCONNER		
Isaac	Rich	291	Ann	Lora	195
McCOLLUM			McCONONEY		
Isaac	Monr	226	Margaret	Wood	359
Miller	Guer	120	McCONOUGHEY		
Nancy	Cler	051	Elizabeth	Jeff	169
William	Mont	236	McCONOUGHY		
McCOMAS			Dolly	Cuya	076
Love P	Morg	258	McCOOL		
McCOMBS			Agnes J	Dark	078
Hester	Wood	363	McCORD		
Samuel T	Guer	119	Elias Ogden	Clar	045
McCOMMON			Thomas J	Pike	281
William	Ross	298	McCORKHILL		
William H	Star	317	Geo	Ross	301
McCONAHA			McCORKLE		
Edward	Guer	117	Susan	Pike	281
McCONAHY			McCORMACK		
Jos	Wyan	364	William H	Madi	202
McCONAUGHEY			McCORMICK		
Duncan	Guer	118	Allen R	Harr	149
McCONAUGHKEY			And W	Hami	126
Pat	Jeff	170	Charlotte	Wayn	352
McCONAUGHLEY			George	Guer	117
Alex	Musk	265	Henry	Wyan	366
McCONAUGHY			Isaiah H	Jack	168
Henry C	Belm	030	James	Mont	236
McCONG			James C	Colu	056
Robert James	Guer	118	James H	Gall	109
McCONKEY			John	Erie	086
Andrew P	Defi	081	Margaret	Cuya	068
McCONNAHA			Margaret	Rich	294
Delia	Star	318	Mary	Belm	028
McCONNAUGHEY			Mary A	Cuya	068
Diana	Miam	218	Nancy	Butl	036
McCONNAUGHY			Timothy	Mont	254
Moses	Maho	207	McCOST		
McCONNEL			Edward	Perr	277
Hugh	Hanc	140	McCOURT		
Joseph II	Wood	360	Mary	Cuya	068
Miller	Luca	202	McCOURTNEY		
McCONNELL			Francis	Hami	138
Alex F	Loga	189	McCOWAN		
Cyrus	Ashl	011	Isaac S	Wash	350

McCOWEN		
Nancy J	Dark	077
McCOY		
Aaron	Colu	058
Alex R	VanW	339
Alfred	Fran	102
Charles	Mont	236
Daniel W	High	156
Elizabeth A	Adam	004
Elizabeth A	Scio	308
Henry W	Guer	120
Hugh	Colu	058
Jacob L	Augl	025
James	Rich	294
Joseph H	Mont	249
Maria	Ross	296
Mary	Hami	124
Milton	Ross	300
Nancy	Butl	036
Patience	Jeff	172
Sarah E	Cuya	068
Susan	Guer	117
Susan	Pike	282
William	Medi	211
William H	Harr	149
McCRACKEN		
Jas E	Cuya	072
John L	Sene	311
William W	Morr	260
McCRAIT		
John	Putn	289
McCRAMNON		
Robert	Monr	226
McCRATE		
Joseph	Putn	289
McCRAY		
Job	Mont	227
John	Carr	039
John	Mont	233
McCREADY		
Margaret	Harr	148
Samuel J	Huro	163
Harrison L	Asht	018
McCREARY		
Matilda	Knox	175
Somelia	Unio	335
McCREERY		
William	Sand	304
McCROBY		
John W H	Fran	099
McCRORY		
Jesse	Wood	362
McCROSSIN		
Thomas	Mont	249
McCRUM		
Elizabeth	Lick	186
Samuel	Belm	030
McCUE		
James	Star	319
McCULIA		
Nancy J	Fran	103
McCULLOCH		
Barney F	Loga	191
McCULLOCK		
William S	Athe	021
McCULLOUGH		
Anna	Mont	230
David N	Jeff	171
Harvey	Craw	064
John R	Colu	058
McCULLY		
Virginia	Athe	022
McCUNE		
Alexander	Mont	248
Hannah	Guer	117
James	Holm	160
John	Guer	119
Washington	Cosh	061
McCURDY		
Elizabeth P	Wash	347
Ellen	Paul	272
Jas N	Craw	062
John T	Mont	244
Lucius	Wash	346
Rachel	Clin	052
McCUTCHAN		
William	Mont	254
McCUTCHEN		
Abraham F	Star	317
John	Fran	099
William	Craw	062
McDANIEL		
Andrew	Perr	277
Daniel	Lawr	179
Daniel	Lawr	181
Eliza	Scio	305
Fanny B	Merc	217
James H	Sene	313
James M	Clin	054
John E	Gall	107
Joseph	Brow	032
Sally	Gall	107
Wester A	Fran	097
(alias Wester A Barnes)		
William	Gall	110

McDANIEL (cont)		
William R	Jack	167
McDANIELD		
John W	Lick	188
McDANIELS		
Jacob	Fair	089
Jas Tiss	Asht	018
McDAVITT		
Lydia	Jeff	170
McDERMET		
David	Scio	305
McDERMOTT		
Francis	Mont	255
John	Mont	254
Lawrence	Fran	099
Milly	Adam	004
McDEVITT		
Thomas	Harr	150
McDEWITT		
Austin	Colu	057
McDIVITT		
Samuel S	Unio	334
McDONAL		
Austin	Maho	206
McDONALD		
Andrew C	Mont	255
Angus	Wash	345
Ann E	Star	320
Basiel	Mont	255
Chas	VanW	339
Elias	Perr	276
Elphonzo	Clin	053
Eve	Maho	207
Granville F	Clin	052
Harriet	Nobl	270
Isaac	Guer	118
James	Mont	240
James	Mont	252
James F	Nobl	268
James S	Perr	276
Johanna	Hami	124
John	Wash	345
John J	Jeff	171
John V	Athe	021
Leander	Miam	222
Lottridge	Clar	045
Margaret	Hock	158
Maria	Warr	343
Michael	Belm	027
Owens	Cuya	066
Patrick	Cuya	072
Peter	Jack	166
Philip	Fair	089

McDONALD (cont)		
Rachel	Medi	211
Rebecca	Cham	042
Samuel	Fran	099
William	Fran	099
William	Knox	175
William	Mont	246
McDONELL		
Hugh	Ross	298
McDONIEL		
Elizabeth	Scio	305
McDONNAL		
Jane E	Star	316
McDONNEL		
Jane	Preb	287
McDONNELL		
Daniel	Madi	204
McDONOUGH		
Ferd	Hami	126
Jno	Mont	254
Mary E	Cler	050
Thomas	Mont	255
McDOWELL		
Austin	Gree	115
Edward	Belm	028
Gustavess A	Madi	203
Isabell	Warr	343
James	Mont	249
William F	Scio	307
William T	Fran	096
McDULIN		
Charles	Cler	050
McELDERRY		
Margaret	Unio	333
McELFRESH		
William A	Monr	226
McELHANEY		
Samuel O	Gall	109
McELRAVY		
Thomas C	Harr	149
McELROY		
Charles H	Dela	082
Elmira	Sand	302
James	Brow	033
Samuel	Lora	196
Thomas D	Hard	144
William	Wayn	353
McELVAINE		
Robert G	VanW	337
McELWAIN		
Edwin W	Geau	113
Emily	Mont	230

McEWEN			McGAHEY		
Daniel	Cuya	073	James P	Rich	294
William S	Fran	099	McGANN		
McEWING			Michael	Mont	240
Thomas C	Wood	360	McGARRAN		
McFADDEN			Eli T	Colu	055
Albert	Harr	149	McGATH		
Alexander	Mont	255	Samuel W	Pick	280
Alice	Vint	340	McGAUGHEY		
Daniel	Maho	207	Thomas	Gree	116
Geo W	Clin	053	McGEE		
James C	Lawr	181	Ellen	Cuya	073
Martha	Hock	159	Henrietta	Wash	350
Mary J	Will	357	Henry	Mont	244
Rachel	Wayn	352	James H	Lawr	182
Silas	Unio	334	Morris	Putn	288
Taylor	Carr	040	Patrick	Musk	265
McFALL			Pressley	Warr	342
Andrew J	Miam	221	Thirza E	Unio	335
Anna	Asht	017	William	Wash	348
Geo W	Wood	361	William E	Athe	022
Malcom	Maho	207	McGHEE		
Simon P	Trum	328	Rebecca	Gall	111
McFARLAND			McGILL		
Abram P	Belm	028	James H	Fran	099
Allen	Hami	128	James W	Geau	112
Allen	Rich	293	Mary	Clar	045
Andrew J	Alle	010	Mary	Paul	274
Christina J	Wash	345	Stewart	Hami	138
Eliza	Hard	146	McGILLIVANY		
Elizabeth	Maho	205	Eliza	Colu	056
Geo	Belm	031	McGIN		
James	Jeff	171	Mary	Adam	003
Jane	Belm	030	McGINLEY		
Jane	Jeff	171	Samuel E	Hanc	142
John J	Vint	341	McGINN		
Joseph	Adam	006	Barney	Mont	245
Joseph W	Cler	050	McGINNIS		
Julia	Fair	089	Cath	Unio	335
Mathew	Cuya	072	Cerilla	Belm	030
Robert	Scio	306	Elizabeth	Ross	300
Robert C	Rich	294	Frances	Clar	046
Samuel R W	Wash	345	James F	Loga	189
Sarah M	Guer	119	John B	VanW	339
William	Guer	118	John R	Nobl	270
William	Mont	233	Michael	Hard	147
William H	Cuya	072	Sarah A	Gree	116
McFARLIN			Thomas B	Jack	166
Elizabeth	Maho	207	McGINNISS		
McFARLING			William S	Hock	159
Robert	Lick	188	McGINTY		
McFEE			James	Gree	114
John	Nobl	268			

McGIRR		
Alexander C	Wash	348
McGIVEN		
Lawrence	Mont	238
McGLADE		
Geo A	Musk	262
McGLAUGHLIN		
Jacob	Clar	047
McGLOUE		
Hiram W	Henr	153
McGLOYD		
Phebe	Luca	199
McGOHAN		
Elijah	Brow	033
McGONAGLE		
Hugh	Perr	276
McGOVERN		
Ellen	Musk	265
Peter	Mont	229
McGOWAN		
Alex	Fair	090
Ann	Ross	298
Sarah	Geau	112
McGOWN		
Clarissa	Cham	042
McGRANE		
Henry J	Mont	239
McGRATH		
Alpheus	Athe	022
Henry W	Gall	109
Hiram	Morg	258
James	Fran	099
John	Cuya	072
Mary	Cuya	073
Thomas	Wash	348
McGRAW		
John	Huro	162
McGRAY		
Bridget	Jeff	171
McGREARY		
Michael	Mont	254
McGREEN		
Edward	Hami	128
McGREGOR		
George M	Hard	144
James P	Star	316
Mary Ann	Port	283
McGREW		
Oliver	Belm	030
McGROARTY		
Cath	Hami	124
Mary	Hami	138

McGUCKIN		
David	Huro	162
McGUIRE		
Clinton S	Holm	161
Cornelius	Rich	293
Edward	Mont	248
George	Guer	118
Mary	Ashl	012
Michael	Cuya	066
Michael A	Hami	126
Middleton	Lawr	182
Patrick	Maho	207
Rebecca E	Cler	050
Thomas	Jack	169
William	Cler	050
William L	Hami	128
William W	Alle	009
McGUNNIGLE		
Charles	Hami	126
McHARMON		
John	Rich	293
McHENRY		
Henry	Henr	152
Joseph	Mont	254
McILREE		
Jas	Butl	036
McILVAIN		
Francis	Fran	099
John Q	Rich	293
Ruth	Rich	294
William H	Hard	147
McINTIRE		
Darius	Unio	334
Jefferson H	Athe	023
Lovisa W	Dela	082
Stephen S	Jeff	169
McINTOSH		
George L	Lake	178
Robert	VanW	339
Susan	Port	285
McINTURF		
Eli	Morg	257
McINTYRE		
Rosalthe	Fult	106
McIRION		
Sarah A	Faye	094
McJUNKIN		
Mary	Scio	308
McKABE		
Ann	Cuya	073
McKAIN		
Elvira O	Meig	215

McKASSON			McKENZIE			
Martin	Butl	038	Charles C	Hami	128
McKAY			Duncan	Mont	255
Florentine	Asht	018	Eliza	Pick	279
Geo A	Cuya	072	John	Brow	032
Hugh B	Dela	084	Joseph C	Knox	175
John W	Dark	078	Joseph L	Holm	160
Rosetta L	Cuya	068	Laughlin	Colu	058
McKEAG			Louis	Mont	254
Hannah	Hami	135	Mary C	Meig	213
McKEAN			Robert Z	Wood	359
Aseneth	Gall	108	McKEON		
John	Gall	108	Michael	Mont	255
McKEE			McKERNAN		
Alfred	Jack	168	William	Fran	099
Andrew B	Cler	049	McKESSON		
Chas W	Ross	299	Lester V	Huro	162
Charles W	Shel	315	McKEVITT		
Francis J	Holm	160	Chas A	Hami	137
Francis M	Clin	054	McKIBBAN		
Georgia	Lora	196	Chockley	Dela	085
Jas	Jeff	172	McKIBBEN		
John	Preb	287	James W	Cler	051
John W	Colu	056	Rachel	Henr	153
Joseph	Adam	006	Samuel	Putn	290
Joseph N	Lawr	183	William	Fult	107
Milan	Knox	173	William H	Morg	257
Rebecca	Dark	078	McKIBBINS		
Samuel	Lawr	183	Jesse M	Morg	259
Sarah	Dark	078	McKIBBON		
Sarah J	Butl	036	Mary	Athe	023
Thomas J	Shel	316	McKIESSON		
Thomas J	Trum	326	Geo F	Belm	030
William	Henr	152	McKIM		
McKEEVER			Eliza	Colu	057
John W	High	154	Isabella	Belm	030
Reuben B	Ross	296	Margaret	Maho	206
Susannah	Unio	334	McKINLEY		
McKELLY			Baylis V	Meig	215
Electa	Huro	165	David S	Belm	028
McKELOY			Eliza	Sand	302
Mary A	Colu	056	Jesse L	Brow	031
McKELVEY			Mary	Miam	218
Nancy	Belm	029	Matilda	Augl	025
McKENDRY			Nancy	Jeff	171
Albert	Nobl	268	William	Trum	326
McKENLEY			Zelotes	Will	356
Amelia	Musk	264	McKINNEL		
McKENNA			Walter S	Cler	051
Maria	Wash	347	McKINNEY		
Patrick	Fult	105	Joseph	Musk	264
McKENNEY			Theodore T	Harr	149
Rebecca A	Musk	262	William	Fran	102

McKINNIE			McLAUGHLIN (cont)		
David K	Trum	327	Isaac	Hard	147
Hannah	Maho	207	Jos	Colu	059
McKINNIS			Lawrence	Brow	032
William	Hanc	141	Levi	Nobl	268
McKINO			Marcy	Hami	135
Robert	Huro	162	Samuel	Nobl	268
McKINSTRY			Sarah	Fair	089
Casanda	Athe	022	Thomas	Hami	128
McKINZIE			Thomas	Merc	218
Julia	Ross	297	McLEAN		
McKIRAHAN			Edwin F	Cuya	072
John R	Belm	029	Jos C	Ross	300
McKISSON			McLEFRESH		
James B	Perr	275	Joseph	Cler	048
Jane	Belm	028	McLEISH		
McKITRICK			John	Cuya	072
David F	Unio	334	McLELLAN		
Jas	Wash	346	Mercy	Pike	281
John W	Wash	346	McLEOD		
Mahlon L	Wash	346	Donald N	Butl	039
Robert	Ross	299	William	Mont	254
McKITUCK			McLIN		
Abram	Belm	031	Victor	Mont	240
McKNIGHT			McMAHAN		
Adaline	Warr	343	John H	Wood	361
Benj F	Wash	351	Mary J	Wash	345
Hayden	Meig	213	McMAHON		
Samaria	Meig	213	Ellen	Wood	361
Thomas	Belm	029	Henry	Augl	026
McKONKEY			Jas	Cuya	072
Cath	Belm	028	John W	Cler	048
Nancy B	Guer	120	Margaret	Faye	093
McKUNE			Mathew	Preb	287
David	Loga	191	Melissa V	Fult	105
McLAIN			Michael	Mont	242
Anna	Preb	286	William	Mont	241
Charles	Ashl	011	McMAINS		
Edward	Cuya	072	James J	Athe	024
Eli N	Will	355	McMANIGEHL		
Flora	Trum	327	Lavina	Lawr	180
James	Loga	189	McMANIS		
Peter	Madi	203	Greenleaf N	Adam	003
McLANE			McMANN		
John	Vint	341	John	Pick	278
McLAREN			McMANNIS		
Susan	Musk	262	Elmer	Wayn	352
McLAUGHLIN			McMANUS		
Alex	Craw	062	Cath	Preb	288
Ann	Perr	278	Harriet	Ross	301
Elijah	Hami	139	Jas	Cuya	066
Harriet	Rich	294	Mary	Brow	033
Henry J	VanW	338	Owen	Mont	255

McMARRAH			McNAGHTIN			
Cath	Faye	093	James	Fair	091
McMARRELL			McNAIR			
John	Wayn	353	Archibald	Cler	051
McMASTERS			Mary E	Gree	116
Mary F	Hanc	142	McNALLY			
Thomas	Athe	021	Peter	Mont	254
William	Meig	214	McNAMAR			
McMEEN			Alvira	Scio	307
David W	Sene	310	McNAMARA			
McMEENS			Honora	Erie	087
Ann	Erie	087	John	Lick	186
McMICHAEL			Joseph	Mont	249
Charles	Cosh	060	William	Wash	346
John A	Craw	062	McNANEE			
McMILLAN			Bartholomew	Perr	278
Eve	Tusc	332	McNEAL			
Mary	Belm	029	John	Morr	260
William	Harr	150	John W	Hard	148
McMILLEN			Laura	Lora	192
Harriet N	Knox	174	William	VanW	337
John A	Rich	293	McNEELY			
Mary J	Guer	119	Charles C	Hami	128
Miranda	Tusc	331	Martin	Miam	220
Susannah	Jeff	169	McNEIL			
Theophilus C	Cler	049	Lydia A	Athe	022
Polly	Gall	111	Samuel A	Unio	335
McMINNIS			McNEMEE			
Eli	Cler	050	Nancy	Fair	092
William	Unio	334	McNERLAND			
McMONIGAL			James	Lick	185
Sarah E	Wayn	354	McNITT			
McMOORAN			Maria Ann	Fult	106
Samuel T	Cham	042	McNULTY			
McMORROW			Anthony	Mont	245
Susan	Meig	213	Hugh T	Fran	104
McMULLAN			James	Holm	160
Samuel	Mont	254	John G	Hami	126
McMULLEN			McNUT			
Ann M	Mont	230	John H	Adam	003
Archibald A	Mont	241	McNUTT			
Margaret	Guer	119	Henry J	Athe	023
Noah	Guer	120	Samuel	Preb	287
William	Summ	324	William J	Unio	333
McMURRAY			McPECK			
Jane	Hami	139	Ezekiel A	Monr	225
William H	Ashl	011	John E	Harr	150
McMURRY			McPEEK			
John A	Scio	306	Christiana	Guer	117
McMURTEY			Mary	Maho	206
Alex C	Cuya	066	Mary A	Monr	225
McNABB			McPHERSON			
Jno B	Mont	254	Benj	Dela	082

McPHERSON (cont)			McWHORTER			
Cynthia	Sand	301	James	Athe	022	
Geo D W	Belm	028	McWILLIAMS			
John H	Athe	024	Elizabeth	Nobl	268	
Mary E	Clin	055	Lavina	Belm	030	
Sarah	Cosh	060				
McPIGUE						
Patrick	Putn	288	MABEE			
McQUADE			Alphonso	Rich	292	
David	Vint	342	MABRA			
Eliphalet	Ross	296	Albert	Belm	027	
John	Mont	249	MABRY			
McQUATE			Dorcas	Gall	109	
Samuel	Ashl	011	MACCABEE			
McQUAY			John	Clar	045	
Anna	Dark	078	MACE			
McQUEEN			Margaret	Ross	297	
George W	Lick	184	MACEY			
McQUILLAN			Obed(?)	Miam	221	
Bryan	Butl	038	MACHER			
McQUILLON			Ambrose	Mont	230	
Lucretia	Gree	113	MACHLING			
McQUINIFF			Barbara	Unio	334	
Henry	Ross	299	MACK			
McQUISTON			Israel S	Asht	018	
Fanny	Trum	325	Sigfried	Hami	122	
McRANY			MACKEY			
Lucinda	Dela	084	David L	Guer	118	
McROBERTS			Jos W	Pick	278	
Albert	Lora	195	Mary J	Wood	362	
McSHANE			Robert A	Trum	326	
Edward	Perr	276	MACKIN			
Joseph	Mont	254	Thaddeus	Erie	087	
McSHAY			MACKINAM			
Sarah	Putn	289	Englebeth	Mont	255	
McTHOMAS			MACKINTOSH			
Reuben	Lick	187	Alex R	Lawr	180	
McVAY			MACKLEY			
William J	Faye	094	Jacob	Rich	292	
McVETTA			Jeremiah	Rich	294	
Thomas	Wood	359	MACKLIN			
McVEY			Judith	Fair	091	
Esau	Wash	346	MACOMBER			
Thomas	Shel	315	Geo W	Sand	303	
McVICKER			MADDE			
Sarah Ann	Athe	022	Sarah A	Mont	231	
William	Lick	186	MADDEN			
McWAIN			Cornelius	Cham	043	
Wallace	Cuya	066	John	Holm	161	
McWHIRTER			John	Mont	241	
Mary	Musk	264	Nelson D	Belm	030	
McWHISTER			MADDOCK			
Robert	Musk	265	Joseph	Lora	194	

MADDUX			**MAGUIRE (cont)**		
Lucinda M	Hami	138	John	Mont	243
MADEARY			**MAHAFFEY**		
Francis	Hami	131	Grace A	Miam	219
MADEIRA			Milton	Knox	176
Mary C	Ross	297	Rebecca A	Adam	007
MADGE			**MAHAN**		
Wreford	Mont	246	Andrew	Port	283
MADIGAN			John D	Maho	207
Johanna	Brow	031	Patrick H	Fran	100
William	Mont	241	Samuel S	Hard	148
MADISON			**MAHANEY**		
Frank	Brow	034	Cornelius	High	155
Irena	Sene	312	**MAHANNAH**		
James	Clin	055	Haney	Trum	325
James	Colu	058	**MAHANY**		
William	Clar	047	Adam	Lick	189
MADOLE			**MAHER**		
Margaret	Athe	024	Michael	Mont	255
MADOX			William	Mont	254
Malinda E F	High	156	**MAHLON**		
MAENLE			August	Sand	303
Chas	Putn	289	**MAHON**		
MAEULEN			Patrick	Mont	255
Carl	Otta	272	William B	Paul	273
MAEYER			**MAHONEY**		
Henry	Mont	252	Frances	Trum	325
MAGEE			Jeremiah	Geau	111
Dolly W	Huro	162	John	Wood	359
Geo C	Tusc	331	Mary	Clar	044
Isaac J	Pike	282	**MAHR**		
MAGERS			Dorothy	Clar	046
James W	Morg	258	**MAHRLEIN**		
Nathan	Knox	175	Caroline	Hami	131
MAGG			**MAIER**		
George	Mont	248	Cath	Will	356
MAGGS			**MAIERS**		
Eliza	Cosh	061	Godfrey	Star	319
MAGHER			**MAIL**		
Michael	Mont	255	Nancy E	Monr	226
MAGILL			**MAILE**		
Francis	Erie	087	Kasper	Hami	122
MAGLY			**MAIN**		
Andrew	Hami	121	Margaret	Dela	084
Juliana	Hami	131	**MAINES**		
MAGNER			Abiram	Wash	350
Adele S	Gall	109	Jacob	Hanc	142
Isaiah	VanW	340	**MAIZE**		
William	Maho	205	Lewis E	Ashl	011
MAGRUDER			**MAJOR**		
John W	Cosh	062	Henry A	Hard	145
MAGUIRE			Thomas	VanW	340
Jas G	Meig	216	William O	Maho	205

MALCOMB			MANCK			
James M	Athe	020	Lewis W	Gall	108
MALEY			MANDELL			
Margaret	Hami	129	Wilhelmine	Hami	131
MALICK			MANDERBACH			
Isma H	VanW	339	Anna M	Summ	323
MALLARY			MANECKE			
Oliver H P	Mari	208	William	Sene	311
MALLERY			MANELIUS			
Hiram W	Medi	211	Cornelius	Mont	245
MALLETT			MANGEN			
Eliza	Paul	273	John	Hami	126
MALLIN			MANGER			
Bridget	Cuya	068	Rosina	Hami	131
MALLONEE			MANGOLD			
John J	VanW	339	Geo	Fran	100
MALLORY			MANINGTON			
Martha F	Fair	091	William	Clar	045
Sarah	Gree	116	MANION			
MALLOTT			Thomas	Hami	122
Lawner	Brow	032	MANKIN			
MALLOY			Henry C	Colu	056
Stephen	Mont	254	Judith	Colu	056
MALONE			Mary A	Colu	055
Hugh	Jack	169	MANKINS			
James	Unio	335	Francis	Wash	345
Julia	Belm	031	MANLEY			
Mary	Hami	131	Christiana	Musk	267
Rebecca	Ross	297	Columbus	Mari	208
MALONEY			Jacob R	Perr	277
James S	Cuya	066	Julia A	Gree	116
John	Lick	188	Mahlon K	Wood	360
Mary	Star	320	Seth	Lake	178
Michael	Hami	122	MANLY			
Michael	Perr	276	Malinda	Athe	023
Thomas H	Sene	310	MANN			
MALOTT			Cath A	Morr	261
Caroline	Hami	135	David	Mont	230
Oliver	Brow	033	Delana	Huro	165
MAM			Edward M	Asht	015
William A	Putn	290	Elizabeth	Morr	259
MAN			Elizabeth E	Cuya	069
Rebecca	Lick	183	George	High	155
MANAHAN			Horace G	Maho	205
Caroline	Huro	165	MANNING			
John W	Pick	280	Anna V	Belm	027
Mary A	Huro	164	Clarkson	Miam	218
MANCHE			Geo W	Erie	086
Mary	Butl	037	John J	Maho	207
MANCHESTER			John W	Colu	058
Rachel	Brow	032	Lorenda	Musk	267
William L	Brow	032	Nancy	Cler	051
			Patrick	Hami	136

MANNING (cont)			MARBERTH		
Thomas	Mont	244	Joseph	Mont	254
Thomas B	Clar	045	MARBLE		
William	Lake	177	Grace A	Lick	187
MANNON			Lydia	Lake	176
Samuel B	Brow	032	MARCEAR		
MANOR			Henry H	Guer	118
Elizabeth	Dark	078	MARCH		
Joseph	Ashl	014	Daniel W B	Port	285
MANS			James E	Asht	017
John	Mont	248	John	Mont	246
MANSFIELD			Sarah	Warr	343
Henry O	Harr	149	MARCHAL		
Job	Defi	079	John	Putn	290
Johiel	Defi	081	John F	Ross	298
William W	Harr	149	MARCUM		
MANSON			Horace G	Dark	077
William H	Wayn	353	MARGENTHALER		
MANTER			Mary	Mont	230
David	VanW	338	MARGUART		
MANTOR			Russell	Fran	100
Lydia	Dela	084	MARHART		
MANTZ			Gotthold	Hami	139
Jacob	Mont	235	MARIETTA		
MANUEL			John	Miam	220
William	Butl	038	Mason H	Ashl	011
MANVILLE			MARIHUGH		
Rebecca	Ross	296	Henry	Defi	080
MANYAN			MARINER		
Geo R	Tusc	333	Mary	Hami	131
MAPES			MARING		
Abigail	Cuya	075	Geo W	Belm	028
Margaret	Maho	205	James S	Sene	311
Sally	Erie	088	MARION		
Samuel R	Will	355	Daniel	Morg	257
Thomas	Cuya	075	MARK		
William	Gall	108	Sarah A	Wayn	354
William	Putn	290	MARKEE		
MAPLE			Maranda A	Tusc	331
Nancy	Jeff	169	MARKER		
Rezin B	Jack	168	Alice Ann	Jeff	171
MAPLES			Margaret	Summ	324
Sarah	Jeff	169	MARKET		
MAPPS			Jacob	Lawr	181
David	Clar	045	MARKIN		
MARA			Cornelius	Lawr	182
Margaret	Hami	131	Lorenzo D	Lawr	181
MARANVILLE			William H	Gall	110
Nancy	Summ	321	MARKINS		
MARAT			Delitha	Lawr	179
Cath A	Mont	230	MARKLEY		
MARATTA			Cyrus	Ashl	011
John	Mont	237	Geo W	Pick	280

MARKLEY (cont)			MARSH (cont)		
Margaret	Medi	211	Milton	Mari	208
Martin V	Cler	050	Sarah	Unio	334
Orlando	Ashl	011	Sarah A	Erie	086
Truman C	Cler	052	Sarah E	Fult	106
MARKS			William D	Musk	265
Alonzo	Fult	106	MARSHALL		
Emeline E	Hami	124	Daniel S	Wayn	351
George J	Mont	252	Elinor	Pick	279
Isaac H	Fair	092	Frank	Brow	032
John	Will	355	Hugh	Brow	035
Richard Jr	Colu	057	James	Rich	292
Samuel	Erie	086	Jasper	Miam	221
Samuel	Mont	233	John	Dark	079
Samuel	Tusc	330	John	Mont	228
Samuel J	Wayn	352	Joseph R	Alle	009
MARKWARD			Joseph T	Erie	087
William C	Rich	294	Luther	Luca	197
MARLATT			Marion	Lawr	181
Josephus	Guer	119	Mary E	Gree	115
William A	Rich	291	Nancy	Perr	276
MARLOW			Samuel J	Hard	147
Mary	Guer	119	Sarah	Dark	078
Moses	Rich	293	Sarah E	Augl	026
MARMON			William B	Gall	108
Joseph E	Loga	192	William F	Rich	295
MARQUART			William H	Alle	009
Werner	Dela	083	William L	Mont	254
MARQUIS			MART		
Samuel	Hard	145	Eliza	Clin	055
MARRIGON			MARTIN		
Ross C	Jeff	170	Abram	Athe	021
MARRIOTT			Alba G	Wash	348
Julia A	Lick	186	Albert	Harr	149
MARROW			Alexander	Gall	108
Margaret T	Hami	135	Alexander	Hock	158
MARSEILLES			Alice	Perr	275
M Caroline	Huro	164	Angeline	Erie	086
MARSH			Ann	Knox	175
Ann	Fran	097	Ann	Medi	210
Ann B	Luca	200	Benj	Fair	090
Benj	Colu	056	Benj F	Ashl	011
Chauncey D	Athe	022	Bloomfield U		
Enos L	Huro	162		Morr	261
Hiram J	Asht	016	Calvin B	Monr	226
Hudson C	Luca	201	Cath	Pick	279
Joel	Erie	086	Cath	Preb	286
Joseph	Guer	120	Charles	Madi	204
Lyman W	Lick	185	Charlotte	Miam	222
Margaret	Guer	119	Christopher C		
Marshall	Athe	022		Putn	290
Mary R	Loga	192	Chs G	Huro	165
Milton	Madi	204	David	Geau	112

MARTIN (cont)

David	Lawr	182
Delilah D	Belm	030
Drusilla H	Wyan	366
Elizabeth	Ashl	011
Elizabeth	Scio	305
Elvira A	Lake	178
Frank M	Augl	026
George	Athe	024
George	Belm	030
George	Hami	126
George	Warr	343
(alias George Clay)		
Harman H	Morr	259
Henry	Wash	346
Horace H	Adam	003
Isaac	Mont	232
Jacob	Wash	350
Jacob W	Sene	310
James	Brow	032
James	Knox	173
James	Mont	240
James H F	Sene	312
James P	Summ	322
Jane	Colu	056
Jeremiah	Pick	279
Jeremiah M	Dark	077
Johannah	Loga	190
John	Wayn	354
John B	Hami	126
John C	Hanc	141
John H	Pike	282
John T	Fran	100
John W	Lawr	181
Louis	Mont	240
Mary	Hami	124
Mary	Jack	167
Mary	Knox	173
Mary	Perr	276
Mary	Putn	291
Mary	Wash	345
Mary	Wash	350
Mary A	Scio	304
Mary E	High	154
Mary E	Miam	219
Otis	Maho	205
Phebe W	Morr	259
Philip	Ashl	011
Reuben	Ashl	013
Reuben	Defi	081
Richard	Lawr	179
Robert	Holm	160
Robert	Mont	256

MARTIN (cont)

Ross M	Morr	261
Samuel	Harr	149
Samuel	Henr	152
Samuel G	Jack	167
Sarah	Belm	030
Sarah	Fran	097
Sarah E	Musk	265
Silas	Hami	122
Thomas	Meig	214
Washington	Alle	010
William	Adam	007
MARTINDALE		
Luther	Geau	111
Susan	Gall	110
MARTS		
John C	Knox	173
MARTY		
Randolph	Monr	226
MARTZ		
Elisha	Merc	218
Mary A	Maho	205
MARVIN		
Cath	Hanc	142
George R	Hanc	141
Mearrison J	Henr	152
Ulysses L	Summ	322
MARZ		
Burkhart	Wyan	364
MASE		
Benj	Rich	293
MASON		
Cyrus A	Port	285
Edwin F	Asht	017
Jas	Morr	261
John	Clin	054
Joshua S	Medi	211
Lewis W	Wood	360
Mary Ann	Fult	106
Milton A	Summ	324
Rachel	Belm	026
Reuben S	Morg	256
Robert B	Jack	168
Stephen A	Huro	163
William	Mont	236
William B	Wash	348
MASSEY		
Henry C	Cuya	066
William	Lora	193
MASSIE		
Edmond	Lawr	179
Gaines P	Lawr	179
Harrison	Scio	308

MASSIE (cont)			MATHEWS (cont)		
Joseph L	Adam	007	Hannah M	Guer	117
Loudon	Lawr	179	Jackson	Adam	005
Peter	Scio	305	John T	Fran	100
MAST			Mary	High	156
Serenous	Paul	273	Mary W	Huro	164
MASTEN			Philip	Gall	109
David	Mont	238	Sarah	Adam	004
James H	Hami	126	Sarah	Brow	032
MASTERS			Susannah	Scio	307
Aquilla	Luca	199	MATHIAS		
Dorcas	Cler	049	Albert C	Putn	289
Eliza	Fair	091	Ann M	Craw	062
Eliza	Fran	103	Frederick	Lora	193
Geo	Musk	264	Jacob	Mont	252
Henry	Guer	119	John	Ross	298
Jane	Ashl	014	Mahon	Luca	196
John	Trum	329	Martin L	Fran	103
Joseph	Nobl	269	Walter	Mont	229
Miriam	Wash	346	William	Mont	246
Richard	Nobl	269	MATHIEN		
Robert	Athe	023	Lucinda	Fran	097
Samuel C	High	157	MATHIESEN		
Sarah	Guer	119	Sonker	Hami	122
Thomas A	Wash	346	MATHYS		
MASTERSON			John	Clar	047
Thomas J	Morg	259	MATLOCK		
MASTIN			Mary	Harr	148
Clements J	Preb	287	MATSON		
MATCHETT			Almira K	Luca	201
Augusta E	Dark	078	Eliza M	Merc	218
MATHAI			James M	Musk	265
Charles	Mont	255	John	Merc	218
MATHENY			John S B	Rich	295
James C	Hock	157	William D	Cler	050
Jane	Ross	299	MATTERN		
Lucy N	Adam	004	Jacob	Hami	140
Stephen W	Athe	021	MATTERS		
Theodore J	Nobl	268	Calysta C	Fult	105
MATHER			MATTESON		
Daniel D	Unio	335	Philip	Wayn	353
Daniel S	Knox	176	MATTHEWS		
Donnelly	Huro	165	Betsey	Asht	019
Penny F	Lake	177	Chas W	Will	357
MATHERS			Delia	Fran	097
Margaret	Wash	347	Geo K	Wood	363
Mary J	Butl	036	Geo W	Dela	085
MATHEWS			Isaac W	Clin	053
Chas W	Asht	018	Louis W	Mont	236
Dyer R	Henr	151	Lydia	Wayn	353
Eliza	Maho	205	Orlo C	Cuya	064
Elizabeth	Morr	261	Rebecca H	Ross	297
Geo W	Will	355	Sarah	Jack	168

MATTNEY			MAY (cont)		
Jeffrey J	Lawr	182	Hiram	Sand	302
MATTOCK			John	Pick	279
Hester	Pick	279	John G	Fran	103
MATTOCKS			Malinda	Lawr	180
James J	Luca	196	Margaret	Sand	302
MATTOX			Martha B	Ross	297
Eliza	Cler	049	Nancy J	Adam	007
Levi L	Cler	048	MAYALL		
Levina	High	157	Ann	Cosh	061
MAUCHE			Charles	Mont	255
Barbara	VanW	340	MAYBERRY		
MAUCK			Jane	Clar	044
Anthony	Wyan	366	MAYBURY		
MAUK			Joseph	Lick	186
Julia A	Perr	276	MAYBUSH		
Samuel S	Hock	159	Conrad	Butl	036
MAURER			MAYER		
Annie	Star	321	Adam	Mont	231
Jacob	Cuya	071	William A	Fran	100
William	Sand	303	MAYERS		
MAUS			John	Luca	199
Barbara	Hami	124	William H	Sene	313
MAVIS			MAYES		
Abraham J	Defi	081	Jacob	Cham	043
Linas	Knox	173	MAYHEW		
MAXFIELD			Hannah A	Lake	178
Isaac	Lake	176	MAYLAND		
MAXHAM			Margaret	Cuya	068
Phebe	Trum	325	MAYLONE		
MAXON			Hannah	Colu	059
Mary A	Wash	349	MAYNARD		
Olcott P	Lawr	181	Henry	Butl	036
MAXWELL			Margaret	Ross	300
John	Musk	266	MAYO		
John B	Jeff	170	Allen G	Faye	094
John C	Jeff	172	Edith	Dela	083
John D	Morr	259	Geo W	Fran	100
John T	Athe	024	MAYSE		
Joseph	Ashl	012	Harrison	Loga	191
Mary	Alle	009	MAZE		
Nancy	Colu	056	Alfred	Clin	054
Rebecca	Mont	227	Nelson	Will	355
Robert	Clar	045	MEACHAM		
Samuel	Harr	149	Fanny	Trum	327
Sarah	Cler	049	MEACHEN		
Sarah A	Adam	003	William	Wood	360
William H	Dela	084	MEAD		
MAY			Alfred	Clar	045
Andrew	Summ	321	Alfred	Knox	173
Edward D	Merc	216	Chas H	Asht	018
Elizabeth	Will	356	Isaac	Scio	306
Hiram	Cham	041	Joseph M	Warr	344

MEAD (cont)			MEEKS			
Rowena	Huro	163	Newton M	Nobl	270	
Silas	Asht	019	Oliver M	Lawr	181	
Sylvia C	Huro	164	MEESE			
MEADER			Geo	Tusc	332	
Nathan B	Hami	126	MEFFORD			
MEALLS			Jacob M	Knox	175	
James O	Putn	289	MEGRAIL			
MEALY			Geo E	Jeff	170	
Franklin K	Harr	149	MEHAFFEY			
MEANEY			James	Guer	118	
Edward	Rich	293	MEHAN			
MEANS			Sarah	Fair	090	
Francis M	Loga	190	MEHARRY			
Huldah S	Loga	189	James	Fran	103	
Lyman N	Augl	026	MEIDIG			
MEARS			Elizabeth	Star	317	
James R	Mari	208	MEIEN			
MEBZNER			Jacob	Mont	231	
Albert	Mont	248	MEIER			
MECAY			August	Hami	121	
Maria B	Dela	084	MEIKLE			
MECHLING			David	Mont	244	
William L	Alle	009	MEIMER			
MECKLING			John	VanW	340	
Lewis	Warr	342	MEINEKE			
MEDICK			Henry	Hami	126	
Geo W	Fran	095	MEINHART			
Peter	Fran	100	John	Mont	249	
MEDILL			MEINSHADT			
Margaret	Star	318	Gertrude	Hami	124	
MEDLEY			MEIRES			
Gilbert L	Trum	327	William	Hami	127	
MEEDS			MEISENHELDER			
Henry E	Dark	078	Amelia	Wash	349	
MEEK			MEISER			
Elisha P	Athe	022	Herman	Maho	205	
Henry	Belm	030	MEISNER			
John W	Defi	081	Charles	Mont	235	
Seth	Colu	056	MEISTER			
Washington	Will	355	Barbara	Hami	140	
MEEKER			MEITZLER			
Aaron	Fair	092	John H	Sene	314	
David E	Trum	327	MELCHER			
Elvirah	Fair	092	Nancy	Scio	307	
Harriet L	Trum	328	MELCHOIR			
Henry M	Maho	205	Charles H	Huro	162	
Jas S	Augl	024	MELFORD			
John	Alle	010	Sophia D	Augl	025	
Rolla	Luca	199	MELHEIM			
Stephen	Dela	085	John	Ashl	013	
Stephen B	Cuya	069	MELICH			
Thomas J	Hami	127	Henry H	Musk	264	

MELICK			MENTZ			
Alfred B	Fair	092	Fred	Fran	100
Andrew	Rich	295	MENZ		
MELINE			Jacob	Hami	121
Mary E	Hami	131	MENZE		
MELISSA			Henry	Mont	252
Warner	Asht	016	MEQUILLET		
MELL			David	Morr	260
Andrew J	Alle	010	MERCER		
MELLAGE			Chas	Mont	230
Frederick	Hami	126	David H	Morg	257
MELLEN			Edwin A	Luca	196
Chas A	Wayn	351	Eliza	Musk	267
Lydia	Wood	358	Eliza A	Monr	226
MELLER			Eliza J	Ross	296
Caroline	Sene	313	Elizabeth A	Faye	094
MELLON			Henley H	Meig	213
August	Mont	249	James	Merc	216
Jacob C	Craw	063	Job F	Nobl	268
Nancy	Wyan	366	John T	Harr	150
Samuel	Wash	346	John T	Jeff	170
MELLOTT			Leo	Star	320
John S	Monr	223	Lydia A	High	155
MELLVILLE			Madison	Ashl	011
Margaret	Erie	086	Mathias	Morg	259
MELVILLE			Matilda	Monr	223
Jaques	Rich	295	Reason	Wood	362
MELVIN			Sarah A	Adam	004
Madison M	Clar	045	Thomas	Nobl	268
MEMIE			William D	Morg	257
Ignatz	Hami	126	William W	Belm	030
MENDEL			MERCHAM		
William	Scio	307	Frank W	Hami	136
MENDENHALL			MERCHANT		
Elizabeth	Dark	079	Geo B	Rich	293
John	Preb	286	Isaac T	Tusc	332
William T	Wash	346	Walter J	Sene	312
MENELEY			MEREDITH		
Susan	Fran	096	Ann	Wash	348
MENKER			Henry G	Morr	260
Henry	Hami	125	Isaac	Cosh	061
MENNER			Isaiah W	Star	320
Frederick	Mont	252	Joseph W	Fran	100
MENNS			Thomas E	High	154
Joseph	Mont	254	MERGEL		
MENTAL			George	Hami	126
Conrad	Erie	088	MERICA		
MENTEL			John	VanW	337
Daniel	Mont	231	MERION		
John A	Hami	122	Hannah E	Otta	272
MENTHOIN			MERIVAN		
Sarah	Monr	225	Gilbert	Port	286

MERKEL			MESEUGER		
Mathew	Mont	249	Lydia	Lick	184
MERKER			MESNARD		
Adam	Clin	055	Lewis	Sene	314
MERKLE			Luther B	Huro	165
Cath M	Cuya	075	MESSENGER		
MERKLEIN			David	Lick	188
Cath	Hami	124	Everett	Putn	290
MERLING			Harriet A	Huro	163
Chas	Ashl	011	Sophia E	Jack	167
MERLY			William K	Mari	209
Hiram	Fran	100	MESSENHEIMER		
MERRELL			Mat A	Star	316
David W	Hami	126	MESSMEYER		
MERRIAM			August	Hami	121
Edward T	Musk	267	MESSMORE		
MERRICK			Harvey	Knox	173
Isaac	VanW	339	METCALF		
MERRIFIELD			Daniel	Wayn	353
Jane	Wayn	354	Geo	Sene	313
Julia A	Huro	163	William M	Perr	278
MERRIHEW			METCALFE		
Emma L	Craw	062	Arthur	Mont	255
MERRILL			METHENY		
Ezra W	Mont	245	David	Lick	187
John W	Fran	100	METTER		
Robert	Adam	004	Hannah	Hock	158
Sylvester	Lora	195	METTLE		
William W	Nobl	270	Sarah	Fran	096
MERRIMAN			METZ		
Henry L	Geau	111	Alan T	Mont	255
MERRITT			Elizabeth	Sene	313
Atwood	Medi	211	Frederick	Wood	363
Frederick	Gree	116	Mercy	VanW	336
Geo W	Luca	198	Philippine	Augl	025
Martha E	Unio	335	William	Monr	225
MERROW			METZEN		
Samuel	Wash	347	Jacob	Hami	126
MERRY			METZGER		
Earl W	Wood	358	Elizabeth	Hami	124
Lemuel E	Huro	161	Whalon	Brow	032
MERRYMAN			METZLER		
Anna	Ross	296	Eliza	Wayn	354
MERSHINER			Michael	Mont	242
George	Mont	252	MEUNSON		
MERTZ			Shubal	Luca	202
James	Hard	145	MEYER		
John F	Cler	050	Anthony	Mont	255
MERWIN			Barbara	Cuya	068
David P	Star	319	Charles	Mont	256
George W	Star	319	Elizabeth	Cuya	068
Henry	Trum	329	Gottfried	Carr	039
			John	Mont	247

MEYER (cont)			MIDLAM			
Joseph	Hami	126	Harvey	Dark	077	
Joseph	Mont	254	Martha	Wyan	366	
Kate	Fran	104	MIEGER			
Louis	Mont	240	Peter	Maho	205	
Susan	Dark	078	MIER			
William	Hami	126	Dietrick	Hami	126	
MEYERS			MIGHT			
Ebenezer	Fran	100	Mary	Athe	022	
Henry	Mont	238	MIKE			
Jno	Mont	254	Elizabeth	Wash	350	
MICHAEL			MIKESELL			
Mary	Clin	053	David A	Dark	077	
Sarah	Fran	102	Ephriam Jr	Preb	286	
William	Mont	254	MIKLE			
William	Warr	342	Peter	Musk	265	
MICHAELS			MILA			
John	Hanc	141	Gottleib	Morr	259	
Michael	Mont	243	MILBURN			
Theo	Fair	090	Isaac N	Putn	290	
William	Wyan	366	MILES			
MICHEL			Ann	Musk	265	
Frederick	Holm	160	Barbara	Lick	189	
Frederick	Mont	244	Gideon M	Fran	100	
MICHELBACH			MILEY			
Henry	Dela	082	Jesse W	Fult	107	
MICHELS			William C	Fult	107	
Anton	Hami	121	MILHUF			
MICHENER			Jeremiah	Hanc	141	
Anna E	Lora	195	MILK			
John J	Belm	029	David	Huro	162	
MICK			MILKS			
Henry	Hard	147	Gideon H Jr	Summ	325	
Ruth	Clin	053	MILLAN			
Simeon	Ross	301	Hannah M	Trum	328	
MICKEY			MILLAR			
Clay	Mont	255	Walter	Hami	127	
Florence L	Rich	295	MILLARD			
MIDDAGH			John D	Rich	295	
Enos	Perr	278	MILLE			
MIDDAUGH			Eve	Fair	092	
Benj	Holm	160	MILLER			
John	Alle	009	Abram	Butl	035	
MIDDLETON			Adam	Hami	121	
Ardon P	High	154	Adam B	Augl	024	
Basil	Henr	152	Aliander C	Loga	191	
Edward	Cler	049	Alvin M	Faye	094	
James	Ross	300	Amos E	Wyan	366	
John H	High	154	Andrew S	Luca	199	
Martha	High	156	Annie P M	Dark	078	
MIDGHALL			Anthony W	Fult	106	
Emily	Brow	031	Anton	Hami	139	
			Asenath	Wash	349	

MILLER (cont)			MILLER (cont)		
Austin	Jeff	171	George C	Mont	228
Beneville	Asht	015	George M	Hock	157
Benj	Mont	255	George W	Ashl	011
Benoni	Alle	010	George W	High	154
Cath	Guer	119	George W	Huro	165
Cath	Hanc	140	George W	Rich	291
Cath	Ross	296	George W	Rich	293
Cath A	Mont	231	Hannah	Cham	041
Charles	Cuya	072	Hannah	Loga	190
Charles	Mont	240	Hannah	Preb	288
Charles D	Lick	187	Hannah	Ross	297
Christian	Monr	226	Harriet	Mont	231
Christina	Trum	326	Harrison D	Alle	009
Christopher	Star	319	Henry	Cham	041
Constantine	Mont	255	Henry	Sene	311
Cornelius	Pike	281	Henry	Tusc	332
Cyrus	Preb	288	Henry	VanW	337
Dan J	Fult	107	Henry C	Gall	108
Daniel	Cosh	061	Henry J	Wash	348
Daniel	Cuya	071	Hester	Wash	346
Daniel	Holm	160	Hiram B	Wyan	367
Daniel	Holm	161	Ira A	Ross	300
Daniel	Mari	209	Isaac	Rich	296
Daniel F	Mont	233	Isaac	VanW	337
David	Butl	035	Israel	Rich	296
David A	Hock	158	Jacob	Brow	034
David L	Jeff	169	Jacob	Hock	157
Dicey	Preb	288	Jacob	Monr	225
Edward E	Fran	104	Jacob	Ross	298
Eleanor	Lake	178	Jacob C	Wyan	366
Eli	Alle	010	Jacob G	Vint	341
Elias	Miam	220	James	Carr	039
Eliza	Brow	032	James	Port	285
Eliza A	Trum	327	James	Wyan	364
Elizabeth	Cosh	060	James A	Unio	336
Elizabeth	Dark	078	James B	Vint	341
Elizabeth	Fair	091	James M	Loga	191
Elizabeth	Hanc	140	James R	Fran	099
Elizabeth	Miam	219	James W	Jack	166
Ellen	Sand	302	Jane	Henr	152
Enoch	Fran	102	Jesse	Star	316
Ephraim C	Lake	177	John	Butl	035
Ferdinand	VanW	337	John	Cuya	075
Francis W	Gree	116	John	Fran	100
Frank	Mont	252	John	Guer	120
Frank R	Madi	204	John	Hami	126
Fred	Cuya	071	John	Mont	241
Frederick	Hami	125	John	Mont	241
Frederick	Mont	252	John	Sand	303
George	Cuya	071	John	Sene	313
George	Hami	126	John	VanW	339
George	VanW	338	John	Warr	344

MILLER (cont)			MILLER (cont)		
John	Wash	349	Mitchell	Cuya	072
John Jr	Vint	341	Moses	Gall	108
John B	Fair	092	Nancy	Hard	144
John B	Fran	100	Nicholas	Hami	122
John B	Fran	100	Oliver	Wash	345
John B	Trum	326	Owen J	Wayn	352
John C	Alle	009	Perry	VanW	338
John C	Mont	241	Peter	Hami	124
John E	Hami	126	Peter	VanW	337
John F	Star	319	Peter W	Mont	238
John G	Mont	254	Philip	Cosh	059
John H	Fran	095	Polly	Cham	041
John H	Wyan	366	Quincy	Cuya	071
John J	Musk	263	Rebecca W	Butl	036
John L	Colu	058	Rhoda	Monr	223
John W	Craw	064	Richard	Hami	135
John W	Preb	286	Richard S A B		
John W	Sene	309		Gall	109
Johnson	Defi	080	Riley D	Trum	328
Jonathan	Luca	199	Rodney	Trum	330
Joseph	Hami	122	Ruth A	Dela	084
Joseph	Rich	293	Samuel	Cuya	071
Joseph B	Trum	326	Samuel	Fult	106
Joseph H	Summ	322	Samuel	Huro	162
Joseph S	Nobl	269	Samuel	Miam	222
Josephus	Harr	151	Samuel	Mont	232
Julius	Mont	254	Samuel	Morg	258
Julius G	Mont	229	Samuel C	Butl	039
Levi	Pike	282	Samuel J	Alle	010
Levi L	Craw	064	Samuel O	Otta	271
Lorenz	Hami	125	Sarah	Ashl	012
Louis	Mont	254	Sarah A	Scio	304
Louisa	Wood	362	Sarah C	Mont	230
Lydia	Gree	114	Sarah J	Lawr	183
Manville	Wood	364	Stephen H	High	154
Margaret	Knox	174	Stewart	Summ	321
Margaret	Ross	297	Susan	Hanc	142
Maria	Hami	124	Susan	Star	317
Martha	Knox	174	Susannah	Holm	160
Martha J	Preb	287	Thomas	Loga	191
Mary	Butl	038	Thomas	Trum	325
Mary	Clin	053	Thomas	Wood	364
Mary	Defi	079	Webster	Cuya	066
Mary	Hard	147	Wells W	Erie	086
Mary	Huro	164	Wendline	Mont	254
Mary	Morr	261	William	Fran	100
Mary A	Harr	148	William	Luca	199
Mary A	Lawr	179	William	Wash	347
Mary A	Shel	316	William A	Sand	303
Mary Jane	Dark	079	William B	Will	357
Mathew G	Mari	209	William D	Wayn	354
Michael	Miam	218	William H	Adam	003

MILLER (cont)			MILLS (cont)		
William H	Craw	062	Margaret	Star	317
William H	Fran	099	Margaret	Tusc	331
William H H	Sene	309	Mary A	Cuya	068
William J	Asht	018	Mary S	Jeff	170
William M	Fair	092	Mary S	Lora	195
William M	Sene	314	Nancy	Clin	052
MILLES			Nathaniel B	Cosh	060
Lucinda	Ashl	013	Orlando C	Otta	271
MILLHEM			Stephen	Nobl	268
James	Mont	252	Wilmot A	Sene	313
MILLHOFF			MILNER		
Philip J	Mont	231	Isaac	Clin	053
MILLIGAN			Isaac	Jack	166
Alexander	Guer	119	Lyman H	Star	316
Mary M	Port	285	MILNOR		
William	Wash	347	Sidney	Hami	122
MILLIKEN			MILTENBERGER		
Julia A	Port	286	Elizabeth	Warr	344
Mary B	Lake	176	MILTON		
MILLIKIN			Edward	Mont	248
Leonora	Madi	204	MILVERSTEDT		
MILLIMANN			Christian	Luca	199
Mary	Cuya	068	MINARD		
MILLINGTON			Lenza M	Lora	193
Angeline	Unio	334	MINEAR		
MILLIONS			Alex W S	Athe	020
Homer	Sand	303	Alfred D	Athe	022
Marcellus	Sand	303	MINEHANE		
Mary A	Sand	303	Hester	Belm	030
MILLIROUS			MINER		
Geo W	Gall	108	Geo A	Cuya	076
Martha	Pike	282	Hester A	Perr	277
MILLIS			Mary	Colu	059
James	Musk	267	Samuel	Asht	017
MILLISON			MINES		
Aaron	Scio	306	Thomas M	Perr	275
MILLMAN			MINGUS		
Andrew J	Mont	255	Samuel P	Morg	257
MILLNER			MINICK		
Nathaniel	Loga	190	Low J	Shel	315
MILLS			MINIER		
Asenanth	Fult	106	Christopher	Otta	271
Charles F	Athe	020	John	Otta	271
Francis M	Warr	344	MINIHEN		
Gordon	Mont	232	Andrew	Mont	239
Henry D C	Erie	088	MINKE		
Henry M	Asht	019	Jacob	High	155
James	Preb	286	MINNER		
James L	Madi	203	Chas C	Musk	262
Jefferson C	Fult	106	MINNICK		
John	Colu	056	Geo W	Clar	045
Josiah T	Asht	015	Valentine	Miam	221

MINNIS			MITCHELL (cont)		
James S	Tusc	332	Joseph	Lora	193
MINOR			Joseph M	Wash	350
Abner C	Hard	145	Josiah L	Adam	005
Absalom	Gall	109	Lydia	Knox	174
Charles E	Huro	166	Martin V B	Defi	080
Julia	Preb	287	Peter	Cuya	075
Leah	Tusc	330	Philip	Mont	249
MINSER			Rebecca	Hami	121
John W	Ross	299	Richard	Paul	274
MINSHALL			Robert	Butl	039
Sarah	Hard	147	Robert A	Sand	304
MINTEN			Rosannah	Ross	297
Henry J	Hami	126	Sarah	Mont	230
MINTON			Simon	Musk	264
James O	Miam	221	Thomas	Clin	055
Mary	Brow	033	Thomas	Musk	267
MINTUN			Uriah	Sand	304
Jonathan	Madi	203	William	Colu	056
MIRACLE			William	Musk	263
William	Wash	347	William H	Scio	306
MIRANDA			MITCHELSON		
Katharine J	Adam	003	Levi	Wyan	365
MIRER			MITMAN		
John	Sene	309	Elizabeth	Gree	114
MISAMORE			MITTEN		
Henry	Hanc	142	William A	Wyan	364
MISER			MITTIGER		
Henry	Harr	149	George	Mont	249
John W K	Gree	114	MITTS		
Washington	Wyan	367	Thomas J	Ross	298
MISLER			MIXON		
Anton	Huro	161	Samuel	Hami	135
MISNER			MIXTARD		
David R	Meig	216	Honora	Dela	083
MISSIG			MIZEN		
Conrad	Erie	087	Henry	Mont	252
MITCHELL			MIZER		
Aaron B	Gall	110	Amos	Carr	040
Andrew	Madi	203	Henry	Cosh	059
Augustus P	Cosh	061	MOAKLER		
Cath	Trum	327	Nancy	Lick	187
David	Wayn	353	MOATS		
Eleanor	Jack	168	Alonzo	Knox	174
Elizabeth	Jack	166	Ezra	Will	357
Elizabeth	Wood	363	George N	Lawr	181
Frances M	Perr	276	John M	Lick	188
James	Hami	138	Jonathan	Fran	100
James A	Butl	038	MOBBERLY		
James L	Perr	277	Rebecca J	Monr	225
John T	Cham	043	MOBLER		
Jonas	Pick	280	John H	Sene	311
Joseph	Adam	003			

MODERWELL			MOLLOY			
Jas Q	Craw	062	Martha	Hami	136	
MODIC			MOLYNEAUX			
Martin	Morr	261	Joseph B	Cuya	072	
MOE			MOMENY			
Lorinda	Asht	015	Geo	Otta	272	
Lyman W	Putn	290	MONAGHAN			
Perry	Lora	194	William	Colu	057	
MOENINGER			MONAHAN			
Charles	Mont	236	James	Butl	038	
MOERZ			MONDY			
William	Ashl	013	Geo W	Will	357	
MOFF			MONE			
Adam	Mont	255	James	Pike	282	
MOFFATT			MONEGHAM			
John	Tusc	330	Cath	Star	319	
MOFFET			MONESMITH			
Benj C	Unio	335	Isaac	Preb	286	
MOFFETT			MONEY			
William H	Putn	290	John	Gall	110	
MOFFIT			MONEYSMITH			
Andrew J	Meig	212	Solomon R	VanW	338	
MOFFITT			MONFORT			
Elizabeth	Unio	333	Elias	Alle	010	
Hannah	Trum	326	Jennetta	Hami	137	
MOFFORD			MONGER			
John	Cler	049	Isaac	Asht	015	
MOGLE			Sarah A	Lora	194	
Sarah	Dark	079	MONIG			
MOHERMAN			Theresia	Hami	131	
Cath	Maho	206	MONK			
MOHLER			John	Lawr	181	
William H	Perr	276	MONKS			
MOHR			Martha	Summ	324	
Alvin D	Mari	209	Zera C	Cuya	071	
Charles	Mont	255	MONOHAN			
Jas F	Mari	209	Louisa	Hami	124	
John	Mont	249	MONROE			
Mandes M	Mari	209	Adoniram J	Loga	191	
MOIST			Alfred H	Cuya	071	
William H	Dela	082	Alfred R	Lake	176	
MOLAHAN			James M	Maho	207	
Nancy	Vint	341	Jesse	Scio	308	
MOLAN			Lewis	Port	285	
Jemima	Adam	005	Louisa M	Morr	260	
MOLBASH			Mary E	Brow	034	
Mary	Holm	161	Richard M J	Mari	208	
MOLER			Royal	Augl	024	
David	Mont	229	Samuel	Fult	105	
Thomas	Meig	213	MONSMITH			
MOLLENKOPF			Frank	Craw	063	
Jos	Craw	062	MONTAGNIER			
			Clementia	Hami	131	

MONTAGUE			MOONEY (cont)		
Geo H	Rich	293	James P	Huro	166
Martha A	Wyan	364	Mary A	Hami	131
MONTEITH			MOONSHINE		
William	Wyan	366	Joseph	Lora	193
MONTFORT			MOORE		
Elias R	Hami	126	Aaron B	Knox	176
MONTGOMERY			Albert	Musk	264
Albert A	Colu	058	Alfred F	Gall	109
Bartlett	Mont	248	Ambrose	Jeff	169
Chas H	Augl	026	Andrew	Craw	064
Elizabeth	Morr	261	Caleb B	Rich	294
Geo	Alle	008	Carey W	Adam	006
Geo W	Guer	118	Caroline	Luca	200
Geo W	Vint	341	Cath	Tusc	332
Hannah	Rich	294	Chas	Mont	228
James	Scio	308	Chas H	Paul	273
James H	Gall	108	Chas L	Musk	265
John	Mont	239	Clarissa	Luca	202
Lewis	Ross	299	Cornelia S	Cuya	074
Mary A	Scio	308	Cornelius	Musk	266
Patience	Butl	035	Cyrena	Adam	005
Robert	Mont	241	David B	Tusc	331
Thomas H	Jeff	172	Edward W	Trum	329
William	Monr	224	Eliza A	Hanc	142
William C	Lick	184	Eliza Ann	Craw	062
William T	Brow	035	Eliza E	Cler	048
MONTIS			Eliza J	Meig	215
John	Knox	175	Elizabeth	Guer	119
MOODIE			Elizabeth	Lick	187
Oscar	Mont	231	Elizabeth	Musk	263
MOODY			Elizabeth	Musk	263
Caroline	Hami	138	Elizabeth	Nobl	269
Dorliska E	Port	285	Elleanor	Pick	279
James	Mont	240	Ellen	Augl	024
James C	Maho	205	Fannie	Mont	231
Jane	Unio	333	Frances	Meig	215
Thomas	Mont	254	Frances	Musk	263
MOOMAN			Francis M	High	154
John	Ross	297	George W	Trum	329
MOON			George W	Wayn	353
Andrew J	Colu	055	Gideon R	Colu	058
Clarissa	Port	286	Harriet	Belm	029
Daniel C	Clin	055	Henry G	Wayn	352
Eliza	Medi	210	Hugh	Unio	334
George	Luca	196	Hylas S	Unio	335
Irwin C	Clin	054	Isaac	Fran	103
Orlando	Warr	342	Jacob	Adam	005
MOONEY			Jacob	Fran	095
Edward	Miam	219	James	Perr	276
Francis	Lawr	180	James	Will	357
George	Jeff	169	James A	Gall	109
James	Mont	252	James B	Trum	325

MOORE (cont)			MOORE (cont)		
James C	Sene	309	Thomas P	Mont	246
James W	Guer	120	Washington	Athe	024
Jane E	Summ	321	Wesley	Lick	184
John	Maho	205	William	Henr	152
John M	Colu	058	William	Meig	214
Joseph	Hami	125	William F	Nobl	269
Joseph	Scio	305	William H	Luca	202
Joseph J	Monr	226	William L	Maho	205
Joseph N	Adam	003	William P	Belm	030
Joseph T	Maho	207	William R	Shel	315
Laura	Fran	102	William S	Perr	276
Le Roy	Sand	302	Wilson C	Musk	267
Lewis	Musk	265	MOOREHEAD		
Lorenzo B	Wash	348	William	Hami	127
Louisa A	Unio	333	MOORHEAD		
Lucius	Lick	187	Erastus S	Cler	051
Lydia	Medi	211	Sarah	Harr	148
Margaret A	Belm	026	Thomas W	Cler	051
Maria L	Athe	020	MOORMAN		
Mary	Clar	046	Henry	Hami	126
Mary	Merc	217	MORAN		
Mary A	Gree	115	Anthony	Cuya	071
Mary Ann	Scio	307	John	Hami	137
Mary E	Belm	027	John	Lick	184
Martha J	Maho	204	John	Mont	238
Mitchell	Scio	305	Martha	Lawr	180
Nancy	Musk	264	Mary	Luca	200
Nancy	Scio	308	Patrick	Luca	199
Nancy A	Hanc	142	MORATT		
Nancy J	Adam	004	Geo W	Fran	102
Nathan	Wash	350	MOREE		
Nathan K	Nobl	268	Anna E	Knox	173
Nathaniel	Butl	038	MOREHART		
Orfo(?) A	Lora	192	John	Hanc	143
Philip H	Cosh	060	MOREHEAD		
Robert	Madi	203	David	VanW	336
Robert A	Loga	189	MOREHOUSE		
Robert L	Harr	150	Alfred	Dela	082
Robert S	Adam	007	Stanley S	Dela	082
Robert S	Tusc	331	Theda B	Gree	115
Robert T	Wash	348	MORELAND		
Samuel C	Wayn	353	Dan A	Jeff	169
Sarah	Port	283	James	Guer	118
Sarah C	Cler	049	John	Madi	203
Sarah C	Wash	350	Lucretia	Carr	040
Sarah M	Loga	190	Magdalena	Wayn	351
Sarah M	Putn	289	MOREN		
Sarah M	Summ	321	Jesse P	Butl	037
Silas	Gree	114	Mary	Hami	130
Susannah	Adam	006	Mary A	Pick	279
Thomas	Hami	137	MORETZ		
Thomas J	Pike	280	Balitzer	Hami	136

MOREY			MORIAT		
Delano	Hard	145	David	Perr	275
Rebecca	Augl	026	MORLAN		
Sylvanus T	Augl	026	Jacob S	Hock	157
MORFOOD			MORLEY		
John R	Fran	100	Alfred W	Lake	178
MORFORD			MORLING		
Julian R	Scio	308	Ann S	Musk	265
MORGAN			MORRELL		
Ann	Jack	166	Martha C	Colu	058
Benj	Warr	342	Moses	Lake	177
Burgess	Fran	102	MORRETT		
Charles	Mont	236	Jacob	Cham	041
Charles B	Fran	104	John H	Clar	045
Daniel J	Pick	280	MORRILL		
Elizabeth	Gall	110	James H	Sand	302
Elizabeth	Tusc	331	MORRIS		
Francis	Geau	113	Andrew J	Monr	226
George	Pick	278	Andrew J	Mont	237
George E	Star	317	Anna M	Wayn	354
Isaac	Miam	220	Barizllah F	Rich	295
James	Butl	038	Benajah P	Wash	350
James W	Harr	149	Benj F	Knox	176
Jno	Meig	213	Cath	Wyan	366
John F	Clar	045	Eleanor	Harr	150
Joyce	Scio	308	Eliza	Brow	031
Leonard	Madi	204	Eliza Y	Wayn	354
Loomis	Fran	100	Elizabeth	Pick	280
Lucretia J	Cuya	068	Ellen R	Star	320
Mack	Hami	122	George	Augl	026
Mary A	Brow	035	George M	Wash	346
Michael	Mont	249	George R	Luca	197
Richard	Adam	007	Henry	Ashl	012
Samuel	Rich	294	Henry	High	154
Silloughly	Monr	223	Henry M	Augl	026
Susan	Dela	083	Isaac	Clar	045
Thomas	Maho	207	James M	Fair	089
William	Rich	293	John	Cler	051
William A	Fran	100	John	Shel	316
William H	Clin	055	John A	Belm	029
William M	Fran	103	John B	Gree	115
MORGANSTEIN			John H	Defi	080
John H	Mont	254	John P	VanW	339
MORGANTHALER			Jno R	Wash	346
Cath	Butl	036	Jno W	Wash	346
MORGAREIDGE			Jonathan	Huro	162
Ransford	Wash	348	Lydia A	Cler	048
MORGARIDGE			Margaret	Cosh	060
William	Wash	348	Mary	Craw	062
MORIARTY			Mary N	Miam	222
Cath	Hami	124	Matilda	Hami	138
Patrick	Mont	249	Nancy K	Maho	206
			Noah	Wash	350

MORRIS (cont)			MORSE (cont)		
Owen	VanW	339	Jael	Asht	019
Rebecca	Preb	287	Lewis	Huro	165
Rosannah	Star	320	Marvin	Asht	019
Sarah	Belm	027	MORT		
Sarah	Fair	090	Sarah	Alle	009
Stout	Fran	100	MORTAL		
Susannah	Ross	299	Albert B	Fair	092
Thomas J	Athe	020	MORTEN		
Thomas N	Putn	291	Jos	Miam	222
Thomas P	Madi	204	MORTIMER		
William H	Pick	279	William	Mont	238
William R	Ross	299	MORTLEY		
MORRISON			David H	Cosh	060
Charles	Mont	255	MORTON		
Eliza	Adam	004	Eliza	Fran	095
Francis W	Dela	082	Eliza	Ross	300
George	Mont	252	John H	Cler	050
Harriet	Colu	057	John H	Craw	063
Harriet L	Augl	025	Leander L	Medi	210
Henry	Colu	059	Mary	Scio	307
Henry C	Merc	218	Matilda	Monr	226
James E	VanW	338	Michael	Mont	249
James H	Summ	322	Philip	Erie	086
Jane	Fran	097	Rachel	Craw	062
Jane	Huro	165	Rosannah	Craw	062
John	Vint	340	Sarah	Musk	267
Joseph	Athe	020	Stephen	Clar	045
Mary	Asht	018	Thomas	Alle	010
Mary	Guer	120	William	Rich	295
Mary J	Adam	004	MOSEL		
Robert	Star	317	William	Mont	246
Samuel D	Clar	047	MOSELEY		
Samuel P	Trum	325	Ellen	Nobl	270
Sarah A	Carr	040	MOSER		
Morrow			Fred	Monr	225
Bazel	Mont	230	Geo	Cham	043
Chas	Fair	092	Henry	Hami	139
Elisha W	Cosh	060	Henry S	Rich	296
Ellener	Meig	213	James H	Rich	292
James A	Colu	056	Nicholas	Cuya	075
John	Monr	226	MOSES		
Julia A	Mari	209	Henry	Asht	016
Lewis N	High	154	Henry S	Star	317
Lydia	Clin	052	MOSHOLDER		
Martha	Cham	042	David E	Lick	184
Oscar C	Clar	045	MOSIER		
Robert M	Colu	059	Joseph T	Meig	214
William H	Hard	144	MOSS		
William M	Preb	286	Charles	Mont	255
MORSE			Fred T	Summ	323
Betsey	Defi	080	Joseph	Athe	021
Chas P	Unio	335	Mary J	Ross	297

MOSS (cont)			MOWERS		
Sarah	Clar	044	Henry H	Rich	292
William	Ross	298	MOWON		
MOSSBROOKS			Thomas	Erie	088
Geo W	Lick	186	MOWREY		
MOSSGROVE			Anna	Wayn	354
Ann	Musk	263	Emily T	Hock	159
MOSSHOLDER			MOWRY		
William	Wayn	351	Caroline	Hock	157
MOSSMAN			David	Sene	310
Nancy	Lick	183	John N	Rich	292
MOSURE			Sarah	Gall	110
Samantha	VanW	339	MOXWELL		
MOTE			Rebecca C	Warr	343
Casville	Dark	077	MOY		
Harvey	Merc	217	Benedict	Hard	147
John H	Mont	228	MOYER		
Nelson	Dark	077	Jacob O	VanW	336
MOTHSHEAD			Jeremiah	Fair	089
John	Mont	236	Samuel W	Maho	207
MOTT			Tobias N W	Summ	323
Chester	Will	356	MOYERS		
Elijah	Lawr	182	Mary C	Paul	273
Elizabeth	Fair	091	MOZENA		
Samuel R	Paul	274	Rachel	Monr	224
MOTTS			MUCHE		
John	Mont	243	William	Mont	254
MOULTON			MUCHLER		
Dallas	Port	283	Mary	Cuya	076
George W	Port	285	Matilda	Musk	263
MOULTZ			MUCHMORE		
Mary A	Star	319	Thomas H	Miam	220
MOUND			MUELLER		
Sarah J	Musk	263	Herman	Fran	100
MOUNDAY			Joseph	Hami	125
William	Erie	086	Martin	Otta	272
MOUNT			MUENZING		
Amey	Cler	048	Gottlieb	Geau	113
Phebe D	Knox	173	MUFFORD		
Thompson	Cham	041	William H	Hanc	141
MOUNTS			MUIR		
Susan	Fair	091	James	Wood	363
MOUSER			John	Wood	363
Mary C	Cham	041	MUISHALL		
MOWAN			Stephen K	Hami	122
Baltzar	Hard	144	MULCHY		
Cath	Hard	144	Margaret	Cuya	068
MOWBRAY			MULFORD		
James	Ross	297	Enos C	Meig	214
MOWDER			Sarah E	Fran	097
Henry	Monr	226	MULHALL		
MOWEN			Michael	Mont	243
David C	Sene	311			

MULHOLLAND			MUNCASTER		
Mary	Hami	129	Chas H	Star	317
MULL			MUNCHENHAGEN		
David O	Fran	100	David	Lora	193
Henry	Warr	343	MUNCY		
MULLALY			Elizabeth	Musk	267
John	Cuya	075	MUND		
(alias John Hall)			Henry	Mont	252
MULLANE			MUNDORFF		
John	Hami	127	Sarah	Wayn	352
MULLEN			MUNDY		
Albert C	Warr	344	Reuben B	Wood	362
Anna	Hanc	140	MUNGEN		
Bethnel	Warr	344	William	Hanc	141
Cath	Hami	132	MUNGER		
Eliza W	Brow	031	Andrew J	Paul	273
Hugh	Fran	102	Hiram A	Otta	271
Jehu	Warr	344	MUNK		
Joseph T	Brow	032	Elizabeth	Shel	315
Theo	Unio	334	MUNN		
William A	Alle	010	Eliza A	Lake	176
MULLENIX			Fanny M	Geau	112
Thomas B	Defi	081	MUNNELL		
MULLER			Joseph H	Rich	295
Charles	Mont	236	MUNS		
Magdalena	Hami	131	William	Athe	020
Maria S	Tusc	330	MUNSELL		
Mary	Hami	131	William E	Paul	273
Otto	Hami	122	MUNSHOWER		
MULLET			Nathan	Lawr	181
Samuel	Tusc	331	MUNSON		
MULLIGAN			Alneda	Hami	131
James	Mont	245	Hessel P	Rich	292
John	Craw	062	William	Cuya	075
MULLINS			William O	Musk	266
John	Mont	236	Wilmot	Hard	145
Patrick	Mont	238	MURDOCK		
Richard A	Mont	236	David	Harr	149
MULLVEAN			David	Wood	363
Elizabeth J	Tusc	331	George	Trum	326
MULVANEY			George W	Musk	267
Patrick	Mont	255	Thomas A	Hami	121
MUMEA			MURDOCKS		
Elizabeth	Star	320	Jackson C	Morg	258
MUMFORD			MURGRAGE		
Annie V	Lora	195	Fred N	Nobl	268
James	Musk	264	MURLEY		
MUMMELL			Mary	Hami	131
Rachel	Musk	265	MURNAHAM		
MUMMY			Hiram	Lawr	179
Anne	Harr	150	MURNEY		
MUMPER			Cornelius	Mont	237
Andrew	Ashl	012			

MURPHEY			MURRAY (cont)		
Lucy L	Putn	289	Hannah	Wash	345
MURPHY			Harriet	Colu	056
Adaline M	Warr	344	Henry W	Geau	111
Ann	Summ	323	Isaac P	Musk	266
Barbara	Preb	287	James	Meig	213
Bridget	Wash	346	John	Mont	249
Cath	Fran	097	John D	Hami	126
Cath	Gree	113	John R	Guer	118
Cath	Jack	168	Joseph N	Scio	306
Cornelius	Mont	244	Levanda	Ashl	013
Daniel	Loga	191	Luke	Fran	100
David	Morg	258	Michael	Mont	245
Dennis	Mont	253	Peter	Mont	255
Dennis	Ross	297	Robert B	Madi	202
Edward	Mont	255	Samuel A	Musk	267
Edward	Mont	255	Samuel P	Butl	038
Eleanor	Warr	343	William H	Cuya	072
Francis M	Brow	034	MURRY		
Hannah	Hard	146	Atwill	Fult	105
Honora	Gree	116	Chas	Colu	056
James	Mont	252	Edward	Jeff	171
John	Gree	114	John	Ross	299
John	Mont	237	Lavina	Sand	304
John	Trum	329	Mary	Madi	203
Marcena M	Knox	175	William	Cham	043
Margaret	Hami	124	MUSCROFT		
Margaret	Hami	131	Samuel J	Rich	292
Margaret	Lawr	180	MUSGRAVE		
Mary	Luca	197	Maria P	Hami	131
Matthew	Mont	234	Sarah	Cosh	061
Michael	Mont	230	MUSHRUSH		
Michael	Mont	235	Hiram	Jeff	172
Michael	Mont	249	MUSSALMAN		
Owen	Mont	246	Henry W	Wayn	352
Patrick	Mont	241	MUSSELMAN		
Phebe A	Defi	081	Martin	Gree	116
Rebecca A	Monr	225	MUSSER		
Sarah A	Trum	329	Elizabeth	Wood	358
Thomas	Paul	273	Mary	Hami	131
Thomas	Warr	344	Nancy	Augl	026
Wesley	Lawr	181	MUSSEY		
Wilfred F	Mont	246	Francis B	Hami	125
William A	Morg	257	MUSSULMAN		
William L	Mont	234	Abram L	Merc	218
MURRAY			MUST		
Adam C	Sene	314	Christian	Mont	229
Bridget	Hami	131	MUSTAIN		
Dorcas	Alle	008	Berry	Faye	094
Elizabeth	High	154	MUTE		
Elizabeth M	Maho	206	Geo P	Fran	100
Emeline	Henr	152	MUTH		
George	Holm	160	Maria	Sand	302

MUZZEY			MYERS (cont)		
Geo	Fran	103	John F	Wyan	365
MYER			Jonathan Jr	Star	316
Charles	Star	320	Joseph	Mont	235
Christiana	Erie	086	Joseph P	Luca	199
John	Faye	094	Joseph P	Sene	314
Jonathan E	Cuya	071	Margaret	Putn	289
MYERS			Maria	Wash	346
Aaron	Putn	290	Michael	Mont	233
Adam J	Monr	223	Rachel	Will	356
Alfred T	Hard	147	Rebecca	Dark	078
Amanda	Butl	036	Rebecca E	Putn	289
August	Mont	229	Rhoda	Hock	158
Augustine	Jeff	172	Ruth	Scio	307
Barbara	Miam	219	Samuel	Clar	047
Benj	Loga	192	Samuel	Tusc	331
Benj F	Defi	080	Sarah	Gree	113
Cath	Carr	040	Siddy	Scio	307
Cath	Will	355	Susannah	Lora	192
Charles W	Hami	121	Telitha A	Rich	291
David	Carr	040	Thornton D	Putn	289
David D	Rich	295	Wayne	VanW	339
Edward	Hami	126	William	Hami	138
Edward	Sand	301	William	Hanc	143
Edwin C	Port	283	William L	Wash	351
Elizabeth	Knox	174	MYRICE		
Franklin R	Lick	184	William	Wood	363
Frederick	Port	284	MYTINGER		
Frederick	Sene	314	John	Colu	056
Frederick A	Hami	121			
George	Lick	185			
George	Sand	303			
George L	Monr	225	NAAS		
George M	Fair	090	Eliza	Butl	035
George W	Cler	049	NABER		
George W	Fair	092	Mary	Hami	136
George W	Sene	309	NABRING		
Gilbert L	Paul	273	Henry	Erie	086
Gottleib	Tusc	332	NACE		
Hannah	Belm	029	William M	Fran	098
Henry	Fran	100	NAGEL		
(recorded as Henry Wyers)			Christopher	Defi	081
Henry	Miam	221	NAGLE		
Henry R	Maho	206	Augustus	Colu	056
Hury	Luca	201	John E	Dela	085
Jabez	Mont	232	Margaret	Fran	097
Jackson	Alle	009	NALL		
Jacob	Paul	273	Henry	Mont	227
James W	Sene	314	NALLY		
Jane	Defi	079	John	Monr	225
Jane	Rich	292	William	Mont	255
John	Hami	127	NANCE		
John	Merc	217	William	High	157

NANCE (cont)		
Wilson	Lawr	182
NANGLE		
Margaret A	Henr	153
NANNA		
William	Henr	151
NAPP		
Cath	Summ	324
Henry L	Summ	324
NARACONG		
Patience	Lora	194
NARAGON		
Alfred C	Tusc	330
NARGNEY		
Jane M	Tusc	331
NARIGON		
Mary	Tusc	331
NARMEY		
Isabell	Tusc	331
NASH		
Adaline	Loga	190
Felix	Jack	167
James M	Maho	205
Jane	Dela	082
Lydia A	Cosh	062
William D	Lick	187
NASMYTH		
Alexander H	Miam	222
NATCHER		
Martha	Loga	190
NATHANS		
Hannah	Fran	101
NATION		
Franklin	Preb	286
NAU		
John	Hami	134
NAUGHTON		
James	Mont	241
NAUMAN		
Lewis	Wayn	355
NAUS		
Aaron F	Hanc	143
John A	Fran	098
John P	Hard	146
Samuel	Augl	026
William	Hard	145
NAVARRE		
Daniel	Luca	199
Robert C	Luca	199
NAYLOR		
Jonathan	Morg	258
Thomas	Mont	246
William	Luca	202

NAYLOR (cont)		
William P	Sand	304
NEAL		
Anna E	Hami	131
Clarissa	Clar	044
Elizabeth	Gall	110
Francis M	Cler	050
John T	Shel	316
Nancy	Wood	361
Robert D	Gall	109
Rosanna	Belm	030
Simeon	Lawr	182
NEARON		
Adam	Merc	217
NEASE		
Washington	Meig	216
NEASON		
Anvinette B	Sand	302
NEDROW		
John	Paul	274
NEEDLES		
Enoch A	Faye	094
NEEDRY		
John F	Senc	312
NEEHOUSE		
John	Otta	271
NEELY		
Elizabeth	Luca	197
Martha	Carr	040
NEER		
Cynthia A	Craw	063
Joseph F	Cham	041
Matthew	Clar	044
NEERIEMER		
James	Tusc	332
NEESE		
Caroline	Hami	131
NEFE		
Elizabeth	Morr	262
NEFF		
Abby A	Sene	311
Adam C	Preb	286
Cornelius	Otta	270
Cynthia E	Sene	309
Eliza P	Scio	307
John D	Alle	009
John S	Ross	296
Obedience	Scio	305
NEGELE		
William	Sene	313
NEGLEY		
Mary	Mont	232

NEGUS		
Mary E	Colu	058
Sarah A	Colu	059
NEHREW		
Joseph	Mont	246
NEIB		
Anna	Hami	131
NEIBERT		
Joseph	Mont	228
NEIBLING		
Elizabeth A	Hanc	142
Sarah	Fair	090
NEICE		
Daniel	Dark	077
NEIDHORDT		
Frederick	Otta	272
NEIDIG		
Valentine	Wyan	367
NEIGHBOR		
David	Tusc	331
Jacob W	Tusc	331
NEIGHBORS		
Abel C	Carr	040
NEIKIRK		
David	Sene	312
NEIL		
William S	Unio	334
NEILL		
Foster F	Erie	088
NELL		
Mary	Alle	010
NELLIGAN		
Hannah	Cuya	068
NELLIS		
Adelaide	Tusc	330
NELSON		
Alex W	Athe	023
Andrew H	Meig	212
Benj F	Jeff	170
Benj R	Guer	117
Clarissa	Vint	341
David L	Luca	202
Esther	Guer	119
George	Mont	254
Isabella	Pike	282
James	Cosh	059
James N	Wyan	367
John	Defi	081
John	Lick	187
Julius C	Asht	018
Nancy	Morr	260
Peter	Medi	211
Philemia	Athe	023

NELSON (cont)		
Samuel	Faye	094
Sophronia	Geau	112
Thomas	Colu	057
Washington	Fair	089
William W	Fran	098
NEPHEW		
Robert	Trum	327
NEPTUNE		
Selina C	Nobl	269
NESBET		
Lucinda	Summ	324
NESBIT		
James	Sand	302
Samuel	Sene	309
NESBITT		
Mary	Adam	006
NESSELROADE		
Robert	Wash	348
NESSLE		
Isaiah J	Maho	205
NESSLEY		
Jonas	Fran	098
NEST		
Maximillian	Maho	207
NETMORE		
Elbridge	Wood	359
NETTLETON		
Augustus	Asht	016
NEVILLE		
Caroline M	Dela	082
Sarah A	Brow	035
NEVIN		
Henry C	Ross	300
John	Tusc	330
Matilda	High	155
NEWALL		
Huldah	Geau	111
NEWBEGIN		
Chas M	Hami	134
NEWBERGER		
Anna M	Wash	349
NEWBERRY		
William R	Lick	184
NEWBY		
Elsey	Belm	028
James W	Merc	216
NEWCOM		
Gottlieb	Cuya	067
NEWCOMB		
Cyrenius L	Asht	019
Nathan L	Cuya	067

NEWCOMBER		
Henry	Sene	310
NEWELL		
Abraham V	Putn	288
Adelbert	Luca	199
Chas W	Colu	056
Jeremiah	Mont	235
John A	Musk	264
Nancy	Defi	079
Polly M	Lora	194
Richard	Carr	040
William M	Hard	148
NEWHARD		
George A	Trum	329
NEWHART		
Geo	Monr	225
NEWHOUSE		
James H	Dela	085
Michael	Craw	064
NEWKIRK		
Mary A	Cler	050
NEWKUM		
Margaret	Hard	147
NEWLAN		
Rachel	Rich	294
NEWLAND		
Allen	Ross	296
Andrew	Augl	026
Edward K	Alle	010
Eliza	Augl	026
John	Gall	110
John H	Paul	272
NEWLEN		
David	Wash	350
Eliza J	Wash	347
Sarah	Wash	350
NEWLER		
Ira	Wash	350
NEWLING		
James E	Mont	235
NEWMAN		
Adam	Mont	238
Cath	Warr	344
Geo	Morg	258
Guilford A	Pike	282
James	Loga	189
James	Mont	254
James K P	Adam	003
Jeremiah	Mont	243
Jno	Lawr	183
John	Wash	345
Joseph	Mont	236
Joseph J	Cuya	067
NEWMAN (cont)		
Louis	Mont	253
Lucinda	Wash	346
Maria J	Gree	116
Mary	Adam	004
Michael	Hanc	141
Richard	Scio	305
Sarah J	Geau	113
Veturia	Will	357
William	Luca	199
William L	Ashl	011
NEWMANN		
Erdmann G	Mont	246
NEWPORT		
Susannah	Fran	103
NEWSON		
Chas E	Fran	098
William	Sene	311
NEWSTEAD		
Benj	Mont	238
NEWTON		
Alfred L	Fult	106
Alonzo	Athe	023
Cath	Cuya	066
Charles A	Maho	206
Gresham	Athe	023
Malissa J	High	156
Martha	Nobl	268
Mary A	Lora	194
Robert	Luca	199
Sarah	Huro	165
Townsend E	Luca	199
William M	Otta	272
Winson A	Hami	137
Zilpha	Brow	031
NICE		
Isaac	Athe	023
NICHAUS		
Herman	Mont	249
NICHIZER		
Matilda	Pick	279
NICHOLAS		
Jas F	Butl	037
Oscar F	Cuya	076
NICHOLS		
Amos	Musk	264
Amos J	Putn	290
Benj F	Fran	098
Charles	Lick	188
Daniel W	Wyan	367
Elizabeth A	Guer	120
Frank C	Hami	134
Geo	Perr	277

NICHOLS (cont)			NIGHSWANDER		
George J	Mont	239	Andrew	Cler	050
James	Scio	307	Martin	Sene	310
John W	Medi	211	NIHILL		
Mahlon	Belm	030	John	Mont	236
Malinda	Ross	297	NIHUFF		
Martha	Harr	149	Jos	Medi	210
Nancy	Monr	223	NILLS		
Thomas	Knox	172	Sarah E	Adam	005
Thomas	Morg	257	NIMS		
Thomas	Vint	340	Ruel	Geau	112
William	Madi	202	NIROTE		
William C	Jeff	172	Christian	Holm	160
NICHOLSON			NISWONGER		
Hannah J	Warr	343	David E	Dark	077
William	Mont	246	Frederick	Nobl	268
William	Rich	293	NITSCHELM		
NICK			Salomi	Cuya	068
William S	Medi	210	NIXON		
NICKEL			David	Adam	007
Julia A	Merc	218	John	Jeff	172
Philip	Butl	038	Richard	Butl	038
NICKELS			Thomas	Mont	252
James A	Cham	041	William	Luca	196
NICKERSON			NOBLE		
Franklin B	Huro	162	Alexander	Henr	151
Samuel R	Warr	344	Ann	Belm	028
NICKEY			George	Guer	117
Sarah A	Wayn	353	Henry	Morr	259
NICKLES			Henry S L	Pick	280
Jacob	Tusc	332	Isaac	Huro	165
NICODEMUS			Jaques	Clar	047
Harrison	Miam	219	Johnson	Trum	326
Meredith H	Madi	203	Mary E	Fran	103
NICOL			Robert	Perr	276
Mary	Musk	265	Sarah	Huro	163
NICOLL			NOBLET		
Jas	Belm	027	Thomas	Craw	064
NIEBAUER			NODINE		
John	Cuya	076	Jacob	Lake	178
NIEBEL			NOE		
Elijah	Sene	310	David P	Fran	104
NIENHUSER			NOEL		
John L	Cler	049	Ernest	Mont	254
NIERMANN			Margaret	Wood	363
Chas A	Mont	244	Nancy	Scio	307
NIGH			William	Hard	146
Mary J	Wyan	364	NOEPEL		
Sarah	Fair	092	Frederick	Mont	246
Sarah	Pick	279	NOGGLES		
NIGHMAN			Hiram	Mari	208
Lydia	Star	317	NOHL		
			John A	Luca	199

NOLAN			NORRIS (cont)		
Cath	Erie	087	John W	Brow	032
Jane	Hami	132	Josiah	Monr	223
Michael	Hami	134	Lucian W	Fran	098
Thomas	Mont	239	Marquis	Musk	264
NOLAND			Ormar P	Wood	358
Alfred	Morg	257	Rachel	Belm	027
Burris M	Summ	323	Thomas B	Clar	046
Joseph	Wash	346	William	Scio	306
Reuben	Athe	021	William E	Rich	293
Ruel	Perr	276	NORTH		
Silas	Perr	277	Amos	Miam	221
Sylvester	Wash	345	Chas	Hami	134
Thomas	High	153	Elizabeth	Miam	222
William	Mont	242	Susan	Mont	256
William A	Wash	346	William H	Wood	359
NOLDER			NORTHCUTT		
James	Clin	054	Jos P	Cham	042
NOLL			NORTHROP		
Adam	Hami	134	Malissa	Clar	047
NOLLER			NORTHRUP		
John	Hanc	140	Henry B	Cuya	076
NOLTE			Hiram R	Huro	162
Frederick	Mont	235	NORTHWAY		
NOLZE			Abbie P	Trum	328
Fredrica	Ross	301	Sherman B	Trum	326
NONAN			William H	Ashl	012
Martin	Mont	245	NORTON		
NONNAMAKER			Ellen	Vint	340
Jacob A	Alle	008	Experience	VanW	339
NOONAN			Horace	Lake	178
Thomas	Mont	237	James A	Sene	314
NORCRASS			Jesse S	Luca	199
William C	Henr	151	John	Hami	134
NORMAN			John W	Sene	310
Amos I	Morg	257	Lorenzo	Asht	016
Angelina	Lick	187	Loretta S	Cuya	065
Elizabeth	Lick	185	Michael	Vint	340
Henry C	Hard	146	Sally	Cuya	076
John	Musk	263	Samuel H	Trum	328
NORRICK			William H	Summ	324
Mary F	Rich	293	NOSKON		
NORRIS			Chas	Mont	233
Albert	Musk	262	NOTESTINE		
Alexander	Dela	083	Cath	Loga	190
Amaziah	Scio	308	NOTT		
Chas C	Asht	017	Jane	Wash	347
David R	Cosh	061	Oscar B	Morg	257
Dorcas C	Athe	022	Vandevere	Morg	259
Elisha B	Wyan	367	NOTTER		
Hadasah E	Asht	019	Sarah S	Gall	110
James L	Morg	258	NOTTINGHAM		
John J	Athe	022	Amanda	Merc	218

NOUSE			OBEALY		
George	Holm	161	Frank L	Wood	363
NOWE			OBERHOLTZ		
Nicholas	Mont	240	Eli	Medi	211
NOYES			OBERLIN		
Alvin A	Huro	162	Orlando	Will	357
Edward F	Hami	134	William K	Rich	294
NUBER			OBERLY		
Jacob	Fran	098	Daniel	Miam	221
NUGENT			OBERMIER		
Amanda	Ross	297	Simon P	Hanc	142
Patrick	Mont	246	O'BOYLE		
NULL			Michael	Mont	241
Elizabeth	Dela	083	OBRACK		
James W	Lawr	182	Henry	Cuya	074
John	Dela	083	O'BRIANT		
John W	Lawr	183	Lewis	Ross	300
Laura A	Medi	211	O'BRIEN		
Samuel R	Lawr	179	Cath	Huro	161
NUNNEMAKER			Cath	Putn	289
Daniel J	Vint	340	James	Luca	199
NURNBERGER			John	Cuya	072
Henry	Butl	036	John	Mont	242
NUSHANG			John	Mont	250
Mary	Mont	233	Michael	Ashl	011
NUSSBAUNER			Michael	Luca	200
Benja	Huro	165	Michael	Mont	247
NUTT			Patrick	Mont	256
Edmund E	Shel	315	William	Fran	100
NUTTER			OBRINGER		
Isaac	Wyan	365	Nicholas	Merc	216
Thomas S	Hock	158	O'BRYAN		
NUTTING			Mary	Hami	124
Josiah	Mont	239	O'CALLAGHAN		
NYDEYGER			Frank M	Luca	199
Charles W	Holm	161	OCHS		
NYE			Henry	Hard	147
John A	High	155	Henry G	Mont	238
John H	Scio	306	OCKULY		
Mary M	Lora	193	John	Hami	125
			O'CONNARD		
			Timothy	Mont	241
			O'CONNELL		
OAKLEY			Bridget D	Jeff	169
Henry H	Summ	324	Jeffrey	Mont	244
Seth D	Medi	211	Michael	Mont	247
OAKS			Peter D	Jeff	169
Nelson A	Clar	045	O'CONNER		
OATES			Jacob	Ross	298
John A	Mont	247	John	Luca	199
OATLEY			O'CONNOR		
Edwin	Trum	326	Bridget	Hami	127
			James	Jeff	169

O'CONNOR (cont)		
James	Mont	250
Thomas	Mont	249
Timothy	Mont	243
O'DANIELS		
Edward	Warr	342
O'DAVIS		
John	Craw	063
ODELL		
Bennager	Wood	362
Cyrus	Sand	304
Emeline W	Lake	177
Hannah	Hock	157
Nancy	Gall	108
Phebe	Fran	103
ODEN		
Charles	Fran	100
(alias Charles Odenthal)		
Elias	Lick	188
ODENTHAL		
Charles	Fran	100
(alias Charles Oden)		
ODLE		
James	Scio	307
Martha A	Augl	025
ODLIN		
Speice	Mont	231
O'DONAHOE		
Florance	Mont	255
O'DONALD		
Mary	Jeff	171
O'DONNELL		
Bridget	Cosh	060
John A	Musk	265
Sarah	Hami	124
Sarah	Hami	127
O'DOWD		
Eliza	Hami	124
Michael M	Mont	243
O'DRISCOLL		
Daniel	Mont	240
OECKEL		
Charles	Luca	199
OELTER		
John	Mont	235
OERTEL		
Geo P	Cuya	072
O'FLYNG		
Lydia	Craw	062
OGAN		
John Q	Cosh	061
Noah W	Putn	289
William H H	Trum	329

OGBORN		
David H	Clin	055
OGDEN		
Dean	High	153
Francis M	High	156
Hannah	Ross	301
Herbert G	Sene	309
John T	Lora	196
Martha	Morr	260
Sarah	Hock	158
Sarah A	Cler	051
OGG		
Geo P	Wyan	365
Jerome	Hanc	143
Lewah	Perr	277
OGIER		
James H	Vint	340
Julius	Mont	229
OGLE		
Benj C	Nobl	268
Elisha M	Will	355
Elizabeth	Musk	263
Elizabeth	Port	284
Mary	Colu	057
OGLEVEE		
Hugh	Harr	150
OGLEVIE		
Cath	Putn	289
Jas	Cosh	061
O'HANLAN		
Daniel	Mont	250
O'HARRA		
John T	Fran	097
O'HERN		
Mary	Defi	079
OHL		
John	Hami	128
OHLINGER		
Jno	Meig	215
OHLMER		
John	Butl	036
OHMART		
Sarah	Dark	078
OHR		
Henry	Butl	036
OILER		
Andrew J	Vint	341
James	Gall	107
O'KANE		
Simon	Mont	249
O'KEEFE		
Michael	Mont	243

O'KELLY			OLMSTEAD		
Thomas	Cuya	072	Ann E	Trum	329
OKEY			Anna C	Pick	279
Gardner	Monr	225	Sanford A	Dela	085
Levin O	Monr	224	OLMSTED		
OLCOTT			Lucius J	Morr	261
Chas P	Medi	210	Lydia B	Lake	176
OLDEN			OLNEY		
Lydia A	Shel	315	Otis	Alle	009
OLDER			OLSHLAGER		
Barnett	Wood	359	Christian	Merc	217
Henry	Colu	058	O'MAHLEY		
OLDFATHER			Patrick	Mont	250
Samuel	Preb	286	O'MALLEY		
OLDFIELD			Thomas	Mont	250
Elizabeth A	Scio	306	OMAN		
Geo B	Defi	081	Ellen	Hanc	143
OLDHAM			O'MARAH		
Christenah	Musk	267	Belinda	Cuya	073
Joshua G	Dela	082	O'MEARA		
OLDS			Jas	Hami	138
Abigail	Morr	261	OMWEG		
Gilbert O	Sene	309	Cath A	Wayn	351
Hubert B	Sene	309	ONAWEG		
Theda	Morr	261	Jacob	Huro	162
William C	Tusc	333	O'NEAL		
OLDT			Martha A	Clin	055
Geo	Mont	232	Samuel	Scio	306
O'LEARY			Thomas	Hami	137
Edward	Madi	204	O'NEIL		
OLER			Charles	Mont	239
Henry	Tusc	332	Johnson	Lawr	183
OLINGER			Michael	Cler	050
Chas	Ross	299	William H	Mont	244
George	Mont	246	O'NEILL		
Lucinda	Clar	044	Daniel	Mont	250
OLIVER			ONG		
Chas E M	Wyan	366	Oliver C	Musk	265
David	Wash	348	ONSTOTT		
Esther A	Hami	127	Mary E	Ashl	012
George W	Trum	326	ONWELLER		
James	Lake	176	Amanda B	Fult	105
John	Jack	168	OOT		
Louisa	Star	318	Amento	Luca	200
Mary	Morg	258	OPPENHOF		
Rebecca	Star	319	Herman	Maho	205
Sarah	Lick	186	OPPER		
Sarah	VanW	339	Geo	Morr	259
Thomas	Hami	129	John	Lora	193
William	Fran	100	OPPLINGER		
Zerna A	Morr	259	Anna O	Monr	224
OLLINGER			OPPY		
Sarah	Holm	161	Elizabeth	Scio	307

243

ORAHOOD			OSBORN (cont)		
Hiram	Unio	335	Joel	Sene	311
ORAM			John	Warr	343
Hester	Putn	290	Jonas	Clin	055
ORAWFORD			Joseph	Lora	193
Sarah	Lawr	183	Josiah	Pick	278
(possibly Sarah Crawford)			Milton	Lick	185
ORCUTT			Ralph N H	Huro	165
William E	Asht	015	Sarah M	Butl	038
O'REILLEY			Seth W	Clin	054
Richard	Mont	247	Walter C	Clar	047
ORESTA			William E	Paul	272
Henry	Erie	086	OSBOUR		
ORMSBY			Susannah	Wyan	366
Morris S	Hard	148	OSBOURN		
ORMSTED			Sarah	Cler	051
Jane	Lawr	180	OSBUN		
O'ROURKE			Ransom I	Rich	294
Richard	Cuya	072	OSBURN		
ORR			David	Meig	216
Abraham	Unio	334	John	Putn	290
Harvey	Ross	297	John N	Mont	250
Jacob	Nobl	268	Rosannah	Meig	215
Julia F	Wash	349	OSGOOD		
William H	Belm	030	Susan E	Lora	193
William H	Faye	094	OSLER		
ORTH			Francis A	Nobl	268
Louis D	Cuya	072	John H	Belm	027
ORTLAUF			OSLING		
Adam	Holm	160	Sophia	Hami	124
ORTMAN			OSMAN		
James S	Fran	100	Zibia	Wood	363
Joseph	Hami	125	OSMER		
William	Mont	247	Addison F	Trum	326
ORTNER			OSMUN		
Martin	Erie	088	Colesman	Will	355
ORTT			OSMUS		
Mary	Otta	272	Cath	Hami	124
ORWICK			OSTERHOLD		
Rebecca	Jeff	169	William	Hami	125
ORWIG			OSTERMEYER		
Hannah	Sene	313	Mathew	Cuya	072
OSBORN			OSTIRHOLD		
Abraham	VanW	338	Derick D	Sene	309
Eliza	Cham	041	OSTRANDER		
Elliott	Scio	307	Geo M	Henr	151
Emory	Star	316	Jacob	Dela	085
Enos	Lick	185	Solomon	Lake	176
Eugene A	Huro	165	O'SULLIVAN		
George	Hard	148	Serena	Belm	027
George W	Maho	205	OSWALT		
Harmon B	Trum	326	John	Paul	273
Huldah T	Cuya	069			

OTIS			OVERPACK		
Geo	Defi	081	Geo	Clar	044
O'TOOL			Nancy	Clar	046
Margaret	Huro	161	OVERS		
O'TOOLE			David	Monr	225
Patrick	Clar	045	OVERSTREET		
OTT			Greenbury	Mont	255
Charles A	Mont	239	OVIALT		
Christian	Mont	250	John F	Cuya	075
Philip	Luca	199	OVIATT		
Valentine	Sand	302	Sarah J	Trum	327
OTTERBACHER			OWEN		
John	Wood	359	Bartley	Wash	346
OTTGEN			Chas W	Morr	259
John C	Fult	106	John J	Fran	100
OTTO			Joseph P	Lora	194
Andrew	Mont	227	Levi	Miam	221
John H	Star	319	Mary E	Wash	347
Margaret	Otta	271	OWENS		
OUG			Archibald	Rich	291
Jacob B	Hami	125	David	Fran	100
OUTCALT			Elizabeth	Jack	167
Chas S	Clin	055	Elizabeth	Warr	342
Clarkson	Fair	089	Elizabeth J	Gree	113
Henry W	Morg	259	Harrison H	Ashl	013
Judson A	Fran	100	James	VanW	338
Thomas	Fran	100	John A	Asht	017
OVARMIER			Julia A	Monr	224
Hiram	Paul	273	Malinda	Gree	115
OVEN			Mary Ann	Hard	145
John	Mont	238	Mary R	Geau	112
OVER			Moses	Port	284
Eli L	Cosh	060	Phebe	Morr	260
OVERBY			Sarah	Belm	028
Andrew J	Jack	167	OXLEY		
OVERHOLSER			John M	Mont	233
Jeremiah	Loga	189	OYER		
Mary	Colu	055	John	Pick	278
OVERHOLT			John E	Star	320
Joseph	Rich	292	OZBILL		
OVERHOLTZER			Lorenzo	Henr	153
Rebecca	Clar	044	OZIER		
OVERHULSE			Gaylord	Craw	063
Jesse	Henr	152	OZMUN		
OVERLY			Maria	Summ	324
Samuel W	Hard	147			
Thomas P	Mont	247			
OVERMAN					
William	Dark	077			
OVERMIER					
Samuel	Henr	151			
OVERMYER					
Homer	Sand	304			

PACE				**PALM (cont)**		
Elias	Perr	277		Margaret	Rich	292
Henry	Mari	209		**PALMER**		
James	Fran	098		Benj F	Wash	345
Mary	Perr	277		Cath	Jack	166
Nathan	Loga	191		Charles T	Fran	098
PACKARD				David	Carr	039
John M	Fran	098		David	Fult	105
Slary	Huro	162		Elizabeth	Ashl	013
PACKER				Elizabeth	Hard	148
Storer	Belm	030		George H	Luca	199
PADDOCK				George W	Defi	081
Daniel J	Mont	245		Hannah	Monr	226
PADEN				Harrison	Adam	003
Jas	Clar	046		Henry	Huro	162
Sarah	Trum	328		James	Cuya	076
PAESSLER				Jewett Jr	Wash	349
Theophilus	Carr	040		John	Cuya	074
PAFT				John C	Cuya	067
Betsey M	Trum	330		John D	Summ	322
PAGE				Jonathan	Putn	290
Francis M	Wash	345		Martha A	Lick	188
Jas G	Medi	211		Mary Ann	Hami	127
Jesse	Tusc	331		Mason H	Fran	099
Joseph	Mont	245		Melvin	Sene	311
Nancy	Meig	216		Reuben	Lawr	181
Thomas	Unio	336		Robert W	Belm	029
William	Mont	228		Sally	Asht	017
PAGUE				William H	Defi	081
Alfred	Hard	146		William H	Jack	167
PAIGE				**PALMERTON**		
Job	Mont	245		Benj F	Wood	360
PAIN				James N	Henr	152
Margaret	Faye	094		**PALSGROVE**		
PAINE				Tilman	Miam	221
Franklin	Lake	177		**PANCAKE**		
Melissa E	Wood	358		Andrew	Lawr	180
PAINS				**PANCOAST**		
Sarah	Sene	314		Ohio	Ashl	011
PAINTER				Polly	Faye	093
Emeline	Wayn	352		**PANGLE**		
Peter S	Wood	358		Rebecca	VanW	336
Robert M	Loga	192		**PANSLER**		
Samuel	Musk	262		Rachel	Musk	263
PAINTON				**PARCELL**		
George W	Summ	322		John	Wayn	351
PAKE				**PARCHER**		
Henry L	Musk	265		Geo	Will	355
Melissa A	Meig	213		Sally	Craw	062
PALEN				**PARDEE**		
Louisa	Mari	208		Allen	Medi	212
PALM				Eben L	Cuya	066
John G	Pick	278				

PARDUE			PARKER (cont)		
Harrison L	Miam	220	Lucy H	Hami	126
PARENT			Manville F	Asht	017
Harriet M	Fult	105	Margaret	Brow	032
Nathaniel	Fult	105	Mary	Hami	124
PARIDO			Mary J	Loga	190
Mary H	Fair	091	Rachel	Gall	110
PARIS			Rufus B	Geau	111
Lewis	Warr	344	Samuel	Knox	174
Mercie H	Warr	344	Sarah J	Trum	327
Stephen	Adam	005	Sewell S	Luca	200
PARISH			Sheldon	Athe	024
Anna	Preb	287	Silas T	Adam	006
Charlotte	Trum	327	Thomas	Mont	240
John E	Sand	302	William	Summ	322
PARK			William H	Warr	344
David P	Fran	103	PARKINSON		
Delilah	Wood	358	Martha	Musk	262
George A	Hard	145	Thomas K	Guer	118
James	Wayn	353	William	Mont	246
Thomas C	Lick	188	PARKISON		
Tyler D	Ashl	014	Cath	Lick	188
PARKE			Robert	Faye	093
William	Mont	243	Thomas	Rich	294
PARKER			William M	Lick	187
Adam B	Clar	046	PARKS		
Albert C	Summ	323	Almena	Geau	112
Albertus N	Asht	017	Cath J	Lick	188
Andrew C	Trum	327	Charles A	Geau	112
Anne	Meig	216	Charles T	Summ	322
Betsey	Cuya	064	James	Harr	150
Cath	Augl	024	James H	Scio	305
Clarissa	Fran	096	Mary E	Morr	261
De Forest	Summ	323	Matilda	Trum	328
Edwin	Hanc	141	Wesley	Monr	225
Elihu	Erie	086	PARLET		
Eliza	Knox	174	Isaiah	Butl	038
Eliza Jane	Wash	349	PARLETT		
Elizabeth	Cler	050	Ann	Guer	119
Ellen	Ross	298	PARMMER		
Ephraim	Madi	203	Cyrus	VanW	336
Erastus H	Athe	021	PARNETT		
Geo	Gree	113	Mary	Fran	103
(alias George Sandusky)			PARR		
Hartwell A	Summ	323	Andrew	Ashl	013
Henry G	Guer	117	Barbara	Augl	026
Isaac	Port	284	William A	Lick	188
James D	Hami	133	PARRET		
James M	Otta	272	James H	Hami	133
James O	Clar	046	PARRETT		
James S	Wash	349	Geo M	Clin	053
Joseph S	Ashl	013	William J	Ross	300
Lucy A	Putn	288			

PARRISH		
Henry	Lick	184
Isaac	Sand	302
John	Fran	103
Mary A	Musk	262
Rebecca E	Perr	276
Sarah	Paul	273
PARROTT		
Jacob	Hard	146
PARROW		
Charles	Mont	244
PARRY		
Sarah	Harr	149
Thomas	Craw	063
PARSHALL		
Belle E	Warr	343
PARSON		
Hannah	Jeff	171
Sarah	Rich	295
PARSONS		
Amanda	Cosh	062
Amy	Port	283
Chas B	Morg	257
Charlotte E	Wood	363
David	Gree	114
Elizabeth	Morr	261
Hardison	Wash	345
Henry	Meig	215
Jno A	Maho	206
John G	Cuya	069
Lorin G	Trum	326
Loverne E	Lora	195
Mary M	Luca	201
Sarah	Pick	278
Warren W	Huro	166
PARTEE		
John E	Will	356
PARTHEMORE		
Adelina	Unio	334
Erastus	Unio	334
PARTIONS		
Samuel	Ross	300
PARTLOW		
Mary A	Meig	215
Sarah	Lawr	180
PARTRIDGE		
Chas	Unio	336
Elvira P	Trum	329
Wesley	Scio	305
William	Cuya	067
PARVIS		
Alfred	Butl	035

PATCH		
Harmon	Madi	204
Jackson D	Asht	019
PATCHEN		
Thaddeus	Geau	112
PATCHIN		
Edward	Geau	111
James W	Asht	019
PATMOR		
Mary A	Hami	140
PATRICK		
Martha A	Hard	147
Minerva J	Hami	137
Nathan E	Dela	085
Theodore J	Mont	236
William	Cham	042
PATTEN		
George M	VanW	337
William T	Fran	099
PATTERSON		
Andrew C	Rich	293
Angelina	Athe	020
Barbara	Dark	077
Benj	Otta	272
David	Miam	218
Geo B	Geau	112
Geo P	Warr	343
James M	Guer	120
Jane	Harr	150
Jesse E	Luca	201
John	Colu	059
John D	Putn	290
John W	Lick	185
Jos M	Miam	220
Louisa	Cler	050
Margaret	Meig	212
Mary A	Summ	324
Rachel P	Dark	077
Rebecca	Tusc	330
Robert N	Rich	293
Ruth	Cosh	060
Seth D	Asht	014
Thomas M	Mont	242
Wesley L	Mont	243
William	Otta	272
William E	Colu	056
William F	Scio	305
William H	Dark	077
William H	Rich	294
William M	Cler	049
Wilson	Wood	364
PATTINSON		
Robert	Madi	203

PATTISON			PAYNE (cont)		
Robert D	Hami	133	James	Gree	116
PATTON			John B	Lawr	179
Elijah	Athe	022	Joshua	Knox	176
Elizabeth S	Faye	095	Lavina	Warr	344
George M	Harr	150	Lawrence	Ross	299
George W	Scio	305	Maria	Hami	124
James	Brow	032	Oren V	Wash	348
James F	High	155	Orris T	Asht	019
Jane	Harr	150	Polly B	Mont	232
Joseph A	Hami	133	True P	VanW	337
Mary K	Ross	297	William	Rich	293
Michael J	Hami	133	PAYSON		
Nancy	Butl	039	David F	Belm	029
Nancy	Putn	288	PAYTON		
Nancy M	Hami	137	William F	Jack	166
Phebe S	Hock	157	PEABODY		
Sophia L	Wash	350	Elias	Lora	192
William	Mont	228	Mary	Lora	195
PATTY			Rachel	High	156
William H	Miam	221	PEACH		
PAUL			Charles	Scio	308
Anna B	Miam	222	Sarah	Loga	192
Forstner	Cuya	066	PEACOCK		
Geo B	Mont	246	Charlotte	Wood	358
Michael	Cler	049	John N	Ross	299
PAULEY			Margaret	Pike	281
James W	Pike	283	PEAK		
PAULHAMUS			Chas C	Mari	210
Daniel H	Mont	240	PEALER		
PAULIC			Susan	Knox	173
Henry	Mont	241	William	Hard	144
PAULLIN			PEARCE		
Ruth V	Gree	114	Albert	Cler	050
PAULLUS			Charles	Huro	163
Mariah E	Preb	287	Elizabeth	Cosh	061
PAVEY			Frederick	Cuya	067
Amanda	Clin	053	John S	Harr	149
PAXSON			Mary E	Lick	184
William	Meig	215	Nancy M	Guer	118
PAXTON			PEARCH		
Eliza M	Cler	049	Elizabeth	Carr	040
Hannah K	Gree	115	PEARSE		
Samuel	Gree	114	Jane	Fair	089
PAYLER			John	Unio	334
George W	Hami	134	PEARSON		
PAYNE			Calvin	Preb	286
Burton H	Asht	017	Elizabeth	Harr	149
Elizabeth	Hami	124	George W	Putn	289
George	Madi	203	Leah	Preb	287
George H	Summ	323	Melinda	Guer	119
George L	Clar	046	Richard	VanW	338
Huldah	Knox	175	William S	Asht	018

PEASE		
Milly	Mont	256
Phineas	Fran	096
Sally J	Cuya	075
Samuel	Mont	229
Susan A	Summ	324
PEASLEY		
Edward A	Faye	093
PEAVY		
Caroline	Athe	020
PECHINEY		
Peter F	Hami	134
PECK		
Anna	Lora	194
Fannie	Medi	210
Henophon	Lora	193
Hiram	Huro	163
James C	Madi	203
Jemima	Summ	324
John	Cler	048
John	Madi	203
John B	Belm	028
Lawrence	Hami	133
Loman	Vint	341
Louisa	Asht	019
Nancy	Asht	019
Uriah W	Dark	078
William	Vint	340
PECKHAM		
Geo F	Lora	193
PEDRICK		
William E	Cuya	067
PEEBLES		
Ransellor R	Cuya	067
PEEPER		
Elizabeth	Rich	292
PEEPLES		
James	Colu	059
PEESO		
Charlotte	Wyan	366
PEET		
Chas C	Otta	271
Geo H	Hami	134
Mary	Hami	124
PEFFY		
Alfred	Dark	077
PEGG		
Elias	Fran	101
PEIPHER		
Peter	VanW	337
PEIUTY		
Mary A	Hami	139

PELKEY		
John	Fult	106
PELLOW		
Mathias	Star	320
PELS		
Alfred	Hami	134
PELTON		
Augustus	Trum	326
Henry J	Wood	363
John	Wood	359
PEMBER		
Dallas S	Wood	362
PEMBERTON		
Clinton	Lawr	182
Jane	Lawr	183
PENCE		
Cath	High	155
Cath	High	156
David M	Dela	084
Eli	Cham	042
Elizabeth	Warr	344
Henry A	Craw	064
Isaac	Perr	278
John S	Butl	037
Mary A	Wayn	352
Peter K	Butl	037
Rhoda	Cham	040
Samuel	Luca	200
Samuel	Scio	305
PENDERGRASS		
Ed D	Pike	281
PENDLETON		
Lewis	Fran	104
PENFIELD		
Henry B	Mont	227
PENN		
Ellen	Harr	150
Ezekiel C	Morr	261
Joseph	Belm	029
PENNELL		
Berny	Sene	310
Sylvenus	Trum	325
William D	Monr	225
PENNEY		
Cath	Miam	222
Jason H	Dark	077
PENNIMAN		
James M	Mont	239
PENNINGTON		
Margaret	Madi	203
PENNOCK		
Mary	Harr	149
Richard	Tusc	332

PENNY		
Geo A	Butl	038
Isaac	Fult	105
Jno T	Hami	139
Joshua A	Brow	033
Lafayette	Brow	033
Lewis	Brow	033
Louisa	Brow	033
Richard	Mont	245
PENROD		
Mary	Adam	005
Sarah	Summ	321
PENROSE		
Susannah	Knox	175
PENRY		
Elizabeth	Dela	083
Hannah	Miam	223
John P	Mari	209
PENTECOST		
Thomas	Butl	035
William	Butl	035
PEOPLES		
Jemima	Tusc	332
John	Hard	144
Mary	Vint	340
PEPPER		
Edward	Morr	259
Gottlieb	Hami	134
James	Jack	169
PEPPINGER		
Cornelius	Miam	221
PEPPLE		
Susanna	Ross	296
PERCELL		
William	Mont	237
PERCIVAL		
William	Fult	105
PERDUE		
Mason	Pike	281
William W	Tusc	330
PEREIRA		
Doningos M	Cuya	067
PERIN		
Austin G	Sene	312
Robert A	Star	319
PERKINS		
Celina A	Will	357
David W	Faye	093
James W	Lora	193
Jennie	Asht	014
Jeptha	Morr	259
John	Jack	166
John	Wash	345

PERKINS (cont)		
Maria	Trum	328
Martha	Wash	345
Mary A	Hami	126
Mayron B	Cuya	067
Sarah M	Cuya	073
William C	Lake	179
PERKISER		
Marth J	Cler	050
PERNELL		
Hugh	Gree	114
PERNIER		
Francis	Mont	236
PERRIN		
Adelaide	Clar	044
James	Knox	176
Livingston T	Hami	133
Phebe M	Sand	301
Walter R	Huro	165
PERRINE		
Emma L	Hami	139
John V	Cosh	061
PERRINGER		
Michael	Trum	325
PERRY		
Albert H	Fran	096
Alex	Lora	194
Alvah	Fran	096
Arnold H	Scio	308
Caleb E	Cuya	076
Cath C	Cuya	069
Chas	Mari	208
Elijah K	Clin	055
Eliza	Fran	102
Fanny	Port	283
Frances	Scio	306
Geo	Asht	016
John	Cler	048
John	Fair	092
Joseph S	Hami	134
Lucius H	Hanc	142
Philemon	Trum	328
Polly	VanW	337
Roland	Athc	020
PERSON		
Geo	Huro	165
Henry M	Erie	088
PERSONS		
Eli	Athe	022
James L	Belm	030
Loren S	Meig	212

PERTERSON		
Samuel K	Gree	114
PERYN		
William F Sr	Luca	200
PETEE		
Louis	Luca	196
PETER		
Muss	Star	317
PETERBAUGH		
Alexander	Mont	253
PETERMAN		
John	Hanc	142
Susan	Tusc	331
PETERS		
Athelinda	Wash	345
Charlotte A	Musk	267
David S	Wayn	352
Ebenezer	Mari	208
Elizabeth	Asht	016
Elizabeth	Pike	281
India	Brow	034
Jacob F	Star	318
Joseph D	Sene	308
Mary	Scio	305
Samuel A	Star	320
Sarah Bell	Hami	124
PETERSON		
Caroline	Fran	103
Chas	Mont	242
Christopher	Fair	092
Elizabeth	Ross	299
Jacob D	Colu	057
James	Paul	274
James J	Fult	105
John K	Lawr	181
Lewis	Gree	115
Sarah A	High	153
Shadrack B	Holm	160
Wiley	Wood	359
PETKINS		
Theodore S	Knox	174
PETREE		
Cath	Tusc	333
PETRY		
William	Mont	237
PETTICORD		
John G	Sene	312
PETTIER		
John W	Alle	009
PETTIFORD		
Parkey	Ross	297
Sally	Meig	215
PETTIJOHN		
Granville O	Brow	035
PETTINGILL		
Cyrus	Mont	244
PETTIT		
Eleazor W	Hami	134
Hattie C	Hami	126
Joseph	Mont	233
Nancy	Otta	272
Rebecca	Brow	033
Samuel S	Wyan	367
PETTY		
James L	Athe	022
Margaret	Wash	346
Mary A	Belm	027
Samuel	Monr	225
Watterman L	Athe	024
PETTYS		
Hubert	Sene	312
PETZER		
Samuel J	Brow	032
PEW		
Achsa	Cosh	060
PEYSHA		
Albert	Cuya	069
PFAFF		
Geo	Cuya	065
PFAFFENBEIGER		
George	Mont	238
PFARR		
Jacobb	Pike	281
PFARRER		
Notburga	Aug1	026
PFEIFER		
Peter	Fran	098
William	Fran	095
PFEIFFER		
Geo	Hami	134
John G	Wash	349
PFIEFER		
Jacob	Lick	186
PFINGSTAG		
Peter	Rich	294
PFIRMAN		
Valentine	Star	319
PFISTER		
George	High	155
Regula	Hami	127
PFLUG		
Jacob w	Maho	207
PFOUTS		
Edward	Trum	326

PFROM		
John M	Hami	133
PHALEM		
Patrick	Gree	115
PHARES		
James	Mont	253
PHEFFER		
William T	Fult	106
PHEILS		
Jacob	Wood	362
PHELAN		
Cath	Rich	293
PHELPS		
David	Rich	291
Derastus J	Unio	333
Eliza	Fran	104
Eliza	Meig	216
Fanny	Medi	211
James E	Mont	227
Lemuel	Unio	336
Martha P	Geau	111
Nancy M	Guer	119
Richard D	Asht	018
Sarah	Asht	016
William	Hami	134
PHENIS		
Rebecca	Butl	035
PHERSON		
Mary J	Perr	275
PHIFER		
Caroline	Knox	175
PHILBES		
Nancy	Lick	185
PHILE		
Henry E	Otta	270
William	Knox	176
PHILIPS		
John	Mont	240
Lawrence	Mont	235
Sarah Ann	Asht	018
William H	Hard	146
PHILIS		
Elsie	Wash	345
PHILLIPPI		
Jeremiah	Lick	188
PHILLIPS		
Alfred R	Monr	227
Ann	Port	285
Chas E	Otta	271
David	Athe	020
David	Trum	328
Elizabeth	Cler	050
Ellen	Luca	198

PHILLIPS (cont)		
Emily	Jack	168
Ezra	Clin	053
Harriet J	Loga	189
Hiram C	Morg	257
Isaac C	Nobl	268
Jacob	Cuya	069
James	Cuya	067
Jas H	Hami	136
Jerusha	Trum	329
John	Madi	203
John A	Maho	207
John M	Dark	078
John S	Huro	162
Joseph	Butl	036
Joseph	Fair	092
Lyman	Luca	197
Martha Ann	Adam	005
Mary L	Maho	206
Milford	Unio	335
Milton	Jack	168
Nancy	Meig	215
Orlando	Morr	260
Oscar B	Fran	104
Perce M	Vint	341
Peter	Mont	233
Robert	Geau	112
Robert E	Meig	214
Thomas G	Morg	256
William	Hami	133
William B	Meig	213
William B	Port	285
William H	Loga	191
William P	Luca	197
PHILO		
Sarah	Otta	272
PHILSON		
Cynthia E C	Meig	215
PHIPPS		
Edward	Mont	239
PIATT		
Cath	Guer	118
Nancy	Dark	078
PICHEL		
Bernard	Hami	133
PICK		
Philipp	Hami	133
PICKARD		
William	Defi	080
PICKELHEIMER		
William D	Cler	050
PICKENS		
Amos J	Musk	267

PICKENS (cont)		
Austin R	Wash	348
PICKERING		
William	Defi	080
William	Gree	114
PICKETT		
James	Cler	050
Samuel	Wyan	367
William H	Fran	099
PIDGEON		
Chas B	Clin	053
PIEFENBRINK		
Cath	Hami	126
PIEFFER		
William H	Mont	254
PIEHL		
Simon	Hami	134
PIERCE		
Allison J	Port	285
Anne	Dela	083
Arthur H	Asht	015
Christopher	Hock	157
Columbus D	Morr	261
Elizabeth	Holm	160
Ermina S	Lick	187
Frederick B	Asht	015
Isaac	Knox	173
James R	Athe	024
Jane	Craw	063
John C	Lawr	183
Martha	Dela	084
Nancy W	Morr	259
Nathaniel T	Hami	134
Orriel C	Summ	324
Rachel	Cler	048
Richard	Dela	083
Silas	Mont	244
Wilbur F	Hard	145
William G	Luca	200
William H	Huro	166
William W	Vint	341
Zachariah	Morg	258
Zebina S	Trum	329
PIERMAN		
Polly	Putn	290
PIERSON		
Alex	Fult	105
Frank W	Rich	293
Harriet	Cham	043
Isabella	Nobl	270
Mary	Preb	288
Thomas J	Hami	138

PIERUCCI		
Celse	Clar	046
PIESTER		
Adam	Monr	223
PIETRO		
Brunelle	Faye	094
PIGMAN		
Mary	Lawr	179
PIGOTT		
John	Faye	094
PIKE		
Cath	Miam	219
Harvey	Port	284
Horace Jr	Mont	246
James S	Port	284
PILCHER		
Thomas M D	Athe	020
PILES		
Abina	Scio	306
Delilah	Jeff	170
Elizabeth	Scio	308
Jacob	Ross	301
John M	Dark	077
Samuel	Lawr	179
Zachariah	Craw	064
PILLIOD		
Francis	Shel	316
PILOTT		
Dasy	Star	319
PIM		
Rhoda E	Colu	056
PIMLOT		
Anna	Medi	211
PINE		
Elizabeth	Lawr	179
George W	Pike	282
Jacob B	Lawr	179
John A	High	154
Sarah	Hami	138
William	Lawr	179
PINGREE		
Geo A	Fran	104
PINKERMAN		
William	Lawr	182
PINKERTON		
Richard P	High	155
PINKNEY		
Julia	Cuya	069
PINKS		
Thomas R	Trum	326
PINNEY		
Henry C	Huro	165
Smith	Trum	326

PINNEY (cont.)
William	Fran	104

PIPER
Albert	Mont	246
Flavilla C	Asht	015
Francis	Mont	243
Martin M	Mont	233
Sarah Van Dyke		
	Hami	127

PIPES
Robert	Mont	239

PIPPENGER
William	Mont	256

PISEL
Edward	Wood	358
Thomas	Hard	145

PISTNER
Leo	Hami	134

PITCHER
Ezra	Madi	204
Gundon	Wood	359
Sarah	Nobl	269

PITCOCK
Eli	Musk	264

PITKIN
John	Knox	175

PITMAN
James M	Preb	288

PITNER
Francis A	Belm	027

PITT
Sarah J	Morr	261

PITTENGER
Henry O	Rich	296

PITTINGER
Henry C	Wood	362
James H	Rich	292
Thomas	Wayn	352

PITTMAN
Benj D	Luca	196

PITTS
Henry	Mont	245

PITTSENBARGER
Sina L	Dark	079

PITZER
Lorenzo	Maho	207

PIXLEY
Peter A	Huro	162
Phineas	Lake	178
William W	Wash	349

PLACE
Horace	Huro	162
James	Knox	176

PLAIN
Delilah	Lora	195

PLANK
Cyrus	Ashl	011

PLANTS
Daniel	Maho	207

PLANTZ
Franklin	Otta	271

PLATT
Lida S	Luca	199
Robert	Cosh	061

PLATZGRAFF
Cath	Gree	115

PLEITGEN
Joseph	Mont	244

PLETT
Mary A	Knox	175

PLIMELL
Geo W	Unio	333

PLINDABLE
John	Mont	238

PLOOT
Lewis	Merc	217

PLOW
Elizabeth	Hami	126

PLUE
David	Huro	162

PLUM
John W	Wayn	352
Josephus	Meig	215
William	Fran	103

PLUMB
Samuel	Pike	281

PLUMMER
Caroline	Sene	309
Elizabeth	Jack	166
Emily	Fran	095
Mary J	Harr	150
Susan	Ashl	012
William A	Mont	228

PLUNKETT
Mary	Colu	056
Richard	Dela	083

PLYMALE
Junius	Gall	110

POCKMIRE
William H	Alle	009

POCOCK
Edgar J	Cosh	060

POE
James	Ross	298
Sarah	Brow	033

POINT			**PONTIONS**			
James	Alle	010	Wesley	Fult	107	
James	VanW	337	**PONTIUS**			
POINTER			David	Fult	107	
Robert	Morr	260	Wilson	Fult	107	
Susan A	Adam	003	**POOL**			
POLAN			Edward M	Huro	163	
James H	Cosh	061	Ira L	Will	356	
POLAND			Isaac	Meig	215	
Absalom	Cham	042	James B	Hard	146	
Alex	Rich	292	Mary J	Hami	127	
Nathaniel	Cler	048	Polly	Will	356	
Rebecca	Cham	041	Sarah A	Sand	301	
POLEN			**POOR**			
Jacob	Monr	224	Jewett B	Port	284	
John	Jeff	169	Sarah	Jack	166	
POLHEMUS			**POORMAN**			
Harriet W	Gree	116	Barnard	Henr	152	
POLING			Cath	Ashl	011	
Elizabeth	Fair	089	John F	Musk	263	
Margaret	Pick	279	Mary	Wayn	352	
POLITE			William	Sand	302	
Joseph	Luca	200	**POPE**			
POLK			Nancy	Wash	350	
Margaret N	Loga	191	Thomas	Fran	099	
POLLARD			William	Butl	039	
John K	Adam	007	William H	Otta	271	
(alias John K Kibby)			**POPP**			
POLLEY			John	Hami	121	
Amos W	Hanc	140	**POPPLETON**			
Jay A	Asht	014	Susannah	Rich	291	
POLLICK			**PORT**			
William	Mont	237	John	Butl	038	
Henry L	Morr	259	**PORTER**			
POLLOCK			Albert H	Cuya	074	
James S	Loga	189	Atlanta	Summ	324	
John C	Guer	118	Cath	Cuya	074	
Thomas M	Rich	293	Cath	Knox	175	
POLLY			Chauncey	Summ	322	
Otis	Geau	112	Geo M	Miam	219	
POMERENE			Harriet	Nobl	270	
Permelia	Holm	160	Henry N	Huro	162	
POMEROY			James	Hanc	142	
Geo A	Mont	228	James	Summ	323	
Justine M	Putn	290	James C	Mari	208	
Orange	Geau	111	John W	Lawr	181	
POND			Martha	Maho	205	
Francis B	Morg	258	Mary	Alle	010	
Horace R	Erie	087	Mary A	Knox	174	
Matilda	Paul	272	Mary A	Pick	280	
PONDS			Mary P	Rich	295	
Tempa	Paul	274	Melville C	Cuya	065	
			Richard N	Miam	219	

PORTER (cont)		
Samuel	Maho	205
Sarah Ann	Musk	265
Stephen B	Fran	098
William	Lawr	179
William	VanW	340
PORTS		
Israel A	Dela	085
PORTZ		
Eva	Sene	310
PORSCHNER		
Maria	Hami	127
POSEY		
Benj	Morg	257
Henry	Wash	350
POST		
Charles J	Loga	189
Mathew B	Athe	020
Peter	Butl	037
William	Sene	313
POSTLE		
Alex H	Wayn	352
William Y	Fran	099
POTH		
Adam	Mari	209
POTTENGER		
Cyrus	Preb	286
POTTER		
Americus V	Asht	017
Betsey A	Lake	178
Calvin	Hami	133
Chas H	Lora	194
Daniel	Lake	176
Daniel	Paul	273
Elbridge	Asht	017
Harrison	Hard	148
Henry	Scio	306
Henry A	Trum	329
James	VanW	338
Jeremiah A	Sand	302
Juliana	Wayn	353
POTTINGER		
Samuel W	Preb	286
POTTS		
Israel	Summ	323
John M	Carr	039
Jonathan	Preb	286
Joseph	Morr	259
William	Adam	007
POULSON		
Albert	Holm	160
POULTON		
Ella	Luca	201

POULTON (cont)		
Rachel	Fair	090
POVENMIRE		
Mahlon	Hard	144
POWELL		
Alexander	Mont	255
Andrew J	Lick	187
David W	Summ	322
Delilah	Trum	326
Edward G	Cuya	067
Elanor	Lawr	179
Eliza L	Cham	042
Harriet	Wayn	352
Isaac	Nobl	269
Jeptha H	Cham	042
Jno	Perr	275
John W	Miam	221
John W	Wood	362
Levi	Mont	243
Lovina A	Butl	036
Malinda	Perr	278
Mary	Cham	042
Mary	Monr	224
Nancy A	Augl	025
Rachel	Putn	289
Samuel P	Wood	359
Watt E	Mont	238
William B	Mont	254
POWELSON		
Lewis	Holm	160
POWER		
James B	Asht	017
John	Miam	220
Mary J	Adam	005
POWERS		
Cath	Scio	308
James	Port	285
James A	Gree	114
John W	Rich	293
Margaret	Clar	044
Maria	Fult	107
Martha	Perr	275
Martin	Perr	275
Mary	Fran	096
Michael	Mont	241
Nicholas	Mont	239
Philander	Morr	259
Pierce	Mont	243
(alias Pierce Bowers)		
Rhoda	Gall	110
Sarah	Jack	167
William A	Gree	114

POWLEY				PRICE (cont)		
Samuel	Huro	163		Barbara E	Preb	288
POWNALL				Benj F	Meig	215
John W	Adam	006		Cath A	Wood	363
POWSER				Elizabeth	Cler	050
Elijah	Lick	186		Elizabeth	Summ	324
PRATHER				Evan	Trum	327
Amanda	Fair	090		Ezekiel	Rich	292
John H	Adam	006		George W	Nobl	269
PRATT				Gerard	Ross	298
Amanda A	Musk	266		Henry	Mont	243
Benj R	Mont	248		Isaac	Monr	226
Edward W	Guer	118		Isaac D	Trum	325
Eleanor	Huro	162		James	Clin	055
Franklin	Gree	114		Jesse	Butl	035
James N	Loga	189		John C	Unio	334
Nancy	Henr	152		Joseph	Mont	254
Rhoda	High	155		Joseph	Sene	314
William N	Hanc	143		Levi	Wyan	365
PREBLE				Louisa E	Lick	188
Edward	Sene	311		Lydia	Star	317
Joshua S	Hanc	142		Mary	Cuya	073
PREDMORE				Matilda	Lawr	180
Daniel	Hard	144		Nancy	Morg	256
PREEH				Naomi	Hami	127
Henry	Luca	200		Nathan	Cosh	061
PREGIZER				Rachel	Star	316
Willis	Fult	106		Rebecca A	Brow	032
PRENTER				Richard M	Alle	008
Thomas W	Putn	289		Samuel B	Cham	042
PRENTICE				Samuel W	Mont	231
Albert D	Trum	325		Sarah	Cler	051
PRENTISS				Sarah	Craw	062
Hester Ann	Morr	261		Sarah	Rich	294
John C	Luca	200		Sarah	VanW	339
PRESLER				Sarah A	Jack	167
Jacob	Will	356		Sarah E	Athe	022
PRESLEY				Solomon	Mont	232
Charles L	Lake	179		Susana J	Monr	223
PRESSING				Thomas	Cuya	066
Leonard	Cuya	067		Thomas K	Carr	040
PRESSINGER				William H H	Harr	148
Edward	Gree	116		PRICER		
PRESSLER				Elizabeth M	Clar	044
Jacob	Defi	081		William H	High	154
PRESTON				PRIDE		
Edward	Meig	216		Jacob F	Cler	048
Martin L	Asht	019		Joseph	Brow	033
Sarah	Port	285		PRIEST		
William H	Miam	220		Delilah	Ashl	013
PRICE				Jane	Lick	183
Alexander K	Cler	049		Jane	Musk	265
Alice	Monr	225		Mary A	Lick	188

PRIEST (cont)			PRUDEN		
William	Miam	222	Charles F	Huro	163
PRIMMER			Geo E	Sene	309
Andrew J	Paul	274	PRUDY		
PRINCE			Eliza J	Holm	160
Jane	Star	320	PRY		
Mary	Unio	334	Elanor	Pike	282
Mary Ann	Clar	046	PRYOR		
William	Cham	042	William A	Wood	362
William H	Lora	194	PUCKETT		
PRINDLE			Nathan J	Brow	032
Maria	Guer	117	Sylverius	Ross	299
PRINE			PUFFENBERGER		
Joel	VanW	337	Blair H	Maho	207
PRINZ			PUFFER		
August	Mont	253	Calista	Pike	282
Geo	Mont	228	PUGH		
PRIOR			David J	Cuya	066
Jno	Perr	274	Henry L	Wash	345
Mary	Sand	303	John H	Wood	359
PRITCHARD			Moses N	Paul	272
Aaron	Putn	289	Samuel A	Hard	144
Alcinda	Musk	262	Thomas	Wash	347
John A	Gall	108	William M	Loga	191
John R	Craw	063	PULLAR		
PRITCHETT			Jos C	Cham	041
Silas S	Gall	109	PUMMEL		
PRITZUCH			William	Pike	281
Jos	Mont	254	PUMMIL		
PROCHES			Margaret	High	156
Nancy E	Alle	008	PUMPHREY		
PROCTOR			Tacy	Wyan	365
Abigail	Scio	308	PURCELL		
Haskell F	Cuya	067	Jas T	Morr	261
John D	Butl	038	Jno	Mont	253
William	Mont	246	Maria	Wood	361
William S	Guer	119	Martha	Adam	004
PRONTO			Michael	Mont	254
Benj	Otta	271	Michael	Mont	254
PROPHATER			PURCILL		
Margaret	Hami	124	Patrick	Erie	087
PROSSER			PURDUM		
Elizabeth S	Huro	163	Jesse L	Cler	049
Hannah	Jeff	171	PURINE		
Thomas	Unio	336	James R	Summ	322
PROTZMAN			PURKEY		
Sarah	Merc	217	Joseph	Guer	119
PROUT			PURNEY		
Jno	Mont	253	Clemence	Luca	198
PROUTY			Rosett	Luca	198
Royal	Lake	176	PURSELL		
PROVOST			John H	Wayn	352
Cath R	Gree	114			

259

PURTEE			QUICK (cont)		
Ann	Adam	006	Robert	Adam	006
Elizabeth	Adam	004	QUICKEL		
Maria	Adam	004	Marinda	Meig	215
PURVIANCE			QUICKLE		
Elizabeth	Miam	219	Alex R	Meig	215
Marcus D	Preb	288	QUIGLEY		
PUSEY			James	Medi	212
William	Fair	089	(alias James Flynn)		
PUTHOFF			James	Mont	239
Francis H	Mont	245	James	Wash	349
PUTNAM			QUILLAN		
Andrew	Wood	362	James M	Mont	232
David E	Fran	098	QUILLEN		
Jas F	Wash	347	Thomas	Fran	098
Newell	Asht	016	QUILLIN		
William D	Wash	347	Maggie R	Preb	288
PUTT			QUINCY		
Richard	Cuya	067	David	Lake	177
PUTZ			QUINLAN		
Amelie	Cuya	073	James A	Mont	233
PYLE			Patrick	Mont	235
Hezekiah D	Cham	042	QUINN		
PYLES			Cath	Star	316
Charlotte	Jack	167	James	Mont	237
William	Musk	262	James W	Ross	296
PYNE			John	Mont	236
John W	Hami	133	John	Mont	255
			John C	Cuya	067
			Mary	Lake	177
			Peter	Mont	242
QUAIL			QUINNACHETT		
Thomas	Colu	059	William	Fran	098
QUALLS			(alias William		
James H	Athe	020	Quynichee)		
QUAMBY			QUINTRELL		
Frederick	Hami	134	Emma	Cuya	071
QUANCE			QUIRK		
Albert	Mont	256	John	Mont	239
QUAYLE			QUIZZLE		
Samuel H	Cuya	076	Louisa	Fult	105
QUEAL			QUOAIN		
John O	Cler	050	Matilda	Gree	114
QUEAR			QUONN		
Henry	Colu	059	Sarah L	Faye	093
QUEDENFELD			QUYNICHEE		
Mary	Cuya	073	William	Fran	098
QUEEN			(alias William		
Elizabeth	Scio	304	Quinnachett)		
John	Vint	341	QYNANE		
Mary	Colu	058	Michael	Mont	244
QUICK					
Martin V B	Jack	167			

RAAB		
Peter	Athe	023
RAABE		
Henry	Hami	127
RABE		
Beyan	Cuya	073
RABOURN		
Allen	Fair	090
RABURN		
Francis M	Ross	300
RACE		
Geo C	Wayn	352
Geo F	Rich	293
RACHLEY		
Alex	Will	357
RADABAUGH		
Mary A	Alle	008
RADCLIFF		
William	Mont	228
RADCLIFFE		
Thomas	Mont	233
RADER		
Henry	Hanc	140
Henry J	Putn	288
John	Star	317
Samantha	Fair	091
RADZINSKY		
Joseph	Mont	245
RAETCHE		
George	Mont	246
RAFF		
William H	Star	317
RAFFERTY		
Ann	Lawr	180
Richard	Hami	132
RAFTER		
Frank	Cuya	066
RAGAN		
Edward	Luca	196
Elizabeth	Luca	196
John	Hard	147
Martha	Miam	220
Martha B	Jeff	171
RAGLAND		
Clinton	Hami	139
RAGON		
Geo W	Unio	334
RAHBACK		
John	Mont	250
RAHEA		
Joseph	Fair	088
RAHSKOPF		
Louisa	Hami	127

RAIDAIE		
John	Medi	210
RAINER		
Janet	Gall	110
RAINEY		
Diana	Hock	159
Elijah	Lick	184
RAINS		
Nancy	High	156
Rose A	Pick	279
Sarah	High	155
RAINSBURY		
Robert	Mont	235
RAIRDEN		
Amos G	Athe	022
RAIRDON		
Eliza E	Loga	190
RALF		
Mary	Hami	125
RALLS		
William J	Cler	048
RALLSTON		
Margaret A	Guer	118
RALPH		
Curtis B	Cuya	066
William G	Gall	111
RALSTON		
James A	Ashl	012
Rachel	Miam	219
Smith R	Rich	295
RAMAGE		
John J	Dela	083
William E	Harr	151
RAMBO		
Andrew	Perr	275
Josiah	Perr	276
Mary A	Morg	258
Peter	Star	319
Thomas	Alle	011
William	Perr	276
RAMEY		
William H	Rich	295
RAMSAY		
Solomon	Hami	128
RAMSBOTTOM		
William	Wood	364
RAMSDELL		
Horace V	Erie	086
William R	Wyan	365
RAMSEY		
Andelia	Fran	101
Daniel	Hanc	142
David C	Preb	287

RAMSEY (cont)		
Eleanor C	Fran	101
James	Brow	034
Jesse	VanW	336
Joseph H	Preb	287
Lydia Ann	Jeff	170
Maggie A	Harr	149
Martin L	Brow	034
Nancy	Brow	034
Phillip	Pike	280
Thomas	Gall	109
William	Mont	250
RAMSOWER		
Isaac	Guer	118
RAMSTETTER		
Albert	Hami	128
RAN		
Caroline	Mont	231
Samuel	Colu	055
RANCH		
Cath	Sene	313
Franz Peter	Mont	250
Mary	Hanc	142
RAND		
Silas M	Lake	176
RANDAL		
Adolphus	Tusc	332
John	Guer	117
RANDALL		
Amanda	Cuya	073
Edwin D	Alle	010
Felix	Defi	081
James G	Fair	090
John C	Mont	256
Orlin	Mont	249
Theo B	Medi	210
William H	Hami	123
RANDANTZ		
John	Mont	250
RANDOLPH		
Elenor	Erie	086
James	Gall	110
John F	Erie	086
Josiah C	Mont	243
RANDON		
Eli	Morg	259
RANGER		
Francis W	Hami	127
RANK		
Mary A	Tusc	331
RANKIN		
James	Jeff	169
James L	Lick	186

RANKIN (cont)		
Margaret	Belm	027
Richard C	Brow	034
Samuel	Loga	189
Sarah A	Belm	027
Simon	Luca	197
RANNELS		
Thomas G	Clin	053
William J	Vint	341
RANOR		
Lucinda	Nobl	269
RANSHAHOUS		
Fred F	Scio	308
RANSLEY		
John R	Mont	245
RANSOM		
Amanda J	Guer	120
RANSY		
Samuel M	Hanc	142
RAPER		
Charles W	Cler	051
Fanny	Cler	048
John M	Monr	224
RAPP		
Ann Barbara	Hami	125
Courtland W	Mont	243
Elijah M	Miam	218
William C	Mari	209
RAQUETT		
Geo	Cuya	073
RARDEN		
Aaron	Gall	108
RARDON		
Elizabeth	Meig	213
RAREY		
Alfred K	Hard	147
RASCO		
William	Monr	225
RASCOPH		
Geo	Butl	036
RASE		
Sarah	Mont	256
RASELY		
John	Athe	022
RASTETTER		
Joseph	Star	319
RATCIL		
Mary E	Lora	193
RATEKIN		
Electa J	Gall	110
Sarah E	Gall	111
RATENICK		
John	Hami	127

RATHBUN		
Elizabeth	Madi	204
RATHBURN		
Edmund	Cuya	075
Jno A	Perr	277
RATLIFF		
Daniel	Lawr	181
RATTLE		
Thomas A	Cuya	074
RAUB		
Mary J	Maho	206
RAUCH		
Adolph	Hami	128
RAUS		
Maria A	Hami	127
RAUSCHERT		
John	Mont	242
RAVENAUGH		
John	Wood	360
RAW		
Regina	Fran	101
RAWDON		
William H	Trum	329
RAWLINS		
Sarah	Scio	305
RAWSON		
Elizabeth	Lora	194
Fanny	Sand	303
Mary J	Huro	165
RAY		
Andrew	Hami	127
Caroline	Gall	108
Cath	Nobl	269
Celia	Jack	168
Eleanor	Butl	035
Hannah	Jack	168
John	Erie	088
John	Jack	168
Joseph	Dark	078
Joseph B	Colu	057
Louis	Huro	161
Peter	Athe	021
Ruth	Lake	176
Samuel	Asht	017
Sarah	Ross	301
William D	Holm	160
Zachariah	Wayn	353
RAYBURN		
David C	Clar	045
RAYL		
Boston	Wayn	354
RAYMOND		
Augustus	Hock	157

RAYMOND (cont)		
Elizabeth B	Asht	016
Gisbert	Erie	087
Helen	Wood	358
Merritt	Fult	107
RAYNER		
William S	Gree	115
RAYNOR		
William H	Cuya	066
REA		
Daniel W	Perr	276
James	Adam	007
Mary E	Guer	117
William	Clar	045
William	Loga	190
William P	Harr	149
READ		
Sally W	Sene	312
READER		
John M	Knox	174
Thomas A	Rich	292
REAM		
Daniel A	Alle	009
Eli	Hard	145
Henry	Paul	274
Israel R	Paul	273
John A	Alle	010
John T	Summ	323
Jonathon	Sand	304
Joseph H	Star	317
REAMER		
Sophia	Wayn	353
REAMS		
Abraham	Wood	364
Jasper N	Hard	147
Jeremiah	Loga	192
Rebecca	Loga	192
REANY		
Zachariah	Wash	348
REAPER		
William W	Luca	202
REARDON		
Mary	Clin	053
Patrick	VanW	336
REARICK		
Edward	Lora	194
Isaac L	Adam	005
John E	Sand	303
Samuel	Geau	112
REASE		
Samuel	Wash	348
REASON		
Lewis F	Madi	204

REASON (cont.)			**REDING**		
William H	Fran	104	Chs L	Huro	165
REASONER			**REDINGER**		
Nancy A	Musk	264	Rebecca J	Dark	079
REAVIE			**REDKY**		
Hepsey E	Star	319	Cath	Brow	035
REB			**REDLER**		
Elias	Mont	240	Geo	Fran	103
REBEL			**REDMAN**		
Joseph	Hami	126	Emily J	Adam	005
REBER			James C	Warr	343
Cath	Cuya	071	John	Adam	005
Geo L	Fran	100	Joseph	Pike	282
REBOUT			Samuel	Henr	152
Margery	Guer	117	William	Adam	005
REBSTOCK			**REEB**		
Englehart R	Ross	299	Cath	Loga	190
RECHEL			**REED**		
Conrad	Hami	129	Alex D	Unio	334
RECK			Amanda E	Asht	019
Daniel	Mont	231	Amos T	Fair	090
Luther M	Craw	063	Andrew	Madi	203
RECTOR			Anson	Fult	106
Ann	Clar	047	Caroline	Cler	050
James L	Lick	187	Cath	Wayn	351
William W	Port	284	Charlotte C	Clar	044
RED			Clarissa	Clar	046
Mary	Fair	088	Columbus	Meig	215
REDD			Content	Geau	113
Mary L	Fair	091	Edward O'G	Hami	128
REDDICK			Eldridge	Maho	207
Elisha	Cler	050	Elizabeth	Fair	090
Samuel	Miam	222	Elizabeth	Guer	117
REDDIN			Elizabeth	Henr	152
Michael	Butl	036	Elnathan H	Unio	333
REDDING			Ezekiel	Adam	006
Chas A	Fran	104	Fredericka	Star	320
James	Gree	116	George W	Medi	211
John	Putn	290	George W	Mont	250
Lovena	Ross	296	George W	Morg	257
Nancy	Madi	203	Gustavus P	Port	285
REDDON			Hannah	Maho	204
Sarah	Scio	308	Hanson M	Sene	309
REDFERN			Hiram	Jeff	171
Ira A	Jack	167	Hiram	Unio	334
REDFIELD			Horace L	Rich	294
Sarah L	Port	285	Jane	Guer	119
REDHEAD			Jane	Scio	308
Elizabeth	Lick	187	Jane	Wash	348
REDICK			John	Unio	334
Wesley	Hock	159	John	Will	356
REDINBAUGH			John B	Hami	126
Nancy	Miam	220	John W	Maho	207

REED (cont)			REESE (cont)		
John W	Mont	250	Thomas	Fair	091
Joseph	Wash	346	William J	Medi	210
Joseph W	Augl	024	REEVE		
Josephus	Cler	051	Benj	Asht	018
Levi B	Sand	302	Mary J	Lora	193
Louisa	Huro	162	Sarah	Trum	327
Major	Meig	215	REEVES		
Mary A	Tusc	331	Abram	Wash	348
Mary E	Ross	297	Cath E	Asht	018
Mary H	Wyan	365	David M	High	155
Mary J	Pike	283	Elizabeth	Meig	212
Minerva D	Trum	329	Henry C	Vint	341
Myers	Maho	206	John J	Colu	057
Ralph S	Clin	054	Mabel	Huro	164
Richard F	Medi	210	Margaret	Asht	018
Robert M	Wyan	366	Maria A	Belm	027
Samuel N	Luca	199	Moses Jr	Wyan	366
Sarah	Adam	006	Peter	Fran	103
Sarah	Fran	096	Samuel Sr	Vint	342
Sarah	Wyan	365	William C	Meig	213
Sarah J	Tusc	331	REGAN		
Seymour S	Cuya	071	Daniel	Mont	250
Syrena	Summ	321	Johanna	Port	284
Thomas C	Butl	037	Thomas	Butl	038
Thurston	Mont	250	Timothy	Mont	231
William A	Wyan	364	William	Mont	235
William W	Wyan	366	REGNER		
REEDER			Eliza	Fran	101
Daniel B	Brow	031	REGULA		
Elias	Mari	210	John	Star	319
Isabell	Pick	279	REHM		
Nancy A	Warr	342	Henry	Henr	153
REEHER			REHS		
Mary	Trum	329	John	Tusc	330
REEMAN			REI		
Gustave	Musk	262	Geo	Fair	090
REEME			REIBARD		
Daniel E	Sene	313	John	Dark	077
REES			REIBER		
James	Lawr	180	Jacob	Miam	221
Thomas	Wash	346	REICH		
REESE			George A	Mont	244
Armine T	Fran	104	REICHARD		
George	Mont	242	Ann	Star	319
Hester	Mont	232	Benton	Mont	233
Isaiah C	Cosh	061	Calvin	VanW	340
Jacob	Mont	229	REICHART		
Jacob S	Sene	313	George	Henr	152
John	Loga	189	REICHERD		
Joseph	Jeff	171	Frederick	Luca	199
Joseph	Sene	312	REICHERT		
Mary	Preb	287	Francis	Mont	246

REICHERT (cont)			REINOEHL			
John S	Mont	255	John W	Star	320
REID			REIS			
David M	Wayn	353	John	Ross	298
Duncan	Mont	233	REISER			
Hannah	Gree	113	Elizabeth	Hami	127
Homer C	Trum	329	REISINGER			
John	Maho	205	Louisa	Cuya	068
John H	Wood	358	Samuel	Wayn	353
Lizzie	VanW	337	REISS			
Mariah	Lick	188	Joseph	Scio	306
Matilda	Hock	158	REISSE			
Ruth	Adam	005	Christian	Cuya	073
REIDEL			REISSER			
Ernst	Hami	127	Josephine	Hami	127
REIDER			REITELSPACHER			
Cyrus	Wayn	354	Fredericka	Musk	263
Eliza A	Wayn	351	REITER			
REIDI			Adolph	Mont	246
Jacob	Cuya	071	Augustus	Hanc	142
REIDY			John H	Trum	329
Irena	Sand	301	REITHER			
REIES			John T	Wood	362
John M	Mont	243	REIZLEN			
REIF			Conrad	Mont	239
Edward	Fair	090	RELUE			
REIGER			John	Defi	080
Philip	Henr	152	REMENSCHMEIDER			
REIGLE			Eliza	Fran	096
Martin	Hanc	141	REMINGTON			
REILEY			Elizabeth	Holm	160
Caroline	Hami	127	REMLEY			
REILLY			Jacob A	Hami	126
Perry S	Hard	148	Joseph R	Ashl	012
REILY			William S	Brow	033
John	Loga	191	REMM			
John	Mont	238	Fritz A	Asht	019
Patrick	Clin	053	REMMER			
REIMEL			August	Mont	229
A	Huro	164	REMS			
REINCH			Thomas A	Cham	041
Mary	Guer	118	RENAND			
REINER			Charles	Mont	250
Eliza	Hami	125	RENCH			
REINHARDT			David E	Hanc	141
William	Hami	128	Electa A	Fran	097
REINHART			RENNARD			
Andrew	Fran	100	John J	Belm	029
Jacob	Otta	271	RENNELS			
REINHEIMER			Samson	Tusc	330
Alfred	Dark	078	RENNER			
REINHOLT			Anthony	Mont	244
Henry	Sene	309	Jacob	Mont	231

RENNER (cont)			**REYBURN (cont)**		
Margaret	Fair	090	Jane	Scio	307
RENO			**REYFF**		
Peter	Luca	198	Eusibius	Defi	081
RENOR			**REYNARD**		
Grace	Hami	137	Electa	Lora	195
RENSHAW			**REYNOLDS**		
John A	Putn	288	Betsey A	Cuya	071
RENSSER			Cath	Pick	280
John W	Monr	226	Cornelius	Mont	235
RENTER			Eliza A	Cham	043
Sophia	Hami	127	Elizabeth	Fult	106
RENTZ			Espy	Wayn	354
Veronica	Hami	125	James	Gall	108
REPP			Job	Trum	327
Joseph	Geau	112	John	Erie	086
Sarah	Mont	256	Jno	Wash	350
RERCY			John W	Mont	250
Elizabeth	Mont	230	Joshua H	Wyan	366
RESCH			Julia A	Hami	136
Jacob	Cuya	073	Laura M	Lora	193
RESER			Leander J	Harr	150
John C M	Lora	195	Malber	Jeff	171
Shield	VanW	338	Martin	Hami	137
RESS			Mary A	Tusc	332
Geo	Miam	220	Richard	Jeff	169
RETAN			Rush	Miam	219
Henry C	Fult	106	Sarah M	Huro	162
RETTER			William C	Huro	162
Francis C	Hami	140	William H	Craw	064
RETTIG			William H	Jeff	171
Anton	Hami	138	Zylpha	Brow	035
REUL			**RHAMY**		
Mary J	VanW	337	John W	Defi	080
REUTER			**RHEA**		
Nicholas	Mont	246	Nancy	Preb	287
REUTHLER			**RHINEHALT**		
Martin	Dark	077	Joseph W	Rich	291
REVELS			**RHINEHAMER**		
John	Loga	189	Emily	Hanc	142
REX			**RHINEHART**		
Daniel	Alle	010	Joseph	Nobl	269
Daniel	Trum	328	**RHOADES**		
John D	Hanc	141	Angeline	High	154
Joseph	Star	317	Elizabeth	Fult	105
William	Alle	010	Gilbert	Eric	085
William A	Defi	081	James	Mari	208
REXFORD			**RHOADS**		
John	Huro	165	John A	Fair	091
REY			**RHODA**		
Thomas H	Asht	018	Chas	Wood	359
REYBURN			**RHODEN**		
Ann S	Miam	221	John R	Miam	221

INDEX TO 1883 PENSIONERS OF OHIO

RHODES			**RICE (cont)**			
Alva M	Mari	209	Nimrod E	Merc	217	
Asa	Augl	026	Zemie M	Mont	239	
Charles	Jack	167	**RICH**			
Charles F	Geau	112	William	Ashl	011	
Daniel	Sene	314	William W	Cler	049	
Eden	Lawr	180	**RICHARD**			
George W	Summ	322	Joseph	Mont	256	
Hannah	Knox	173	Mary	Carr	039	
Isaac S	Merc	217	William	Sene	309	
Jane A	Clin	053	**RICHARDS**			
Jane S	VanW	339	Anna C	Knox	174	
John J	Dela	085	Edgar (see Richards Edgar)			
John S	Monr	225	Eliza	Belm	028	
Joseph H	Rich	294	Frank W	Mont	238	
Letita	Brow	032	Franklin S	Alle	009	
Margaret	Rich	291	Frederick	Luca	199	
Robert B	Fran	100	Henry A	Clar	045	
Sarah	Colu	057	James W	Mont	241	
RIAL			John	Carr	039	
Josephus F	Mont	250	John A	Will	357	
RIBLER			John Lorrine			
William W	Trum	326		Geau	111	
RICE			Judith	Preb	288	
Adam A	Preb	287	Lewis Y	Henr	152	
Americas V	Putn	290	Mahlon A	Colu	059	
Ancel G	Luca	199	Maria E	Wash	349	
Andrew	Hami	127	Martin	Shel	314	
Ann	Alle	008	Mary	Colu	057	
Anna	Jack	168	Mary J	Tusc	330	
Annar	Erie	086	Myron	Port	284	
Aquilla	Fair	092	Rebecca	Fair	088	
Calvin M	Asht	016	Rebecca	Guer	120	
Eliza	Brow	035	Thomas	Trum	327	
Elizabeth	Otta	271	Wesley	Ashl	013	
Esau	Fran	103	William B	Alle	008	
Ezekiel	Wood	360	William W	Guer	120	
Geo H	Otta	271	**RICHARDSON**			
Geo J	Meig	214	Adams'n B	Morr	259	
Geo W	Nobl	269	Cath	Wash	345	
Harmon A	Fult	106	Cath	Will	357	
Hiram F	Defi	081	Daniel	Dark	078	
Israel	Luca	197	Eleanor	Wyan	367	
Jacob	Hami	126	Eliza	Ross	299	
Jacob	Meig	213	Elizabeth	Gree	115	
James H	Fran	100	George	Lick	185	
John	Rich	295	Jesse	Lake	177	
John F	Tusc	331	John	Cler	047	
Jno H	Butl	038	John E	Defi	080	
Lawrence	Erie	087	John G	Loga	189	
Lydia J	Wayn	352	Joseph	Cuya	065	
Mary	Fult	106	Julia	Asht	016	
Nancy	Sene	309	Laland	Wood	360	

RICHARDSON (cont)			RICKETS			
Maria	Cosh	060	William C	Faye	093
Mary	Scio	306	RICKETSON			
Mary A	Monr	225	Chas	Sene	312
Ruth	Belm	026	RICKETTS			
Sam	Jeff	171	Francis A	Hock	158
Susan	Brow	033	Jane	Athe	021
William	Pike	282	Keziah	Perr	275
William H	Alle	009	Mary	Fair	091
William P	Wash	348	RICKEY			
RICHART			Annie M	Luca	199
Cath	Will	356	Mathew C	Adam	004
William K	Trum	328	RICKNER			
RICHCREEK			Harriet	Lick	184
Jonas	Cosh	061	RICKNOR			
RICHEL			Lusetta	Fult	107
Thomas	Mont	245	RIDDELL			
RICHESON			Robert	Asht	015
Benj F	Belm	030	RIDDLE			
RICHEY			Geo	Cham	043
John	Athe	023	Henry L	Dark	078
Lewellen	Athe	022	Margaret	Rich	291
Mary	Ashl	013	Stephen W	Clar	045
Mary	Hami	127	Thomas J	Port	285
Naomi	Ashl	012	RIDENOUR			
Sarah	Brow	033	Ann	Fran	097
RICHISON			Barbara	Butl	035
Maria	Cosh	060	Cyrus	Clar	045
RICHMOND			Dorcas E	Alle	010
Amos	Adam	003	Elizabeth	Perr	275
Henry C	Luca	199	Jacob F	Preb	286
Rosa Ann	Luca	198	Magdalena	Perr	275
Temperance	Geau	113	Martin	Perr	275
Zerina	Athe	020	Mary	Alle	008
RICHNER			Mathias	Alle	010
Rudolph	Mont	248	RIDER			
RICHSTUG			George	Harr	150
Rudolph	Mont	239	Oramel L	Cuya	076
RICHTER			Peter	Cuya	073
John	Merc	217	William	Jack	169
RICHWINE			RIDGEWAY			
Lewis	Fair	090	Frances	Butl	038
RICKARD			RIDGLEY			
Andrew J	Wood	360	Hibard R	Ashl	011
Augusta E E	Ashl	011	RIDGWAY			
John	Wood	360	Joseph	Hard	147
Nancy	Wash	349	RIDIMANN			
RICKENBACHER			John	Hami	126
Adam	Fran	102	RIDLE			
RICKER			Alfred A	Wayn	352
Benj J	Cler	049	RIED			
RICKET			William	Mont	236
Abel	Perr	276				

RIEFF			RIGHTSELL			
Eliza	Fran	097	John	Madi	203	
RIEGEL			RIGNSWALD			
Elias	Hard	145	Joseph	Mont	245	
RIEGER			RIGRISH			
Franklin	Mont	233	Philip	Lick	186	
George	Mont	235	RIKE			
RIEGLE			Christian S	Mont	250	
Philip A	Hanc	140	George W	Mont	250	
RIEHARD			John L	Miam	220	
Lewis	Luca	201	RIKER			
RIEHL			Ennis	Warr	344	
Henry	Mont	227	Lafayette	VanW	339	
RIEHLE			RIKEY			
Martin	Mont	229	Joseph	Knox	174	
RIEKE			RILEA			
Sophia	Hami	125	Richard M	Clin	052	
RIER			RILEY			
Nancy	Luca	197	Caroline	Ross	297	
RIES			Daniel	VanW	336	
John H	Dark	078	David M	VanW	336	
Maria	Hami	127	Diana	Port	283	
Maria E	Hami	127	Eliza	Belm	027	
Sarah A	Alle	010	George W	Athe	024	
RIESTERER			Henry	Mont	244	
Balbine	Hami	127	James	Mont	250	
RIFE			James W	Merc	217	
John H	Ross	297	John	Mont	245	
Mary	Meig	212	John P	Pick	279	
RIFENBERICK			John R	Mont	228	
Richard P	Athe	020	Julius	Port	283	
RIFF			Margaret	Hami	127	
Alexander B	Wood	363	Mary	Hami	127	
RIFFNER			Mary	Hami	138	
Sarah	Hami	138	Mary A	Hami	127	
RIGBY			Nancy	Butl	036	
Benj F	Luca	199	Peter	Scio	308	
Major	Craw	063	Thomas	Lawr	183	
RIGDON			RIMEL			
Benj	Colu	058	John	Mari	209	
Marion	VanW	337	RIMPLER			
Samuel B	Star	319	George	Hami	128	
Sarah	VanW	336	RINE			
RIGGLE			Mary	Jeff	170	
Frances	Cuya	073	Nancy	Cosh	061	
RIGGLEMAN			RINEHART			
David H	Morg	257	Agnes	Clar	046	
RIGGS			Amenia E	Sand	301	
David	Belm	028	Barnet	Ross	298	
Ibby	Adam	005	Jesse	Morr	260	
Sterling	Belm	030	RINELY			
RIGHTER			Emily E	Ross	301	
John	Cuya	065				

RINEMAN			RITCHARD		
John	Sene	314	William H	Sene	311
RINER			RITCHEY		
Eve	Musk	265	Alexander	Wash	346
John J	Musk	265	Chas	Mont	231
RINEY			Lorinda	Asht	019
Cath	Musk	264	William A	Rich	292
Louis	Luca	199	RITTENHOUSE		
RING			Henry H	Butl	038
Anna	Star	319	Joseph	Dela	085
RINGER			RITTENOUR		
Gertrude	Hami	127	Adam	Defi	081
Mary A	Vint	340	Jacob	Ross	300
Nancy	Ross	301	RITTER		
RINGERSON			Arthur C	Cler	050
John	Belm	030	Jacob G	Dark	079
RINGLE			John	Star	319
Geo	Sene	309	John J	Hami	126
John	Sene	309	Levi	Rich	292
RINGLEE			Martin	Hami	126
Henry	Mont	237	Reuben	Cuya	073
RINIKER			Stephen M	Unio	335
Frederick	Shel	314	RITZ		
RINK			Christian S	Rich	294
Frederick	Hami	127	Elias M	Sene	313
RINNER			Geo	Erie	087
John	Mont	250	Louisa	Erie	086
RINO			Susan R	Mont	230
Anna	Wayn	352	RITZERT		
RIORDON			Philip	Mont	244
Sarah D	Fran	096	RIVER		
RIPLEY			Adam	Adam	005
Chas	Asht	016	RIVERS		
Hannah	Tusc	330	Ethelbert D	Athe	020
RIPPLE			James	Asht	015
Joseph	Perr	276	RIZAR		
RISHER			John J	Hock	158
Manassa	Dela	082	RNAU		
RISK			Abel M	Dela	083
Robert M	Port	283	ROACH		
RISLEY			Ann	Fair	091
Albert C	Hami	137	George	Luca	196
Ezra B	Brow	032	Henry M	Nobl	268
RISON			James	Mont	246
David	VanW	339	John T	Dela	082
Elizabeth	VanW	339	Mary	Star	316
RISSER			Pracilla	Monr	225
Christian	Putn	289	Salathiel	Vint	341
RISSLER			ROADS		
Margery	Fair	092	Eliza	Fran	097
RIST			Henry	High	156
Rachel J	Brow	031	John W	Pike	281
			Randolph B	Loga	191

ROAN			ROBERTS (cont)			
Grizzy	Wayn	353	Harriet	Belm	026
ROATCH			Henry	Mont	236
David E	Carr	039	Henry C	Lawr	182
ROATH			Henry H	Perr	277
Elizabeth	Geau	113	Henry P	Hard	144
Mathew W	Star	317	Jacob	Faye	093
ROBB			James	Gall	110
Charles	Mont	241	John	Adam	007
Elizabeth	Hami	127	John	Mont	239
Margaret A	Tusc	331	John A	Merc	218
Samuel O	Morg	257	Joseph	Athe	021
William H	Unio	334	Juliann	Fair	092
Wylie	Miam	219	Lloyd	Scio	307
ROBBER			Louis E	Mont	250
Christna	Sand	301	Lucy	Lora	193
ROBBERTS			Margaret	Gall	110
Sarah	Lick	185	Mary	Loga	190
ROBBINS			Mary	Morg	258
Cath B	Pick	279	Mary E	Warr	343
Daniel	Dark	077	Nancy	Fran	096
Elizabeth	Lake	177	Samuel	Belm	028
Hannah	Adam	007	Samuel	Sene	310
Hiram L	Preb	286	Susan	Lawr	183
Joseph	Lora	194	William	Mari	208
Mary L	Maho	207	William	Perr	276
Rosannah	Trum	325	William C	Pick	280
Sarah C	Wyan	367	ROBERTSON		
Vincent	Brow	033	Alley	Augl	026
Wesley C	Clin	052	Cath	Fran	095
ROBENALT			Eliza	Wayn	351
William	Sene	313	Frederick	Mont	231
ROBERTS			Frederick	Mont	249
Absalom	Perr	275	John	Mont	250
Amos	Faye	094	John	Sene	310
Andrew G	Nobl	270	Julia A	Vint	341
Andrew J	Gall	109	Mose J	Vint	341
Angeline	Hami	124	Philip E	Morr	261
Anna	Rich	295	William	Fran	095
Benj F	Huro	164	ROBESON		
Calvin	Cham	041	Sophia	Mont	256
Chas	Clar	045	ROBINETT		
Chas C	Madi	203	Marion P	Ross	299
Chas H	Mont	246	Sarah	Athe	022
Cynthia A	Loga	191	ROBINS		
David	Butl	038	Jas	Colu	058
Eliza J	Knox	175	Jane	Fult	105
Elizabeth	Craw	064	Matilda	Rich	294
Everard D	Warr	344	ROBINSON		
Geo	Jeff	170	Aaron	Musk	264
Geo H	Luca	199	Alex	Mari	208
Geo P	Huro	165	Alexander	Mont	244
Geo W	Musk	265	Alexander Y	Guer	120

ROBINSON (cont)		
Amelia	Pike	282
Anderson	Gree	116
Ann	Preb	286
Ansel D	Hami	127
Benj C	Fran	100
Bryant	Clin	054
Charles	Luca	199
Charles M	VanW	337
Chloe	Fran	095
Coffman	Morr	259
Cyrus W	Lora	194
David	Pike	282
Delia E	Sene	312
Edwood M	Colu	056
Eli	Hami	136
Eliza	Cham	042
Eliza	Cuya	069
Elizabeth	Hami	135
Elizabeth	Sand	302
Elmira	Brow	035
Emeline	Huro	165
Enos P	Mont	239
Frances A	Summ	321
George	Musk	262
George F	Port	285
George W	Nobl	269
Henry	Lora	192
Henry B	Pike	282
Henry H	Hanc	141
Henry S	Hami	126
Hiram	Belm	031
Isaac R	Paul	273
Israel C	Musk	262
James	Clar	047
James	Mont	246
James H	Hard	147
James S	Hard	147
James W	Gall	108
James W	Sene	312
Jane M	Rich	294
John	Cosh	060
John	Rich	292
John	Ross	297
Joseph G	Mont	239
Lucy J	Cuya	071
Margaret	Lick	185
Martha	Gree	115
Mary	Hami	139
Mary E	Sene	312
Nancy	Trum	329
Nathan	Jeff	169
Phebe	Mari	208

ROBINSON (cont)		
Rebecca J	Alle	009
Samuel T	Cosh	061
Sarah	Athe	021
Sarah	Craw	063
Thomas J	Athe	024
Thomas J	Wayn	353
Thomas K	Tusc	331
William	Musk	264
William H	Sene	313
William J	Mont	234
ROBISON		
Branson D	Asht	018
Cath A	Musk	267
Eliza	Wayn	354
Henry H	Maho	205
Rachel	Rich	294
ROBOSON		
Utley	Dela	082
ROBUCK		
Mary E	Adam	005
Rachel E	High	156
ROBY		
Harriet	Maho	206
Henry C	Fair	091
John H	Carr	039
ROCHE		
John H	Mont	237
ROCK		
Anton	Mont	250
George	Sand	301
Henry Sr	Defi	082
Lydia A	Erie	087
William F	Cuya	074
ROCKEL		
Adam	Clar	047
ROCKENBACK		
Christ	Mont	236
ROCKERMAN		
Louise	Hami	127
ROCKEY		
Lewis L L	Mont	230
William H	Fair	090
ROCKHILL		
Sarah	Hard	144
ROCKHOLD		
Flora	Butl	038
John W	Scio	308
Nancy A	Dark	076
ROCKWELL		
David	Fult	107
William	Knox	173

ROCKWOOD			ROETTGER		
Ammiel H	Medi	210	Charles	Mont	235
Byron	Wood	361	ROGALL		
Diantha	Lora	193	Albert	Hard	144
RODDE			ROGER		
Elise	Hami	132	David C	Miam	222
RODDY			ROGERS		
John	Henr	152	Caroline	Pike	281
RODE			Cath	Guer	120
Conrad	Erie	088	Clarissa A	Asht	019
RODENBERG			Daniel D	Huro	162
Amelia	Hami	127	Dennis	Mont	242
RODENMILLER			Frank	Otta	271
Geo	Luca	201	George F	Lake	178
RODES			George H	Paul	273
Russell	Gree	114	Gilbert J	Asht	017
RODGERS			Hiram	Musk	266
Ann	Nobl	270	Israel	Hard	147
Charles A	Pike	281	James P	Sene	312
Daniel	Erie	088	Joseph	Scio	308
Edward P	Wash	346	Lewis	Wayn	353
Jacob M	Cosh	060	Lodem	Asht	015
James	Mont	250	Lucy G	Paul	272
James H	Paul	274	Mary	Athe	020
John	Mont	246	Moses	Sand	303
Joseph L	Faye	094	Otis N	Huro	164
Samuel J	Adam	003	Richard H	Port	285
Washington	Meig	214	Samuel	Unio	335
William	Mont	246	Seneca C	Nobl	269
RODMAN			Simon	Tusc	332
David B	Hami	137	Wesley M	Tusc	333
Samuel J	Hock	158	William	Cuya	066
Susan	Lick	189	William A	Rich	294
RODNEY			William F	Colu	057
Sophia	Clar	047	William H	Fult	106
ROE			ROHDE		
Alexander	Jeff	171	Frederick	Henr	152
James McDermott			ROHN		
	Luca	199	Charlotte O	Defi	081
Scott	Jeff	170	John	Summ	323
ROEDEL			ROHNER		
John	Meig	215	Casper	Luca	196
ROELLER			ROHR		
John	Hami	126	Christiana	Maho	206
ROESCH			J Madison	Dark	079
Geo L	Mont	245	William	Dark	079
Louis	Mont	250	ROHRER		
ROESTROP			Elizabeth	Mont	232
Jno Peter	Mont	250	ROK		
ROETHER			Frederick	Mont	244
Isaac	Morr	261	ROLAND		
William B	VanW	338	Henry W	Cham	042
			Mary	Huro	162

ROLFE			ROONEY (cont)		
Darius D	Huro	162	James	Mont	245
ROLL			Malachi	Mont	240
Joseph	Wyan	364	Margaret	Hami	125
ROLLAND			Michael	Sand	303
Joseph	Ashl	013	ROOP		
ROLLER			Susannah	Knox	173
Augustus	Guer	118	ROOSA		
ROLLINS			Abraham	Hami	139
Lydia	Paul	273	Alex W	Mont	233
Mary	Jack	166	Henry	Lora	194
Thomas H	Cuya	071	ROOT		
William	Sene	311	Belinda	Huro	163
ROLOFF			Edson A	Fult	107
William	Fran	100	Emery J	Fult	107
ROLOSON			Emily	Fult	105
Jerome	Morr	260	Hiram	Summ	322
Wesley H	Dela	082	Margaret	Mont	233
ROLPH			Martin	Fran	095
Stephen	Medi	211	Mary	Fult	104
ROMAN			Nelson	Trum	327
Fred	Cuya	073	William R	Brow	032
ROMANS			ROPE		
Joseph	Harr	149	Nancy	Adam	005
ROMER			ROPER		
Ann Matilda	Hami	127	Jas H	Cuya	071
ROMEY			ROPP		
Henry	Alle	008	Bethia	Wayn	351
Henry L	Alle	008	ROSBROUGH		
ROMICK			Charles	Hami	127
Jacob	Fran	103	ROSCOE		
ROMIG			Jehial P	Asht	015
Isaac E	Tusc	333	William H	Belm	030
ROMINE			ROSE		
Sarah	Meig	216	Amelia	Defi	081
Thaddeus S	Meig	213	Amos	Vint	340
Uriah W	Defi	081	Benj	Loga	189
RONE			Charles B	Huro	164
William	Musk	266	Charles J	Dela	082
RONEY			Cynthia Ann	Asht	019
Enoch E	Hami	126	Isaiah	Wash	345
Geo	Brow	034	Jesse E	Ashl	013
Hiram	Unio	334	John	Scio	305
Silas	Miam	221	John J	Mont	250
ROOD			Margaret E	Fran	104
Edwin L	Asht	016	Mary E	Lora	194
Emily J	Ross	301	Polly A	Lora	193
ROOK			Robert	Maho	204
Daniel C	Hami	126	Salathiel A	Loga	191
Robison S	Knox	173	Susan B	Clar	047
ROONEY			Sylvester	Scio	304
Alex	Cuya	066	Thankful	High	157
Cinderella	Brow	032	Thomas	Mont	250

ROSE (cont)

Thomas W	Fran	100
Thompson	Guer	119
Uz	Loga	189
William	Erie	088
William A	Knox	176
William T	Lawr	183

ROSEA

Frederick	Mont	250

ROSEBOOM

Abraham	Ross	299
Jacob J	Ross	299
Phebe	Hami	140
William H	Ross	300

ROSEBROOK

David	Loga	190

ROSECRANS

Rosey	Hami	138
(alias Sarah A Rosecrans)		
Sarah A	Hami	138
(alias Rosey Rosecrans)		

ROSEMAN

Clemens	Hami	128

ROSENBERGER

Sarah	Sene	309

ROSENCRANTZ

Albert	Wood	363

ROSENPLENTER

Charles	Hami	127

ROSER

John	Fran	100
Lucy	Dark	077
Margaret	Harr	150

ROSETTER

William	Sene	311

ROSEY

Joseph	Fult	105
Sarah A	Hami	138
(alias Sarah A Rosecrans)		

ROSHON

Isaac	Medi	211

ROSS

Amanda	Lawr	183
Chas C	Clar	045
Chas P	Athe	020
David S	Dela	084
Edward	Mont	238
Eli	Paul	273
Elizabeth	Musk	262
Elizabeth	Unio	335
Franklin	Morg	258
Harriet	Maho	206
Henry	Musk	262

ROSS (cont)

Hiram	Medi	211
Ingham C	Mont	232
Jacob H	Cosh	060
James	Clin	052
James Y	Hard	147
John A	Alle	008
John D	Lick	185
John W	Jack	169
John W	Otta	271
Joseph	Paul	273
Justice	Maho	204
Lourancy	Lora	192
Mary	Gall	110
Mary	Wood	361
Mellsena	Warr	344
Nancy	Gall	108
Orville A	Cuya	072
Richard T	Paul	274
Robert	Mont	255
Theo M	Merc	217
Thomas	Perr	275
Thomas C	Paul	274
William	Sene	312
William H	Wayn	351
William M	Holm	160

ROSSER

John M	Trum	326
Richard A	Athe	023

ROSSON

Hattie J	Butl	038
William	Cler	048
(see also Rosson William)		

ROST

Henry	Hami	139

ROTH

Cath	Medi	210
Eliza	Brow	032
Elizabeth	Morr	260
George	Jeff	170
Jacob	Hami	127
John	Mont	240
John	Tusc	332
William	Star	317

ROTHACHER

John	Monr	225

ROTHAN

Joseph N	Hami	126

ROTHENBUSCH

Peter	Brow	031

ROTHERMEL

Frank	Cuya	075

ROTHROCK		
Ner	Warr	342
ROTHWELL		
Nancy J	Adam	004
ROTTERSTEIN		
Susannah	Star	318
ROUGHTON		
Thomas B	Henr	153
ROUKE		
Michael	Mont	255
ROUSCH		
Jacob	Miam	220
ROUSE		
Cath M	Knox	173
Hannah	Pick	280
Rebecca E	Cuya	069
Simeon	Ross	296
ROUSH		
Cath	Carr	039
Henry J	Sand	304
Jacob	Rich	294
John	Gall	108
Martin	Lawr	179
Mary	Star	318
Newton J	Gall	110
Purnell	Adam	003
ROUSTON		
Sarah	Loga	191
ROVABAUGH		
Sophrony	Wayn	352
ROVER		
John	Alle	010
ROW		
John	Lawr	180
ROWE		
Chas E	Mont	229
Christian	Wyan	364
Frances A	Hami	127
Frederick W	Mont	238
Isaac N	Faye	094
Lydia	Faye	094
Richard W	Mont	243
Susan	Sand	304
William S	Cler	051
ROWELL		
Martha	Shel	314
Sarah L	Will	357
ROWLAND		
Cath	VanW	339
Millie C	Lora	193
Rebecca	Geau	112
Samuel	Huro	166

ROWLES		
Elizabeth S	Wash	350
Harriet	Belm	029
ROWLEY		
Angeline	Belm	027
Horace	Luca	199
Jane B	Fran	097
Melville B	Knox	173
Samuc	Gall	110
William H	Knox	173
ROWSE		
Henry M	Madi	204
ROWSEY		
Charles A	Luca	199
ROY		
Alexander	Musk	265
Andrew	Fran	100
Charles	Henr	151
ROYCE		
Abbie M	Knox	173
Amos H	Knox	173
George S	Sand	304
ROYER		
Cath	Sene	310
Geo W	Wayn	353
Jno	Loga	190
Joseph	VanW	338
Philip	Colu	058
Samuel	Sand	302
Susannah	Will	357
ROZELLE		
Esther	Ross	301
RUARK		
Morris	Cuya	075
RUBBINS		
John	Port	284
RUBENOUR		
Ernst	Hami	126
RUBERT		
Samuel W	Medi	210
RUBINS		
Edward H	Wyan	365
RUBLE		
Lydia	Monr	223
Nancy	High	153
RUBY		
William	Miam	219
RUCK		
Geo	Augl	024
RUCKER		
Edward Taylor		
	Nobl	270
Rachel	Nobl	268

RUDD			RUMMELL			
Benj M	Wayn	353	Riner V	Wyan	367	
Sophia	Port	286	RUMOR			
RUDESILL			Geo W	Fran	103	
Elizabeth	Trum	325	RUMPEL			
RUDIG			William	Alle	010	
Margaret	Wash	349	RUMPF			
RUDISELL			John	Mont	235	
Susan	Hami	127	RUNDELL			
RUDOLPH			Frank	Otta	271	
Eliza	Lick	184	RUNION			
John	Lawr	181	Jacob	Loga	189	
Martha G	Port	284	Jas M	Clar	044	
Willson N	Fair	092	John	High	156	
RUDY			Serena	Clar	047	
Jacob Jr	Loga	191	RUNNEBAUM			
John	Star	320	Henry	Hami	126	
RUECKEL			RUNNION			
Geo	Cuya	075	Milo M	Athe	022	
RUEMMELE			RUNTZ			
Mary	Erie	087	Mare	Hami	136	
Rosa M	Erie	087	RUNYAN			
RUFFIN			Emily	Warr	342	
Fannie	Hami	138	Isaac	Hami	140	
RUFFING			Johnson J	Morr	260	
Eliza	Fran	101	Thomas B	Knox	176	
RUGEL			RUNYON			
Susan L	Clar	047	Alex C	Mari	209	
RUGG			Martha C	Loga	190	
Geo N	Lick	187	Mary	Putn	289	
Samuel	Perr	275	Theo C	Cham	043	
RUGGLES			RUPERSBERGER			
John	Morr	261	Henry	Craw	062	
Martha A	Morr	260	RUPLE			
RUGSEGGER			Tryphena M	Cuya	074	
Levi	Monr	224	RUPLEY			
RUHL			Mary	Will	357	
Thomas	Preb	288	RUPP			
RUHMAN			Conrad	Butl	036	
Heinrich C	Mont	250	Joseph	Mont	250	
RULE			Lemon W	Rich	294	
Deborah	Summ	321	RUPPERT			
RULEY			Jacob W	Maho	206	
Thornton F	Pike	282	RUPPRECHT			
RULL			Geo	Hami	126	
Conard	Ross	299	RUPRIGHT			
RUMBAUGH			John G	VanW	339	
Nicholas	Wood	363	RURSON			
Thomas H	Hard	144	Sarah	Morr	260	
RUMFIELD			RUSH			
Rachel	Meig	213	Abigail	Morr	259	
RUMMEL			Andrew	Wood	359	
Amelia	Hanc	143	Ceylon F	Summ	322	

RUSH (cont)			RUSSELL (cont)		
David	Clar	045	Joseph	Wood	359
David	Merc	216	Lucia	Mari	209
John R	Monr	226	Lyman W	Lake	177
John W	Mont	250	Malissa E	Gall	110
Martha	Clar	044	Margaret	Adam	004
Peter H	Cuya	075	Mary	Cham	041
RUSHONG			Mary	Craw	064
Thomas H	Hanc	143	Mary	Hami	138
RUSK			Mary A	Vint	341
Asa S	Morg	258	Mary J	Colu	059
Eliza	Cuya	069	Mary L	Meig	216
Samantha	Perr	275	Obid C	Sand	304
Sarah H	Morg	258	Peter P	Belm	029
RUSS			Robert J	Colu	056
Geo F	Mont	228	Sarah	Morr	261
Stephen	Hami	140	Sheffield	Meig	214
RUSSEL			Thomas	Mont	240
Anthony	Meig	215	Thomas	Wayn	351
RUSSELL			Thomas N	Otta	271
Alvin	Gall	108	William A	Wood	360
Amanda	Ross	297	William H	Jeff	171
Amanuel	Wash	346	William H	Perr	278
Anna	Fult	106	William H	Rich	292
Anna M	Cham	041	William W	Athe	022
Anthony C	Clar	045	RUSSY		
Briton	Wood	363	Elizabeth	Fair	091
Cecilia	High	156	RUST		
Celia	Loga	190	Jane	Cler	050
Charles	Clar	044	Nathaniel	Clar	044
Charles D	Vint	341	RUTAN		
Charlotte	Musk	267	Harriet	Brow	034
Converse P	Henr	152	RUTH		
Daniel	Mont	238	Jesse	Ashl	013
David	Athe	024	Samuel	Preb	288
Edward	Summ	324	RUTHER		
Eli	Pike	281	Eugene	Mont	256
Eliza	Athe	021	RUTHERFORD		
Emanuel	Jack	167	David	Jack	167
Emily C	Asht	018	Isabella	Fair	089
Eunice M	Luca	199	John H	Miam	218
George	Hock	159	Louis	Lick	186
George A	Athe	024	Melzer J	Meig	213
Hannah E	Henr	151	Robert	Cosh	059
Hezekiah	Pike	282	William	Luca	198
Hiram	Meig	214	RUTLEDGE		
James	Ross	301	Rachel	Alle	010
James	Will	357	Thomas J	Hard	144
James	Wood	358	RUTLER		
John	Wood	358	Elizabeth	Gall	111
John D	Musk	266	RUTT		
John H	Huro	166	Sarah	Wayn	353
John W	Craw	063			

RUTTER			SACKETT (cont)			
Jacob	Mont	246	James H	Putn	291	
Jane	Loga	190	Mark	Asht	016	
Saloma J	Wayn	353	Mary	Huro	163	
William B	Ross	299	Sarah E	Summ	324	
RYAN			SACKMAN			
Albert	Cuya	073	Phebe A	Dark	078	
Amanda M	Gree	115	SACKS			
Ann	Pick	280	Casper	Luca	200	
Elizabeth	Preb	287	SACO			
Ellen	Dark	078	Henry	Luca	200	
Ellen	Hami	127	SADLER			
Gavin W	Miam	222	George	Port	285	
Geo	Adam	006	William	Mont	245	
James	Mont	246	SAFFELL			
John	Cuya	075	William O	Perr	276	
John	Hami	137	SAGE			
John	Mont	237	George	Luca	197	
Mary E B	Cler	050	Mary	Trum	328	
Michael P	Hami	126	William	Lora	193	
Patrick	Hami	128	SAGER			
Perry	Asht	014	Benj F	Geau	113	
Peter	Tusc	331	Jacob A	Trum	328	
Thomas	Fran	103	SAGESER			
Uriah V	Preb	286	Barbara	Hard	147	
William	Hami	137	SAID			
William	Miam	218	Abner	Dela	085	
RYANE			SAILOR			
Nathan	Sand	302	Elizabeth J	Loga	190	
RYBOLT			Geo W	Pike	281	
Wilson S	Clar	045	Mary	Belm	030	
RYLATT			SAIN			
James	Shel	315	James F	Fair	092	
RYMERE			William H	Fair	092	
William	Otta	270	ST CLAIR			
RYND			James	Musk	262	
John Louis	Lake	177	ST JOHN			
(alias Louis Rynd)			Amanda	Morr	260	
Louis	Lake	177	Edwin	Hami	130	
(alias John Louis Rynd)			Emily	Lake	177	
			Harrison H	Erie	088	
			James H	Warr	343	
			Prudence	Asht	019	
SABAKER			Sarah	Monr	226	
Rebecca	Wayn	353	ST ONGE			
SABERTON			Michael	Trum	328	
Jas	Mont	243	SAKEMILLER			
SABIN			Harmon L	Putn	288	
Chas E	Wood	362	SALA			
SABINS			Benj	Luca	198	
William	Wood	359	SALISBURY			
SACKETT			Adin W	Morr	261	
Chas H	Summ	324	Elizabeth	Unio	335	

SALISBURY (cont)				SANDERS		
Samuel R	Rich	293		Benj F	Scio	305
William N	Luca	198		Daniel	Lora	195
SALLEE				Emris M	Wood	361
William	Butl	038		Eunice R	Pike	281
SALLS				James W	Jeff	171
Priscilla P	Mont	231		Jesse	Gree	114
SALMON				John H	Fran	102
Geo E	Mari	209		Jos W	Mont	249
Isaiah	Carr	040		Mary J	Loga	190
SALSBERRY				Mary Jane	Hami	132
Stanethlas	Wood	359		Mortimer E	Loga	190
SALSBURY				Rachel	Tusc	331
John W	Adam	005		Susan	Gall	110
SALT				SANDERSON		
Elizabeth	Hanc	142		Ellen	Clar	045
SALTER				Frederick M	Cuya	070
William G	Luca	198		Hannah	Fair	089
SALTERS				Isabella	Fair	089
James M	Athe	020		James	Hami	130
SALTMAN				Mary	Faye	093
John W	Otta	271		Nancy	Faye	093
SALTSMAN				Nathaniel	Wood	362
Maria	Perr	276		Sarah	Faye	093
SALTZGABER				William N	Unio	333
Thomas J	Paul	274		SANDFORD		
SAMIL				Mary	Asht	016
Plumer	High	156		SANDMEIER		
SAMMONS				Frederick	Mont	229
Elizabeth	Musk	265		SANDRIDGE		
SAMPLE				Paul	Mont	235
Jno R	Mont	252		SANDS		
SAMPSON				Almeron	Madi	203
Colby P	Lawr	182		Ann	Morg	258
Daniel S	Hanc	142		Geo	Augl	026
Thomas	Fran	102		Geo I	Morg	258
William	Lawr	180		Joel	Fran	098
SAMS				(alias Jos Sands)		
John D	Athe	022		John R	Morg	258
Jos	Cham	041		Jos	Fran	098
Nehemiah	Adam	007		(alias Joel Sands)		
SAMSON				Martha A	Jack	168
David N	High	154		Mary	Nobl	269
George W	Lick	184		Richard	VanW	337
SANBORN				Simeon	Fair	091
Chas M	Asht	014		SANDUSKY		
Jason J	Mont	229		Geo	Gree	113
Jno O	Meig	214		(alias Geo Parker)		
SANDEL				SANER		
John	Musk	264		Geo	Miam	221
SANDER				Henry	Wash	349
Herman	Butl	037		SANFORD		
John	Fran	095		Asa E	Geau	113

SANFORD (cont)		
Darius W	Lora	194
Elizabeth A	Erie	085
George P	Meig	212
Jerry D	Geau	113
Oliver P	Nobl	270
SANNER		
William	Mont	251
SANNIER		
Jos A	Clin	054
SAPP		
George W	High	154
Joseph R	Summ	323
Madison N	Knox	175
(alias Napoleon M Sapp)		
Napoleon M	Knox	175
(alias Madison N Sapp)		
SARAZEN		
Peter	Wood	363
SARBACK		
David	Star	320
SARBER		
Geo W	Adam	004
SARGENT		
Margaret C	Clin	053
SARNS		
Eli	Otta	270
SARRIC		
Benj S	Vint	341
SARWILL		
Nancy Q	Wayn	354
SASSER		
Benj F	Dark	078
SATER		
Char's C	Dark	077
SATTERTHWART		
William H	Belm	027
SAUCERMAN		
Daniel	Knox	173
SAUER		
Henry	Butl	038
Susan	Jeff	172
Theresia	Huro	165
SAUL		
Geo	Sene	310
SAULSBURY		
Daniel	Monr	225
SAULTER		
Jacob	Wood	364
SAUM		
Cath	Sene	310
Solomon	Sene	310

SAUNDERS		
Edward S	Brow	032
Eliza	Ashl	011
John S	Jeff	171
Maria	Harr	150
Mary D	Madi	204
William D	Trum	328
Zachariah R	Clin	054
SAUTER		
Helena	Wood	361
SAUTTER		
Caroline E	Wood	363
Charles F	Star	319
Jacob	Pike	282
SAVAGE		
Bennett	Paul	274
Charles M	Fran	096
David A	Huro	165
Franklin	Paul	272
Mary	Ross	297
Robert	Clin	054
Valentine	Meig	215
William B	Meig	213
SAVEY		
John	Cuya	069
SAVIERS		
Milton	Rich	295
SAVOY		
Franklin	Mont	229
SAWMILLER		
Geo W	Alle	008
SAWWELL		
Louisa J	Brow	031
SAWYER		
Demita E	Loga	190
Emory F	Luca	197
Franklin	Huro	164
Henry A	Dark	078
Horace B	Luca	200
Jacob	Sene	314
Louise	Lick	188
Sabina	Cuya	068
Samuel	Luca	202
Simon	Lake	177
SAXTON		
James	Scio	305
James H	Ross	297
SAYE		
Samuel	Guer	120
SAYER		
Noah	Hard	148
SAYLER		
Lewis R	Clar	046

SAYLES			SCHARLOTT		
Jane	Cuya	064	James	Jeff	172
SAYLOR			SCHARRINGHAUSEN		
Elizabeth	High	153	H'N'Y(Henry?)	Mont	242
SAYRE			SCHATZMAN		
Elizabeth	Lawr	183	Isabel	Fran	097
SCALLAN			SCHAUB		
Mary	Perr	278	Elizabeth	Erie	087
SCALOVER			SCHAUM		
Asher	Musk	266	Philip	Cuya	070
SCAMMON			SCHAURER		
Geo	Will	357	Simon	Butl	037
SCANLON			SCHAUZ		
Cath	Summ	321	Frederick	Mont	254
John	Sand	302	SCHEAF		
Mary	Cuya	073	John	Fran	098
SCANNELL			SCHECKLER		
James	Mont	233	William H	Craw	063
SCARBOROUGH			SHEFFEL		
William H	Knox	175	Paul	Mont	246
SCARBROUGH			SCHEID		
David M	Guer	118	Philip	Mont	254
SCARBURG			Theodore	Merc	217
Jas F	Mont	244	SCHEIDECKER		
SCHAADS			Anna M	Summ	323
Benj	Craw	063	SCHEIDLE		
SCHAADT			Frederick	Pike	280
Nicholas	Mont	246	SCHEINHART		
SCHABLE			Louis	Mont	253
Chas T	Butl	037	SCHELL		
SCHACHT			Fredericka	Belm	027
Amelia	Hami	127	William	Fult	106
SCHAEFER			SCHELLART		
Frederick	Mont	229	Geo	Jeff	172
Henry	Augl	025	SCHENCH		
John	Cuya	069	Nancy J	Dark	078
Philip	Cham	043	SCHENCK		
Philipp	Mont	230	Julius C	Hami	140
SCHAEFFER			SCHENZ		
Cath	Mont	232	Mathias	Cler	050
Heinrich	Mont	244	SCHERER		
SCHAERGES			Michael	Butl	037
Caroline	Hami	127	SCHEUERMAN		
SCHAFER			John	Defi	080
Agnes	Hami	123	SCHIELY		
Frank	Nobl	268	Charles M	Luca	202
John	Cler	050	SCHIESS		
William	Mont	251	Fredericka	Hami	124
William A	Nobl	269	SCHIESSWOHL		
SCHAFFER			Frederick	Mont	246
Isaac H	Luca	200	SCHILL		
SCHAFFTER			John	Sand	302
Charles	Mont	252	Regina	Hami	132

SCHILTZ			SCHMIDT (cont)		
Frank	Star	320	Mary	Miam	220
Michael	Shel	315	Peter	Mont	254
SCHIMMOLLER			Philip	Fran	098
Mina	Hami	132	William	Mont	251
SCHIMPF			SCHMINK		
Jacob	Mont	252	Cath	Hanc	143
SCHINDLER			SCHMIT		
Barbara	Cuya	074	Salomena	Hami	121
SCHISLER			SCHMITH		
Samuel	Maho	206	William H	Fran	102
SCHIVERS			SCHMITT		
George	Wash	345	Frances	Musk	267
SCHLABACH			Michael	Mont	249
Sarah	Medi	211	SCHMITZ		
SCHLEGEL			Christina	Hami	132
John L	Fran	102	John	Hami	121
SCHLESINGER			SCHMITZLER		
Michael	Hami	130	John	Lora	194
SCHLICKER			SCHMOUTZ		
Frederick	Wash	349	Cath	Shel	315
SCHLONECKER			SCHMUTTHEIMER		
Rebecca	Cham	042	Michael	Hami	130
SCHLOSSER			SCHMUTZ		
Adam	Jack	166	Nancy	Sene	313
Samuel	Mont	227	SCHNABEL		
SCHLOTTERBACK			Jane C	Summ	324
John	Hock	159	SCHNEBLY		
SCHLUDER			Eliza	Mont	232
Charlotte	Hami	132	SCHNEIDER		
SCHMAL			Cath	Hami	127
Frederick	Mont	230	Frederick	Cuya	070
SCHMERZ			Frederick	Mont	237
Jacob	Fran	098	Geo	Hami	130
SCHMETZEE			Gottleib	Cuya	070
Christian	Mont	239	Henry	Mont	246
SCHMICK			Jacob	Lora	193
Henry	Defi	080	Margaretha	Hami	124
SCHMID			Mary	Tusc	331
Louisa	Hami	124	Moritz	Butl	037
SCHMIDT			Victor	Butl	037
Alvis	Mont	252	William	Mont	239
Bruno	Sene	313	SCHNEITER		
Charles	Hami	123	Christiana	Will	356
Charles	Mont	241	SCHNELL		
Charles H	Mont	255	Barbara	Augl	026
Cornelia K	Cuya	068	Charles	Miam	221
Jacob	Mont	233	George	Mont	247
James	Mont	241	SCHNELLRISDER		
Louis	Mont	253	David	Mont	233
Louis	Wash	349	SCHNETZ		
Margaret	Butl	036	Henry	Brow	034
Martin	Hami	136			

SCHNETZER		
Maria	Warr	343
Mary	Hami	124
SCHNIDER		
Geo	Craw	063
SCHOBEY		
William	Miam	222
SCHOCH		
Conrad	Summ	324
SCHOCKNESEY		
Michael	Clar	046
SCHOELKOFF		
Frederick	Hami	123
SCHOEN		
John	Mont	228
SCHOFIELD		
Edward	Belm	030
Ruth	Nobl	268
Sarah I	Henr	153
William	Wash	348
SCHOLLY		
Sargeant E	Medi	211
SCHOLZ		
Constantine	Mont	243
SCHOMMERS		
Mathias	Mont	234
SCHONDERMARK		
Elizabeth	Hami	132
SCHONDORF		
Conrad V	Mont	254
SCHOOLEY		
Samuel	Gree	116
SCHOONNOVER		
John	Cosh	059
SCHOONOVER		
Eliza	Scio	304
James	Pike	281
Jonas	Summ	322
SCHORNDORF		
Charles	Mont	243
SCHORP		
John	Mont	237
SCHORTT		
Elizabeth	Hami	140
SCHOTTMULLER		
Carls	Hami	130
SCHOULLER		
Nicholas	Mont	253
SCHRADER		
Sophia	Pike	280
SCHRAER		
Henry	Hami	136

SCHRAM		
Frederick F	Hami	130
SCHRAMM		
Elizabeth	Clar	045
SCHRAMME		
Lewis	Belm	027
SCHRAN		
Peter	Pike	281
SCHRANTZ		
Urias	Star	320
SCHREIBER		
David	Hami	123
SCHREINER		
Andrew	Sene	314
Ann Maria	Hami	127
Eva	Fran	101
Henry	Fran	102
Louis	Wayn	354
SCHRENKEISEN		
Rosa	Fran	099
SCHREYER		
George	Mont	253
SCHRIVER		
Henry	Hard	145
John C	Cosh	059
SCHROCK		
William	Fran	095
SCHRODER		
Frederick	Jeff	171
SCHROEDER		
Chas	Fult	105
Franziski	Hami	124
Richard	Augl	025
William	Summ	321
SCHROTZ		
John	Mont	246
SCHROWE		
Margaret C	Hami	132
SCHRUNDERE		
Mary A	Butl	036
SCHUARTZ		
Cath	Wayn	352
SCHUBERT		
William	Huro	164
SCHUCK		
Elizabeth	Hami	124
SCHUERENBERGER		
Jos	Mari	209
SCHUFFENECKER		
Crusoe	Cuya	069
SCHUHMACHER		
Leon	Will	355

SCHULER			SCHWAGER		
John	Cler	050	Elizabeth	Hami	132
SCHULL			SCHWANTNER		
Elizabeth D	Lora	195	John	Mont	244
SCHULLIAN			SCHWARTZ		
Gustave	Cuya	070	Dorothea	Merc	217
SCHULTE			Erhard	Cuya	069
Elizabeth	Clar	045	Gustav	Mont	252
Henry	Butl	037	Jno	Mont	252
SCHULTHEIS			Joseph	Sand	302
Adam	Wash	350	Julian	Mont	233
Jacob	Wash	349	Mary	Mont	231
SCHULTHIES			Otto	Luca	198
Frederick W	Hami	130	Peter H	Star	316
SCHULTZ			SCHWEGLER		
Charles	Mont	252	Philip	Butl	037
Henry	Mont	239	SCHWEIGERT		
Jacob	Hami	130	Simon	Mont	244
John M	Morr	260	SCHWEIKERT		
John W	Hami	130	Cath	Mont	230
Joseph	Mont	246	SCHWEIN		
William	Luca	198	Peter	Hami	123
SCHULTZE			SCHWEITZER		
Adam	Holm	161	Cath	Fran	101
Anna B	Cuya	074	Henry	Tusc	332
Lewis	Hami	130	SCHWENK		
SCHULZE			Henrietta	Butl	036
August	Hami	136	SCHWERZLER		
Henry	Mont	246	Martin	Otta	270
SCHUMACHER			SCHWESSINGER		
Anna	Hami	124	Henry	Hami	130
Geo	Erie	087	SCHWIND		
SCHUMAKER			Frederick	Wood	361
John M	Luca	198	SCHWINDEWOLF		
SCHUNPF			William	Hard	147
Gustavus A	Mont	241	SCHWOERRER		
SCHUPP			Philip	Hami	123
John G	Sene	309	SCHWOP		
SCHURR			Philip C	Henr	153
Christena M	Shel	316	SCHYLANDER		
SCHUSTER			John A	Cuya	070
Chas	Hami	130	SCOGGAN		
Jacob	Sene	309	Margaret	Wash	345
John	Sene	311	SCOGIN		
SCHUTTENHELM			Elisha	Mont	246
Andrew	Hami	123	SCOLES		
SCHUYLER			John	Belm	026
Rachel	Brow	032	SCOTT		
Wilson	Henr	151	Alexander	Mont	235
SCHWAB			Andrew G	Guer	118
Caroline	Sene	311	Ann M	Cler	050
Henry	Mont	252	Asa S	Loga	192
Michael	Hami	126	Daniel W	Lick	188

SCOTT (cont)		
David M	Jeff	170
Edward	Cler	048
Elijah	Sand	302
Eliza	Fran	095
Eliza E	Huro	164
Eliza W	Cham	043
Elizabeth	Asht	015
Elizabeth	Wash	345
Ernest	Musk	266
Francis	Guer	118
George C	Mont	245
Henry E	Fran	102
Hiram	Mont	241
Isaac K	Mari	208
James	Adam	005
James	Guer	118
James	Mont	246
James A	Gree	115
James A	Morg	259
James H	High	154
James M	Harr	148
Jennie	Cuya	065
Jeremiah	Lake	176
Joann	Erie	087
John	Colu	056
John	Tusc	332
John A	Adam	003
John C	Adam	004
John S	Hard	146
John W	Adam	003
John W	Monr	224
John W	Preb	287
Levi P	Guer	120
Lewis F	Scio	306
Louisa	Trum	329
Lucinda J	Huro	162
Lucy	Meig	215
Margaret	Fair	091
Martin	Gall	111
Mary	Jeff	171
Mary	Mont	231
Mary J	Morr	261
Mathew	Luca	200
Moses A	Adam	003
Nancy G	Star	318
Nancy J	Hami	132
Oliver H P	Wash	345
Orlando M	Unio	334
Parnelia A	Harr	150
Rebecca	Cosh	061
Samuel	Clar	044
Sarah A	Geau	113

SCOTT (cont)		
Sarah A	Hami	132
Sarah A	Unio	335
Sarah J	Lora	193
Sarah W	Hami	132
Sophia	Geau	113
Susan	Ross	296
Susan	Sene	311
Thomas A	Geau	113
Thomas B	Hanc	141
William	Athe	024
William	Loga	189
William	Miam	222
William	Miam	222
William	Putn	290
William	Wyan	365
William L	Cosh	060
William P	Knox	172
Winey	Gall	108
Winfield	Athe	020
SCOVELL		
Thomas J	Cuya	074
SCOVILLE		
Elizabeth	Hock	158
John	Asht	019
SCRANTON		
Alonzo C	Erie	088
Edwin E	Star	317
SCRIBNER		
Hannah	Asht	018
Mary	Dark	077
Samuel	Morr	260
SCROGGY		
John B	Warr	342
Thomas E	Gree	115
SCULLY		
Cath	Fran	095
John	Mont	240
Thomas	Colu	057
SCURLOCH		
James M	Jack	168
SCURLOCK		
Armenia	Jack	168
Isaac	Jack	167
SEABURY		
William	Wayn	354
SEACRIST		
William	Star	317
SEAGER		
Francis M	Luca	197
SEAL		
John H	Cler	050
St Clair	Monr	223

SEALS		
Ambrose	Meig	216
Rachel	Monr	225
Rebecca	Belm	030
Sarah	Perr	276
SEAMAN		
Ann M	Huro	165
Ellen	Ross	297
John	Sene	312
Lillis	Clin	052
Winfield	Hami	129
SEAMON		
Conrad	Fair	091
SEAPER		
John	Gall	109
John W	Gall	109
SEARBERRY		
James	Lawr	179
SEARCH		
Elizabeth	Musk	267
Ira	Jack	166
SEARES		
Mary	Morg	258
SEARFOSS		
Rebecca E	Putn	289
SEARIGHT		
Rebecca	Colu	056
SEARL		
Louisa	Geau	112
Pamelia	Geau	112
SEARLES		
Harriet	Lake	178
Henry C	Summ	325
SEARLS		
Philander	Fran	101
SEARS		
Ethelinda	Brow	032
Henry W	Port	283
John H	Fair	089
Rachel	Mari	209
SEAS		
Henry	Dark	078
(alias Henry Crase)		
SEATON		
Lafayette	Trum	328
SEAY		
Mildred	Jack	168
SEBASTIAN		
Benj	Hami	136
Lucas	Mont	234
SEBEXEN		
Louisa	Cler	050

SEBOLD		
John	Sene	309
SEBRING		
Aaron	Fult	106
Casander	Musk	262
Martha	Fran	102
SECHEVERELL		
Hamilton	Asht	017
SECOR		
Lauretta	Sand	302
SECOY		
Jasper	Athe	024
Matilda	Athe	021
SEDARS		
William	Hard	146
SEEDS		
Margaret	Fran	104
SEEGER		
Frank	Mont	246
SEELEY		
Andrew	Lake	177
SEELIG		
Jacob	Mont	241
SEELY		
Hamon J	Medi	210
Mahala	Asht	017
Morrell	Lora	196
William	Asht	016
SEEMAN		
John	Butl	037
John	VanW	339
SEERY		
Christopher	Star	318
John	Hami	130
SEEVERS		
Sarah	Wash	347
SEGARS		
Willard	Hami	129
SEGAULT		
Erville	Hami	136
SEIBERT		
Ann	Cham	042
SEIFERD		
Martin	Butl	037
SEIGFRIED		
Ann E	Medi	211
Caroline	Mari	208
Samuel	Ashl	013
SEILER		
Susan	Mont	232
SEIPLE		
John	Asht	015

SEITZ			SEMPLE			
Adam	Cuya	070	Eliza A	Hami	126
Emanuel	Lick	188	SENBERT			
John A M	Belm	030	Margaret	Erie	087
SELBACH			SENCE			
Chas	Fran	102	Jacob	Henr	153
SELBY			SENG			
Dennis	Fran	096	John Q	Morg	257
Edward M	Athe	020	SENNET			
Emily	Lick	185	Michael	Mont	233
Harriet	Ross	301	SERENA			
Jane C	Morr	260	Jacob H	Hami	126
Nehemiah	Fran	095	SERGENT			
SELDERS			Amos	Harr	149
William	Guer	119	SERGRAVES			
SELDOMRIDGE			Michael	Dark	077
Geo W	Gree	116	SERKS			
SELDONRIDGE			David	Hard	144
Abbey J	Alle	010	SERNFER			
SELIG			Caspar	Mont	236
Mary A	Cuya	075	SERVICE			
SELIGER			William H	Mont	228
Maria	Huro	163	SESSOR			
SELKER			Sarah E	Lick	187
Henry G	Erie	088	SETTLE			
SELKIRK			Sarah A	Morg	258
Nicholas	Trum	329	SETTLEMIRE			
SELL			Rachel	Warr	342
Elizabeth	Asht	018	SETZLER			
Lucy	Morr	262	Mary A	Huro	163
SELLARS			SEUF			
Elizabeth	Gree	114	Barbara	Luca	199
Henry	Gree	114	SEUFERT			
SELLER			William	Cuya	070
John	Mont	242	SEVER			
SELLERS			Sarah	Clin	052
Oliver P	Cuya	070	SEVERE			
Phebe	Monr	225	Jefferson W	Unio	334
SELLMAN			SEVERNS			
Ritta A	Adam	007	Samuel	Cosh	061
SELLS			SEVERS			
Orange	Fran	103	Jacob	VanW	337
SELLYETT			Jesse	Clin	054
Augusta A	Cler	050	SEVEY			
SELTSAM			Benj L	Lora	196
John G	Fran	102	SEVY			
SEMASTERS			Jeremiah	Hami	136
Abraham R	Defi	081	SEWARD			
SEMCKE			Clinton W	Butl	038
Albert	Mont	229	Edward	Ross	299
SEMKLE			Mary	Port	285
Nicholas	Mont	240	SEWELL			
			Anderson	VanW	337

SEWING		
Adolph	Mont	246
SEXTON		
Amos C	Cuya	074
Lawrence	Augl	026
Stephen M	Colu	058
Wash	Maho	206
SEYFORTH		
Adolphus	Mari	209
SEYMOUR		
Joseph	Cuya	075
Margaret	Fran	095
Rebecca	Ross	299
Spencer	Lick	186
William B	Henr	152
SEYS		
Clement T	Clar	046
SHACKLEFORD		
Fern'do W	Warr	344
SHADE		
Amos K	Wyan	364
Elijah	Dela	085
William H	Rich	293
SHADLE		
William H	Sene	310
SHADWICK		
Eliza	Fran	095
SHAEFFER		
Ezra	Pick	280
John H	Fair	089
Joseph F	Maho	206
SHAFER		
Barbara	Shel	315
Geo B	Hami	130
Henry	Rich	292
Jacobs	Trum	328
James H	Loga	190
James W	Huro	166
Joseph	Knox	173
Julia A	Scio	306
Mary	Morr	260
Mary A	Butl	036
Mary A	Hanc	143
Peter	Dark	079
Peter	Scio	305
Sarah J	Preb	287
William	Mont	251
William J	Trum	329
SHAFF		
Daniel H	Trum	327
SHAFFER		
Adam	Will	357
Alexander H	Loga	192

SHAFFER (cont)		
Barbara	Putn	290
Cath	Maho	206
Christian	Lora	195
Conrad	Maho	205
Fred W	Cuya	074
Hiram	Trum	325
Isaiah	Vint	340
Jack	Lick	185
James K	Lake	176
John	Hami	138
John M	Fran	102
Levi	Fran	102
Lewis	Port	283
Margaret	Dela	082
Margaret	Rich	291
Mary	Star	320
Perry	Lick	184
Robert C	High	154
Samuel	Clar	046
Samuel	Fran	102
Samuel A	Hard	145
Samuel M	Wayn	352
SHAFFSTALL		
Josiah	Wyan	365
SHAFFT		
Louis	Mont	241
SHAFOR		
William	Butl	038
SHAFT		
Charles F	Sand	302
Jacob V	Otta	271
SHAHAN		
Mary	Belm	027
SHAKLEE		
Francis M	Nobl	269
SHAM		
Elizabeth	Putn	290
SHAMBAUGH		
Maria J	Gree	116
Nancy	Cosh	062
SHAMBS		
Clara C	Cuya	073
SHAMEL		
Benj F	Athe	024
SHANE		
Louisa	Colu	058
Rachel A	Jeff	169
Sarah	Gree	115
SHANER		
Ebenezer	Athe	020
John S	Wyan	367
William	Athe	024

SHANK			SHARP (cont)		
Christian	Holm	161	Edwin	Wood	362
Peter	Mont	232	Henry H	Mari	208
William B	Hard	145	Henry M	Gall	111
SHANKLAND			Jane E	Carr	040
John H	Nobl	270	John	Luca	200
S W	Lake	178	John C	Gall	111
SHANKLIN			Martin	Rich	291
David H	Wayn	354	William M	Fran	103
SHANKS			SHARPE		
Caroline	Athe	021	Mary	Cham	042
Cath	Holm	161	SHARROW		
Clarinda	Augl	026	Daniel	Trum	327
Peter	Miam	219	SHATTLER		
William H	Lora	195	Lydia	Hami	132
SHANNON			SHATTON		
Cath A	Hami	126	Frank	Lora	192
Enos	Hard	145	SHATTUCK		
Henry N	Mont	246	Samuel A	Pike	281
James F	Putn	289	SHATZEL		
John B	Cosh	061	Ann	Pick	279
Mary A	Lick	188	SHATZER		
Mary E	Lick	186	Henry A	Wood	359
Sarah B	Tusc	333	John	Belm	028
Thomas	Guer	119	SHAUAFELT		
William J	Butl	037	Harriet	Star	318
William M	Meig	212	SHAUER		
SHANON			Fred	Clin	055
Frederick	Wood	361	SHAUF		
SHAPE			Henry	Star	319
Jas	Unio	334	SHAULL		
SHAPER			Mary	Sene	313
Samuel A	Clin	054	SHAUP		
SHAPPEE			Eliza	Colu	057
William A	Gree	115	SHAVER		
SHAPPELL			William	Gall	110
Nelson	Alle	009	SHAW		
SHAPPERT			Amelia	Dela	084
Louis	Mont	253	Andrew	Mont	245
SHAPPUT			Chambers S	Brow	032
John	Monr	223	Elizabeth	Morr	260
SHARDELOW			Harriet	Fran	101
Jos	Wayn	351	Harrison	Nobl	268
SHARER			James	Dela	085
Jasper N	Ashl	012	James M	Colu	057
SHARKEY			James R	Cuya	076
Labold	Star	319	James S	Warr	342
SHAROLD			Jesse W	Star	320
Geo F	Hami	139	Jestin	Lake	178
SHARP			John W	Sene	312
Caleb	Pike	281	Junius B	Morr	261
Cath E	Craw	063	Lester	Preb	287
Clinton E	Fran	104	Mary S	Brow	034

SHAW (cont)		
Susan	Augl	025
Thomas D	Wayn	351
Thomas S	Augl	026
William	Sene	314
William D	Hami	123
SHAWEN		
Martha	Mont	231
SHAWHAN		
Frederick K	Hard	146
SHAY		
Jno	Mont	255
Olive A	Lora	193
SHEA		
John	Huro	164
Thomas F O	Hami	128
SHEADS		
Sallie E	Rich	296
SHEAFER		
Frederick	Butl	036
SHEAFFER		
Henry B	Defi	080
SHEAHAN		
Cath	Hami	127
SHEARER		
Jacob	Mont	233
Michael	Alle	010
SHEARS		
Edwin	Asht	018
SHECKLER		
Lydia	Carr	039
SHEDD		
Mary F	Hami	121
SHEEDY		
John	Warr	342
Patrick	Mont	254
SHEEHAN		
William	Mont	240
SHEEHAND		
Elizabeth A	Ashl	013
SHEELER		
Adam	Brow	033
SHEELEY		
Mary A	Guer	117
SHEELY		
Sarah	Guer	119
SHEEP		
Jacob	Hami	140
SHEERAN		
Peter J	Perr	276
SHEERER		
John	Mont	245

SHEETS		
Albert A	Wood	360
Cath	Morg	257
Christian	Colu	058
Eliza	Morg	257
Isabel	Fran	104
James H	Gall	108
Jane M	Cuya	066
John R	Fran	098
Mary	Morg	257
Mary	VanW	336
Sarah	Hanc	142
Sibni P	Gall	110
Solomon	Ashl	012
William	Ashl	012
William H	Cosh	061
SHEFFER		
Geo	Fult	106
SHEFFIELD		
George	Fult	105
George W	Geau	112
William E	Huro	161
SHEFLER		
Conrad	Wood	362
SHEHAN		
Margaret	Luca	199
SHEHY		
Daniel J	Maho	207
SHEIBEL		
Ludwig	Fran	098
SHELBY		
Margaret	Cuya	073
Thomas	Adam	006
SHELDEN		
Chas W	Asht	017
SHELDON		
Chas	Summ	325
Edith	Asht	018
Esther A	Hami	138
Henry G	Dela	084
Horace S	Port	283
Mary	Asht	014
SHELHART		
William	Will	357
SHELL		
Absalom	Sand	302
Henry H	Miam	221
Jonathan	Sand	302
Lydia	Wood	359
Mary	Morg	258
SHELLABERGER		
De W H	Miam	219

SHELLEY			SHEPHERD			
Henry	Medi	212	David W	Dark	077	
SHELLHAMMER			Dorcas	Lake	177	
Sarah	Pick	279	Elenore	Ross	299	
SHELLHOUSE			Elizabeth	Carr	040	
Elizabeth A	Warr	343	Esther	Wood	359	
Julia A	Butl	036	Geo W	Dark	079	
SHELLMAN			James	Cuya	066	
Jacob	Putn	288	Mary	Loga	190	
SHELLY			Nancy	Ross	299	
John	Clar	046	Richard	Belm	026	
SHELT			William E	Summ	325	
John	Henr	152	SHEPLER			
Sabina	Sene	311	William T	Hami	126	
SHELTON			SHEPPARD			
Alex M	Adam	005	Elizabeth	Morg	258	
Benj	Adam	003	Emma D	Musk	264	
Charles	Lawr	182	Leah	Musk	264	
Darius	Adam	003	Phebe	Cuya	069	
Eliza	Brow	031	William A	Cuya	066	
Lewis	Adam	003	SHEPPERD			
Malissa	Brow	031	Sarah	Perr	275	
William J	Adam	003	SHERARD			
SHENAULT			Samuel	Butl	039	
Malinda	Ross	299	Susannah	Butl	037	
SHENEFIELD			SHERER			
Celestine	Meig	216	Peter	Erie	088	
SHENGLE			SHERMAN			
John B	Cuya	070	David	Gree	115	
SHENKEL			Don Carlos	Mont	229	
Chas	Colu	056	Eldridge	Sene	314	
SHENKEY			Eliza	Cuya	073	
Andrew	Luca	197	Frederick	Henr	151	
SHEPARD			William N	Cler	047	
Andrew	VanW	337	SHERMER			
Andrew J	Jeff	170	Eden H	Mont	256	
Elizabeth	Morg	259	SHERRARD			
Emily	Monr	226	Elvirah	Musk	263	
Hester A	Gree	114	Hannah	Musk	263	
Jane R	Cham	041	SHERRIN			
SHEPERD			Jeanetta	Hock	157	
Eliza	Cuya	073	SHERRITT			
Sarah	Monr	224	Eli	Cham	041	
SHEPFER			SHERRY			
Jacob	Wood	361	James	Dela	085	
SHEPFIELD			SHERTZER			
Alex	Asht	017	Silas	Hard	147	
SHEPHARD			SHERWOOD			
Alvin O	Lake	178	Isaac R	Luca	198	
Ann H	Jack	166	Jacob	Ross	300	
Geo W	Belm	027	John G	Belm	031	
John A	Jack	168	William D	Sand	303	
			William R	Madi	203	

SHERWOOD (cont)			SHIN			
Zebediah	Hard	148	America	Brow	035
SHETTERLY			SHINABERG			
James K	Sene	312	John	Merc	218
SHETZMAN			SHINABERY			
Jacob	Hami	130	Benj	VanW	338
SHEUMAN			SHINDOFF			
William	Preb	287	Joseph	Sand	301
SHEURER			SHINE			
David	Henr	151	Eliza	Star	320
SHEW			SHINER			
Cath	Mont	231	Henry G	Hami	130
SHEWALTER			Jane	Meig	216
Chas W	Clar	047	Jno A	Mont	233
SHEWELL			Mary E	Athe	022
Benj F	Wyan	366	SHINGLE			
SHICK			Barney	Mont	230
Paul	Mont	254	SHINKLE			
SHIDLER			Deborah	Brow	032
Elmore J	Clar	047	SHINN			
SHIEAR			Celia B	Wash	347
William	Hami	129	Chas P	Wash	350
SHIELDS			SHINNWAY			
Adrian A	Clin	052	Chas	Summ	325
Celina	Dark	077	SHIP			
John	Mont	243	Louisa	Cuya	067
Mary A	Scio	306	SHIPE			
Mary J	Adam	007	David	Lick	188
Payton	Morr	259	SHIPLEY			
William	Hock	157	Adam	Jeff	170
William	Mont	241	Camden B	Pick	278
SHIERS			Lewis M	Mont	230
Geo	Clar	046	Otho M	Guer	119
Robert	Wash	349	Samuel S	Merc	217
SHIFFER			Sarah	Hami	135
Jacob P	Wayn	355	SHIPMAN			
SHIFFLER			Chas	Madi	204
Christian	Will	355	Horatio N	Erie	087
SHIFFLETT			Kate	Hami	132
Harrison	Pick	280	SHIPPEY			
SHIFFLET			Nathaniel	Mont	246
Jemima	Mont	256	SHIPS			
SHIFLET			Margaret A	Clar	047
Ira	Fran	102	SHIRE			
Levi	Vint	340	Henry	Holm	161
SHIFLETT			SHIRES			
Elizabeth S	Pick	280	John	Mont	240
SHIGLEY			SHIRK			
Lewis	Loga	190	Brittania	Unio	335
SHILLEY			SHIRLEY			
Laurin C	Mont	238	Charles	Otta	272
SHIMP			Maria	Athe	021
John	Fair	089	Stephen M	Defi	080

SHISLEY		
William	Will	356
SHIVELY		
Andrew J	Trum	325
Jacob	Morr	261
Mary A	Hanc	143
Nancy	Rich	291
SHIVERDECKER		
Michael	Mont	256
SHIVERS		
Robert E	High	154
SHOALTS		
Jacob	Sand	302
SHOBE		
Matilda	Faye	094
SHOBER		
Malinda	Sene	308
SHOCKEY		
Elizabeth	Clar	044
SHOCKLEY		
Henry	Belm	027
John W	Ross	299
Mary	Wash	347
SHOE		
David	Will	355
Jacob	Colu	058
SHOEMAKER		
Amzi	Colu	056
Christena	Star	316
Edward M	Hami	126
Geo A	Wood	362
Henry	Madi	203
Isaac J	Henr	152
Isaac K	Mont	229
James	Luca	202
John	Scio	306
John W	Dela	082
Margaret	Hock	158
Mary	High	154
Rebecca	Fair	089
Sophia	Hami	121
William H	Dela	082
William W	Mont	228
SHOEMATE		
Thomas	Adam	003
SHOFFSTALL		
Richard	High	155
SHOLES ˙		
Eliza	Cuya	065
Hiram	Mont	244
Lucy	Fran	096
SHOLL		
David W	Mont	229

SHOLTY		
Christian B	Putn	288
SHOMBERG		
Justus	Erie	087
SHOOK		
Jacob	Fair	090
John	Maho	207
SHOOP		
Eliza	Fran	101
James P	Athe	020
SHOPE		
Betsey	Alle	008
William	Scio	305
William C	Port	285
SHOPWELL		
Jacob	Ashl	011
SHORT		
Charles	Mari	209
Levi W	Cler	047
Lydia	Loga	192
SHORTESS		
Asbury	Rich	292
SHORTS		
David	Trum	328
Hubert	Sand	302
SHORTWELL		
Isaac	Harr	151
SHOTWELL		
Hudson B	Morr	260
John C	Carr	039
John W	Vint	341
SHOUB		
Amy	Dela	083
SHOUBE		
Theophilus	Hami	130
SHOUKWILER		
Ezra	Pike	281
SHOUP		
Elizabeth	Defi	080
John	Wood	362
Martin	Augl	025
SHOVER		
Alva J	Fran	096
Rhoda	Wayn	354
SHOWE		
Uzziah	Hard	145
SHOWMAN		
Elias W	Lick	186
SHRALL		
Barsheba	Miam	220
SHREVE		
Emanuel	Holm	161
Hyempsel J	Holm	161

SHREVE (cont)		
William H	Wayn	353
SHREWSBURY		
Jno	Meig	214
SHRIVER		
Aaron F	Adam	007
Ann	Sene	313
Daniel R	Adam	005
Sarah	Guer	117
SHROCK		
William A	High	154
SHROPSHIRE		
Gilbert R	Pike	281
SHROUD		
Ellen	Rich	294
SHROYER		
Samuel	Wood	362
SHRUM		
Jas C	Cham	043
SHUART		
Squair M	Asht	014
SHUCK		
John L	Hard	147
SHUE		
Benj	Miam	221
Joseph W	Wood	362
Mary A	Wood	362
Miriam F	Wood	358
SHUFELT		
Peter J	Asht	018
SHUFF		
Margaret	Lawr	180
SHUGERT		
Zachariah	Fair	090
SHULER		
Alexander H	Meig	212
Andrew J	Wyan	365
Conrad	Miam	220
William A	Miam	222
William A	Unio	335
SHULL		
Edward F	Hard	145
Henry	Shel	316
Hiram H	Star	317
Isaiah	Will	357
SHULTERS		
William D	Defi	080
SHULTZ		
David	Mari	209
Geo	Ashl	012
Henry	Hard	148
Joseph	Mont	246
Lawrence	Mont	233

SHULTZ (cont)		
Moses	Asht	017
Sabina	Hock	158
Sarah A	Colu	057
SHUMA		
Jacob A	Knox	173
SHUMAKER		
Cath	Rich	291
SHUMAN		
Amos C	Sene	312
Elizabeth A	Scio	306
John	Sand	302
SHUMARD		
Joseph	Cler	048
Mary	Cler	049
SHUMATE		
Abigail	Pike	281
SHUMLEFEL		
Henry	Fran	098
SHUMOKER		
Henry	Dark	077
SHUMWAY		
Dwight	Summ	323
Homer	Fran	098
John Q	Scio	308
Louisa J	Meig	212
SHUPE		
John	Henr	151
SHURE		
Margaret	Wood	363
SHUSSER		
Geo	Wayn	351
SHUSTER		
Elihu	Paul	274
Elizabeth	Jeff	172
Theodore	Mont	246
SHUTT		
Rachel A	Alle	008
SHUTTLEWORTH		
Samuel	Dark	078
SHUTTS		
Christopher	Luca	202
SIBLE		
Geo	Fult	105
SIBLEY		
Byron L	Guer	118
Hiram L	Wash	349
Ruth	Luca	199
SIBOLD		
Casper	Sene	314
SIBREL		
Geo W	Adam	007

SICKELS			SILAS			
Isaiah	Athe	022	Cath	Hami	124
Lafayette	Scio	305	SILER			
William	Jack	168	Warren S	Putn	289
SICKER			SILL			
Maria	Hami	124	Geo W	VanW	340
SICKLES			Martha	Wyan	365
Daniel P	Cosh	060	SILLETT			
Judith	Scio	305	James	Hami	130
SIDDERS			SILLS			
Daniel	Athe	022	Barbara	Tusc	331
SIDEL			SILVER			
Jacob	Sene	310	Isaac N	Preb	286
SIDLES			William	Wood	364
Nancy	Clin	052	SILVERMAIL			
SIDNER			Amon H	Trum	330
David	Fran	096	SILVERTHORN			
SIDONBENDER			Polly	Lora	194
Geo	Ross	299	SILVERWOOD			
SIEBERT			Thomas	Otta	272
Abel	Cuya	067	SILVESTER			
SIEBRECHT			William	Hami	139
Henry B	Butl	037	SILZEL			
SIEDKIE			William	Mont	228
Henry	Erie	087	SIMBER			
(alias Henry Dehnel)			John	Gree	114
SIEG			SIMERSON			
Jacob	Hard	148	Alonzo	Sand	301
SIEGEL			SIMES			
Cath	Hami	127	Edward D	Miam	219
John A	Hami	126	Thomas J	Miam	219
Michael	Mont	237	SIMION			
SIEGLEY			Levi	Wood	358
John	Hard	145	SIMKINS			
SIEREN			John H	Fran	098
Peter	Defi	081	Rachael S	Knox	176
SIERING			SIMLEY			
Henri	Asht	017	Nancy	Fran	095
SIEVE			SIMMERMANN			
Henry	Hami	139	John D	Putn	290
SIGHS			SIMMLER			
Archy F	Cler	047	Anton	Mont	239
SIGLER			SIMMONDS			
Cornelia	Athe	023	Cath	Harr	150
John	Gall	110	SIMMONS			
SIGLING			Esther	Scio	307
Margaret	High	155	Frederick	Hami	136
SIGMAN			Harvey	Lick	185
Julia A	Guer	117	John	Ashl	013
Margaret	Guer	117	Joshua	Harr	150
Martha	Guer	117	Margaret	Harr	150
Rolla	Guer	118	Sophia	Jack	167
			Thomas C	Cler	049

297

SIMMONS (cont)			SINCLAIR		
Wesley C	Alle	009	Alonzo	Colu	057
SIMMS			David	Colu	057
Abijah H	Athe	020	James A	Belm	028
Hester	Gree	115	Maria C	Sand	302
SIMON			Mary Y	Monr	226
Alex	Rich	296	Sarah A	High	156
Florentine M	Maho	207	SINDELBACH		
William	Cler	050	Andrew	Hami	123
SIMONDS			SINES		
Alice	Wood	358	Christena	Guer	117
SIMONS			SINGER		
Benj F	Wood	363	Gilbert L	Knox	175
Philotus	Cler	050	SINGERS		
SIMONTON			Ellen	Guer	117
Finley I	Harr	149	SINGLETON		
Ode C	Warr	343	Robert F	Hami	130
SIMPKINS			SINKS		
Otis J	Maho	207	Ira	Mont	256
SIMPKINSON			John F	Mont	228
Charlotte	Holm	160	SINNARD		
SIMPSON			Thomas W	Mont	251
Arthur D	Musk	265	SINNELL		
Charlotte	Hami	123	Wealthey	Lick	184
Frances	Fran	101	SINNET		
George	Guer	120	Edwin	Lick	184
Isaac N	Dark	078	Lucinda	Lick	185
James P	High	155	SINSABAUGH		
John	Madi	202	Joseph B	Lick	188
Lovina R	Trum	325	SINUS		
Maria D	Fran	104	William H	Musk	265
Sarah J	Lawr	179	SIPE		
Silas M B	Mont	229	Christopher	Morr	259
Thomas H	Wash	346	Levi	Rich	292
Townsend L	Morg	257	SIPLE		
William H	Musk	266	Benj F	Sene	309
William L	Morr	260	SIPLES		
William M	Mont	228	Lewis	Mari	210
SIMS			Samuel	Mari	210
Ann	Musk	262	SIPPLE		
Barnet	VanW	340	Harriet	Will	355
Belinda	Putn	289	Richard	Sene	311
Ellen	Knox	175	SIRRAN		
Israel	Musk	262	John S	Mont	228
Israel W	Morg	256	SISCO		
James	Jack	169	Mary J	Maho	205
John S	Star	319	William	Fair	090
Johnson	Knox	174	SISE		
Margaret F	Cler	051	Nancy	Cham	042
Mary	Meig	215	SISK		
Nancy	Gall	110	Verlinda	Pick	279
Olive	Mont	231	SISLER		
Ruth	Fran	101	Nancy A	Loga	190

SISNEY			SKINNER (cont)		
Hannah	Ashl	014	Isaac N	Geau	112
SISSON			James	Perr	275
Benj W	Gall	109	James N	Fran	104
Nelson B	Gall	110	Jno	Perr	275
SISTON			Jno	Preb	287
Elizabeth	Gall	109	John T	Belm	030
SISTY			Lemuel	Perr	277
Ann E	Henr	151	Matilda	Lick	188
SITES			SKIPPER		
Jacob	Perr	278	Chas A	Fran	102
Robert	Lawr	183	SKIPTON		
Sylvester C	Lawr	183	Jno	Wash	350
SITLEY			SKIVER		
Joseph B	Mont	240	Hester	Hock	157
SIVERS			SKULLEY		
Emily A	Fult	105	Henry	Musk	266
SIVITS			SKYNN		
Daniel	Cham	043	John	Cuya	075
SIX			SLACK		
Abraham	Athe	021	Albert L	Mari	208
Benj	Athe	021	George	Dela	082
Delilah	Sene	313	SLADE		
Hester	Athe	022	Edwin P	Cuya	066
SIZER			Hamilton	Dark	077
Mary W	Luca	198	Joanna	Cler	048
SKATES			SLAGLE		
William	Dela	083	Joseph	Mari	208
SKEELS			Sarah	Warr	343
Chas E	Madi	203	Sullivan W	Mont	254
SKELLEY			Tamar	Brow	031
Hannah	Holm	161	SLATER		
SKELLY			Anthony	Musk	262
Sarah	Holm	160	Edward	Will	356
SKELTON			Frances	Lawr	180
James	Madi	204	Mary Ann	Asht	019
SKESHAN			Sarah	Asht	019
Richard	Luca	200	Zalmon B	Huro	163
SKIDMORE			SLATESER		
Chapin J	Hami	137	James K	Hock	157
SKILES			SLATTERY		
Mary	Will	355	Patrick	Mont	246
SKILTON			SLAUGHBACK		
Alva S	Huro	163	Thomas	Cuya	070
SKIMNER			SLAUGHTER		
Geo F	Luca	200	Adams	Pike	283
SKINNER			Evaline	Cham	043
Adaline	Cuya	069	William H	Mont	242
Adolphus	Hami	137	SLAUGHTERBACK		
Cath E	Huro	162	G W	Wood	358
Eunina	Luca	198	J A	Wood	358
Henry	Musk	266	Samuel	Wood	361
Herman G	Huro	164			

SLAVENS				SLOOP (cont)		
Rachel	Pike	282		Eliza Jane	Hami	132
SLAWSON				Joshua	Craw	063
Anna E	Wood	359		SLOSS		
SLAYMAKER				Andrew	Mont	246
Rufus H	Sene	312		SLOUGH		
SLAYTON				Charles J	Dela	082
William T	Lake	178		SLOYER		
SLEIGH				Edw	Wood	359
Henry C	Hock	159		SLUSSER		
SLEIGHT				Frank	Fran	103
Benj	Mont	246		Joseph	Putn	290
SLEIRN				Mary	Mont	256
Patrick S	Luca	200		SLY		
SLEMMER				Henry C	Fran	095
William R	Wyan	364		Samuel	Huro	162
SLEMMONS				SLYE		
John P	Fran	098		Geo N	Clar	046
SLENKER				SMALL		
William A	Loga	191		Edward G W	Mont	229
SLENTZ				Geo	Cuya	070
William H	Will	356		Mary A	Miam	220
SLERLING				Mary E	Mont	230
Asa F	Luca	200		Priscilla J	Miam	220
SLEYMAKER				William P	Gall	109
John	Hami	123		SMALLEN		
SLICK				Patrick	Mont	234
Joseph T	Hanc	143		SMALLEY		
SLICKER				Chas	Cuya	069
Lewis	Star	318		SMALLWOOD		
SLICKMAN				Isaac W	Mont	229
August	Fair	090		SMART		
SLIFE				Isabelle	Hock	157
John	Merc	217		John W	Lick	185
SLITOR				Joseph W	Dela	085
Richard V	Geau	113		Leander	Hami	123
SLIVER				Mary J	Musk	263
Levi J	Preb	286		William H	Meig	215
SLOAN				SMATHER		
Hilliard H	Otta	271		Henry	Vint	341
James	Loga	190		SMEDLEY		
Leah	Preb	287		Hannah	Lawr	180
SLOCUM				SMELLIE		
William	Ashl	012		William R	Cuya	070
SLOCUMB				SMELZER		
Isaac	Lick	185		Anselm	Fair	092
SLONE				SMETHERS		
Cath	Cler	050		Daniel F	Fran	104
Susan	Cler	049		SMETTS		
SLONEKER				George W	Summ	322
David R	Loga	191		SMILES		
SLOOP				Reuben	Hanc	143
Eli	Unio	335				

SMILEY			SMITH (cont)		
Jay	Rich	295	Cynthiannetta	Loga	192
Sarah	Adam	003	Daniel	Star	316
Theodore	Loga	191	Daniel A	Asht	018
Wellington	Morr	261	Daniel A	Lick	185
William	Mont	236	Daniel H	Erie	086
William F	Preb	286	Daniel O	Mari	208
SMITH			David	Belm	029
Abijah	Morg	258	David	Loga	192
Abram	Asht	017	David	Lora	196
Abram	Cham	043	David	Monr	226
Adelbert A	Summ	322	David	Ross	300
Alanson	Will	356	David C	Luca	200
Albert S	Will	356	Diocleseare A	Meig	215
Alexander	Monr	224	Dorinda A	Lake	176
Alice	Cosh	062	Edward	Faye	094
Amelia A	Lawr	180	Edward	Mont	235
Amos	Fair	089	Edward S	Lora	194
Amos R	Musk	262	Elias	Huro	162
Andrew	Defi	081	Elisha D	Huro	162
Andrew	Hami	130	Eliza	Butl	035
Andrew M	Merc	218	Eliza	Perr	276
Andrew R	Loga	189	Eliza A	Asht	017
Andrew T	Mont	246	Eliza J	Brow	035
Andrew Y	Jeff	172	Eliza J	Lawr	180
Anna	Faye	095	Eliza Jane	Star	320
Anson	Monr	224	Elizabeth	Cuya	066
Asa	Geau	112	Elizabeth	Defi	079
Asahel P	Luca	197	Elizabeth	Lake	179
Benj	Hami	135	Elizabeth	Sand	303
Benj	Scio	307	Elizabeth	Shel	315
Betsey	Wood	363	Elizabeth A	Clar	045
Caroline	Mont	232	Elizabeth C	Huro	162
Caroline A	Trum	327	Elizabeth L	Loga	192
Caroline M	Sand	303	Ellen	Mont	231
Cath	Fair	091	Ellen T	Hami	137
Cath	Hock	159	Eluathan C	Cosh	061
Cath	Lick	185	Emily	Faye	093
Cath	Miam	219	Emsley D	Loga	191
Charles	Cler	051	Enoch N	Cler	051
Charles	Mont	246	Eugene	Huro	165
Charles P	Faye	095	Eugene M	Mont	242
Charles W	VanW	337	Fairfax W	Medi	210
Charlotte	Perr	274	Florian	Sand	302
Charlotte	Wayn	354	Francis B	Will	355
Christopher	Summ	322	Francis F	Meig	215
Christopher F			Frederick	Wood	361
	Fran	096	Frederick C	Lora	193
Clement D	Hami	130	George	Athe	021
Clements	Athe	022	George	Hami	130
Conrad	Ashl	011	George	Mont	255
Cynthia F	Lake	176	George	Otta	270
			George	Ross	299

301

SMITH (cont)		
George	Summ	322
George A	Athe	020
George N	Fran	098
George T	Trum	329
George W	Cuya	070
George W	Hami	130
George W	Morr	259
Georgianna	Musk	265
Gilbert	Fult	106
Hannah	Colu	059
Hannah	Meig	216
Harriet H	Cuya	075
Henry	Fran	103
Henry	Hock	158
Henry	Mont	252
Henry	Sene	309
Henry	Wayn	352
Henry C	Fair	091
Henry D	Morr	259
Hiram	Butl	037
Howell G	Alle	010
Huldah	Monr	225
Isaac	Gree	114
Isaac	Mont	238
Isaac	Preb	287
Isaac M	Madi	203
Isabella	Star	319
Jachariah	Monr	224
Jacob	Cuya	070
Jacob	Cuya	075
Jacob	Hami	126
Jacob	Monr	227
Jacob L	Alle	010
Jacob V	Gall	110
Jacob W	Fair	091
James	Jeff	169
James	Madi	203
James	Mont	244
James	Ross	301
James	Warr	344
James A	Wash	350
James B	Ashl	012
James H	Lick	186
James H	Miam	220
James L P	Mont	227
James M	Gree	114
James P	Miam	219
James T	Gall	111
James W	Mont	235
Jane	Loga	191
Jane	Ross	297
Jane M	Hard	147

SMITH (cont)		
Jane V	Meig	214
Jedidiah D	Wood	358
Jeremiah	Faye	095
Jeremiah	Mont	230
Jerome	Hanc	143
Jerusha	Geau	112
John	Cuya	069
John	Luca	200
John	Mont	237
John	Mont	239
John	Mont	246
John	Wash	350
John A	Mont	246
John A	Musk	266
John B	Ross	298
John C	Clin	055
John C	Preb	286
John C	Rich	294
John D	Dark	077
John G	Clin	052
John G	Maho	207
John M	Trum	327
John M	Wayn	351
John O	Dela	084
John O	Sand	302
John S	Belm	030
John W	Wood	363
John W B	Brow	032
Jonathan U	Mont	242
Joseph	Geau	112
Joseph	Loga	191
Joseph	Mont	245
Joseph	Nobl	269
Joseph	Wash	347
Joseph E	Mont	253
Joseph H	Faye	093
Joseph L	Nobl	268
Joseph R	Mont	228
Josias	Wood	363
Judith P	Maho	205
Julia	Lake	177
Keziah	Adam	005
King	Defi	079
Laura C	Wood	358
Leneous O	Port	284
Leon S	Sene	312
Levi	Sand	301
Lewis H	Lawr	182
Lucinda	Faye	094
Lucinda	Unio	335
Lucinda A	Hami	132
Lucretia	Wash	348

SMITH (cont)			SMITH (cont)		
Lucy	Loga	191	Peter W	Perr	275
Lydia S	Mari	209	Petetiah	Asht	016
Lyman C	Asht	018	Philip	Miam	219
Malinda	Hami	132	Polly N	Summ	321
Manuel	Cuya	066	Rachel	Lick	188
Margaret	Cler	051	Raleigh	Clin	053
Margaret	High	156	Ralph J	Mont	243
Margaret	Lick	184	Randolph E	Miam	220
Margaret H	Lawr	180	Rebecca	Knox	174
Margaretta L	Warr	344	Reuben J	Asht	019
Marion	Fran	102	Rhoda	Hard	148
Marshall	Mont	231	Rice	High	155
Marshall M	Will	357	Robert	Monr	226
Martha	Clar	044	Robert J	Wayn	354
Martha E	Cuya	066	Rudolphus	Mont	254
Martin	Craw	064	Russell	Geau	112
Mary	Athe	020	Ruth A	Knox	173
Mary	Harr	148	Samantha	Dela	082
Mary	Monr	224	Samuel	Clin	054
Mary	Wayn	354	Samuel B	Loga	192
Mary A	Lora	196	Samuel B	Unio	333
Mary A	Summ	324	Samuel L	Huro	163
Mary C	Scio	306	Samuel M	Miam	222
Mary E	Guer	119	Samuel W	Adam	003
Mary E	Hard	146	Samuel W	Lake	176
Mary E	Holm	160	Sarah	Hock	159
Mary H	Lora	195	Sarah	Knox	174
Mary J	Cham	040	Sarah	Monr	226
Mary J	Cham	041	Sarah	Trum	326
Mathias	Trum	328	Sarah	Wayn	352
Mathias W	Vint	341	Sarah A	Hami	132
Matthew	Hami	123	Sarah A	Knox	173
Merrick C	Huro	162	Sarah Ann	Meig	214
Michael A	Lawr	180	Sarah Ann	Will	357
Milton	Hard	145	Sarah Eliza	Clin	052
Modena	Pike	281	Sarah M	Geau	113
Moses	Wash	349	Savilla	Lora	194
Nancy	Cler	051	Sherman	Huro	163
Nancy	Jeff	172	Sinah	Clar	044
Nancy	Morr	261	Stewart	Dela	084
Nancy A	Ross	299	Susan	Cosh	061
Nancy A	Ross	300	Susan F	Brow	033
Nancy M	Cuya	065	Susannah	Hock	157
Naomi	Dela	085	Susannah	Jeff	169
Nathan	Guer	117	Susannah	Mont	231
Nathan B	Harr	151	Susannah	Will	356
Nathan M	Fair	090	Theodore	Madi	204
Newton W	Butl	037	Thomas	Fran	096
Norman J	Summ	322	Thomas	Mont	242
Orvil D	Faye	095	Thomas	Trum	328
Peter	Clar	047	Thomas	Trum	328
Peter	Mont	233	Thomas J	Hard	147

SMITH (cont)		
Thomas J	Loga	190
Thomas J	Perr	276
Thomas T	Perr	278
Thomas V	Jack	169
Washington	Clar	044
William	Cuya	070
William	Guer	119
William	Jack	167
William	Knox	175
William	Lick	188
William	Loga	190
William	Luca	198
William	Unio	334
William	Will	356
William B	Erie	086
William C	Mont	235
William E	Cuya	070
William E	Wood	364
William F	Fair	092
William F	Luca	201
William H	Asht	016
William H	Cuya	070
William H	Warr	342
William L	Knox	174
William L	Mont	256
William O	Asht	018
William W	Loga	192
SMITHER		
Ursula	Cuya	069
SMITHMAN		
William H	Miam	222
SMITLEY		
Charles W D	Lawr	180
SMITTLE		
Cath	Miam	221
Margaret	High	154
SMOCK		
Peter T	Fran	098
SMOOTS		
Sarah	Morr	261
SMYTH		
William H	Carr	040
SNAUFER		
John H	Cham	043
SNAVELY		
John W	Mont	228
SNEADAKER		
Jane	Clar	045
SNEARY		
John	Carr	040
Lemuel	Putn	289
William S	Carr	040

SNEDAKER		
* Margaret	Adam	006
SNEIDER		
Morris	Cuya	076
SNELL		
Joseph	Mont	253
SNELTZER		
Joseph	Gall	110
SNEVELY		
Gco W	Mont	228
SNIDER		
Alfred J	Craw	064
Anna B	Cuya	074
Carolina F	Brow	035
Daniel	Fair	090
Daniel S	Perr	276
Jos C	Wyan	364
Leonard	Dela	083
Mary	Cosh	060
Sarah	Cler	048
William	Cler	050
SNIFFEN		
Jno W	Wash	349
SNITKER		
Henry	Hami	130
SNITT		
Mary J	Guer	118
SNIVELY		
Robert A	Wood	359
***SNNEED (possibly SNEED ?)**		
Edwin	Wood	361
SNODGRASS		
David	Craw	063
David	Hard	146
Elizabeth	Gree	114
George	Wash	346
Harrison	Huro	164
James	Gree	114
John N	Jeff	171
Samanda	Cham	041
Susan W	Colu	057
William O	Belm	029
SNOOK		
Ann	Paul	273
Cornelius	Augl	025
Irwin	Warr	344
John H	Clar	046
Maria	Faye	095
SNOW		
Cath	Luca	199
Freeman	Knox	173
Jonathan L	Athe	020
Lucy	Medi	210

SNOW (cont)		
Matilda	Knox	173
Polly B	Athe	021
Samuel	Mari	210
Sylvia	VanW	336
SNOWDEN		
George	Athe	021
SNURR		
Lydia	Putn	290
SNYDER		
Abdella	Alle	009
Abner	Huro	163
Asa	Merc	218
Barbara	Hami	124
Carian	Nobl	269
Cath	Wyan	367
Chas W	Mont	227
Christopher	Lora	192
David	Rich	295
David W	Sene	311
Eli	Sene	310
Elias	Port	283
Elizabeth	Maho	206
Elizabeth A	Hanc	143
Francis A	Alle	010
Francis M	Clar	044
Frank	Mari	209
George	Port	284
George W	Dela	083
George W	Holm	160
Harriet	Cham	041
Henry	Henr	153
Henry F	Merc	217
Jas	Clin	053
Jas M R	Craw	063
Jas W H	Summ	323
Jeremiah	Rich	295
Jesse	Morr	259
John	Cuya	075
John Jr	Huro	164
John W	Sene	309
John W	Trum	325
Joseph	Cuya	076
Joseph B	Perr	277
Levi	Alle	010
Maranda	Hami	132
Martha	Pike	281
Mary	Wayn	354
Peter	VanW	338
Peter L	Star	320
Peter S	Mont	235
Riley W	Summ	322
Samuel A J	Sand	303

SNYDER (cont)		
Simeon	Huro	162
Susannah	Medi	211
Susannah	Sand	302
Thomas C	Star	318
Trecey	Pike	282
Valentine	Craw	063
William	Fult	105
William	Lake	177
SOALS		
William L	Defi	080
SOEFFING		
Frank L	Erie	088
SOHN		
James A	Sene	313
SOKUP		
Joseph	Hami	130
SOLADY		
Cath	Lick	187
SOLE		
Isaac	Monr	226
SOLES		
Warren J	Ashl	012
SOLETHER		
Charles	Wood	360
SOLLORS		
Wells B	Faye	094
SOLOMON		
Isaac	Wash	349
Joseph	Hanc	141
SOLON		
Richard	Mont	239
SOLTMAN		
Cath	Jeff	169
SOMERS		
Elizabeth B	Hami	124
John	Cuya	066
SOMIESKY		
Andreas	Mont	235
SOMMER		
Andreas	Hami	126
SOMMERS		
George	Hard	148
SOMMERVILLE		
William	Hami	136
SON		
Jacob	Mont	238
SONGER		
Ruth	Craw	062
SOPHER		
Frances J	Morg	258
Julia A	Morg	258

SORBER			SOWERS			
Leander	Butl	036	Amy	Musk	264	
SORG			Cath	Musk	264	
Lisette	Sene	313	Chas	Musk	266	
Maria	Sene	309	Chas H	Cuya	069	
SORGE			David	Alle	010	
William	Cuya	070	Frank S	Rich	295	
SORGEN			Henry	Brow	034	
Edward	Hard	147	Mathias	Cosh	061	
SORIN			Susan	Rich	292	
Caroline	Hami	127	SOWREY			
SORTER			Mary Ann	Summ	321	
Sarah L	Lora	195	SPACE			
SOTHORON			David	Mont	238	
Virginia R	Dark	078	SPACH			
SOUDER			Josephine	Tusc	332	
William P	Fran	102	Leonard L	Putn	288	
SOUL			SPAFFORD			
Peter D	Alle	010	Harrison	Ashl	012	
SOULE			SPAGUE			
Rachel	Hard	145	Mary	Monr	224	
Sally	Trum	329	SPAHN			
SOULT			Maria L	Cuya	066	
Thomas	Hami	129	SPAIN			
SOUNANSTINE			Ella R	Cham	043	
Joseph F	Morg	257	Enoch	Unio	335	
SOUTH			Henry	Rich	291	
Andrew J	Athe	020	John W	Rich	291	
Geo W	Unio	334	SPALDING			
Margaret	Brow	033	James E	Otta	272	
Philip T	Cler	048	John	Fran	102	
Thomas	Clin	055	Mariah	Lake	177	
SOUTHACK			SPANGLER			
Evelina	Cuya	066	Aaron	Gree	114	
SOUTHARD			Calvin W	Luca	197	
Priscilla A	Lick	186	Eliza	Cuya	069	
Robert W	Hard	146	Francis M	Henr	152	
SOUTHERN			John	Pick	280	
William P	Cuya	075	Martha W	Musk	267	
SOUTHGATE			Simon B	Hard	145	
Mary	Hami	132	SPARKMAN			
SOUTHWICK			Kinnin	Fran	096	
Maria	Mari	209	SPARKS			
Olive P	Mari	208	Abi	Clin	055	
SOVERNS			Geo W	Fran	098	
Andrew J	Knox	175	Jane	Brow	034	
SOWDERS			Layman E	Will	356	
Elizabeth A	Vint	341	SPARLIN			
S_OWE (letter missing ?)			John S	Shel	316	
Mary Amy	Trum	325	SPARLING			
SOWELL			George W	Lawr	180	
Elizabeth	Clar	045	SPARR			
			John	Wayn	354	

SPARROW			SPEELMAN (cont)		
Julia	Clar	044	Isaac M	Dark	079
Richard	Gree	114	Jacob	Holm	160
SPATCH			SPEELMANN		
Jacob	Otta	272	Geo W	Miam	219
SPATROHR			SPEES		
Jacob	Mont	246	Lizzie M	Star	320
SPAULDING			SPEICE		
Albert J	Musk	266	Geo	Paul	274
Frances	Dela	083	SPEIDEL		
John	Luca	197	John C	Hami	130
SPAUN			SPEIER		
Samuel	Meig	213	William	Sene	313
SPEAKER			SPEIGEL		
Experience	Paul	272	Cath	Henr	152
Geo W	Cosh	061	SPEIGHT		
SPEAKMAN			John F	Colu	056
David A	Ross	296	SPEISER		
Ebenezer	Ross	299	Christian	Defi	080
Lydia	Ross	297	SPELLING		
Thomas	Hami	129	Conrad	Luca	200
SPEALMAN			Patrick	Hami	130
Silas	Holm	160	SPELLMAN		
SPEAR			William W	Lick	184
Daniel	Morr	259	SPELLMYER		
John A	Trum	329	Margaret A	Hami	132
Maurice L	Mont	251	SPELMAN		
Sophronia	Nobl	268	Calista	Cosh	060
Wesley W	Wayn	354	Fanny	Summ	323
William R	Trum	329	George N	Summ	321
SPEARMAN			Timothy	Lick	187
John	Dela	084	Timothy	Lick	188
SPEARS			SPENCE		
Anderson	Lawr	179	David	Clar	046
Henry	Lawr	179	Hannah	High	156
Ida J	Lawr	180	James M	Hanc	142
Isaac	Scio	308	Michael H	Nobl	268
John P	Will	356	Milton	Warr	344
Josiah	Fair	088	Milton M	Mont	251
Peter	Lawr	181	SPENCER		
William H	Summ	324	Aaron P	Fran	102
SPECHT			Allen	Will	357
Noah	Fult	106	David D Jr	Alle	010
SPECK			Eliza	Wayn	353
Henry	Dark	078	Geo B	Wood	364
SPECKMAN			Geo W	Ashl	012
John	Cosh	059	Harriet L	Medi	210
SPEDDY			James	Hock	157
Joseph	Cuya	070	John	Wyan	366
SPEEDY			Nelson	Ross	296
Jane	Jeff	171	Pierson	Athe	023
SPEELMAN			Priscilla M	Miam	222
Benj F	Miam	219	Samuel	Morr	260

SPENCER (cont)			SPITNALE		
Samuel	Perr	277	Jacob W	Putn	289
Samuel	Sene	309	SPITZER		
Samuel Boyd	Holm	161	Cath A	Wayn	352
Sylvester M	Musk	263	SPITZLER		
Thomas P	Fran	102	Samuel	Perr	277
Victoria J	Brow	033	SPIVES		
William H	Scio	305	John	Brow	033
Wiseman	Musk	262	SPLITSTONE		
SPERLING			Sarah	Trum	327
Cath	Tusc	332	SPOHN		
SPERRY			David	Perr	275
Chloe L	Asht	018	Jeremiah K	Perr	275
DeWitt C	Asht	019	Joel	Sand	302
Huldah	Faye	093	SPOKN		
Martha A	Musk	263	Daniel	Sand	304
SPETNAGLE			SPONSLER		
Ann M	Ross	298	William C	Defi	080
SPICE			SPOON		
Ellen	Star	317	Daniel	Wyan	367
SPICER			Jacob	Wyan	367
Amanda	Unio	333	Solomon	Wyan	366
Benj	Merc	217	SPOONER		
Geo	Hami	136	Henry K	Sene	312
John E	Vint	341	Jesse M	Sene	312
SPIDEL			SPRAGUE		
John	Gree	114	Ara	Lake	177
SPIDLE			Calvin	Cuya	069
Sarah	Ashl	013	Charity	Tusc	331
SPIEGEL			Frank D	Wash	349
Geo	Erie	088	Joshua W	Augl	025
SPIELDENNER			Julia C	Cuya	066
Frank	Sand	301	Levi	Augl	025
SPIELMAN			Nehemiah	Paul	274
Frances	Mont	231	Oscar L	Asht	014
SPIERY			Samuel	Meig	214
Amelia S	Wash	348	Thomas J	Meig	214
SPIES			SPRANKLE		
Philip	Cuya	076	Chas W	Star	317
SPIGGLE			SPRAY		
Samuel	Craw	063	Joseph C	VanW	337
SPIKER			SPRIGER		
Charles W	Nobl	267	John C	Port	284
SPILLMAN			SPRIGG		
James	Hami	123	William	Adam	006
Samuel	Fran	103	SPRIGGS		
SPINNER			Cyrus	Monr	223
Joseph	Hami	130	William	Scio	306
SPIRES			SPRING		
George M	Gall	110	Chas B	Lora	193
Jacob C	Meig	212	Edward V	Cuya	075
SPITLER			John C	Holm	160
Peter	Wood	360	Neal C	Fult	106

SPRING (cont)		
Watson A	Geau	112
SPRINGER		
Elizabeth	Athe	023
James	Ashl	012
John C	Sene	311
Margaret	VanW	340
Mathias M	Craw	064
Reuben B	Colu	057
Rufus	Athe	023
Sarah J	Colu	057
SPRINGMEYER		
Henrietta	Hami	124
SPRINGSTEEN		
Wallace S	Cuya	074
SPRINKLE		
Samuel M	Butl	038
Simon	Cosh	060
SPROUL		
Robert M	VanW	337
SPROULE		
Joseph	VanW	338
SPROUSE		
Polly	Gall	107
Rebecca	Pike	281
Sally	Vint	341
SPROUT		
Benj F	Sene	312
Samuel	Sand	304
SPRY		
Julia A	Loga	190
Mary	Knox	173
Thomas B	Merc	218
SPULER		
Jacob	Star	319
SPUMG		
Lazarus	Morg	258
SPURGEON		
Drusilla	Unio	335
Eli	Perr	275
Eliza A	Fair	091
Elizabeth A	Warr	343
Mary	Musk	262
Reuben	Hock	157
Susanna	Holm	160
SPURLOCK		
Eliza	Hard	148
SPURRIER		
Cath	Huro	162
Edward G	Perr	277
William	Jack	166
SQUIBB		
David C	Mont	234

SQUIBB (cont)		
Geo W	VanW	338
SQUIER		
Justus	Faye	094
SQUILT		
Lydia W	Mari	208
SQUIRE		
Cath	Madi	202
Jennie	Star	320
SQUIRES		
Heber	Huro	163
Luman	Cuya	070
SROFE		
Timothy	Brow	035
William J	High	156
SROUFE		
Mary	Brow	033
STAATS		
Abraham G	Clar	047
Elizabeth	Nobl	269
STABLER		
Benj F	Cler	050
Christian	Paul	274
Eugene	High	155
Lucy A	Paul	273
STACHER		
Samuel	Ashl	012
STACHLER		
Martin	Mont	244
STACK		
William	Wash	348
STACKHOUSE		
Eliza T	Colu	057
Harriet W	Wash	347
Lucy	Monr	224
Sarah J	Morr	261
STACKS		
Sarah J	Lora	196
STACY		
Miles A	Wash	348
STADJI		
Thursnelda	Hami	123
STADLEBAUAR		
Mary	Sene	313
STAFFINGER		
Henry	Athe	021
STAFFORD		
Cecelia C	Cuya	074
Homer O	Erie	088
James	Monr	223
James	Mont	236
John	Cosh	060
John	Mont	244

STAFFORD (cont)			STANBERY			
Margaret M	Cosh	060	Philemon B	Meig	215	
Mary	Hami	132	STANDEN			
Rebecca	Star	319	John A	Lora	194	
STAGE			STANDENMAIN			
Andrew	Wash	347	Bernhard	Mont	249	
William M	Guer	118	STANDISH			
STAGGS			Ellen S	Cham	043	
Nancy	Defi	081	STANEART			
STAGNEY			Ansel C	Tusc	333	
Harriet E	Cuya	066	STANFFER			
STAHL			Daniel	Hami	130	
Barbara	Star	320	STANFIELD			
Cath	Summ	322	Ferdinand	Hami	130	
Ephraim	Belm	028	Horatio C	Mont	227	
Jacob	Wood	359	STANFORD			
Julian	Wayn	352	James A	Knox	175	
Mary A	Wayn	352	Joseph	Cosh	061	
Susan	Miam	219	Ruth	Wyan	367	
STAHLEY			STANGLER			
Elias	Hami	130	Philip	Merc	216	
STAHLIN			STANHOPE			
Frederick	Mont	235	Charles W	Lake	178	
STAINBROOK			STANLEY			
Samuel	Perr	277	Jackson	Meig	213	
STAIRS			John	Hami	130	
Elizabeth	Rich	295	Nelson	Pick	278	
STAKE			(alias Nelson Foster)			
Geo W	Rich	294	Rufus P	Athe	024	
STALDER			William	Wash	348	
Elizabeth	Augl	025	STANSBERRY			
STALEY			Rebecca	Brow	035	
Bridget M	Mont	231	STANSBURY			
Jacob C	Mont	229	Jacob W	Carr	040	
John	Paul	274	STANTON			
Malinda	Mont	256	Cath	Morr	261	
STALL			Hugh	Fran	095	
Andrew H	Fair	090	Lewis	Cuya	070	
Christiana	Cler	051	Martin	Cuya	070	
Christina	Cuya	068	Samuel	VanW	339	
Sarah	Morg	257	STAPLETON			
Susannah	Maho	206	Arnold	Mont	247	
STALLINGS			STAR			
Cornelius	Monr	226	Merrill L	Erie	088	
STAMBROOK			STARING			
Leth	Perr	277	William H	Mont	251	
STAMMER			STARK			
Fredericka	Hami	124	Asa	Adam	003	
STAMP			Betsey	Dela	082	
Emily	Madi	203	Emma	Sand	302	
John H	Star	316	Reed A	Erie	086	
STANBERG			STARKEY			
Jonas M	Luca	202	Mary	Monr	225	

STARKEY (cont)		
Richard	Mont	237
Robert A	Hami	123
Robert R	Lawr	182
William	Geau	112
STARKS		
Chas G	Meig	215
STARKWEATHER		
Cela M	Fran	098
Henry	Asht	015
STARLING		
John	Athe	024
STARNER		
Elizabeth	Will	355
STARR		
Sarah N	Hock	157
Susan	Colu	058
William N	Ashl	012
STARRY		
Levi D	Miam	220
STATE		
Eli	Mont	242
STATER		
William M	Luca	200
STATES		
Rebecca	Carr	040
STATLER		
Elizabeth	Rich	291
Mary	Will	357
Samuel K	Miam	220
Sarah	Miam	222
STAUB		
Otis G	Star	320
STAUM		
Jacob	Wyan	366
STAYNER		
John W	Alle	010
STAYTON		
Verney	Brow	032
STEAD		
Booth F	Butl	037
STEAGALL		
John W	Hard	146
STEARNES		
Mary C	Cuya	065
STEARNS		
Alonzo M	Ashl	013
Cynthia	Asht	017
Garden	Cuya	070
Orrin	Sene	310
Radamanthus	Unio	336
Sylvester	Sene	310

STEBBENS		
Nelson	Port	283
STEBBINS		
Edwin	Hami	130
James K	Asht	014
STEBEAR		
Mary	Gall	108
STEDEM		
John B	Hock	158
STEDMAN		
Geo W	Lora	195
Malender B	Lick	186
STEECE		
James	Mont	238
STEED		
Abraham	Wash	347
STEEDMAN		
James B	Luca	198
STEEL		
Harriet E	Dark	078
Henry	Guer	119
Margaret J	Colu	058
Mary	Hard	148
Sarah Ann	Guer	120
Sarah E	Nobl	268
Simon	Rich	295
STEELE		
Allen P	Medi	212
Calvin F	Asht	017
Clemens F	Fair	090
Eli	Adam	007
Eliza H	Clar	044
Ellen A	High	155
James	Mont	232
John W	Lora	195
Reuben M	Wayn	352
Thomas	Brow	034
William	Hami	129
William	Madi	202
William H	Hami	123
STEEN		
Ely W	Wash	349
James	Wash	350
James B	Mont	241
John A	Brow	034
STEERE		
John R	Mont	238
STEESE		
Charles	Summ	322
John	Summ	321
STEEVER		
Wesley	Cuya	066

STEFFE			STEPHENS (cont)		
Jacob	Tusc	331	Alfred	Dark	078
STEFFY			Daniel	Defi	080
Susannah	Tusc	333	Elizabeth	Adam	003
STEGER			George	Henr	153
Joseph	Mont	229	George L	Adam	003
STEGMAN			Ira	Ross	299
Francis G	Mont	242	Margaret	Defi	079
STEGMILLER			Mary	Colu	056
George C	Mont	253	Salsbury	Cham	043
STEGNER			Thomas	Dela	083
Philip	Hami	126	STEPHENSON		
STEIGELMEIER			Eliza	Belm	029
Mary L	Cuya	067	Elizabeth	Madi	204
STEIGER			Harrison	Jack	168
Jacob	Dark	079	John H	Jack	166
STEIN			Louisa G	Wash	349
Charlotte	Hami	124	Mary	Brow	034
John	Fran	102	Mary E	Medi	212
STEINAUR			Oney	Geau	111
Benedict	Hami	136	STERK		
STEINER			Joseph H	Mont	246
Jacob	Hami	129	STERMER		
Josephine	Star	318	Harriet	Fair	091
STEINERT			STERN		
Charles	Fran	096	Herman	Cuya	070
STEINHEIZER			STERNS		
Philip	Summ	321	Rachel	Cuya	076
STEINHOFF			STERRETT		
Henry	Mont	237	James	Mont	234
STEINLEIN			William	Fran	102
Bernhard	Fran	096	STERRY		
STEINMETZ			Henry F	Hami	123
Simon	Dark	077	STESTON		
STELLER			Charles	Monr	224
John C	Mont	240	STETSON		
STELLERS			Edward	Monr	224
William H	Jeff	172	Nancy	Gall	108
STEM			STETZER		
Amanda	Sene	313	Christian	Fran	096
STEMEN			STEUART		
Norah W	Alle	008	Robert	Lawr	182
STENCER			STEVENS		
John	Jeff	172	Aaron	Guer	117
STENZEL			Alice C	Summ	324
Frank	Hami	138	Benj	Trum	329
STEPENUS			Chas C	Cuya	070
Lydia	Dark	077	Chas L	Fult	106
STEPHEN			Douglass H	Fran	095
Frederick	Monr	224	Eleanor	Guer	119
Snyder	Tusc	332	Elias	Wayn	353
STEPHENS			Eliza	Warr	343
Abednego	Otta	271	Elizabeth	Carr	040

STEVENS		
Elizabeth	Hami	124
Elizabeth	Mont	232
Fannie	Hami	132
Geo	Luca	200
Geo C	Clar	046
Geo H	Lake	179
Geo W	Cler	051
Geo W	Cuya	070
Horace	Trum	329
James	Cham	042
James M	Sand	304
John	Clin	052
John	Otta	271
John H	Will	356
Jos N	Clin	054
Joshua	Carr	040
Levi A	Hami	123
Marcus D	Huro	163
Martin	Wood	361
Mary	Lora	193
Polly	Gall	108
Rosannah	Brow	035
Royal C	Fult	106
Sally	Lake	176
Sarah	Cuya	067
Sarah	Star	319
Sarah C	Musk	264
Sarah P	Butl	038
William	Vint	340
William H Jr	Fult	107
Winfield S	Sand	304
STEVENSON		
Geo	Wood	360
Geo W	Guer	118
Gillett V	Hami	130
Hazia	Butl	036
Jacob	Alle	009
John	Brow	032
John G	Knox	175
Joseph M	Hami	123
Lewis M	Loga	189
Matilda	Putn	288
Otho P	Brow	033
Rebecca L	Fran	099
Robert K	Gree	115
Sarah	Cosh	060
Sarah A	Hard	146
Thomas G	Colu	057
Thomas R	Musk	264
William	Brow	034
William	Sand	302
William H	Cuya	075

STEVER		
Abram I D	Alle	008
STEVISON		
Mary Ann	Jack	167
STEWARD		
Demetrius M	Hami	130
Jane	Cler	049
Mary	Fult	106
Thomas L	Mont	232
STEWART		
Adolphus E	Summ	323
Alex	Brow	031
Alexander	Meig	214
Alexander	Mont	252
Alonzo	Butl	038
Andrew D	Wood	358
Archibald	Pike	283
Augustus	Asht	015
Chas M	Lick	187
Charlotte	Wyan	364
Charlotte	Wyan	364
Elanor	Shel	315
Elizabeth	Defi	079
Elizabeth	Hock	158
Elsie J	Hami	137
Francis R	Sene	310
Frederick	Huro	163
Geo H	Craw	063
Geo W	Clin	055
Harriet	Trum	329
Isabella	Morr	262
James	Hard	147
James	Port	283
James A	Wyan	365
James H	Mont	237
James M	Jack	166
James R	Sene	314
Jane	Cham	042
Jane	Lawr	183
Jefferson	Morg	257
John	Clin	054
John	Lawr	182
Jno B	Mont	252
John C	Erie	087
John T	Fran	096
Kate B	Lick	185
Lavina	Mont	232
Luther	Perr	276
Margaret E	Monr	223
Maria	Carr	039
Maria	Vint	341
Marvin A	Meig	213
Mary	Guer	118

STEWART (cont)			STILES (cont)		
Mary	Port	285	William H H	Scio	308
Mary L	Sand	303	STILL		
Nixon B	Jeff	170	Cath A	Tusc	331
Phebe	VanW	339	Samuel	Jeff	171
Rebecca	Cler	050	STILLIONS		
Rebecca	Nobl	269	Lemuel	Guer	119
Robert J	Trum	328	STILLIOUS		
Robert W	Hanc	141	Sarah H	Guer	117
Sarah A	Luca	202	STILLWAGON		
Seneca	Meig	213	Mary	Rich	294
Susana	Hami	121	Peter	VanW	338
Thomas	Jeff	171	STILLWALL		
William	Clar	044	Sam	Jeff	172
William	Lawr	182	STILLWELL		
William A	Cosh	060	Nelson P	High	157
STEWPHEUS			STIMLER		
Thomas	Gall	109	August	Huro	164
STICKEL			STIMMEL		
Chas	Perr	278	Michael M	Hard	146
John	VanW	339	STIMPSON		
STICKLE			John	Sene	310
Wilbur F	Summ	321	STINE		
STICKLEMAN			Cath	Monr	223
Nancy	Vint	341	Diana	Tusc	333
STICKLES			Reuben	Sand	302
John	Mont	231	William	Belm	028
STICKLEY			William M	Monr	224
Jacob	Henr	153	STINEBAUGH		
STICKNEY			Jacob	Cosh	059
Eleanor	Unio	335	STINEMETZ		
STICKRATH			Truman	VanW	337
Lewis	Wash	348	STINER		
STIER			Calvin W	Cham	041
Edward	Wash	349	STINGER		
STIERS			John	Defi	081
Ebenezer	Guer	120	STINSON		
Frederick L	Musk	262	Garner	Huro	163
Martha	Musk	262	STIPES		
Polly	Guer	120	Mary	Clar	044
STIFFLER			STIRES		
Andrew J	Holm	161	Julia A	Lick	184
Serena	Jack	168	STISKEL		
STIGALL			Benj	Clar	046
James S	Fair	091	STITES		
STIGGERS			Mary E	Butl	038
Lewis W	Unio	336	STITH		
STIGLEMAN			Aseneth	Faye	094
John A	Maho	207	STITLE		
STILES			William	Wayn	351
Jacob	Hanc	141	STITT		
John P	Hami	137	James	Colu	058
Thomas B	Clar	046			

STITZEL			STOLER		
Harvey A	Butl	037	Jacob	Loga	189
STIVER			STOLIKER		
Rebecca	Colu	058	Lester C	Asht	017
STIVERSON			STOLL		
Edward	Port	284	John	Sand	302
STOAT			STOLLINGS		
William	Alle	009	Martin	Pike	282
STOCK			STOLTZ		
Christiana	Craw	064	Lewis	Fair	092
Rebecca	Wood	358	Sarah J	Perr	275
STOCKDALE			STOLTZE		
Moses	Guer	117	Frederick W	Mont	254
Thomas	Guer	120	STOLZ		
STOCKHAM			Jacob	Mont	232
Elias G	Dela	085	Mary A	Mont	231
STOCKING			STOLZER		
Henry A	Port	283	John	Otta	271
STOCKLE			STOM		
Terese	Huro	163	Samuel	Wyan	364
STOCKLIN			STONE		
Jacob	Hami	130	Almira	Lick	185
STOCKTON			Chester	Port	285
Job	Luca	201	Electa	Cuya	068
Joseph R	Trum	325	George H	Trum	327
Mary	Preb	286	Hannah J	Wash	346
STOCKWELL			Harriet	Sene	312
Lurancy	Summ	325	Henry	Colu	056
William J	Colu	059	James F	Belm	029
STODDARD			John	Musk	266
Sophronia S	Defi	080	John F	Rich	291
STODGHILL			Jonathan	Wash	345
Martha	Hami	138	Margaret	Rich	291
STOEPPEL			Nancy	Asht	018
August	Hami	140	Olivia M	Wash	345
STOFER			Rachel	Athe	022
Joseph	Ashl	012	Samuel R	Holm	160
STOFFEL			Sarah	Athe	022
John	Hami	130	William	Cuya	070
STOFFER			STONEBREAKER		
William	Tusc	332	Cath	Mont	232
STOHL			STONEBROOK		
Geo W	Fult	105	Elizabeth	Summ	323
STOKELY			STONEBURNER		
Rufus P	Hock	159	Eliza	Alle	008
William H	Preb	287	Rachel	Fair	090
STOKER			STONEMAN		
Darius R	Hanc	141	Susan	Morg	257
STOKES			STONER		
Francis	Cuya	069	George W	Tusc	330
Harriet	Loga	190	STONEROCK		
John	Jeff	169	Aaron	Dark	079
Sarah	Cham	043			

STONETROCKER			STOVE			
Mary A	Cosh	059	William	VanW	339
STOOKEY			STOVER			
John W	Pick	280	Alfred	Cler	051
STOOPS			Joel	Butl	037
John B	Hami	130	John	Mont	227
Rebecca W	Faye	093	John	Morg	258
STORER			Lydia	Knox	174
Charles	Hard	144	Nancy M	Dark	077
Dianna	Scio	306	STOWDER			
Edward S	Loga	189	Henry	Fran	096
James B	Summ	322	STOWE			
Samuel M	High	153	Henry E	Mari	208
STORES			STOWERS			
Robert	Mont	229	Emma	Hami	124
STORM			STRACKE			
John	Ross	297	Fredericka	Fair	090
STORMS			STRACY			
William H	Cuya	070	Mattie	Trum	329
STORY			STRADER			
Lucy A	Lake	177	Levi T	Fran	098
Margaret	Asht	016	STRAHL			
Thomas	Cler	049	Benj J	Craw	063
STOTLER			Nathan P	Wash	345
William	Fran	102	STRAIGHT			
STOTT			Alexander	Monr	226
Geo	Rich	293	Edward F	Shel	316
STOTTLEMGER			Lewis	Lawr	183
Daniel	Dela	085	Sophia	Luca	198
STOUDT			William R	Cler	048
John W Jr	Summ	324	STRAIN			
STOUFFER			Mary	Brow	033
Henry J	Wayn	351	STRAIT			
STOUGH			Matilda	Brow	032
Christ	Lick	187	STRANAHAN			
Samuel	Rich	292	Ellen	Luca	200
Thomas C	Wayn	353	STRANBRIDGE			
William	Will	355	Henry	Madi	203
STOUGHTON			STRANGE			
Omar L	Knox	175	Juliana	Otta	271
Sumner	Asht	019	William	High	156
STOUT			STRASSER			
Christena	Henr	153	Andrew Sr	Erie	087
Eliza	Summ	324	STRATTON			
Isaiah	Otta	271	Aaron	Cler	050
John	Will	356	Cath	Brow	033
John A	Hard	145	Eliza	Ross	301
Joseph R	Scio	305	Gilmer	High	156
Orlando B	Henr	151	Henry	Mari	210
William	Hard	146	Henry G	Trum	329
William H H	Hanc	141	Maria	Cuya	065
STOUTER			Mary E	High	156
John M	Putn	290	Minard F	Augl	026

STRAUB		
Geo	Wyan	365
John	Mont	240
Reinhard	Monr	226
Theo	Hami	136
STRAUSBAUGH		
William G	Sene	313
STRAUSS		
Jas	Wayn	354
STRAWMAN		
John G	Sene	311
STRAWSER		
John	Ross	299
Lydia	Vint	340
STRAYER		
Ellen M	Fair	092
Joseph	Rich	291
STREET		
Mary A	Hami	121
Nancy A	Miam	220
Samuel R	Lick	185
William H	Clin	054
STREETER		
Chas B	Huro	164
STRENTZ		
John W	Hock	158
STRENVING		
Henry	Hami	123
STRESSING		
Chas	Cuya	065
STRETCHBERY		
James	Wood	363
STREUM		
Arnold	Tusc	332
STRICKER		
Amos	Henr	151
STRICKLAND		
Harriet	Erie	086
Mark	Cler	051
Simon C	Asht	014
STRICKLER		
Louis M	Fair	092
STRICKLING		
Isiah J	Shel	316
STRIKER		
George G	Port	284
Julia	Hami	123
Milly	Craw	064
STRIMPEL		
Benj	Hard	147
STRINGFELLOW		
Richard	Warr	344
STROBEL		
Charles	High	154
STROBLE		
Geo	Mont	227
STROCK		
David	Cham	042
Edward	VanW	339
STRODE		
Allen B	Loga	191
William H	Clin	053
William H	Fair	090
STROEDTER		
Charles	Mont	243
STROHL		
Cath	Perr	275
STROLIPER		
Maria	Sene	313
STROMAN		
Joseph A	Adam	007
Sidney R	Adam	007
STRONG		
Abner D	Asht	014
Benj T	Huro	166
Elvira	Knox	173
Emma G	Defi	079
Francis	Port	283
Geo W	Will	355
Harriet	Huro	164
Luther M	Hard	146
Mary B	Fran	097
Newton G	Loga	191
Reason C	Fran	102
Rebecca	Sene	312
Rhoda	Asht	014
Wesley A	Hard	146
STROSNIDER		
Rachel	Monr	223
STROTHER		
Ellen	Monr	226
STROUD		
John	Jeff	171
STROUP		
Jerina	Cler	049
Lawrence K	Augl	026
Lovina	Trum	327
Philip B	Knox	175
Thomas	Belm	029
STROUSE		
Wesley	Gree	114
STROUT		
William H	Warr	344
STROW		
Daniel	Putn	289

STRUBLE			STUMP		
Abraham	Craw	063	Cath	Mont	232
Jasper	Trum	325	James H	Hock	158
Lewis G	Shel	315	John A	Wood	362
STRUNCK			Mary	Fair	091
J Franklin	Hard	144	Mary	Hock	159
STRUTT			Noah E	Wood	362
Anna	Pike	281	STUMPF		
STRYKER			Christian	Fran	102
Hannah	Fult	106	STUPP		
STUART			Jacob C	Pike	281
David	Mont	246	STURDEVANT		
Elijah R	Asht	017	Horace	Lick	184
James A	Mont	244	Phebe	Clar	044
Jane	Wayn	353	STURGEON		
John J	Unio	335	James K	Fair	090
Margaret	Cuya	066	Jeremiah	Clin	052
Mary	Cler	051	STURM		
STUBB			Joseph	Hami	130
Lizzie S	Dark	077	STURR		
STUBBS			William G	Hami	136
James	Belm	026	STURTEVANT		
STUBE			Antonette	Sand	301
Matilda	Hami	132	Russell Z	Sand	302
STUBER			STUTSMAN		
Elizabeth	Tusc	332	Eliza L	Mont	232
STUBLE			STUTTER		
Rachel	Hanc	142	Margaret J	Fair	090
STUCKY			STUTTS		
John	Defi	080	Louis W	Asht	015
STUDER			STUTZEL		
Eliza	Cuya	073	George	Mont	244
STUDY			STYER		
Thomas	Hami	126	Francis M	Wayn	351
STUHLMAN			STYERS		
Henry	Miam	221	Jerry	VanW	337
STUKEY			STYMETTS		
Abigail	Monr	223	Francis W	Cler	051
Anna	VanW	337	SUBLER		
STULL			August	Dark	079
Henry	Cler	051	SUCK		
Lewis	Rich	291	William	Cuya	070
Martha	Musk	266	SUDDUTH		
William	Knox	176	William	Alle	008
STULLER			SULLIGER		
Alex	Carr	039	Theo W	Wyan	366
STULTS			William R H	Hard	145
Mary Jane	High	154	SULLINGER		
STULTZ			Sarah	Defi	081
Harvey	Hock	158	SULLIVAN		
Marshall	Musk	266	Ann	Dela	085
STUMM			Ann	Hami	127
Philip W	Paul	274	Anthony	Mont	244

SULLIVAN (cont)		
Bridget	Lawr	180
Cath	Cuya	068
Cath M	Musk	264
Daniel	Cham	041
Daniel	Fran	102
Denis	Musk	266
Elizabeth	Mont	256
Florence O	Luca	201
Frances	Merc	218
James (1st)	Fran	102
James	Mont	237
James	Musk	266
Jeremiah	Mont	229
Jeremiah	Mont	252
Jerry	Lawr	180
John	Fult	107
John	Hami	136
John	Mont	242
John	Summ	323
John L	Ross	300
John W	Hami	139
Julia	Hami	124
Lorenzo D	Loga	191
Martin	Musk	264
Mary	Asht	016
Mary	Musk	265
Michael	Mont	255
Nancy	Maho	206
Parthena	Monr	225
Patrick	Fran	098
Peter J	Hami	130
Sarah	Guer	119
Sarah	Lick	188
William	Cham	043
SULPHIN		
Chas	Butl	037
Darius L	Butl	037
SULSAR		
Malissa	Fran	101
SULTNER		
Geo W	Colu	057
Henry	Colu	056
SUMMER		
Conrad	Cuya	069
Jacob	Mont	246
SUMMERFIELD		
Henry	Mont	245
SUMMERS		
Abram	Asht	019
Francis W	Hard	148
Hannah	Adam	004
Henry M	Jack	169

SUMMERS (cont)		
James	Mont	236
Jane D	Faye	093
Mary A	Madi	202
Rosanna	Belm	027
SUMMERSVILLE		
Susan	Hard	144
SUMMERTON		
Frances E	Wayn	351
SUMMONEY		
Jane	Holm	160
SUMMONS		
Ann D	Luca	197
SUMNERS		
Cath	Madi	202
SUNDMACHER		
Johann D	Augl	025
SUNKAS		
Jacob	Luca	197
SUNKER		
John	Fran	102
SUPER		
Geo H	Rich	293
SUPPLEE		
Albert F	Athe	023
SURLS		
Elizabeth	Jeff	170
SUSORE		
John B	Otta	272
SUSS		
Charles	Mont	238
SUTERMISTER		
Godfrey	Hard	146
Jacob	Hard	147
SUTHERLAND		
Aggie	Clar	044
Geo	Craw	064
Margaret	Hard	147
SUTLER		
John	Monr	225
SUTLEY		
Geo	Mari	210
SUTLIFF		
James P	Port	285
Joseph J	Trum	325
SUTTLE		
Maxwell P	Adam	006
Sherman	Asht	018
SUTTLES		
Benj	Musk	265
Thomas	Perr	277
SUTTON		
Adaline A	Port	285

SUTTON (cont)			SWARTZ		
Albert G	Huro	164	Cath	Augl	025
Cath A	Guer	120	Elizabeth	Fran	101
Guier	Morr	261	George W	Hard	145
Harvey W	Cler	051	George W	Perr	278
James	Huro	162	John W	VanW	338
John D	Mont	238	Jonathan	Wood	361
Lois A	Luca	201	Joseph	Dela	084
Margaret	Trum	325	Margaret	Fran	095
Peter	Lick	184	Sarah G T	Monr	225
Robert	Fult	105	SWARTZFAGER		
Samuel J	Lawr	183	Henry F	Paul	274
Sarah J	Athe	024	SWARTZLANDER		
William	Cuya	070	Mathias	Wood	360
SUVERLY			Sarah	Wood	360
Adam	Madi	204	SWASICK		
SWABLE			James C	Ashl	013
Mary A	Clar	044	SWATZ		
SWACKHAMMER			Frederick	Wood	363
Mary A	Hock	158	SWEANY		
SWADNER			Daniel	Tusc	332
William	Clar	046	SWEENEY		
SWAGER			Jas	Cuya	069
Isaac	Trum	329	Rose	Perr	276
SWAIN			Thomas	Mont	236
Bennonah	Guer	120	SWEENY		
Ellen	Butl	036	John	Mont	249
SWALLOW			Mary	Hami	132
John	Loga	189	Patrick	Hami	130
Jos W	Cosh	061	SWEET		
SWALLUMS			Bermelia	Cuya	075
John	Morr	259	Charles	Asht	014
SWAN			Cordean	Asht	015
Horace	Meig	213	Dan	Sand	304
Joseph	Jack	166	Eunice	Sand	304
Susan	Guer	120	George W	Hock	157
Susan B	Cham	043	Hannah	Rich	295
SWANEY			Harry	Defi	081
Francis M	Hami	130	Jesse M	Asht	014
SWANGER			Narcissa	Asht	019
Alex J	Rich	296	Perces	Perr	275
SWANK			William K	Mont	235
David E	Fult	106	Zur	Asht	014
Elias L	Rich	291	SWEETLAND		
Sarah	Sand	303	Andrew F	Huro	166
Wilhelminar	Musk	267	Chas B	Musk	266
William	Fran	102	Daniel	Huro	162
SWANSON			Lorenzo	Huro	162
Jane	Jack	167	SWEETMAN		
SWARM			Michael A	Pick	278
Franklin J	Wood	360	Richard	Clin	053
SWARTWOOD			SWEGHEIMER		
Ira A	Cuya	070	Jacob	Dela	083

SWEITZER		
James	Asht	017
SWENY		
James R	Warr	342
SWETLAND		
Leonard	Lake	177
SWICK		
Henry F	Mari	210
Martin V B	Fair	092
SWICKARD		
Christina	Fran	103
SWIFT		
Alfred	Hami	140
Geo F	Meig	214
Nelson E	Hami	130
SWIGART		
Barbara A	Rich	292
Jesse L	Rich	292
John M	Rich	293
William H	Sene	309
SWIGER		
Lewis	Pike	281
SWHIHART		
Christena	VanW	339
SWINDELL		
Amanda A	Lick	187
SWINDLER		
Harry H	Miam	221
Margaret	Hanc	142
SWINEFORD		
Curtis	Ashl	012
Minor W	Ashl	012
SWINEHART		
Cath	Medi	210
SWINK		
Sarah	Clin	055
SWINSON		
James	Hami	130
SWINT		
Henry	Sand	303
SWINTON		
John	Mont	256
SWISHER		
Absalom C	Adam	007
Alexander	Miam	219
Alfred M	Maho	207
James	VanW	337
Joseph T	Lick	188
Rebecca	Alle	008
Solomon	Preb	288
SWITZER		
Christian	Mont	252
David A	Wayn	352

SWITZER (cont)		
Jacob	Cuya	074
Jacob	Fult	105
Jacob	Paul	273
Julia A	Dark	077
Lydia	Ashl	013
Samson	Wood	360
SWONGER		
Emer L	Craw	064
James M	Rich	291
Reuben	High	153
SWOOELAND		
Peter	Holm	160
SWOPE		
Franklin G	Musk	266
SWORDS		
James W	Wash	345
John C	Scio	307
William	Wash	345
SWORTWOOD		
Thomas	Monr	226
SWYTSER		
John	Morg	257
SYKES		
Otis	Huro	162
Ransom F	Asht	019
SYLVESTER		
Marcus B	Lick	186
Stephen	Morg	257
SYNOTT		
Thomas	Mont	235
SYPHER		
Mary	Summ	321
TAAFE		
Jaseph	Mont	234
TAAFF		
Mary A	Hami	132
TABLER		
Michael	Athe	021
Sarah A	Alle	009
TABORN		
Minerva	Lora	195
TAES		
Lydia	Fair	089
TAFEL		
Gustav	Hami	125
TAFT		
Irena	Lora	195
TAGGART		
Cath	Jeff	170

TAGGART (cont)			TATEM		
Leonard W	Gree	114	Sarah A	Hami	132
TALBITZER			TATHWELL		
Anna	Trum	328	Ellen	Knox	175
Chas W	Trum	328	TAULMAN		
TALBOT			Eliza	Hami	139
Allen	Putn	290	TAUTLINGER		
Audrie	Mont	240	Mary A	Star	319
Richard C	Perr	277	TAYLOR		
TALBOTT			Addison A	Wood	360
Eliza	Lawr	180	Allen	High	156
Joseph P	Pike	281	Amelia	Star	321
TALIZE			Amelia M	Port	284
Frederick	Mont	233	Andrew	Belm	029
TALLMAN			Ann	Hock	159
Alfred T	Unio	333	Ann Minerva	Belm	030
Almira	Knox	175	Barbara H	High	154
Eleanor T	Loga	192	Cath	Fult	106
TAMME			Chandler P	Belm	030
Albin	Brow	034	Charles A	Hanc	143
TAMPENAN			Charles W	Vint	341
Theodore	Mont	233	Charlotte	Cuya	069
TANCETT			Cornelius P	Will	356
Rebecca	Wash	350	David H	Asht	019
TANNEHILL			Eliza	Brow	034
Angeline	Rich	292	Eliza	High	154
Nathaniel	Hock	158	Elizabeth	Faye	095
TANNER			Elizabeth C	Miam	219
Augustus	Sene	309	Ellen	Monr	223
Benj	Huro	164	Francis M	Wyan	365
Cath A	Gall	111	Geo	Asht	015
John	Musk	267	Geo K	Hami	125
William A	Alle	009	Griffin	Star	320
TANNHAUSEN			Harrison P	Star	320
Moses	Mont	242	Harvey	Clin	055
TAP			Henry	Knox	174
Jennie	Hami	132	Henry D	Hanc	141
TAPPAN			Isaac	Meig	213
Mary	Cuya	069	Isaac	Mont	240
TAPSCOTT			Isaac	Wood	361
John	Warr	342	James	Erie	087
TARBELL			James	Scio	305
Eli M	Asht	014	James E	Mari	210
TARPENNING			James E	Vint	340
James	Madi	204	Jane	Lora	194
TARR			Jane	Rich	294
Eliza	Wayn	351	Jane E	Maho	205
TARTTER			Joel B	Colu	057
Daniel	Cuya	075	John	Adam	007
TATE			John	Cosh	061
Cath E	Athe	021	John	Hami	138
Henry H	Gree	117	John	Loga	190
			John	Wayn	354

TAYLOR (cont)			TEDROW (cont)		
John	Wood	360	Elizabeth	Jeff	170
John A	Scio	308	Jacob W	Athe	022
John B	Huro	163	TEED		
Jno W	Wash	345	Sarah J	Jack	167
Joseph M T	Cosh	060	TEEGARDIN		
Kate D	Hami	132	Margaret	Pick	280
Lucinda A	Colu	058	TEEL		
Lucretia	Fran	104	Henry	Guer	119
Lydia M	Meig	214	John A	Sene	312
Margaret	Colu	059	William A	Sene	309
Margaret	Wayn	354	TEEPLE		
Margaret	Will	356	Edward J	Wood	362
Martha B	Fran	096	TEETER		
Mary	Adam	004	Henry	Scio	306
Mary	Cosh	060	TEETS		
Mary	Lawr	179	David M	Adam	007
Mary Ann	Perr	275	Margaret	Alle	009
Mary E	Guer	117	TEFORT		
Mary E	Meig	216	Charlotte	Fair	092
Nancy J	Clin	054	TEGARDINE		
Orpha	Gall	108	Jacob	Cuya	075
Racel B	Maho	206	TEHAN		
Richard V	Lake	178	Eugene	Alle	009
Samuel	Adam	007	TEICHMANN		
Samuel W	Loga	192	Charles	Hami	126
Sarah	Cuya	073	TELFER		
Sarah	Cuya	076	Margaret C	Carr	039
Sarah A	Perr	277	TELL		
Sarah Ann	Pike	282	Geo	Musk	265
Sarah R	Knox	175	TEMMENS		
Stephen M	Lora	195	Jno	Mont	234
Thomas B	Wayn	352	TEMPEL		
Thomas J	Asht	015	John	Will	356
Thomas W	Rich	294	TEMPERENCE		
William	Brow	033	Dennis	Loga	189
William	Wood	363	TEMPLAR		
William M	Meig	216	Austin	Wash	345
William V	Cham	043	TEMPLE		
TEACH			Andrew J	Cler	049
Elijah	Clar	044	Bynum	Cler	047
TEACHMAN			George W	Cler	049
John B	Fult	106	Taylor	Ross	299
TEAGADEN			TEMPLETON		
Moses	Paul	274	James	Jeff	169
TEARE			John S	Fult	106
William	Hami	125	TENER		
TECH			Caroline D	High	157
Mary	Hami	132	Dynes	Adam	004
TEDAKER			Elizabeth	Monr	223
Emerson F	Paul	273	Jas W	Clin	054
TEDROW			Sarah B	Adam	004
Douglass W	Pike	281			

TENERTY		
Patrick	Mont	244
TENEYCK		
David	Wayn	351
Lewis	Luca	198
TENNEY		
Isaac W	Athe	023
Latham	Hami	137
Newton F	Mont	240
TENNIS		
Cath	Loga	190
TENNISON		
Andrew	Paul	273
TEPLADY		
Robert	Luca	196
TEPOOL or TEPOOLE		
Ennis J	Hami	125
TERHUNE		
Nathan D F	Mont	229
TERMIN		
Elizabeth	Hanc	142
TERPANY		
Samantha	Mari	208
TERREL		
Leroy S	Hock	159
TERRELL		
Daniel A	Meig	215
Eleanor J	Perr	277
Eppy	Loga	191
TERRIL		
Daniel	Meig	215
TERRILL		
Elizabeth	Morr	261
TERRY		
Franklin P	Hami	138
John	Jack	168
John H	Carr	040
Mary A	Wyan	365
Rebecca	Mont	232
Richard	Ross	300
Sarah	Cham	041
Thomas	Athe	022
TERWILLEGAN		
Stuard L	Hami	136
TERWILLIGER		
Chas J	Jack	167
John M	Sene	310
TESCHER		
John F	Colu	058
TEST		
Lucy	Colu	058
TETRICK		
William E	Guer	119
TEVERBAUGH		
Solomon	Miam	220
TEXTER		
David P	Star	318
THACHER		
Daniel	Scio	305
THACKER		
Henry H	Jack	168
William S	Lick	186
THAIR		
James	Scio	307
THALER		
Henry	Fran	104
THARP		
Benj	Pick	278
Caleb B	Wayn	353
Job	Morr	261
Lucy J	Lick	184
Mary J	Gall	109
Reuben	Perr	275
THATCHER		
Eliza	Fran	101
John W	Trum	327
Jonathan	Loga	192
Orrin S	Craw	064
Rosanna	Adam	007
Susannah	Jack	168
William P	Sene	313
THAXTON		
Benj F	Mont	242
Martha	Gall	110
THAYER		
Alfred A	Knox	175
Ephraim	Lora	193
Mathilda	Hami	139
Newton	Fran	102
Peter	Geau	112
Roswell E	Lora	196
THEAKER		
Mary	Belm	028
THEIS		
Eva Cath	Hami	132
THENNE		
Herman	Mont	237
THEOBALD		
Frederick	Clin	054
Mariah	Gree	114
Valentine	Fult	107
THEOBOLD		
Cath	Pike	283
THIEKE		
Cath E	Hami	132

THOBURN			THOMAS (cont)		
Hattie L	Fran	101	John H	Clar	046
Kate A	Jeff	170	Jonathan	Dark	078
THOMAS			Jonathan E	Gall	111
Alexander	Wash	346	Joseph	Hanc	141
Allen B	Wash	350	Joseph E	Dela	085
Alvah C	Henr	151	Joseph S	Hard	147
Andrew J	Preb	288	Louisa	Guer	119
Benj	Meig	213	Margaret	Madi	204
Benj H	Fair	092	Mary	Erie	087
Byron	Fran	102	Mary J	Mont	227
Byron	Loga	190	Noah	Fran	101
Cadwell	Scio	304	Oliva S	Port	285
Cath	Gree	115	Oliver	VanW	338
Cath	Nobl	268	Peter	Hami	125
Charles R	Mari	210	Phebe M	Will	357
Cornelius	Pick	280	Rebecca	Dela	083
Daniel	Scio	306	Rebecca	Perr	276
Daniel W	Cuya	071	Reuben	Gall	109
David	Adam	007	Robert M	Fran	101
Ebenezer	Wayn	351	Samuel	Hami	136
Edmund	Lora	195	Samuel	Hanc	141
Eliza	Madi	204	Samuel	Wash	346
Eliza A	Preb	288	Seth M	Summ	323
Eliza J	Dark	078	Thomas	Belm	028
Elizabeth	Dark	078	William	Cuya	074
Elizabeth	Gree	114	William A	Trum	327
Elizabeth	Mont	232	William H	Mont	228
Ellen M	Geau	111	William R	Gree	117
Frank M	Shel	315	THOMASON		
Frederick	Athe	022	Charles	Vint	340
George M	Trum	326	THOMASSON		
George S	Jeff	171	Richard H	Mari	208
Glenn	Hock	158	THOMBERGH		
Harriet	Meig	215	Thomas H	Luca	198
Henry	Craw	063	THOMEN		
Henry	Hami	139	Alvis	Hami	136
Henry E	Mont	250	THOMPSON		
Henry E	Star	317	Aaron	Warr	344
Herbert	Sand	304	Agnes	Jeff	171
Hugh	Morg	258	Albert C	Scio	306
Isaac L	Fair	092	Alexander H	Mont	236
J B	Meig	215	Allen S	Brow	033
Jacob	Sene	309	Alvin	Unio	334
Jacob	Star	320	Anne	Colu	056
Jacob E	Wyan	365	Aurilla	Trum	326
James M	Mont	234	Calvery M	Athe	023
Jane	Guer	117	Cath	Hock	158
Jane	Scio	307	Cath	Nobl	269
John	Lawr	182	Chas E	Mont	242
Jno	Meig	214	Chas H	Mont	250
John	Monr	224	Danforth B	Butl	038
John A	Cosh	059	David	Henr	152

THOMPSON (cont)			THOMPSON (cont)		
David	Will	356	Mary	Mari	208
David B	Brow	032	Mary	Miam	219
Emery	Hami	121	Mary	Summ	324
Emily E	Fair	091	Mary E	Mont	256
Francis D	Jeff	171	Mary E	Wood	361
Francis M	Scio	304	Mary S	Hock	158
Frederick W	Hami	125	Nancy	Wood	362
George	Athe	020	Nancy E	Brow	034
George	Hock	158	Nelson	Butl	037
Hannah J	Jack	166	Newton	Butl	037
Harvey L	Harr	150	Orson	Mont	239
Harvey M	Fran	102	Oscar F	Warr	343
Henry	Mont	240	Rebecca	Gree	114
Hiram	Medi	210	Rebecca S	Fran	097
Jacob	Hami	125	Reuben	Miam	221
Jacob A	Warr	344	Richard	Mari	210
Jacob E	Mont	238	Robert J	Jeff	171
James	Harr	150	Rosannah	Belm	029
James	Lick	185	Rosetta R	Hami	139
James A	Fair	092	Ruth	Loga	192
James D	Guer	117	Samuel	Miam	220
James D	Trum	327	Sarah	Carr	040
James F	Warr	342	Sarah	Loga	191
James L	Miam	220	Sarah	Preb	287
James M	Clin	052	Sarah	Rich	291
James S	Hard	145	Sarah	Wash	346
James W	Belm	029	Susan	Morr	261
James W	Hock	159	Susan	Port	285
Jane	Hard	148	Tamma	Adam	003
Jane	Trum	329	Thomas	Adam	003
John	Putn	290	Thomas	VanW	338
John	Sene	314	William	Guer	120
Jno B	Mont	233	William	Hock	158
John E	Colu	056	William	Scio	306
John W	Cler	048	William H	Nobl	268
Jno W	Mont	234	William J	Mont	233
John W	Mont	243	William M	Wyan	366
Joseph L	Brow	033	THOMS		
Joseph M	Jeff	169	Sarah	Knox	174
Joseph S	Unio	336	William H	Cler	049
Levi P	Hami	125	THOMSBURG		
Lois	Fran	102	Margaret A	Cler	050
Lucinda	Clin	054	THOMSON		
Lucretia	Hanc	142	Charles M	Hami	121
Margaret	Cler	050	Cornelius	Monr	223
Margaret	Shel	315	William H	Mont	228
Margaret A	Preb	288	THORMILY		
Maria	Hami	140	Jas	Wash	349
Marinda	Belm	027	THORN		
Martha	Sand	303	Cassandra	Hard	144
Martha	Sand	303	Cath	Sene	313
Mary	Brow	032	Joshua S	Gall	109

THORN (cont)				THURMAN (cont)		
Samuel S	Luca	198		William S	Cham	041
THORNBERRY				THURSTON		
Frank	Monr	225		Abraham	Preb	286
THORNBURG				Benoi	Fran	104
Lois	Will	355		Clara	Warr	343
Zade	Madi	204		THWING		
THORNBURGH				Henry	Geau	111
Rebecca	Adam	007		TIBBS		
THORNTON				Qualls	Fair	090
James	Pick	279		TICE		
Mary E	Defi	079		Aaron G	Fran	102
Nancy	Gall	110		Benj	Hanc	141
Reuben T	Nobl	269		Lewis	Wash	345
THOROMAN				Maria	Cler	048
Samuel H	Adam	005		Melissa	Cler	048
Thomas	Adam	004		Sherwood	Wash	345
William B	Adam	004		TIDD		
William R	Adam	004		Elijah	Gree	113
THORP				Jeremiah M	Trum	329
Bezaled	Cuya	076		TIEBE		
David M	Luca	202		Theodore	Faye	093
Franklin T	Lick	186		TIENY		
James	Lora	195		John	Mont	243
Maria J	Vint	341		TIERNEY		
Thomas J	Star	320		Thomas	Mont	242
THORUSKY				TIFFANY		
Dorcas	Cosh	060		Geo W	Clar	046
THRAILKILL				Polly A	Erie	086
Nancy J	Hard	147		TIFFT		
Richard H	Defi	081		Geo G	Sene	311
THRALL				TIGNER		
Henry L	Lick	184		Charles	Hock	159
John E	Fran	102		TILL		
Sarah	Gree	115		William A	Erie	087
Walter	Fran	097		TILLETT		
THRAPP				Jiles	Belm	027
John	Henr	153		Samuel	Belm	031
THRASLER				TILLEY		
Leonidas L	Mont	234		William A	Jack	167
THRIFT				TILLINGHAST		
Sinah	Putn	289		Francis M	Clin	055
THROCKMORTON				TILLISTON		
Brewer	Jack	168		Martha	Cuya	068
THROPP				TILLMAN		
William B	Putn	289		Henry J	Hami	125
THUM				TILLOTSON		
Augusta	Hami	132		Christopher C	Huro	163
THURINGER				Edward H	Mont	250
Joseph	Mont	235		Sophia	Sand	301
THURMAN				TILLSON		
Eveline	Clin	053		William D	Butl	038
Francis M	Clin	053				

TILTON			**TITTLER**		
Benj B	Nobl	268	Allen	Fair	090
Frances M	Pick	279	**TITUS**		
Frances W	Pick	279	Frank M	Hami	125
TIMANUS			Giles J	Sand	304
Richard H	Sand	301	Harlam E	Clar	046
TIMBERLAKE			Samuel N	Mari	209
John E	Belm	029	**TIVERRELL**		
Samuel	Hock	158	William	Lora	195
TIMBERS			**TLAMSA**		
Eli	VanW	337	Joseph	Hami	125
TIMM			**TOBER**		
Henry C	Musk	265	Philip W	Fult	107
TIMME			**TOBERGATE**		
Henry	Warr	342	Augustus	Mont	250
TIMMES			**TOBIN**		
John	Fran	101	Martin	Tusc	333
TIMMONS			Morris	Colu	057
Daniel	Faye	093	Sarah E	Knox	173
TIMMS			**TOD**		
John	Summ	324	William D	Mont	243
TINCKLER			**TODD**		
Charles H	Star	319	Celia Ann	Asht	018
TINDALL			Emily E	Trum	328
John C	VanW	339	Emma	Clar	045
TINER			George T	Luca	198
Richard	Cuya	071	George W	Lick	188
TINGLE			George W	Wood	363
James	Mont	232	James E	Musk	266
Joseph	Putn	289	Samuel A	Guer	117
TINGLEY			Sarah	Cham	042
Isaac	Clar	046	William	Tusc	330
TINKER			**TODHUNTER**		
Henry H	Hami	125	James E	Faye	093
TINKHAM			**TOHEY**		
Lewis	Athe	021	Cath	Hami	132
TINKLER			**TOLAND**		
John	Mont	239	Benj	Tusc	331
TIPPIE			**TOLBOT**		
John M	Athe	020	Joseph	Musk	262
TIPTON			**TOLIN**		
James E	Belm	029	William W	Cler	049
John	Scio	306	**TOLL**		
Jonathan	Holm	160	William G	High	157
TISDALE			**TOMBOW**		
Chas C	Sene	312	Sarah	Star	318
Hiram	Erie	088	**TOMER**		
TISDELL			Thomas J	Star	318
Edward	Mont	250	**TOMLIN**		
TITSWORTH			John	Clin	055
Richard L	Hard	147	Lewis	Clin	052
TITTLE			**TOMLINSON**		
Joseph	Athe	023	Ann M	Ross	300

TOMLINSON (cont)			TORRENCE (cont)		
Hager	Mont	239	Mary A	Craw	064
Nancy M	Hami	139	Sarah B	Meig	215
Norton	Ross	300	TORREY		
Richard L	Ross	300	Martha	Morr	261
TOMPKINS			TORRIE		
Geo	Cuya	071	John K R	High	155
Jos W	Mont	244	TOTTEN		
Lyman	Fult	104	Susan	Carr	040
William	Cuya	071	TOULKS		
TOMS			Acksa	Warr	343
Edward	Lawr	179	TOUNES		
Geo O	Miam	221	Margaret	Hami	132
TONAR			TOUT		
Sinah	Morg	258	Artimicy	Brow	033
TONKINSONS			TOUVEL		
John	Huro	163	Jackson	Rich	294
TONSING			TOUVELLE		
Fred H	Cuya	071	Mary W	Merc	217
TOOHY			TOWELL		
Michael	Cham	043	Sarah	Gree	114
TOOL			TOWELSON		
David	Geau	111	Olvier C	Tusc	331
Susan	Hock	158	TOWER		
TOOLE			Isaiah F	Hami	125
Robert E	Fair	092	TOWERS		
TOOLEN			Margaret	Luca	200
James	Mont	245	TOWN		
TOOLY			Margaret	Cham	042
Sarah A	Madi	202	TOWNER		
TOOMEY			Elizabeth	Erie	086
John	Otta	272	Emeline	Cler	050
TOOMIRE			TOWNLEY		
Aaron	Cham	043	William W	Dela	085
TOOTLE			TOWNSEND		
Owen B	Fran	102	Elizabeth	Faye	094
TOPE			Ferris	Summ	321
Hiram G	Carr	040	Hiram W	Huro	163
Margaret	Meig	213	Hosea	Huro	163
TORBET			Isaac N	Wash	345
James	Hami	125	Margaret	Huro	163
TORMELTY			Sarah Jane	Athe	022
Melvin	Mont	240	William	Star	316
TORRANCE			William C	Musk	266
Aaron W	Unio	334	Wilson	Lawr	179
Geo W	Fran	102	TOWNSLEY		
John W	Lora	195	Innis A	Gree	115
TORRENCE			James L	Mont	234
Aaron	Meig	212	John F	Cler	049
Evaline	Lora	195	Lovenia M	Cler	048
Geo W	Hami	137	Margaret	Gree	113
(alias Jas W Clifton)			TOWSLEE		
Lewis W	Jack	167	Margaret	Medi	210

TOWSLEY		
Jane A	Cuya	066
TRABER		
Mary A	Adam	005
TRACE		
Aery E	Musk	264
Mathias	Lick	186
TRACY		
Abraham	Perr	275
Benj N	Cosh	060
Daniel	Monr	223
Emeline	Preb	287
Harriet E	Luca	198
Isaiah	Madi	202
James	Mont	234
John S	Loga	191
Joshua H	Cham	043
Linus	Trum	327
Peter	Alle	009
Sarah	Perr	275
TRADER		
Sarah A	Clar	046
TRAGER		
Henry E	Summ	321
TRAGO		
Samuel W	Craw	064
TRAIL		
Mary	Henr	153
TRANSUL		
Samuel	Summ	324
TRAPP		
Alonzo	Erie	087
Peter M	Shel	315
Sarah	Wayn	353
TRASK		
James R	Putn	289
TRAVEL		
Serens	Fran	100
TRAVER		
Alvaro V	Asht	014
TRAVIS		
Chancy E	Trum	325
Dudley R	Geau	113
George W	Madi	204
Hannah	Tusc	332
Magdalena	Cuya	069
Mary	Merc	217
TRAWSH		
Leonard	Hami	125
TRAXLER		
Jacob	Will	355
Lester	Rich	291
William	Summ	324

TREACE		
Michael S	Ashl	013
TREADWELL		
Nathan	Huro	164
TREAP		
Christian	Summ	324
TREAT		
Alonzo L	Medi	212
John	Trum	328
Labin	Cuya	069
Ruth A	Fran	095
TREEN		
James	Summ	321
TREMBATH		
Thomas G	Cuya	071
TREMBLY		
David N	Monr	226
TREN		
Dorothea	Cuya	068
TRENARY		
Christina	Adam	005
TRENHAM		
Harriet A	Dela	082
TRENSCHEL		
Frederick	Wood	362
TREPKY		
Alex	Cham	041
TRESCOTT		
William D	Nobl	269
TRESS		
Ruhamah	Knox	174
TRESSEL		
George C	Hard	147
Leonard R	Star	318
TRESSELL		
Elizabeth	Holm	161
TREVOR		
Baxter	Cuya	071
TREYMAN		
Sarah E	Wood	363
TRIBBY		
Elizabeth A	Cler	048
TRICKEY		
Hartwell M	Fran	096
TRICKLE		
Edward H	Wash	346
TRIGER		
Maria	Ross	297
TRIMBLE		
Margaret	Wash	350
Mary A	Clar	046
Sarah	Nobl	270
Simeon D	Mont	230

TRIMBLE (cont)		
Stewart	Star	316
William H	High	155
TRIMMER		
Edwin	Huro	162
TRINE		
David	Butl	038
TRIPP		
Edwin	Merc	217
Nancy A	Vint	340
Sylvester	Carr	039
TRIQUART		
Peter	Mont	241
TRITCH		
James	Mont	231
TROBRIDGE		
Ruth	Gall	108
TRODE		
Fred	Cuya	071
TROOP		
Jacob	Mont	231
TROP		
Susannah	Unio	335
TROPE		
Geo	Cuya	071
TROST		
Mary B	Musk	267
TROT		
Paulus	Fran	101
TROTH		
Biddy	Gall	110
Isma	High	155
TROTT		
William	Knox	174
TROTTER		
James	Jeff	171
Mary Jane	Hami	132
TROUP		
Hannah E	Ashl	014
Ann E	Musk	262
Anthony	Musk	262
George	Maho	206
Jane	Morg	257
TROUTMAN		
Peter	Mont	234
TROVER		
John C	Carr	039
TROVILLO		
Hannah F	Clin	052
TROW		
Henry F	Mont	227
TROWBRIDGE		
Henry	Cuya	076

TROWBRIDGE (cont)		
Mehitable	Cuya	076
Sylvester E	Fult	105
Willard	Fult	105
TROXELL		
Mary	Hami	132
TROXLER		
Elizabeth	Dela	083
TROY		
Anna	Hami	121
TRUAX		
Ralph	Luca	198
TRUBE		
Jane	Putn	289
Mary	Will	357
TRUBEE		
Mary E	Gree	114
TRUBY		
Abram M	Merc	218
TRUE		
John	Knox	175
Melvin C	Wash	348
Wilber L	Wash	348
TRUEMAN		
Mary J	Belm	027
TRUER		
Nathaniel	Belm	030
TRUESDALE		
Henry S	Trum	328
John C	Mont	246
Olive A	Asht	018
TRUEX		
Jasper	Ross	296
TRUITT		
Caroline V	Dark	078
Elizabeth	Ross	300
John K	Adam	003
Samuel B	Adam	005
TRUMAN		
Chas Y	Fran	102
Sybil T	Medi	211
TRUMBO		
Pliny	Sene	311
TRUMBULL		
Jane	Medi	211
Rufus H	Luca	197
TRUNK		
Frances	Wayn	354
TRUSHEL		
Cath	Tusc	332
TRUSLIEL		
Ann	Harr	149

TRUSNAN			TULIAN		
James	Hami	125	Joseph	Otta	271
TRUX			TULK		
George	Monr	223	Katharine	Ross	297
John A	Monr	223	TULLIS		
TRUXELL			Err H	Colu	057
Jacob	Huro	163	James W	Merc	218
TRYMAN			Richard B	Colu	055
Eliza	Brow	035	Thomas	Alle	008
TRYON			TULLOSS		
Ezra	Port	284	Eliza A	Colu	055
John	Cuya	064	TUMAN		
John M	VanW	337	Margaret	Medi	210
Robert G	Mont	230	TUNIS		
TUAAY			Sarah A	Lake	177
Thomas	Mont	234	TUNISON		
TUBBS			William	Luca	197
Geo	Sene	312	TUOHEY		
Smith S	Meig	214	John	Mont	235
TUCK			TURKE		
William	Huro	162	Nathan M	Unio	333
TUCKER			TURLEY		
Charles	Knox	174	John A	Scio	306
Daniel	Athe	020	William	Luca	198
David	Rich	292	TURNACE		
Elizabeth	Hard	147	Joshua	Dark	079
Ellanor	Athe	020	TURNBULL		
Hester	Butl	036	Francis	Cosh	059
John F	Paul	273	James	Jeff	171
John M	Craw	063	TURNER		
John W	Merc	218	Cornelius M	Geau	111
Joseph	Guer	118	Cyrus H	Fran	102
Josephus	Athe	022	Daniel	Musk	265
Louisa M	Cuya	065	Daniel M	Lake	178
Paris	Paul	274	Edward	Fair	092
Samuel	Athe	021	Edward	Maho	207
Telitha	Carr	040	Elanor C	Warr	342
Walter	Monr	225	Eliza Ann	Asht	019
Wesley S	Knox	174	Eliza J	Guer	117
William	Brow	034	Evander V	Medi	211
William E	Vint	340	Geo	Paul	273
William J	Mont	231	Geo W	Belm	030
TUCKERMAN			Henry	Clin	053
John	Sand	302	Henry P	Trum	330
TUDHOPE			James N	Scio	305
Esther	Wyan	365	Jesse G	Lora	192
TUDOR			John	Cler	051
Clarissa J	Cuya	065	John P	Fair	092
TUFTS			John W	Vint	340
Anthony F	Star	317	Jos	Morr	260
TULE			Jos S	Fair	089
Elwood T	Will	357	Leaven	Musk	265
			Lewis	Morg	258

TURNER (cont)				TWILLING		
Mary C	Shel	314		Mary	Hami	132
Mary E	High	154		TWINEM		
Milton	Guer	118		Charles	Monr	223
Pamelia	Mont	232		TWINING		
Rachel	Lora	193		Johanna	Lick	186
Rachel K	Sene	309		Laetitia	Wood	359
Randolph M	Fair	092		TWITCHELL		
Reddon	Lawr	183		Charles	Asht	019
Rees H	Putn	291		TWOMEY		
Samuel	Hard	144		Bridgett	Dela	083
Samuel W	Clin	054		TYLER		
Sarah	Preb	288		Aaron	Miam	220
Sarah N	Pike	282		Geo E	Cuya	074
William	Mont	232		Jno C	Lake	178
TURNEY				John W	Sand	302
John	Fult	107		Morris E	Sand	302
Mary A	Fran	097		Olive	Gall	111
TURNIPSEED				Royal	Port	284
Allen	Mont	234		Warren	Luca	201
David	Carr	039		William D	Wyan	366
John L	Guer	120		TYLOR		
TURNPAUGH				Selleck K	Butl	037
Joseph H	Hami	125		TYNER		
TURPEN				James	Wood	360
John H	Merc	218		TYRILL		
TURRILL				Martin	Trum	327
William P	Wash	345		TYRRAL		
TUSSING				Daniel L	Belm	030
David	Hanc	141		TYRRELL		
Harmon	Hard	147		Tracy R	Lake	178
TUSTISON						
Lucinda	Morr	260				
TUTTLE						
Chester	Trum	326		UDELL		
Emily F	Clar	045		Benj F	Asht	017
Harriet	Asht	015		UFFORD		
Henry H	Clar	046		Elizabeth	Dela	083
Jerome	Lake	176		UHL		
Mary Ann	Ashl	013		Conrad	Mont	245
Nancy	Meig	212		George	Hanc	143
Philemon H	Cuya	066		Jacob	Craw	064
Sally	Lora	194		John Frank	Holm	160
William	Jack	166		Mary	Lick	187
TWADDLE				UHLER		
Mary	Jeff	170		Samuel	Wayn	351
Thomas	Monr	223		UHRBACH		
TWEED				Christian F	Mont	233
Polley	Brow	034		UHRICH		
Samuel A	Tusc	333		Philip	Fran	102
TWEEDY				ULGENER		
Sarah	Jeff	170		Peter	Luca	201
				ULLERY		
				David S	Miam	221

ULLERY (cont)			**UPDEGROVE**			
Elizabeth	Miam	222	Edm'd B	Clar	044	
Jos C	Hami	137	Joseph R	VanW	338	
ULLMAN			**UPDIKE**			
Chas	Hami	137	John A	Wood	358	
ULLOM			**UPHOLD**			
Elihu M	Monr	223	Benj	Musk	266	
ULLUM			**UPTON**			
Drusilla	Vint	341	William	Summ	323	
Ellis	Dark	077	**URELL**			
Hannah	Lawr	183	Michael	Mont	234	
ULM			**URIAS**			
Edward	Mont	244	Cely	Cuya	066	
Hezekiah B	Mont	227	**URICH**			
ULREY			Christopher	Holm	160	
George B	Cler	048	John	Lora	193	
ULRICH			**URIE**			
Cath	Wyan	366	Ellinda	Wood	358	
Mary	Dela	084	Rachel	Ashl	011	
UMBAUGH			**URQUHART**			
Rachel A	Fran	097	Moses J	Jeff	171	
UMENSTETTER			**URTON**			
Elizabeth	High	155	Josiah	Warr	342	
UMMELMAN			**USHER**			
Henry	Clar	047	James	Cler	049	
UMPLEBY			Joel C	Asht	018	
Tamson A	Jack	167	**USTICK**			
UMSTEAD			Abner	Morr	260	
Samantha	Colu	058	**USURY**			
UNDERHILL			Nancy	Gall	109	
Geo C	Lora	194	**UTLEY**			
Harlow	Sand	304	Amos	Dela	082	
UNDERWOOD			Delia	Erie	087	
Adolph H	Madi	203	**UTTZ**			
Chas	VanW	336	Jacob C	Craw	064	
Hannah	Butl	038	**UTZ**			
Joseph	VanW	338	Wendel	Butl	035	
Mary E	Alle	009				
Obediah	Knox	176				
Robert	Ashl	012				
William	Clin	055	**VAHUE**			
William	VanW	338	Eli J	Paul	273	
UNION			**VAIL**			
Eliza	Hami	132	Barbara C	Dela	083	
UNKART			Charlilans	Summ	324	
Geo	Wood	360	Eliza	Wood	358	
UNKEFER			Geo W	Wood	358	
Alvin C	Star	320	Henry M	Colu	057	
UNKELHOLZ			Mary	Tusc	331	
Frederick	Shel	316	**VAINS**			
UNTERREINER			Sarah	Perr	277	
Christian	Mont	234	**VALENTINE**			
			Amelia	Guer	120	

VALENTINE (cont)				VANCE (cont)		
Elizabeth	Unio	336		Hannah	Fran	097
Jordan	Ross	298		James W	Hami	137
Milton	Fran	095		James W	Loga	191
Rebecca	Tusc	332		Jerome B	Fran	096
Weil	Cuya	066		John B	Lick	187
William H	Fran	096		John S	Gall	109
VALIQUETTE				Lewis	High	156
Theresa	Otta	272		Loyal C	Lick	188
VALLENDER				Mary P	Adam	005
Anthony	Mont	234		Reuben A	Cuya	066
VALLET				Richard W	Alle	010
Andrew	Cuya	066		Thomas W	Dark	077
VALLEY				William	Mont	234
Henry	Cuya	066		William H	Craw	064
VALLO				VAN CLEAF		
Anthony	Hami	137		Cath	Mont	227
VALZ				John M	Mont	228
Nicholas	Mont	238		VANCOISE		
VANALST				Jesse R	Wood	362
Arvilla	Wood	361		VANCUREN		
VAN ANDA				Geo W	Belm	030
Susan	Brow	032		Wilson S	Belm	028
VANANKER				VANCYOC		
John W	Maho	206		Lafayette	Scio	307
VANANSDALE				VANDEMAN		
Isaac	Preb	286		Amelia	Adam	003
VANASDEL				Sarah	Dela	083
Mary	Knox	174		VANDENBURG		
VANASTREM				John	Cuya	066
Joseph	Musk	263		VANDERGRIFF		
VANATA				Ellen	Lick	187
Henry	Hanc	140		VANDERGRIFT		
VANATTA				Stricklin	Mont	244
Elizabeth	Fair	092		VANDERHOOF		
VAN BIBBER				Caroline	Star	317
Jonathan	Meig	213		VANDERHULE		
VAN BLOW				Geo W	Mont	242
John	Sene	314		VANDERPOOL		
VAN BRIGGLE				Geo	Sene	313
Eugene	Cler	049		VAN DERVEER		
VAN BRINAER				Henry E	Butl	035
Curley	Morr	260		VANDERWORT		
VAN BUREN				Elizabeth	Warr	342
Martin	Mont	255		Martha	Cler	049
VAN BURLINGHAM				VAN DEUSEN		
A	Wood	362		Don C	Medi	210
VANCE				VANDIGN		
Alexander	Gall	109		Mary	Belm	026
Chloe	Gall	110		VANDIKE		
David	Merc	217		Henry	Sand	303
Euphemia A	Lick	187		VANDIVORT		
Geo	Lick	187		Anna	Scio	305

VANOSDOL			VAN WINKLE (cont)		
John W	Cler	048	Henry C	High	157
VANOSTRAND			Margaret	High	155
Cynthia	Wayn	354	VAN WOERT		
VANOTTA			William T	Mont	246
John	Musk	263	VAN WORMER		
VAN PEARSE			William	Luca	201
Dianah	Fair	091	VANY		
John	Unio	334	Elizabeth	Wash	350
VANPELT			VAN ZANDT		
Jas L	Colu	056	John	Mont	236
VAN SCHOYCK			VANZANT		
S	Fran	103	Morris	Hami	137
VANSCODER			VARIAN		
Israel	Ashl	012	Truman W	Fran	096
VAN SCYOE			VARLEY		
Geo W	Belm	027	Benj E	Cler	051
VAN SHOCK			VARNER		
Peter	Asht	018	George	Maho	204
VAN SICKLE			VARNEY		
A M	Cuya	066	Margaret T	Medi	211
VANSICKLEN			VASBERGER		
Samuel	Mont	234	Herman	Mont	240
VANSKIVER			VASKA		
Alvaro	Defi	080	Joseph	Mont	234
VAN SKORK			VASSER		
Anna V	Asht	018	Thomas G	Loga	191
VANSKY			VAUGHAM		
Silas	Hard	147	Rebecca	Gall	108
Zachariah	Hard	147	VAUGHAN		
VAN SLACK			Elizabeth	Mont	256
Ellen	Sene	310	Geo W	Fran	103
VAN TASSEL			Ruth Ann	Adam	005
Reuben	Wood	359	VAUGHN		
Sarah A	Sene	311	Albert J	Star	317
VANTILBURGH			John F	Gall	111
Mary	Rich	294	Mahala	Pick	279
VAN VALKENBERG			Samuel	Hami	137
Isaac	Wood	363	Thomas H	Mont	231
VAN VALKENBURG			Watson B	Mont	256
Cyrenius	Lake	177	William	Adam	006
VAN VLEET			William E	Wash	345
Garnett	Fult	105	VAUROY		
Mary Ann	Fult	105	Camron	Will	356
VAN VLIET			VAUSKY		
Mary J	Sene	313	John	Vint	341
VAN VOORHIS			VEACH		
Mary E	Loga	191	Charlotte	Ross	301
VAN VORHES			VEATCH		
Nelson H	Athe	020	Sarah K	Morg	257
VAN WINKLE			VEITTER		
Eliza	Clin	054	Mary	Hami	132

VENHAM			VIERS (cont)		
Wilson S	Belm	029	Zilpah	Summ	321
VENOAH			VIEW		
Chas	Will	357	Peter	Luca	201
VENSEL			VIGNOS		
Elizabeth	Musk	264	Augustus	Star	317
VENSON			VINCENT		
Samuel J	Putn	288	Marion	Wash	345
VEO			Mary	Lora	194
Lafayette	Luca	196	Nancy	Pick	280
VEON			Winfield S	Hami	137
John F	Sene	314	VINE		
Tammy	Otta	271	Harriet M	Fult	106
VERITY			VINES		
James	Athe	023	Adaline	Butl	036
VERMILLION			VINET		
Hannah	Guer	120	Morris	Hami	137
John	Lawr	179	VINEY		
Mary Ann	Lick	186	Lewis	Star	319
William H	Guer	117	VINING		
VERMON			Clarinda	Dela	083
Elizabeth	Asht	019	Joseph	Putn	289
VERNER			Philena	Dela	083
Jas E	Fran	096	William G	Putn	289
VERNON			VINNEDGE		
Jesse	Alle	008	Lewellen H	Butl	035
Nancy	Musk	267	VOETH		
Peggy	Musk	262	Anton	Fran	096
VERT			VOGHT		
Edward	Mont	238	William	Mont	236
VERWOLD			VOGT		
Sophia	Mont	231	Christiana	Musk	266
VESEY			Frederick W	Musk	263
William	Trum	328	VOIGHT		
VESPER			Caspar	Hami	137
Mary J	Mont	230	Herman	Mont	243
VESTAL			VOLK		
Marshal	Unio	335	Cath	Luca	202
VEZINA			VOLKER		
Octave	Mont	240	John	Cuya	066
VIALL			VOLKMAN		
Benj	Defi	080	Chas	Mont	256
Sarah	Summ	323	VOLLMAN		
VICK			John	Pike	282
Holland E	Star	316	VOLMOUTH		
VICKERS			Jno	Mont	234
Frederick H	Port	284	VOLZER		
Joseph	Lawr	180	Christian	Star	317
Mary	Ross	299	VONDENBENDEN		
VIERS			Joseph	Gall	108
James E	Fult	107	VONDERAN		
John B	Henr	152	John	Unio	334
Wilson S	Adam	006			

338

VOORHEES			WADDICK		
Thomas B	Hock	157	James M	Luca	200
VOORHES			WADDINGTON		
Elizabeth	Guer	117	Mercer	Hami	131
James	Guer	120	WADDS		
Mary W	Guer	120	Anton	Mont	233
Richard M	Cosh	060	WADE		
VORHES			Cath	Hami	132
Chas D	Butl	025	Edward	Craw	063
VORHIS			John W	Miam	219
John J	Wood	359	William	Fran	096
Lewis E	Butl	037	William A	Athe	023
Samuel D	Hami	139	WADEN		
VORIS			Samuel	Hami	138
A C	Summ	323	WADENPOHL		
VORNS			Henry	Mont	253
Mary M	Loga	190	WADSWORTH		
VOSBURGH			Fanny	Lick	184
Harmon J	Sene	310	WAFFLE		
VOSE			John	Medi	211
David L	Miam	222	WAGAR		
VOSLER			John L	Trum	327
Margaret	Cuya	075	WAGEMAN		
Michael	Cuya	075	John H	Cler	049
VOSS			WAGER		
Gartrue	Ross	299	Geo M	Erie	087
VOTTELER			WAGERS		
Henry J	Cuya	066	Martha	Belm	029
VREELAND			Mary	VanW	336
Mary A	Perr	277	WAGGONER		
VROMAN			Chas C	Augl	026
Jno A	Hami	137	Elizabeth	Faye	093
VROOMAN			Elizabeth	Sene	308
George W	Luca	201	Susanna	Luca	197
VYARS			WAGNER		
Martha	Gall	107	Chas	Wayn	354
			Christian	Lora	193
			Daniel	Sene	314
			David	Dela	084
WABLE			Frederick	Sene	314
Jacob	Adam	007	Geo H	Wayn	352
WACHENDORF			John	Defi	082
Frederick	Mont	239	John	Hami	140
WACHTER			Jno	Meig	213
Joshua	Fair	090	John	Wash	349
William	Fair	090	Joseph	Hami	131
WADAMS			Levi	Fran	096
Lucretia	Sene	312	Louis	Fran	096
WADDELL			Maria K	Ross	297
James H	Fult	107	Martha	Asht	015
John	Trum	325	Mary E	Hami	124
Sarah	Belm	028	Mary M	Huro	164
			Michael	Wayn	351

WAGNER (cont)				WAKERS		
Peter	Augl	025		Geo	Fult	107
Samuel	Mont	254		WAKLYN		
William	Madi	202		John C	Hami	136
William	Mont	235		WALBURN		
William C	VanW	336		Edward J	Lawr	181
WAGONER				Matilda	Cham	041
Eliza	Wood	363		WALCHER		
Enoch	Athe	024		Michael	Hami	131
Fred	Cuya	070		WALCK		
James	Musk	263		Israel	Athe	024
Jesse	Wood	361		WALCUTT		
John	Jeff	170		Ann E	VanW	340
Joseph	VanW	337		WALDEN		
Mary	Star	318		Bathsheba	Gall	108
Nancy	Gree	116		Charles H	Scio	307
Philip	Fran	096		WALDMANN		
Simon M	Henr	151		Herman	Otta	270
William W	Jeff	170		WALDO		
WAGY				Fred H	Hami	124
John H	Lick	186		WALDORF		
WAHL				Aly	Wayn	352
Anton	Mont	243		James P	Fran	096
John	Huro	164		Joseph M	Will	357
WAHRER				WALDREN		
Frank	Sene	313		Francis P	Brow	031
WAIBEL				Thomas	Pike	281
John	Colu	056		WALDRON		
WAID				Cordelia L	Lora	195
Ellen	Trum	327		Eliza A	Summ	322
WAINMAN				Katherine	Dela	084
Chas P	Cuya	070		WALFORD		
WAIT				John D	Luca	196
Isaac	Mont	234		WALKER		
WAITE				Anderson	Scio	307
Clinton C W	Ross	296		Andrew	Lake	178
Elizabeth	Adam	004		Cath	Adam	004
Ruth Ann	Guer	120		Charles	Mont	244
WAITLEY				Druzilla	Scio	307
John C	Mari	208		Edward	Cuya	065
WAITS				Elizabeth	Pick	279
Aaron	Holm	161		Frederick	Fair	090
Cath	Cler	049		Geo W	Dark	077
Elizabeth	Cler	048		Harlan F	Clin	054
Mary	Brow	032		Henrietta	Meig	214
Mary	Cler	051		Henry C	Miam	221
Mathias	Cler	047		Hiram D	Port	286
WAKEFIELD				James W	Rich	291
Franklin B	Hami	131		Jane	Hami	140
John	Cuya	064		Jesse	Lick	187
WAKELEE				John	Cosh	062
Arthur B	Cuya	070		John M	Harr	148
Oscar R	Lake	178		John S	Colu	059

WALKER (cont)		
John W	Clin	054
Jonathan	Mont	230
Jonathan	Summ	322
Joshua R	Clin	054
Lewis	VanW	337
Lynan	Wood	358
Margaret	Vint	340
Martha	Hami	132
Mary E	Wyan	367
Nancy	Hami	135
Nancy	Ross	300
Nancy A	Brow	032
Nancy C	Morg	257
Robert	Brow	035
Robert P	Gree	113
Sarah	Hami	135
Sarah	Shel	315
Seth	Medi	211
Smith A	Rich	292
Susannah	Loga	190
Thomas	Mont	234
Townends	Cham	041
Walter R	Hard	144
William	Lawr	180
William	Otta	271
William	Scio	307
William H	Fair	090
William R	Cuya	075
Wilson R	Brow	033
WALKEY		
John	Knox	173
WALKINS		
William H	Cuya	070
WALKLEY		
Lovina	Asht	015
WALL		
Eliza	Brow	033
Jas H	Unio	334
John	Lora	195
Joseph	Defi	080
Susanna	Putn	290
Tabitha J	Sene	312
William F N	Mont	251
WALLACE		
Anthony	Brow	033
Chas	Fran	096
David P	Loga	192
Eli	Mont	256
Eliza	Colu	059
Geo W	Wash	346
Gillespie	Mont	229
Henrietta R	Star	318

WALLACE (cont)		
Henry B	Cuya	065
Hiram N	Brow	033
James Sr	Jeff	170
James A	Dark	077
Jane	Guer	118
Jared	Hami	131
John	Colu	058
Joseph L	Jack	166
Margaret A	Rich	294
Martha A	Loga	190
Mary	Guer	117
Nancy	Guer	118
Robert	Wood	360
Samuel H	Monr	226
Sylvester	Carr	040
William	Asht	017
William	Butl	038
William F	Belm	028
WALLAHAN		
Charlotte	Meig	214
WALLAM		
Eliza J	Colu	059
WALLER		
Benj B	Nobl	268
George M	Jack	167
Peninah	Lawr	182
Silas P	Port	283
WALLING		
Hiram A	Asht	017
Sarah	Lick	188
WALLS		
Jeremiah	Scio	306
William	Putn	290
WALN		
Ann	Faye	093
WALRATH		
Wallace	Cuya	076
WALRAVEN		
Rachael	Morg	258
WALSH		
Andrew B	Maho	205
Ann	Cuya	068
Fannie	Mont	232
James	Mont	237
James	Mont	247
Lambert	Craw	063
Michael	Hami	131
Owen	Mont	234
Owen	Mont	245
Patrick	Mont	234
William	Mont	234

341

WALTEMATH			**WALTON** (cont)		
Cath	Hami	132	Thomas J	Colu	058
WALTER			William M	Fran	103
Caroline	Star	319	Zimri W	Clin	053
Cath	Hami	132	**WALTZ**		
Geo	Cuya	070	Joseph	Butl	039
Herny C	Cham	043	Moses	Hock	159
John C	Loga	191	**WALWORTH**		
John F	Mont	245	Warren F	Cuya	070
Joseph	Wayn	354	**WALZ**		
Levi	Maho	207	Jacob	Hami	131
Mary	Wayn	354	**WAMICA**		
Thomas	Cuya	065	Frederick	Scio	307
Thomas R	Gall	108	**WAMSHER**		
William	Wood	362	John	Luca	200
William C	VanW	337	**WANBAUGH**		
WALTERS			Jacob	Hanc	143
Adam	Hanc	141	**WANDLE**		
Angelette	Jeff	169	Christena	Dark	077
Anna Maria	Hami	132	**WANK**		
Benj S	Mari	208	John	Cham	042
Clement	Monr	226	**WANRER**		
David	Hanc	143	Samuel	Sand	304
Edward	Shel	316	**WANSEL**		
Elizabeth	Gall	110	Jacob	Luca	200
Elizabeth	Hanc	143	**WANTZ**		
George	Mont	234	Rebecca	Dark	077
George E	Musk	266	**WARBINTON**		
Hannah	Miam	219	John	Cler	051
Henry H	Fair	090	Samuel	Shel	315
Isaac S	Musk	266	**WARD**		
Jane	Jeff	169	Betsey A	Fran	103
John	Hami	131	Byron	Knox	175
Jno	Perr	277	Cornelius	Athe	021
John W	Sene	310	Cyrus M	Warr	344
John W	Wayn	354	Daniel S	Gall	110
Joseph	Sand	303	Durbin	Hami	131
Maria	Meig	212	Eliza	Cuya	069
Sylvanus	Fult	105	Eliza J	Alle	010
Thomas	Wood	362	Ella	Colu	057
Zipporah	Hard	148	Geo W	Will	356
WALTHER			Isaac	Gall	108
Henry	Mont	227	James G	Hanc	143
WALTMAN			Jeremiah	Warr	342
William H	Henr	151	Joel M	Knox	175
WALTON			John	Hanc	143
Andrew	Asht	019	John	Lawr	180
Elizabeth	Cosh	060	John	Vint	340
Frederick W	Miam	220	John H	Defi	080
Jonathan	Port	283	Jonathan	Colu	055
Malinda	Lick	188	Joseph	Alle	009
Mary	Meig	215	Mahala	Wash	350
Mathew	Wyan	367	Mary	Gall	109

WARD (cont)			WARNER (cont)		
Mary	Mari	208	Edward C	Hard	145
Mary A	Hami	139	Eliza	Erie	086
Mary E	Lick	184	Ephraim P	Will	357
Moses	Monr	224	Esther	Sand	302
Nelson J	Meig	213	Geo E	Meig	214
Patrick	Mont	246	Geo S	Musk	266
Richard M	Putn	290	Irwin	Cuya	065
Samuel	Pike	282	Jacob	Erie	088
Sarah	Tusc	330	Jacob	Hami	131
Stephen A	Paul	274	James M	Jack	167
Susannah	Ross	297	John B S	Vint	341
Sylvina	Hanc	142	Lewis	Clar	047
William S	Sand	302	Magdalena	Colu	058
Zacharial	Wood	363	Mary E	Medi	212
Zippora	Hami	135	Melissa	Asht	016
WARDEN			Phillip	Dark	077
Nathan C	Craw	063	Polly	Medi	211
William F	Fran	104	Rachel	Unio	334
William P	Craw	064	Sarah	Preb	287
WARE			Sophia	Tusc	332
Charles M	Mont	244	Thomas C	Lora	193
Kimble	Hami	136	Thornton J	Madi	203
Mariah	Pike	282	Wilhelmina	Tusc	331
WAREHIME			William H	Mont	241
Joseph	Vint	342	WARNICK		
WARHEIGHT			Robert	Mont	234
Barbara	Huro	162	WARNICKER		
WARICH			Lydia	Loga	191
Jacob	VanW	336	WARNOCK		
WARLE			James	Lora	193
James E	Knox	175	WARREN		
WARMAN			Chas D	Mari	208
Caleb	Mont	232	Ellen L	Huro	164
Charles V	Lick	188	Geo	Asht	015
George G	Lick	186	Geo H	Hami	131
John	Hami	137	Jane	Fran	101
WARNE			Jno B	Colu	058
Ezra G	Musk	263	John B	Knox	175
James W	Pike	282	Jonathan	Madi	203
WARNEKE			Joseph W	Athe	021
John Henry	Hami	131	Mary Ann	Lake	176
WARNER			Nancy H	Clar	045
Adoniram J	Wash	349	William P	Mont	238
Albert J	Hanc	143	WARRETT		
Almon M	Hami	129	James C	Ashl	013
Ann C	Knox	175	WARRINER		
Benj	Tusc	332	Silo P	Geau	111
Charles	Hami	129	WARRINGTON		
Charles E	Lora	193	Emily E	Cuya	069
Charles M	Trum	327	John W	Hami	131
Christopher C	Ashl	012	Sarah	Mari	208
David	Miam	221			

WARSON			WATKINS			
Rachel	High	155	George W	Athe	023
WARSTLER			John W	Dela	085
Aaron	Star	320	Judith	Scio	307
WARTENBE			Rebecca	Knox	173
Francis	Jack	167	Wells	Fult	105
John	Jack	167	WATRONS			
WARTY			Julia M	Asht	014
Jacob	Cuya	070	WATROS			
WARWICK			Joseph H	Huro	164
John O	Dark	077	WATROUS			
Laura	Jeff	170	George H	Madi	202
WASCHER			George W	Madi	203
Henry	Wyan	367	WATSON			
WASEM			Anna	Musk	265
Margaret	Fair	089	Asenath M	Fran	102
WASHBURN			Eliza	Sene	310
Abraham	Adam	007	Eliza J	Harr	150
Alabine	Jack	167	Enoch B	Sene	309
Amason	Erie	088	Geo B	Dela	085
Eliza	Hock	159	James	Adam	006
Ellis W	Adam	007	James	Monr	226
George H	High	155	James G	Colu	057
Guy H	Asht	014	Jane	Cosh	060
Harriet G	Lora	193	John H	Butl	037
Rachel A	High	154	John M	Loga	191
William C	Lawr	180	John W	Luca	200
WASHINGTON			Josiah P	Miam	221
York	Paul	274	Mary	Cler	048
WASMUND			Mary A	Merc	217
Bernhard	Mont	252	Nancy	Cuya	074
WASTALL			Porter	Maho	205
Grace	Gall	108	Prudence	Ross	297
WATERHOUSE			Rose A	Fran	097
Elizabeth	Hami	138	Ruth	Sene	310
Thomas J	Tusc	331	Thomas	Holm	161
WATERMAN			Thomas A	Sene	309
Homer C	Musk	266	William	Mont	233
Mary J	Erie	086	William S	Morg	256
WATERS			WATT			
Abigal	Colu	058	Barbara	VanW	339
Alonzo M	Miam	219	Francis	Guer	118
Cath	Cosh	061	Geo	Gree	116
Enos	Belm	031	Marietta B	Hard	146
Lester	Asht	014	Samuel	Hard	143
Louisa	Fran	101	WATTERS			
Lucius W	Asht	018	Julia	Hami	123
Margaret A	Brow	033	Mary	Holm	160
Mary	Cosh	060	Robert	Cosh	061
Mary Jane	Dela	082	WATTERSON			
Philena	Cuya	076	Carrie T	Cuya	068
Rachel C	Jeff	170	Cornelia A	Sand	302
William	Dela	085				

WATTS			WEAVER (cont)		
Ann	Hock	158	Elizabeth	Miam	222
Arthur H	Musk	266	Elizabeth	Wood	363
Cassey	Athe	024	Henry	Ashl	012
James	Gree	114	Jacob	Hock	158
John S	Gree	115	John	Alle	008
John S	Gree	116	John	Colu	058
Margaret	Gree	115	Lydia A	Colu	056
Michael B	Gall	108	Mahala	Hock	159
William W	Clin	054	Mary	Cosh	060
WAUGH			Mary	Dark	079
Sylvester W	Lawr	182	Rachel M	Brow	035
WAY			Rebecca	Wayn	352
David L	Clin	054	Rebecca A	Tusc	330
Eliza A	Guer	120	Washington C	Craw	064
Jno C	Wash	350	WEBB		
Joseph	Rich	295	Alexander	Lawr	181
Mary	Erie	087	Almon	Trum	330
Milton	Mont	237	Darwin O	Asht	015
Nathan	Mont	247	Elias	Lawr	183
WAYLAND			Eliza	Butl	036
Alvidas	Cler	048	Eliza L	Port	284
WAYNE			Elizabeth	Lick	185
Cath E	Wayn	354	Frances	Lawr	183
WAYT			Geo A	Maho	205
Mary E	Belm	028	Herny J	Asht	015
WEACHAM			John	Miam	218
Homer	Paul	274	John	Star	318
WEAIL			Jonathan	Cosh	061
John	Ross	297	Nancy	Hami	139
WEAKLY			Sophia C	Fair	091
Harrison	Pick	278	Thomas G	High	156
WEAKS			William	Maho	205
Jacob	Putn	288	WEBBER		
WEARIN			Albert	Mont	231
Edmund	Athe	023	Caroline	Nobl	270
WEATHERBEE			Christopher C	Port	285
Mary Jane	Athe	020	Geo W	Paul	272
WEATHERBY			Howard J	Port	283
Jackson W	Athe	022	James	Port	283
WEATHERHEAD			John	Monr	226
Elizabeth	Miam	222	Levi D	Nobl	270
Margaret	Miam	222	WEBER		
WEAVER			Anna M	Lora	193
Adam	Port	284	Barbara	Cuya	074
Alpheus	Sene	310	Geo	Fran	102
Benj	Meig	212	Henry	Cuya	073
Cath	Musk	264	Henry	Jack	168
Cath	Pick	279	John	Fult	104
Christian	Hami	137	Marcus	Luca	200
Daniel	Nobl	269	WEBERT		
Daniel	Sene	310	Henry	Mont	246
Eliza	Jack	168			

WEBLEY				**WEIDMAN**		
Betsey	Brow	033		Webster	Star	318
WEBSTER				**WEIDNER**		
Amanda	Hami	138		Fred	Fair	090
Charles D	Mont	241		William A	Butl	035
Charles W	Dela	084		**WEIGAND**		
Dennis	Butl	037		Barbara	Augl	026
Elias H	Guer	120		**WEIGEL**		
George P	Dela	084		Barney	Erie	088
Gilbert G	Meig	213		Cath	Fult	106
Margaret A	Morr	260		Charles	Luca	202
Mary	Dela	082		Ephraim	Fult	106
Samuel H	Sand	303		**WEIGLE**		
William S	Mont	249		William	Cuya	066
WEDDLE				**WEIGLER**		
Olive	Miam	221		Charles	Mont	242
WEDMANN				**WEIHR**		
Gottlieb	Hami	131		Jacob	Athe	020
WEED				**WEIKER**		
David S	Sene	309		Jacob	Wayn	353
WEEDON				**WEIKERT**		
Alfred	Guer	119		Jacob	Maho	205
WEEDS				**WEIL**		
Kate	Hami	137		Anna M	Hami	123
WEEKER				**WEILER**		
Barbara	Loga	191		Jacob	Augl	026
WEEKS				John	Cuya	070
Eliza H	Hami	135		**WEILMAN**		
Horace L	Jack	167		Elizabeth	Erie	086
Lyman	Fult	106		**WEIMER**		
Nancy R	Ashl	011		Mary	High	155
Oliver M	Mari	209		**WEINGATE**		
Phebe M	Lora	195		James	Jack	169
WEEMAN				**WEIR**		
Lydia	Luca	202		James	Hami	131
WEGSTEIN				William	Fult	107
Magdaline	Cham	043		**WEIRICH**		
WEHMANN				James L	Knox	173
Christian	Hami	129		**WEIRICK**		
WEHRUNG				Albert G	Trum	327
Henry	Meig	214		Sally A	Craw	064
WEIBER				**WEIS**		
John J	Wayn	353		Geo	Mont	228
WEICH				**WEISER**		
Theresia	Hami	123		Chas W	Wayn	351
WEICHARER				Elizabeth	Cosh	060
Carl	Mont	244		**WEISGERBER**		
WEICHEIMER				Charles	Mont	252
Henry	Wayn	352		**WEISLER**		
WEIDERRICHO				Dorothea	Hami	132
Martin	Hami	136		**WEISNER**		
WEIDLE				August	Mont	240
John F	Mont	238				

WEISS			WELLEN		
Ernest	Mont	234	Rachel	Fran	104
Jno N	Mont	234	WELLER		
Philip	Mont	255	Jerome B	Miam	222
William G	Mont	238	Jos	Clar	046
WEISSIGERN			Mary M	Morg	257
George C	Shel	315	Sarah A	Gree	114
WEIST			Telitha	Hami	139
Gabriel M	Fair	088	WELLING		
WEITMAN			John	Cuya	070
Henry	Mont	249	Mary Jane	Cosh	062
WEITZEL			William C	Fran	096
Elizabeth	Pick	280	WELLMAN		
Henry	Dark	076	Hiram W	Luca	197
Joseph	Star	319	Jonas G	Hami	137
WELCH			WELLS		
Adolphus	Geau	111	Ann	Ashl	011
Daniel	Hard	148	Benj	Wood	360
Daniel	Ross	297	Benj S	Wayn	351
Daniel J	Morr	261	Chas	Fair	091
Dennis	VanW	338	Daniel A	Medi	211
Ellen	Cuya	069	Edward	Port	284
Frank	Asht	014	Elizabeth	Unio	335
Geo P	Cuya	070	Emily E	Huro	162
James	Jack	168	Geo	Merc	218
James	Mont	246	Jacob	Wayn	351
John	Jeff	171	James B	Hami	131
John	Luca	197	Jane T	Unio	335
Jno	Meig	213	John A	Hard	145
Julia A	Lawr	180	John F	Clin	053
Luther A	Ashl	013	Judson	Fult	107
Mary Ann	Summ	322	Julia A	Musk	263
Noah	Meig	213	Mary	Defi	079
Patrick	Cuya	070	Mary A B	Wayn	354
Sally	Fult	104	Mary H	Gree	116
Sally	Huro	164	Matilda J	Hami	123
Sarah	Colu	059	Nathan M	Wayn	351
Stephen	Hami	136	Owen D	Ross	299
William	Mont	251	Richard H	Pike	281
William O	Dela	084	Robert G	Meig	212
WELDAY			Royal T	Summ	322
Mary	Jeff	170	Samuel	Dela	084
Nancy	Jeff	172	Sarah	Faye	094
WELDY			Silas H	Mont	234
Hazel	Miam	222	Theodore	Guer	118
WELKER			William	Hanc	140
Elizabeth	Knox	174	William	Wash	349
George	Sand	302	William W	Huro	164
Isaac H	Adam	005	WELSH		
Mary	Hard	145	Crawford E	Belm	026
Oscar D	Knox	174	Geo W	Fair	090
Rebecca	Defi	081	Harrison	Fult	106
			Henry M	Wyan	367

WELSH (cont)			WERNER (cont)		
John C	Pick	278	Lydia A	Alle	009
Margaret	Clar	045	Rebecca	Sand	304
Margaret	Cuya	069	William	Sene	311
Margaret A	Pick	279	WERTENBERGER		
Pinckney J	Hami	131	Isaac	Ashl	013
Sarah	Sene	311	WERTS		
William B	Hami	138	Israel	Dark	076
Zehamiah B	Knox	175	Mary A	Miam	218
WELSHBILLIG			WERTSBAUGHER		
John	Hami	131	Jno G	Star	319
WELSHEIMER			WERTZ		
Elmer W	Faye	095	Caroline	Cham	042
WELTMAN			WESCO		
Rachel	Medi	211	Henry	Miam	218
WELTON			Mary	Preb	286
Andrew	Wood	358	WESLER		
Louis L	Mont	250	John J	Miam	221
Stephen	Summ	325	WESLEY		
WELTY			Donaldson	Adam	007
Abraham C	Hock	158	Michael	Cuya	070
Henry G	Rich	292	WESSENDORF		
Nathaniel	Perr	275	Mary E	Scio	305
WELTZ			WESSLING		
Mary A	Hock	158	Anna Maria	Hami	132
WENAT			WEST		
Caroline	Cuya	074	Alonzo R	Asht	015
WENDEL			Benj F	Warr	344
Augustus	Hami	129	Cath E	Fran	104
WENDELKEN			Charles	Mont	238
Henry	Wash	349	Elizabeth	High	154
Martin	Wash	349	Elizabeth	Jack	167
WENDELL			Enoch	Dark	078
Ferdinand J	Mont	249	Fred E	Huro	164
Hannah L	Nobl	268	Harrison	Lawr	179
WENDLING			Henry B	Jeff	169
Adam	Star	319	Henry C	Wash	349
Theresa	Sene	312	Henry O	Ashl	013
WENER			Herny R	Monr	226
John A	Hanc	143	Hugh H	Hock	158
WENGER			James M	Morg	257
Christian	Merc	217	Jeremiah	Mont	227
Hannah	Dark	077	Johnston G	Mont	244
WENTWORTH			Jos	Clin	052
William R	Mont	251	Jos G	Adam	006
WENTZ			Leander	Perr	276
John	Wyan	367	Levi	Wash	349
WENZEL			Lydia	Monr	225
Conrad	Mont	233	Mary J	Mont	230
WERNER			Philina A	Cuya	068
Charles	Mont	252	Rachael	Fran	103
Frederick	Sene	310	Rebecca J	High	154
John	Trum	330	Richard C	Pike	281

WEST (cont)		
Roxanna	Sand	302
Sarah	Cosh	060
Sylvester	Rich	293
WESTENBARGER		
Jas T	Fair	090
Mary J	Fair	091
WESTENBERGER		
Amaziah	Hock	159
WESTERFIELD		
Sarah E	Mont	256
WESTERKAMP		
Christ	Hami	129
WESTERMAN		
Elizabeth	Hami	123
Jacob	Henr	153
Joseph	Henr	153
WESTFALL		
Daniel M	Preb	286
Hannah	Luca	198
Harva	Vint	341
Helen A	Star	320
Henry W	Pike	280
WESTLAKE		
Lydia	Hock	158
WESTON		
Ethan A	Butl	038
John	Craw	064
William P	Rich	295
WESTOVER		
Sheldon	Sene	309
WETECAMP		
Henry G	Mont	227
WETHERBEE		
Emory G	Lake	177
WETHERELL		
Joseph	Fran	095
WETHERILL		
James G	Hard	146
WETMORE		
David	Otta	270
Maria	Asht	014
WETRO		
Henry	Rich	294
WETTERHAM		
Adam	Hami	131
WETZ		
Chas	Mont	227
WETZEL		
Francis	Butl	039
John	Lake	177
Susanna	Butl	036
WETZELL		
George	Mont	236
Oswald	Cuya	070
WEVELL		
Geo	Hami	139
WEYER		
William H	Alle	008
WEYMER		
John M	Mont	242
WHALEN		
Alice	Pick	279
Bridget	Cham	042
Martin	Gree	114
Patrick	Cham	043
WHALER		
Ira	Star	318
WHALEY		
Elizabeth	Jack	168
John	Huro	162
Lucius D	Cuya	074
WHALING		
Olive	Asht	019
WHALON		
John	Luca	200
WHAM		
John	Cham	041
WHARF		
Oliver	Wash	351
WHARFF		
Herny H	Athe	023
WHARTON		
Arthur	Nobl	270
Jacob A	Jack	169
James	Guer	120
Jason	Augl	026
Lucy	Musk	263
Mary Ann	Lick	185
Nathan	Nobl	268
Samantha	Lick	185
William H	Nobl	269
WHEALAN		
John	Sene	314
WHEALON		
Patrick S	Sene	313
WHEATCRAFT		
Chloey A	Cosh	061
WHEATLEY		
Margaret	Madi	204
WHEATON		
Barbara	Mont	232
Benj B	Miam	218
James	Fult	104

WHEATSTONE			**WHISTLER**		
Daniel	Wood	358	Aaron	Clar	047
WHEELAND			**WHITACRE**		
Jonathan	Ross	298	Benj F	Warr	344
WHEELER			Jacob G	Dark	079
Anna M	Lake	176	John	Star	320
Benj S	Henr	153	John N E	Clin	052
Chas C	Morr	261	**WHITAKER**		
Enos	Nobl	268	Hannah	Morg	259
Geo W	Lick	186	John	Cuya	070
Gilbert	Musk	263	John H	Morg	257
Harrison	Paul	273	Jos R	Clin	052
Harvey	VanW	338	Levi W	Miam	219
Isaac L	Augl	024	Lydia	Loga	192
Jesse C	Lora	195	Maranda	Wayn	352
Jonathon	Belm	030	William	Henr	151
Julia	Cuya	068	**WHITBECK**		
Mary J	Fran	096	Horatio W	Cuya	065
Mary J	Luca	198	**WHITCOMB**		
Porter	Lora	195	Ann Ellen	Hami	123
Rebecca I	Erie	087	David M	Ashl	013
Samuel	Nobl	270	Rich	Mont	228
Samuel C	Erie	088	William	Wayn	353
Thomas	Madi	203	**WHITCRAFT**		
William P	Erie	088	David B	Hock	157
Zephaniah	Henr	151	**WHITCROFT**		
WHERFEL			Henry H	Carr	039
Jacob B	Miam	222	**WHITE**		
WHETSTONE			Addison	Trum	328
David C	Maho	205	Alfred	Brow	034
Joseph	Wash	350	Alfred	Colu	058
Margaret J	Guer	120	Andrew	Fran	096
WHIDDEN			Andrew J	Lawr	179
Joseph	Luca	197	Ann K	Athe	021
WHIPKEY			Anna	Guer	117
Josiah	Athe	020	Anne E	Colu	056
WHIPP			Armedian	Fran	104
William G	Rich	294	Arthur B	Harr	150
WHIPPLE			Barbara	Huro	165
Jerome B	Luca	200	Carlos L	Cuya	070
WHIPPS			Chrisdeltha	Belm	028
Joshua F	Perr	276	Ciria C	Hami	123
Susannah	Perr	276	Cornelius C	Fran	096
WHIPS			Dares	Lick	186
Ann	Perr	277	Edward L	Star	318
Francis M	Mari	209	Edwin D	VanW	339
WHISAMORE			Eliza	Cuya	068
Abram	Ashl	013	Esther	Hard	145
WHISLER			Esther	Mont	232
Cath	Wood	358	Fanny M	Asht	014
Elam	Fult	105	Franklin L	Perr	275
Ephraim	Will	357	Geo	Belm	029
Samuel	Star	318	Geo	Belm	030

WHITE (cont)

George	Jack	169
George O	Mont	234
Grafton	Ashl	012
Hamilton	Monr	224
Hannah O	Asht	017
Henry M	Cham	041
Horatio	Musk	266
Jackson G	Wyan	365
James	Mont	255
James W	Musk	264
John	Cler	051
John	Mont	243
John	Mont	244
Jno	Mont	255
John	Morg	259
John A	Rich	296
John B	Morr	260
John E	Brow	032
Joseph	Clin	052
Joseph	Hard	148
Joseph P	Musk	264
Joseph W	Mont	228
Josiah W	Luca	200
Lemuel H	Lick	186
Letita	Ashl	011
Lewis B	Unio	335
Lewis P	Trum	328
Lydia	Putn	290
Margaret	Cuya	068
Margaret C	Perr	276
Mary	Gall	109
Mary F	Sand	302
Mary M	Morg	257
Matilda J	Fran	101
Melita E	Brow	032
Nancy E	Butl	038
Nancy J	Sand	301
Oscar F	Fult	107
Patrick	Mont	241
Peter	Belm	030
Rachel	Guer	119
Rebecca	Pick	279
Rebecca	Pick	279
Richard H	Unio	335
Robert	Rich	295
Robert	Sene	309
Rosannah	Geau	112
Samuel	Lawr	182
Samuel A	Cosh	062
Samuel J	Lick	187
Sarah A	Faye	094
Sarah E	Unio	335

WHITE (cont)

Thomas	Asht	018
Thomas B	Dark	076
Thomas K	Mont	237
Thomas M	Wyan	367
Warner	Huro	163
William H	Belm	028
William H	Jeff	169

WHITED

Belinda	Dark	079
Elizabeth	Loga	190

WHITEFIELD

Alfred	Mont	236

WHITEHEAD

Chas	Huro	164
Edward B	Cham	041
Elizabeth	Lick	188
John H	Wood	358
Martha E	Belm	029
William W	Lick	185

WHITEHORN

Myron	Fult	105

WHITEHURST

John W	Hanc	141

WHITELEATHER

Louisa	Colu	057

WHITELEG

Joshua C	Fair	090

WHITELOCK

William	Hami	121

WHITEMAN

Harman	Sene	313

WHITENIGHT

Philip C	Mont	235

WHITESIDE

Franklin W	Miam	221
James	Faye	093

WHITESIDES

Jonathan	Cham	043

WHITESMAN

William H H	Warr	342

WHITFIELD

Andre	Cham	043
Smith A	Hami	131

WHITING

Margaret W	Warr	342
Robert W	Dela	085

WHITLEY

Eliza	High	155
Ziba	Mont	251

WHITMAN

Elizabeth	Wood	363

WHITMAN (cont)			WICK			
Louis	Wood	363	Cyrus	Mont	241	
Theodore	Wood	362	Phillip	Hami	135	
WHITMER			WICKELL			
Geo W	Miam	221	Francis A	Madi	203	
Jno	Perr	278	WICKER			
WHITMORE			Mary A	Summ	324	
Elijah	Luca	196	William	Clar	044	
Emily	Wood	360	WICKERHAM			
John A	Sene	310	Elizabeth J	Sene	310	
Rebecca	Sene	313	WICKES			
William P	Lawr	182	William C	Huro	164	
WHITNEY			WICKEY			
Abigail	Summ	322	Daniel S	Cham	043	
Almira	Port	285	WICKHAM			
Ann	Knox	175	Almira	Asht	015	
Ann E	Wash	349	Clarinda H	Athe	021	
Charles M	Port	285	Elizabeth	Nobl	269	
Elisha S	Luca	202	Fred C	Huro	164	
Fanny A	Lora	195	Hadley H	Athe	021	
Frank R	Wood	360	Jacob	Nobl	269	
Henry	Alle	009	John W	Erie	086	
Henry M	Luca	200	WICKIZER			
Martha	Lick	185	Eliza	Mari	210	
McClure	Fran	096	WIDDOES			
Oscar F	Will	355	Louisa E	Belm	030	
Roxanna J	Mont	231	WIDEMAN			
William	Lick	188	Cath	Hami	123	
WHITSELL			Mary B	Belm	027	
Anna	Hock	157	WIDMER			
WHITTAKER			Ellen	Miam	222	
Louisa	Miam	222	WIEDERICHT			
Richard	Mont	246	John	Hami	131	
WHITTECAR			WIEHLE			
Francis M	Fran	103	Margaretha	Scio	305	
WHITTEN			WIELAND			
Chas M	VanW	338	Andrew	Hami	136	
Solomon C	Trum	328	WIEMER			
William	Dela	084	Jacob	Paul	273	
WHITTENBERGER			WIEN			
H	Maho	205	John	Alle	010	
WHITTLE			WEISER			
Jas G	Belm	029	Henry	Augl	025	
WHOLLAN			WIET			
Margaret	Hami	137	Ann	Cham	042	
WHORLEY			WIGER			
Huldah W	High	155	Conrad	Henr	151	
WHYMAN			WIGGIN			
Samuel	VanW	337	Emily	Monr	224	
WIARD			WIGGINS			
Lewis W	Carr	039	Ann M	Jeff	171	
WIBRALSKI			Hannah F	Harr	148	
David	Mont	237	Isaac Q	Cosh	062	

WIGGINS (cont)			WILDES			
William H	Hami	138	Thomas F	Summ	322	
WIGHT			WILDEY			
Elizabeth	Shel	315	Hannah	Asht	019	
WIGHTMAN			Jeremiah	Mont	234	
Geo	Mont	233	WILDMAN			
Harriet T	Asht	014	Mary J	Asht	015	
WIGTON			WILEMAN			
Charlotte	Morr	260	Mary	Faye	093	
WIKEL			WILES			
Mary	Preb	288	Eliza	Brow	034	
WIKOFF			John W	Brow	034	
William C	Hami	140	Perry	Musk	265	
WILBER			WILEY			
Albert M	Will	357	Aquila	Wayn	354	
Lewis	Wood	358	David G	Fult	107	
Martin V	Erie	086	Josiah N	Clar	044	
WILBOUR			Mary E	Belm	029	
John A	Ashl	012	Mary J	Lick	185	
WILBUR			Oren M	Gall	109	
Anthony W	Belm	031	Thomas J	Mont	254	
Bradford	Fult	105	WILHELM			
Herman L	Luca	198	Daniel	Summ	322	
WILCOX			Ignatz	Mont	242	
Ann	Loga	189	John	Wayn	354	
Elizabeth	Jack	168	WILKERSON			
Elizabeth	Unio	335	Elizabeth	Warr	344	
Ellen	Cuya	068	Isaiah	Clin	054	
Emily A	Asht	014	WILKIN			
George W	Hard	148	Grace	Belm	029	
Hiram	Gall	111	John	Carr	039	
Irving F	Port	285	Lydia	High	156	
Jno	Mont	234	Philip	High	154	
John E	Luca	197	WILKINS			
John W	Trum	326	Cooley M	Asht	014	
Lorain	Hami	135	Geo A	Colu	058	
Louisa	Fran	101	Hettie A	Butl	036	
Luther L	Henr	151	John	Alle	009	
Martha	Dela	083	John	Fran	096	
Mary	Port	284	John A	Fult	105	
Orphia Almira	Dela	085	Sarah	Belm	029	
Phebe	Hami	136	Sophia	Medi	210	
Sarah A	Fult	106	Thomas J	Loga	189	
Thomas	Medi	211	William P	Mari	209	
William J	Will	357	WILKINSON			
WILCOXEN			Eli	VanW	338	
Anthony	Gall	110	Joseph	Butl	038	
WILD			Oliver	Belm	027	
Anton	Craw	063	William S	Mont	227	
WILDER			WILKISON			
Daniel S	Fran	096	John M	Wayn	351	
Marion	Asht	018	Mary	Star	318	

WILKS			WILLIAMS (cont)		
Franklin	Lawr	179	Daniel	Mont	253
William D	Mont	251	Daniel	Wash	346
WILL			David	Hami	129
Eliza J	Meig	216	David	Mont	239
George H	Sand	303	David	Trum	325
John	Fair	088	David S	Wood	361
Richard B	Rich	291	Dinah	Morr	262
WILLABY			Drusilla	Tusc	333
Mary Ann	Lick	186	Ebenezer	Cham	041
WILLARD			Edmund	Wood	364
Frederick	Lick	187	Eliza	Asht	014
Manfred	Faye	095	Ellis M	Loga	192
WILLBAUM			Emeline	Dela	084
George P	Mont	234	Emily E	Adam	006
WILLEAMSON			Emily M	Cuya	075
George S	Lick	186	Frederick	Port	285
WILLENER			Geo	Craw	063
Christ	Star	317	Geo F	Sand	303
WILLET			Geo J	Maho	207
Joseph	Hami	131	Geo W	Dela	084
WILLEY			Geo W	Hard	148
Almira	Asht	014	Geo W	Loga	192
Chas T	Musk	267	Geo W	Vint	341
Ethan A	Alle	009	Grafton	Knox	174
Frances M	Defi	080	Hannah	Pick	279
John J	Lick	186	Hannah	Pick	279
Levi	Nobl	270	Harriet	Medi	210
William H H	Medi	211	Helen	Hami	123
WILLGARD			Henry	Craw	063
Edwin C	Port	285	Henry	Dark	079
Sylvester	Port	285	Henry B	Warr	342
WILLIAM			Henry H	Miam	221
Rosson	Cler	048	Henry L	Lora	192
WILLIAMS			Isaac	Miam	222
Albert C	Meig	216	Isaac D	Hami	138
Alonzo L	Wash	349	Jackson	Adam	006
Ann	Clin	052	James	Merc	217
Anna	Lake	178	James	Pike	282
Anton	Wood	363	James	Summ	324
Benj F	Mont	236	James K	Gall	107
Benj F	Vint	341	James M	Fran	096
Bennett	Erie	086	James W	Butl	037
Bentley	Loga	190	Jeffrey	Loga	192
Charity	Mari	209	Jerome	Wyan	364
Chas	Adam	004	John	Jeff	169
Chas	Cuya	070	John	Sene	312
Chas	Lora	194	John G	Gall	111
Chas E	Cham	041	John P	Dela	085
Chas J	Jeff	170	Jonas	Lick	187
Chas O	Warr	343	Joseph	Madi	204
Chas W	Dela	085	Joseph	Mont	228
Conrad	Mont	238	Joseph	Mont	236

WILLIAMS (cont)		
Joseph	Putn	289
Kennedy	Scio	307
Kinsey S	Clin	054
Laura F	Fran	101
Laura M	Summ	323
Leah J	Jack	166
Lewis	Lick	184
Loren	Asht	016
Louisa F	Geau	112
Lucinda E	Gall	108
Lucy L	Knox	174
Luther	Hock	157
Martha	Loga	190
Martha	Port	285
Martin L	Hami	140
Mary	Carr	039
Mary	Luca	200
Mary	Morg	256
Mary	Musk	265
Mary	Tusc	331
Mary A	Hard	146
Mary A	Luca	196
Mary Ann	Warr	342
Mary Ann	Will	356
Mary E	Hami	132
Mary L	Cuya	068
Melissa B	Wash	346
Michael W	Rich	295
Morris	Dela	085
Nancy	Mont	231
Nancy	Wyan	365
Napoleon J	Tusc	332
Nicholas	Loga	191
Oliver W	Huro	164
Richard R	Sene	311
Robert	Lick	185
Samuel	Star	318
Samuel G	Craw	063
Sarah	Clin	053
Sarah	Pike	282
Sarah	Trum	328
Sarah	Will	355
Simon	Lick	187
Sophia	Cosh	061
Susan	Clin	054
Susan	High	156
Susan J	Musk	263
Susannah	High	156
Theo S	Huro	164
Thomas	Hard	143
Thomas	Mont	240
Thomas	Mont	254

WILLIAMS (cont)		
Thomas	Mont	254
Thomas D	Jack	168
Thomas F	Lora	192
Thomas G	Summ	322
Wallace R	Asht	016
Wilber A	Wood	359
William	Mont	228
William	Mont	228
William B	Scio	307
William G	Hock	158
William H	Shel	315
William J	Morg	258
William S	Merc	217
William T	Nobl	269
William W	Cuya	070
William W	Mont	244
Woodsen D	Clin	053
WILLIAMSON		
Albert M	Brow	034
Elizabeth	Lora	195
Elmira	Warr	342
Henry	Miam	218
Henry C	Fair	092
Henry P	Dark	076
Hugh	Wash	346
James	Jeff	169
John	Wash	349
Margaret	Hanc	142
Mary E	Sand	303
Peter	Hanc	141
Richard M	Shel	316
Sarah	Hami	140
Stephen D	Hami	132
William	Butl	039
William H	Mont	237
WILLIAN		
Elizabeth	Cler	048
WILLIARD		
Abigail F	Summ	325
Thomas	Trum	328
WILLIER		
Barbara	Wood	361
WILLIFER		
Alfred D	Musk	265
WILLIS		
Abram	Huro	165
Benona E	Musk	266
Chas	Fran	096
Edmund	Lawr	181
Eliza	Cler	051
Elizabeth	Lawr	183
George H	Lawr	179

WILLIS		
George W	Lawr	180
Henry	Mont	239
Jesse	Hard	145
Julia A	Meig	212
Levi W	Belm	029
Susan	Summ	321
Thomas M	Cler	050
William	Shel	315
WILLISON		
Amos	Belm	026
Sarah	Lick	185
WILLISTON		
John H	Craw	063
John R	Port	284
WILLKING		
Jacob	Lick	188
WILLOCK		
Stephen	Maho	207
WILLOUGHBY		
Amos	Hami	129
Edgar	Perr	277
Levi P	Wyan	365
WILLS		
Edmond W	Ross	300
John	Brow	032
John W	Brow	034
Joseph A	Henr	152
Julia A	Ross	300
Ottomar	Hami	135
Richard	Clin	054
WILLSEY		
Moses D	Asht	016
WILLSON		
Edwin S	Wyan	366
Minerva A	Unio	334
WILLYARD		
Frederick	Holm	161
WILMOTH		
Esther	Wash	346
WILSON		
Adaline	Wash	347
Alfred	Craw	063
Alfred B	Augl	025
Ann	Trum	329
Arvin	Port	284
Calvin H	Erie	087
Cath	Gree	115
Cath	Hard	146
Chas	Loga	191
Chas M	Faye	095
Christina	Brow	031
Cynthia	Jack	166

WILSON (cont)		
Daniel M	Fair	092
David	Fair	090
Dias N	Musk	264
Edward	Unio	334
Eli C	Fult	105
Elizabeth	Hard	144
Elizabeth	Nobl	270
Ellen	Brow	033
Emily	Rich	296
Ephraim	Cuya	070
Ezekiel	Sand	304
Finley V	Athe	020
Francis M	Fran	096
Frank	Tusc	331
Freeland C	Wash	348
George	Cosh	061
George	Cuya	070
George	Fran	103
George	Trum	329
George F	Lawr	182
Hannah	Musk	262
Hannah A	Hami	123
Hannibal	Lawr	181
Harvey L	Mont	237
Helen S	Cosh	060
Henrietta M	Vint	341
Henry	Craw	064
Henry	Morg	259
Henry V	Shel	315
Hiram	Cosh	060
Hiram G	Star	319
Hugh	VanW	337
Hugh C	Hami	131
Isaac	Adam	005
Isaac	Pike	282
Isabella A	Asht	014
James	Fran	096
James	Lawr	179
James	Lawr	179
James	Wash	349
James A	Huro	164
James C	Wash	345
James M	Brow	033
James M	Cuya	070
James P	Adam	007
James R	Musk	264
Jane A	Rich	295
Jesse J	Musk	266
John	Belm	028
John	Dela	084
John	Musk	264
John N	Lake	178

WILSON (cont)		
John R	Loga	189
Jno W	Belm	030
Joseph	Fair	089
Joseph	Hanc	141
Joseph	Scio	304
Joseph	Wash	345
Joseph A	Mari	208
Joseph H	Cosh	060
Joseph H	Nobl	270
Louisa	Asht	017
Lydia	Jack	166
Lydia A	Brow	032
Margaret	Cuya	075
Martha	Fran	097
Martin	Wash	346
Martin S	Wash	348
Mary	Musk	263
Mary	Unio	333
Mary A	Fran	101
Mary A	Mari	209
Morris	Ross	298
Nancy	Maho	206
Nancy	Pike	282
Nancy	Scio	306
Nancy	Scio	307
Nancy A	Perr	278
Oliver H	VanW	337
Patrick H	Loga	189
Peter D	Morr	262
Philander E	Will	356
Philip H	Clar	044
Rachel	Belm	030
Robert	Paul	274
Samuel J	Nobl	269
Samuel W	Clar	047
Sanford	Gree	113
Sarah	Butl	038
Sarah	Ross	300
Sarah	Shel	316
Sarah C	Ashl	012
Stephen	Mont	234
Thomas	Belm	031
Thomas	Monr	226
Thomas A	Huro	162
Wesley W	Trum	329
William	Mont	228
William	Mont	238
William	Rich	292
William	Wash	345
William G	Maho	206
William H	Harr	150
William S	Ashl	012

WILSON (cont)		
William T	Fran	096
William W	Cham	043
Willis	Cosh	061
Wright	Brow	033
WILT		
Jacob	Hard	146
James P	Perr	277
Sarah	Fran	104
WILTY		
William H	Mont	234
WIMBEY		
Joseph	Asht	014
WIMER		
Henry C	Faye	093
John W	Faye	093
WINANS		
Benj L	Alle	010
Elizabeth	Trum	330
John C	Miam	221
William H	VanW	339
WINBIGLER		
Mary	Ashl	012
WINCH		
Francis F	Sene	312
WINCHELL		
Eli	Fult	104
Geo H	Geau	111
Sarah	Ross	297
WINCHESTER		
Jonadab	Lake	176
Mary	Wash	347
Olive	Erie	086
Rosella	Cuya	064
WINDELSPECHT		
Jacob	Cuya	075
WINDER		
Ferdinand	Mont	233
WINDHAM		
Aquilla	Nobl	270
Thomas M	Nobl	270
WINDLE		
Cath	Lawr	179
John H	Jack	168
WINDRAM		
Robert	Trum	328
WINDSOR		
Sallie	Brow	033
WINE		
Sarah A	Colu	056
WINEBRENNER		
Jos B	Wayn	353

WINELAND			WINTER (cont)		
David	Defi	081	James B	Gree	113
David	Wood	358	WINTERBOTTOM		
WINEMAN			William	Summ	322
William	Monr	226	WINTERINGER		
WINES			John W	Fran	103
Geo W	Meig	216	WINTERMUTE		
Hedgman	Colu	057	Margery	Musk	265
WINFIELD			WINTERS		
Sallie	Warr	344	Amaziah	Lawr	183
Sarah J	Cuya	065	Andrew J	Trum	329
Thomas B	Rich	293	Chas H	Gree	116
WING			Chas H	Lawr	183
Eliza	Lora	194	Christian	Mont	237
Hannah	Cuya	076	Eliza	Jeff	171
WINGER			Elizabeth	Hami	131
Maria	Star	318	Isaiah S	Colu	058
WINGFIELD			Jas	Medi	212
Felix	Cham	041	Jane	Jeff	172
WINIAN			Mary L	Rich	293
Justus	Fair	090	Winfield S	Unio	335
WINKLE			WINTERSTEEN		
John	Wood	361	James	Defi	080
WINKLER			James E	Geau	113
Isaac N	Scio	308	Manville	Miam	222
Leonard	Erie	087	WINTON		
Louisa	Putn	290	Justice	Ashl	011
WINN			Rolson	Wood	358
Ann J	Musk	266	Sarah	Rich	295
Eliza	Musk	262	WINTRICK		
Jane	Mont	230	Peter	Cuya	068
WINNE			WINZENRIED		
Magdalena	Defi	081	Ralph	Cuya	070
WINNER			WIRES		
Isaac	Star	316	Warren	Athe	022
WINNING			WIRNER		
Jonathan	Maho	206	Adam	Maho	205
Nicholas	Colu	055	WIRTHS		
WINSLER			Mathias	Mont	255
Anna	Luca	197	WIRTS		
WINSLOW			John R	Fult	104
Fanny J	Dela	084	WISE		
Susan	Madi	202	Alice	Cosh	061
WINSOR			Amelia	Knox	173
Lydia W	Asht	016	Cath	Mont	230
Sidney	Henr	152	Daniel	Hanc	140
WINST			Daniel W	Belm	029
Anna C	Mont	230	David	Cuya	074
WINSTON			Elisha R	Trum	329
Spencer A	Lawr	180	Eliza	Sene	313
WINTER			Eva	Loga	191
Geo C	Cuya	076	Ezra	Lawr	181
Henry	Mont	234	Franklin	Lick	187

WISE (cont)		
Henry	Sene	311
Henry A	Mont	256
Joanna	Hanc	142
Jno	Dark	079
John W	Summ	324
Levi	Sene	310
Lucinda	High	156
Mary A	Nobl	268
Michael	Clar	047
Peter	VanW	336
Rosetta	Rich	294
Sarah	Lick	187
Sarah A	Mont	231
Valentine A	Mont	234
Watson	Star	318
William	Mont	251
William	Tusc	331
William A	Hanc	142
WISECUP		
Harrison	Adam	004
Jacob	High	155
Lavina	High	154
WISEMAN		
Adam P	Star	319
Andrew	Sene	310
Thomas	Wash	345
WISENER		
Elizabeth	VanW	339
WISHARD		
Samuel G	Nobl	268
WISHON		
Charlotte	Ross	300
Franklin	Pick	280
WISICK		
Samuel S	Shel	315
WISLER		
John	Defi	080
WISNER		
Samuel N	Lawr	181
WISSER		
Amelia	Warr	343
WISSINGER		
Augustus	Miam	223
WISSWESSER		
Geo	Augl	025
WISWELL		
John L B	Fran	096
Lucinda	Dela	084
Oliver II	Alle	010
WITCAMP		
Anna M	Hami	124

WITCOMB		
John	Mont	245
WITER		
Samuel	Star	320
WITHAM		
Jeddediah	Athe	021
William N	Warr	343
WITHERELL		
Daniel W	Asht	017
WITHERICK		
Christian	Huro	162
WITHERILL		
John H	Cuya	070
WITHEROW		
Ann E	Jeff	170
Mary	Colu	059
WITHERS		
Amanda	Musk	265
WITHERSPOON		
John S	Vint	341
Mary	Vint	341
WITHGOTT		
Mary	Ross	297
WITHROW		
James	Madi	203
WITLER		
Jonathan	Sene	312
WITMER		
Harriet	Sand	303
Henry	Wayn	351
WITT		
Esther	Dark	078
WITTE		
Henry	Fran	096
WITTER		
Alfred	Unio	335
WITTGENFIELD		
Rudolph	Hami	131
WITTICH		
William	Mont	237
WITTMEIER		
Ernst	Brow	033
WITZEL		
Henry	Athe	021
William	Wyan	367
(or Wm Wizel ?)		
WOESNER		
Richard	Hami	135
WOESSNER		
Dorothea	Sene	310
WOHLFORD		
Jacob	Wayn	354

WOHLGAMUTH			WOLFE (cont)		
Isaac	Hanc	143	Newton J	Fran	095
WOKATI			Richard E	Putn	289
Anna	Cuya	074	Ruth	Guer	120
WOLARY			Sarah	Ross	300
Andrew	Clin	054	WOLFF		
WOLBERT			Cline J	Mari	210
Christian	Lawr	181	Geo	Monr	224
WOLCOTT			Gottfried	Mont	234
Henrietta	Lora	194	John	Hard	146
Henry C	Luca	197	Samuel M	Rich	293
Huldah	Huro	164	Sylvester	Cham	041
John	Asht	015	WOLFORD		
Philander	Trum	326	Charles W	Cosh	060
Sarah	Miam	218	WOLFRUM		
Willis A	Asht	018	Andrew	Shel	316
WOLERY			WOLOVER		
David	Mont	236	John	Lick	187
WOLF			WOLTERS		
Adolph	Wood	358	August	Mont	244
Charles A	Ross	297	WOLTZ		
Charles M	Dark	077	Peter L	Hock	159
Daniel B	Rich	296	WOLVERTON		
Elizabeth	Hami	123	John A	Will	357
Ellen	Holm	161	John B	Knox	175
Frederick	Mont	253	WOMELDORFF		
Frederick	Sene	309	Sarah	Gall	110
Henry	Summ	323	WONDERS		
Jacob	Sene	314	Lafayette	Star	316
James M	Clin	052	WONNELL		
John	Gall	108	Thomas J	Otta	271
Joseph	Cuya	070	WOOD		
Joseph	Mont	233	Alfred H	Hami	129
Joseph	Tusc	331	Alpheus H	Cuya	070
Margaret	Fran	096	Archer	Fair	090
Margaret	Hami	123	Bridget L	Sene	311
Maria E	Hanc	142	Cath J	Fran	101
Markus	Sand	303	De Wilton	Otta	270
Mary	Defi	081	Francis	Hami	123
Mary A	Hanc	142	Francis V	Otta	271
Matilda	Meig	214	Frederick M	Hami	131
Michael	Fran	096	Geo	Belm	028
Rebecca	Gree	113	Geo	Hami	135
Valentine	Dark	079	Geo W	Cuya	070
William W	Mont	228	Gustavus A	Wash	349
WOLFE			Hannah	Colu	057
Ann	Rich	292	Hannah	Gall	108
Charles E	Scio	305	Harrison	Asht	016
Christiana	Otta	272	Henry	Summ	324
George R	High	156	Isaiah	Clar	044
John C	Hock	159	James J	Hard	144
John R	Rich	295	Jane A	Cuya	069
John W	Putn	290	Jos N	Mari	208

WOOD (cont)			WOODRUFF		
Julius V	Morr	260	Henry	Wood	362
Loren	Lora	193	Jesse	Huro	166
Marilla	Luca	197	Joel G	Sene	312
Martha	Augl	025	John M	Mont	235
Martha	High	155	Joseph H	Hami	131
Mary	Meig	216	Mary M	Hami	124
Mildred	Jeff	171	Merril	Athe	020
Myron	Maho	207	Moses C	Putn	289
Nancy J	Unio	335	Sarah	Summ	321
Nancy S	Pike	282	Sarah A	Fran	095
Nathan	Vint	340	Susan	Lick	187
Nathan	Warr	343	William	Athe	020
Osmar J	Nobl	270	WOODS		
Perry A	Will	355	Aaron	Mont	255
Richard O	High	156	Benj	Scio	307
Robert	Cler	047	Edward	Mont	255
Samuel	Ross	300	Edwin	Port	283
Samuel T	Otta	271	Eliza	Belm	028
Semion P	Monr	225	George	Faye	095
Sidney	Knox	175	Harlan	Madi	203
Soranus S	Wash	349	James	Athe	023
Star B	Cuya	070	Jno	Mont	255
Susan	Asht	018	John R	Butl	037
Thomas H	Erie	088	Kate	Maho	206
Wade	Erie	087	Luther	Miam	220
William	Cham	043	Sarah	Butl	036
William	Colu	057	Sylvester	Musk	266
William W	Star	316	Virginia	Scio	306
Zernah	Warr	344	Walter O	Lawr	181
WOODARD			WOODSON		
William	Summ	322	William	Jack	169
WOODBORNE			WOODSWORTH		
Geo W	Tusc	333	John	Wood	364
WOODBURN			WOODWARD		
Louisa	Warr	344	Aaron	Morg	259
WOODBURY			Chas L	Hock	159
Robert	Asht	018	Joseph	Fult	107
Sarah E	Medi	211	Luther	Morg	258
WOODCOCK			Martin	Meig	214
Diantha D	Lick	184	Orpheus	Maho	206
WOODCOX			WOODWORTH		
Sarah	Defi	081	Carolina	Cuya	066
WOODEN			Diodate	Asht	019
Jeremiah	Hock	159	E Smith	Port	286
WOODFORD			Edwin C	Asht	019
Cath	Morr	259	Jas P	Asht	016
WOODIN			Maria	Asht	019
Alfred	Cuya	070	Olive	Asht	017
WOODLAND			WOODYARD		
Minerva E	High	153	Jas L	Meig	212
WOODMAN			Joshua	Athe	022
William	Madi	203			

WOOLEVER			WORTHINGTON	(cont)		
John	Hock	157	Betsey	Huro	164
WOOLEY			Susannah	Harr	149
David B	Mont	234	Thomas	Warr	344
Stephen	Hard	144	WORTMAN		
WOOLF			Elizabeth	Morg	257
James G	Mont	256	Geo W	VanW	338
Samuel	Colu	058	Henry D	Vint	340
WOOLUMS			James L	Musk	264
Rachel	High	157	WORTS		
WOOSTER			Richard	Cuya	075
Almira F	Huro	164	WOTTER		
Henrietta M	Cuya	069	Hiram	Miam	218
Joseph B	Mont	240	(alias Hiram Fairbanks)		
WOOTEN			WOX		
Louisa	Preb	287	Jane E	Fran	104
Marshall B	Gall	108	WRAY		
WORDEN			Eliza	Fran	101
Anna	Rich	293	James L	Fran	096
Lucia	Loga	190	WREN		
Sanford	Paul	272	Mary M	Aug1	025
WORK			WRENN		
Warren S	Brow	032	Alfred H Jr	Morr	261
WORKMAN			Richard L	Morr	261
Cath A	Hanc	142	WRESTLER		
Hammett	Putn	289	William B	Brow	035
James	Paul	273	WRIGHT		
John M	Putn	291	Aaron W	Wood	360
Nancy	Carr	039	Abigail	Port	284
WORLEY			Adah	Morr	261
Eli Perry	High	155	Almira	Lick	183
Elizabeth	Miam	219	Alonzo	Lora	192
Geo	Rich	291	Andrew J	Cuya	066
WORMAN			Anna M	Cuya	066
John J	Sene	311	Aseneth	Musk	263
WORNSTAFF			Benj B	Erie	086
Elsey	Ross	299	Chas	Belm	028
WORRELL			David	Clin	054
Mary	Faye	094	Eliza	Brow	034
WORSLEY			Eliza	Cuya	065
Nancy E	Hanc	142	Emily J	Summ	324
WORST			Francis	Dela	082
Hannah	Sand	303	Franklin	Sand	304
WORSTELL			Geo C	Huro	164
Ann	Morg	257	Hannah C	Gree	115
WORTH			Hannah M	Asht	016
Thomas	Lick	186	Henry C	High	155
WORTHEN			Hiram D	Port	283
Charles	Meig	213	Hiram H	Gall	110
WORTHING			Isaac	Hami	138
William	Dela	085	Jacob	Fran	102
WORTHINGTON			James	Unio	333
A A	Geau	112	James K	Cuya	076

WRIGHT (cont)				WYANT		
Jesse	Gree	116		Mary	Star	320
John A	Monr	223		WYATT		
John C	Fran	096		Francis M	Scio	307
John L	Musk	262		Frank	Huro	165
John W	Cosh	062		Lizzie	Pick	279
Jonathan W	Holm	160		Mary S	Mari	210
Jos H	Mont	255		Nathaniel	Cham	043
Josiah J	Summ	322		WYBURN		
Lafayette	Sand	302		Joseph	Mont	255
Lavina	Brow	032		WYCKOFF		
Levi	Meig	216		Hannah T	Cuya	065
Lorenzo D	Unio	336		Susannah	Musk	264
Lot	Warr	343		WYERS		
Lovina	Hami	140		Henry	Fran	100
Lucius P	Meig	216		WYGUM		
Maria	Luca	198		Geo J	Fair	090
Martha E	Asht	016		WYLAND		
Mary	Augl	025		John H	Fran	096
Mary	Fair	092		WYLIE		
Mary	Loga	190		Francis H	Fran	096
Mary	Mont	232		WYMAN		
Mary B	Gree	114		Henry	Luca	197
Melissa	Lake	176		WYMER		
Nathan B	Fran	103		Cath	Brow	033
Oliver O	Summ	322		John F	Sene	311
Prescott P	Putn	290		Rachel	Lawr	180
Rhoda	Clin	052		WYNN		
Sarah A	Clin	054		Hannah	Pike	282
Sarah C	Fair	089		John Y	Colu	057
Silas	Henr	153		Jos D	Wash	350
Stephen E	Fair	090		WYSS		
Susan P	Port	283		Ann	Monr	225
Susanna	Lora	194		Mary	Shel	315
Sylvina	Henr	152		WYTHE		
Thomas	Lick	184		George	Knox	175
William	Wash	346		WYTT		
William L	Tusc	333		Marvin B	Sand	302
Winnefred	Colu	057				
WRIKEMAN						
John S	Carr	040		no X's		
WROTEN						
William H	Miam	221				
WRYIARCH				YAGER		
James H	Lick	185		Garrett	Gall	107
WUMMER				YAKEY		
William A	Mont	249		Margaret	Perr	276
WUNMEY				YALE		
Charles	Morg	259		Ann	Lora	196
WURSTER				YALEY		
Susan	Holm	160		Mary A	Craw	064
WURZBACHER				YARGER		
Fred	Brow	033		Jacob	Carr	039

YARGER (cont)			YOHA			
Margaret	Fair	091	Anne	Will	357
YARNELL			YOHO			
George	Morg	257	Peter	Nobl	269
Hannah	Warr	342	YONKER			
YATES			Chas	Gree	115
David G	Maho	207	YORK			
John A	Mont	248	Andrew	Hami	137
Joseph	Jack	166	Renjamin	Cler	047
Porter	Sene	312	(possibly Benjamin ?)			
YATSEY			YOSS			
Henry	Hami	121	Levi	Monr	226
YEAGER			YOST			
Absalom	Defi	080	Chas	Summ	323
Cath	Rich	294	David J	Wood	359
Geo W	Hami	138	Francis M	Belm	027
Jacob C	Sene	313	Lovisa	Star	320
Jacob F	Sene	314	Peter	Monr	224
Permelia	Jack	168	YOUNG			
YEAMANS			Adelia A	Lake	178
Elisha Jr	Fult	104	Albert	Hard	147
John L	Fult	104	Anderson	Putn	289
YEARHOUSE			Ann	Huro	163
Maria	Pick	278	Ann	Meig	214
YEAST			Anthony	Sand	304
Gertrude	Musk	265	Cath	Hami	132
YEAZEL			Cath	Luca	200
Samuel	Cham	041	Chas J	Mont	234
YELDEN			Charles L	Luca	201
Martha	Morg	257	Charles T	Jeff	172
YENCER			Christopher C	Ashl	012
Joseph	Fair	089	David W	Madi	202
YEOMAN			Douglas H	Wash	348
Stephen B	Faye	094	Edward B	Harr	149
YEOMANS			Eliza	Miam	219
Albert	Trum	328	Eliza	Morr	261
Elizabeth	Trum	327	Eliza J	Wayn	351
YERGER			Elizabeth	Musk	264
Isaac L	Maho	207	Emily	Luca	196
YINGOT			Henry W	Fair	089
Jos	Miam	218	Homer H	Asht	017
YOAKUM			Jacob	Fair	090
Margaret	Pick	279	Jacob	Hami	136
YOAST			Jacob	VanW	339
Jas S	Hami	137	James	Luca	197
YOCKEY			James	Mont	237
Philip	Star	317	Jane E	Lora	194
YOCORM			Jennetta	Miam	219
Nathan	Musk	266	John E	Wood	363
YOCUM			Jno L	Wash	347
Joseph	Belm	028	Jno S	Mont	252
Silas	Jeff	171	Jno T	Mont	252
			Joseph P	Mont	239

YOUNG (cont)			YOUSE (cont)		
Leonard	Adam	006	Mary E	Cler	052
Lucinda	Hami	137	YOUST		
Lucy	Huro	165	Hannah C	Knox	175
Lydia	Wash	347	YOUTZ		
Maria E	Madi	203	Mary	Fair	091
Martha	Brow	033			
Mary	Cham	043			
Mary	Nobl	270			
Mary A	Unio	335	ZACHMAN		
Mary J	Clin	052	Solomon	Mari	208
Mary J	Faye	094	ZAENGER		
Nancy	Harr	148	Christian	Wood	362
Nancy	Miam	222	ZAGER		
Nancy	Ross	297	Amanda	Augl	026
Peter F	Cuya	066	ZAHN		
Philip W	Shel	314	John	Cuya	066
Rachel M	Adam	004	Veronika	Erie	087
Richard	Scio	308	ZAHNER		
Robert J	Brow	034	Josiah	Hard	145
Sally S	Lake	177	ZAHRINGER		
Sarah M	Hard	143	Engelbert	Mont	234
Silas D	Shel	315	ZAISER		
Stephen M	Shel	316	William	Hami	137
Thomas	Loga	189	ZANE		
Thomas J	Cuya	066	Corban	Fran	095
Walter	Sene	310	John	Colu	056
Washington	Wood	361	ZAPP		
William	Augl	025	Jacob	Ashl	011
William	Brow	033	ZARBAUGH		
William H	Star	320	John B	Wood	361
William T	Warr	342	ZARTMAN		
YOUNGBLOOD			Henry	Perr	278
Matilda	Ashl	013	Simon P	Pick	278
YOUNGBLUTE			ZEARING		
Margaret	Nobl	269	Lizzie D	Mont	231
YOUNGER			ZEDAKA		
William C	Musk	266	Matilda	Maho	206
YOUNGLING			ZEDAKER		
Mary M	Holm	160	Absalom	Maho	207
YOUNGMAN			ZEEB		
Mary	Craw	062	Geo	Will	356
YOUNGS			ZEEK		
John	Colu	058	Garland	Dark	078
YOUNKINS			ZEHRUNG		
Harriet A	Athe	023	Peter B	Ross	299
YOUNT			ZEIGLER		
Hannah	Sand	304	Benj F	Will	356
Jos	Miam	219	Geo W	Huro	165
Samuel	Miam	221	Henry	Fult	106
Solomon	Miam	219	James	Wood	363
YOUSE			Lewis	Sand	303
Arthur L	Will	357	Philip	Luca	201

ZEIHER			ZIMMERMAN (cont)		
Peter	Meig	214	John	Lawr	183
ZEISE			John B	Sene	314
Peter F	Meig	214	John P	Mont	252
ZELB			Joseph	Athe	024
Jacob	Hami	137	Joseph	Huro	165
ZELLER			Josephine	Hami	124
Elizabeth	Hami	132	Josiah	Sene	312
Joseph	Luca	201	Lewis	Sand	303
Lewis	Hami	137	Rebecca	Sene	311
Martin	Ross	299	Sarah L	Fult	105
Sarah A	VanW	337	William	Ashl	011
ZELLNER			William	Faye	094
Edwin	Craw	064	William H	VanW	336
ZEMAN			ZIN		
William	Lora	194	Clarinda	Jack	166
ZENDHER			ZINGLING		
Chas	Mont	252	Emanuel	Tusc	331
ZENTMYER			ZINK		
Ellen	Butl	038	John H	Fair	089
ZEPPERLIM			ZINMERLY		
Cary	Jeff	170	Samuel	Monr	223
ZERCHER			ZINNBRUN		
Add W	Wayn	352	Susan	Mont	256
ZERKEL			ZINTL		
Aaron	Alle	010	Anton	Mont	237
ZERLY			ZIPPERER		
John H	Summ	323	Maria Agnes	Lick	187
ZERMAN			ZITTEL		
Margaret	Huro	161	Conrad	Summ	323
ZETLER(?)			ZIVIESLER		
Joseph	Mont	252	Edward	Mont	229
ZETNER			ZOELLER		
Christian	Fran	096	Samuel	Mont	243
ZIEGENHARDT			ZOLL		
Marcus	Hami	137	Felix	Huro	163
ZIELINSKI			ZOLLER		
Chas	Hami	137	Adam	Mont	235
ZIGLER			ZONVERS		
Philip	Tusc	332	Caleb	Rich	296
William	Hard	145	ZOOK		
ZIMMER			Albert	Colu	056
David	Musk	266	ZOPFI		
William	Clin	052	Henry	Hami	137
ZIMMERMAN			ZUBER		
Andrew	Mont	227	John G	Will	356
Barbara	Jeff	172	ZUCK		
Chas	Maho	207	David	Miam	220
Edward	Luca	201	Elisha	High	156
Elizabeth	Sand	304	ZUELCH		
Henry	Fair	090	Conrad	Mont	252
Henry	Mont	227	ZUERN		
Henry C	Lawr	183	Geo	Sene	313

ZUGSCHWERT		
Albert	Hard	147
ZUICK		
Jacob	Hami	137
ZURCHER		
Frederick	Tusc	332
ZURICKER		
Ernest	Otta	270
ZUVER		
William H	Adam	007
ZWEZ		
Julius F	Augl	025
ZWICKY		
Conrad	Will	356

Cynthia	Clar	044

Esther	Clar	044

www.ingramcontent.com/pod-product-compliance
Lightning Source LLC
Chambersburg PA
CBHW070544270326
41926CB00013B/2193